The cost of social security
Thirteenth international inquiry, 1984-1986
Comparative tables

Le coût de la sécurité sociale
Treizième enquête internationale, 1984-1986
Tableaux comparatifs

El costo de la seguridad social
Decimotercera encuesta internacional, 1984-1986
Cuadros comparativos

The cost of social security
Thirteenth international inquiry, 1984-1986
Comparative tables

Le coût de la sécurité sociale
Treizième enquête internationale, 1984-1986
Tableaux comparatifs

El costo de la seguridad social
Decimotercera encuesta internacional, 1984-1986
Cuadros comparativos

INTERNATIONAL LABOUR OFFICE   GENEVA
BUREAU INTERNATIONAL DU TRAVAIL   GENÈVE
OFICINA INTERNACIONAL DEL TRABAJO   GINEBRA

ILO, BIT, OIT

The cost of social security. Thirteenth international inquiry, 1984-1986: Comparative tables

Le coût de la sécurité sociale. Treizième enquête internationale, 1984-1986: Tableaux comparatifs

El costo de la seguridad social. Decimotercera encuesta internacional, 1984-1986: Cuadros comparativos

Geneva, International Labour Office. Genève, Bureau international du Travail. Ginebra, Oficina Internacional del Trabajo, 1992

/Report/, /Comparative study/, /Statistical table/s, /Social security/, /Cost/s, /Social security financing/, /Developed country/s, Developing country/s 02.03.1

/Rapport/, /Etude comparative/, /Tableau statistique/, /Sécurité sociale/, /Coût/, /Financement de la sécurité sociale/, /Pays développé/, /Pays en développement/. 02.03.1

/Informe/, /Estudio comparativo/, /Cuadros estadísticos/, /Seguridad social/, /Costo/, /Financiamiento de la seguridad social/, País desarrollado/, /País en desarrollo/. 02.03.1

ISBN 92-2-006430-8
ISSN 0538-8295

ILO Cataloguing in Publication Data
Données de catalogage du BIT
Datos de catalogación de la OIT

The designations employed in ILO publications, which are in conformity with United Nations practice, and the presentation of material therein do not imply the expression of any opinion whatsoever on the part of the International Labour Office concerning the legal status of any country, area or territory or of its authorities, or concerning the delimitation of its frontiers.
The responsibility for opinions expressed in signed articles, studies and other contributions rests solely with their authors, and publication does not constitute an endorsement by the International Labour Office of the opinions expressed in them.
Reference to names of firms and commercial products and processes does not imply their endorsement by the International Labour Office, and any failure to mention a particular firm, commercial product or process is not a sign of disapproval.

ILO publications can be obtained through major booksellers or ILO local offices in many countries, or direct from ILO Publications, International Labour Office, CH-1211 Geneva 22, Switzerland. A catalogue or list of new publications will be sent free of charge from the above address.

Les désignations utilisées dans les publications du BIT, qui sont conformes à la pratique des Nations Unies, et la présentation des données qui y figurent n'impliquent de la part du Bureau international du Travail aucune prise de position quant au statut juridique de tel ou tel pays, zone ou territoire, ou de ses autorités, ni quant au tracé de ses frontières.
Les articles, études et autres textes signés n'engagent que leurs auteurs et leur publication ne signifie pas que le Bureau international du Travail souscrit aux opinions qui y sont exprimées.
La mention ou la non-mention de telle ou telle entreprise ou de tel ou tel produit ou procédé commercial n'implique de la part du Bureau international du Travail aucune appréciation favorable ou défavorable.

Les publications du Bureau international du Travail peuvent être obtenues dans les principales librairies ou auprès des bureaux locaux du BIT. On peut aussi se les procurer directement, de même qu'un catalogue ou une liste des nouvelles publications, à l'adresse suivante: Publications du BIT, Bureau international du Travail, CH-1211 Genève 22, Suisse.

Las denominaciones empleadas, en concordancia con la práctica seguida en las Naciones Unidas, y la forma en que aparecen presentados los datos en esta publicación no implican juicio alguno por parte de la Oficina Internacional del Trabajo sobre la condición jurídica de ninguno de los países, zonas o territorios citados o de sus autoridades, ni respecto de la delimitación de sus fronteras.
La responsabilidad de las opiniones expresadas en los artículos, estudios y otras colaboraciones firmados incumbe exclusivamente a sus autores, y su publicación no significa que la OIT las sancione.
Las referencias a firmas o a procesos o productos comerciales no implican aprobación alguna por la Oficina Internacional del Trabajo, y el hecho de que no se mencionen firmas o procesos o productos comerciales no implica desaprobación alguna.

Las publicaciones de la OIT pueden obtenerse en las principales librerías o en oficinas locales de la OIT en muchos países o pidiéndolas a: Publicaciones de la OIT, Oficina Internacional del Trabajo, CH-1211 Ginebra 22, Suiza, que también puede enviar a quienes lo soliciten un catálogo o una lista de nuevas publicaciones.

Printed by the International Labour Office, Geneva, Switzerland

FOREWORD

This volume gives the results of the 13th international inquiry into the cost of social security, in the series initiated by the International Labour Office after the Second World War. The 13th inquiry comprises two parts: a basic inquiry and a supplementary inquiry. The basic inquiry follows the lines adopted in the earlier inquiries in so far as the definition, classification and content of the data are concerned. It is recalled, however, that the figures relating to medical care provided under public health services have no longer been included as from the 11th international inquiry. The supplementary inquiry covers special schemes for central government employees; its results are presented in a separate section at the end of this volume.

The data in the present volume were derived mainly from the replies to a questionnaire sent in December 1988 to all member States of the International Labour Organisation. Governments were requested to submit statistical information on the financial operations of their national social security systems for each of the calendar years 1984-86, or for the financial years of which the greater part falls in these calendar years. They were also asked to submit or supplement, wherever appropriate, the data for the years 1949-83 in order that data not previously submitted – or changes in the data already submitted – could be taken into account in the comparative tables. It may be mentioned here that from the fifth inquiry onwards governments were requested to group the data by risk or contingency according to the definitions given in the different parts of the ILO Social Security (Minimum Standards) Convention, 1952 (No. 102).

The International Labour Office would like to thank the national authorities for replying to the questionnaire and providing the information requested.

CONTENTS

AVANT-PROPOS

Ce volume présente les résultats d'une enquête internationale sur le coût de la sécurité sociale, treizième de la série consacrée à cette question par le Bureau international du Travail depuis la fin de la seconde guerre mondiale, ainsi que ceux d'une enquête complémentaire sur les régimes spéciaux des agents de l'Etat. Il se conforme, pour l'enquête de base, au modèle suivi pour les enquêtes précédentes en ce qui concerne les définitions, la classification et le contenu des données (rappelons cependant que les chiffres sur les soins médicaux fournis dans le cadre de la santé publique ne sont plus retenus depuis la onzième enquête). Les résultats de l'enquête complémentaire sont présentés séparément à la fin de l'ouvrage.

Les données figurant dans ce volume proviennent principalement des réponses à un questionnaire envoyé en décembre 1988 à tous les Etats Membres de l'Organisation internationale du Travail. Les gouvernements étaient invités à communiquer des informations statis-tiques sur les opérations financières du système national de sécurité sociale pour les années civiles de la période 1984-1986 ou pour les exercices financiers compris en majeure partie dans ces années. Ils étaient aussi invités à communiquer ou à compléter, le cas échéant, les données relatives aux années 1949-1983, afin qu'on puisse tenir compte, dans les tableaux comparatifs, des données non communiquées précédemment ou des modifications dans des données déjà communiquées. Précisons ici qu'à partir de la cinquième enquête les gouvernements ont été priés de grouper les données par éventualité selon les définitions apparaissant dans la convention (n° 102) concernant la sécurité sociale (norme minimum), 1952, de l'OIT.

Le Bureau international du Travail tient à exprimer sa reconnaissance aux autorités nationales pour avoir bien voulu répondre au questionnaire et fournir les données demandées.

TABLE DES MATIÈRES

PROLOGO

En este volumen se presentan los resultados de la decimotercera encuesta internacional sobre el costo de la seguridad social, en la serie que la Oficina Internacional del Trabajo dedica a esta cuestión desde el fin de la Segunda Guerra Mundial. La decimotercera encuesta comprende dos partes: una encuesta básica y una encuesta suplementaria. La encuesta básica sigue los lineamientos adoptados en las encuestas anteriores con respecto a las definiciones, la clasificación y el contenido de los datos. Sin embargo, conviene recordar que las cifras sobre la asistencia médica proporcionada por los servicios de salud pública han dejado de incluirse a partir de la undécima encuesta internacional. La encuesta suplementaria abarca regímenes especiales para funcionarios del gobierno central; los resultados se presentan en una sección separada, al final de este volumen.

Los datos de este volumen provienen principalmente de las respuestas a un cuestionario enviado en diciembre de 1988 a todos los Estados Miembros de la Organización Internacional del Trabajo. En él se solicitó a los gobiernos que enviaran datos estadísticos sobre las operaciones financieras del sistema nacional de seguridad social con respecto a cada año del período 1984-1986, o a los ejercicios financieros cuya mayor parte corresponde a estos años. Se les pidió también que, cuando correspondiera, facilitaran o completaran los datos relativos a los años 1949-1983 a fin de que se pudieran tener en cuenta en los cuadros comparativos los datos que no hubieran enviado anteriormente o los cambios registrados en datos ya enviados. Conviene señalar que a partir de la quinta encuesta se solicitó de los gobiernos que agruparan los datos por contingencia conforme a las definiciones dadas en las diversas partes del Convenio sobre la seguridad social (norma mínima), 1952 (núm. 102), de la OIT.

La Oficina Internacional del Trabajo aprovecha la oportunidad para expresar su agradecimiento a las autoridades nacionales por haber respondido al cuestionario y haber facilitado las informaciones solicitadas.

INDICE

Basic inquiry
All social security schemes

Enquête de base
Ensemble des régimes de sécurité sociale

Encuesta básica
Todos los regímenes de seguridad social

INTRODUCTION

This part gives the results of the 13th international inquiry into the cost of social security conducted by the International Labour Office since the Second World War.[1]

I. Objectives of the inquiry

These inquiries aim, first, at establishing a consolidated statement of the financial operations of all the social security schemes falling within the scope of the inquiry; and, second, at providing an international comparison of the data in order to identify trends in receipts and expenditure during the period under review, as well as the distribution of the receipts according to their origin and that of expenditure among the different schemes. In order to assess the importance of social security in the national economy, the data are related to various national accounts aggregates and to population data.

As in the last five inquiries, the results are issued in two separate publications, namely the comparative tables in this volume and the basic tables in a companion volume.

The present volume, containing the international comparative tables, generally follows the pattern set in the latest editions, in particular by giving country entries by region in order to facilitate comparison.

Two additional tables, however, have been added, expressing the main results for all countries in a common currency (the US dollar). The results of the supplementary inquiry are presented in four separate tables.

The set of basic tables gives detailed statistical data, on a disaggregated basis in absolute terms, of receipts and expenditure of social security schemes in each of the countries covered by the inquiry. Copies of the basic tables, which on this occasion have been issued in two volumes (the main volume, containing 81 countries, and the supplement, containing 32 countries) are available in English only and can be obtained from the ILO Social Security Department on request.[2]

In view of the importance of social security in the economy of nearly every country, there is great interest in obtaining precise, detailed, homogeneous and comprehensive statistical series on social transfers. This publication and its companion set aim at fulfilling that need.

Extensive social security statistics are necessary in order to provide the input for the computation and development of social indicators. In the field of social security, meaningful indicators are needed, on the one hand, to serve the general purpose of social and economic planning, notably in an integrated system of social indicators and, on the other hand, for social security policy formulation, planning, decision-making and evaluation.[3]

II. Scope of the inquiry

In order to maintain direct comparability of the data collected in the course of the 13th inquiry with those obtained in the preceding inquiries, the definitions and methods previously adopted have been retained.

The scope of the inquiry is such as to obtain for each country as complete a picture as possible of social security receipts and expenditure, that is, relating to all the schemes or services which meet the following criteria:

(1) The objectives of the system must be –

   (a) to grant curative or preventive medical care;

   (b) to maintain income in case of involuntary loss of earnings or of an important part of earnings; or

   (c) to grant a supplementary income to persons having family responsibilities.

(2) The system must have been set up by legislation which attributes specified individual rights to, or which imposes specified obligations on, a public, semi-public or autonomous body.

(3) The system should be administered by a public, semi-public or autonomous body.

However, where the liability for the compensation of employment injuries is imposed directly on the employer, schemes of employment injury compensation are included in the inquiry even if they do not meet criterion 3 above.

1. Schemes covered by the inquiry

In accordance with the criteria listed above, the following types of scheme are in general covered by the inquiry:

(i)   compulsory social insurance;

(ii)   voluntary social insurance, in so far as it meets criterion 2;

(iii)   universal non-contributory schemes;

(iv)   provident funds, within the limits of criterion 3;

(v)   employers' liability in respect of employment injury;

(vi)   family benefit schemes;

(vii)   national health services that are established by legislation and confer on all citizens rights to prescribed services and benefits;

(viii) special schemes or arrangements for public employees[4] (pensions, family benefits, sickness, employment injury compensation, etc., whether they are contributory or not);

(ix)   public assistance, within the limits of criterion 1;

(x)   benefits for war victims, within the limits of criterion 1;

(xi)   industrial or occupational schemes, or schemes and arrangements established as a result of agreements between employers and workers, provided the obligation on the employers has been made compulsory by law and these schemes or arrangements meet criteria 1, 2 and 3.

Thus, even if the provision of benefits is made compulsory by law, the inquiry does not cover benefits paid directly by employers in respect of such contingencies as sickness, maternity and retirement. The exception in respect of employment injury compensation (see (v) above) is made because it is the oldest branch of social security – one for which virtually all countries have made some legal provision – and because, from the practical point of view, in most countries it has been possible to obtain significant data since machinery usually exists for enforcing the relevant legislation. This is less often the case in respect of other employers' liability benefits. Finally, in countries where social insurance is introduced by gradual extension, the legislation on employment injury compensation is still in force in those areas, industries and enterprises that have not yet been brought under the social insurance scheme; if the benefits payable under employers' liability were not taken into account, the data on employment injury benefits would be incomplete and distorted.

The same can, of course, be said in respect of other social security benefits; but the existence of such benefits under employers' liability is not so widespread, and the practical problems of obtaining the relevant data are greater. It should be borne in mind, however, that in some cases direct payments by employers can attain quite considerable amounts, particularly in respect of the payment of wages and salaries during sickness and the payment of termination indemnities. It should also be noted that when such benefits are paid directly to their employees by public bodies, they do come within the scope of the inquiry.

The most important schemes of social security protection excluded under the three criteria mentioned above are probably the so-called "non-statutory schemes", in other words schemes that have not been established by legislation and that provide protection against the usual risks in accordance with criterion 1, e.g. non-statutory pension schemes, or medical care schemes established within enterprises. In some countries such schemes account for a considerable part of the resources devoted to social security. Indeed, the growth of non-statutory employee benefit schemes which supplement statutory schemes means that the figures given in the present volume for countries such as the United Kingdom or the United States considerably understate the real coverage provided.

2. Definition of benefits

The definition of benefits corresponding to criterion 1 above conforms to that of the ILO Social Security (Minimum Standards) Convention, 1952 (No. 102), which distinguishes between nine branches of social security as follows:

(1) medical care (Part II);
(2) sickness benefit (Part III);
(3) unemployment benefit (Part IV);
(4) old-age benefit (Part V);
(5) employment injury benefit (Part VI);
(6) family benefit (Part VII);
(7) maternity benefit (Part VIII);
(8) invalidity benefit (Part IX);
(9) survivors' benefit (Part X).

This definition does not always correspond to that applied under the national systems in the countries covered by the inquiry, since in a number of them social security includes benefits in respect of other contingencies. Such benefits have as far as possible been excluded from the tables. This is the case, for example, for Israel and Switzerland, where special allowances compensate for loss of earnings during military service.

Conversely, there are schemes which, although not strictly falling within the definition of social security, are nevertheless included in the inquiry as they provide benefits or services to persons who otherwise may have to rely on social security. Examples are the sheltered employment allowances in Australia and the kindred scheme in the Netherlands.

In addition, there are certain benefits and services which fall outside the definition of social security as laid down in Convention No. 102 but which are nevertheless included for practical reasons, as it has been considered too difficult (if not impossible) to separate the relevant data from other data relating to the social security institutions administering these benefits. Examples are the emergency benefits in New Zealand, particularly allowances to deserted wives, and recreation and physical training allowances in the USSR and other Eastern European countries. As a rule, the inclusion of benefits and services which, strictly speaking, fall outside the scope of the inquiry does not significantly affect the total figures for the schemes and branches concerned.

3. Medical care previously classified under "public health services"

As from the year 1978 – the first year of the 11th inquiry (1978-80) – medical care provided under public health services was excluded from the inquiry. Such data are therefore no longer included in the comparative tables.[5]

However, the miscellaneous medical care provided under public health services should not be confused with the medical care provided as a statutory right, and often on a contributory basis, under social security schemes covering the entire population. That is the case of the National Health Service in the United Kingdom, of the national health service in Italy and of similar services that operate, for example, in the countries of Eastern Europe. Those schemes have been included within the scope of the inquiry under the heading "social insurance and assimilated schemes", like sickness insurance schemes. (In the publication of the 10th and earlier inquiries, the receipts and expenditures of these social security schemes came under the heading "public health services", which are no longer in the tables.) Because the change affects the comparability of chronological series, a line has been inserted wherever appropriate in the tables in order to warn the reader.

III. Scope of the inquiry and of other statistical surveys

Various international or regional bodies collect and publish statistics in which social security, as defined for the purpose of the ILO inquiry, occupies a more or less important place depending on their objective.

1. United Nations System of National Accounts

The System of National Accounts (SNA) aims at providing a comprehensive and detailed framework for the systematic and integrated recording of all the flows and stocks of an economy. The social security financial operations presented in *The Cost of Social Security* are necessarily included in the various flows recorded in the SNA, although they may not all be classified under the heading "social security" as defined under that system. Under the new SNA "social security arrangements" are defined as follows:

> The social security arrangements to be included are those which are imposed, controlled or financed by the government. Schemes imposed by the government will involve compulsory contributions by employees and/or employers and cover the whole community or particular sections of the community. These arrangements may, in addition, allow certain sections of the community to join the scheme voluntarily. Schemes formulated by the government solely in its role as an employer of personnel, for example schemes which differ significantly from social security arrangements for the community or which are the subject of negotiation with government employees, are not to be included here. Such schemes are considered to be pension arrangements. Even if a scheme does not involve compulsory contributions imposed by the government, it should nevertheless be included as a part of general government services if, by way of public regulation and supervision, or by virtue of the existence of a system of government grants, the scheme clearly forms part of the social policy of the government in respect of the community as a whole.[6]

This definition covers to some extent the schemes classified under "social insurance and assimilated schemes" and "family benefits" in the ILO inquiry. Schemes for public employees (military and civilian) are, as far as pensions are concerned, included under "pension funds and other financial institutions" in the SNA; that category also includes private pension funds, which fall outside the scope of the ILO inquiry. Sick leave and other short-term benefits to public employees appear under "wages and salaries" in the SNA. "Public assistance" and "benefits for war victims" appear under "general public services".

2. Social protection statistics of the European Communities

The Statistical Office of the European Communities (EUROSTAT) carries out an annual survey on current expenditures relating to social protection benefits, within the framework of the European System of Integrated Social Protection Statistics (ESSPROS).[7] This system is fully coordinated with the European System of Integrated Economic Accounts.

Social protection benefits are defined as all benefits in cash and in kind provided to households through the intervention of a third party in respect of certain specified risks and contingencies, which extend beyond those covered by the ILO inquiry (e.g. benefits in respect of placement, vocational guidance, resettlement and housing are included). The EUROSTAT survey aims at measuring total social protection expenditure and at making it possible to analyse the destination of such expenditure and the way it is financed.

The survey distinguishes between basic schemes and complementary or supplementary schemes, and within each category it divides schemes into (1) national schemes, (2) general schemes, (3) special schemes and (4) voluntary schemes. Special schemes are further subdivided into: (i) statutory schemes, (ii) other occupational schemes, (iii) schemes in favour of victims of political events and natural disasters, and (iv) other special schemes. There is also a residual category, viz. schemes relating to other forms of social protection. The scope of the survey is somewhat wider than that of the ILO inquiry, in particular because of the inclusion of non-statutory schemes. It may be added, however, that a degree of coordination has been established between the ILO inquiry and the EUROSTAT survey, with a view to enabling the preparation of replies to the ILO questionnaire on the basis of the data furnished for the survey.

3. Nordic Statistics on Social Security

The Nordic Statistics on Social Security, published at two-yearly intervals since 1949 and covering the five Nordic countries (Denmark, Finland, Iceland, Norway and Sweden), are based on a definition which to some extent differs from that of the ILO inquiry: for example, these statistics include items such as safety and accident prevention services, employment and placement services, public works and retraining of the unemployed, advance payment of maintenance for children, and estimated tax relief in respect of children. On the other hand, the Nordic Statistics do not include schemes for public employees.

IV. Collection and presentation of data

On the basis of the replies submitted, together with data collected from various other national or international sources, the Office has been able to compile overall tables for a total of 113 countries, listed by region below. The eight countries that appear for the first time in this publication are shown in italics.

In accordance with the usual practice in ILO statistical publications, throughout the tables the name of each country appears in English, French or Spanish when the national language of the country, or the language commonly used in it, is one of the three; in other cases the name of the country is given in the language used in official correspondence between the country in question and the ILO. Appendix 2 provides a key to country names in the three languages.

The regions and countries covered in the tables are as follows:

Africa (33 countries): Benin, Burkina Faso, Burundi, Cameroon, Cape Verde, Central African Republic, Chad, Côte d'Ivoire, *Egypt*, Ethiopia, Gabon, Guinea, Guinea-Bissau, Kenya, Madagascar, Mali, Mauritania, Mauritius, Morocco, Mozambique, Niger, Nigeria, Rwanda, Sao Tome and Principe, Senegal, Sudan, Swaziland, the United Republic of Tanzania, Togo, *Tunisia*, Uganda, *Zaire* and Zambia.

America (28 countries): Argentina, Bahamas, Barbados, Belize, Bolivia, Brazil, Canada, Chile, Colombia, Costa Rica, Cuba, Dominica, *Dominican Republic*, Ecuador, El Salvador, Grenada, Guatemala, Guyana, Honduras, Jamaica, Mexico, Panama, Peru, Saint Lucia, Trinidad and Tobago, United States, Uruguay and Venezuela.

Asia (19 countries): Bahrain, Bangladesh, Cyprus, India, Indonesia, the Islamic Republic of Iran, Israel, Japan, Jordan, Kuwait, Malaysia, Myanmar, Pakistan, Philippines, *Qatar*, Singapore, Sri Lanka, *the Syrian Arab Republic* and Thailand.

Europe – market economy countries (20 countries): Austria, Belgium, Denmark, Finland, France, the Federal Republic of Germany,[8] Greece, *Iceland*, Ireland, Italy, Luxembourg, Malta, the Netherlands, Norway, Portugal, Spain, Sweden, Switzerland, Turkey and the United Kingdom.

Europe – centrally planned economy countries[9] (9 countries): Bulgaria, the Byelorussian Soviet Socialist Republic, Czechoslovakia, the German Democratic

Republic,[8] Hungary, *Poland*, the Ukrainian Soviet Socialist Republic, the Union of Soviet Socialist Republics and Yugoslavia.

Oceania (4 countries): Australia, Fiji, New Zealand and the Solomon Islands.

Every effort has been made to compile comprehensive data for each country. However, for some countries it was not possible to obtain information on certain schemes, in particular public employees' and workers' compensation schemes, and public assistance.

The basic tables [2] show which schemes and services have been included. In a few cases, where the information was not available for the current year, but was available for a previous year, an estimate was made on that basis. Attention has been drawn in the footnotes of table 1 to these countries and to others where it appears that the data provided are incomplete. In some cases the data for years prior to those covered by the current inquiry may not be strictly comparable with the data collected for this inquiry. This may be due to a change in the database or legislation. An example is Chile, where a new social insurance system has been introduced and a transition from the old social insurance system began in March 1981.

The collection of data on all the schemes and services covered creates a heavy burden for government departments, in particular because the various schemes are often administered by a number of different bodies under the supervision of different departments. Moreover, the coordination of the work entailed at the national level represents a considerable undertaking for the government department (usually the ministry of labour) responsible for relations with the ILO, especially if the administration of the various social security schemes is decentralised or run by provincial or local bodies.

Thus the collection of complete data takes a considerable time. The final data for most schemes are usually not available until about one-and-a-half to two years after the end of the year to which they relate, and sometimes a longer period is needed. For many countries the complete data are obtained by the ILO only after correspondence with the national authorities, and sometimes additional extensive research into national sources is necessary.

An electronic data processing system was developed to store and process the data from the 12th inquiry after verification. Data from previous rounds of the inquiry have been entered into the system. The opportunity has been taken to revise the calculations for previous years to take into account, in particular, revisions to the data on gross domestic product, population or price indices. The historical figures published in this edition may therefore differ slightly from the past editions of the inquiry.

The questionnaire which served as a basis for the inquiry requests governments to furnish data on receipts and expenditure according to the following framework:

Receipts	Expenditure
Contributions –	Medical care
from insured persons from employers	Benefits in kind other than for medical care
Levies and special taxes allocated to social security	Cash benefits
	Total benefits
State participation	Administrative expenses

Participation of other public authorities

Income from capital

Transfers from other schemes covered by the inquiry

Other receipts

Total receipts

Transfers to other schemes

Other expenditure

Total expenditure

The last column in the questionnaire should give the positive or negative difference between total receipts and expenditure.

The following comments may facilitate the interpretation of the data.

1. Receipts

Under "contributions from insured persons" and "contributions from employers" are included the amounts which are usually understood as such contributions. However, there are a number of borderline cases and cases where the distinction between the two types of contribution is not very clear. Social security contributions are very often paid by the employer, who then deducts the insured persons' contributions from their wages or salaries. It seems fairly clear that these two types of contribution should be classified in their respective columns. However, depending on the methods of accountancy employed, the type of contribution is not always specified, and therefore estimates have had to be made. This can easily be done with sufficient accuracy if the law specifies uniform rates of employers' and workers' contributions. It becomes more complicated when different rates are applied in respect of different categories of insured persons (e.g. by wage level or branch of insurance). Furthermore, if the scheme covers self-employed and unemployed persons or allows voluntary insurance (all cases in which the insured person has to pay the entire contribution), the task of distributing the amounts between the two columns becomes very difficult.

The two columns for contributions should in principle include any special taxes collected through the taxation machinery when they are deemed to be contributions rather than true taxes. For example, until 1968 in New Zealand there was a special social security income tax, which was entered in the column "contributions from insured persons". This tax was abolished by the Finance Act of 1968 and the financing made out of general revenue. Consequently, the amounts for financing the scheme are now entered in the column "state participation".

The social security schemes in Eastern European countries [9] are to a large extent financed out of the resources of enterprises or establishments. The sums involved are therefore entered in the column "contributions from employers". However, in the Byelorussian SSR, the Ukrainian SSR and the USSR as a whole, social security payments from state enterprises and state organisations are fully incorporated in the state budget, and the amounts concerned are entered, together with other payments from the State, in the column "state participation".

In many countries employment injury protection is based on the direct liability of the employer, who is legally responsible for the payment of benefits to any of his or her employees who suffer employment injuries. In that case the amount paid by the employer is entered in the column "contributions from employers". Insurance premiums paid by employers to insure their obligations

6

with an insurance company are similarly treated, irrespective of whether such insurance is voluntary or compulsory.

With regard to special schemes for public employees, the payments made by the State or other public authorities in their capacity as employers are considered to be employers' contributions for the purpose of this inquiry, and are therefore entered as such.

The column "levies and special taxes allocated to social security" should include taxes which cannot be assimilated to social security contributions but the proceeds of which are specifically earmarked for social security purposes. For example, in France the scheme for occupiers of agricultural holdings is partly financed by various resources of a semi-fiscal nature.

The two columns "state participation" and "participation of other public authorities" should include all payments made for the financing of social security by central and local governments respectively, irrespective of whether the payments take the form of part of the contributions in respect of all insured persons or of certain categories only, or of part of benefit expenditure or administrative expenses. For countries with a federal Constitution the "state participation" column includes the amounts spent by the federal government, whereas the receipts from constituent states or provincial governments are entered in the column "participation of other pubic authorities".

The column "income from capital" should in principle show interest on invested capital net of expenses relating to investments.

With a view to eliminating double-counting of transfers from one scheme to the other, two columns in the questionnaire relating to the inquiry apply to transfers between schemes. In the totals presented in this volume, such transfers are excluded. The data received in this respect are, however, noted in the basic tables.[2] In principle the totals of the two columns should be equal; however, owing to differences between the schemes as regards accounting procedures and financial years, this is not always the case and some differences (usually of a minor nature) may appear.

2. Expenditure

On the expenditure side a distinction has been made between medical care benefits, benefits in kind other than for medical care, and cash benefits.

In the column "medical care" all expenditure in respect of personal medical care (e.g. general practitioner and specialist care, hospital care (including treatment and board), pharmaceuticals, dental care, laboratory examinations, rehabilitation, provision of prosthetic appliances, etc.) is entered. The amounts relating to such benefits are entered under "medical care" irrespective of whether the benefits are in kind or in cash (e.g. reimbursement of medical care expenses borne directly by insured persons). Where the beneficiary has to bear part of the cost of medical care the amounts paid by the beneficiary towards cost-sharing, either directly to the person or service providing the care or to the social insurance institution reimbursing the cost, have been considered as being outside the scope of the inquiry and are consequently entered on neither the receipts nor the expenditure side.

A separate column for "benefits in kind other than for medical care" has been included as from the 8th inquiry, mainly to meet the needs of economic analysis. Numerous social security and social assistance and welfare schemes offer many types of services and benefits in kind which do not come under "medical care". For example, the family benefit schemes in many French-language countries in Africa provide a range of services and benefits under the heading of "health and welfare services" *(action sanitaire et sociale)*. These may take the form of medical care (operation of dispensaries and health centres for mothers and children, subsidies towards hospitalisation, etc.), benefits in kind (provision of milk and other foodstuffs, layettes, children's clothing) or services (nursery schools, children's holiday camps, housing). Again, in the Nordic countries certain benefits and services are provided under various social welfare schemes (old people's and pensioners' homes, home-help services, holidays for children and housewives, etc.). In the Eastern European countries also the social security schemes provide benefits such as recreational facilities, rest homes and health foods.

As regards "cash benefits", generally speaking there are no problems of classification. With regard to the column "total benefits", a problem arose in connection with benefits for migrant workers under bilateral or multilateral conventions and instruments. The procedures followed may vary from country to country, but as a rule the amounts concerned are shown as benefit payments for the country of the institution which has borne the cost of the payments, even though the actual payments may have been made through an institution in another country. The settlement between institutions and countries may result in a positive or negative difference which as a rule has been entered, as the case may be, in the columns "other receipts" or "other expenditure" respectively.

In the column "administrative expenses", the data may not always be accurate or complete. The administration of a social security scheme may be entrusted to a government department which also administers other schemes not coming within the scope of the ILO inquiry (as, for example, when unemployment insurance and placement services are administered by the same body and the method of accountancy employed does not make it possible to distinguish the administrative expenses relating to unemployment insurance). As regards public assistance, it is not always possible to distinguish between expenditure relating to benefits and expenditure on administration. In many cases only estimates can be given, and sometimes it is not even possible to make estimates. For some countries, therefore, the amounts entered in this column may not always give a complete and accurate picture of the administrative expenses, and caution should be exercised when interpreting the figures. The basic tables show the schemes and services for which administrative expenses have been included and those for which they were not available.[2]

The column for the difference between receipts and expenditure over the financial year should in principle represent, for each country, the net surplus or deficit of the total of all schemes and services included in the inquiry. However, it should be noted that the column may include allocations to technical reserves or guarantee or contingency funds.

3. Financial years

In the earlier publications, data were presented for the calendar year, or the financial year ending in the calendar year mentioned, irrespective of the number of months contained in the respective calendar year. In the present inquiry, data are presented for the calendar year, or the financial year of which the greater part falls in the calendar year concerned.

For some countries, however, the period covered may differ from one scheme to another. For example, a government financial year may differ from the calendar year and the data for some schemes and services may relate to the calendar year (usually the calendar year beginning in the financial year). For example, in Singapore the Government's financial year ends on 31 March, whereas for the Central Provident Fund the financial year coincides with the calendar year.

V. The comparative tables

The comparative tables consist mainly of a compilation of relative measures. As indicated above, the present volume follows the pattern set in the previous editions, in particular the listing of countries by region in order to facilitate comparison.

As a rule, data are given for the years 1970, 1975, 1980 and 1983-86. For some countries the data for the specific earlier years are not available, and in those cases the figures relate to the first year for which data are available or the year closest to 1970, 1975, 1980 or 1983.

The objective of the presentation of relative measures is, first, to show the trend of social security benefits and expenditure and their distribution within individual countries and, second, to make international comparisons. However, caution should be exercised when drawing conclusions from the figures in the tables since the relative measures are based on overall totals for each country.

There is much diversity in the degree of protection from country to country, and great variations within each country among sectors of the population covered. Hence an overall average is not an adequate measure of the social protection afforded, particularly in many developing countries, where the main items in the social security system that fall within the scope of this inquiry may be a social insurance scheme covering limited groups of the employed population (mainly in the modern sector) and a special scheme for public employees. Also, the economic, social, and political development and structure of different countries determine the development of their social security systems, and account for the substantial variations that exist as regards the nature and degree of social security protection given. Thus in one country the emphasis may be on sickness insurance, in another on pensions, and so on.

In many countries the social security system is not yet fully developed and, as the various elements determining the cost can differ basically between different branches of the system, the financial data set out in the present volume must be treated with reserve. For example, a sickness or employment injury insurance scheme covering substantial parts of the population may result in relatively low figures per head, and because limited or no funds have been accumulated, receipts and expenditure may be practically equal. On the other hand, a pension scheme with the same degree of protection may, because of the nature of the contingency, show much higher figures per head, and if the degree of funding is high there will be a substantial difference between receipts and expenditure.

Again, the cost of protection against a given contingency varies with the incidence: for example, a country with a high level of unemployment or which has suffered several epidemics and has thus incurred heavy expenditure on unemployment benefit or health services cannot be considered more advanced in social security – other things being equal – than another country in which the total cost of social security forms a smaller percentage of the gross domestic product simply because the level of unemployment is lower or the health situation more favourable.

It should also be noted that the definition of social security adopted for the purpose of the ILO inquiry may exclude important features of the social protection afforded to the population in some countries, particularly where a substantial part of the protection is provided through non-statutory schemes [10] or through schemes providing benefits of a statutory nature (payment of wages during sickness, medical care, maternity benefits) that are to be paid or provided directly by the employer and therefore do not come within the scope of the inquiry.

In some of the tables it has not been possible to include all the countries listed in the previous section. This is either because some of the basic data to which the social security figures are related (gross domestic product, population figures, etc.) are not available or because the necessary breakdowns are lacking. In some cases the figures for one or more years have been omitted because they are not comparable with the data for other years. For example, figures for Chad, Guinea and Guinea-Bissau could not be presented in table 3, because the relevant data on gross domestic product were not available; Benin and Cuba could not be included in table 6 because the data on cost-of-living indices were not available. Qatar is not included in tables 7 and 10 because only data on social assistance were provided. Whenever "100%" is indicated against one of the heads of classification in those tables which give a percentage distribution of receipts or expenditure (tables 7 to 10), caution should be exercised as this could be due to incomplete reporting.

Table 1: Total social security receipts and expenditure by main item (in millions of national currency units), pp. 40-71

The overall totals for the various columns of receipts and expenditure appearing in the questionnaire are shown in table 1, except for transfers from or to other schemes. As already explained, those amounts should in principle cancel each other out, and for the purpose of the comparative tables the net totals only, after deduction of transfers, should be taken into account. The significance of the figures in each column is explained in section IV above.

The figures enable one to trace the trends in the different kinds of receipts and expenditure, as well as in total receipts and expenditure, over the period of 17 years (1970-86) which in principle is covered by the tables. The figures are quoted in the monetary unit in use at the time of the last year covered by the inquiry. In cases where a country has had a reform of the currency in the period covered, the necessary conversions have been made.

The trends that can be discerned may be due to various factors which can work in the same or in opposite directions; these factors may be extensions of the scope of the social security schemes in terms of both persons covered and benefits provided, or they may result from the introduction of new schemes. As seen in appendix table 1, "National accounts data, population data, consumer price indices and exchange rates", the cost-of-living index has in most cases shown a rapid increase which is reflected in the amounts in table 1.

Other differences result from changes in administrative or financial arrangements, leading to sudden changes from one year to the other in the relative importance of the amounts in one or another column – for example, when a special tax assimilated to social security contributions has been discontinued and replaced by general revenue, this will be shown in the table as a sudden drop in, or complete disappearance of, the figures in the column "special taxes allocated to social security" and a corresponding increase of the amounts in the column "state participation". Further information on the reasons underlying the movements of the figures in table 1 may be deduced from the relative figures in later tables and the comments on them.

The main footnotes relating to the social security data for various countries are given in table 1 only and are not repeated in the other tables.

Table 2: Total social security receipts and expenditure (in millions of US dollars) pp. 72-78

For comparative purposes, this table gives an indication of total social security receipts, total expenditure and benefit expenditure in US dollars. The conversions are based on the exchange rates given in appendix table 1. The foreign exchange rates in units of national currency per US dollar refer to end-of-year period quotations taken from publications of the International Monetary Fund and the United Nations. In certain instances, where the rates are not given in these sources, country sources are used.

Attention is drawn to the limitation of such comparisons due to the practice of multiple exchange rate systems, e.g. in the USSR, or in countries where the currency unit changed over a period of years, e.g. Bolivia, Brazil, Israel and Peru.

Table 3: Receipts and expenditure of social security schemes (as percentages of gross domestic product in purchasers' values), pp. 79-85

Table 3 demonstrates the relative importance of social security in the national economy. The total receipts, total expenditure and expenditure on benefits (columns 10, 17 and 14 of table 1) have therefore been related to gross domestic product (GDP) or net material product (NMP) at current prices drawn as a rule from the United Nations *Yearbook of National Accounts Statistics* and given in appendix table 1. For countries whose financial years do not correspond to calendar years, the GDP or NMP for the calendar year where the greater part of the financial year falls has been used.

The GDP can be roughly defined as the total of the contributions to production of each resident producer. Since this measure includes indirect taxes net of subsidies, the resulting total is expressed in purchasers' values. Gross valuation implies that the consumption of fixed capital has not been deducted.[11]

The new System of National Accounts (SNA) was adopted by the Statistical Commission of the United Nations at its 15th Session, in 1968, and is a revision and extension of the earlier system expanded in a publication issued in 1953.[6] As a rule, the figures in table 3 are based on GDP according to the new system. In a few cases, only data produced under the old system are available; in such cases the fact is indicated in a note. Comparisons made for countries where data are available according to both the new and the old system

revealed very little difference between the total gross domestic products arrived at under the two systems. The variations between the two systems should therefore not affect the comparability of the data in table 3 to any substantial extent.

The system used in countries with centrally planned economies [9] (the system of Material Product Balances – MPS) differs basically from the SNA in that it aims primarily at measuring the production of goods in the so-called sphere of material production, i.e. excluding the non-material sphere, which is that of services. The aggregate generally used is the net material product, which is defined as the total net value of goods and productive services (including turnover taxes) produced by the economy. By productive or material services are understood services such as transport, storage, commodity circulation, etc., which are considered to be a continuation of material production.[11] The net material product does not include economic activities that do not contribute directly to material production, such as public administration and defence, personal and professional services and similar activities. Consequently, the figures in table 3 based on net material product according to the MPS are not comparable with those based on the GDP according to the SNA. As the latter aggregate includes a series of activities not included in the former, the cost of social security may be expected to constitute a somewhat higher proportion of the net material product than of the GDP.

Irrespective of whether in principle the figures are calculated in accordance with the SNA or the MPS, there are great variations between countries as regards the quality of the basic data, methods of estimating the value of the various elements entering into the calculations, and so on. The figures are also often subject to adjustments which may sometimes be substantial. Consequently, the figures given in this table should be interpreted with caution. In addition, and as already mentioned above, on the basis of the overall totals presented in this volume it is difficult to draw conclusions regarding, for example, the relative standard of protection in different countries, since such conclusions cannot be drawn from financial data alone.

Subject to those reservations and the limitations of comparability, the figures in table 3 indicate the relative magnitude of social security in the national economy within each country and in comparison with other countries and regions. In most countries there is no notable difference between the percentages based on receipts and those based on expenditure. There are, however, some countries where substantial differences may be noted; as explained in connection with table 1, they reflect the degree of capital accumulation of the social security system.

Tables 4 and 5: Average annual social security receipts and expenditure per head of population, pp. 86-95 and pp. 96-105

Whereas table 1 presents the receipts and expenditure for the schemes included in the inquiry in absolute figures for each country, in tables 4 and 5 total receipts, total expenditure and expenditure on benefits (columns 10, 17 and 14 of table 1) are related to the total population and the population aged between 15 and 64 years ("the working-age population"). The figures in table 4 are in national currency units. These are converted into US dollars in table 5 at the same exchange rates as those used in table 2 in order to facilitate international comparisons.

The figures on total population (given in appendix table 1) are based on the series of mid-year estimates or census figures. The sources are as a rule the United Nations *Demographic Yearbook* and recent issues of the United Nations *Monthly Bulletin of Statistics*. Data on the working-age population are generally not available on a year-to-year basis, and therefore recourse was had to estimates, by calculating the ratio of the estimated working-age population to the estimated total population at five-year intervals between 1970 and 1990 and then interpolating to obtain the intermediate values. For estimates of the ratio of the working-age population to the total population (medium variant) for interpolation, reference has been made to the United Nations publication, *Global Estimates and Projections of Population by Sex and Age, the 1988 Revision* (New York, 1989).

The reservations about overall averages expressed above should be borne in mind – in particular the fact that if the scope of protection is fairly limited, as is generally the case in the developing countries, an average per head of total population alone does not give a true indication of the average level of social security costs and benefits for the persons covered by the scheme.

The main use of these tables is to make it possible to discern national trends in social security receipts and expenditure when the effect of demographic increase has been eliminated. Thus, if the increases in table 4 and table 1 are compared it can be seen how demographic trends and structure affect the data. The most interesting exercise, however, is to discern the rate at which social security costs have progressed as compared with population figures. It should be repeated that the figures are influenced by several factors including, in particular, the rise in the cost of living during the period covered.

Table 6: Indices of annual average benefit expenditure per head of the total population (values adjusted according to cost-of-living indices), pp. 106-108

Mention has just been made of the effect that the rise in the cost of living has on the figures per head, which makes it rather difficult, and in some cases practically impossible, to compare figures based on national currency units. To improve comparability, the average annual amounts of benefit expenditure per head of the total population (in column 5 of table 4 and column 5 of table 5) have been deflated by the consumer price indices, and a series of indices has been calculated on the basis of the year 1980. The exclusion of medical care provided under the public health services in the latest three inquiries requires, however, the establishment of two different series for the countries affected. Thus countries with consistent data throughout have a single series of indices with 1980 as the base year; countries with a break of continuity due to the exclusion of public health services have two series: the old series based on data including public health services, with 1970 as the base year, and the new series without public health services, with 1980 as the base year. In either case, if data for the base year (i.e. 1970 or 1980) are not available, the nearest year for which data are available is taken as the base year. The new series is separated from the old one by a vertical bar.

The figures for the consumer price indices used for these calculations are given in appendix table 1. As a rule these are the general indices for all groups published in the ILO *Year Book of Labour Statistics*, the quarterly ILO *Bulletin of Labour Statistics* and the *International Financial Statistics Yearbook* of the International Monetary Fund.

When examining the data in this table, and in particular when making inter-country comparisons, the explanation of the concept of the consumer price indices given in the *Year Book of Labour Statistics* should be kept in mind:

> The consumer price indices are designed to show changes over time in the price level of certain goods and services which are selected as representatives of the consumption patterns of the population concerned. ... The method employed in calculating the indices varies somewhat from one country to another. ... The weights, which represent the relative importance of each item, are usually derived from family expenditure surveys conducted to obtain the pattern of consumer expenditure and the relative importance of each item for a particular population group. ... Owing to differences in scope and in methods used for the compilation of the indices, the statistics for the different countries shown are not uniformly representative of changes in price levels and vary in reliability from one country to another.[12]

It may also be added that the consumption pattern relating to social security benefits may differ substantially from that on which the consumer price index is based. Furthermore, the latter may be based on consumption and prices in certain locations (often the capital of the country), whereas the social security data relate in principle to the whole country.

Table 7: Distribution of social security benefit expenditure among the different schemes (as percentages of total benefit expenditure), pp. 109-122

Table 7 shows the distribution of social security benefit expenditure among different types of scheme. It illustrates the differences in the relative importance of the different types of scheme in various countries, as well as the changes that may have occurred within each country over the period under review. The schemes covered are the same as in the previous edition, namely social insurance and assimilated schemes; family allowances; special schemes for public employees; public assistance and assimilated schemes; and war victims.

It is not always easy to distinguish between the various types of scheme, as in some countries the same institution may operate schemes that fall under two or more headings, without there being any possibility of separating the data. For example, in most of the Eastern European countries there are integrated social security schemes covering social insurance and social assistance, and sometimes war victims as well.

There are no specific criteria for classifying a scheme under one or other of the main types but certain practices have developed over the years.

Non-contributory pension (or other benefit) schemes have been included under "social insurance and assimilated schemes" rather than under "public assistance and assimilated schemes", even though the payment of all or part of the benefits may be subject to a means test. It was felt that for the purposes of international comparison this procedure was more appropriate, as in many cases the non-contributory benefits form an integral part of a general contributory system (e.g. supplements granted subject to a means test in addition to the general contributory benefits), while in others the entire system is on a non-contributory basis.

Employment injury compensation schemes based on private insurance or on the principle of the direct liability of the employer have also been included under "social insurance and assimilated schemes".

Under "special schemes for public employees" are included the schemes for such employees which are distinct from the general or other specific social security schemes. When public employees are covered by the general scheme, as in Finland and Sweden, the respective data are included under "social insurance and assimilated schemes".

It should be noted that the column "public health services" has been maintained only to present data prior to the 11th inquiry; this column has been blocked by the symbol "x" wherever it does not apply. Schemes providing medical care to the entire population as of right, which remain within the scope of the inquiry, are grouped under "social insurance and assimilated schemes".

Since the figures are expressed as percentages of the total, increases under one heading may be accompanied by decreases under another even though the benefit expenditure under the second heading may show an increase in absolute terms. Other changes have occurred because the data available were more complete than in earlier inquiries, or conversely because data available for previous inquiries were not provided for the present one; in the latter case, wherever appropriate, in order to provide at least the order of magnitude, the figure for the last year available has been repeated, and this has been indicated in a footnote. Again, some changes may be attributed to changes in legislation or improvement of benefits.

Table 8: Distribution of social security receipts according to origin (as percentages of total receipts), pp. 123-136

Table 8 shows how the national social security system, as defined for the purpose of the inquiry, is financed in each country. It shows the distribution of receipts by origin, expressed as percentages of the total, and indicates the changes in that distribution during the period covered.

The reservations expressed in connection with table 7 regarding increases and decreases in relative figures and the completeness of the data are equally valid here. Other changes may be due to modified accounting procedures or to the use of different sources of information.

Table 9: Distribution of receipts relating to social insurance and assimilated schemes and family allowances (as percentages of total receipts), pp. 137-149

Whereas table 8 related to the entire social security system, as defined for the purpose of the inquiry, table 9 gives the same information regarding only the schemes classified under the two main headings "social insurance and assimilated schemes" and "family allowances". A number of countries do not have family allowance schemes or did not provide the relevant data; the fact is indicated in footnotes. It should be noted that this table includes data in respect of public employees in so far as they are covered by the general social security schemes, as in Finland and Sweden.

Table 10: Distribution of benefit expenditure by social security branch, relating to schemes classified under the headings "social insurance and assimilated schemes" and "family allowances" (as percentages of total benefit expenditure), pp. 150-169

In order to make it possible to rearrange the data on the cost of social security by risk or contingency, the questionnaire requested governments to break down the data for each scheme or service by branch of social security, following the classification adopted for the various parts of the Social Security (Minimum Standards) Convention, 1952 (No. 102). This rearrangement is given in table 10. Its scope is the same as that of table 9 (i.e. social insurance and assimilated schemes and family allowances). It is difficult to rearrange the data for the schemes classified under "special schemes for public employees" (in the countries of Eastern Europe and a few others the data pertaining to them are included under the item "social insurance and assimilated schemes" and they are not separable from them), "public assistance and assimilated schemes" and "benefits for war victims". The table is limited to benefit expenditure only.

Although data were requested for all nine branches of social security as classified in Convention No. 102, it was found preferable to break the data down by five main branches, namely sickness-maternity, employment injury, pensions, unemployment benefit and family allowances. These main branches correspond in large measure to the administrative and financial organisation of a great number of social security schemes. For these five branches benefit expenditure is expressed as percentages of total benefit expenditure for all the schemes and services coming within the scope of the table, with a breakdown by kind of benefit for sickness-maternity and employment injury. With regard to the classification by branch, it may be noted that "provident funds" and "death grants" have been classified under "pensions". Sometimes the data provided overlapped two or more branches and were not separable; in this case the data were shown against one of the branches concerned and noted in a footnote.

In many countries it was not possible to draw a clear-cut line between the various branches, and benefits which are classified under one branch in one country may be classified under another branch in another country. Numerous examples could be quoted,[13] and obviously the comparability of the figures is affected. Where the effect is serious the fact is mentioned in a note.

As regards special schemes which generally provide the whole range of social security benefits and for which no breakdowns were available, the data were classified under the heading where previous experience had shown that the main part of the benefits belong (in most cases this was under the heading "pensions"). This heading is therefore overestimated, with corresponding underestimation for other headings.

Exceptionally, it has not always been possible to separate the figures relating to schemes which come within the scope of this particular table because of the manner in which the reply to the inquiry was provided.

In spite of some unavoidable inconsistency in presentation, which calls for caution in interpretation, the table does provide information on the overall structure of the social security system in the different countries, the relative importance attached to individual branches of social security and the stage of development they have reached. To permit an assessment of the importance of the schemes, the absolute amount of benefit expenditure in millions of national currency units is shown in column 14.

VI. Appendix tables

1. National accounts data, population data, consumer price indices and exchange rates, pp. 172-181

The reference data used in the comparative tables are given for each country.

2. Key to country names in three languages, pp. 182-183

Notes

[1] For a summary of the activities of the International Labour Office in this field before the Second World War see International Social Security Association (ISSA): *The Cost of Social Security, 1949-1951: International Inquiry prepared by the International Labour Office* (Geneva, ILO, 1955).

The results of the previous inquiries have been published as follows:

First inquiry: "The cost of social security", in *International Labour Review* (Geneva, ILO), June 1952, pp. 726-791, and "A comparative analysis of the cost of social security", ibid., Mar. 1953, pp. 292-303;

Second inquiry: ISSA: *The Cost of Social Security, 1949-1951...*, op. cit., and ILO: *The financing of social security*, Report III, First European Regional Conference, Geneva, 1955;

Third inquiry: ILO: *The Cost of Social Security, 1949-1954* (Geneva, 1958);

Fourth inquiry: idem: *The Cost of Social Security, 1949-1957* (Geneva, 1961);

Fifth inquiry: idem: *The Cost of Social Security, 1958-1960* (Geneva, 1964);

Sixth inquiry: idem: *The Cost of Social Security: Sixth international inquiry, 1961-1963* (Geneva, 1967);

Seventh inquiry: idem: *The Cost of Social Security: Seventh international inquiry, 1964-1966, with a supplement on the scope of social security schemes* (Geneva, 1972);

Eighth inquiry: idem: *The Cost of Social Security: Eighth international inquiry, 1967-1971, with a supplement on the cost of non-statutory schemes* (Geneva, 1976), and *The Cost of Social Security: Eighth international inquiry, 1967-1971: Basic tables* (Geneva, 1976);

Ninth inquiry: idem: *The Cost of Social Security: Ninth international inquiry, 1972-1974* (Geneva, 1979), and *The Cost of Social Security: Ninth international inquiry, 1972-1974: Basic tables* (Geneva, 1978);

Tenth inquiry: idem: *The Cost of Social Security: Tenth international inquiry, 1975-1977* (Geneva, 1981), and *The Cost of Social Security: Tenth international inquiry, 1975-1977: Basic tables* (Geneva, 1981);

Eleventh inquiry: idem: *The Cost of Social Security: Eleventh international inquiry, 1978-1980* (Geneva, 1985), and *The Cost of Social Security: Eleventh international inquiry, 1978-1980: Basic tables* (Geneva, 1985).

Twelfth inquiry: idem.: *The Cost of Social Security: Twelfth international inquiry, 1981-1983: Comparative tables* (Geneva, 1988), and *The Cost of Social Security: Twelfth international inquiry, 1981-1983: Basic tables* (Geneva, 1988).

[2] ILO: *The Cost of Social Security: Thirteenth international inquiry, 1984-1986: Basic tables, main volume* (Geneva, 1990), and *Supplementary volume* (Geneva, 1991).

[3] idem: *Report of the Committee of Experts on Social Security* (Geneva, 26 Nov.-3 Dec. 1975) (doc. CSSE/D.14.1975 (Rev.); mimeographed), Annex II: "Second item on the agenda: Social security indicators: First appraisal of their development".

[4] Special schemes for public employees are social security schemes or arrangements for these employees, separate from the general and other specific social security schemes. For the purpose of this inquiry, public employees are those who work in public administration and in public education, health, social and cultural services. Both civilian and military employees are to be included.

[5] See ILO: *The Cost of Social Security: Eleventh international inquiry...*, op. cit., p. 3.

[6] United Nations, Department of Economic and Social Affairs, Statistical Office: *A system of national accounts*, Studies in methods, Series F, No. 2, Rev. 3 (New York, 1968; Sales No. E.69.XVII.3), p. 75, para. 5.27.

[7] See Statistical Office of the European Communities: *European System of Integrated Social Protection Statistics: Methodology*, Vol. I (Luxembourg, 1981; ISBN 92-825-2066-8).

[8] Data refer to the period 1970-86 before the reunification of Germany in 1990.

[9] Data refer to the period 1970-86 when the economies of these countries were still of a centrally planned nature. The country names used are those which were current during the period in question.

[10] See ILO: *The Cost of Social Security: Eighth international inquiry...*, op. cit., supplement.

[11] United Nations, Department of Economic and Social Affairs, Statistical Office: *Yearbook of National Accounts Statistics, 1981*, 3 vols. (New York, 1981; Sales No. E.83.XVII.3), and earlier issues; the definitions cited are in Vol. I, pp. XV and XVII.

[12] For further details of the contents and methods of computation of the consumer price indices, see the various explanatory notes in ILO: *Year Book of Labour Statistics, 1981*, p. 511, as well as the various specialised publications quoted in it.

[13] See ILO: *The Cost of Social Security: Seventh international inquiry...*, op. cit., p. 10.

INTRODUCTION

Cette partie présente les résultats de la treizième enquête internationale sur le coût de la sécurité sociale menée par le BIT depuis la fin de la seconde guerre mondiale [1].

I. Objet de l'enquête

Les enquêtes du BIT doivent permettre, d'une part, de dresser, par pays, un état complet et coordonné des opérations financières de tous les régimes de sécurité sociale qui entrent dans leur champ; d'autre part, de procéder à une comparaison internationale des données montrant notamment l'évolution des recettes et des dépenses pendant la période considérée, la répartition des recettes d'après leur provenance et la répartition des dépenses selon les régimes. Pour que l'on puisse juger de l'importance de la sécurité sociale dans l'économie des pays, les données sont rapportées à différents agrégats de la comptabilité nationale et aux données démographiques.

De même que pour les cinq dernières enquêtes, l'ensemble des résultats fait l'objet de deux publications distinctes: les tableaux comparatifs inclus dans le présent volume et les tableaux de base publiés séparément.

Ce volume présente une comparaison internationale des données et suit le modèle des dernières éditions, notamment dans le regroupement des pays par région en vue de faciliter les comparaisons. Il comprend cependant deux nouveaux tableaux, donnant les recettes et les dépenses de la sécurité sociale de tous les pays dans une même monnaie: le dollar des Etats-Unis.

Les tableaux de base présentent des données statistiques détaillées, en chiffres absolus non agrégés, sur les recettes et les dépenses des régimes de sécurité sociale pour chacun des pays couverts par l'enquête. Ces tableaux sont publiés cette fois en deux volumes (volume principal, comprenant quatre-vingt-un pays, et supplément, comprenant trente-deux pays), uniquement en anglais. On peut se les procurer auprès du Département de la sécurité sociale du BIT [2].

Les résultats de l'enquête complémentaire sur les régimes spéciaux des agents de l'Etat sont donnés dans quatre tableaux distincts à la fin du présent volume.

Compte tenu de l'importance prise par la sécurité sociale dans l'économie de presque tous les pays, il est d'un grand intérêt de pouvoir disposer de séries statistiques précises, homogènes et complètes sur les transferts sociaux. Cette publication, ainsi que les tableaux de base qui l'accompagnent, répond à cet objectif.

Il est également nécessaire de disposer de statistiques détaillées de la sécurité sociale pour l'élaboration d'indicateurs sociaux. Quant à la sécurité sociale, on a besoin d'indicateurs, d'une part, aux fins générales de la planification économique et sociale, en particulier dans le cadre d'un système intégré d'indicateurs sociaux, d'autre part, dans le domaine même de la sécurité sociale, pour formuler la politique générale, élaborer les plans, prendre les décisions et les évaluer [3].

II. Champ de l'enquête

Pour sauvegarder la comparabilité directe des données recueillies au cours de la treizième enquête et de celles qui ont été recueillies lors des enquêtes antérieures, on a conservé avec le minimum de modifications les définitions et les méthodes adoptées jusqu'ici.

Le champ de l'enquête doit permettre d'obtenir, pour chaque pays, une image aussi complète que possible des recettes et des dépenses de la sécurité sociale, c'est-à-dire des régimes ou services qui répondent aux critères suivants:

1) le système doit avoir pour objet:

 a) soit d'accorder des soins médicaux curatifs ou préventifs;

 b) soit de garantir les moyens d'existence en cas de perte involontaire du revenu du travail ou d'une partie importante de celui-ci;

 c) soit encore d'accorder un revenu supplémentaire aux personnes ayant des charges de famille;

2) le système doit être institué par un acte législatif qui attribue des droits individuels déterminés ou qui impose des obligations définies à un organisme public, paraétatique ou autonome;

3) le système doit être administré par un organisme public, paraétatique ou autonome.

Toutefois, les régimes de réparation des accidents du travail et des maladies professionnelles sont englobés dans l'enquête même s'ils ne répondent pas au critère 3 lorsque la réparation est directement imposée à l'employeur.

1. Régimes couverts par l'enquête

De l'application des critères indiqués ci-dessus, il résulte que l'enquête couvre d'une manière générale les types de régimes suivants:

i) régimes d'assurance sociale obligatoire;

ii) régimes d'assurance sociale volontaire ou facultative, s'ils satisfont au critère 2 ci-dessus;

iii) régimes universels non contributifs;

iv) fonds de prévoyance, dans les limites du critère 3 ci-dessus;

v) régimes de responsabilité de l'employeur en matière d'accidents du travail et de maladies professionnelles;

vi) régimes de prestations familiales;

vii) services nationaux de santé établis par la loi et assurant des services et des prestations déterminés à tous les citoyens;

viii) régimes spéciaux pour les agents publics (retraite, prestations familiales, prestations de maladie, prestations en cas d'accidents du travail ou de maladies professionnelles), contributifs ou non [4];

ix) assistance publique, dans les limites du critère 1 ci-dessus;

13

x) prestations aux victimes de guerre, dans les limites du critère 1 ci-dessus;

xi) régimes applicables à certaines branches d'activité ou à certaines professions ou régimes établis par voie d'accord entre employeurs et travailleurs, à condition que les obligations qui en découlent pour les employeurs aient été sanctionnées par la loi et que ces régimes répondent aux critères 1, 2 et 3 ci-dessus.

L'enquête laisse de côté les régimes de prestations servies directement par l'employeur au titre de la maladie, de la maternité, de la retraite, etc., même si ces prestations sont instituées par la loi. L'exception faite en ce qui concerne la réparation des accidents du travail et des maladies professionnelles (voir rubrique v) ci-dessus) s'explique par le fait qu'il s'agit là de la branche la plus ancienne de la sécurité sociale, sur laquelle la quasi-totalité des pays ont légiféré et pour laquelle, d'un point de vue pratique, il a été possible d'obtenir de la plupart des pays des données significatives du fait qu'il existe habituellement des procédures et des organismes assurant l'application de la législation. Il en va moins souvent ainsi dans le cas des autres prestations qui sont de la responsabilité de l'employeur. Enfin, dans les pays où l'assurance sociale est introduite par paliers successifs, la législation qui régit la réparation des accidents du travail et des maladies professionnelles reste en vigueur dans les régions, les secteurs d'activité et les entreprises qui ne sont pas encore intégrés au système d'assurance sociale; si l'on ne prenait pas en compte les prestations payables en vertu de la responsabilité incombant à l'employeur, les données sur les prestations au titre des accidents du travail et des maladies professionnelles se trouveraient incomplètes et comporteraient une distorsion.

Certes, on peut en dire autant d'autres prestations de la sécurité sociale, mais il est moins courant que ces prestations résultent d'une obligation imposée à l'employeur, et les problèmes pratiques qui se posent lorsqu'on veut obtenir des données sont plus difficiles à résoudre. Il convient cependant d'avoir à l'esprit que, dans certains cas, les paiements effectués directement par les employeurs peuvent représenter des montants importants, par exemple lorsqu'il s'agit du versement du salaire en cas de maladie ou du versement d'indemnités de départ. Il faut noter, d'autre part, que, lorsque les prestations de ce genre sont payées directement par des organismes publics à leurs salariés, elles entrent effectivement dans le champ de l'enquête.

Les régimes de protection sociale les plus importants qui se trouvent éliminés de l'enquête par l'application des trois critères indiqués ci-dessus sont probablement les régimes privés, c'est-à-dire ceux qui ne sont pas établis en vertu de la loi et qui offrent une protection contre les éventualités courantes conformément au critère 1, par exemple les régimes privés de pensions ou les régimes d'entreprise pour les soins médicaux. Ces régimes peuvent représenter parfois une part importante des ressources consacrées à la sécurité sociale. L'extension prise dans certains pays par les régimes privés de protection sociale des salariés qui complètent les régimes légaux signifie que les chiffres donnés dans le présent volume pour des pays comme les Etats-Unis ou le Royaume-Uni sont sensiblement inférieurs à la réalité.

2. Définition des prestations

La définition des prestations qui résulte du critère 1 ci-dessus est conforme à celle qui est donnée dans la convention (n° 102) concernant la sécurité sociale (norme minimum), 1952, laquelle distingue neuf régimes de sécurité sociale:

1) soins médicaux (partie II);
2) indemnités de maladie (partie III);
3) prestations de chômage (partie IV);
4) prestations de vieillesse (partie V);
5) prestations en cas d'accidents du travail et de maladies professionnelles (partie VI);
6) prestations aux familles (partie VII);
7) prestations de maternité (partie VIII);
8) prestations d'invalidité (partie IX);
9) prestations de survivants (partie X).

Cette définition des prestations ne correspond pas toujours à celle qui est appliquée dans les systèmes nationaux des pays soumis à l'enquête, la sécurité sociale englobant, dans un certain nombre d'entre eux, des prestations au titre d'autres éventualités. Dans la mesure du possible, il n'est pas fait état des prestations de ce genre dans les tableaux. Tel est le cas, par exemple, pour Israël et pour la Suisse, où des indemnités spéciales sont payables pour compenser le manque à gagner pendant le service militaire.

En revanche, l'enquête tient compte de certains régimes qui ne relèvent pas de la sécurité sociale proprement dite mais qui fournissent des prestations ou des services à des personnes qui, sans cela, devraient avoir recours à la sécurité sociale. On citera à titre d'exemple le régime d'indemnités d'emploi protégé en vigueur en Australie et le régime de même nature institué aux Pays-Bas.

Reste enfin le cas de certaines prestations et de certains services qui, bien que ne relevant pas de la définition de la sécurité sociale établie par la convention n° 102, sont pris en compte dans l'enquête pour des raisons d'ordre pratique, car il serait trop difficile, voire impossible, de les isoler dans les statistiques des institutions de sécurité sociale qui administrent ces régimes. Citons, à titre d'exemples, les prestations payables en cas de difficultés imprévues en Nouvelle-Zélande, notamment celles qui sont accordées aux épouses abandonnées, ainsi que les indemnités de loisirs et d'entraînement physique payables en URSS et dans divers pays de l'Europe de l'Est. Dans l'ensemble, le fait de tenir compte de prestations et de services qui ne rentrent pas, à proprement parler, dans le champ de l'enquête ne modifie pas sensiblement les totaux afférents aux régimes et aux branches considérés.

3. Soins médicaux antérieurement libellés «services publics de santé»

A partir de l'exercice 1978 (première année de la onzième enquête 1978-1980), les soins médicaux fournis au titre de la santé publique n'ont plus été retenus dans l'enquête. Les données correspondantes ne figurent donc plus dans les tableaux comparatifs [5].

Il ne faut pas confondre, toutefois, les soins divers fournis au titre de la santé publique et les soins médicaux assurés par des régimes de sécurité sociale qui couvrent l'ensemble de la population, en vertu d'un droit consacré par la loi, souvent sur une base contributive. Tel est le cas du Service national de santé au Royaume-Uni, du Service sanitaire national en Italie ou des régimes analogues qui fonctionnent, par exemple, dans les pays de l'Est de l'Europe. Ces régimes ont été inclus dans le champ de l'enquête dans la rubrique «assurances sociales et régimes assimilés», au même titre que les régimes d'assurance maladie (dans les publications antérieures à la onzième enquête, les recettes et les dépenses de ces régimes de sécurité sociale figuraient sous la rubrique «services publics de santé», désormais supprimée dans les tableaux). Le changement décidé se répercutant sur la comparabilité des séries historiques, une ligne de séparation figure dans les tableaux aux endroits appropriés, de façon que l'utilisateur en soit averti.

III. Champ de l'enquête du BIT et champ d'autres enquêtes statistiques

Diverses organisations internationales ou régionales établissent et publient des statistiques dans lesquelles la sécurité sociale, telle qu'elle est définie pour l'enquête du BIT, occupe une place plus ou moins importante selon l'objectif visé.

1. Le Système de comptabilité nationale des Nations Unies (SCN)

Le SCN vise à fournir un cadre complet et détaillé pour l'enregistrement systématique et intégré des flux et des stocks d'une économie. Les opérations financières de la sécurité sociale présentées dans *Le coût de la sécurité sociale* font nécessairement partie des différents flux enregistrés dans le SCN, même si elles n'entrent pas toutes dans la rubrique «sécurité sociale» prévue dans ce système. Dans le nouveau SCN, les «régimes de sécurité sociale» sont définis en ces termes:

Les régimes de sécurité sociale qui doivent être compris... sont ceux qui sont imposés, contrôlés ou financés par l'Etat. Les régimes imposés par l'Etat exigent des cotisations obligatoires des salariés et (ou) des employeurs; ils s'appliquent à l'ensemble de la collectivité ou à des groupes particuliers. Ces régimes peuvent, de plus, admettre la participation volontaire d'autres groupes de la collectivité. Les systèmes adoptés par les administrations publiques uniquement à titre d'employeurs – par exemple ceux qui diffèrent notablement du régime général ou qui font l'objet de négociations avec le personnel de l'Etat – ne rentrent pas dans cette catégorie. De tels systèmes doivent être considérés comme des systèmes de pensions. Même si l'Etat n'impose le paiement d'aucune cotisation, un régime devra néanmoins figurer dans les branches non marchandes des administrations publiques si, en raison de la réglementation et du contrôle officiels ou d'un jeu de subventions, ce régime est manifestement l'expression de la politique sociale envers l'ensemble de la collectivité [6].

Cette définition couvre dans une certaine mesure les régimes classés sous «assurances sociales et régimes assimilés» et «prestations familiales» de l'enquête du BIT. Les régimes destinés aux agents publics (civils et militaires) figurent, en ce qui concerne du moins les pensions, sous la rubrique «caisses de pensions et autres institutions financières» du SCN; cette rubrique englobe également les caisses de pensions privées, qui ne sont pas comprises dans l'enquête du BIT. Les congés de maladie et les autres prestations à court terme dont bénéficient les agents publics figurent sous «traitements et salaires» dans le SCN. L'«assistance publique» et les «prestations aux victimes de guerre» sont rangées sous la rubrique «services publics généraux».

2. Les statistiques de la protection sociale des Communautés européennes

L'Office statistique des Communautés européennes (Eurostat) entreprend chaque année une enquête sur les dépenses courantes de protection sociale dans le cadre du Système européen de statistiques intégrées de la protection sociale (SESPROS) [7]. Ce système est coordonné avec le Système européen de comptes économiques intégrés.

Les prestations de protection sociale comprennent toutes les prestations en espèces ou en nature versées aux ménages grâce à l'intervention d'un tiers pour la couverture de certains risques, éventualités ou besoins. La gamme en est plus étendue que dans l'enquête du BIT (les «fonctions de protection sociale» comprennent par exemple le placement, l'orientation, la mobilité et le logement). Le système a notamment pour objet de fournir une mesure globale des dépenses de protection sociale ainsi que des décompositions qui permettent de les analyser du point de vue de leur destination et de celui des conditions de leur financement.

Les régimes sont classés en régimes de base et en régimes complémentaires ou supplémentaires. Dans chacune de ces deux catégories, ils se répartissent en: 1) régimes nationaux; 2) régimes généraux; 3) régimes spéciaux; 4) régimes volontaires. Les régimes spéciaux sont subdivisés eux-mêmes en: *a)* régimes statutaires; *b)* autres régimes professionnels; *c)* régimes en faveur de victimes d'événements politiques ou de calamités naturelles; *d)* autres régimes spéciaux. Le système englobe en outre une troisième catégorie de régimes: les régimes d'autres actions de protection sociale. Le champ de l'enquête est plus étendu que celui de l'enquête du BIT, en raison notamment de la prise en compte de régimes qui n'ont pas une base légale. Une certaine coordination a pu être instaurée cependant entre les deux enquêtes, afin qu'il soit possible de répondre au questionnaire du BIT à partir des données fournies pour l'enquête Eurostat.

3. Statistiques de la sécurité sociale des pays nordiques

Les statistiques de la sécurité sociale des pays nordiques, publiées tous les deux ans depuis 1949, concernent les cinq pays nordiques (Danemark, Finlande, Islande, Norvège, Suède) et sont fondées sur une définition qui s'écarte dans une certaine mesure de celle qui est utilisée pour l'enquête du BIT. Elles comprennent par exemple des postes tels que les services de sécurité et de prévention des accidents, les services de l'emploi et du placement, les travaux publics et le recyclage pour les chômeurs, les avances pour l'entretien des enfants (en cas de défaut de paiement des pensions alimentaires) et les exonérations fiscales au titre des enfants. Elles ne tiennent pas compte, par contre, des régimes destinés aux agents publics.

IV. Rassemblement et présentation des données

A partir des réponses reçues et de données provenant de différentes sources nationales ou internationales, le BIT a été en mesure d'établir des tableaux synthétiques pour un total de cent treize pays, qui sont énumérés ci-dessous, groupés par région. Les noms des huit pays qui figurent pour la première fois dans la présente publication sont en italique.

Conformément à la pratique suivie par le Bureau dans ses publications statistiques, les noms des pays sont donnés en anglais, en français ou en espagnol lorsque la langue nationale du pays ou la langue usuellement utilisée est une de ces trois langues; dans les autres cas, le nom est donné dans la langue utilisée dans la correspondance officielle entre le pays et le BIT. On trouvera dans le tableau 2 de l'annexe l'index des noms des pays dans les trois langues.

15

Les régions et les pays apparaissant dans les tableaux sont les suivants:

Afrique (trente-trois pays): Bénin, Burkina Faso, Burundi, Cameroun, Cap-Vert, République centrafricaine, Côte d'Ivoire, *Egypte*, Ethiopie, Gabon, Guinée, Guinée-Bissau, Kenya, Madagascar, Mali, Maroc, Maurice, Mauritanie, Mozambique, Niger, Nigéria, Ouganda, Rwanda, Sao Tomé-et-Principe, Sénégal, Soudan, Swaziland, République-Unie de Tanzanie, Tchad, Togo, *Tunisie*, *Zaïre*, Zambie;

Amérique (vingt-huit pays): Argentine, Bahamas, Barbade, Belize, Bolivie, Brésil, Canada, Chili, Colombie, Costa Rica, Cuba, *République dominicaine*, Dominique, El Salvador, Equateur, Etats-Unis, Grenade, Guatemala, Guyana, Honduras, Jamaïque, Mexique, Panama, Pérou, Sainte-Lucie, Trinité-et-Tobago, Uruguay, Venezuela;

Asie (dix-neuf pays): Bahreïn, Bangladesh, Chypre, Inde, Indonésie, République islamique d'Iran, Israël, Japon, Jordanie, Koweït, Malaisie, Myanmar, Pakistan, Philippines, *Qatar*, Singapour, Sri Lanka, *République arabe syrienne*, Thaïlande;

Europe: pays à économie de marché (vingt pays): République fédérale d'Allemagne [8], Autriche, Belgique, Danemark, Espagne, Finlande, France, Grèce, Irlande, *Islande*, Italie, Luxembourg, Malte, Norvège, Pays-Bas, Portugal, Royaume-Uni, Suède, Suisse, Turquie;

Europe: pays à économie planifiée [9] (neuf pays): RSS de Biélorussie, Bulgarie, Hongrie, *Pologne*, République démocratique allemande [8], Tchécoslovaquie, RSS d'Ukraine, URSS, Yougoslavie;

Océanie (quatre pays): Australie, Fidji, Iles Salomon, Nouvelle-Zélande.

Tous les efforts ont été faits pour rassembler des données complètes pour chaque pays. Cependant, pour plusieurs, il n'a pas été possible d'obtenir des informations sur certains régimes, notamment les régimes des agents publics, les régimes de réparation des accidents du travail et des maladies professionnelles et les régimes d'assistance publique.

Les tableaux de base indiquent quels sont les régimes et les services dont il a été tenu compte [2]. Dans quelques cas, lorsque les données n'étaient pas disponibles pour l'année en cours mais l'étaient pour une année précédente, une estimation a été faite à partir de ces données. Les notes du tableau 1 signalent ces pays ainsi que d'autres pour lesquels les données fournies paraissent incomplètes. Dans certains cas, il peut arriver que les données relatives aux années précédant la période couverte par la treizième enquête ne soient pas exactement comparables aux données recueillies pour celle-ci, ce qui peut être dû à un changement dans la base des données ou à des modifications de la législation. Le Chili en est un exemple: dans ce pays, un nouveau système d'assurances sociales a été introduit, avec une phase de transition à partir de mars 1981.

Le rassemblement de données sur l'ensemble des régimes et des services considérés impose une lourde tâche aux administrations nationales, d'autant que les divers régimes sont souvent administrés par des organismes distincts dépendant de ministères différents. La coordination de l'opération au niveau national n'est pas une mince affaire pour le ministère (généralement le ministère du Travail) chargé des relations avec l'OIT, surtout lorsque l'administration des régimes est décentralisée ou confiée à des organismes provinciaux ou locaux.

On conçoit donc que le rassemblement de données complètes prenne beaucoup de temps. Pour la plupart des régimes, les chiffres définitifs ne sont généralement guère disponibles moins de dix-huit mois ou de deux ans après la fin de l'année à laquelle ils se rapportent; il arrive même que le délai soit plus long. Pour de nombreux pays, le BIT ne peut obtenir des données complètes qu'à la suite d'échanges de correspondance avec les autorités nationales, et il lui faut parfois procéder encore à de longues recherches dans les sources nationales.

Un système informatisé a été mis en place pour enregistrer et traiter, après vérification, les données de la douzième enquête. Les données des enquêtes précédentes ont été introduites dans ce système. On a revu les calculs des années précédentes afin de prendre en compte, notamment, les chiffres révisés pour le produit intérieur brut, la population ou les indices de prix. De ce fait, les chiffres des séries publiées dans cette édition peuvent différer légèrement de ceux qui apparaissent dans les éditions précédentes.

Le questionnaire qui a servi de base à l'enquête demandait aux gouvernements de fournir des données sur les recettes et les dépenses dans le cadre suivant:

Recettes	*Dépenses*
Cotisations:	Soins médicaux
– des assurés	
– des employeurs	Prestations en nature à d'autres titres que les soins médicaux
Taxes et impôts spéciaux affectés à la sécurité sociale	Prestations en espèces
Participation de l'Etat	Total des prestations
Participation d'autres pouvoirs publics	Frais d'administration
Revenu des capitaux	Transferts à d'autres régimes couverts par l'enquête
Transferts provenant d'autres régimes	Autres dépenses
Autres recettes	Total des dépenses
Total des recettes	

La dernière colonne du questionnaire doit donner la différence entre le total des recettes et le total des dépenses, positive ou négative.

Les explications qui suivent pourront aider à l'interprétation des chiffres.

1. Recettes

On a fait figurer sous les rubriques «cotisations des assurés» et «cotisations des employeurs» les montants qui sont considérés généralement comme constituant les cotisations en question. Cependant, il existe un certain nombre de cas marginaux et de cas où la distinction entre les deux types de cotisations n'est pas très claire. Les cotisations de sécurité sociale sont très souvent payées par l'employeur, qui déduit ensuite les cotisations des assurés des salaires de ceux-ci. Il va de soi que ces deux catégories de cotisations devraient être rangées dans les colonnes qui les concernent. Or, selon la méthode de comptabilité employée, le type de cotisation n'est pas toujours précisé, d'où la nécessité de procéder à des estimations. On peut y parvenir aisément avec une précision suffisante lorsque la loi prévoit des taux uniformes de cotisation pour les employeurs et les travailleurs. Les choses se compliquent lorsque des taux différents sont applicables aux différentes catégories d'assurés (du point de vue du niveau de salaire, de la branche

16

d'assurance, etc.). De plus, si le régime s'étend aux travailleurs indépendants et aux chômeurs ou admet l'assurance volontaire, l'assuré acquittant en pareils cas le montant total de la cotisation, il devient très difficile de répartir les montants entre les deux colonnes.

Les deux colonnes réservées aux cotisations devraient en principe comprendre les impôts spéciaux perçus par les services fiscaux lorsque ces impôts peuvent être considérés comme des cotisations plutôt que comme des impôts proprement dits. En Nouvelle-Zélande, par exemple, il existait, jusqu'en 1968, un impôt spécial de sécurité sociale qui figurait dans la colonne «cotisations des assurés». La loi de finances de 1968 a aboli cet impôt, et le financement est assuré depuis sur les recettes générales. En conséquence, les montants affectés au financement de la sécurité sociale figurent dans la colonne «participation de l'Etat».

Dans les pays de l'Europe de l'Est, les systèmes de sécurité sociale sont, dans une large mesure, financés sur les ressources des entreprises ou des établissements. Aussi les sommes correspondantes figurent-elles dans la colonne «cotisations des employeurs». Cependant, en RSS de Biélorussie, en RSS d'Ukraine et en URSS, les paiements effectués au titre de la sécurité sociale par les entreprises et les organismes d'Etat font partie intégrante du budget de l'Etat, si bien qu'ils figurent, avec les autres paiements effectués par l'Etat, dans la colonne «participation de l'Etat».

Dans bien des pays, la protection contre les risques professionnels est fondée sur la responsabilité directe de l'employeur, à qui il incombe, aux termes de la loi, de verser des prestations aux salariés qui sont victimes d'un accident du travail ou d'une maladie professionnelle. En pareil cas, le montant versé par l'employeur figure dans la colonne «cotisations des employeurs». Il en va de même des primes payées par les employeurs aux compagnies d'assurances auprès desquelles ils contractent une police couvrant leurs obligations, que l'assurance soit volontaire ou obligatoire.

Pour les régimes spéciaux des agents publics, les paiements effectués par l'Etat ou des autorités publiques en tant qu'employeurs sont considérés comme des cotisations des employeurs aux fins de l'enquête, et les montants correspondants figurent dans la colonne réservée à celles-ci.

La colonne «taxes et impôts spéciaux» affectés à la sécurité sociale doit comprendre les impôts que l'on ne peut assimiler à des cotisations et dont le produit est spécifiquement destiné à la sécurité sociale. En France, par exemple, dans le régime agricole, la sécurité sociale des non-salariés est partiellement financée par une série de ressources parafiscales.

Les deux colonnes «participation de l'Etat» et «participation d'autres pouvoirs publics» doivent englober tous les paiements faits à la sécurité sociale par l'Etat central et les autorités locales, qu'ils correspondent à la prise en charge d'une partie des cotisations pour tous les assurés ou certaines catégories d'entre eux ou à celle d'une partie des dépenses en prestations ou des frais d'administration. Pour les pays fédératifs, la colonne «participation de l'Etat» comprend les montants versés par l'Etat fédéral, et la colonne «participation d'autres pouvoirs publics», les montants versés par les Etats constituants ou les provinces.

La colonne «revenu des capitaux» doit en principe indiquer les intérêts des capitaux investis, déduction faite des dépenses relatives aux investissements.

Dans le questionnaire qui a servi de base à l'enquête, deux colonnes sont réservées aux transferts entre régimes, l'intention étant d'éliminer une double prise en considération des transferts d'un régime à un autre. Les totaux figurant dans ce volume ne prennent plus en compte ces transferts. On trouvera dans les tableaux de base les données reçues à ce sujet [2]. En principe, les totaux des deux colonnes devraient être égaux. Cependant, étant donné les différences qui peuvent exister entre les régimes en ce qui concerne les méthodes de comptabilité et les exercices financiers, il n'en est pas toujours ainsi et il existe parfois, entre les deux colonnes, une différence, généralement mineure.

2. Dépenses

Du côté des dépenses, une distinction a été établie entre les prestations au titre des soins médicaux, les prestations en nature à d'autres titres que les soins médicaux et les prestations en espèces.

Dans la colonne «soins médicaux» figurent toutes les dépenses au titre des soins médicaux personnels (par exemple les soins de praticiens de médecine générale ou de spécialistes, les soins hospitaliers (traitements médicaux et frais de pension), les produits pharmaceutiques, les soins dentaires, les examens de laboratoire, la rééducation, la fourniture de prothèses, etc.), cela, qu'il s'agisse de prestations en nature ou de prestations en espèces payées aux bénéficiaires (par exemple remboursement des frais médicaux réglés directement par les assurés). Lorsque les bénéficiaires doivent supporter une partie du coût des soins, les montants payés par eux (en vertu du système dit du «ticket modérateur»), soit directement à la personne ou au service qui fournit les soins, soit à l'institution d'assurance sociale qui en rembourse le coût, ont été considérés comme hors du champ de l'enquête et ne figurent par conséquent ni du côté des recettes, ni du côté des dépenses.

A partir de la huitième enquête, on a réservé une colonne séparée aux prestations en nature à d'autres titres que les soins médicaux, surtout pour répondre aux besoins de l'analyse économique. Beaucoup de régimes de sécurité ou d'assistance sociale ou de services sociaux assurent toutes sortes de prestations ou de services en nature que l'on ne peut classer sous «soins médicaux». C'est ainsi que les régimes de prestations familiales de nombreux pays francophones d'Afrique fournissent, au titre de l'action sanitaire et sociale, toute une gamme de services et de prestations qui peuvent se présenter sous la forme soit de soins médicaux (dispensaires et centres sanitaires pour les mères et les enfants, subventions d'hospitalisation, etc.) – auquel cas les montants correspondants figurent dans la colonne «soins médicaux» –, soit de prestations en nature (fourniture de lait et d'autres denrées alimentaires, de layette, de vêtements d'enfants), soit encore de services (jardins d'enfants, colonies de vacances, logements). De même, dans les pays nordiques, certaines prestations et certains services sont assurés dans le cadre de divers régimes sociaux (foyers pour personnes âgées et retraités, services d'aide ménagère, vacances pour les enfants et les ménagères, etc.). Enfin, dans les pays de l'Europe de l'Est, la sécurité sociale touche des domaines tels que les loisirs organisés, les foyers de repos et la fourniture de produits diététiques.

Pour les prestations en espèces, il ne se pose généralement pas de problèmes de classification. Mentionnons cependant, en ce qui concerne la colonne «total des prestations», le cas des paiements et des prestations aux travailleurs migrants en vertu de conventions et d'instruments bilatéraux ou multilatéraux. Les procédures peuvent en effet différer d'un pays à l'autre, mais, dans l'ensemble, les montants correspondants sont consignés en tant que paiements de prestations dans le pays auquel appartient l'institution qui en supporte le coût, même si, dans la réalité, les paiements sont effectués par les soins d'une institution d'un autre pays. Après règlement de ces comptes entre les institutions et les pays concernés, il peut apparaître une différence positive ou négative, que l'on a fait figurer généralement, selon le cas, dans la colonne «autres recettes» ou «autres dépenses».

Les données consignées dans la colonne «frais d'administration» ne sont pas toujours exactes ou complètes. L'administration d'un régime de sécurité sociale peut être confiée à un département ministériel chargé également de l'administration d'autres services qui n'entrent pas dans le champ de l'enquête du BIT (tel est le cas, par exemple, lorsque les services de l'assurance chômage et les services de placement relèvent administrativement du même organisme, sans que les méthodes de comptabilité permettent d'isoler les frais d'administration de l'assurance chômage). En ce qui concerne l'assistance publique, il n'est pas toujours possible de faire la distinction entre les dépenses en prestations et les frais d'administration. Dans de nombreux cas, on ne peut donner que des estimations, et parfois c'est même impossible. On interprétera avec prudence les chiffres figurant dans cette colonne, qui, pour certains pays, peuvent ne pas fournir une indication complète et exacte des frais d'administration. Les tableaux de base montrent quels sont les régimes et les services pour lesquels on connaît les frais d'administration et quels sont ceux pour lesquels les données manquent [2].

La colonne réservée à la différence entre les recettes et les dépenses au cours de l'exercice doit en principe présenter, pour chaque pays, l'excédent ou le déficit net de l'ensemble des régimes et des services relevant de l'enquête. On notera cependant qu'elle comprend, le cas échéant, les montants destinés aux réserves techniques et aux fonds de garantie.

3. Exercices financiers

Les données présentées dans les publications antérieures se rapportaient aux années civiles ou aux exercices financiers se terminant au cours des années civiles indiquées, quelle que fût la fraction de l'exercice comprise dans l'année. En ce qui concerne la présente enquête, les données se rapportent aux années civiles ou aux exercices compris en majeure partie dans les années civiles indiquées.

Pour certains pays, la période couverte peut différer d'un régime à l'autre. L'exercice financier du gouvernement peut ne pas coïncider avec l'année civile, alors que les données relatives à certains régimes et à certains services se rapportent à celle-ci (en général à celle qui commence au cours de l'exercice financier). Par exemple, à Singapour, l'exercice financier du gouvernement se termine le 31 mars tandis que, pour le Fonds central de prévoyance, l'exercice financier coïncide avec l'année civile.

V. Les tableaux comparatifs

L'information présentée dans les tableaux comparatifs consiste essentiellement en mesures relatives. Comme on l'a déjà indiqué, le présent volume reprend le modèle suivi dans les éditions précédentes, notamment le regroupement des pays par région, en vue de faciliter les comparaisons.

Les chiffres se rapportent, en règle générale, aux années 1970, 1975, 1980 et 1983-1986. Pour certains pays, les données font défaut pour les premières de ces années; on a indiqué alors les chiffres de la première année pour laquelle on dispose de statistiques ou de l'année la plus proche de 1970, 1975, 1980 ou 1983.

La présentation de mesures relatives doit permettre, en premier lieu, de faire apparaître l'évolution des recettes et des dépenses de la sécurité sociale et la manière dont elles se répartissent dans chaque pays et, en second lieu, de procéder à des comparaisons internationales. Il faut toutefois se montrer prudent dans les conclusions que l'on tire des chiffres figurant dans les tableaux car les mesures relatives sont fondées sur des totaux globaux pour chaque pays.

On observe en effet, selon les pays, des différences considérables dans l'étendue de la protection, et des différences sensibles aussi, à l'intérieur des pays, dans la protection assurée à différents secteurs de la population. Les moyennes, dans ces conditions, renseignent très imparfaitement sur la protection garantie, notamment dans beaucoup de pays en voie de développement, où le système de sécurité sociale, du point de vue de l'enquête du BIT, sera essentiellement constitué peut-être par un régime d'assurance couvrant des catégories limitées de la population salariée (surtout dans le secteur moderne) et par un régime spécial pour les fonctionnaires. Les structures et l'évolution économiques, sociales et politiques déterminent le développement des systèmes de sécurité sociale – tel pays privilégiant l'assurance maladie, par exemple, tel autre le régime de pensions – et expliquent les grandes différences que l'on constate dans la nature et l'étendue de la protection.

Etant donné que, dans beaucoup de pays, le système de sécurité sociale n'a pas encore atteint son développement définitif et que les facteurs qui déterminent le coût peuvent varier beaucoup selon les branches, il convient de considérer les données financières présentées ici de façon critique. Prenons par exemple un régime d'assurance maladie ou de protection contre les risques professionnels couvrant une grande partie de la population et un régime de pensions au champ d'application comparable; il est fort possible qu'on obtienne des chiffres par personne relativement faibles pour le premier, beaucoup plus élevés pour le second, en raison de la nature de l'éventualité, et, conséquence d'une faible accumulation de fonds dans le premier, d'une forte accumulation dans le second, une quasi-égalité des recettes et des dépenses ici et une importante différence là.

Autre facteur à signaler: le coût de la protection contre un même risque varie selon l'incidence de ce risque. Prenons un pays qui souffre d'un fort chômage ou qui connaît une série d'épidémies et qui doit consacrer des sommes considérables à la protection des chômeurs ou aux services de santé; on ne peut dire que ce pays a un système de sécurité sociale plus avancé, toutes choses égales d'ailleurs, qu'un autre où les dépenses représentent un pourcentage plus faible du produit national simplement parce que le chômage est moindre ou la situation sanitaire meilleure.

On rappellera enfin que la définition de la sécurité sociale adoptée pour l'enquête du BIT peut écarter, dans certains pays, d'importants éléments de la protection sociale, notamment lorsque cette protection est assurée pour une grande part par des régimes privés [10] ou lorsqu'elle fait intervenir des régimes de prestations instituées par la loi mais servies directement par l'employeur (paiement du salaire en cas de maladie, soins médicaux, prestations de maternité) qui, de ce fait, n'entrent pas dans le champ de l'enquête.

Dans certains tableaux, il n'a pas été possible de faire figurer tous les pays dont on a donné la liste ci-dessus, soit que certaines des données de base auxquelles sont rapportés les chiffres de la sécurité sociale (produit intérieur brut, effectif de la population, etc.) fassent défaut, soit qu'on n'ait pas obtenu les ventilations nécessaires. Dans certains cas, les chiffres pour une ou plusieurs années ont été omis car ils n'étaient pas comparables aux chiffres donnés pour les autres années. Dans le tableau 3, on n'a pas pu présenter de chiffres pour la Guinée, la Guinée-Bissau et le Tchad, faute de données sur le produit intérieur brut. Dans le tableau 6, on ne trouvera pas de chiffres pour le Bénin et Cuba, faute de données sur l'indice du coût de la vie. Le Qatar n'apparaît pas dans les tableaux 7 et 10, car les données reçues concernaient uniquement l'assistance sociale. En ce qui concerne les tableaux qui présentent la répartition en pourcentage des recettes et des dépenses (tableaux 7 à 10), il convient de se montrer prudent quand le pourcentage 100 apparaît dans une colonne, les informations pouvant être incomplètes.

Tableau 1: Recettes et dépenses totales de la sécurité sociale par rubrique principale (en millions d'unités monétaires nationales), pages 40-71

Le tableau 1 donne, pour les recettes et les dépenses, les totaux généraux des différentes colonnes du questionnaire, abstraction faite des transferts provenant d'autres régimes et des transferts à d'autres régimes couverts par l'enquête; comme on l'a déjà indiqué, ces montants doivent en principe s'annuler et, dans les tableaux comparatifs, seuls les totaux nets, après élimination des transferts éventuels, doivent entrer en ligne de compte. La signification des chiffres qui apparaissent dans chaque colonne est expliquée ci-dessus dans la section IV.

Les chiffres permettent de suivre l'évolution des différents types de recettes et des différents types de dépenses, ainsi que celle du total des recettes et du total des dépenses au cours de la période de dix-sept ans (1970-1986) qui est en principe couverte. Ils sont donnés dans les unités monétaires en usage la dernière année couverte par l'enquête; au cas où un pays aurait procédé à une réforme monétaire au cours de la période considérée, les conversions nécessaires ont été effectuées.

Les tendances qui apparaissent peuvent être dues à différents facteurs, qui peuvent agir dans le même sens ou en sens opposés, notamment à l'élargissement des régimes de sécurité sociale (champ d'application et prestations) ou à la création de nouveaux régimes. Comme on le verra dans le tableau 1 de l'annexe – «Données de la comptabilité nationale, données démographiques, indices des prix à la consommation, taux de change» –, l'indice du coût de la vie a, dans la plupart des cas, accusé une hausse rapide, qui se répercute sur les chiffres du tableau 1.

D'autres différences peuvent avoir été déterminées par des modifications apportées aux dispositions administratives ou financières, qui entraînent de brusques changements d'une année à l'autre dans l'importance des chiffres de telle ou telle colonne. Ainsi, lorsqu'un impôt spécial assimilable à une cotisation de sécurité sociale cesse d'être perçu et que le financement correspondant est assuré sur les recettes générales de l'Etat, on observera, dans le tableau, une brusque diminution, voire la

disparition des chiffres figurant dans la colonne «taxes et impôts spéciaux» affectés à la sécurité sociale et une augmentation correspondante des montants figurant dans la colonne «participation de l'Etat». On pourra par déduction, à partir des chiffres relatifs donnés dans les autres tableaux et des explications fournies, se faire une idée plus précise des causes des mouvements des chiffres figurant au tableau 1.

On trouvera à la fin du tableau 1 une série de notes concernant les chiffres donnés pour différents pays. Les notes d'application générale ne sont pas répétées dans les autres tableaux.

Tableau 2: Recettes et dépenses totales de la sécurité sociale (en millions de dollars des Etats-Unis), pages 72-78

Pour permettre les comparaisons, ce tableau donne le total des recettes de la sécurité sociale, le total des dépenses et le chiffre des dépenses en prestations en dollars des Etats-Unis, sur la base des taux de change indiqués dans le tableau 1 de l'annexe. Ces taux, qui sont ceux qui étaient applicables à la fin de la période considérée, sont tirés des publications du Fonds monétaire international ou de l'Organisation des Nations Unies; dans certains cas, quand les taux n'étaient pas donnés dans ces publications, on a utilisé des sources nationales.

Il convient d'être attentif aux problèmes que soulèvent les comparaisons qui peuvent être faites, sur cette base, notamment pour les pays qui avaient un système de taux de change multiples, telle l'URSS, ou ceux qui ont changé d'unité monétaire au cours des années, comme la Bolivie, le Brésil, Israël et le Pérou.

Tableau 3. Recettes et dépenses de la sécurité sociale (en pourcentage du produit intérieur brut aux valeurs d'acquisition), pages 79-85

Le tableau 3 indique le poids relatif de la sécurité sociale dans l'économie nationale. Le total des recettes, le total des dépenses et les dépenses en prestations (colonnes 10, 17 et 14 du tableau 1) sont rapportés à cette fin au produit intérieur brut (PIB) ou au produit matériel net (PMN) aux prix courants, tirés, en règle générale, de l'annuaire de statistiques de la comptabilité nationale de l'Organisation des Nations Unies et donnés dans le tableau 1 de l'annexe [11]. Pour les pays dont l'exercice financier ne coïncide pas avec l'année civile, on a utilisé le PIB ou le PMN de l'année civile dans laquelle est comprise la plus grande partie de l'exercice financier.

Le produit intérieur brut peut être défini de façon approximative comme le total des contributions à la production de tous les producteurs résidant dans le pays. Cette mesure englobant les impôts indirects déduction faite des subventions, le total qui en résulte est exprimé aux valeurs d'acquisition. Le fait qu'il s'agit d'une évaluation brute signifie que l'on n'a pas déduit la consommation de capital fixe [11].

Adopté par la Commission de statistique de l'Organisation des Nations Unies à sa 15e session en 1968, le nouveau Système de comptabilité nationale (SCN) est une version révisée et augmentée de l'ancien système publié en 1953 [6]. Les chiffres donnés au tableau 3 sont en général fondés sur le produit intérieur brut selon le nouveau système. Dans quelques cas, on ne dispose que de données produites selon l'ancien système; une note de bas de page le précise alors. Les comparaisons faites pour les pays où l'on dispose de données établies selon l'un et l'autre système ne font apparaître que de très faibles écarts en ce qui concerne le produit intérieur brut; ainsi, les différences entre les deux systèmes ne devraient pas avoir de conséquences notables sur la comparabilité des données figurant dans le tableau 3.

Le système utilisé dans les pays à économie planifiée – système de comptabilité du produit matériel (CPM) – se distingue essentiellement du SCN en ce qu'il vise avant tout à mesurer la production de biens dans ce qu'il est convenu d'appeler le domaine de la production matérielle, à l'exclusion du domaine non matériel, c'est-à-dire le secteur des services. L'agrégat généralement utilisé est le produit matériel net, défini comme la valeur nette totale des biens et des services productifs (y compris les taxes sur le chiffre d'affaires) produits par l'économie. On entend par services productifs, ou matériels, les services tels que les transports, les entrepôts, la circulation des biens, etc., considérés comme la suite de la production matérielle [11]. Le produit matériel net ne comprend pas les activités économiques qui ne contribuent pas directement à la production matérielle, par exemple l'administration et la défense, les services personnels, les services des professions libérales ainsi que les activités analogues. En conséquence, les chiffres du tableau 3 fondés sur le produit matériel net selon la CPM ne sont pas comparables avec ceux qui prennent comme grandeur de référence le produit intérieur brut selon le SCN. Ce dernier agrégat comprenant toute une série d'activités que l'autre laisse de côté, on peut s'attendre que le coût de la sécurité sociale représente un pourcentage un peu plus élevé du produit matériel net que du produit intérieur brut.

Que les chiffres soient calculés en principe d'après le SCN ou selon la CPM, on constate de grandes différences d'un pays à l'autre dans la qualité des données fondamentales, les méthodes d'évaluation des différents éléments dont il est tenu compte pour les calculs, etc. Les chiffres font souvent aussi l'objet d'ajustements qui peuvent être considérables. Il convient donc d'interpréter avec prudence les chiffres qui figurent dans ce tableau. En outre, comme nous l'avons signalé plus haut, il est difficile d'en tirer des conclusions en ce qui concerne, par exemple, le niveau relatif de la protection dans les divers pays, car les seules données financières sont insuffisantes pour cela.

Compte tenu de ces réserves et des limites de la comparabilité, les chiffres du tableau 3 renseignent sur l'importance relative de la sécurité sociale dans l'économie nationale, au sein de chaque pays et par comparaison avec les autres pays et les autres régions. Dans la plupart des cas, il n'y a pas de différence notable entre les pourcentages obtenus pour les recettes et pour les dépenses. Pour certains pays, toutefois, on observe des différences importantes, qui traduisent le degré d'accumulation de capital du système de sécurité sociale, comme nous l'avons indiqué à propos du tableau 1.

Tableaux 4 et 5: Moyennes annuelles des recettes et des dépenses de la sécurité sociale par habitant (en unités monétaires nationales et en dollars des Etats-Unis), pages 86-95 et pages 96-105

Alors que, dans le tableau 1, les recettes et les dépenses des régimes relevant de l'enquête sont exprimées en chiffres absolus pour chaque pays, elles sont rapportées dans les tableaux 4 et 5 – pour le total des recettes, le total des dépenses et les dépenses en prestations (colonnes 10, 17 et 14 du tableau 1) – à la population totale et à la population âgée de quinze à soixante-quatre ans («population en âge de travailler»). Donnés en unités

monétaires nationales dans le tableau 4, les chiffres le sont, dans le tableau 5, en dollars des Etats-Unis, sur la base des taux de change appliqués dans le tableau 2, de façon à faciliter les comparaisons.

Les chiffres de la population totale, indiqués dans le tableau 1 de l'annexe, sont fondés sur des séries d'estimations de milieu d'année ou sur les données de recensement. Ils sont tirés, en général, de l'*Annuaire démographique* et de numéros récents du *Bulletin mensuel de statistique* de l'Organisation des Nations Unies. Les données sur la population en âge de travailler ne sont généralement pas disponibles en séries annuelles, et il a fallu procéder à des estimations en calculant le rapport de la population en âge de travailler à la population totale de cinq en cinq ans entre 1970 et 1990 et en obtenant par interpolation les valeurs intermédiaires. Les résultats sont donnés dans le tableau 1 de l'annexe. Pour les estimations du rapport de la population en âge de travailler à la population totale (variante moyenne), on s'est servi de la publication de l'Organisation des Nations Unies *Global estimates and projections of population by sex and age. The 1988 revision* (New York, 1989).

Il convient ici de garder en mémoire les réserves exprimées plus haut au sujet des moyennes globales. Notons en particulier que, si la protection offerte par la sécurité sociale est relativement peu étendue, comme c'est généralement le cas dans les pays en voie de développement, une moyenne calculée sur la population totale ne donne pas une indication correcte du niveau des dépenses ou des prestations de la sécurité sociale par personne pour la population protégée.

L'intérêt de ces tableaux est qu'ils permettent d'observer, à l'échelon national, l'évolution des recettes et des dépenses de la sécurité sociale une fois éliminé l'effet de l'accroissement démographique. Si l'on compare la progression des chiffres dans le tableau 4 et dans le tableau 1, on peut se rendre compte de l'influence de l'évolution et de la structure démographiques. Il est particulièrement intéressant d'avoir une idée de la progression du coût de la sécurité sociale au regard de celle de la population. Répétons que les chiffres subissent l'influence de plusieurs facteurs, notamment de la hausse du coût de la vie au cours de la période considérée.

Tableau 6: Indices des moyennes annuelles des dépenses en prestations par habitant (population totale) (valeurs ajustées d'après l'indice du coût de la vie), pages 106-108

On vient de rappeler l'effet de la hausse du coût de la vie sur les chiffres par habitant, effet qui rend difficiles, et dans certains cas presque impossibles, les comparaisons de chiffres fondés sur les unités monétaires nationales. Pour améliorer les possibilités de comparaison, on a corrigé les moyennes annuelles des dépenses en prestations par habitant pour la population totale (colonne 5 des tableaux 4 et 5) en fonction des indices des prix à la consommation et on a établi une série d'indices dont la base est l'année 1980. L'exclusion des soins médicaux fournis au titre de la santé publique dans les trois dernières enquêtes a nécessité l'établissement de deux séries différentes pour les pays concernés. En conséquence, pour les pays pour lesquels les données sont homogènes pour toute la période considérée, on a une série unique d'indices dont la base est l'année 1980; au contraire, pour les pays pour lesquels s'est produite une rupture de la continuité des données du fait de l'exclusion des soins fournis au titre de la santé publique, on a deux séries d'indices: l'ancienne série, basée sur des données incluant ces soins, avec 1970 comme année de base, et la nouvelle série, excluant ces soins, avec 1980 comme année de base. Dans l'un et l'autre cas, si les données pour l'année de base (1970 ou 1980) ne sont pas disponibles, on a pris comme base l'année la plus proche pour laquelle on a des données. Les anciennes et les nouvelles séries sont séparées par un filet vertical.

Les chiffres des indices des prix à la consommation utilisés pour le calcul sont indiqués dans le tableau 1 de l'annexe. Il s'agit en principe des indices généraux pour tous les groupes publiés dans l'*Annuaire des statistiques du travail* du BIT, le *Bulletin des statistiques du travail* du BIT (trimestriel) et l'annuaire des *Statistiques financières internationales* du Fonds monétaire international.

Il convient de tenir compte, en examinant le tableau 6, surtout si l'on fait des comparaisons entre pays, des caractéristiques des indices des prix à la consommation; comme le dit l'*Annuaire des statistiques du travail* du BIT:

Les indices des prix à la consommation ont pour objet de mesurer les changements dans le temps des prix de détail d'une liste fixe de certains biens et services choisis de façon à représenter les habitudes de consommation de la population considérée... Les méthodes suivies lors du calcul des indices varient d'un pays à un autre... Les coefficients de pondération, qui permettent de tenir compte de l'importance relative des dépenses de consommation, sont généralement fondés sur les résultats d'enquêtes sur les dépenses familiales reflétant la structure des dépenses de consommation et leur importance relative pour un groupe de population donné... Vu les différences existant dans la portée des indices et dans les méthodes utilisées pour les établir, les statistiques figurant dans le tableau pour les différents pays ne sont pas uniformément représentatives des variations des niveaux de prix et elles n'ont pas la même précision d'un pays à un autre [12].

Ajoutons que la structure de la consommation, dans le cas des prestations de la sécurité sociale, peut être fort différente de celle sur laquelle est fondé l'indice des prix. De plus, celui-ci est établi parfois d'après la consommation et les prix dans certaines localités (souvent la capitale du pays), tandis que les données de la sécurité sociale se rapportent en principe à l'ensemble du pays.

Tableau 7: Répartition des dépenses de la sécurité sociale en prestations entre les différents régimes (en pourcentage du total des dépenses en prestations), pages 109-122

Le tableau 7 indique la répartition des dépenses de la sécurité sociale en prestations entre les régimes. Il montre les différences qu'on observe, quant à l'importance relative des divers régimes, selon les pays, de même que les modifications qui ont pu se produire à cet égard dans chaque pays pendant la période considérée. Les régimes envisagés sont les mêmes que dans la précédente édition: assurances sociales et régimes assimilés, prestations familiales, régimes spéciaux pour les agents publics, assistance publique et régimes assimilés, prestations aux victimes de guerre.

Il n'est pas toujours facile de distinguer les divers régimes. Dans certains pays, la même institution peut en administrer plusieurs sans qu'il soit possible de ventiler les données. Ainsi, dans la plupart des pays de l'Europe de l'Est, il existe des régimes qui regroupent les assurances sociales, l'assistance sociale et, parfois, les prestations aux victimes de guerre.

Aucun critère précis n'est appliqué pour le classement d'un régime dans telle ou telle catégorie, mais, au fil des ans, certaines pratiques se sont imposées.

Les régimes de pensions (ou d'autres prestations) non contributifs sont rangés sous «assurances sociales et régimes assimilés» plutôt que sous «assistance publique et régimes assimilés», même si le paiement des prestations ou d'une partie d'entre elles est subordonné au cri-

tère des ressources. Cette méthode semble celle qui convient le mieux pour les comparaisons internationales, car, dans de nombreux cas, les prestations non contributives font partie intégrante d'un système général contributif (cas des prestations supplémentaires accordées, sous condition de ressources, en plus des prestations générales contributives), tandis que, dans d'autres cas, c'est le système tout entier qui est de nature non contributive.

Les régimes de réparation des accidents du travail et des maladies professionnelles fondés sur l'assurance privée ou sur le principe de la responsabilité directe de l'employeur sont aussi compris dans la rubrique «assurances sociales et régimes assimilés».

Les régimes spéciaux pour les agents publics sont les régimes institués pour ces agents qui sont distincts du régime général et des autres régimes spéciaux de la sécurité sociale. Lorsque les agents publics relèvent du régime général, comme en Finlande et en Suède, leurs prestations sont comprises dans la rubrique «assurances sociales et régimes assimilés».

La colonne «services publics de santé» a été maintenue uniquement pour la présentation des données antérieures à la onzième enquête. Le signe «x» dans cette colonne indique que la rubrique est devenue sans objet du moment que les soins médicaux fournis au titre de la santé publique ne sont plus pris en considération. Les régimes qui assurent des soins médicaux accessibles de droit à l'ensemble de la population demeurent dans le champ de l'enquête et sont regroupés sous la rubrique «assurances sociales et régimes assimilés».

Les chiffres étant exprimés en pourcentage du total, une augmentation dans une rubrique s'accompagnera d'une diminution dans une autre rubrique, bien que les dépenses en prestations, pour cette dernière, puissent avoir augmenté en chiffres absolus. D'autres modifications pourront être observées du fait que les données disponibles étaient plus complètes que lors des enquêtes précédentes ou, à l'inverse, que des données disponibles lors des enquêtes précédentes n'ont pas été fournies pour celle-ci; en pareil cas, en vue d'indiquer un ordre de grandeur, on a répété, chaque fois qu'il y avait lieu, le chiffre de la dernière année pour laquelle on avait des renseignements et on l'a signalé en note. Certains changements, enfin, peuvent être attribués à des modifications de la législation ou à des améliorations des prestations.

Tableau 8: Répartition des recettes de la sécurité sociale d'après leur provenance (en pourcentage du total des recettes), pages 123-136

Le tableau 8 montre comment est financé, dans chaque pays, le système de sécurité sociale, tel qu'il est défini aux fins de l'enquête; il indique la répartition, d'après leur provenance, des recettes en pourcentage du total et fait apparaître les modifications de cette répartition au cours de la période considérée.

Les réserves faites à propos du tableau 7 en ce qui concerne les augmentations et les diminutions des chiffres relatifs et le caractère plus ou moins complet des données valent également pour le tableau 8. Des changements dans les méthodes de comptabilité ou l'utilisation de sources d'informations différentes peuvent être à l'origine d'autres modifications.

Tableau 9: Répartition des recettes au titre des assurances sociales et régimes assimilés et des prestations familiales (en pourcentage du total des recettes), pages 137-149

Le tableau 9 donne les mêmes informations que le tableau 8, non plus pour l'ensemble du système de sécurité sociale, tel qu'il est défini aux fins de l'enquête, mais pour les seuls régimes classés sous les rubriques principales: «assurances sociales et régimes assimilés» et «prestations familiales».

Un certain nombre de pays ne possèdent pas de régime de prestations familiales ou n'ont pas fourni d'informations à ce sujet; le fait est signalé en note. Il faut remarquer que ce tableau inclut les données relatives aux agents publics quand ceux-ci sont couverts par le régime général de sécurité sociale, comme en Finlande et en Suède.

Tableau 10: Répartition des dépenses en prestations par branche de la sécurité sociale, pour les régimes entrant dans les rubriques «assurances sociales et régimes assimilés» et «prestations familiales» (en pourcentage du total des dépenses en prestations), pages 150-169

Pour permettre un regroupement des données sur le coût de la sécurité sociale par risque ou par éventualité, le questionnaire invitait les gouvernements à ventiler les données pour chaque régime ou chaque service par branche de la sécurité sociale conformément à la classification adoptée pour les différentes parties de la convention (n° 102) concernant la sécurité sociale (norme minimum), 1952. Le tableau 10 présente les résultats de ce regroupement. Les régimes qu'il englobe sont les mêmes que dans le tableau 9: assurances sociales et régimes assimilés et prestations familiales. Il est malaisé en effet de regrouper les données relatives aux régimes spéciaux pour les agents publics (dans les pays de l'Europe de l'Est comme dans quelques autres, les chiffres correspondants sont inclus dans la rubrique «assurances sociales et régimes assimilés», et on ne peut les isoler), à l'assistance publique et aux régimes assimilés et aux prestations aux victimes de guerre. Seules sont prises en considération les dépenses en prestations.

Bien que les données aient été demandées pour les neuf branches distinguées dans la convention n° 102, on a jugé préférable d'établir la répartition pour cinq branches principales: maladie-maternité, accidents du travail et maladies professionnelles, pensions, prestations de chômage, prestations familiales. Ces cinq branches correspondent largement, en effet, à l'organisation administrative et financière d'un grand nombre de systèmes de sécurité sociale. Les dépenses en prestations sont données, pour ces cinq branches, en pourcentage du total pour les régimes considérés, avec une ventilation par type de prestations pour la maladie-maternité et pour les accidents du travail et les maladies professionnelles. En ce qui concerne la répartition par branche, il faut noter que les prestations des fonds de prévoyance et les allocations de décès ont été classées sous la rubrique «pensions». Quelquefois, les informations fournies se rapportent à plusieurs branches à la fois et ne peuvent être ventilées; en pareil cas, elles ne figurent que sous l'une des rubriques concernées, et le fait est signalé en note.

Pour bien des pays, il n'est pas possible d'établir une distinction nette entre les diverses branches, et des prestations qui, dans tel pays, sont classées dans une branche peuvent, dans tel autre, être classées dans une autre branche. On pourrait citer de nombreux cas de ce genre,

ce qui évidemment influe sur la comparabilité des chiffres [13]; lorsque celle-ci s'en trouve très diminuée, une note le signale.

Pour certains régimes spéciaux qui servent généralement toute la gamme des prestations de la sécurité sociale et pour lesquels aucune ventilation n'était donnée, les chiffres ont été indiqués dans la rubrique qui, d'après l'expérience passée, représente la majeure partie des prestations (dans la plupart des cas, il s'agit de la rubrique «pensions»). Les chiffres de cette rubrique se trouvent alors surestimés, alors que sont sous-estimés en proportion les chiffres des autres rubriques.

Dans quelques cas, il n'a pas été possible d'isoler les chiffres relatifs aux régimes considérés dans ce tableau en raison de la manière dont étaient présentées les réponses au questionnaire.

Malgré un inévitable défaut d'uniformité dans la présentation, qui impose la prudence dans l'interprétation des chiffres, le tableau 10 peut renseigner sur la structure d'ensemble du système de sécurité sociale dans les différents pays, sur la place faite aux diverses branches et sur le stade de développement qu'elles ont atteint. Afin d'indiquer l'importance des régimes, on a fait figurer dans la colonne 14 le montant total des dépenses en prestations en millions d'unités monétaires nationales.

VI. Tableaux annexes

1. Données de la comptabilité nationale, données démographiques, indices des prix à la consommation, taux de change, pages 172-181

Ce tableau présente, par pays, les différentes données de référence utilisées dans les tableaux comparatifs.

2. Index des noms des pays dans les trois langues, pages 182-183

Notes

[1] Pour un résumé des travaux du BIT avant la guerre, voir Association internationale de la sécurité sociale (AISS): *Le coût de la sécurité sociale, 1949-1951: Enquête internationale préparée par le Bureau international du Travail* (Genève, BIT, 1955).

Les résultats des précédentes enquêtes ont été publiés comme suit:

Première enquête: «Enquête sur le coût de la sécurité sociale», *Revue internationale du Travail* (Genève, BIT), juin 1952, pp. 773-843, et «Analyse comparée du coût de la sécurité sociale», *ibid.*, mars 1953, pp. 314-326.

Deuxième enquête: AISS: *Le coût de la sécurité sociale, 1949-1951..., op. cit.*, et BIT: *Le financement de la sécurité sociale*, Conférence régionale européenne, Genève, 1955, rapport III (doc. polycopié).

Troisième enquête: BIT: *Le coût de la sécurité sociale, 1949-1954* (Genève, 1958; trilingue).

Quatrième enquête: Idem: *Le coût de la sécurité sociale, 1949-1957* (Genève, 1960; trilingue).

Cinquième enquête: Idem: *Le coût de la sécurité sociale, 1958-1960* (Genève, 1964; trilingue).

Sixième enquête: Idem: *Le coût de la sécurité sociale: sixième enquête internationale, 1961-1963* (Genève, 1967; trilingue).

Septième enquête: Idem: *Le coût de la sécurité sociale: septième enquête internationale, 1964-1966, avec un supplément sur le champ d'application des systèmes de sécurité sociale* (Genève, 1972; trilingue).

Huitième enquête: Idem: *Le coût de la sécurité sociale: huitième enquête internationale, 1967-1971, avec un supplément sur le coût des régimes privés* (Genève, 1976; trilingue), et *The cost of social security: eighth international inquiry, 1967-1971 – Basic tables* (Genève, 1976; en anglais seulement).

Neuvième enquête: Idem: *Le coût de la sécurité sociale: neuvième enquête internationale, 1972-1974* (Genève, 1979; trilingue), et *The cost of social security: ninth international inquiry, 1972-1974 – Basic tables* (Genève, 1978; en anglais seulement).

Dixième enquête: Idem: *Le coût de la sécurité sociale: dixième enquête internationale, 1975-1977* (Genève, 1981; trilingue), et *The cost of social security: tenth international inquiry, 1975-1977 – Basic tables* (Genève, 1981; en anglais seulement).

Onzième enquête: Idem: *Le coût de la sécurité sociale: onzième enquête internationale, 1978-1980* (Genève, 1985), et *The cost of social security: eleventh international inquiry, 1978-1980 – Basic tables* (Genève, 1985; en anglais seulement).

Douzième enquête: Idem: *Le coût de la sécurité sociale: douzième enquête internationale, 1981-1983 – Tableaux comparatifs* (Genève, 1988) et *The cost of social security: twelfth international inquiry, 1981-1983 – Basic tables* (Genève, 1988; en anglais seulement).

[2] BIT: *The cost of social security: thirteenth international inquiry, 1984-1986 – Basic tables* (Genève, 1990; en anglais seulement); *The cost of social security: thirteenth international inquiry, 1984-1986 – Basic tables,* supplementary volume (Genève, 1991; en anglais seulement).

[3] BIT: *Rapport de la Commission d'experts pour la sécurité sociale*, Genève, 26 novembre-3 décembre 1975 (doc. polycopié CSSE/D.14 1975 [Rév.]; annexe II: «Deuxième point à l'ordre du jour: Les indicateurs de sécurité sociale; première évaluation de leur développement».

[4] Régimes ou arrangements spéciaux de sécurité sociale pour les agents publics, distincts du régime général et des autres régimes spéciaux. Aux fins de l'enquête, sont considérés comme agents publics les agents des administrations publiques et ceux des services publics de l'éducation et de la santé ainsi que des services publics sociaux et culturels, qu'il s'agisse de personnel civil ou militaire.

[5] Voir BIT: *Le coût de la sécurité sociale: onzième enquête internationale, 1978-1980, op. cit.*, p. 13.

[6] Nations Unies, Département des affaires économiques et sociales, Bureau de statistique: *Système de comptabilité nationale*, Etudes méthodologiques, série F, n° 2, rév. 3 (New York, 1970; numéro de vente: F.69.XVII.3), p. 79, paragr. 5.27).

[7] Office statistique des Communautés européennes (Eurostat): *Système européen de statistiques intégrées de la protection sociale (SESPROS): méthodologie*, vol. I (Luxembourg, 1981).

[8] Les données portent sur la période 1970-1986, antérieure à la réunification de l'Allemagne (1990).

[9] Les données portent sur la période 1970-1986, antérieure aux transformations économiques en cours. Les pays sont désignés par les noms qui étaient en usage à l'époque.

[10] Voir BIT: *Le coût de la sécurité sociale: huitième enquête internationale, 1967-1971, avec un supplément sur le coût des régimes privés, op. cit.*

[11] Nations Unies, Département des affaires économiques et sociales, Bureau de statistique: *Yearbook of national accounts statistics, 1981*, 3 vol. (New York, 1981; numéro de vente: E.83.XVII.3) et éditions antérieures (publié en anglais seulement depuis 1966); définitions citées: vol. I, pp. XV et XVII.

[12] Pour plus de détails sur le contenu et les méthodes de calcul des indices des prix à la consommation, voir BIT: *Annuaire des statistiques du travail, 1981* (Genève, 1981), notes explicatives, p. 512, ainsi que les publications spécialisées qui y sont citées.

[13] Voir BIT: *Le coût de la sécurité sociale: septième enquête internationale, 1964-1966..., op. cit.*, p. 23.

INTRODUCCION

En esta parte se presentan los resultados de la decimo-tercera encuesta internacional, de la serie comenzada por la Oficina Internacional del Trabajo al finalizar la Seguda Guerra Mundial [1].

I. Objetivos de la encuesta

Las encuestas de la OIT deben permitir, por una parte, establecer un estado completo y coordinado, por países, de las operaciones financieras de todos los regímenes de seguridad social comprendidos en el campo de dichas encuestas, y, por otra parte, proceder a una comparación internacional de los datos que muestre, en particular, la evolución de los ingresos y los egresos durante el período considerado, la repartición de los ingresos según su proveniencia y la repartición de los egresos según los regímenes. Para que se pueda justipreciar la importancia de la seguridad social en la economía de cada país, los datos se relacionan con los diversos totales de las cuentas nacionales y con estadísticas demográficas.

Al igual que para las cinco encuestas anteriores, los resultados constan en dos publicaciones separadas: los cuadros comparativos, incluidos en el presente volumen, y los cuadros básicos, editados en volumen aparte.

En el presente volumen – donde figura la comparación internacional de los datos – se sigue en general el modelo de las últimas ediciones, en particular en la clasificación de los países por regiones a fin de facilitar las comparaciones. Se han incluido, no obstante, dos cuadros adicionales en donde se consignan los resultados para todos los países en una moneda común (dólar estadounidense). Por otra parte, los resultados de la encuesta suplementaria se presentan en cuatro cuadros separados.

Los cuadros básicos contienen datos estadísticos detallados, en valores absolutos disgregados, sobre los ingresos y egresos de los regímenes de seguridad social de cada uno de los países abarcados por la encuesta. Esos cuadros básicos, que en esta oportunidad se han publicado en dos volúmenes (el volumen principal, con 81 países, y el suplementario, con 32 países), se publican solamente en inglés y pueden obtenerse ejemplares solicitándolos al Departamento de Seguridad Social de la OIT [2].

A causa de la importancia adquirida por la seguridad social en la economía de numerosos países, es muy interesante poder disponer de series estadísticas precisas, detalladas, homogéneas y lo más completas posible sobre las transferencias sociales. El presente volumen, como los cuadros básicos que lo acompañan, procura colmar la necesidad de tales informaciones.

También es necesario disponer de amplias estadísticas de seguridad social con objeto de utilizarlas en la elaboración y el desarrollo de indicadores sociales. En el campo de la seguridad social, se requieren indicadores significativos tanto para contribuir a la planificación económica y social en general, sobre todo mediante un sistema integral de indicadores sociales, como para que, en el propio ámbito de la seguridad social, se disponga de mejor información a fin de formular la política general, elaborar los planes, tomar las decisiones y evaluar los resultados [3].

II. Alcance de la encuesta

Para permitir la comparación directa de los datos estadísticos obtenidos mediante la decimotercera encuesta con los recopilados en las encuestas precedentes, se han conservado las definiciones y los métodos adoptados anteriormente.

Se trata de obtener para cada país una imagen lo más completa posible de los ingresos y egresos de la seguridad social, o sea del conjunto de los regímenes o servicios que respondan a los criterios siguientes:

1) el sistema debe tener por objeto:

   a) conceder asistencia médica curativa o preventiva;

   b) garantizar medios de subsistencia en caso de pérdida involuntaria del ingreso proveniente del trabajo o de una parte importante de tal ingreso, o

   c) conceder un ingreso suplementario a las personas con carga de familia;

2) el sistema debe haber sido instituido por un acto legislativo en virtud del cual se conceden derechos individuales determinados o se imponen determinadas obligaciones a un organismo público, semiestatal o autónomo;

3) el sistema debe estar administrado por un organismo público, semiestatal o autónomo.

Sin embargo, los regímenes de indemnización por accidentes del trabajo y enfermedades profesionales se incluyen en la encuesta aun si no respondieran al criterio 3, cuando la obligación de indemnizar los accidentes del trabajo y las enfermedades profesionales es impuesta directamente al empleador.

1. Regímenes que abarca la encuesta

De conformidad con los criterios citados anteriormente, están comprendidos en la encuesta, en términos generales, los siguientes tipos de regímenes:

i) regímenes de seguro social obligatorio;

ii) regímenes de seguro social voluntario o facultativo, a reserva de que se ajusten al criterio 2;

iii) regímenes universales no contributivos;

iv) cajas de previsión, en la medida en que se les aplique el criterio 3;

v) regímenes de responsabilidad del empleador en caso de accidentes del trabajo y de enfermedades profesionales;

vi) regímenes de prestaciones familiares;

vii)	servicios nacionales de salud establecidos por ley que otorguen a todos los ciudadanos el derecho a servicios y prestaciones prescritos;

viii)	regímenes especiales para los empleados públicos [4], contributivos o no (de pensiones, prestaciones familiares, enfermedad, indemnización de accidentes del trabajo y de enfermedades profesionales, u otras contingencias);

ix)	asistencia pública, dentro de los límites del criterio 1;

x)	prestaciones a las víctimas de guerra, dentro de los límites del criterio 1;

xi)	regímenes para determinadas ramas de industria o profesiones, o regímenes y planes instituidos por acuerdo entre empleadores y trabajadores, con la condición de que las obligaciones impuestas en virtud de ellos a los empleadores lo hayan sido por ley y que dichos regímenes o planes respondan también a los criterios 1, 2 y 3.

Así, no están comprendidos en la encuesta los regímenes de prestaciones pagadas directamente por el empleador en caso de enfermedad, maternidad, jubilación, etc., aunque la ley obligue al empleador a concederlas. La excepción que se hace en el apartado v) respecto de la indemnización por accidentes del trabajo y enfermedades profesionales se explica por el hecho de que, siendo ésta la rama más antigua de la seguridad social, casi todos los países poseen normas legales al respecto y, desde un punto de vista práctico, en el caso de la mayoría de los países resultó posible obtener datos ilustrativos, ya que por lo común existen instituciones que hacen cumplir la legislación pertinente. No ocurre lo mismo con igual frecuencia en el caso de las demás prestaciones que incumben a los empleadores. Finalmente, en los países donde el seguro social se implanta por extensión gradual, la legislación que rige la indemnización por accidentes o enfermedades de origen profesional sigue en vigencia en las zonas, empresas y ramas de industria a las que no se ha extendido todavía el seguro social; por tanto, si no se tuvieran en cuenta las prestaciones que el empleador está obligado a pagar, las estadísticas sobre las prestaciones por accidentes del trabajo y enfermedad profesional quedarían truncas y viciadas.

Claro está que lo mismo podría decirse de otras prestaciones, pero no es tan corriente que su pago sea responsabilidad legal del empleador, y los problemas prácticos que se presentan cuando se quiere obtener las cifras pertinentes son más difíciles de resolver. Sin embargo, conviene tener presente que en algunos países las cantidades abonadas directamente por los empleadores pueden ser considerables; por ejemplo, en el caso del pago de sueldos y salarios durante las enfermedades o debido a la terminación de la relación de trabajo. Por otro lado, cabe observar que las prestaciones de este tipo están comprendidas en la encuesta cuando son pagadas por organismos públicos directamente a su personal.

Los regímenes de seguridad social más importantes que quedan excluidos de la encuesta a raíz de la aplicación de los tres criterios mencionados anteriormente son quizá los regímenes privados, es decir, los no instituidos por ley y que ofrecen protección contra las contingencias corrientes de conformidad con el criterio 1; por ejemplo, los regímenes de pensiones privados o los planes de empresa en materia de asistencia médica. En algunos países tales regímenes pueden representar una parte importante de los recursos destinados a la seguridad social. El desarrollo en algunos países de los regímenes voluntarios de prestaciones a los trabajadores, que complementan a los regímenes instituidos por ley, es suficiente indicio de que las cifras consignadas en este volumen acerca de países como los Estados Unidos y el Reino Unido son bastante inferiores a las reales.

2. Definición de las prestaciones

La definición de las prestaciones que deriva del criterio 1 mencionado anteriormente se ajusta a la del Convenio sobre la seguridad social (norma mínima), 1952 (núm. 102), de la OIT, que distingue nueve ramas de seguridad social:

1)	asistencia médica (parte II);
2)	prestaciones monetarias de enfermedad (parte III);
3)	prestaciones de desempleo (parte IV);
4)	prestaciones de vejez (parte V);
5)	prestaciones en caso de accidente del trabajo y de enfermedad profesional (parte VI);
6)	prestaciones familiares (parte VII);
7)	prestaciones de maternidad (parte VIII);
8)	prestaciones de invalidez (parte IX);
9)	prestaciones de sobrevivientes (parte X).

Esta definición de las prestaciones no siempre coincide con la aplicada por los sistemas nacionales de los países comprendidos en la encuesta, pues en algunos de ellos la seguridad social abarca prestaciones pagaderas por otras contingencias. Los datos estadísticos referentes a tales prestaciones se han excluido en lo posible de los cuadros. Así se hizo, por ejemplo, con respecto a Israel y a Suiza, países en los cuales se pagan prestaciones especiales para compensar la pérdida de ingresos durante el servicio militar.

A la inversa, la encuesta comprende ciertos regímenes que no encajan estrictamente dentro de la definición de la seguridad social pero que ofrecen prestaciones o servicios a personas que, de lo contrario, quizá tendrían que recurrir a la seguridad social. Sirvan de ejemplo los sistemas de empleo protegido de Australia y de los Países Bajos.

Por último, ciertos servicios y prestaciones que caen fuera de la definición de la seguridad social del Convenio núm. 102 se han incluido, no obstante, en la encuesta por razones prácticas porque sería muy difícil, si no imposible, desglosar los datos correspondientes a ellos en las estadísticas de las instituciones de seguridad social que administran tales servicios y prestaciones. A título de ejemplo cabe citar las prestaciones pagaderas en caso de dificultades imprevistas en Nueva Zelandia, en particular las que se conceden a las esposas abandonadas, y los subsidios de recreo y adiestramiento físico que se abonan en la URSS y en algunos otros países de Europa oriental. Como regla general, la inclusión de prestaciones y servicios que en rigor deben excluirse de la encuesta no altera mayormente las cifras totales correspondientes al respectivo régimen o rama.

3. Asistencia médica que figuraba anteriormente en «Servicios públicos de salud»

A partir del ejercicio de 1978, primer año de la undécima encuesta, 1978-1980, se excluyó la asistencia médica facilitada a título de la salud pública. Por consiguiente, los datos correspondientes ya no figuran en los cuadros comparativos [5].

Sin embargo, hay que cuidar de no confundir la asistencia médica diversa facilitada a título de la salud pública con la asistencia médica proporcionada por regímenes de seguridad social que protegen al conjunto de la población, en virtud de un derecho reconocido por ley, a menudo sobre una base contributiva. Este es el caso del Servicio Nacional de Salud del Reino Unido, del Servicio Sanitario Nacional de Italia y de regímenes análogos existentes, por ejemplo, en los países de Europa oriental. Estos regímenes han sido incluidos en la encuesta bajo la rúbrica «Seguros sociales y regímenes asimilados», asimilándolos a los regímenes de seguro de enfermedad. (En las ediciones de las encuestas anteriores a la undécima de esta serie, los ingresos y los egresos de estos regímenes de seguridad social figuran bajo «Servicios públicos de salud», rúbrica ahora suprimida en los cuadros.) Como este cambio tiene consecuencias para la comparabilidad de las series históricas, en los lugares apropiados de los cuadros aparece una raya de separación para que se tenga en cuenta este hecho.

III. Alcance de la encuesta de la OIT y de otras compilaciones estadísticas

Diversos organismos internacionales o regionales compilan y publican estadísticas en las que la seguridad social, tal como está definida a los efectos de la encuesta de la OIT, ocupa un lugar más o menos importante según el objetivo de la compilación.

1. Sistema de cuentas nacionales de las Naciones Unidas (SCN)

El propósito de este sistema es ofrecer una estructura completa y detallada para registrar en forma sistemática y articulada todos los movimientos y existencias de una economía. Las operaciones financieras de la seguridad social expuestas en *El costo de la seguridad social* están necesariamente comprendidas en los diversos movimientos contabilizados en el SCN, aunque tal vez no todas estén clasificadas en la rúbrica «seguridad social», tal como se la define a los efectos del SCN. En el nuevo SCN, los «regímenes de seguridad social» se definen de la manera siguiente:

Los sistemas de seguridad social que han de incluirse son aquellos impuestos, controlados o financiados por las administraciones públicas. Los regímenes impuestos por las administraciones implicarán contribuciones obligatorias de los asalariados, de los empleadores, o de ambos, y abarcarán a toda la comunidad o a determinados sectores de la misma. Además, estos sistemas pueden permitir que algunos sectores de la comunidad se adhieran a los mismos voluntariamente. No se incluirán los regímenes establecidos por las administraciones públicas como empleador de personal; por ejemplo, los regímenes que difieren significativamente de los sistemas de seguridad social en favor de la comunidad o que son objeto de negociaciones con los empleados de las administraciones públicas. Se considera que tales regímenes son sistemas de pensiones. Aunque un régimen de seguridad social no implique contribuciones obligatorias impuestas por las administraciones públicas, deberá, no obstante, incluirse como parte de las administraciones públicas si, a través de la supervisión y reglamentación públicas o en virtud de la existencia de un sistema de donaciones de las administraciones públicas, forma parte claramente de la política social del gobierno para con el conjunto de la comunidad [6].

Esta definición abarca hasta cierto punto los regímenes clasificados como «seguros sociales y regímenes asimilados» y «prestaciones familiares» en la encuesta de la OIT. Los regímenes destinados al personal del sector público (funcionarios civiles y militares) están comprendidos, en lo que a las pensiones se refiere, entre las «cajas de pensiones y otras instituciones financieras» del SCN, categoría que también engloba a las cajas privadas de pensiones, las cuales están fuera del ámbito de la encuesta de la OIT. Las prestaciones de los empleados públicos durante las licencias de enfermedad y otros períodos de corta duración figuran en el SNC como «sueldos y salarios». La «asistencia pública» y las «prestaciones para las víctimas de guerra» aparecen bajo «servicios públicos generales».

2. Estadísticas de protección social en las Comunidades Europeas

La Oficina Estadística de las Comunidades Europeas (OECE) lleva a cabo cada año una encuesta sobre gastos corrientes relativos a las prestaciones de protección social; esa encuesta se realiza en el marco del Sistema Europeo de Estadísticas Integradas sobre Protección Social [7], en plena coordinación con el Sistema Europeo de Cuentas Económicas Integradas.

Se entiende por prestaciones de protección social todas las prestaciones en efectivo y en especie otorgadas a los hogares a raíz de determinados riesgos y contingencias, gracias a la intervención de un tercero; tales riesgos y contingencias abarcan más materias que las comprendidas en la encuesta de la OIT, tales como las prestaciones relacionadas con la colocación, la orientación profesional, el reasentamiento y la vivienda. La encuesta de la OECE procura medir los gastos sociales totales por concepto de protección social y permitir el análisis de los fines perseguidos con dichos gastos y el modo en que se financian.

A los fines de esta encuesta se consideran separadamente los regímenes generales y los regímenes complementarios o suplementarios; dentro de cada una de estas categorías se presentan diferenciadamente los siguientes: 1) regímenes nacionales; 2) regímenes generales; 3) regímenes especiales, y 4) regímenes voluntarios. Los regímenes especiales son objeto de subdivisiones más detalladas según se trate de: i) regímenes establecidos por ley; ii) otros regímenes de orden profesional; iii) regímenes en favor de las víctimas de trastornos políticos o catástrofes naturales, y iv) otros regímenes especiales. También se desglosa, con carácter residual, la categoría relativa a otras formas de protección social. La encuesta de la OECE es más amplia que la encuesta de la OIT, sobre todo porque abarca regímenes no creados en virtud de una ley. Sin embargo, se ha logrado cierta coordinación entre ambas encuestas con miras a que se puedan contestar las preguntas del cuestionario de la OIT a partir de los datos recogidos con motivo de la encuesta de la OECE.

3. Estadísticas de seguridad social de los países nórdicos

Estas estadísticas, que se publican cada dos años desde 1949, abarcan a los cinco países nórdicos (Dinamarca, Finlandia, Islandia, Noruega y Suecia) y se basan en una definición que difiere algo de la aplicada en la encuesta de la OIT. Comprenden, por ejemplo, partidas como los servicios de seguridad y de prevención de accidentes, los de empleo y colocación, las obras públicas y la capacitación profesional de los desempleados, los anticipos para el mantenimiento de los niños (en caso de falta de pago de la pensión alimentaria) y las exenciones fiscales estimadas por concepto de los hijos. En cambio, no abarcan los regímenes para los empleados públicos.

IV. Reunión y presentación de los datos estadísticos

Basándose en las respuestas recibidas y en datos extraídos de fuentes nacionales o internacionales, la Oficina ha podido compilar cuadros sintéticos para un total de 113 países, que se enumeran más abajo, agrupados por regiones. Figuran en bastardilla los nombres de los 8 (ocho) países incluidos por primera vez en la presente edición.

Conforme a la práctica seguida en las publicaciones estadísticas de la Oficina, en los cuadros los nombres de los países figuran en español, francés o inglés cuando su idioma nacional o de uso general es una de estas tres lenguas; en los demás casos figuran en la lengua utilizada en la correspondencia oficial entre el país y la Oficina.

Las regiones y los países que figuran en los cuadros son los siguientes:

Africa (33 países): Benin, Burkina Faso, Burundi, Cabo Verde, Camerún, República Centroafricana, Côte d'Ivoire, Chad, *Egipto*, Etiopía, Gabón, Guinea, Guinea-Bissau, Kenya, Madagascar, Malí, Marruecos, Mauricio, Mauritania, Mozambique, Níger, Nigeria, Rwanda, Santo Tomé y Príncipe, Senegal, Sudán, Swazilandia, Tanzanía, Togo, *Túnez*, Uganda, *Zaire* y Zambia.

América (28 países): Argentina, Bahamas, Barbados, Belice, Bolivia, Brasil, Canadá, Colombia, Costa Rica, Cuba, Chile, Dominica, *República Dominicana*, Ecuador, El Salvador, Estados Unidos, Granada, Guatemala, Guyana, Honduras, Jamaica, México, Panamá, Perú, Santa Lucía, Trinidad y Tabago, Uruguay y Venezuela.

Asia (19 países): Bahrein, Bangladesh, Chipre, Filipinas, India, Indonesia, República Islámica del Irán, Israel, Japón, Jordania, Kuwait, Malasia, Myanmar, Pakistán, *Qatar*, Singapur, *Republica Arabe Siria*, Sri Lanka y Tailandia.

Europa: países con economía de mercado (20 países): República Federal de Alemania [8], Austria, Bélgica, Dinamarca, España, Finlandia, Francia, Grecia, Irlanda, *Islandia*, Italia, Luxemburgo, Malta, Noruega, Países Bajos, Portugal, Reino Unido, Suecia, Suiza y Turquía.

Europa: países con economía centralmente planificada [9] (9 países): RSS de Bielorrusia, Bulgaria, Checoslovaquia, Hungría, República Democrática Alemana [8], *Polonia*, RSS de Ucrania, URSS y Yugoslavia.

Oceanía (4 países): Australia, Fiji, Nueva Zelandia e Islas Salomón.

Se ha hecho todo lo posible para compilar datos completos acerca de cada país. Sin embargo, en algunos casos fue imposible obtener informaciones acerca de ciertos regímenes, especialmente los relativos a los empleados públicos y la indemnización de accidentes del trabajo y enfermedades profesionales o la asistencia pública.

En los cuadros básicos [2] se aclaran los regímenes y servicios incluidos. En algunos casos en que no se contó con informaciones sobre algún año del período se incluyó una estimación basada en las cifras disponibles para un año anterior. En las notas del cuadro 1 se indican los nombres de los países correspondientes y de otros cuyos datos parecen ser incompletos. Puede ocurrir en ciertos casos que los datos disponibles para la decimotercera encuesta no sean estrictamente comparables con los de años anteriores. Esto puede deberse a cambios de la base de los datos o a modificaciones de la ley. En Chile, por ejemplo, se introdujo un nuevo sistema de seguro social y la transición a partir del sistema antiguo comenzó en marzo de 1981.

La compilación de datos estadísticos sobre el conjunto de los regímenes y servicios abarcados por la encuesta constituye una pesada carga para las administraciones públicas nacionales, sobre todo porque los diversos regímenes suelen estar administrados por organismos diferentes que dependen de ministerios distintos. La coordinación de la tarea en cada país representa un esfuerzo considerable para el ministerio encargado de las relaciones con la OIT (habitualmente el ministerio de trabajo), en particular cuando la administración de los regímenes está descentralizada o se ha dejado en manos de organismos provinciales o locales.

Es fácil comprender, pues, que la compilación de estadísticas completas lleve mucho tiempo. Para la mayor parte de los regímenes, generalmente no se dispone de los datos definitivos antes de que transcurran dieciocho meses o dos años después de finalizar el año al que se refieren, y en ocasiones el retardo es mayor aún. En el caso de numerosos países, la Oficina sólo puede obtener datos completos después de un prolongado intercambio de correspondencia con las autoridades nacionales, y a veces debe estudiar una serie de fuentes nacionales.

Para almacenar y reconstituir, una vez verificadas, las informaciones recogidas con motivo de la duodécima encuesta se ha creado un sistema electrónico de tratamiento de datos al que se añadieron estadísticas provenientes de anteriores encuestas. Durante estas operaciones se aprovechó la oportunidad de revisar cálculos realizados en años anteriores con objeto de reflejar, en particular, datos revisados sobre producto interno bruto, población o índices de precios. En consecuencia, las cifras de series históricas que figuran en esta edición de la encuesta pueden ser ligeramente distintas de las que se publicaron en ediciones anteriores.

En el cuestionario en que se basa la encuesta se solicitaba a los gobiernos que presentaran datos estadísticos sobre los ingresos y los egresos conforme al siguiente esquema:

Ingresos	*Egresos*
Cotizaciones:	Asistencia médica
de los asegurados	Prestaciones en especie,
de los empleadores	excepto asistencia médica
Impuestos y derechos especiales	Prestaciones monetarias
Participación del Estado	Total de prestaciones
Participación de otras	Gastos de administración
entidades públicas	
Renta del capital	Transferencias a otros
	regímenes cubiertos
Transferencias a otros	por la encuesta
regímenes cubierto	
por la encuesta	Otros egresos
Otros ingresos	Total de egresos
Total de ingresos	

En la última columna del cuestionario debía figurar la diferencia, positiva o negativa, entre el total de ingresos y el total de egresos.

Las explicaciones siguientes ayudarán a interpretar las cifras.

1. Ingresos

En las partidas «Cotizaciones de los asegurados» y «Cotizaciones de los empleadores» están incluidas las sumas que corresponden habitualmente a esos dos conceptos. Ahora bien, hay ciertos casos marginales y otros en que no se puede hacer claramente la distinción entre unas cotizaciones y otras. Es corriente que el empleador pague las cotizaciones de seguridad social y descuente después los aportes de los asegurados de su remuneración. No cabe la menor duda de que cada tipo de cotización debe clasificarse en su respectiva columna. Sin embargo, según el método de contabilidad aplicado, no siempre se especifica el tipo de cotización, y es preciso entonces hacer estimaciones. Estas últimas son fáciles de efectuar con suficiente exactitud cuando la ley establece tasas uniformes de cotización para los empleadores y los trabajadores, respectivamente, pero se complican cuando rigen tasas diferentes para las distintas categorías de asegurados (por ejemplo, por nivel de salario, rama del seguro, etc.). Es más: si el régimen ampara a los trabajadores independientes y a los desempleados o permite la afiliación voluntaria, con la cotización pagada íntegramente en tales casos por el asegurado, se dificulta mucho la operación de distribuir las cantidades entre las dos columnas.

Las dos columnas relativas a las cotizaciones deberían comprender teóricamente cualquier gravamen especial recaudado por el fisco cuando se deba considerar como cotización, más bien que como un verdadero impuesto. Por ejemplo, hasta 1968 había en Nueva Zelandia un impuesto especial sobre la renta destinado a la seguridad social, que se imputaba a la columna «Cotizaciones de los asegurados». Ese impuesto fue abolido por la ley de finanzas de 1968, y los fondos necesarios fueron provistos por las rentas generales del Estado. Por consiguiente, las sumas empleadas se imputan ahora al rubro «Participación del Estado».

Los regímenes de seguridad social de los países de Europa oriental se financian en gran parte con los recursos de los establecimientos o empresas. Las cantidades utilizadas con ese fin se inscriben en la columna «Cotizaciones de los empleadores». Sin embargo, en la RSS de Bielorrusia, en la RSS de Ucrania y en la URSS los aportes de las empresas y organizaciones del Estado a la seguridad social están enteramente incorporados en el presupuesto del Estado, por lo que se imputan, junto con otros pagos del Estado, a la columna «Participación del Estado».

En muchos países, la protección contra los riesgos profesionales se basa en la responsabilidad directa del empleador, que está obligado por la ley a pagar las prestaciones a cualquiera de sus obreros o empleados que sufra un accidente del trabajo o contraiga una enfermedad profesional. En este caso, el importe abonado por el empleador se indica en la columna «Cotizaciones de los empleadores». También se sigue ese criterio con las primas pagadas por el empleador para asegurarse en una compañía contra tales eventualidades, sin establecer distinciones según que el seguro sea voluntario u obligatorio.

En lo que respecta a los regímenes especiales para los funcionarios y empleados públicos, se considera que las sumas pagadas por el Estado u otras autoridades públicas en su calidad de empleadores son «aportes patronales» a los efectos de la encuesta y se registran, pues, en la columna «Cotizaciones de los empleadores».

La columna «Impuestos y tasas especiales» debería comprender los tributos que no pueden asimilarse a cotizaciones de seguridad social, pero cuyos proventos están expresamente reservados para la seguridad social. En Francia, por ejemplo, el régimen para los no asalariados de la agricultura se financia parcialmente con una serie de recursos parafiscales.

Las columnas «Participación del Estado» y «Participación de otras entidades públicas» deben comprender todos los pagos efectuados a la seguridad social por el gobierno central y las autoridades locales, respectivamente, sin que importe que se pague una parte de las cotizaciones correspondientes a todos los asegurados o sólo a algunas categorías, o de los gastos por prestaciones o los gastos de administración. Tratándose de países con régimen federal de gobierno, en la columna «Participación del Estado» están incluidas las sumas desembolsadas por el gobierno federal, mientras que los ingresos procedentes de los gobiernos de los estados o provincias se incluyen en la columna «Participación de otras entidades públicas».

La columna «Renta del capital» debe comprender, en principio, los intereses del capital invertido, netos de los gastos relacionados con las inversiones.

En el cuestionario en que se basa la encuesta, dos columnas se refieren a las transferencias entre regímenes, a fin de eliminar la doble contabilización de los traspasos de un régimen a otro. Esos traspasos no están englobados en los totales que figuran en este volumen. Los datos estadísticos recibidos a su respecto constan en los cuadros básicos [2]. Teóricamente, los totales de las dos columnas deberían coincidir, pero no siempre lo hacen (aunque las diferencias son habitualmente de poca cuantía), debido a los distintos procedimientos contables y ejercicios financieros de los diversos regímenes.

2. Egresos

En cuanto a los egresos, se ha establecido una distinción entre las prestaciones de asistencia médica, las prestaciones en especie, excepto asistencia médica, y las prestaciones monetarias.

En la columna «Asistencia médica» deben figurar todos los gastos por concepto de asistencia médica personal (es decir, asistencia por médicos generalistas y especialistas, asistencia hospitalaria (tratamiento y hospitalización inclusive), productos farmacéuticos, asistencia odontológica, exámenes de laboratorio, readaptación funcional, aparatos de prótesis, etc.), tanto si se trata de prestaciones en especie como de prestaciones en efectivo pagadas a los beneficiarios (por ejemplo, para reembolsarles los gastos de asistencia médica costeados directamente por ellos). Cuando el beneficiario tiene que soportar parte del costo, se ha considerado que los importes pagados por él, ya se abonen directamente a la persona o servicio que proporciona la asistencia o a la institución de seguro social que reembolsa los gastos, quedan fuera del ámbito de la encuesta y, por consiguiente, no se consignan ni como ingresos ni como egresos.

A partir de la octava encuesta se reservó una columna a las prestaciones en especie distintas de la asistencia médica, sobre todo para atender las necesidades del análisis económico. Muchos regímenes de seguridad social, de asistencia social o de servicios sociales ofrecen múltiples prestaciones o servicios en especie no clasificables como asistencia médica. Por ejemplo, los regímenes de prestaciones familiares de muchos países africanos de lengua francesa brindan una gama de servicios y prestaciones bajo el rubro de «servicios de salud y bienestar» *(action sanitaire et sociale)*. Estos pueden adoptar la forma de asistencia médica (dispensarios y centros materno-infantiles, subsidios de hospitalización, etc.), prestaciones en especie (distribución de leche y otros alimentos, ropa para los recién nacidos y para otros niños) o servicios (guarderías, colonias de vacaciones infantiles, vivienda). En forma análoga, en los países del norte de Europa existen prestaciones y servicios proporcionados por diversos regímenes de previsión social (asilos de ancianos y jubilados, servicios de asistencia doméstica, vacaciones para los niños y para las amas de casa, etc.). En los países de Europa oriental, la seguridad social proporciona centros de recreo, hogares de vacaciones y productos dietéticos.

Las prestaciones monetarias no plantean en general problemas de clasificación. Cabe mencionar, sin embargo, en lo que atañe al total de las prestaciones, el caso de las sumas pagadas y los servicios concedidos a los trabajadores migrantes en cumplimiento de convenios y de instrumentos bilaterales o multilaterales. Los procedimientos pueden variar de un país a otro, pero en general las cantidades de que se trata se consignaron como prestaciones pagadas por el país de la institución que sufragó el costo, aun cuando el pago haya sido hecho por la institución de otro país. La liquidación entre instituciones y entre países puede dejar un saldo positivo o negativo, que normalmente se ha registrado, según el caso, bajo «Otros ingresos» o bajo «Otros egresos», respectivamente.

En la columna «Gastos de administración» es posible que los datos no siempre sean exactos ni completos. La administración de un régimen de seguridad social puede estar a cargo de un organismo que administra al mismo tiempo otros regímenes no comprendidos en el ámbito de la encuesta de la OIT (como ocurre cuando los servicios del seguro de desempleo y los servicios de colocación dependen administrativamente del mismo organismo y los métodos contables no permiten desglosar los gastos de administración imputables al seguro de desempleo). En lo que atañe a la asistencia pública, no siempre es posible hacer la distinción entre los gastos por concepto de prestaciones y los gastos de administración. En muchos casos sólo se pueden dar cifras aproximadas, y a veces incluso esto es imposible. Por tanto, para algunos países las sumas pueden pecar por defecto, y los datos que figuran en esta columna deben interpretarse con prudencia, pues pueden no constituir una indicación completa y exacta de los gastos de administración. Los cuadros básicos muestran para qué regímenes y servicios se conocen los gastos de administración y aquellos para los cuales se carece de estos datos [2].

La columna relativa a la diferencia entre los ingresos y los egresos en el curso del ejercicio debe reflejar en principio el superávit o déficit neto del conjunto de los regímenes y servicios comprendidos en la encuesta. Sin embargo, hay que señalar que comprende, cuando procede, las sumas asignadas a las reservas técnicas o a los fondos de contingencia.

3. Ejercicios financieros

En las publicaciones precedentes, los datos se referían al año civil o al ejercicio financiero terminado en el respectivo año, con independencia del número de meses del año civil. En la presente encuesta, los datos se refieren al año civil o al ejercicio financiero cuya mayor parte corresponde al respectivo año civil.

En algunos países, el período considerado varía de un régimen a otro. Puede ocurrir que el ejercicio financiero del Estado no coincida con el año civil, pero que las estadísticas de algunos regímenes o servicios se ajusten a dicho año (habitualmente al que empieza durante el ejercicio financiero). En Singapur, por ejemplo, el ejercicio financiero del Estado termina el 31 de marzo, pero el de la Caja Central de Previsión coincide con el año civil.

V. Los cuadros comparativos

Los cuadros comparativos consisten principalmente en compilaciones de medidas relativas. Como se señaló anteriormente, la presentación general de este volumen se ajusta a la de ediciones anteriores, en especial en las agrupaciones de países por regiones, a fin de facilitar las comparaciones.

Como regla general, los datos se refieren a los años 1970, 1975, 1980 y 1983-1986. En lo referente a algunos países, como no se dispone de estadísticas para determinados años, se han dado los datos del primer año para el cual existen o del año más próximo a 1970, 1975, 1980 o 1983.

El objeto de presentar medidas relativas es, en primer lugar, mostrar la tendencia de los ingresos y los egresos de la seguridad social y su distribución dentro de cada país, y, en segundo lugar, dar la posibilidad de establecer comparaciones internacionales. Sin embargo, hay que obrar con prudencia al sacar conclusiones de las cifras de los cuadros, pues las medidas relativas se basan en totales globales para cada país.

En efecto, según los países, se observan diferencias considerables en el alcance de la protección y también, dentro de un mismo país, diferencias notables en la protección que se ofrece a diferentes sectores de la población. En estas condiciones, los promedios informan de manera muy poco satisfactoria sobre la protección ofrecida, en particular en muchos países en desarrollo, en los cuales, desde el punto de vista de la encuesta de la Oficina, el sistema de seguridad social puede consistir esencialmente en un régimen de seguro que cubre sólo a algunas categorías de la población asalariada (sobre todo en el sector moderno) y un régimen especial para los empleados públicos. Las estructuras y los cambios económicos, sociales y políticos determinan el desarrollo de los sistemas de seguridad social – un país da preferencia, por ejemplo, al seguro de enfermedad y otro tal vez al régimen de pensiones – y explican las grandes diferencias que es dable observar en la índole y el alcance de la protección.

Dado que en muchos países el sistema de seguridad social no ha alcanzado todavía su pleno desarrollo y que los diversos elementos determinantes del costo difieren a veces fundamentalmente según las ramas de la seguridad social, es conveniente considerar con espíritu crítico los datos financieros que aquí se presentan. Tomemos, por ejemplo, el caso de un régimen de seguro de enfermedad o de protección contra las lesiones profesionales que cubre a una gran parte de la población y de un régimen de pensiones con un campo de aplicación comparable; en este caso es muy probable que las cifras por persona sean relativamente reducidas para el primero y mucho más elevadas para el segundo, a causa de la naturaleza de las respectivas contingencias, y que los ingresos y los egresos sean casi iguales en aquél como consecuencia de una reducida acumulación de fondos y considerablemente diferentes en éste de resultas de una acumulación muy importante.

Hay otro factor que es menester señalar: el costo de la protección contra un mismo riesgo varía según la incidencia de éste. Consideremos el caso de un país que sufre de un fuerte desempleo o soporta una serie de epidemias y que, por esta razón, debe gastar cuantiosas sumas por concepto de prestaciones de desempleo o de servicios de salud; sin embargo, a igualdad de los demás factores, lo crecido de esas sumas no autoriza a afirmar que ese país posee un sistema de seguridad social más adelantado que otro en el cual los gastos representan un porcentaje menor del producto nacional, simplemente porque el desempleo no es tan grande o la situación sanitaria no es tan desfavorable.

Por último, debe recordarse que la definición de la seguridad social que se adoptó para la encuesta de la Oficina puede excluir importantes aspectos de la protección social otorgada a la población en algunos países, sobre todo cuando una parte apreciable de esa protección está a cargo de regímenes privados [10] o de regímenes que conceden prestaciones instituidas por ley pero concedidas directamente por el empleador (pago de salarios durante las enfermedades, asistencia médica, prestaciones de maternidad) y que por esta razón no entran en el ámbito de la encuesta.

En algunos cuadros no se han podido incluir todos los países enumerados anteriormente, sea porque no se disponía de algunos de los datos básicos a que se refieren las cifras de la seguridad social (producto interno bruto, cifras de la población, etc.), sea porque se carecía de los desgloses necesarios. En algunos casos se omitieron las cifras de uno o varios años porque no eran comparables con las de otros años. Así, por ejemplo, las cifras correspondientes al Chad, Guinea y Guinea-Bissau no se han presentado en el cuadro 3, porque no se disponía de datos relevantes sobre producto interno bruto; en el cuadro 6 no se han incluido Benin y Cuba, porque no se disponía de datos sobre índices del costo de la vida. En los cuadros 7 y 10 no se ha incluido Qatar, ya que sólo se suministraron datos de asistencia social. Los cuadros 7-10, donde se presenta la distribución porcentual de ingresos y egresos, deben utilizarse con prudencia en aquellos casos en que se ha indicado que el porcentaje es de 100 por ciento, pues esto puede deberse a informes incompletos.

Cuadro 1. Ingresos y egresos totales de la seguridad social por rúbricas principales (en millones de unidades monetarias nacionales), páginas 40-71

En el cuadro 1 aparecen, para los ingresos y los egresos, los totales generales de las diversas columnas del cuestionario, salvo de las referentes a las transferencias provenientes de otros regímenes y a las transferencias a otros regímenes comprendidos en la encuesta. Como ya se explicó, en principio estos importes deben anularse mutuamente, y en los cuadros comparativos deben tenerse en cuenta únicamente los totales netos, es decir, previa eliminación de las transferencias, si existen. El significado de las cifras de cada columna se explicó en la sección IV.

Las cifras permiten seguir los movimientos de los diferentes tipos de ingresos y los diferentes tipos de egresos, así como del total de ingresos y del total de egresos, en el curso del período de 17 (diecisiete) años (1970-1986) que los cuadros abarcan en principio. Se dan en las unidades monetarias que se utilizaban en el último año abarcado por la encuesta; cuando un país efectuó una reforma monetaria en el período considerado, se hicieron las conversiones necesarias.

Las tendencias que se perciben pueden deberse a diversos factores, que pueden conjugar sus efectos o anularse mutuamente, y en particular a la extensión de los regímenes (campo de aplicación y prestaciones) o a la creación de otros nuevos. Como puede verse en el cuadro anexo [1], «Datos sobre las cuentas nacionales y la población e índices de los precios del consumo», el índice del costo de la vida ha aumentado rápidamente en la mayor parte de los casos, con las consiguientes repercusiones en las cantidades del cuadro 1.

Otras diferencias pueden deberse a modificaciones de las disposiciones administrativas o financieras, que provocan cambios bruscos de un año a otro en los montos de las cifras de una u otra columna. Así, cuando deja de percibirse un impuesto especial asimilable a una cotización de seguridad social y la respectiva financiación pasa a hacerse con cargo a las rentas generales del Estado, en el cuadro se observa una brusca disminución, e incluso la desaparición, de las cifras de la columna «Impuestos y tasas especiales» y un aumento equivalente de las cantidades consignadas en la columna «Participación del Estado». Gracias a deducciones que pueden inferirse de las cifras relativas que se dan en otros cuadros y de las explicaciones proporcionadas, es posible hacerse una idea más exacta de las causas de los movimientos que registran las cifras del cuadro 1.

Las notas principales relativas a los datos de la seguridad social en distintos países sólo figuran al pie del cuadro 1 y no se repiten en los demás cuadros.

Cuadro 2. Ingresos y egresos totales de la seguridad social (en millones de dólares de los Estados Unidos), páginas 72-78

Con fines comparativos, en este cuadro se presentan el total de ingresos, el total de egresos y los gastos por concepto de prestaciones, en dólares de los Estados Unidos. Las conversiones se basan en las tasas de cambio indicadas en el cuadro anexo 1. Los tipos cambiarios del mercado de divisas expresados en unidades monetarias nacionales referidas al dólar de los Estados Unidos corresponden a las cotizaciones de fin de ejercicio financiero mencionadas en publicaciones del Fondo Monetario Internacional y de la Organización de las Naciones Unidas. En los casos en que estos tipos de cambio no figuran en dichas publicaciones, se han utilizado fuentes de documentación nacionales.

Conviene señalar la limitación de tales comparaciones, debida a la existencia de varios sistemas de tipos de cambio, por ejemplo en la URSS, o en países en donde la unidad monetaria ha cambiado en un período de años, por ejemplo Bolivia, Brasil, Israel y Perú.

Cuadro 3. Ingresos y egresos de los regímenes de seguridad social (en porcentaje del producto interno bruto a precios de comprador), páginas 79-85

El cuadro 3 muestra la incidencia relativa de la seguridad social en la economía nacional. A tal fin, el total de ingresos, el total de egresos y los gastos por concepto de prestaciones (columnas (10), (17) y (14) del cuadro 1) se relacionan con el producto interno bruto (PIB) o el producto material neto (PMN) a precios corrientes, tomados por regla general del *Yearbook of National Accounts Statistics*, de la Organización de las Naciones Unidas, y que figuran en el cuadro anexo [1]. En el caso de aquellos países cuyos ejercicios financieros no coinciden con el año civil, el PIB o el PMN respectivo es el del año civil en que transcurrió la mayor parte del ejercicio financiero.

El PIB puede definirse de manera aproximada como el total de las contribuciones a la producción de todos los productores residentes en el país. Como esta medida incluye los impuestos indirectos una vez deducidas las subvenciones, el total resultante se expresa a precios de comprador. El hecho de que se trata de una valoración bruta significa que no se ha descontado el consumo de capital fijo [11].

El nuevo sistema de cuentas nacionales (SCN), adoptado por la Comisión de Estadística de la Organización de las Naciones Unidas en su 15.º período de sesiones, en 1968, es una versión revisada y aumentada del sistema anterior, publicado en 1953 [6]. Como regla general, las cifras del cuadro 3 se basan en el PIB según el nuevo sistema. En algunos casos sólo se dispone de datos compilados según el antiguo sistema, y entonces ello se indica en una nota. Las comparaciones efectuadas en el caso de países para los cuales se dispone de cifras calculadas tanto con arreglo al antiguo sistema como al nuevo mostraron sólo pequeñas diferencias por lo que atañe al producto interno bruto; por tanto, las diferencias entre un sistema y otro no deben alterar mayormente en principio la comparabilidad de los datos del cuadro 3.

El sistema utilizado en los países con economías centralmente planificadas[9] – sistema del producto material neto (SPMN) – se distingue en lo esencial del SCN por el hecho de que tiene el propósito primordial de medir la producción de bienes en la denominada esfera de la producción material, con exclusión de la esfera no material, es decir, el sector de los servicios. El agregado generalmente utilizado es el producto material neto, que se define como el valor neto total de los bienes y de los servicios productivos (incluidos los impuestos sobre las cifras de negocios) producidos por la economía. Por servicios productivos o materiales se entiende servicios como transporte, almacenamiento, circulación de mercaderías, etc., que se conceptúan como continuación de la producción material [11]. El producto material neto no comprende las actividades económicas que no contribuyen directamente a la producción material, como la administración pública y la defensa, los servicios personales, los servicios de las profesiones liberales y actividades semejantes. Por consiguiente, las cifras del cuadro 3 basadas en el producto material neto conforme al SPMN no son comparables con las que toman como referencia el PIB conforme al SCN. Como éste comprende una serie de actividades no incluidas en aquél, cabe esperar que el costo de la seguridad social represente un porcentaje algo mayor del producto material neto que del producto interno bruto.

Tanto cuando las cifras se calculan en principio con arreglo al SCN como según el SPMN, puede haber grandes diferencias de un país a otro en la calidad de los datos básicos, los métodos de evaluación de los diversos elementos que entran en los cálculos, etc. A menudo las cifras son también objeto de reajustes, a veces considerables. Por tanto, las cifras de este cuadro deben interpretarse con prudencia. Además, como ya se señaló, es difícil sacar de ellas conclusiones en lo que atañe, por ejemplo, al nivel relativo de protección en los diversos países, puesto que los datos financieros por sí solos no son suficientes para ello.

Las cifras del cuadro 3 dan, teniendo en cuenta estas reservas y las limitaciones de su comparabilidad, informaciones sobre la importancia relativa de la seguridad social en la economía nacional dentro de cada país y en comparación con otros países y otras regiones. En la mayor parte de los casos no hay diferencias notables entre los porcentajes basados en los ingresos y los fundados en los egresos, pero para algunos países se observan diferencias apreciables que reflejan el grado de acumulación de capital del sistema de seguridad social, como se explicó a propósito del cuadro 1.

Cuadros 4 y 5. Ingresos y egresos anuales medios de la seguridad social por habitante, páginas 86-95 y páginas 96-105

Mientras que en el cuadro 1 los ingresos y egresos de los regímenes comprendidos en la encuesta se presentan en cifras absolutas para cada país, en los cuadros 4 y 5 el total de ingresos, el total de egresos y los gastos por concepto de prestaciones (columnas (10), (17) y (14) del cuadro 1) se relacionan con la población total y la población entre 15 y 64 años de edad (población en edad de trabajar). Las cifras en el cuadro 4 corresponden a unidades monetarias nacionales. Estas se han convertido en dólares de los Estados Unidos en el cuadro 5, con las mismas tasas de cambio que las utilizadas en el cuadro 2, a fin de facilitar comparaciones internacionales.

Las cifras de la población total (que aparecen en el cuadro anexo 1) se basan en estimaciones de mediados de año o en los datos de censos. Proceden, por regla general, del *Demographic Yearbook* y de números recientes del *Monthly Bulletin of Statistics*, de la Organización de las Naciones Unidas. Los datos sobre la población en edad de trabajar no suelen existir para cada año, y hubo que recurrir casi siempre a estimaciones calculando la razón entre la población en edad de trabajar y la población total en intervalos de cinco años entre 1970 y 1990 y obteniendo por interpolación los valores intermedios. Para estimaciones de la razón entre la población en edad de trabajar y la población total (variable intermedia) en la interpolación, se ha utilizado como referencia la publicación de la Organización de las Naciones Unidas *Global estimates and projections of population by sex and age, the 1988 revision* (Nueva York, 1989).

También aquí conviene tener presentes las reservas formuladas anteriormente acerca de los promedios generales. En particular, hay que observar que, cuando la protección que ofrece la seguridad social abarca un campo relativamente reducido, como ocurre a menudo en los países en desarrollo, un promedio por habitante calculado basándose sólo en la población total no da ninguna indicación sobre el costo de la seguridad social por habitante para la población protegida.

La utilidad de estos cuadros es que permiten percibir, en cada país, las tendencias de los ingresos y egresos de la seguridad social una vez eliminado el efecto del crecimiento demográfico. Si se compara la progresión de las cifras en el cuadro 4 y en el cuadro 1, es posible darse cuenta de la influencia de la evolución y la estructura demográficas. Particularmente interesante es tener una idea de la progresión del costo de la seguridad social en relación con la de la población. Cabe reiterar que las cifras sufren la influencia de varios factores, entre los que conviene destacar el aumento del costo de la vida durante el período examinado.

Cuadro 6. Indices de promedios anuales de egresos en prestaciones por habitante (población total) (valores ajustados de acuerdo con los índices del costo de la vida), páginas 106-108

Se acaba de señalar el efecto que tiene el aumento del costo de la vida sobre las cifras por habitante, lo que hace difíciles, y en algunos casos casi imposibles, las comparaciones de cifras basadas en unidades monetarias nacionales. Para mejorar las posibilidades de comparación, se corrigieron los promedios anuales de egresos en prestaciones por habitante para la población total (columna 5 del cuadro 4 y columna 5 del cuadro 5) teniendo en cuenta los índices de los precios del consumo y se calculó una serie de índices que tienen como base el año 1980. Sin embargo, a raíz de la decisión de excluir de las tres encuestas más recientes la asistencia médica proporcionada a título de la salud pública, fue necesario establecer dos series distintas según los países de que se trate. En consecuencia, aquellos países para los que existen datos firmes y consecuentes durante todo el período llevan una serie de índices única, con base 1980; cuando hay países en los que se interrumpe la continuidad a causa de la exclusión de los servicios de salud pública, aparecen dos series: la antigua, basada en datos que incluyen esos servicios, con base 1970, y una nueva serie, de la que se eliminan los servicios de salud pública, con base 1980. En uno u otro caso, puede ocurrir que no haya datos para el año de base (1970 o 1980), por lo que entonces se toma como base el año más reciente para el que se dispone de datos. La serie anterior está separada de la nueva por una raya vertical.

Los índices de los precios del consumo utilizados en los cálculos se mencionan en el cuadro anexo 1. En principio, se trata de los índices generales para todos los grupos publicados en el *Anuario de Estadísticas del Trabajo*, así como en el *Boletín de Estadísticas del Trabajo*, de la OIT, y el *International Financial Statistics Yearbook*, del Fondo Monetario Internacional.

Al examinar este cuadro conviene tener presente, sobre todo si se hacen comparaciones entre países, la explicación del concepto de índices de precios del consumo, tal como aparece en el *Anuario de Estadísticas del Trabajo*, de la OIT:

Los índices de los precios del consumo tienen por objeto medir los cambios que sufren, en el tiempo, el nivel de los precios al por menor de una lista fija de un conjunto de bienes y servicios que se considera representativo de los hábitos del consumo de una población determinada... Los métodos utilizados para calcular los índices varían de un país a otro... Los coeficientes de ponderación, que permiten tener en cuenta la importancia relativa de los gastos del consumo, se basan generalmente en los resultados de encuestas sobre los gastos de las familias que reflejan la estructura de los gastos del consumo y su importancia relativa para un grupo dado de la población... Dadas las diferencias en el alcance de los índices y en los métodos que se utilizan para calcularlos, las estadísticas que se presentan en este cuadro para los diferentes países no representan de modo uniforme las variaciones de los niveles de los precios, y la exactitud de los datos varía de un país a otro [12].

Cabe agregar que el esquema del consumo en materia de prestaciones de seguridad social puede diferir apreciablemente del esquema en que se basa el índice de precios. Además, este último se calcula a veces según el consumo y los precios de ciertos lugares (a menudo la capital del país), mientras que las estadísticas de seguridad social se refieren en principio a todo el país.

Cuadro 7. Distribución de los egresos de la seguridad social en prestaciones entre los distintos regímenes (en porcentaje del total de gastos en prestaciones), páginas 109-122

El cuadro 7 indica la distribución entre los regímenes de los egresos en prestaciones de la seguridad social. Muestra las diferencias que es dable observar según los países en lo que se refiere a la importancia relativa de los diversos regímenes, al igual que las modificaciones que pueden haberse producido al respecto en cada país

durante el período objeto de la encuesta. Los regímenes considerados son los mismos que en las ediciones anteriores: seguros sociales y regímenes asimilados, asignaciones familiares, regímenes especiales para empleados públicos, asistencia pública y regímenes asimilados, y víctimas de guerra.

No siempre es fácil distinguir entre los diversos regímenes. En algunos países, la misma institución puede administrar varios regímenes sin que exista la posibilidad de desglosar los datos. Por ejemplo, en la mayor parte de los países de Europa oriental existen regímenes unificados de seguridad social que comprenden los seguros sociales, la asistencia social y, a veces, las prestaciones a las víctimas de guerra.

No hay criterios precisos para clasificar un régimen en una categoría más bien que en otra, pero con el transcurso del tiempo se han impuesto ciertas prácticas.

Los regímenes de pensiones (o de otras prestaciones) no contributivos se incluyen en «Seguros sociales y regímenes asimilados», y no en «Asistencia pública y regímenes asimilados», aun cuando el pago de las prestaciones o de una parte de ellas se supedite a una comprobación de recursos. Este procedimiento parece ser el más conveniente para las comparaciones internacionales, ya que en muchos casos las prestaciones no contributivas forman parte integrante de un sistema general contributivo (caso de los suplementos concedidos, además de las prestaciones contributivas generales, si se demuestra la insuficiencia de recursos), mientras que en otros todo el sistema es no contributivo.

Los regímenes de protección contra los accidentes del trabajo y las enfermedades profesionales basados en los seguros privados o en el principio de la responsabilidad económica directa del empleador también figuran en la rúbrica «Seguros sociales y regímenes asimilados».

En «Regímenes especiales para empleados públicos» se incluyen los regímenes para tales empleados que difieren del régimen general o de otros regímenes específicos de seguridad social. Cuando los empleados públicos están protegidos por el régimen general, como en Finlandia y Suecia, los datos respectivos figuran en «Seguros sociales y regímenes asimilados».

Cabe señalar que la columna «Servicios públicos de salud» subsiste con el único objeto de presentar datos anteriores a la undécima encuesta; el signo «x» denota cada caso en que esto no rige. Los regímenes en virtud de los cuales se proporciona asistencia médica a toda la población que ejercita su derecho a ella siguen siendo abarcados por la encuesta y están agrupados en la rúbrica «Seguros sociales y regímenes asimilados».

Dado que las cifras se expresan en porcentaje del total, un aumento en una rúbrica debe ir acompañado de una disminución en otra, aun cuando los gastos en prestaciones correspondientes a esta última hayan aumentado en cifras absolutas. Otros cambios pueden deberse a que los datos de que se dispuso eran más completos que los de encuestas anteriores o, a la inversa, a que no se dispuso ahora de datos que habían existido en ocasiones anteriores; en este último caso, a fin de proporcionar un orden de magnitud, se repitió la cifra correspondiente al último año en que se dispuso de informaciones, aclarándose esto en la nota pertinente. Por último, algunos cambios pueden atribuirse a modificaciones de la legislación o al mejoramiento de las prestaciones.

Cuadro 8. Distribución de los ingresos de la seguridad social según su procedencia (en porcentaje del total de ingresos), páginas 123-136

El cuadro 8 muestra cómo se financia en cada país el sistema de seguridad social, tal como se define a los efectos de la encuesta. Da la distribución de los ingresos según su procedencia, expresándolos en porcentaje del total de ingresos, e indica los cambios que ha experimentado la distribución durante el período de referencia.

Las reservas formuladas con respecto al cuadro 7 en lo concerniente a los aumentos y disminuciones de las cifras relativas y al carácter más o menos completo de los datos son también válidas para el cuadro 8. Otros cambios pueden deberse a reformas de los procedimientos contables o a la utilización de otras fuentes de información.

Cuadro 9. Distribución de los ingresos relativos a los seguros sociales y regímenes asimilados y a las asignaciones familiares (en porcentaje del total de ingresos), páginas 137-149

El cuadro 9 proporciona las mismas informaciones que el cuadro 8, pero no para todo el sistema de seguridad social tal como se define a los efectos de la encuesta, sino únicamente para los regímenes clasificados en los epígrafes principales «Seguros sociales y regímenes asimilados» y «Asignaciones familiares». Algunos países no poseen regímenes de asignaciones familiares o no proporcionaron informaciones pertinentes, y en tales casos ello se indica en una nota. Obsérvese que este cuadro incluye datos sobre empleados públicos toda vez que están amparados por regímenes generales de seguridad social, como en Finlandia y Suecia.

Cuadro 10. Distribución de los egresos por prestaciones por ramas de la seguridad social, en lo relativo únicamente a los regímenes clasificados en las rúbricas «Seguros sociales y regímenes asimilados» y «Asignaciones familiares» (en porcentaje del total de egresos por prestaciones), páginas 150-169

Para posibilitar la agrupación de los datos sobre el costo de la seguridad social por riesgo o contingencia, en el cuestionario se pedía a los gobiernos que desglosaran los datos relativos a cada régimen o servicio por ramas de la seguridad social según la clasificación adoptada para las diversas partes del Convenio sobre la seguridad social (norma mínima), 1952 (núm. 102). En el cuadro 10 se presentan los resultados de esta agrupación de los datos. Están comprendidos en él los mismos regímenes que en el cuadro 9: seguros sociales y regímenes asimilados, y asignaciones familiares. Ello se debe a que es difícil agrupar los datos referentes a los regímenes clasificados en «Regímenes especiales para empleados públicos» (en los países de Europa oriental y en algunos otros, las cifras correspondientes figuran en «Seguros sociales y regímenes asimilados», y no pueden desglosarse), «Asistencia pública y regímenes asimilados» y «Víctimas de guerra». Unicamente se tienen en cuenta los gastos por concepto de prestaciones.

Aunque se habían solicitado datos sobre las nueve ramas que distingue el Convenio núm. 102, se juzgó preferible desglosarlos en cinco ramas principales: enfermedad y maternidad, riesgos profesionales, pensiones, desempleo y asignaciones familiares, pues estas grandes categorías corresponden bastante bien a la organización administrativa y financiera de un gran número de sistemas de seguridad social. Los gastos en prestaciones se dan, para las cinco ramas aludidas, en porcentaje del total para los regímenes considerados, con un desglose por tipo de prestaciones para la rama de enfermedad y maternidad y para la de riesgos profesionales.

Cabe hacer observar que, en esa clasificación, los datos relativos a las «cajas de previsión» y a los «subsidios en caso de muerte» figuran bajo la rúbrica «Pensiones». A veces, los datos proporcionados se refieren a dos o más ramas y no pueden imputarse separadamente, y en tales casos la información aparece en un solo lugar, aclarándose este hecho en la nota correspondiente.

Para muchos países no es posible distinguir netamente entre las diversas ramas: prestaciones que en determinados países se clasifican en cierta rama pueden imputarse en otro país a otra rama. Podrían citarse numerosos ejemplos, y es evidente que ello menoscaba la comparabilidad de las cifras [13]; cuando ésta deja mucho que desear, una nota lo advierte.

En el caso de ciertos regímenes especiales que otorgan en la mayor parte de los casos todas las prestaciones de seguridad social y para los cuales no se proporcionó ningún desglose, las cifras se imputaron a la rúbrica que, según la experiencia adquirida, representa la mayor proporción de las prestaciones (casi siempre «Pensiones»). Las cifras de la respectiva rúbrica pecan, pues, por exceso y las de las demás por la subestimación equivalente.

En ciertos casos excepcionales, no siempre ha sido posible desglosar las cifras correspondientes a regímenes comprendidos en este cuadro, y ello se debe a la forma en que se ha respondido a la encuesta.

Pese a ciertas inevitables faltas en la presentación, que imponen prudencia en la interpretación de las cifras, el cuadro informa acerca de la estructura global del sistema de seguridad social de los respectivos países, de la importancia relativa atribuida a cada rama y de la etapa de desarrollo que ha alcanzado cada una de ellas. Con miras a la evaluación de la importancia de los regímenes, en la columna 14 se indica el monto total de egresos por prestaciones en millones de unidades monetarias nacionales.

VI. Cuadros anexos

1. Datos sobre las cuentas nacionales y la población e índices de los precios del consumo, páginas 172-181

Se proporcionan, para cada país, los datos de referencia utilizados en los cuadros comparativos.

2. Clave de nombres de países en tres idiomas, páginas 182-183

Notas

[1] Para un resumen de la labor de la OIT en los años anteriores a la guerra, véase Asociación Internacional de la Seguridad Social (AISS): *El costo de la seguridad social en 1949-1951: Encuesta internacional realizada por la Oficina Internacional del Trabajo* (Ginebra, OIT, 1955).

Los resultados de las encuestas anteriores a la presente se publicaron de la siguiente manera:

Primera encuesta: «El costo de la seguridad social», en *Revista Internacional del Trabajo* (Ginebra, OIT), junio de 1952, págs. 762-834, y «Análisis comparativo del costo de la seguridad social», en *ibíd.*, marzo de 1953, págs. 334-347.

Segunda encuesta: AISS: *El costo de la seguridad social en 1949-1951...*, *op. cit.*, y OIT: *Le financement de la sécurité sociale*, Informe III a la Primera Conferencia Regional Europea, Ginebra, 1955 (mimeografiado; existen también en inglés).

Tercera encuesta: OIT: *El costo de la seguridad social, 1949-1954* (Ginebra, 1958; edición trilingüe).

Cuarta encuesta: Idem: *El costo de la seguridad social, 1949-1957* (Ginebra, 1961; edición trilingüe).

Quinta encuesta: Idem: *El costo de la seguridad social, 1958-1960* (Ginebra, 1964; edición trilingüe).

Sexta encuesta: Idem: *El costo de la seguridad social: Sexta encuesta internacional, 1961-1963* (Ginebra, 1967; edición trilingüe).

Séptima encuesta: Idem: *El costo de la seguridad social: Séptima encuesta internacional, 1964-1966, con un suplemento sobre el campo de aplicación de los sistemas de seguridad social* (Ginebra, 1972; edición trilingüe).

Octava encuesta: Idem: *El costo de la seguridad social: Octava encuesta internacional, 1967-1971, con un suplemento sobre el costo de los regímenes no instituidos por ley* (Ginebra, 1976; edición trilingüe), y *The cost of social security: Eighth international inquiry, 1967-1971: Basic tables* (Ginebra, 1976; en inglés únicamente).

Novena encuesta: Idem: *El costo de la seguridad social: Novena encuesta internacional, 1972-1974* (Ginebra, 1979; edición trilingüe), y *The cost of social security: Ninth international inquiry 1972-1974: Basic tables* (Ginebra, 1978; en inglés únicamente).

Décima encuesta: Idem: *El costo de la seguridad social: Décima encuesta internacional, 1975-1977* (Ginebra, 1981; edición trilingüe), y *The cost of social security: Tenth international inquiry, 1975-1977: Basic tables* (Ginebra, 1981; en inglés únicamente).

Undécima encuesta: Idem: *El costo de la seguridad social: Undécima encuesta internacional, 1978-1980* (Ginebra, 1985; edición trilingüe), y *The cost of social security. Eleventh international inquiry, 1978-1980: Basic tables* (Ginebra, 1985; en inglés únicamente).

Duodécima encuesta: Idem: *El costo de la seguridad social: Duodécima encuesta internacional, 1981-1983: Cuadros comparativos* (Ginebra, 1988; edición trilingüe), y *The cost of social security: Twelfth international inquiry, 1981-1983: Basic tables* (Ginebra, 1988; en inglés únicamente).

[2] OIT: *The cost of social security: Thirteenth international inquiry, 1984-1986: Basic tables, main volume* (Ginebra, 1990; en inglés únicamente) y *Supplementary volume* (Ginebra, 1991; en inglés únicamente).

[3] Idem: *Informe de la Comisión de Expertos en Seguridad Social, Ginebra, 26 de noviembre-3 de diciembre de 1975* (Ginebra, documento CSSE/D.14/1975 [Rev.], mimeografiado), anexo II: «Segundo punto del orden del día: Indicadores de seguridad social: primera evaluación de su desarrollo».

[4] Regímenes o planes de seguridad social para estos empleados, distintos del régimen general o de otros regímenes específicos de seguridad social. Para propósitos de esta encuesta, se consideran como empleados públicos a quienes trabajan en la administración pública y en servicios públicos sociales, culturales, de educación y de salud. En dicha categoría se incluyen tanto los empleados civiles como los militares.

[5] Véase OIT: *El costo de la seguridad social: Undécima encuesta internacional, 1978-1980* (Ginebra, 1985), pág. 25.

[6] Naciones Unidas, Departamento de Asuntos Económicos y Sociales, Oficina de Estadística: *Un sistema de cuentas nacionales*, Estudios de métodos, serie F, núm. 2, rev. 3 (Nueva York, 1970; número de venta: S.69.XVII.3), pág. 78, párrafo 5.27.

[7] Véase Statistical Office of the European Communities: *European System of Integrated Social Protection Statistics: Methodology*, vol. I (Luxemburgo, 1981, IBBN 92-825-2006-8).

[8] Datos correspondientes al período 1970-1986, con anterioridad a la accesión de la República Democrática Alemana a la República Federal de Alemania, en 1990.

[9] Datos correspondientes al período 1970-1986, en que las economías de estos países eran centralmente planificadas. Los nombres de países son los utilizados en ese período.

[10] Véase OIT: *El costo de la seguridad social: Octava encuesta internacional...*, *op. cit.*, suplemento.

[11] Naciones Unidas, Departamento de Asuntos Económicos y Sociales, Oficina de Estadística: *Yearbook of National Accounts Statistics*, 1981, 3 vols. (Nueva York, 1981; número de venta: E.83.XVII.3), y ediciones anteriores (se publica desde 1966, únicamente en inglés); definiciones citadas: vol. I, págs. XV y XVII.

[12] Para más detalles sobre el contenido y los métodos del cálculo de los índices de los precios del consumo, véase OIT: *Anuario de Estadísticas del Trabajo, 1981* (Ginebra, 1981), notas explicativas, pág. 513, así como las publicaciones especializadas allí citadas.

[13] Véase OIT: *El costo de la seguridad social: Séptima encuesta internacional...*, *op. cit.*, págs. 35 y 36.

Comparative tables

Tableaux comparatifs

Cuadros comparativos

Explanation of signs used in the tables

−   = Not applicable *or* magnitude nil.
0, 0.0 = Magnitude less than half the unit used.
·   = Figure unknown *or* not available.
x   = Excluding data on medical care provided under public health services; see introduction (table 7).

Full stops are used for decimal places in the tables.

For some countries the figures may not add up to the totals shown, owing to rounding.

A horizontal rule between two figures or lines of figures indicates a discontinuity in the series.

A vertical bar in a line of figures indicates a transition from an old to a new series; see introduction (table 6).

Explication des signes utilisés dans les tableaux

−   = Sans objet *ou* grandeur nulle.
0, 0.0 = Chiffre inférieur à la moitié de l'unité utilisée.
·   = Chiffre inconnu *ou* non disponible.
x   = Indique, dans le tableau 7, que la rubrique est sans objet, les soins médicaux fournis au titre de la santé publique n'étant plus pris en considération (voir introduction, tableau 7).

Un point sépare les unités des décimales.

Pour certains pays, les chiffres ayant été arrondis, leur somme peut ne pas correspondre au total indiqué.

Un filet horizontal entre deux chiffres ou deux lignes de chiffres indique une discontinuité dans les séries.

Un filet vertical dans une ligne de chiffres indique, dans le tableau 6, le passage d'une ancienne à une nouvelle série (voir introduction, tableau 6).

Explicación de los signos usados en los cuadros

−   = No aplicable *o* cifras nulas.
0, 0.0 = Cifras inferiores a la mitad de la unidad utilizada.
·   = Cifras desconocidas *o* de las que no se dispone.
x   = Excluida la asistencia médica brindada por los servicios de salud pública; véase la introducción (cuadro 7).

En los cuadros, las unidades están separadas de los decimales por un punto.

Como en algunos casos se han redondeado las cifras, los totales no siempre corresponden a la suma de las mismas.

Una raya horizontal entre dos cifras o dos renglones de cifras indica una solución de continuidad en las series.

Una raya vertical en un renglón de cifras significa que se pasa de una serie anterior a una nueva; véase la introducción (cuadro 6).

1. Total social security receipts and expenditure by main item
(in millions of national currency units)

1. Recettes et dépenses totales de la sécurité sociale par rubrique principale
(en millions d'unités monétaires nationales)

1. Ingresos y egresos totales de la seguridad social por rúbricas principales
(en millones de unidades monetarias nacionales)

Country and currency unit *Pays et unité monétaire* País y unidad monetaria	Financial year *Exercice financier* Ejercicio financiero	Receipts *Recettes* Ingresos						
		Contributions *Cotisations* Cotizaciones		Special taxes allocated to social security *Taxes et impôts spéciaux* Impuestos y tasas especiales	State participation *Participation de l'Etat* Participación del Estado	Participation of other public authorities *Participation d'autres pouvoirs publics* Participación de otras entidades públicas	Income from capital *Revenu des capitaux* Renta del capital	Other receipts *Autres recettes* Otros ingresos
		From insured persons *Des assurés* De los asegurados	From employers *Des employeurs* De los empleadores					
(1)	(2)	(3)	(4)	(5)	(6)	(7)	(8)	(9)

AFRICA – AFRIQUE – AFRICA

(1)	(2)	(3)	(4)	(5)	(6)	(7)	(8)	(9)
Bénin (Franc CFA)	1970	41.60	595.20	—	1 186.00	—	—	3.80
	1975	179.40	1 203.90	—	1 531.10	—	23.90	0.00
	1981	1 269.02	4 473.02	—	—	—	—	3.90
	1983	1 492.98	5 505.86	—	—	—	—	2.89
	1984[1]	552.90	2 743.30	—	—	—	290.00	73.60
	1985[1]	619.20	3 070.90	—	—	—	220.00	59.00
	1986[1]	721.70	3 559.60	—	—	—	198.30	59.60
Burkina Faso[2] (Franc CFA)	1975	216.20	1 675.70	—	969.70	—	42.40	0.70
	1980	770.10	3 120.70	—	—	—	65.00	376.00
	1983	2 181.70	6 910.40	7.80	—	—	36.80	—
	1984[1]	1 032.80	4 263.40	—	—	—	1 459.90	4.60
	1985[1]	1 137.10	4 539.30	—	—	—	1 561.40	3.50
	1986[1]	1 259.80	5 200.90	—	—	—	1 624.10	2.70
Burundi[3] (Franc burundais)	1978	76.39	143.18	—	64.94	—	4.42	43.56
	1980	100.37	186.50	—	121.85	—	4.97	61.27
	1983	285.45	364.55	—	99.88	—	130.80	9.33
	1984	314.20	469.20	—	—	—	175.30	1.00
	1985	361.20	547.20	—	—	—	207.60	1.00
	1986	422.80	700.00	—	—	—	244.10	2.00
Cameroun[2, 4] (Franc CFA)	1970	128.00	2 321.70	—	2 809.00	—	16.30	0.10
	1981	3 360.00	21 053.00	—	—	—	—	1.00
	1983	4 760.00	29 556.00	—	—	—	8 500.00	1.00
	1984[1, 5]	6 315.00	31 049.00	—	—	—	1 029.00	—
	1985[1, 5]	6 613.00	34 315.00	—	—	—	9 449.00	—
	1986[1, 5]	7 940.00	38 700.00	—	—	—	10 130.00	—
Cap-Vert[3] (Escudo)	1983	64.41	156.85	—	—	—	0.31	1.72
	1984	94.25	220.50	—	—	—	3.39	1.91
	1985	118.71	275.04	—	6.30	—	10.17	2.10
	1986	137.25	312.45	—	7.70	—	40.22	2.25
Rép. centrafricaine[3] (Franc CFA)	1981	238.80	1 850.30	—	—	—	—	2.60
	1983	225.10	2 025.70	—	—	—	31.40	1.30
	1984	275.00	2 472.00	—	—	—	—	—
	1985	301.00	2 712.00	—	—	—	43.00	28.00
	1986	448.00	4 026.00	—	—	—	61.00	14.00

See notes on page 70. *Voir notes page 70.* Véanse notas pág. 70.

Total receipts (excluding transfers)	Benefits				Administrative expenditure	Other expenditure	Total expenditure (excluding transfers)	Difference between receipts and expenditure	
Total des recettes (non compris les transferts)	*Prestations* / Prestaciones				*Frais d'administration*	*Autres dépenses*	*Total des dépenses (non compris les transferts)*	In absolute figures	As percentage of total receipts
Total de ingresos (excl. las transferencias)	Medical care / *Soins médicaux* / Asistencia médica	Benefits in kind other than for medical care / *Prestations en nature à d'autres titres que les soins médicaux* / Prestaciones en especie, excepto asistencia médica	Cash benefits / *Prestations en espèces* / Prestaciones monetarias	Total	Gastos de administración	Otros egresos	Total de egresos (excl. las transferencias)	*En chiffres absolus* / En cifras absolutas	*En pourcentage du total des recettes* / En porcentaje del total de ingresos
(10)	(11)	(12)	(13)	(14)	(15)	(16)	(17)	(18)	(19)
1 826.60	1 203.80	27.60	440.20	1 671.60	104.00	4.40	1 780.00	46.60	2.6
2 938.30	1 436.10	0.30	1 102.90	2 539.30	225.20	11.40	2 775.90	162.40	5.5
5 745.94	190.00	67.43	4 172.41	4 429.84	386.61	—	4 816.45	929.49	16.2
7 001.73	470.00	92.45	5 328.06	5 890.52	309.66	—	6 200.18	801.55	11.4
3 659.80	71.90	—	2 365.20	2 437.10	906.50	36.80	3 380.40	279.40	7.6
3 969.10	77.50	—	2 495.60	2 573.10	941.80	26.70	3 541.60	427.50	10.8
4 539.20	80.50	—	2 481.40	2 561.90	1 306.80	37.60	3 906.30	632.90	13.9
2 904.70	1 056.80	—	1 112.20	2 169.00	144.00	—	2 313.00	591.70	20.4
4 331.80	36.30	—	1 047.60	1 083.90	460.10	220.40	1 764.40	2 567.40	59.3
9 136.70	41.30	0.60	3 920.10	3 962.00	1 603.00	140.10	5 705.10	3 431.60	37.6
6 760.70	12.30	6.50	1 649.70	1 668.50	—	17.50	1 686.00	5 074.70	75.1
7 241.30	7.30	10.70	1 803.10	1 821.10	—	16.90	1 838.00	5 403.30	74.6
8 087.50	13.70	4.30	2 024.90	2 042.90	—	17.50	2 060.40	6 027.10	74.5
332.49	1.84	—	111.78	113.62	50.07	0.46	164.15	168.34	50.6
474.96	2.65	—	193.30	195.95	69.89	0.85	266.69	208.27	43.9
890.01	191.45	—	200.13	391.58	92.40	18.50	502.49	387.52	43.5
959.70	224.00	—	167.20	391.20	113.90	67.40	572.50	387.20	40.3
1 117.00	296.00	—	202.10	498.10	129.80	35.40	663.30	453.70	40.6
1 368.90	498.00	—	269.10	767.10	137.90	28.10	933.10	435.80	31.8
5 275.10	.	.	.	4 531.40	336.70	12.10	4 880.20	394.90	7.5
24 414.00	408.00	1.00	10 731.00	11 140.00	—	—	11 140.00	13 274.00	54.4
42 817.00	288.00	6.00	14 789.00	15 083.00	—	1.00	15 084.00	27 733.00	64.8
38 393.00	311.00	2.00	13 453.00	13 766.00	—	—	13 766.00	24 627.00	64.1
50 377.00	308.00	—	15 259.00	15 567.00	—	—	15 567.00	34 810.00	69.1
56 770.00	371.00	—	19 498.00	19 869.00	—	—	19 869.00	36 901.00	65.0
223.29	5.17	10.26	45.72	61.15	13.16	20.46	94.77	128.53	57.6
320.05	7.34	17.50	54.52	79.36	19.58	21.16	120.10	199.95	62.5
412.32	13.95	26.24	67.53	107.72	21.62	32.35	161.69	250.63	60.8
499.87	18.50	34.85	77.74	131.09	30.86	48.33	210.29	289.58	57.9
2 091.70	3.30	—	834.80	838.10	738.80	118.60	1 695.50	396.20	18.9
2 283.50	3.80	0.50	1 067.20	1 071.50	690.80	159.40	1 921.70	361.80	15.8
2 747.00	11.00	30.00	2 016.00	2 057.00	853.00	48.40	2 958.40	− 211.40	− 7.7
3 084.00	23.00	23.00	1 915.00	1 961.00	927.00	290.00	3 178.00	− 94.00	− 3.0
4 549.00	28.00	27.00	2 477.00	2 532.00	757.00	2 261.00	5 550.00	− 1 001.00	− 22.00

Table 1 *(cont.)* Tableau 1 *(suite)* Cuadro 1 *(cont.)*

Country and currency unit / Pays et unité monétaire / País y unidad monetaria	Financial year / Exercice financier / Ejercicio financiero	Receipts / Recettes / Ingresos						
		Contributions / Cotisations / Cotizaciones		Special taxes allocated to social security / Taxes et impôts spéciaux / Impuestos y tasas especiales	State participation / Participation de l'Etat / Participación del Estado	Participation of other public authorities / Participation d'autres pouvoirs publics / Participación de otras entidades públicas	Income from capital / Revenu des capitaux / Renta del capital	Other receipts / Autres recettes / Otros ingresos
		From insured persons / Des assurés / De los asegurados	From employers / Des employeurs / De los empleadores					
(1)	(2)	(3)	(4)	(5)	(6)	(7)	(8)	(9)
Côte d'Ivoire[3] (Franc CFA)	1981	8 398.00	12 889.00	—	—	—	4 960.00	—
	1983	9 222.00	13 948.00	—	—	—	5 955.00	—
	1984	3 514.80	17 411.80	—	—	—	7 522.00	3.80
	1985	4 888.50	21 007.30	—	—	—	12 527.80	0.10[6]
	1986	5 478.70	21 377.80	—	—	—	13 419.80	1.10
*Egypt[4] (Pound)	1984	653.10	939.80	—	316.10	—	280.60	149.40
	1985	741.20	1 084.30	—	347.30	—	357.80	249.00
	1986	854.10	1 307.90	—	386.10	—	431.80	305.60
Ethiopia[7] (Birr)	1972	7.83	29.91	—	41.79	—	1.21	0.32
	1975	10.30	44.93	—	59.21	—	1.99	0.62
	1980	25.67	83.22	—	5.28	—	3.50	—
	1983[8]	40.05	82.58	—	—	—	3.91	—
	1984[9]	48.07	98.79	—	—	—	4.59	—
	1985[9]	51.89	102.53	—	—	—	4.28	—
	1986[9]	52.74	102.48	—	—	—	6.86	—
Gabon[2] (Franc CFA)	1980	1 632	16 366	—	—	—	549	410
	1983[10]	6 327	25 812	—	5 080	—	2 162	251
	1984[11]	3 204	31 748	—	—	—	—	2 450
	1985[11]	3 561	35 335	—	—	—	—	2 823
	1986[11]	3 145	32 049	—	—	—	—	2 594
Guinée[3] (Syli)	1981	—	133.65	27.67	—	—	—	—
	1983	—	130.81	35.50	—	—	—	—
	1984	.	.	.	.	.	.	.
	1985[5]	4.79	144.81	—	—	—	—	10.60
	1986[5]	8.90	269.27	—	—	—	—	18.02
Guinée-Bissau[3] (Peso)	1981	8.50	14.87	—	—	—	4.00	7.44
	1983	7.19	12.43	—	—	—	5.50	2.79
	1984	10.40	35.40	—	6.00	—	5.80	—
	1985	15.40	49.00	—	13.50	—	5.20	—
	1986	31.50	87.00	—	14.20	—	5.30	—
Kenya[3, 12] (Shilling)	1970	73.40	153.40	0.20	110.00	—	—	2.80
	1975	136.40	210.80	0.00	338.00	—	91.60	14.80
	1981	160.00	160.00	—	—	—	172.40	—
	1983	152.00	152.00	—	—	—	296.40	—
	1984	380.00	380.00	20.00	—	—	900.00	—
	1985	420.00	420.00	20.00	—	—	1 000.00	—
	1986	460.00	460.00	20.00	—	—	720.00	—
Madagascar (Franc malgache)	1981	527.50	6 858.70	—	—	—	551.00	—
	1983	510.30	6 633.80	—	—	—	2 392.00	—
	1984	1 865.00	6 527.60	—	—	—	—	—
	1985	1 981.30	6 934.80	—	—	—	—	—
	1986	2 286.30	8 001.90	—	—	—	—	—
Mali (Franc CFA)	1972[13]	27.50	548.50	—	1 078.00	—	—	6.50
	1975[13]	87.00	742.50	0.50	1 208.00	—	3.00	134.00
	1980[13]	192.50	1 803.50	—	242.00	—	4.50	28.00
	1983[13]	625.60	3 438.70	—	86.80	—	—	401.50
	1984[14]	1 261.70	4 838.60	—	—	—	—	282.10
	1985[14]	1 266.70	5 255.20	—	—	—	—	282.30
	1986	1 350.20	6 041.00	—	—	—	0.90	736.70

See notes on page 70. *Voir notes page 70.* Véanse notas pág. 70.

42

| | Expenditure / Dépenses / Egresos | | | | | | | Difference between receipts and expenditure / Différence entre les recettes et les dépenses / Diferencia entre los ingresos y los egresos | |
| Total receipts (excluding transfers) / Total des recettes (non compris les transferts) / Total de ingresos (excl. las transferencias) | Benefits / Prestations / Prestaciones | | | | Administrative expenditure / Frais d'administration / Gastos de administración | Other expenditure / Autres dépenses / Otros egresos | Total expenditure (excluding transfers) / Total des dépenses (non compris les transferts) / Total de egresos (excl. las transferencias) | In absolute figures / En chiffres absolus / En cifras absolutas | As percentage of total receipts / En pourcentage du total des recettes / En porcentaje del total de ingresos |
	Medical care / Soins médicaux / Asistencia médica	Benefits in kind other than for medical care / Prestations en nature à d'autres titres que les soins médicaux / Prestaciones en especie, excepto asistencia médica	Cash benefits / Prestations en espèces / Prestaciones monetarias	Total / Total / Total					
(10)	(11)	(12)	(13)	(14)	(15)	(16)	(17)	(18)	(19)
26 247.00	806.09	—	7 759.00	8 565.09	4 516.00	1 494.00	14 575.09	11 671.91	44.5
29 125.00	828.70	—	11 973.00	12 801.70	1 486.00	2 050.00	16 337.70	12 787.30	43.9
28 452.40	2 649.60	—	13 728.00	16 377.60	4 454.30	1 138.10	21 970.00	6 482.40	22.8
38 423.70	2 786.10	—	13 499.90	16 286.00	5 760.80	1 218.70	23 265.50	15 158.20	39.5
40 277.40	3 485.50	—	14 726.20	18 211.70	3 210.80	1 444.00	22 866.50	17 410.90	43.2
2 339.00	29.60	—	825.20	854.80	44.70	14.10	913.60	1 425.40	60.9
2 779.60	29.60	—	893.40	923.00	49.20	14.10	986.30	1 793.30	64.5
3 285.50	31.80	—	1 038.60	1 070.40	56.00	17.10	1 143.50	2 142.00	65.2
81.06	37.00	—	25.23	62.23	0.96	0.26	63.45	17.61	21.7
117.05	54.20	—	47.73	101.93	1.04	0.42	103.39	13.66	11.7
117.67	—	5.28	73.08	78.36	1.41	—	79.77	37.90	32.2
126.54	—	—	104.32	104.32	2.00	—	106.32	20.22	16.0
151.45	—	—	101.67	101.67	2.00	—	103.67	47.78	31.5
158.70	—	—	112.91	112.91	2.00	—	114.91	43.79	27.6
162.08	—	—	114.22	114.22	2.10	—	116.32	45.76	28.2
18 957	8 152	72	5 302	13 526	2 371	2 427	18 324	633	3.3
39 632	13 108	262	13 662	27 032	4 027	2 291	33 350	6 282	15.9
37 402	15 587	1 129	10 152	26 868	4 920	1 802	33 590	3 812	10.2
41 719	17 106	1 791	11 466	30 363	5 790	1 690	37 843	3 876	9.3
37 788	19 224	1 303	13 648	34 175	6 380	1 771	42 326	−4 538	−12.0
161.32	9.89	—	26.97	36.86	9.43	—	46.29	115.03	71.3
166.32	17.11	—	16.23	33.34	11.38	—	44.71	121.60	73.1
160.20	2.77	—	123.52	126.29	1.63	12.47	140.38	19.81	12.4
269.19	12.69	—	216.31	229.00	4.76	34.94	268.70	27.49	9.3
34.81	0.80	0.62	0.01	1.43	9.82	29.41	40.66	− 5.85	−16.8
27.91	1.64	—	—	1.64	9.20	36.95	47.79	−19.88	−71.2
57.60	2.70	5.50	5.48	13.68	11.00	—	24.68	32.92	57.2
83.10	10.80	5.30	11.67	27.77	18.40	—	46.17	36.93	44.4
138.00	13.62	5.30	17.97	36.89	25.00	—	61.89	76.11	55.2
339.80	122.40	—	91.20	213.60	6.00	—	219.60	120.20	35.4
791.60	367.80	—	111.80	479.60	15.40	0.40	495.40	296.20	37.4
492.40	0.40	—	24.90	25.30	13.80	—	39.10	453.30	92.1
600.40	0.40	—	40.00	40.40	15.20	—	55.60	544.80	90.7
1 680.00	—	—	160.00	160.00	34.00	—	194.00	1 486.00	88.5
1 860.00	—	—	220.00	220.00	36.00	—	256.00	1 604.00	86.2
1 660.00	—	—	228.00	228.00	40.00	—	268.00	1 392.00	83.9
7 937.20	.	.	.	4 535.00	—	—	4 535.00	3 402.20	42.9
9 536.10	.	.	.	6 609.00	—	—	6 609.00	2 927.10	30.7
8 392.60	54.40	.	7 300.10	7 354.50	1 172.00	—	8 526.50	−133.90	−1.6
8 916.10	69.90	.	7 681.60	7 751.50	1 292.80	—	9 044.30	−128.20	−1.4
10 288.20	67.50	.	8 697.10	8 764.60	1 310.70	—	10 075.30	212.90	2.1
1 660.50	1 107.50	5.50	497.50	1 610.50	97.50	29.50	1 737.50	−77.00	−4.6
2 175.00	1 240.50	—	619.00	1 859.50	239.00	6.00	2 104.50	70.50	3.2
2 270.50	16.50	—	1 395.50	1 412.00	796.00	210.50	2 418.50	−148.00	−6.5
4 552.60	167.00	52.00	2 644.80	2 863.80	1 538.10	—	4 401.90	150.70	3.3
6 382.40	344.30	—	4 479.80	4 824.10	1 609.30	102.00	6 535.40	−153.00	−2.4
6 804.20	314.00	—	4 778.90	5 092.20	2 308.80	40.00	7 441.00	−636.80	−9.4
8 128.80	184.10	—	4 860.30	5 044.40	2 749.10	131.10	7 924.60	204.20	2.5

Table 1 *(cont.)* **Tableau 1** *(suite)* **Cuadro 1** *(cont.)*

Country and currency unit / Pays et unité monétaire / Pais y unidad monetaria	Financial year / Exercice financier / Ejercicio financiero	Receipts / Recettes / Ingresos						
		Contributions / Cotisations / Cotizaciones		Special taxes allocated to social security / Taxes et impôts spéciaux / Impuestos y tasas especiales	State participation / Participation de l'Etat / Participación del Estado	Participation of other public authorities / Participation d'autres pouvoirs publics / Participación de otras entidades públicas	Income from capital / Revenu des capitaux / Renta del capital	Other receipts / Autres recettes / Otros ingresos
		From insured persons / Des assurés / De los asegurados	From employers / Des employeurs / De los empleadores					
(1)	(2)	(3)	(4)	(5)	(6)	(7)	(8)	(9)
Maroc (Dirham)	1970	25.04	235.79	—	212.83	—	11.72	—
	1975	35.31	431.47	—	218.17	—	7.30	0.61
	1980	1 299.20		—	2.60	—	140.40	4.50
	1983	121.70	1 138.00	—	—	—	191.90	—
	1984	831.70	1 281.10	—	—	—	367.90	130.80
	1985	895.90	1 396.00	—	—	—	471.60	568.50
	1986	1 009.70	1 507.60	—	—	—	538.20	605.20
Mauritanie[2, 15] (Ouguiya)	1970	25.04	116.08	—	97.40	—	3.48	1.64
	1981	90.95	585.78	—	347.02	—	14.44	1.09
	1983	111.04	688.82	—	359.43	—	32.57	1.01
	1984[1, 5]	45.24	592.02	—	—	—	27.42	2.35
	1985[1, 5]	47.92	646.28	—	—	—	34.44	20.44
	1986[1, 5]	36.67	512.51	—	—	—	35.44	—
Mauritius (Rupee)	1970	3.15	18.64	—	51.85	—	3.37	0.82
	1975	9.86	45.38	—	114.29	—	6.27	0.34
	1981	35.60	70.80	—	180.60	—	28.30	5.50
	1983[16]	46.00	92.00	—	246.60	—	62.50	7.30
	1984	.	.	.	.	.	.	.
	1985	84.90	308.60	—	323.30	—	131.50	21.20
	1986	95.60	348.20	—	374.40	—	170.90	4.70
Mozambique[3] (Metical)	1981	—	231.11	—	—	—	0.25	—
	1983	—	153.62	—	—	—	0.34	—
	1984[14]	—	201.70	—	31.30	—	0.20	—
	1985[14]	—	206.70	—	31.30	—	0.35	—
	1986	—	196.70	—	31.30	—	0.19	—
Niger[17] (Franc CFA)	1970	69.10	533.30	—	875.00	—	8.60	4.40
	1975	100.70	837.60	—	1 117.20	—	103.40	—
	1980	319.60	3 076.00	—	—	—	426.80	1.10
	1983	511.20	4 930.10	—	—	—	512.50	0.90
	1984[14]	1 585.20	5 007.40	—	4 875.30	—	862.10	1 500.00
	1985[14]	1 592.70	5 149.10	—	4 875.30	—	1 241.40	1 500.00
	1986	1 584.10	5 053.60	—	4 875.30	—	1 377.60	—
Nigeria[3] (Naira)	1970	4.80[18]	12.48	0.04	26.26	—	4.34	—
	1981	23.38	15.75	—	—	—	31.41	0.13
	1983	22.11	15.80	—	—	—	40.27	0.23
	1984[5]	15.56	23.96	—	—	—	47.68	0.03
	1985[5]	19.03	26.41	—	—	—	53.71	0.40
	1986[5]	19.45	26.42	—	—	—	62.02	0.49
Rwanda[3] (Franc rwandais)	1975	102.60	171.00	—	128.06	—	36.50	3.20
	1981	344.20	573.60	—	—	—	185.10	15.60
	1983	387.70	644.70	—	—	—	377.30	30.80
	1984	461.50	769.20	—	—	—	481.00	18.50
	1985	448.00	746.70	—	—	—	584.70	14.20
	1986	521.80	869.70	—	—	—	703.90	28.40
Sao Tomé-et-Principe[3] (Dobra)	1981	33.34	49.76	—	—	—	—	0.11
	1983	33.12	49.53	—	—	—	—	0.22
	1984	31.17	46.55	—	—	—	—	0.08
	1985	36.05	53.98	—	—	—	—	2.84
	1986	17.48	26.16	—	—	—	—	2.77

See notes on page 70.   *Voir notes page 70.*   Véanse notas pág. 70.

	Expenditure / Dépenses / Egresos								Difference between receipts and expenditure / Différence entre les recettes et les dépenses / Diferencia entre los ingresos y los egresos	
Total receipts (excluding transfers) / Total des recettes (non compris les transferts) / Total de ingresos (excl. las transferencias)	Benefits / Prestations / Prestaciones — Medical care / Soins médicaux / Asistencia médica	Benefits in kind other than for medical care / Prestations en nature à d'autres titres que les soins médicaux / Prestaciones en especie, excepto asistencia médica	Cash benefits / Prestations en espèces / Prestaciones monetarias	Total / Total / Total	Administrative expenditure / Frais d'administration / Gastos de administración	Other expenditure / Autres dépenses / Otros egresos	Total expenditure (excluding transfers) / Total des dépenses (non compris les transferts) / Total de egresos (excl. las transferencias)	In absolute figures / En chiffres absolus / En cifras absolutas	As percentage of total receipts / En pourcentage du total des recettes / En porcentaje del total de ingresos
(10)	(11)	(12)	(13)	(14)	(15)	(16)	(17)	(18)	(19)
485.38	212.00	—	209.85	421.85	14.32	—	436.17	49.21	10.1
692.86	217.00	—	340.53	557.53	22.57	0.19	580.29	112.57	16.2
1 446.70	7.50	—	713.50	721.00	86.10	0.60	807.70	639.00	44.2
1 451.60	—	3.80	759.30	763.10	55.00	—	818.10	633.50	43.6
2 611.50	—	—	1 732.60	1 732.60	62.10	30.40	1 825.10	786.40	30.1
3 332.00	—	—	1 921.30	1 921.30	67.50	35.10	2 023.90	1 308.10	39.3
3 660.70	—	—	2 370.10	2 370.10	88.70	47.70	2 506.50	1 154.20	31.5
243.64	102.34	1.26	108.08	211.68	9.60	1.90	223.18	20.46	8.4
1 039.28	2.38	15.30	768.34	786.02	57.17	15.82	859.01	180.27	17.3
1 192.86	4.50	32.69	907.84	945.03	65.04	48.59	1 058.66	134.20	11.3
667.03	35.31	12.77	365.83	413.91	88.80	7.09	509.80	157.24	23.6
749.08	29.05	13.20	344.56	386.82	75.38	—	462.19	286.88	38.3
584.62	32.03	23.42	421.81	477.27	106.02	—	583.29	1.33	0.2
77.83	24.38	—	44.74	69.12	1.32	0.16	70.60	7.23	9.3
176.14	66.63	—	89.31	155.94	1.07	0.55	157.56	18.58	10.5
320.80	—	—	181.70	181.70	7.80	—	189.50	131.30	40.9
454.40	—	—	247.20	247.20	11.80	0.30	259.30	195.10	42.9
869.50	—	—	539.50	539.50	25.90	6.40	571.80	297.70	34.2
993.80	—	—	621.90	621.90	26.80	5.40	654.10	339.70	34.2
231.36	0.11	0.74	14.39	15.24	46.22	24.65	86.11	145.25	62.8
153.96	0.21	1.09	16.45	17.75	30.72	34.52	82.99	70.97	46.1
233.20	19.00	32.00	93.00	144.00	—	—	144.00	89.20	38.3
238.35	21.00	33.00	108.00	162.00	—	—	162.00	76.35	32.0
228.19	22.00	31.00	92.00	145.00	—	—	145.00	83.19	36.5
1 490.40	880.60	21.10	338.40	1 240.10	71.60	—	1 311.70	178.70	12.0
2 158.90	1 123.20	33.90	588.30	1 745.40	83.70	20.30	1 849.40	309.50	14.3
3 823.50	22.50	7.90	1 311.40	1 341.80	252.70	—	1 594.50	2 229.00	58.3
5 954.70	57.20	28.40	1 682.20	1 767.80	840.50	1 850.00	4 458.30	1 496.40	25.1
13 830.00	1 370.00	3.50	3 022.00	4 395.50	2 994.20	3 141.50	10 531.20	3 298.80	23.9
14 358.50	1 380.40	4.30	2 875.30	4 260.00	3 155.80	3 116.00	10 531.80	3 826.70	26.7
12 890.60	1 417.50	12.70	3 484.80	4 915.00	3 252.90	1 864.20	10 032.10	2 858.50	22.2
47.92	26.20	—	8.52	34.72	0.94	0.02	35.68	12.24	25.5
70.67	—	—	3.52	3.52	5.63	—	9.15	61.52	87.1
78.42	—	—	5.14	5.14	6.13	—	11.27	67.15	85.6
87.23	—	—	6.10	6.10	7.43	—	13.53	73.71	84.5
99.56	—	—	7.72	7.72	8.17	—	15.88	83.68	84.0
108.38	—	—	7.84	7.84	9.69	—	17.53	90.85	83.8
441.36	121.79	—	20.86	142.65	18.31	2.69	163.65	277.71	62.9
1 118.50	25.20	—	71.40	96.60	82.20	—	178.80	939.70	84.0
1 440.50	14.00	—	210.30	224.30	160.60	—	384.90	1 055.60	73.3
1 730.20	—	—	255.60	255.60	177.60	—	433.20	1 297.00	75.0
1 793.60	5.00	—	309.00	314.00	199.00	—	513.00	1 280.60	71.4
2 123.80	13.60	—	367.00	380.60	205.30	—	585.90	1 537.90	72.4
83.21	—	—	18.02	18.02	—	—	18.02	65.19	78.3
82.88	—	—	19.70	19.70	—	—	19.70	63.18	76.2
77.80	—	—	21.47	21.47	—	—	21.47	56.33	72.4
92.87	—	—	28.44	28.44	—	—	28.44	64.43	69.4
46.41	—	—	23.68	23.68	—	—	23.68	22.73	49.0

Table 1 (cont.)   Tableau 1 (suite)   Cuadro 1 (cont.)

Country and currency unit *Pays et unité monétaire* País y unidad monetaria	Financial year *Exercice financier* Ejercicio financiero	Receipts / *Recettes* / Ingresos						
		Contributions / *Cotisations* / Cotizaciones		Special taxes allocated to social security *Taxes et impôts spéciaux* Impuestos y tasas especiales	State participation *Participation de l'Etat* Participación del Estado	Participation of other public authorities *Participation d'autres pouvoirs publics* Participación de otras entidades públicas	Income from capital *Revenu des capitaux* Renta del capital	Other receipts *Autres recettes* Otros ingresos
		From insured persons *Des assurés* De los asegurados	From employers *Des employeurs* De los empleadores					
(1)	(2)	(3)	(4)	(5)	(6)	(7)	(8)	(9)
Sénégal[3] (Franc CFA)	1970[4]	1 250.20	3 364.80	488.40	3 635.90	—	0.10	15.60
	1975[4]	1 119.70	4 982.20	—	5 196.00	—	39.00	301.00
	1980[4]	2 512.00	9 310.00	—	759.00	—	1 087.00	236.00
	1983[4, 19]	—	7 379.00	—	—	—	89.00	236.00
	1984	4 112.00	13 020.00	—	—	—	1 590.00	52.00
	1985	4 420.00	15 092.00	—	—	—	1 733.00	55.00
	1986	4 717.00	15 447.00	—	—	—	1 875.00	55.00
Sudan[3] (Pound)	1980	5.20	10.40	—	—	—	2.98	5.21
	1983	5.59	12.39	—	—	—	4.92	10.29
	1984	6.50	13.00	—	—	—	9.40	26.60
	1985	6.60	13.30	—	—	—	19.10	15.10
	1986	6.00	12.10	—	—	—	15.60	8.40
Swaziland[1, 3, 4] (Lilangeni)	1981	2.65	3.47	—	—	—	1.32	—
	1983	3.27	4.53	—	—	—	3.29	—
	1984	3.27	3.27	—	—	—	3.06	0.05
	1985	3.31	3.31	—	—	—	3.62	0.04
	1986	3.36	3.36	—	—	—	3.93	0.05
Tanzania, United Rep. of[3, 4] (Shilling)	1980	102.10	102.10	—	—	—	108.10	—
	1983	127.10	127.10	—	—	—	140.40	0.20
	1984	271.00	364.30	—	20.73	—	84.30	89.60
	1985	295.70	372.50	—	26.04	—	116.50	122.50
	1986	346.60	433.00	—	25.23	—	265.30	216.50
Tchad[3, 20] (Franc CFA)	1979-81[21]	29.36	181.78	—	—	—	—	—
	1983	31.83	195.86	—	—	—	—	—
	1984	197.33	398.15[22]	19.36	—	—	8.17	46.00
	1985	530.99	1 069.06[22]	—	—	—	22.82	46.00
	1986	321.98	804.72[22]	—	—	—	49.20	46.00
Togo (Franc CFA)	1972	195	984	—	721	—	38	28
	1975	243	1 491	—	1 252	—	39	—
	1980	499	3 744	—	—	—	562	9
	1983	692	5 271	—	—	—	1 045	—
	1984	787	5 999	—	—	—	1 391	—
	1985	867	6 606	—	—	—	2 063	—
	1986	892	6 801	—	—	—	1 895	—
*Tunisie (Dinar)	1984	119.50	205.00	—	—	—	26.90	28.30
	1985	151.80	237.80	—	—	—	35.00	43.90
	1986	152.80	240.40	—	—	—	36.20	33.10
Uganda[3,4] (Shilling)	1980	22.50	22.50	—	—	—	37.10	—
	1983	41.50	41.50	—	—	—	88.00	—
	1984[23]	31.64	31.64	—	—	—	87.51	—
	1985[23]	38.96	38.96	—	—	—	68.00	—
	1986[23]	33.45	33.45	—	—	—	8.16	—
* Zaïre[2] (Zaïre)	1984	83.42	198.72	—	—	—	—	40.21
	1985	183.75	499.67	—	—	—	—	52.91
	1986	354.60	745.08	—	—	—	—	138.57

See notes on page 70.   *Voir notes page 70.*   Véanse notas pág. 70.

Total receipts (excluding transfers) / Total des recettes (non compris les transferts) / Total de ingresos (excl. las transferencias)	Expenditure / Dépenses / Egresos — Benefits / Prestations / Prestaciones				Administrative expenditure / Frais d'administration / Gastos de administración	Other expenditure / Autres dépenses / Otros egresos	Total expenditure (excluding transfers) / Total des dépenses (non compris les transferts) / Total de egresos (excl. las transferencias)	Difference between receipts and expenditure / Différence entre les recettes et les dépenses / Diferencia entre los ingresos y los egresos	
	Medical care / Soins médicaux / Asistencia médica	Benefits in kind other than for medical care / Prestations en nature à d'autres titres que les soins médicaux / Prestaciones en especie, excepto asistencia médica	Cash benefits / Prestations en espèces / Prestaciones monetarias	Total				In absolute figures / En chiffres absolus / En cifras absolutas	As percentage of total receipts / En pourcentage du total des recettes / En porcentaje del total de ingresos
(10)	(11)	(12)	(13)	(14)	(15)	(16)	(17)	(18)	(19)
8 755.00	4 019.60	—	3 674.90	7 694.50	207.10	—	7 901.60	853.40	9.7
11 637.90	4 960.90	—	3 462.00	8 422.90	456.00	545.00	9 423.90	2 214.00	19.0
13 904.00	64.00	49.00	8 731.00	8 844.00	970.00	1 410.00	11 224.00	2 680.00	19.3
7 704.00	27.00	232.00	4 547.00	4 806.00	1 181.00	98.00	6 085.00	1 619.00	21.0
18 774.00	182.00	284.00	12 816.00	13 282.00	2 589.00	—	15 871.00	2 903.00	15.5
21 300.00	182.00	259.00	14 203.00	14 644.00	2 775.00	—	17 419.00	3 881.00	18.2
22 094.00	218.00	259.00	15 481.00	15 958.00	2 869.00	—	18 827.00	3 267.00	14.8
23.79	—	—	0.92	0.92	2.38	—	3.30	20.49	86.1
33.19	—	—	2.70	2.70	4.84	—	7.54	25.65	77.3
55.50	—	—	4.30	4.30	3.90	—	8.20	47.30	85.2
54.10	—	—	4.80	4.80	4.50	—	9.30	44.80	82.8
42.10	—	—	4.20	4.20	4.30	—	8.50	33.60	79.8
7.44	—	—	1.46	1.46	0.73	0.45	2.64	4.80	64.5
11.09	—	—	2.41	2.41	1.13	1.05	4.59	6.50	58.6
9.65	—	—	1.41	1.41	—	—	1.41	8.24	85.4
10.28	—	—	1.57	1.57	1.77	—	3.34	6.94	67.5
10.70	—	—	1.78	1.78	2.11	—	3.89	6.81	63.6
312.30	—	—	61.40	61.40	20.80	—	82.20	230.10	73.7
394.80	—	—	64.70	64.70	44.70	91.90	201.30	193.50	49.0
829.93	—	—	119.43	119.43	67.40	0.40	187.23	642.70	77.4
933.24	—	—	198.74	198.74	95.30	0.50	294.54	638.70	68.4
1 286.63	—	—	231.43	231.43	107.60	148.70	487.73	798.90	62.1
211.14	3.20	0.43	70.56	74.19	307.01	—	381.20	− 170.06	−80.5
227.69	3.90	3.32	39.80	47.03	153.23	—	200.25	27.44	12.1
669.01	0.86	3.48	69.01	73.35	210.53	20.67	304.56	364.45	54.5
1 668.87	0.86	7.06	282.21	290.14	292.11	27.02	609.27	1 059.61	63.5
1 221.90	1.80	30.15	316.50	348.45	465.27	27.68	841.41	380.50	31.1
1 966	728	16	464	1 208	140	2	1 350	616	31.3
3 025	1 256	54	613	1 923	323	48	2 294	731	24.2
4 814	22	104	1 709	1 835	500	15	2 350	2 464	51.2
7 008	44	—	2 265	2 309	873	12	3 194	3 814	54.4
8 177	79	—	2 609	2 688	825	—	3 513	4 664	57.0
9 536	120	—	2 910	3 030	1 007	—	4 037	5 499	57.7
9 588	65	—	3 237	3 302	1 369	—	4 671	4 917	51.3
379.70	41.70	5.50	211.80	259.00	41.60	26.00	326.60	53.10	14.0
468.50	50.00	5.30	250.50	305.80	70.10	38.40	414.30	54.20	11.6
462.50	54.60	9.30	272.10	336.00	63.00	13.10	412.10	50.40	10.9
82.10	—	—	7.50	7.50	45.00	—	52.50	29.60	36.1
171.00	—	—	3.20	3.20	53.00	—	56.20	114.80	67.1
150.78	—	—	2.13	2.13	—[24]	—	2.13	148.65	98.6
145.93	—	—	1.99	1.99	—[24]	—	1.99	143.94	98.6
75.06	—	—	0.52	0.52	—[24]	—	0.52	74.54	99.3
322.36	4.96	2.29	32.27	39.51	166.86	—	206.37	115.99	36.0
736.33	0.26	2.04	90.22	92.52	322.65	—	415.17	321.16	43.6
1 238.25	11.72	—	279.41	291.13	753.06	—	1 044.19	194.06	15.7

Table 1 *(cont.)*   **Tableau 1** *(suite)*   **Cuadro 1** *(cont.)*

Country and currency unit / Pays et unité monétaire / País y unidad monetaria	Financial year / Exercice financier / Ejercicio financiero	Contributions / Cotisations / Cotizaciones		Special taxes allocated to social security / Taxes et impôts spéciaux / Impuestos y tasas especiales	State participation / Participation de l'Etat / Participación del Estado	Participation of other public authorities / Participation d'autres pouvoirs publics / Participación de otras entidades públicas	Income from capital / Revenu des capitaux / Renta del capital	Other receipts / Autres recettes / Otros ingresos
		From insured persons / Des assurés / De los asegurados	From employers / Des employeurs / De los empleadores					
(1)	(2)	(3)	(4)	(5)	(6)	(7)	(8)	(9)
Zambia[3, 25] (Kwacha)	1970	11.47	9.56	—	20.70	—	3.33	0.54
	1975	29.72	16.31	—	48.70	—	9.90	1.60
	1980	26.27	21.09	—	—	—	21.57	0.08
	1983	.	.	.	.	.	.	.
	1984	30.31	30.31	—	—	—	41.17	—
	1985	38.63	38.63	—	—	—	50.79	—
	1986	50.88	50.88	—	—	—	77.45	—

AMERICA – AMÉRIQUE – AMERICA

Country	Year	(3)	(4)	(5)	(6)	(7)	(8)	(9)
Argentina[3, 26] (Austral)	1975	0.002	0.008	—	0.000	—	0.000	0.000
	1980	1.05	1.35	0.08	0.20	—	0.06	0.00
	1983	17.84	14.04	1.50	17.12	—	1.04	0.16
	1984	142.76	138.15	10.16	115.28	—	25.20	1.17
	1985	866.80	1 171.80	—	555.40	—	218.10	19.50
	1986	1 564.90	2 276.40	—	973.60	—	166.00	13.60
Bahamas[3] (Dollar)	1980	8.57	14.52	—	1.00	—	8.50	0.00
	1983	11.23	18.41	—	2.50	—	16.31	0.04
	1984	12.97	21.28	—	2.50	—	17.60	0.13
	1985[27]	19.00	28.73	—	2.40	—	21.19	0.15
	1986[27]	19.73	29.93	—	1.00	—	22.55	0.35
Barbados (Dollar)	1971	8.23	—	—	9.25	—	1.67	—
	1975	6.55	7.67	—	33.73	—	5.69	—
	1980	15.03	19.02	—	20.48	—	11.60	—
	1983[28]	47.36	49.05	—	4.53[29]	—	29.23	5.32
	1984	51.97	54.14	—	7.25	—	23.88	0.84
	1985	54.86	57.14	—	7.24	—	28.58	0.49
	1986	55.76	58.29	—	8.28	—	24.70	0.93
Belize (Dollar)	1981	0.37	5.40	—	0.34	—	0.08	0.01
	1983	0.85	8.92	—	0.34	—	1.05	0.37
	1984[30]	1.29	7.75	—	—	—	1.50	0.04
	1985[30]	1.05	6.32	—	—	—	3.02	0.03
	1986[30]	1.06	6.34	—	—	—	3.81	0.03
Bolivia[31] (Peso)	1972	144.80	207.80	5.80	134.10	—	11.30	74.90
	1975	301.50	743.80	4.20	517.20	—	39.80	86.20
	1980	1 043.40	1 945.40	223.80	—	—	286.50	129.30
	1983	10 536.50	14 382.70	1 366.60	8 646.70	—	5 107.90	1 284.90
	1984	190 341.00	272 148.00	4 954.00	228 391.00	—	56 327.00	8 028.00
	1985	18 083 051.00	27 896 517.00	17 194.00	15 022 016.00	1 558 736.00	5 877 027.00	2 282 467.00
Brasil[32] (Cruzado)	1970	.	.	—	.	—	.	.
	1975	.	.	—	.	—	.	.
	1980	.	.	—	.	—	.	.
	1983	1 033.80	5 096.80	—	545.70	—	2.30	144.80
	1984	4 270.80	13 103.80	—	2 198.00	—	196.40	397.90
	1985	12 367.40	52 059.50	—	3 092.00	—	2 985.40	1 210.70
	1986	77 713.10	107 946.20	—	7 678.40	—	5 580.10	2 889.80

See notes on page 70.   *Voir notes page 70.*   Véanse notas pág. 70.

Total receipts (excluding transfers) *Total des recettes (non compris les transfers)* Total de ingresos (excl. las transferencias)	Benefits *Prestations* Prestaciones — Medical care *Soins médicaux* Asistencia médica	Benefits in kind other than for medical care *Prestations en nature à d'autres titres que les soins médicaux* Prestaciones en especie, excepto asistencia médica	Cash benefits *Prestations en espèces* Prestaciones monetarias	Total *Total* Total	Administrative expenditure *Frais d'administration* Gastos de administración	Other expenditure *Autres dépenses* Otros egresos	Total expenditure (excluding transfers) *Total des dépenses (non compris les transfers)* Total de egresos (excl. las transferencias)	Difference — In absolute figures *En chiffres absolus* En cifras absolutas	As percentage of total receipts *En pourcentage du total des recettes* En porcentaje del total de ingresos
(10)	(11)	(12)	(13)	(14)	(15)	(16)	(17)	(18)	(19)
45.60	20.73	—	8.54	29.27	1.47	—	30.74	14.86	32.6
106.23	48.70	—	26.61	75.31	3.53	0.01	78.85	27.38	25.8
69.01	—	—	20.85	20.85	8.63	—	29.48	39.53	57.3
101.79	.	.	17.02	17.02	19.59	—	36.61	65.18	64.0
128.05	—	—	28.72	28.72	27.22	—	55.94	72.11	56.3
179.21	—	—	27.45	27.45	40.21	—	67.66	111.55	62.2
0.011	0.002	0.000	0.008	0.009	0.000	—	0.01	0.001	9.4
2.74	0.56	0.04	1.91	2.51	0.11	0.02	2.64	0.10	3.6
51.70	12.20	0.41	33.86	46.47	1.99	1.60	50.06	1.64	3.2
432.72	91.14	3.58	265.88	360.60	14.59	8.73	383.92	48.80	11.3
2 831.60	—	—	2 277.20	2 277.20	50.80	11.00	2 339.00	492.60	17.4
4 994.50	—	—	4 384.90	4 384.90	101.80	13.50	4 500.20	494.30	9.9
32.59	—	—	5.41	5.41	2.57	0.14	8.12	24.47	75.1
48.50	0.02	—	15.28	15.30	4.33	0.24	19.86	28.63	59.0
54.48	0.13	—	17.70	17.83	5.61	0.22	23.66	30.82	56.6
71.47	0.03	—	21.36	21.39	6.03	0.20	27.62	43.85	61.4
73.56	0.09	—	23.91	24.00	7.38	0.38	31.76	41.80	56.8
19.15	9.29	—	1.24	10.53	0.11	—	10.64	8.51	44.4
53.64	25.56	0.07	13.10	38.73	0.77	—	39.50	14.14	26.4
66.13	0.10	2.35	32.83	35.28	2.40	—	37.68	28.45	43.0
135.49	0.13	4.06	68.40	72.59	3.62	2.08	78.29	57.20	42.2
138.08	0.04	2.82	85.45	88.31	5.47	0.77	94.55	43.53	31.5
148.31	0.03	2.49	95.29	97.81	6.15	0.56	104.51	43.80	29.5
147.96	0.05	2.84	117.43	120.32	6.69	2.46	129.47	18.49	12.5
6.20	0.02	—	3.61	3.63	0.31	0.02	3.96	2.24	36.1
11.53	0.03	0.01	5.04	5.07	0.61	0.01	5.70	5.83	50.6
10.59	0.05	0.02	0.87	0.94	0.70	0.01	1.65	8.93	84.4
10.43	0.08	—	1.15	1.22	0.95	0.03	2.20	8.22	78.9
11.24	0.08	—	1.17	1.25	1.11	0.04	2.40	8.84	78.7
578.70	345.10	3.20	140.70	489.00	52.50	0.40	541.90	36.80	6.4
1 692.70	988.10	0.50	403.20	1 391.80	141.10	—	1 532.90	159.80	9.4
3 628.40	1 598.70	—	1 353.60	2 952.30	707.80	13.20	3 673.30	−44.90	− 1.2
41 325.30	10 882.70	158.80	15 814.20	26 855.70	4 615.00	208.50	31 679.20	9646.10	23.3
760 189.00	400 943.00	—	270 509.00	671 452.00	156 414.00	2 752.00	830 618.00	−70429.00	− 9.3
70 737 008.00	23 813 618.00	—	19 625 869.00	43 439 487.00	9 292 621.00	226 542 00	52 958 650.00	17778358.00	25.1
11.88	.	.	.	9.85	0.82	1.14	11.81	0.07	0.6
61.46	.	.	.	49.53	7.07	1.02	57.62	3.84	6.2
820.18	174.55	0.44	433.52	608.51	29.86	—	638.37	181.81	22.2
6 823.40	1 329.80	—	4 953.00	6 282.80	462.50	8.00	6 753.30	70.10	1.0
20 166.90	4 149.00	—	13 951.40	18 100.40	1 020.60	864.50	19 985.50	181.40	0.9
71 715.00	17 133.70	—	46 349.00	63 482.70	3 729.50	597.70	67 809.90	3 905.10	5.4
201 807.60	41 350.70	—	128 098.10	169 448.80	11 861.40	3 504.70	184 814.90	16 992.70	8.4

Table 1 *(cont.)*   **Tableau 1** *(suite)*   **Cuadro 1** *(cont.)*

Country and currency unit / Pays et unité monétaire / País y unidad monetaria	Financial year / Exercice financier / Ejercicio financiero	Receipts / Recettes / Ingresos						
		Contributions / Cotisations / Cotizaciones		Special taxes allocated to social security / Taxes et impôts spéciaux / Impuestos y tasas especiales	State participation / Participation de l'Etat / Participación del Estado	Participation of other public authorities / Participation d'autres pouvoirs publics / Participación de otras entidades públicas	Income from capital / Revenu des capitaux / Renta del capital	Other receipts / Autres recettes / Otros ingresos
		From insured persons / Des assurés / De los asegurados	From employers / Des employeurs / De los empleadores					
(1)	(2)	(3)	(4)	(5)	(6)	(7)	(8)	(9)
Canada[25] (Dollar)	1970	1 915.60	1 589.10	1 914.20	4 134.30	4 310.60	729.50	4.30
	1975	2 853.30	3 307.00	—	12 801.90	5 680.00	1 509.70	—
	1980	5 547.60	7 004.10	—	23 058.60	9 490.70	3 762.50	—
	1983	8 949.60	11 885.80	—	31 752.10	14 099.40	6 508.40	122.00
	1984	9 284.80	12 643.70	—	34 155.50	14 734.10	7 632.50	161.20
	1985	10 227.60	14 526.10	—	37 751.80	15 798.30	9 070.90	164.20
Colombia[3] (Peso)	1970	583.16	1 580.44	5.59	1 704.34	—	115.49	7.82
	1975	2 439.00	4 954.00	69.00	5 825.80	—	488.00	928.00
	1980	8 386.20	26 085.50	—	8 492.80	—	3 345.00	6 103.40
	1983	17 889.00	38 481.00	158.00	8 255.00	—	6 104.00	230.00
	1984	21 656.00	56 040.00	—	1 392.00	—	6 154.00	5 504.00
	1985	26 491.00	68 664.00	—	1 748.00	—	9 940.00	8 790.00
	1986	36 558.00	96 035.00	—	2 887.00	—	12 150.00	22 242.00
Costa Rica (Colón)	1970	73.10	113.20	—	91.00	—	33.30	3.90
	1975	273.10	549.00	44.60	186.20	—	74.90	21.00
	1980[34]	941.30	1 563.90	633.40	60.20	—	177.60	31.90
	1983[34]	3 322.70	6 934.70	955.70	586.60	—	622.30	1 126.30
	1984	3 935.70	8 259.90	187.90	482.20	—	1 032.40	1 838.20
	1985	4 890.40	10 507.90	165.70	426.60	—	1 835.47	2 360.50
	1986[34]	5 975.30	11 514.00	234.20	381.80	—	2 641.70	2 640.40
Cuba (Peso)	1980	—	.	—	.	—	—	—
	1983	—	660.90	—	830.60	—	—	—
	1984	—	721.10	—	896.00	—	—	—
	1985	—	748.10	—	990.30	—	—	—
	1986	—	789.20	—	1 098.50	—	—	—
Chile[35] (Peso)	1971	5.15	9.40	0.47	8.86	—	0.28	0.92
	1975	802.20	2 292.70	66.40	1 521.00	—	77.50	169.20
	1980[36]	28 753.30	53 553.30	1 991.40	45 901.20	—	2 786.40	6 964.50
	1983	80 904.60	5 525.60	17.50	127 343.30	—	41 469.90	5 276.70
	1984	101 844.00	6 710.00	—	168 526.00	—	38 542.00	4 534.00
	1985	133 335.00	9 328.00	1.00	222 797.00	—	89 030.00	3 564.00
	1986	176 847.00	11 917.00	3.00	287 845.00	—	107 605.00	3 988.00
Dominica (EC Dollar)	1980	1.46	2.42	—	—	—	1.06	0.04
	1983	1.95	3.24	—	—	—	1.86	0.05
	1984	2.57	4.28	—	—	—	2.03	0.06
	1985	2.48	6.10	—	—	—	2.59	0.09
	1986	2.78	6.26	—	—	—	3.13	0.13
*República Dominicana (Peso)	1984	11.73	43.92	—	0.10	—	1.34	1.23
	1985	11.70	44.60	—	—	—	1.45	0.64
	1986	15.69	56.80	—	—	—	1.00	4.38
Ecuador (Sucre)	1972	795.00	854.00	—	162.00	—	561.00	41.00
	1974	1 268.00	1 352.00	—	859.00	—	686.00	39.00
	1980	5 040.00	5 865.00	—	18.00	—	2 720.00	—
	1983	8 861.00	12 213.00	—	250.00	—	6 285.00	—
	1984[37]	10 045.20	11 068.20	—	2 995.30	—	21 828.30	937.60
	1985[37]	13 340.40	19 043.60	—	4 374.40	—	26 561.00	9 352.10
	1986[37]	16 634.60	24 540.20	—	11 150.80	—	40 236.30	8 575.60

See notes on page 70.   *Voir notes page 70.*   Véanse notas pág. 70.

Total receipts (excluding transfers)	Expenditure / Dépenses / Egresos				Administrative expenditure	Other expenditure	Total expenditure (excluding transfers)	Difference between receipts and expenditure	
	Benefits / Prestations / Prestaciones				Frais d'administration	Autres dépenses		In absolute figures	As percentage of total receipts
Total des recettes (non compris les transferts)	Medical care	Benefits in kind other than for medical care	Cash benefits	Total	Gastos de administración	Otros egresos	Total des dépenses (non compris les transferts)	En chiffres absolus	En pourcentage du total des recettes
Total de ingresos (excl. las transferencias)	Soins médicaux / Asistencia médica	Prestations en nature à d'autres titres que les soins médicaux / Prestaciones en especie, excepto asistencia médica	Prestations en espèces / Prestaciones monetarias	Total / Total			Total de egresos (excl. las transferencias)	En cifras absolutas	En porcentaje del total de ingresos
(10)	(11)	(12)	(13)	(14)	(15)	(16)	(17)	(18)	(19)
14 597.60	6 111.00	226.80	6 131.60	12 469.40	236.80	11.30	12 717.50	1 880.10	12.9
26 151.90	7 274.40	1 288.80	14 426.40	22 989.60	559.50	—	23 549.10	2 602.80	10.0
48 863.50	12 351.70	1 688.20	26 521.00	40 560.90	1 301.80	—	41 862.70	7 000.80	14.3
73 317.30	18 840.10	2 331.00	42 577.60	63 748.70	1 732.80	685.50	66 167.00	7 150.30	9.8
78 611.80	19 962.30	2 498.80	45 840.90	68 302.00	1 858.90	1 316.60	71 477.50	7 134.30	9.1
87 538.90	21 453.80	2 529.50	50 229.60	74 212.90	2 075.20	833.90	77 122.00	10 416.90	11.9
3 996.84	2 120.05	221.61	743.61	3 085.27	204.32	46.41	3 336.00	660.84	16.5
14 703.80	6 498.80	568.00	4 330.00	11 396.80	888.00	134.00	12 418.80	2 285.00	15.5
52 412.90	11 897.30	6 393.60	15 981.30	34 272.20	5 460.10	4 448.30	44 180.60	8 232.30	15.7
71 117.00	31 055.00	—	29 011.00	60 066.00	7 894.00	36.00	67 996.00	3 121.00	4.4
90 746.00	4 388.00	—	38 355.00	42 743.00[33]	39 047.00	360.00	82 150.00	8 596.00	9.5
115 633.00	5 088.00	—	48 422.00	53 510.00[33]	44 722.00	897.00	99 129.00	16 504.00	14.3
169 872.00	6 755.00	—	62 347.00	69 102.00[33]	56 528.00	8 207.00	133 837.00	36 035.00	21.2
314.50	154.40	2.10	33.30	189.80	26.20	4.80	220.80	93.70	29.8
1 148.80	615.80	5.30	149.40	770.50	72.70	21.60	864.80	284.00	24.7
3 408.30	2 040.60	11.30	546.20	2 598.10	201.00	128.30	2 927.40	480.90	14.1
13 548.30	4 811.10	46.30	2 097.10	6 954.50	403.90	487.30	7 845.70	5 702.60	42.1
15 736.30	6 128.20	29.90	3 050.90	9 209.00	501.20	1 750.80	11 461.00	4 275.30	27.2
20 186.57	8 099.10	35.80	3 966.70	12 101.60	601.70	2 021.70	14 725.00	5 461.57	27.1
23 387.40	9 789.00	36.70	4 956.20	14 781.90	702.80	2 595.40	18 080.10	5 307.30	22.7
1 149.50	384.20	35.20	692.00	1 111.40	—	38.10	1 149.50	—	—
1 491.50	571.10	55.90	814.20	1 441.20	—	50.30	1 491.50	—	—
1 617.10	627.10	66.80	863.90	1 557.80	—	59.30	1 617.10	—	—
1 738.40	671.80	70.40	931.30	1 673.50	—	64.90	1 738.40	—	—
1 887.70	746.20	77.60	995.30	1 819.10	—	68.60	1 887.70	—	—
25.08	2.91	—	17.18	20.09	1.70	0.43	22.22	2.86	11.4
4 929.00	541.60	212.80	2 835.50	3 589.90	301.10	9.00	3 900.00	1 029.00	20.9
139 950.10	14 677.50	3 611.90	88 534.00	106 823.40	8 720.90	1.50	115 545.80	24 404.30	17.4
260 537.60	25 756.70	3 343.20	173 564.60	202 664.50	18 515.50	1 418.70	222 598.70	37 938.90	14.6
320 156.00	30 728.00	5 014.00	217 746.00	253 488.00	22 385.00	2 287.00	278 160.00	41 996.00	13.1
458 055.00	42 232.00	5 279.00	268 639.00	316 150.00	27 822.00	2 905.00	346 877.00	111 178.00	24.3
588 205.00	55 761.00	5 776.00	329 581.00	391 118.00	31 302.00	2 679.00	425 099.00	163 106.00	27.7
4.98	—	—	0.57	0.57	0.69	—	1.26	3.72	74.7
7.11	0.14	—	1.02	1.16	0.88	—	2.04	5.07	71.3
8.94	0.61	—	1.55	2.16	1.07	—	3.23	5.71	63.9
11.26	0.69	—	1.89	2.58	1.15	—	3.73	7.53	66.9
12.30	0.72	—	2.25	2.97	1.40	—	4.37	7.93	64.5
58.32	33.19	—	12.00	45.19	9.88	—	55.07	3.25	5.6
58.39	33.62	—	12.73	46.35	10.65	—	57.00	1.39	2.4
77.87	38.02	—	18.35	56.37	17.88	—	74.25	3.62	4.6
2 413.00	497.00	2.00	895.00	1 394.00	167.00	2.00	1 563.00	850.00	35.2
4 204.00	1 294.00	3.00	1 258.00	2 555.00	230.00	3.00	2 788.00	1 416.00	33.7
13 643.00	573.00	—	5 610.00	6 183.00	2 402.00	—	8 585.00	5 058.00	37.1
27 609.00	1 492.00	—	13 580.00	15 072.00	5 265.00	—	20 337.00	7 272.00	26.3
46 874.60	5 001.00	—	15 834.00	20 835.00	3 037.00	—	23 872.00	23 002.60	49.1
72 671.50	6 821.00	—	20 373.00	27 194.00	3 749.00	—	30 943.00	41 728.50	57.4
101 137.50	8 721.00	—	27 937.00	36 658.00	4 967.00	—	41 625.00	59 512.50	58.8

Table 1 *(cont.)*   **Tableau 1** *(suite)*   **Cuadro 1** *(cont.)*

Country and currency unit / *Pays et unité monétaire* / País y unidad monetaria	Financial year / *Exercice financier* / Ejercicio financiero	Receipts / *Recettes* / Ingresos						
		Contributions / *Cotisations* / Cotizaciones		Special taxes allocated to social security / *Taxes et impôts spéciaux* / Impuestos y tasas especiales	State participation / *Participation de l'Etat* / Participación del Estado	Participation of other public authorities / *Participation d'autres pouvoirs publics* / Participación de otras entidades públicas	Income from capital / *Revenu des capitaux* / Renta del capital	Other receipts / *Autres recettes* / Otros ingresos
		From insured persons / *Des assurés* / De los asegurados	From employers / *Des employeurs* / De los empleadores					
(1)	(2)	(3)	(4)	(5)	(6)	(7)	(8)	(9)
El Salvador (Colón)	1970	8.15	35.83	—	51.09	—	0.94	0.23
	1975	18.98	61.71	—	86.65	—	4.82	0.89
	1980	62.23	87.71	—	40.00	—	31.00	2.51
	1983	80.40	103.30	—	23.80	11.30	66.60	2.60
	1984	49.80	108.50	—	—	—	43.20	1.70
	1985	54.20	121.70	—	—	—	51.50	2.90
	1986	66.90	155.10	—	—	—	63.70	1.70
Grenada[2] (EC Dollar)	1981[38]	—	3.09	—	0.36	—	0.05	—
	1983	1.74	5.59	—	0.48	—	0.12	0.01
	1984[39]	2.90	7.32	—	—	—	0.92	0.37
	1985[39]	4.22	9.24	—	—	—	0.70	0.16
	1986[39]	4.19	8.77	—	—	—	1.97	0.22
Guatemala (Quetzal)	1970	9.80	15.70	—	16.60	—	0.30	0.10
	1975	17.30	24.90	—	30.10	—	—	1.00
	1980	42.20	70.80	—	10.90	—	9.20	0.30
	1983	36.60	63.40	—	4.50	—	16.40	3.30
	1984	38.70	76.10	—	—	—	—	23.50
	1985	42.30	82.20	—	—	—	—	26.40
	1986	56.10	116.90	—	—	—	—	36.00
Guyana (Dollar)	1972	6.52	8.65	—	12.85	—	3.10	—
	1975	9.03	12.26	—	15.29	—	6.25	—
	1980	29.17	36.89	—	0.18	—	24.85	0.32
	1983	31.00	38.10	—	1.40	—	59.81	6.01
	1984	31.93	38.14	—	2.66	—	77.20	6.02
	1985	31.45	38.78	—	2.94	—	95.04	6.85
	1986	34.67	42.85	—	1.46	—	113.11	8.14
Honduras (Lempira)	1970	2.06	3.17	—	21.52	—	0.15	0.05
	1971	2.14	3.15	—	12.92	—	0.16	0.03
	1981	18.46	33.57	—	5.50	—	7.56	0.60
	1983	19.82	36.58	—	5.50	—	12.82	1.70
	1984	32.76	59.70	—	5.50	—	35.11	0.36
	1985	36.19	64.36	—	5.50	—	42.50	0.50
	1986	39.77	67.81	—	5.50	—	52.64	0.49
Jamaica[25] (Dollar)	1970	6.07	12.74	—	23.56	2.21	3.73	—
	1975	12.50	14.62	—	99.00	—	11.40	—
	1980	26.06	31.01	—	37.46	—	41.08	0.01
	1983	36.70	43.89	—	61.28	—	45.14	0.15
	1984	37.25	44.96	—	103.09	—	82.78	0.06
	1985	38.35	46.34	—	100.54	—	88.78	0.30
	1986	38.90	47.10	—	119.30	—	124.84	0.23
México (Peso)	1970	10 208.40		—	2 383.23	—	523.00	393.10
	1974	23 255.57		—	6 149.31	—	795.81	1 099.00
	1980	36 046.00	74 804.00	—	10 592.00	—	3 036.00	19 857.00
	1983	107 019.00	326 997.00	—	37 538.00	—	10 161.00	61 928.00
	1984	179 081.00	545 603.00	—	61 824.00	—	17 740.00	78 970.00
	1985	277 108.00	896 965.00	—	103 602.00	—	21 035.00	132 403.00
	1986	483 848.00	1 553 759.00	—	123 884.00	—	45 380.00	256 778.00

See notes on page 70.   *Voir notes page 70.*   Véanse notas pág. 70.

Total receipts (excluding transfers) / Total des recettes (non compris les transferts) / Total de ingresos (excl. las transferencias)	Expenditure / Dépenses / Egresos				Administrative expenditure / Frais d'administration / Gastos de administración	Other expenditure / Autres dépenses / Otros egresos	Total expenditure (excluding transfers) / Total des dépenses (non compris les transferts) / Total de egresos (excl. las transferencias)	Difference between receipts and expenditure / Différence entre les recettes et les dépenses / Diferencia entre los ingresos y los egresos	
	Benefits / Prestations / Prestaciones							In absolute figures / En chiffres absolus / En cifras absolutas	As percentage of total receipts / En pourcentage du total des recettes / En porcentaje del total de ingresos
	Medical care / Soins médicaux / Asistencia médica	Benefits in kind other than for medical care / Prestations en nature à d'autres titres que les soins médicaux / Prestaciones en especie, excepto asistencia médica	Cash benefits / Prestations en espèces / Prestaciones monetarias	Total / Total / Total					
(10)	(11)	(12)	(13)	(14)	(15)	(16)	(17)	(18)	(19)
96.24	39.49	0.16	19.09	58.74	10.06	5.15	73.95	22.29	23.2
173.05	76.16	0.24	29.62	106.02	28.36	15.23	149.61	23.44	13.5
223.45	64.73	1.13	60.31	126.17	22.25	—	148.42	75.03	33.6
288.00	72.40	0.40	80.90	153.70	14.30	—	168.00	120.00	41.7
203.20	80.40	0.30	64.80	145.50	29.50	—	175.00	28.20	13.9
230.30	87.80	0.20	70.60	158.60	24.60	—	183.20	47.10	20.5
287.40	69.90	0.30	87.90	158.10	52.80	—	210.90	76.50	26.6
3.50	—	—	3.43	3.43	—	—	3.43	0.07	2.0
7.94	—	—	4.33	4.33	0.20	—	4.53	3.41	43.0
11.51	—	—	4.82	4.82	0.35	—	5.17	6.34	55.1
14.33	—	—	5.49	5.49	0.47	—	5.95	8.38	58.5
15.15	—	—	5.46	5.46	0.54	—	6.00	9.15	60.4
42.50	26.70	—	9.80	36.50	2.60	1.80	40.90	1.60	3.8
73.30	47.50	—	19.10	66.60	4.30	0.40	71.30	2.00	2.7
133.40	46.90	—	33.40	80.30	10.60	—	90.90	42.50	31.9
124.20	46.70	—	33.30	80.00	10.20	—	90.20	34.00	27.4
138.30	48.30	—	37.20	85.50	12.70	3.30	101.50	36.80	26.6
150.90	51.50	—	40.80	92.30	13.70	3.30	109.30	41.60	27.6
209.00	66.60	—	49.00	115.60	14.70	4.10	134.40	74.60	35.7
31.12	13.36	—	3.39	16.76	3.03	—	19.79	11.33	36.4
42.82	15.65	—	3.15	18.81	3.85	—	22.65	20.17	47.1
91.41	0.60	1.59	11.77	13.97	4.68	0.31	18.96	72.44	79.3
136.32	1.73	—	17.41	19.14	6.99	0.50	26.63	109.69	80.5
155.94	2.20	—	19.95	22.15	7.16	1.10	30.41	125.53	80.5
175.07	2.30	—	21.86	24.16	10.69	0.80	35.65	139.41	79.6
200.22	2.48	—	47.35	49.83	11.29	1.00	62.13	138.10	69.0
26.95	11.52		11.67	23.19	0.74	—	23.93	3.02	11.2
18.40	4.12		12.80	16.92	0.89	—	17.81	0.59	3.2
65.69	30.34	—	6.79	37.13	6.75	0.13	44.01	21.68	33.0
76.42	35.77	—	8.91	44.67	9.78	0.32	54.77	21.65	28.3
133.42	40.29	—	15.70	55.99	12.91	0.65	69.55	63.88	47.9
149.05	41.83	—	18.39	60.22	12.86	0.96	74.04	75.01	50.3
166.23	43.82	—	21.13	64.95	11.85	—	76.80	89.42	53.8
48.31	18.68	—	7.40	26.09	3.68	3.44	33.20	15.11	31.3
137.51	66.55	—	28.32	94.87	11.87	0.01	106.76	30.75	22.4
135.62	0.02	—	61.11	61.13	3.95	0.00	65.08	70.54	52.0
187.16	0.05	—	97.14	97.19	6.36	0.06	103.61	83.55	44.6
268.14	0.07	—	136.70	136.77	7.85	0.07	144.69	123.45	46.0
274.31	0.07	—	138.87	138.94	8.05	1.41	148.40	125.91	45.9
330.37	0.12	—	160.06	160.18	10.25	1.07	171.50	158.87	48.1
13 507.73	6 853.53	252.00	3 540.00	10 645.53	1 420.60	657.70	12 723.83	783.90	5.8
31 299.69	17 070.15	551.00	5 962.52	23 583.67	3 159.60	938.82	27 682.09	3 617.60	11.6
144 335.00	55 286.00	2 418.00	27 409.00	85 113.00	15 533.00	16 165.00	116 811.00	27 524.00	19.1
543 643.00	213 962.00	15 640.00	84 471.00	314 073.00	80 847.00	61 527.00	456 447.00	87 196.00	16.0
883 218.00	349 584.00	113 238.00	129 854.00	592 676.00	120 981.00	85 486.00	799 143.00	84 075.00	9.5
1 431 113.00	518 190.00	179 241.00	236 387.00	933 818.00	196 599.00	60 184.00	1 190 601.00	240 512.00	16.8
2 463 649.00	806 630.00	301 717.00	448 531.00	1 556 878.00	366 655.00	192 041.00	2 115 574.00	348 075.00	14.1

Table 1 (cont.) Tableau 1 (suite) Cuadro 1 (cont.)

Country and currency unit / Pays et unité monétaire / País y unidad monetaria	Financial year / Exercice financier / Ejercicio financiero	Receipts / Recettes / Ingresos						
		Contributions / Cotisations / Cotizaciones		Special taxes allocated to social security / Taxes et impôts spéciaux / Impuestos y tasas especiales	State participation / Participation de l'Etat / Participación del Estado	Participation of other public authorities / Participation d'autres pouvoirs publics / Participación de otras entidades públicas	Income from capital / Revenu des capitaux / Renta del capital	Other receipts / Autres recettes / Otros ingresos
		From insured persons / Des assurés / De los asegurados	From employers / Des employeurs / De los empleadores					
(1)	(2)	(3)	(4)	(5)	(6)	(7)	(8)	(9)
Panamá (Balboa)	1972	22.41	49.61	0.85	26.78	—	8.59	1.93
	1975	40.52	88.51	0.78	35.78	—	11.14	1.14
	1980	82.80	130.67	1.52	11.04	—	27.94	36.00
	1983	124.70	197.40	1.70	12.70	—	57.60	56.90
	1984	131.30	196.90	2.50	13.00	—	59.00	24.30
	1985	139.50	208.40	2.70	13.80	—	61.20	27.60
	1986	150.40	224.50	2.00	14.90	—	76.10	32.60
Perú[40] (Inti)	1981	216.62		—	—	—	27.45	4.12
	1983	502.00		—	—	—	58.00	7.00
	1984	319 048.00	720 576.00	—	—	—	—	—
	1985	992 475.00	2 189 162.00	—	—	—	—	—
	1986	2 189 393.00	4 852 284.00	—	—	—	—	—
St. Lucia[3] (EC Dollar)	1981	3.08	3.08	—	—	—	2.09	—
	1983	2.99	2.99	—	—	—	0.89	—
	1984	2.88	2.88	—	—	—	4.69	0.00
	1985	2.61	2.61	—	—	—	5.46	0.00
	1986	4.18	4.18	—	—	—	6.25	0.01
Trinidad and Tobago[4] (Dollar)	1970	2.32	8.15	—	39.10	4.70	—	—
	1975	20.49	42.21	—	110.30	—	9.26	—
	1980	35.74	70.67	—	52.70	—	37.01	—
	1983	85.96	186.00	—	320.47	—	88.00	0.03
	1984[1]	89.01	178.03	—	163.80	—	94.40	—
	1985[1]	80.73	161.46	—	150.20	—	106.80	—
	1986[1]	79.49	158.97	—	176.20	—	90.77	—
United States[17] (Dollar)	1970	26 960	36 988	—	26 776	14 205	6 003	—
	1975	49 915	74 949	—	56 419	26 745	11 872	—
	1980	86 893	149 770	—	79 325	31 043	23 566	—
	1983	116 287	176 445	—	147 154	32 190	42 112	274
	1984	131 700	184 578	2 526	139 688	32 629	48 337	170
	1985	146 202	203 557	3 708	144 242	35 447	58 614	342
	1986	157 701	217 200	3 945	152 547	38 303	75 281	− 513
Uruguay[3,41] (Nuevo peso)	1975	629.77		52.22	233.38	—	3.48	6.84
	1980	2 454.80	3 328.00	790.10	2 952.40	—	147.20	107.00
	1983[5]	5 710.00	5 680.00	339.00	10 740.00	—	268.00	392.00
	1984[1]	7 626.00	8 206.00	286.00	9 968.00	—	277.00	1 053.00
	1985[1]	14 510.00	16 810.00	492.00	13 765.00	—	448.00	1 936.00
	1986[1]	30 955.00	34 576.00	874.00	21 456.00	—	662.00	4 326.00
Venezuela (Bolívar)	1970	238.10	461.20	—	1 006.40	—	48.90	1.10
	1975	507.20	1 014.30	—	3 540.90	—	261.10	0.20
	1980	1 140.40	2 280.60	—	290.00	—	539.80	8.50
	1983	1 156.80	2 312.90	—	700.90	—	934.30	—
	1984	1 203.20	2 405.60	—	718.30	—	1 033.60	—
	1985	1 243.40	2 485.90	—	777.00	—	1 296.90	—
	1986[43]	1 589.40	3 038.00	—	944.80	—	1 885.40	—

See notes on page 70. Voir notes page 70. Véanse notas pág. 70.

Total receipts (excluding transfers) / Total des recettes (non compris les transferts) / Total de ingresos (excl. las transferencias)	Expenditure / Dépenses / Egresos							Difference between receipts and expenditure / Différence entre les recettes et les dépenses / Diferencia entre los ingresos y los egresos	
	Benefits / Prestations / Prestaciones				Administrative expenditure / Frais d'administration / Gastos de administración	Other expenditure / Autres dépenses / Otros egresos	Total expenditure (excluding transfers) / Total des dépenses (non compris les transferts) / Total de egresos (excl. las transferencias)	In absolute figures / En chiffres absolus / En cifras absolutas	As percentage of total receipts / En pourcentage du total des recettes / En porcentaje del total de ingresos
	Medical care / Soins médicaux / Asistencia médica	Benefits in kind other than for medical care / Prestations en nature à d'autres titres que les soins médicaux / Prestaciones en especie, excepto asistencia médica	Cash benefits / Prestations en espèces / Prestaciones monetarias	Total / Total / Total					
(10)	(11)	(12)	(13)	(14)	(15)	(16)	(17)	(18)	(19)
110.17	44.93	0.03	36.05	81.01	13.33	1.65	95.99	14.18	12.9
177.87	65.74	—	53.05	118.79	18.82	0.79	138.40	39.47	22.2
289.97	92.91	—	96.68	189.59	11.43	9.46	210.48	79.49	27.4
451.00	140.20	—	152.20	292.40	26.40	16.30	335.10	115.90	25.7
427.00	167.20	—	172.90	340.10	22.80	0.70	363.60	63.40	14.8
453.20	169.80	—	196.10	365.90	23.10	0.90	389.90	63.30	14.0
500.50	177.60	—	224.00	401.60	23.60	0.70	425.90	74.60	14.9
248.19	125.62	—	60.79	186.41	20.46	—	206.87	41.32	16.6
567.00	351.00	—	185.00	536.00	69.00	—	605.00	− 38.00	− 6.7
1 039 624.00	—	—	429 008.00	429 008.00	607 609.00	65 558.00	1 102 175.00	−62 551.00	−6.0
3 181 637.00	—	—	1 119 428.00	1 119 428.00	1 417 545.00	242 069.00	2 779 042.00	402 595.00	12.7
7 041 677.00	—	—	2 419 501.00	2 419 501.00	3 169 140.00	548 031.00	6 136 672.00	905 005.00	12.9
8.25	—	—	0.72	0.72	0.85	—	1.57	6.68	81.0
6.87	—	—	0.98	0.98	1.17	—	2.15	4.72	68.6
10.44	1.00	—	1.02	2.02	1.07	—	3.09	7.35	70.4
10.68	—	—	0.87	0.87	1.25	—	2.12	8.56	80.1
14.62	1.00	—	1.07	2.07	1.30	—	3.37	11.26	77.0
54.27	37.70	—	15.30	53.00	—	—	53.00	1.27	2.3
182.26	83.00	—	43.96	126.96	4.84	—	131.80	50.46	27.7
196.12	—	—	94.21	94.21	15.18	0.95	110.34	85.78	43.7
680.46	—	—	417.13	417.13	39.76	—	456.89	223.57	32.9
525.24	—	—	260.02	260.02	44.59	6.10	310.71	214.53	40.8
499.19	—	—	254.92	254.92	43.10	8.70	306.72	192.47	38.6
505.43	—	—	295.29	295.29	45.16	42.74	383.19	122.24	24.2
110 932	21 938	7 130	58 476	87 544	2 769	3 492	93 805	17 127	15.4
219 900	45 311	18 202	126 503	190 016	5 821	6 319	202 156	17 744	8.1
370 597	88 601	20 037	208 046	316 684	10 321	2 577	329 582	41 015	11.1
514 462	101 165	22 600	309 114	432 879	13 899	4 917	451 695	62 767	12.2
539 628	111 178	23 989	309 495	444 662	14 607	6 723	465 992	73 636	13.6
592 112	125 652	24 256	326 388	476 296	15 989	6 021	498 306	93 806	15.8
644 464	135 209	24 758	344 501	504 468	16 542	4 845	525 855	118 609	18.4
925.69	110.14	—	578.61	688.75	71.22	112.38	872.35	53.34	5.8
9 779.50	407.80[42]	—	6 502.80	6 910.60	582.60	57.30	7 550.50	2 229.00	22.8
23 129.00	16.00	—	18 885.00	18 901.00	1 113.00	410.00	20 424.00	2 705.00	11.7
27 416.00	1 760.00	—	27 559.00	29 319.00	1 674.00	530.00	31 523.00	−4 107.00	−15.0
47 961.00	3 743.00	—	39 888.00	43 631.00	2 953.00	462.00	47 046.00	915.00	1.9
92 849.00	7 808.00	—	78 739.00	86 547.00	5 638.00	1 194.00	93 379.00	−530.00	−0.6
1 755.70	1 079.50	—	110.20	1 189.70	238.00	176.80	1 604.50	151.20	8.6
5 323.70	3 883.30	—	471.00	4 354.30	286.90	—	4 641.20	682.50	12.8
4 259.30	1 632.70	—	1 236.10	2 868.80	467.80	—	3 336.60	922.70	21.7
5 104.90	1 821.10	—	1 758.20	3 579.30	700.90	—	4 280.20	824.70	16.2
5 360.70	2 275.70	—	1 864.90	4 140.60	718.30	—	4 858.90	501.80	9.4
5 803.20	2 303.70	—	2 060.00	4 363.70	777.00	—	5 140.70	662.50	11.4
7 457.60	3 339.40	—	2 071.50	5 410.90	944.00	—	6 355.70	1 101.90	14.8

Table 1 *(cont.)* **Tableau 1** *(suite)* **Cuadro 1** *(cont.)*

Country and currency unit / *Pays et unité monétaire* / País y unidad monetaria	Financial year / *Exercice financier* / Ejercicio financiero	Receipts / *Recettes* / Ingresos						
		Contributions / *Cotisations* / Cotizaciones		Special taxes allocated to social security / *Taxes et impôts spéciaux* / Impuestos y tasas especiales	State participation / *Participation de l'Etat* / Participación del Estado	Participation of other public authorities / *Participation d'autres pouvoirs publics* / Participación de otras entidades públicas	Income from capital / *Revenu des capitaux* / Renta del capital	Other receipts / *Autres recettes* / Otros ingresos
		From insured persons / *Des assurés* / De los asegurados	From employers / *Des employeurs* / De los empleadores					
(1)	(2)	(3)	(4)	(5)	(6)	(7)	(8)	(9)
ASIA – ASIE – ASIA								
Bahrain (Dinar)	1978	2.20	7.67	—	3.57	—	1.97	3.69
	1980	3.09	10.71	—	5.18	—	5.38	0.24
	1983	11.74	23.47	—	—	—	11.76	0.10
	1984[1]	7.87	15.74	—	—	—	7.59	0.00
	1985[1]	8.41	16.81	—	—	—	11.66	0.51
	1986[1]	7.54	15.08	—	—	—	13.14	0.00
Bangladesh (Taka)	1975	7.04	7.84	—	273.00	—	5.38	0.22
	1980	—	3.14	—	—	—	—	—
	1983	5.63	12.59	1.24	—	—	9.52	—
	1984	63.25	37.39	1.44	0.30	—	26.13	—
	1985	41.20	40.96	1.96	0.30	—	40.97	—
	1986	57.77	64.42	1.88	0.30	—	29.90	—
Cyprus (Pound)	1970	1.95	2.24	—	3.63	—	0.39	0.17
	1975	3.09	4.11	—	8.60	—	0.43	0.27
	1980	10.20	12.35	—	9.92	—	1.23	0.29
	1983	27.16	40.31	—	19.39	—	7.35	0.55
	1984	34.37	44.57	—	20.01	—	10.28	0.79
	1985	38.65	57.57	—	22.57	—	14.04	1.15
	1986	41.55	56.52	—	24.36	—	18.12	1.04
India[3, 25] (Rupee)	1970	6 049.30	1 891.40	34.90	352.50	3 112.90	953.40	3.60
	1975	20 407.00	—	168.20	872.30	5 998.00	3 365.20	59.70
	1980	5 069.80	25 657.70	139.60	636.10	153.30	4 756.70	230.00
	1983[44, 5]	7 310.95	56 945.35	97.19	2 923.99	5 342.20	9 570.29	403.47
	1984[44, 5]	7 642.39	57 252.04	117.73	2 924.67	5 342.20	9 998.49	407.70
	1985[44, 5]	8 562.06	58 737.50	99.49	3 012.70	5 342.20	11 586.73	466.98
Indonesia[3] (Rupiah)	1981	6 970.00	20 121.00	—	—	—	—	5 963.00
	1983	9 286.00	27 285.00	—	—	—	—	19 753.00
	1984[5]	11 882.82	37 627.71	—	—	—	12 746.84	189.10
	1985[5]	15 451.24	50 860.38	—	—	—	17 832.71	802.41
	1986[5]	16 967.62	56 849.94	—	—	—	23 177.72	899.66
Iran, Islamic Rep. of[3] (Rial)	1981	39 022	111 492	—	33 427	—	11 416	30 335
	1983	52 574	150 214	—	77 935	—	18 762	2 047
	1984[5]	230 602	34	—	25 765	—	35 438	8
	1985[5]	259 387	52	—	29 526	—	15.629	14
	1986[5]	288 190	161	—	28 461	—	29 418	230
Israel[25, 45] (New Shekel)	1970	0.046	0.079	—	0.057	0.016	0.009	0.001
	1975	0.133	0.328	—	0.472	0.016	0.068	0.031
	1980	3.46	7.49	—	4.34	0.40	1.87	0.26
	1983	50.10	97.80	—	87.60	3.60	27.50	3.80
	1984	264.00	520.90	—	438.70	20.60	159.50	9.20
	1985	953.70	1 613.90	—	1 455.10	60.90	440.10	23.40
	1986	1 609.90	2 505.60	—	1 977.70	85.60	516.30	27.90
Japan[25] (Yen)	1970	1 555 818	1 703 671	—	1 442 478	199 689	475 273	388 588
	1975	4 423 075	5 075 102	—	4 852 818	701.294	1 433 458	964 696
	1980	8 884 404	9 726 306	—	9 353 074	1 105 477	3 233 784	1 897 437
	1983	11 275 454	12 449 371	—	10 671 585	1 284 557	4 967 284	2 100 872
	1984	11 886 712	13 202 162	—	11 049 370	1 385 679	5 527 719	828 688
	1985	13 158 346	14 500 947	—	11 243 305	1 811 315	6 167 443	1 050 112
	1986	13 731 012	15 469 993	—	11 455 239	2 088 703	6 848 993	931 785

See notes on page 70. *Voir notes page 70.* Véanse notas pág. 70.

	Expenditure / Dépenses / Egresos							Difference between receipts and expenditure / Différence entre les recettes et les dépenses / Diferencia entre los ingresos y los egresos	
Total receipts (excluding transfers) / Total des recettes (non compris les transferts) / Total de ingresos (excl. las transferencias)	Benefits / Prestations / Prestaciones				Administrative expenditure / Frais d'administration / Gastos de administración	Other expenditure / Autres dépenses / Otros egresos	Total expenditure (excluding transfers) / Total des dépenses (non compris les transferts) / Total de egresos (excl. las transferencias)	In absolute figures / En chiffres absolus / En cifras absolutas	As percentage of total receipts / En pourcentage du total des recettes / En porcentaje del total de ingresos
	Medical care / Soins médicaux / Asistencia médica	Benefits in kind other than for medical care / Prestations en nature à d'autres titres que les soins médicaux / Prestaciones en especie, excepto asistencia médica	Cash benefits / Prestations en espèces / Prestaciones monetarias	Total / Total / Total					
(10)	(11)	(12)	(13)	(14)	(15)	(16)	(17)	(18)	(19)
19.10	0.03	0.06	2.24	2.34	0.48	0.16	2.98	16.12	84.4
24.60	0.05	0.20	2.31	2.56	0.73	0.34	3.63	20.97	85.2
47.08	0.14	0.54	5.01	5.70	1.52	1.94	9.16	37.91	80.5
31.21	0.18	0.38	3.07	3.62	1.04	1.14	5.81	25.40	81.4
37.39	0.18	0.52	3.72	4.43	1.38	0.17	5.97	31.42	84.0
35.77	0.12	0.54	4.87	5.53	1.49	0.54	7.56	28.21	78.9
293.48	273.00	—	3.91	276.91	0.77	—	277.68	15.80	5.4
3.14	—	—	3.14	3.14	—	—	3.14	—	—
28.98	—	—	12.29	12.29	0.66	—	12.95	16.03	55.3
128.51	0.16	—	55.69	55.85	1.52	—	57.37	71.14	55.4
125.39	0.38	—	53.66	54.04	1.83	—	55.87	69.52	55.4
153.66	1.53	—	53.92	55.45	2.43	—	57.88	95.78	62.3
8.38	2.22	0.07	4.77	7.06	0.15	—	7.21	1.17	14.0
16.50	3.96	—	13.78	17.74	0.27	0.02	18.03	− 1.53	−9.3
33.99	0.04	—	27.00	27.04	0.51	0.01	27.56	6.43	18.9
94.76	0.05	—	55.43	55.48	0.96	0.11	56.55	38.21	40.3
110.02	0.10	—	60.80	60.90	0.87	0.11	61.87	48.15	43.8
133.98	0.08	—	69.91	69.99	1.04	0.11	71.15	62.83	46.9
141.59	0.11	—	80.36	80.47	1.14	0.12	81.73	59.86	42.3
12 398.00	3 577.50	0.70	4 283.40	7 861.60	72.40	57.40	7 991.40	4 406.60	35.5
30 870.40	6 715.90	37.40	10 803.60	17 556.90	159.50	126.60	17 843.00	13 027.40	42.2
36 643.20	759.70	65.00	20 223.70	21 048.40	289.10	221.40	21 558.90	15 084.30	41.2
82 593.44	941.46	15.53	37 843.98	38 800.97	570.28	0.48	39 371.73	43 221.71	52.3
83 685.22	868.81	15.03	37 860.08	38 743.92	592.89	—	39 336.81	44 348.41	53.0
87 807.66	1 010.60	11.55	38 680.52	39 702.67	659.62	—	40 362.19	47 445.47	54.0
33 054.00	—	—	2 497.00	2 497.00	2 850.00	491.00	5 838.00	27 216.00	82.3
56 324.00	—	—	4 729.00	4 729.00	10 145.00	989.00	15 863.00	40 461.00	71.8
62 446.47	—	—	5 956.53	5 956.53	13 119.96	32 537.22	51 613.71	10 832.76	17.3
84 946.74	—	—	7 948.56	7 948.56	14 339.12	57 612.12	79 899.80	5 046.94	5.9
97 894.94	—	—	11 515.92	11 515.92	17 935.97	62 762.08	92 213.97	5 680.97	5.8
225 692	37 789	130	44 940	82 859	7 813	—	90 672	135 020	59.8
301 532	47 426	140	52 775	100 341	7 178	—	107 519	194 013	64.3
291 847	48 600	—	—	48 600	8 690	61 000	118 290	173 557	59.5
304 608	58 200	—	—	58 200	9 812	75 772	143 784	160 824	52.8
346 460	73 271	—	—	73 271	10 608	84 000	167 879	178 581	51.5
0.209	0.067	0.009	0.074	0.150	0.011	0.009	0.170	0.039	18.7
1.048	0.248	0.026	0.561	0.835	0.048	0.077	0.960	0.088	8.4
17.82	4.43	1.33	9.29	15.05	1.05	0.84	16.94	0.88	4.9
270.40	59.50	17.70	135.60	212.80	21.20	19.30	253.30	17.10	6.3
1 412.90	397.70	76.30	732.30	1 206.30	76.00	165.00	1 447.30	− 34.40	−2.4
4 547.10	1 096.80	231.40	2 504.40	3 832.60	235.80	495.70	4 564.10	− 17.00	−0.4
6 723.00	1 498.20	336.80	3 689.80	5 524.80	334.80	287.20	6 146.80	576.20	8.6
5 765 517	2 075 735	128 580	1 319 096	3 523 411	124 459	433 158	4 081 028	1 684 489	29.2
17 450 443	5 688 085	504 412	5 480 126	11 672 623	326 081	1 230 434	13 229 138	4 221 305	24.2
34 200 482	10 229 840	934 225	12 956 286	24 120 351	513 988	2 287 880	26 922 219	7 278 263	21.3
42 749 123	12 531 529	1 078 662	17 755 232	31 365 423	581 885	2 605 591	34 552 899	8 196 224	19.2
43 880 330	12 922 706	1 124 264	18 939 658	32 986 628	618 854	1 295 820	34 901 302	8 979 028	20.5
47 931 468	13 645 689	1 189 541	20 218 988	35 054 218	654 709	1 445 751	37 154 678	10 776 790	22.5
50 525 725	14 549 750	1 263 981	22 170 133	37 983 864	680 474	1 481 314	40 145 652	10 380 073	20.5

Table 1 (cont.) Tableau 1 (suite) Cuadro 1 (cont.)

Country and currency unit / Pays et unité monétaire / País y unidad monetaria	Financial year / Exercice financier / Ejercicio financiero	Receipts / Recettes / Ingresos						
		Contributions / Cotisations / Cotizaciones		Special taxes allocated to social security / Taxes et impôts spéciaux / Impuestos y tasas especiales	State participation / Participation de l'Etat / Participación del Estado	Participation of other public authorities / Participation d'autres pouvoirs publics / Participación de otras entidades públicas	Income from capital / Revenu des capitaux / Renta del capital	Other receipts / Autres recettes / Otros ingresos
		From insured persons / Des assurés / De los asegurados	From employers / Des employeurs / De los empleadores					
(1)	(2)	(3)	(4)	(5)	(6)	(7)	(8)	(9)
Jordan (Dinar)	1980	1.60	3.16	—	—	—	0.10	—
	1983	9.31	17.85	—	—	—	2.91	0.20
	1984	12.39	23.77	—	—	—	4.02	0.29
	1985	13.10	25.23	—	—	—	5.44	0.37
	1986	15.40	29.62	—	—	—	8.12	0.44
Kuwait[2,4] (Dinar)	1980	10.10	20.20	—	39.50	—	18.50	1.80
	1983	19.08	37.75	—	85.02	—	43.86	27.33
	1984[39]	20.23	39.93	—	78.34	—	34.38	24.75
	1985[39]	21.03	41.46	—	199.69	—	41.59	19.60
	1986[39]	24.30	47.73	—	210.54	—	81.43	21.77
Malaysia (Ringgit)	1970	107.06	170.19	—	158.42	—	127.12	1.11
	1975	584.79		—	318.09	—	271.22	11.02
	1980	1 354.95		—	7.40	—	732.42	35.48
	1983	1 063.40	1 984.43	—	27.70	—	1 279.08	22.03
	1984	1 153.54	2 150.50	—	149.14	—	1 565.76	12.75
	1985	1 256.28	2 379.08	—	157.03	—	1 879.93	37.49
	1986	1 358.55	2 553.57	—	157.81	—	2 189.33	44.72
Myanmar[3,25,47] (Kyat)	1970	2.96	96.59	—	116.42	—	—	0.07
	1975	4.06	129.43	—	189.22	—	—	0.10
	1980[1]	6.12	18.37	—	5.40	—	0.40	0.10
	1983[1]	7.90	23.70	6.70	—	—	0.50	0.20
	1984[1]	8.20	24.40	7.30	—	—	0.50	0.20
	1985[1]	8.40	25.20	8.10	—	—	0.60	0.20
	1986[1]	8.80	26.40	8.20	—	—	0.70	0.20
Pakistan[3,4] (Rupee)	1965	—	159.50	—	155.30	—	—	—
	1980	—	190.52	—	21.01	—	41.52	1.94
	1983[48]	—	276.87	857.12	1 347.77	—	103.39	2.03
	1984[39]	35.40	371.60	—	2 855.20	—	141.00	3.40
	1985[39]	43.00	428.50	—	5 445.00	—	209.80	2.90
	1986[39]	50.30	518.10	—	4 293.50	—	269.70	3.20
Philippines[49] (Peso)	1970	160.31	224.67	—	231.62	—	122.47	1.30
	1978	962.60	1 378.60	—	—	—	739.00	79.00
	1980	1 358.20	1 895.40	—	—	—	1 148.70	85.20
	1983	1 760.60	2 443.40	—	—	—	2 423.80	135.00
	1984	1 748.60	2 489.00	—	—	—	3 551.00	125.60
	1985	1 882.60	2 690.50	—	—	—	5 982.90	81.80
	1986	1 986.10	2 843.00	—	—	—	5 681.40	194.50
*Qatar[2,50] (Riyal)	1984	—	—	76.22	—	—	—	—
	1985	—	—	79.54	—	—	—	—
	1986	—	—	80.02	—	—	—	—
Singapore[51] (Dollar)	1970	61.17	120.14	—	91.20	—	41.23	0.49
	1975	417.63	507.14	—	143.22	—	169.05	2.56
	1980	1 079.44	1 286.89	—	3.60	—	521.14	12.56
	1983	2 245.88	2 364.30	—	3.40	—	1 104.14	26.58
	1984	2 693.05	2 841.53	—	3.43	—	1 324.21	28.81
	1985	2 997.10	3 180.28	—	3.80	—	1 589.76	26.64
	1986	3 413.22	1 554.79	—	4.04	—	1 693.87	25.05

See notes on page 70. *Voir notes page 70.* Véanse notas pág. 70.

58

	Expenditure / Dépenses / Egresos							Difference between receipts and expenditure / Différence entre les recettes et les dépenses / Diferencia entre los ingresos y los egresos	
Total receipts (excluding transfers) / Total des recettes (non compris les transferts) / Total de ingresos (excl. las transferencias)	Benefits / Prestations / Prestaciones				Administrative expenditure / Frais d'administration / Gastos de administración	Other expenditure / Autres dépenses / Otros egresos	Total expenditure (excluding transfers) / Total des dépenses (non compris les transferts) / Total de egresos (excl. las transferencias)	In absolute figures / En chiffres absolus / En cifras absolutas	As percentage of total receipts / En pourcentage du total des recettes / En porcentaje del total de ingresos
	Medical care / Soins médicaux / Asistencia médica	Benefits in kind other than for medical care / Prestations en nature à d'autres titres que les soins médicaux / Prestaciones en especie, excepto asistencia médica	Cash benefits / Prestations en espèces / Prestaciones monetarias	Total / Total / Total					
(10)	(11)	(12)	(13)	(14)	(15)	(16)	(17)	(18)	(19)
4.86	0.01	—	0.02	0.03	0.28	—	0.31	4.55	93.6
30.27	0.20	0.36	2.01	2.57	0.84	0.03	3.44	26.83	88.6
40.47	0.18	—	3.47	3.65	0.95	2.51	7.11	33.36	82.4
44.14	0.24	—	5.07	5.31	1.45	2.57	9.33	34.81	78.9
53.58	0.28	—	7.10	7.38	1.33	0.82	9.53	44.05	82.2
90.10	—	—	39.80	39.80	2.50	—	42.30	47.80	53.1
213.04	—	—	88.24	88.24	4.29	0.23	92.76	120.28	56.5
197.63	—	—	85.41	85.41	5.77	0.19	91.37	106.26	53.8
323.37	—	—	158.76	158.76	5.45	0.37	164.58	158.79	49.1
385.77	—	—	163.30	163.30	6.21	—	169.51	216.26	56.1
563.90	154.80	—	146.42	301.22	6.56	1.26	309.04	254.86	45.2
1 185.12	313.63	—	308.97	622.60	14.35	39.09	676.04	509.08	43.0
2 130.25	0.90	8.93	427.56	437.39	17.40	57.86	512.65	1 617.60	75.9
4 376.64	1.57	0.12	1 190.70	1 192.39	45.20	0.69	1 238.28	3 138.36	71.7
5 031.69	2.21	0.19	1 340.91[46]	1 343.31	125.55	0.63	1 469.49	3 562.20	70.8
5 709.81	2.37	0.17	1 439.00[46]	1 441.54	76.89	0.71	1 519.14	4 190.67	73.4
6 303.98	2.14	0.12	1 490.52[46]	1 492.78	96.05	0.50	1 589.33	4 714.65	74.8
216.04	113.78	—	90.70	204.48	1.36	0.03	205.87	10.17	4.7
322.81	189.30	—	121.03	310.33	2.05	0.04	312.42	10.39	3.2
30.39	8.85	—	6.00	14.85	3.80	0.50	19.15	11.24	37.0
39.00	11.20	—	6.60	17.80	4.90	6.00	28.70	10.30	26.4
40.60	10.00	—	6.80	16.80	4.90	6.90	28.60	12.00	29.6
42.50	10.10	—	6.40	16.50	5.30	9.40	31.20	11.30	26.6
44.30	11.60	—	6.90	18.50	5.60	11.80	35.90	8.40	19.0
314.80	225.70	—	89.10	314.80	—	—	314.80	—	—
254.99	49.11	—	10.79	59.90	22.45	31.61	113.96	141.03	55.3
2 587.18	88.52	0.11	2 111.20	2 199.83	38.98	10.89	2 249.70	337.48	13.0
3 406.60	1 587.40	—	1 429.60	3 017.00	48.00	26.90	3 091.90	314.70	9.2
6 129.20	4 080.20	—	1 564.30	5 644.50	51.10	14.00	5 709.60	419.60	6.8
5 134.80	2 455.90	—	2 101.80	4 557.70	55.60	16.20	4 629.50	505.30	9.8
740.37	185.42	—	177.18	362.60	44.50	2.94	410.04	330.33	44.6
3 159.20	355.90	—	779.40	1 135.30	217.50	—	1 352.80	1 806.40	57.2
4 487.50	439.00	—	962.80	1 401.80	324.10	—	1 725.90	2 761.60	61.5
6 762.80	420.70	—	1 960.50	2 381.20	400.10	69.00	2 850.30	3 912.50	57.9
7 914.20	438.00	—	2 313.70	2 751.70	558.90	—	3 310.60	4 603.60	58.2
10 637.80	454.00	—	2 708.10	3 162.10	572.50	—	3 734.60	6 903.20	64.9
10 705.00	492.10	—	3 197.90	3 690.00	554.80	—	4 244.80	6 460.20	60.3
76.22	—	—	76.22	76.22	—	—	76.22	—	—
79.54	—	—	79.54	79.54	—	—	79.54	—	—
80.02	—	—	80.02	80.02	—	—	80.02	—	—
314.23	87.70	—	74.23	161.93	2.26	0.55	164.74	149.49	47.6
1 239.60	140.12	—	258.08	398.20	4.89	0.64	403.73	835.87	67.4
2 903.63	—	—	852.32	852.32	12.02	57.00	921.34	1 982.29	68.3
5 744.30	—	—	1 829.44	1 829.44	20.29	1 076.54	2 926.27	2 818.03	49.1
6 891.03	—	—	3 614.09	3 614.09	23.16	1 291.25	4 928.50	1 962.53	28.5
7 797.58	—	—	3 506.69	3 506.69	28.92	1 526.75	5 062.36	2 735.22	35.1
6 690.97	—	—	4 023.19	4 023.19	24.21	1 553.84	5 601.24	1 089.73	16.3

Table 1 *(cont.)*   Tableau 1 *(suite)*   Cuadro 1 *(cont.)*

Country and currency unit *Pays et unité monétaire* País y unidad monetaria	Financial year *Exercice financier* Ejercicio financiero	Receipts *Recettes* Ingresos		Special taxes allocated to social security *Taxes et impôts spéciaux* Impuestos y tasas especiales	State participation *Participation de l'Etat* Participación del Estado	Participation of other public authorities *Participation d'autres pouvoirs publics* Participación de otras entidades públicas	Income from capital *Revenu des capitaux* Renta del capital	Other receipts *Autres recettes* Otros ingresos
		Contributions *Cotisations* Cotizaciones						
		From insured persons *Des assurés* De los asegurados	From employers *Des employeurs* De los empleadores					
(1)	(2)	(3)	(4)	(5)	(6)	(7)	(8)	(9)
Sri Lanka (Rupee)	1970	86.10	178.50	—	256.10	—	43.10	7.80
	1975	120.60	241.80	—	370.40	—	125.90	16.10
	1980	812.40		—	911.80	—	368.30	0.30
	1983	916.70	980.30	—	1 812.00	—	1 074.50	16.50
	1984	1 687.99	1 875.75	—	2 405.29	55.72	1 459.04	3.00
	1985	2 045.19	2 310.03	—	3 078.62	32.99	1 918.33	5.49
	1986	2 179.03	2 527.93	—	3 308.77	48.48	2 362.07	6.56
*Rép. arabe syrienne[2,14] (Livre syrienne)	1984	460.50	859.50	—	—	—	130.00	31.00
	1985	484.50	918.50	—	—	—	130.00	38.00
	1986	496.50	1 030.50	—	—	—	130.00	52.00
Thailand[2] (Baht)	1980[1]	—	152.15	—	5.70	—	45.56	50.30
	1983[52]	—	1 706.36	—	13.19	—	112.94	—
	1984[1]	—	248.99	—	—	—	—	—
	1985[1]	—	268.30	—	—	—	—	—
	1986	—	284.76	—	—	—	—	—

EUROPE – EUROPE – EUROPA

Countries with a market economy – Pays à économie de marché – Países con economía de mercado

Austria (Schilling)	1970	18 079	35 654	—	15 518	125	401	1 007
	1975	35 240	66 237	—	29 737	—	881	2 654
	1980	61 080	109 173	9 249	37 233	598	1 464	6 092
	1983	86 785	141 172	9 598	54 546	1 287	1 453	7 076
	1984	94 054	152 676	13 013	58 123	1 316	1 475	8 363
	1985	102 163	163 653	13 295	59 380	1 348	1 581	7 076
	1986	108 661	172 588	13 488	63 157	1 403	1 608	7 657
Belgique (Franc belge)	1970	50 155.10	112 615.50	—	60 001.40	3 585.60	7 954.10	7 195.60
	1975	108 975.60	242 448.10	—	174 881.70	6 716.20	14 034.10	17 754.40
	1980	162 818.40	382 970.20	6 170.00	292 566.80	13 155.90	20 537.90	7 584.80
	1983	231 391.00	449 279.00	5 648.00	424 705.00	18 155.00	21 343.00	29 252.00[53]
	1984	254 342.00	479 352.00	11 824.00	416 765.00	18 717.00	25 585.00	25 276.00[53]
	1985	308 489.00	503 156.00	7 729.00	388 325.00	19 315.00	26 126.00	29 409.00[53]
	1986	327 996.00	532 715.00	6 701.00	397 733.00	19 855.00	27 874.00	29 196.00[53]
Denmark (Krone)	1970	2 540.20	1 609.70	—	10 322.70	3 374.10	219.80	—
	1975	505.90	2 510.60	—	30 767.30	10 319.20	614.00	2.70
	1980	1 818.30	6 106.50	—	59 366.50	33 759.60	2 218.20	—
	1983	4 857.40	12 064.40	—	79 619.30	48 659.30	4 107.20	—
	1984	5 155.00	9 710.30	—	83 746.10	50 810.90	4 278.60	—
	1985	5 031.60	12 936.40	—	86 881.20	55 174.80	4 930.50	—
	1986	6 257.00	14 256.80	—	95 842.70	57 546.70	5 088.70	—
España (Peseta)	1975	104 172.10	531 282.30	4 632.50	60 407.00	17 172.00	9 669.70	4 474.60
	1980	296 847.20	1 698 483.40	8 114.10	351 626.20	20 175.80	15 225.70	10 468.50
	1983[54]	645 740.00	2 372 697.00	12 954.00	837 962.00	70 467.00	33 594.00	23 652.00
	1984	768 492.00	2 518 761.00	19 287.00	1 137 317.00	84 720.00	32 245.00	72 469.00
	1985	838 192.00	2 854 016.00	20 684.00	1 222 972.00	100 089.00	47 478.00	101 107.00
	1986	966 685.00	3 185 679.00	—	1 495 705.00	100 089.00	48 104.00	97 219.00

See notes on page 70.   *Voir notes page 70.*   Véanse notas pág. 70.

	Expenditure / Dépenses / Egresos							Difference between receipts and expenditure / Différence entre les recettes et les dépenses / Diferencia entre los ingresos y los egresos	
Total receipts (excluding transfers) / Total des recettes (non compris les transferts) / Total de ingresos (excl. las transferencias)	Benefits / Prestations / Prestaciones				Administrative expenditure / Frais d'administration / Gastos de administración	Other expenditure / Autres dépenses / Otros egresos	Total expenditure (excluding transfers) / Total des dépenses (non compris les transferts) / Total de egresos (excl. las transferencias)	In absolute figures / En chiffres absolus / En cifras absolutas	As percentage of total receipts / En pourcentage du total des recettes / En porcentaje del total de ingresos
	Medical care / Soins médicaux / Asistencia médica	Benefits in kind other than for medical care / Prestations en nature à d'autres titres que les soins médicaux / Prestaciones en especie, excepto asistencia médica	Cash benefits / Prestations en espèces / Prestaciones monetarias	Total / Total / Total					
(10)	(11)	(12)	(13)	(14)	(15)	(16)	(17)	(18)	(19)
571.60	239.50	—	146.80	386.30	9.30	37.80	433.40	138.20	24.2
874.80	351.50	—	216.20	567.70	6.90	1.20	575.80	299.00	34.2
2 092.80	—	—	1 094.20	1 094.20	47.00	0.60	1 141.80	951.00	45.4
4 800.00	—	—	2 638.60	2 638.60	47.90	8.50	2 695.00	2 105.00	43.9
7 486.79	—	—	3 137.76	3 137.76	31.00	0.00	3 168.76	4 318.03	57.7
9 390.65	—	—	3 842.42	3 842.42	38.10	0.00	3 880.52	5 510.13	58.7
10 432.84	—	—	3 975.01	3 975.01	42.90	4.65	4 022.56	6 410.28	61.4
1 481.00	—	—	663.50	663.50	29.50	1.00	694.00	787.00	53.1
1 571.00	—	—	739.50	739.50	31.50	1.00	772.00	799.00	50.9
1 709.00	—	—	781.50	781.50	38.50	1.00	821.00	888.00	52.0
253.71	41.51	1.74	55.03	98.28	5.70	—	103.98	149.73	59.0
1 832.49	1 528.96	—	67.27	1 596.23	13.19	—	1 609.42	223.07	12.2
248.99	61.11	—	186.07	247.18	13.90	—	261.08	− 12.09	−4.9
268.30	64.47	—	168.14	232.61	19.50	—	252.11	16.19	6.0
284.76	66.42	—	152.06	218.48	27.50	—	245.98	38.78	13.6
70 784	9 117	2 628	54 778	66 523	2 511	667	69 701	1 083	1.5
134 749	17 417	7 075	102 179	126 671	3 952	2 117	132 740	2 009	1.5
224 889	29 447	12 177	171 161	212 785	5 949	4 732	223 466	1 423	0.6
301 917	37 247	18 984	225 484	281 715	7 359	2 878	291 952	9 965	3.3
329 020	39 294	20 325	247 071	306 690	7 735	3 536	317 961	11 059	3.4
348 496	41 800	22 004	263 187	326 991	8 185	4 972	340 148	8 348	2.4
368 562	44 682	23 821	279 044	347 547	8 608	5 036	361 191	7 371	2.0
241 507.30	45 440.00	563.40	160 707.20	212 789.60	11 480.00	7 306.50	231 576.10	9 931.20	4.1
564 810.10	104 048.10	2 616.70	382 802.00	510 888.30	26 346.90	7 476.80	544 712.00	20 098.10	3.6
885 804.00	166 581.60	5 011.90	680 703.80	852 297.30	38 910.70	13 874.20	905 082.20	− 19 278.20	− 2.2
1 179 773.00	219 945.00	7 074.00	881 437.00	1 108 456.00	49 960.00	13 032.00	1 171 448.00	8 325.00	0.7
1 231 861.00	223 104.00	6 615.00	908 782.00	1 138 501.00	51 047.00	13 436.00	1 202 984.00	28 877.00	2.3
1 282 549.00	227 548.00	6 830.00	949 524.00	1 183 902.00	53 518.00	11 466.00	1 248 886.00	33 663.00	2.6
1 342 070.00	255 927.00	7 011.00	986 437.00	1 249 375.00	56 818.00	16 443.00	1 322 636.00	19 434.00	1.4
18 066.50	5 316.40	2 362.00	9 466.00	17 144.40	433.80	—	17 578.20	488.30	2.7
44 719.70	10 574.30	9 313.70	22 774.30	42 662.30	964.50	23.20	43 650.00	1 069.70	2.4
103 269.10	20 517.80	19 760.00	57 603.70	97 881.50	2 700.50	5.40	100 587.40	2 681.70	2.6
149 307.60	27 667.00	28 840.80	83 201.60	139 709.40	4 140.80	—	143 850.20	5 457.40	3.7
153 700.90	28 483.90	30 401.80	84 642.00	143 527.70	4 554.90	—	148 082.60	5 618.30	3.7
164 954.50	30 222.00	33 277.50	91 255.80	154 755.30	4 839.50	—	159 594.80	5 359.70	3.2
178 991.90	31 250.20	35 247.70	102 800.40	169 298.30	5 051.50	—	174 349.80	4 642.10	2.6
731 810.20	199 928.90	10 495.10	450 476.90	660 900.90	24 519.90	21 510.40	706 931.20	24 879.00	3.4
2 400 940.90	565 986.60	40 569.20	1 715 908.00	2 322 464.60	65 819.20	38 222.50	2 426 506.30	−25 565.40	−1.1
3 997 066.00	907 078.00	50 068.00	2 924 862.00	3 882 008.00	106 260.00	32 095.00	4 020 363.00	−23 297.00	−0.6
4 633 345.00	1 010 443.00	71 800.00	3 273 119.00	4 355 362.00	115 956.00	65.720.00	4 537 038.00	96 307.00	2.1
5 184 538.00	1 108 259.00	58 644.00	3 774 047.00	4 940 950.00	133 813.00	70 862.00	5 145 625.00	38 913.00	0.8
5 893 481.00	1 246 766.00	59 312.00	4 205 806.00	5 511 884.00	155 125.00	134 143.00	5 801 152.00	92 329.00	1.6

Table 1 (cont.)   Tableau 1 (suite)   Cuadro 1 (cont.)

Country and currency unit / Pays et unité monétaire / País y unidad monetaria	Financial year / Exercice financier / Ejercicio financiero	Receipts / Recettes / Ingresos						
		Contributions / Cotisations / Cotizaciones		Special taxes allocated to social security / Taxes et impôts spéciaux / Impuestos y tasas especiales	State participation / Participation de l'Etat / Participación del Estado	Participation of other public authorities / Participation d'autres pouvoirs publics / Participación de otras entidades públicas	Income from capital / Revenu des capitaux / Renta del capital	Other receipts / Autres recettes / Otros ingresos
		From insured persons / Des assurés / De los asegurados	From employers / Des employeurs / De los empleadores					
(1)	(2)	(3)	(4)	(5)	(6)	(7)	(8)	(9)
Finland (Markka)	1970	691.80	2 414.80	—	1 703.30	1 095.00	349.50	1.00
	1975	2 059.40	8 978.60	—	4 092.10	2 813.00	787.80	5.00
	1980	3 183.30	18 166.60	—	10 618.40	6 118.80	2 337.80	10.30
	1983	4 386.90	24 525.80	—	18 904.20	9 833.00	4 174.00	29.20
	1984	5 838.20	28 058.60	—	19 647.80	11 772.80	5 182.10	—
	1985	7 126.00	32 920.50	—	22 026.70	13 917.20	5 874.10	—
	1986	7 524.50	35 888.70	—	24 510.90	15 872.20	6 617.00	—
France (Franc)	1970	22 693.00	81 975.00	3 104.00	9 243.00	—	571.00	2 285.00
	1975	61 406.40	199 122.30	7 719.30	75 492.70	5 394.60	3 414.70	2 707.60
	1980	159 648.90	406 663.50	14 504.30	159 157.60	10 137.20	7 317.60	4 283.10
	1983	255 640.40	598 799.80	31 629.00	254 002.00	15 779.10	17 114.90	15 570.70
	1984	288 761.60	645 128.80	40 891.80	265 064.40	18 447.00	19 558.30	17 683.20
	1985	314 464.50	689 699.40	33 339.80	273 863.40	17 757.00	22 553.70	18 254.80
	1986	334 506.30	724 422.10	30 467.40	280 705.30	18 120.00	23 717.90	19 086.00
Germany, Fed. Rep. of[56] (Deutsche Mark)	1970	34 851	50 948	994	30 220	—	2 335	1 119
	1975	67 985	95 402	1 040	67 753	—	4 335	4 438
	1980	121 561	122 452	—	103 500	—	2 877	7 322
	1983	144 903	138 713	—	111 030	—	2 860	8 282
	1984	151 768	145 245	—	112 535	—	2 715	8 916
	1985	159 285	152 017	—	115 670	—	2 534	9 111
	1986	167 892	160 683	—	118 621	—	2 348	9 796
Grèce (Drachme)	1970	9 833	14 808	4 071	5 090	—	1 531	434
	1975	21 094	36 557	8 320	11 577	—	2 922	1 018
	1980	72 095	114 843	19 874	21 496	—	11 812	2 594
	1983	161 607	239 556	60 302	71 673	—	29 355	7 124
	1984	205 910	301 967	60 113	95 347	—	37 386	12 079
	1985	256 105	371 280	77 927	108 980	—	44 182	14 029
*Iceland (Króna)	1984	—	713	—	4 923	471	73	—
	1985	—	898	—	7 146	643	127	—
	1986	—	1 272	—	9 423	929	92	—
Ireland (Pound)	1970	17.90	38.60	—	88.20	23.00	1.00	0.50
	1975	85.10	163.20	—	434.20	10.50	2.70	21.50
	1980	219.80	499.60	—	1 147.50	10.20	3.50	16.10
	1983	442.90	827.93	—	2 041.00	14.20	7.80	35.40
	1984	490.10	900.92	—	2 211.00	16.40	5.00	30.70
	1985	527.40	990.64	—	2 441.50	17.40	3.60	32.10
	1986	558.20	1 051.00	—	2 651.30	0.60	3.00	35.50
Italie (Lires (milliards))	1970	1 381.90	5 997.82	15.07	1 897.35	—	236.04	228.21
	1975	2 823.00	15 246.00	—	2 539.00	1 374.00	523.00	366.00
	1980	11 139.00	38 836.00	—	19 508.00	1 155.00	1 059.00	912.00
	1983	21 943.00	68 655.00	—	46 492.00	1 846.00	1 693.00	1 452.00
	1984[11]	14 001.00	38 223.00	—	13 060.00	—	219.00	7 916.00
	1985[11]	15 676.00	42 912.00	—	15 004.00	—	257.00	8 137.00
	1986[11]	17 693.00	46 898.00	—	15 935.00	—	240.00	9 880.00
Luxembourg (Franc)	1970	2 377.80	3 470.60	—	2 319.50	112.50	786.80	57.10
	1975	5 002.30	7 772.50	—	4 899.00	198.90	1 320.40	760.90
	1980	8 513.60	13 315.50	—	8 735.10	292.50	2 622.20	2 279.60
	1983	12 443.70	16 399.20	—	12 827.00	408.50	3 635.00	2 247.80
	1984	13 625.80	18 070.60	—	14 866.10	—	4 014.70	299.00
	1985	14 508.30	19 218.40	—	16 985.90	—	2 539.00	1 132.70
	1986	14 710.70	20 301.00	—	20 508.20	—	2 793.50	1 114.50

See notes on page 70.   *Voir notes page 70.*   Véanse notas pág. 70.

Total receipts (excluding transfers) / Total des recettes (non compris les transferts) / Total de ingresos (excl. las transferencias)	Expenditure / Dépenses / Egresos							Difference between receipts and expenditure / Différence entre les recettes et les dépenses / Diferencia entre los ingresos y los egresos	
	Benefits / Prestations / Prestaciones				Administrative expenditure / Frais d'administration / Gastos de administración	Other expenditure / Autres dépenses / Otros egresos	Total expenditure (excluding transfers) / Total des dépenses (non compris les transferts) / Total de egresos (excl. las transferencias)	In absolute figures / En chiffres absolus / En cifras absolutas	As percentage of total receipts / En pourcentage du total des recettes / En porcentaje del total de ingresos
	Medical care / Soins médicaux / Asistencia médica	Benefits in kind other than for medical care / Prestations en nature à d'autres titres que les soins médicaux / Prestaciones en especie, excepto asistencia médica	Cash benefits / Prestations en espèces / Prestaciones monetarias	Total / Total / Total					
(10)	(11)	(12)	(13)	(14)	(15)	(16)	(17)	(18)	(19)
6 255.40	1 516.80	520.00	3 442.20	5 479.00	214.00	9.30	5 702.30	553.10	8.8
18 735.90	4 286.10	1 460.20	10 035.40	15 781.70	587.10	25.00	16 393.80	2 342.10	12.5
40 435.20	8 558.80	3 439.30	21 421.40	33 419.50	1 213.50	13.20	34 646.20	5 789.00	14.3
61 853.10	13 550.10	5 386.50	35 357.10	54 293.70	2 240.70	21.50	56 555.90	5 297.20	8.6
70 499.50	15 324.50	6 505.50	40 300.30	62 130.30	2 228.90	—	64 359.20	6 140.30	8.7
81 864.50	17 749.80	7 770.50	46 383.60	71 903.90	2 406.20	—	74 310.10	7 554.40	9.2
90 413.30	19 521.80	8 500.50	51 473.50	79 495.80	2 669.00	—	82 164.80	8 248.50	9.1
119 871.00	31 249.00	—	79 352.00	110 601.00	4 490.00	4 755.00	119 846.00	25.00	0.0
355 257.60	77 988.70	5 492.70	220 522.00	304 003.40	14 202.80	32 167.50	350 373.70	4 883.90	1.4
761 712.20	155 508.90	11 967.00	535 677.80	703 153.70	28 618.60	7 198.70	738 971.00	22 741.20	3.0
1 188 535.90	257 672.60[55]	17 318.90	825 217.90[55]	1 100 209.40	48 005.70	9 890.80	1 158 105.90	30 430.00	2.6
1 295 535.10	288 328.20[55]	18 035.10	894 120.00[55]	1 200 483.30	52 438.80	12 018.90	1 264 941.00	30 594.10	2.4
1 370 132.60	304 708.80[55]	19 777.20	957 974.60[55]	1 282 460.60	54 120.00	11 731.60	1 348 312.20	21 820.40	1.6
1 431 025.00	330 949.40[55]	18 862.30	1 019 421.70[55]	1 369 233.40	57 286.60	13 268.70	1 439 788.70	− 8 763.70	− 0.6
120 467	26 835		82 085	108 920	3 830	2 966	115 716	4 751	3.9
240 953	67 783		165 535	233 318	7 964	2 134	243 416	− 2 463	− 1.0
357 712	85 859	30 941	225 377	342 177	11 075	1 800	355 052	2 660	0.7
405 788	99 595	38 039	258 126	395 760	10 700	159	406 619	− 831	− 0.2
421 179	106 775	37 376	267 047	411 198	11 151	161	422 510	− 1 331	− 0.3
438 617	112 761	36 421	274 676	423 858	11 729	216	435 803	2 814	0.6
459 340	118 550	37 674	282 834	439 058	12 558	269	451 885	7 455	− 1.6
35 767	5 428	572	24 846	30 846	1 330	145	32 321	3 446	9.6
81 488	14 150	570	53 904	68 624	3 977	285	72 886	8 602	10.6
242 714	33 114	1 849	164 328	199 291	9 385	767	209 443	33 271	13.7
569 617	61 324	9 772	436 089	507 185	32 600	—	539 785	29 832	5.2
712 802	73 770	10 497	573 031	657 298	44 748	—	702 046	10 756	1.5
872 503	87 725	13 937	740 526	842 188	56 626	—	898 814	− 26 311	− 3.0
6 180	3 033	4	2 922	5 959	98	24	6 081	99	1.6
8 814	4 276	5	4 230	8 511	137	58	8 706	108	1.2
11 716	5 819	7	5 432	11 258	193	48	11 499	217	1.9
169.20	51.70	1.10	107.90	160.70	6.00	0.80	167.50	1.70	1.0
717.20	245.60	8.60	438.30	692.50	24.80	2.90	720.20	− 3.00	− 0.4
1 896.70	671.30	27.80	1 088.90	1 788.00	89.10	4.20	1 881.30	15.40	0.8
3 369.23	1 014.40	52.60	2 171.33	3 238.33	166.72	4.60	3 409.65	− 40.42	− 1.2
3 654.12	1 076.10	57.50	2 374.31	3 507.91	169.55	4.00	3 681.46	− 27.34	− 0.7
4 012.64	1 159.60	64.80	2 619.18	3 843.58	172.10	5.10	4 020.78	− 8.14	− 0.2
4 299.60	1 217.90	71.90	2 806.87	4 096.67	199.79	5.70	4 302.16	− 2.56	− 0.1
9 756.39	2 319.01	13.08	6 399.50	8 731.59	408.40	313.00	9 452.99	303.40	3.1
22 871.00	6 018.00	588.00	17 563.00	24 169.00	1 831.00	619.00	26 619.00	− 3 748.00	− 16.4
72 609.00	16 552.00	1 412.00	48 515.00	66 479.00	2 814.00	3 684.00	72 977.00	− 368.00	− 0.5
142 081.00	29 842.00	3 380.00	96 479.00	129 701.00	5 091.00	3 792.00	138 584.00	3 497.00	2.5
73 419.00	—	—	72 682.00	72 682.00	1 627.00	7 598.00	81 907.00	− 8 488.00	− 11.6
81 986.00	—	—	81 309.00	81 309.00	1 896.00	8 186.00	91 391.00	− 9 405.00	− 11.5
90 646.00	—	—	89 522.00	89 522.00	1 971.00	8 758.00	100 251.00	− 9 605.00	− 10.6
9 124.30	1 165.50	—	6 767.90	7 933.40	239.50	6.60	8 179.50	944.80	10.4
19 954.00	3 104.10	59.40	14 414.60	17 578.10	576.90	107.50	18 262.50	1 691.50	8.5
35 758.50	6 340.30	259.30	24 629.40	31 229.00	1 061.10	270.80	32 560.90	3 197.60	8.9
47 961.20	7 851.20	537.80	32 864.00	41 253.00	1 132.30	2 020.00	44 405.30	3 555.90	7.4
50 876.20	9 120.80	124.70	35 477.80	44 723.30	1 297.00	784.20	46 804.50	4 071.70	8.0
54 384.30	9 854.30	124.00	36 748.60	46 726.90	1 276.10	464.90	48 467.90	5 916.40	10.9
59 427.90	10 892.00	125.50	38 986.10	50 003.60	1 370.40	269.00	51 643.00	7 784.90	13.1

Table 1 *(cont.)* **Tableau 1** *(suite)* **Cuadro 1** *(cont.)*

Country and currency unit / Pays et unité monétaire / País y unidad monetaria (1)	Financial year / Exercice financier / Ejercicio financiero (2)	Contributions / Cotisations / Cotizaciones — From insured persons / Des assurés / De los asegurados (3)	From employers / Des employeurs / De los empleadores (4)	Special taxes allocated to social security / Taxes et impôts spéciaux / Impuestos y tasas especiales (5)	State participation / Participation de l'Etat / Participación del Estado (6)	Participation of other public authorities / Participation d'autres pouvoirs publics / Participación de otras entidades públicas (7)	Income from capital / Revenu des capitaux / Renta del capital (8)	Other receipts / Autres recettes / Otros ingresos (9)
Malta (Lira)	1970[22]	0.49	1.65	—	4.40	—	0.09	0.06
	1975[22]	2.99	5.06	—	10.73	—	—	0.15
	1980	14.76	17.81	—	20.04	—	—	—
	1983[44]	19.32	23.27	—	27.50	—	—	—
	1984	18.68	22.46	—	26.94	—	—	—
	1985	19.36	23.28	—	27.71	—	—	—
	1986	19.15	24.02	—	28.41	—	—	—
Netherlands (Guilder)	1970	10 497.90	11 701.70	—	2 345.60	1 007.00	1 692.30	30.40
	1975	24 166.60	25 935.70	—	10 400.10	804.10	4 667.50	308.00
	1980	37 749.00	37 865.30	—	26 572.50	1 504.60	10 116.20	—
	1983	55 880.00	44 351.00	—	24 986.00	28.00	14 714.00	—
	1984	55 419.00	43 990.00	—	26 025.00	27.00	16 265.00	—
	1985	56 556.00	45 537.00	—	23 268.00	25.00	17 635.00	—
	1986	53 481.00	47 036.00	—	21 828.00	24.00	18 365.00	—
Norway (Krone)	1970	2 984.10	4 329.70	35.10	3 304.20	2 112.90	255.30	24.80
	1975	6 875.60	12 034.10	88.10	5 553.70	5 190.30	391.00	8.90
	1980	12 502.10	20 606.00	144.40	15 670.50	9 701.60	860.60	27.40
	1983	19 034.60	29 222.70	203.40	26 208.20	14 733.40	1 693.60	58.70
	1984[5]	20 016.40	31 293.40	201.10	47 012.40	32 306.30	2 013.20	476.00
	1985[5]	23 012.50	34 490.30	208.60	49 992.90	34 729.00	2 446.80	622.00
	1986	27 674.80	38 771.10	222.80	34 873.60	52 818.10	2 871.30	622.00
Portugal (Escudo)	1970	2 895.10	7 789.30	—	590.10	—	1 056.10	1 161.90
	1975	9 961.30	31 011.50	—	3 368.70	—	1 233.60	217.50
	1980	33 238.30	81 473.40	—	7 286.20	4 530.80	40.00	430.00
	1983	63 902.90	140 937.10	—	17 497.90	5 703.20	48.90	777.60
	1984	75 630.40	168 285.70	—	32 338.80	10 526.00	5 454.70	5 404.00
	1985	92 732.10	213 498.70	—	32 126.80	13 900.80	6 179.90	8 417.00
	1986	121 793.10	326 178.70	—	34 800.30	—	412.50	11 342.40
Suisse (Franc)	1970	3 584.10	2 183.40	—	1 292.00	2 252.60	864.90	340.30
	1975	7 987.50	4 806.00	—	2 536.10	4 974.10	1 363.80	541.20
	1980	10 529.00	6 529.10	—	3 547.80	2 973.60	1 540.50	451.10
	1983	13 488.40	7 082.10	—	4 300.60	3 732.30	1 424.80	323.00
	1984	14 824.30	7 626.30	—	4 765.40	4 027.00	1 423.80	400.00
	1985	15 980.80	8 058.50	—	4 873.10	4 356.90	1 519.70	421.40
	1986	16 946.60	8 713.60	—	5 072.70	4 823.50	1 610.20	436.10
Sweden (Krona)	1970	4 549.70	11 054.50	—	11 054.80	10 745.90	2 509.40	32.80
	1975	697.50	30 153.60	—	24 654.20	23 011.10	6 186.00	—
	1980	1 911.20	84 336.70	—	39 457.10	43 825.60	14 321.10	—
	1983	2 456.80	110 401.60	—	49 430.50	66 600.50	23 354.70	—
	1984[5]	2 769.70	101 510.00	—	61 474.20	72 773.90	25 728.90	—
	1985[5]	3 828.10	103 860.00	—	70 644.30	78 249.50	28 668.20	—
	1986[5]	5 571.70	122 636.70	—	72 231.20	84 696.80	33 505.50	—
Turquie (Livre turque)	1970	1 861.70	3 563.30	—	152.20	—	729.70	254.70
	1975	10 319.40	16 051.00	—	1 426.70	1.60	2 464.90	1 581.30
	1980	60 859.00	108 976.00	—	15 537.00	9 232.00	13 853.00	9 808.00
	1983[58]	178 730.00	231 322.00	—	20 401.00	21 830.00	79 809.00	24 327.00
	1984[5, 58]	248 722.00	291 763.00	—	158 962.00	14 832.00	144 338.00	33 772.00
	1985[5, 58]	364 768.00	406 051.00	—	248 067.00	36 225.00	153 930.00	79 407.00
	1986[5, 58]	494 591.00	569 467.00	—	230 917.00	48 276.00	287 403.00	122 640.00

See notes on page 70. *Voir notes page 70.* Véanse notas pág. 70.

Total receipts (excluding transfers)	Expenditure — Dépenses — Egresos				Administrative expenditure	Other expenditure	Total expenditure (excluding transfers)	Difference between receipts and expenditure	
	Benefits — Prestations — Prestaciones				Frais d'administration	Autres dépenses		In absolute figures	As percentage of total receipts
Total des recettes (non compris les transferts)	Medical care	Benefits in kind other than for medical care	Cash benefits	Total	Gastos de administración	Otros egresos	Total des dépenses (non compris les transferts)	En chiffres absolus	En pourcentage du total des recettes
Total de ingresos (excl. las transferencias)	Soins médicaux / Asistencia médica	Prestations en nature à d'autres titres que les soins médicaux / Prestaciones en especie, excepto asistencia médica	Prestations en espèces / Prestaciones monetarias	Total			Total de egresos (excl. las transferencias)	En cifras absolutas	En porcentaje del total de ingresos
(10)	(11)	(12)	(13)	(14)	(15)	(16)	(17)	(18)	(19)
6.68	2.58	—	4.48	7.07	0.06	—	7.13	−0.44	−6.6
18.93	3.06	—	13.39	16.44	2.31	—	18.75	0.18	1.0
52.61	—	—	43.28	43.28	0.36	—	43.64	8.97	17.0
70.10	—	—	66.64	66.64	0.60	—	67.24	2.86	4.1
68.09	16.43	—	70.41	86.84	5.17	—	92.01	−23.92	−35.1
70.35	16.87	—	68.66	85.54	5.07	—	90.61	−20.26	−28.8
71.58	17.79	—	70.94	88.73	5.30	—	94.04	−22.46	−31.4
27 274.90	4 533.40	15.80	17 596.90	22 146.10	805.30	—	22 951.40	4 323.50	15.9
66 282.00	11 495.30	—	42 758.10	54 253.40	1 870.90	8.40	56 132.70	10 149.30	15.3
113 807.60	19 195.00	—	72 872.10	92 067.10	3 258.80	98.00	95 423.90	18 383.70	16.2
139 959.00	23 013.00	—	93 271.00	116 284.00	3 347.00	—	119 631.00	20 328.00	14.5
141 726.00	23 086.00	—	95 725.00	118 811.00	3 455.00	—	122 266.00	19 460.00	13.7
143 021.00	23 810.00	—	94 196.00	118 006.00	3 557.00	—	121 563.00	21 458.00	15.0
140 734.00	24 057.00	—	95 040.00	119 097.00	3 694.00	—	122 791.00	17 943.00	12.7
13 046.10	3 501.90	595.20	7 704.90	11 802.00	359.10	187.60	12 348.70	697.40	5.3
30 141.70	9 073.00	1 888.80	15 497.30	26 459.10	1 011.30	2.90	27 473.30	2 668.40	8.9
59 512.60	17 987.80	5 111.50	33 140.70	56 240.00	1 224.10	3.10	57 467.20	2 045.40	3.4
91 154.60	26 177.30	8 620.50[57]	50 990.50	85 788.30	2 069.40	5.30	87 863.00	3 291.60	3.6
133 318.80	64 403.10	409.00[57]	63 666.30	128 478.40	1 301.40	7.60	129 787.40	3 531.40	2.6
145 502.10	69 023.10	491.00[57]	70 294.20	139 808.30	1 492.00	6.50	141 306.80	4 195.30	2.9
157 853.70	73 222.30	681.00[57]	77 823.10	151 726.40	1 512.80	10.40	153 249.60	4 604.10	2.9
13 492.50	2 689.30	—	5 997.20	8 686.50	1 145.40	190.50	10 022.40	3 470.10	25.7
45 792.60	11 528.50	—	26 769.70	38 298.20	2 794.10	372.90	41 465.20	4 327.40	9.4
126 998.70	2 257.00	4 902.20	102 086.30	109 245.50	11 977.40	—	121 222.90	5 775.80	4.5
228 867.60	6 260.80	9 144.20	204 139.80	219 544.80	12 237.90	—	231 782.70	−2 915.10	−1.3
297 639.60	5 470.10	11 263.40	255 604.60	272 338.10	14 707.60	17.90	287 063.60	10 576.00	3.6
366 855.30	5 936.70	14 723.80	316 709.80	337 370.30	17 725.20	19.50	355 115.00	11 740.30	3.2
494 527.00	9 532.10	19 563.80	408 927.80	438 022.90	21 305.10	25.80	459 353.80	35 173.20	7.1
10 517.30	.	.	.	8 606.20	260.60	279.30	9 146.10	1 371.20	13.0
22 208.70	.	.	.	20 034.80	531.10	581.00	21 146.90	1 061.80	4.8
25 571.10	.	.	.	21 830.60	658.70	926.50	23 415.80	2 155.30	8.4
30 351.20	.	.	.	26 929.10	856.00	1 386.20	29 171.30	1 179.90	3.9
33 066.80	.	.	.	29 467.20	886.30	1 703.80	32 057.30	1 009.50	3.1
35 210.40	.	.	.	30 654.30	942.90	1 924.70	33 521.90	1 668.50	4.8
37 602.70	.	.	.	32 666.50	994.30	2 030.40	35 691.20	1 911.50	5.1
39 947.10	10 651.20	2 971.80	17 787.00	31 410.00	625.80	47.60	32 083.40	7 863.70	19.7
84 702.40	22 322.90	8 567.70	42 908.40	73 799.00	1 431.20	65.50	75 295.70	9 406.70	11.1
183 851.70	38 823.50	28 647.00	95 646.00	163 116.50	4 192.20	7.10	167 315.80	16 535.90	9.0
252 244.10	58 004.70	40 720.30	130 769.50	229 494.50	5 079.90	—	234 574.40	17 669.70	7.0
264 256.70	62 674.30	42 811.80	127 010.40	232 496.50	7 301.00	—	239 797.50	24 459.20	9.3
285 250.10	66 265.30	45 871.20	141 691.90	253 828.40	10 826.60	—	264 655.00	20 595.10	7.2
318 641.90	68 832.50	54 006.60	157 241.40	280 080.50	11 881.60	—	291 962.10	26 679.80	8.4
6 561.60	807.00	—	3 510.90	4 317.90	276.70	77.50	4 672.10	1 889.50	28.8
31 844.00	4 141.20	72.00	10 656.10	14 869.30	2 573.50	386.40	17 829.20	14 015.70	44.0
218 265.00	24 590.00	—	150 982.30	175 572.30	7 468.00	881.00	183 921.30	34 343.70	15.7
556 419.00	48 547.00	82.00	367 381.00	416 010.00	14 868.00	1 980.00	432 858.00	123 561.00	22.2
892 389.00	98 133.00	307.00	584 193.00	682 633.00	19 784.00	2 427.00	704 844.00	187 545.00	21.0
1 288 448.00	146 253.00	282.00	896 595.00	1 043 130.00	26 943.00	4 721.00	1 074 794.00	213 654.00	16.6
1 753 294.00	192 337.00	271.00	1 184 805.00	1 377 413.00	36 084.00	4 443.00	1 417 940.00	335 354.00	19.1

Table 1 *(cont.)* Tableau 1 *(suite)* Cuadro 1 *(cont.)*

Country and currency unit / *Pays et unité monétaire* / País y unidad monetaria	Financial year / *Exercice financier* / Ejercicio financiero	Receipts / *Recettes* / Ingresos						
		Contributions / *Cotisations* / Cotizaciones		Special taxes allocated to social security / *Taxes et impôts spéciaux* / Impuestos y tasas especiales	State participation / *Participation de l'Etat* / Participación del Estado	Participation of other public authorities / *Participation d'autres pouvoirs publics* / Participación de otras entidades públicas	Income from capital / *Revenu des capitaux* / Renta del capital	Other receipts / *Autres recettes* / Otros ingresos
		From insured persons / *Des assurés* / De los asegurados	From employers / *Des employeurs* / De los empleadores					
(1)	(2)	(3)	(4)	(5)	(6)	(7)	(8)	(9)
United Kingdom[25] (Pound)	1970	1 448	1 816	—	3 298	568	147	17
	1975	3 333	5 507	—	8 572	1 361	362	32
	1980	6 837	11 447	—	21 468	2 583	1 186	188
	1983	11 369	15 111	—	31 968	3 193	1 327	286
	1984	12 319	15 939	—	34 470	3 342	1 513	271
	1985	13 383	17 191	—	36 732	3 853	1 667	291
	1986	14 436	18 458	—	39 552	3 803	2 199	289

EUROPE – EUROPE – EUROPA

Countries with a centrally planned economy – Pays à économie planifiée – Países con economía centralmente planificada

RSS de Biélorussie (Rouble)	1970	—	—	—	1 061	—	—	45
	1975	—	—	—	1 547	—	—	90
	1980	—	—	—	2 135	—	—	108
	1983	—	—	—	2 584	—	—	105
	1984	—	—	—	2 642	—	—	181
	1985	—	—	—	2 737	—	—	205
	1986	—	—	—	2 980	—	—	219
Bulgarie[2] (Lev)	1970	15.10	619.60	49.70	696.80	43.30	—	43.70
	1975	13.00	1 285.60	64.10	637.80	6.00	—	335.10
	1980	.	.	.	.	.	.	.
	1983[59]	.	.	.	.	.	—	.
	1984[5, 60, 61]	.	.	.	.	.	—	.
	1985[5, 60, 61]	.	.	.	.	.	—	.
	1986[5, 60, 61]	—	658.50	—	16.00	—	—	—
Czechoslovakia (Koruna)	1970	30	1 559	—	54 158	—	—	253
	1975	15	1 980	—	66 349	—	—	1 126
	1980	9	3 395	—	86 407	—	—	1 556
	1983	10	3 847	—	99 522	—	—	1 811
	1984	10	4 230	—	102 344	—	—	1 857
	1985	10	4 443	—	108 035	—	—	1 943
	1986	10	4 521	—	114 073	—	—	2 088
German Democratic Rep. (Mark)	1970	4 223.20	4 597.00	—	5 547.40	—	—	27.00
	1975	5 450.00	6 023.50	—	10 308.90	—	—	45.40
	1980[62]	6 493.60	8 370.20	—	14 737.80	—	—	25.40
	1983[62]	7 121.80	9 103.60	—	14 579.30	—	—	24.80
	1984[62]	7 288.90	9 334.40	—	14 542.70	—	—	30.90
	1985[62]	7 442.20	9 524.90	—	15 728.20	—	—	28.90
	1986[62]	7 668.00	9 698.10	—	16 919.60	—	—	28.60
Hongrie (Forint)	1970	5 455	16 091	—	8 360	—	40	149
	1975	9 479	23 818	—	25 198	—	30	270
	1980	15 569	43 845	—	46 532	—	6	692
	1983	20 602	65 240	—	52 533	—	—	—
	1984	23 700	97 101	—	—	—	—	—
	1985	27 300	108 000	—	—	—	—	—
	1986	31 600	117 800	—	—	—	—	—
*Pologne (Zloty)	1984	33 945	929 399	72 708	422 279	—	2 514	11 102
	1985	39 222	1 131 653	89 550	510 829	—	5 795	13 856
	1986	58 016	1 361 160	109 474	681 936	—	10 729	21 128

See notes on page 70. *Voir notes page 70.* Véanse notas pág. 70.

Total receipts (excluding transfers) / Total des recettes (non compris les transferts) / Total de ingresos (excl. las transferencias)	Expenditure — Dépenses — Egresos							Difference between receipts and expenditure — Différence entre les recettes et les dépenses — Diferencia entre los ingresos y los egresos	
	Benefits / Prestations / Prestaciones				Administrative expenditure / Frais d'administration / Gastos de administración	Other expenditure / Autres dépenses / Otros egresos	Total expenditure (excluding transfers) / Total des dépenses (non compris les transferts) / Total de egresos (excl. las transferencias)	In absolute figures / En chiffres absolus / En cifras absolutas	As percentage of total receipts / En pourcentage du total des recettes / En porcentaje del total de ingresos
	Medical care / Soins médicaux / Asistencia médica	Benefits in kind other than for medical care / Prestations en nature à d'autres titres que les soins médicaux / Prestaciones en especie, excepto asistencia médica	Cash benefits / Prestations en espèces / Prestaciones monetarias	Total / Total / Total					
(10)	(11)	(12)	(13)	(14)	(15)	(16)	(17)	(18)	(19)
7 294	1 885	438	4 259	6 582	219	211	7 012	282	3.9
19 167	5 001	1 324	10 620	16 945	608	535	18 088	1 079	5.6
43 709	11 125	2 630	25 932	39 687	1 155	839	41 681	2 028	4.6
63 254	14 308	5 841	38 140	58 289	1 768	991	61 048	2 206	3.5
67 854	15 111	6 366	41 075	62 552	1 953	1 121	65 626	2 228	3.3
73 117	16 022	7 204	44 685	67 911	2 027	1 219	71 157	1 960	2.7
78 737	17 207	7 425	47 897	72 529	2 245	1 285	76 059	2 678	3.4
1 106	383	19	704	1 106	—	—	1 106	—	—
1 637	477	35	1 125	1 637	—	—	1 637	−1	−0.1
2 243	635	72	1 536	2 243	—	—	2 243	—	—
2 689	708	83	1 898	2 689	—	—	2 689	—	—
2 823	749	81	1 993	2 823	—	—	2 823	—	—
2 942	790	79	2 073	2 942	—	—	2 942	—	—
3 199	836	98	2 265	3 199	—	—	3 199	—	—
1 468.20	282.10	9.00	1 115.20	1 406.30	1.20	34.30	1 441.80	26.40	1.8
2 341.60	513.80	1.20	1 615.50	2 130.50	1.40	157.00	2 288.90	52.70	2.3
2 506.30[59]	.	.	2 506.30	2 506.30	.	.	2 506.30	—	—
2 953.70[59]	—	—	2 953.70	2 953.70	—	.	2 953.70	—	—
3 331.90	—	—	2 934.80	2 934.80	6.00	—	2 940.80	391.10	11.7
3 331.90	—	—	3 212.90	3 212.90	7.50	—	3 220.40	111.50	3.3
3 707.40	—	—	3 584.80	3 584.80	8.20	—	3 593.00	114.40	3.1
56 000	—	—	—	55 758	242	—	56 000	—	—
69 470	15 409	2 355	51 419	69 183	287	—	69 470	—	—
91 367	20 117	2 698	68 222	91 037	330	—	91 367	—	—
105 190	23 433	3 512	77 913	104 858	332	—	105 190	—	—
108 441	24 682	3 670	79 754	108 106	335	—	108 441	—	—
114 431	26 206	3 894	84 002	114 102	329	—	114 431	—	—
120 692	28 575	4 275	87 491	120 341	351	—	120 692	—	—
14 394.60	4 204.10	—	10 118.90	14 323.00	69.90	1.70	14 394.60	—	—
21 827.80	6 250.70	—	15 464.20	21 714.90	112.10	0.80	21 827.80	—	—
29 627.00	8 308.20	—	21 209.70	29 517.90	107.80	1.30	29 627.00	—	—
30 829.50	9 458.90	—	21 262.40	30 721.30	106.80	1.00	30 829.10	0.40	0.0
31 196.90	9 790.50	—	21 298.00	31 088.50	108.10	0.80	31 197.40	−0.50	0.0
32 724.20	10 225.30	—	22 383.20	32 608.50	115.10	0.70	32 724.30	−0.10	0.0
34 314.30	10 739.80	—	23 448.70	34 188.50	125.10	0.90	34 314.50	−0.20	0.0
30 095	8 299	—	21 666	29 965	304	—	30 269	−174	−0.6
58 795	13 878	—	44 265	58 143	567	—	58 710	85	0.1
106 644	22 508	458	83 103	106 069	577	—	106 646	−2	0.0
138 375	30 533	263	106 918	137 714	661	—	138 375	—	—
120 801	—	267	119 810	120 077	724	—	120 801	—	—
135 300	—	282	131 173	131 455	887	—	132 342	2 958	2.2
149 400	—	312	141 611	141 923	1 016	—	142 939	6 461	4.3
1 471 947	319 631	—	932 470	1 252 101	7 437	107	1 259 645	212 302	14.4
1 790 905	390 256	—	1 066 704	1 456 960	11 521	110	1 468 591	322 314	18.0
2 242 443	495 859	—	1 319 113	1 814 972	15 030	160	1 830 162	412 281	18.4

Table 1 *(concl.)* **Tableau 1** *(fin)* **Cuadro 1** *(fin)*

Country and currency unit Pays et unité monétaire País y unidad monetaria	Financial year Exercice financier Ejercicio financiero	Receipts / Recettes / Ingresos						
		Contributions / Cotisations / Cotizaciones		Special taxes allocated to social security Taxes et impôts spéciaux Impuestos y tasas especiales	State participation Participation de l'Etat Participación del Estado	Participation of other public authorities Participation d'autres pouvoirs publics Participación de otras entidades públicas	Income from capital Revenu des capitaux Renta del capital	Other receipts Autres recettes Otros ingresos
		From insured persons Des assurés De los asegurados	From employers Des employeurs De los empleadores					
(1)	(2)	(3)	(4)	(5)	(6)	(7)	(8)	(9)
RSS d'Ukraine (Rouble)	1970	—	—	—	6 101	—	—	402
	1975	—	—	—	8 430	—	—	620
	1980	—	—	—	11 359	—	—	671
	1983	—	—	—	13 551	—	—	629
	1984	—	—	—	14 005	—	—	893
	1985	—	—	—	14 743	—	—	915
	1986	—	—	—	15 938	—	—	897
URSS[63] (Rouble)	1970	—	—	—	33 397	—	—	1 207
	1975	—	—	—	46 953	—	—	2 285
	1980	—	—	—	62 508	—	—	2 108
	1983	—	—	—	73 676	—	—	2 113
	1984	—	—	—	76 796	—	—	3 173
	1985	—	—	—	80 331	—	—	3 242
	1986	—	—	—	86 049	—	—	3 258
Yugoslavia[2] (Dinar)	1970	16 521.00	2 962.00	—	3 112.00	57.00	—	118.00
	1981	179 946.70[64]	63 584.30	2 147.30	19 877.20	778.30	2 699.40	2 389.10
	1983	308.545.00[64]	113 550.00	3 700.00	29 217.00	682.00	3 973.00	2 923.00
	1984[65]	427 752.00	174 135.00	—	45 937.00	1 704.00	—	9 885.00
	1985[65]	784 628.00	347 045.00	—	54 549.00	2 642.00	—	16 546.00
	1986[65]	1 757 449.00	895 391.00	—	76 035.00	17 105.00	—	31 671.00

OCEANIA – OCÉANIE – OCEANIA

Australia[4] (Dollar)	1969-70	339.10	318.10	—	1 696.80	405.80	105.90	10.70
	1974-75	924.70	988.80	—	4 515.70	1 348.70	226.80	23.30
	1980	2 248.40[66]	2 117.20	—	12 057.00	78.50	685.30	48.90
	1983	3 460.50[66]	3 420.60	—	17 759.20	—	775.80	122.30
	1984[5,67]	371.10	1 631.60	405.00	17 009.10	—	196.50	—
	1985[5,67]	400.00	3 234.60	1 065.00	18 099.60	—	234.20	—
	1986[5,67]	432.30	3 030.90	1 220.00	19 405.40	—	221.90	—
Fiji[2,4] (Dollar)	1975	6.80	6.98	—	10.88	—	2.80	1.70
	1980	16.60	17.78	—	5.47	—	12.32	5.64
	1983	24.60	24.81	—	8.42	—	27.28	0.24
	1984[1]	27.36	27.36	—	—	—	34.19	0.87
	1985[1]	34.14	34.14	—	—	—	41.84	0.90
	1986[1]	29.52	29.52	—	—	—	51.61	0.92
New Zealand[25] (Dollar)	1970	30.50	30.60	—	574.30	—	16.00	—
	1975	83.10	114.90	—	1 586.40	—	37.70	—
	1980	106.70	167.00	—	3 828.50	—	51.90	14.60
	1983	123.50	284.40	—	5 713.30	—	142.00	20.00
	1984	122.80	236.20	—	6 210.20	—	167.20	24.80
	1985	135.40	257.30	—	7 538.70	—	199.70	29.00
	1986	155.50	294.60	—	8 919.40	—	242.80	33.20
Solomon Islands[2,4] (Dollar)	1981	1.50	1.50	—	—	—	0.63	0.17
	1983	2.28	3.42	—	—	—	1.58	0.24
	1984	2.72	4.07	—	—	—	2.34	—
	1985	3.13	4.70	—	—	—	3.06	—
	1986	3.81	5.71	—	—	—	4.14	—

See notes on page 70.   *Voir notes page 70.*   Véanse notas pág. 70.

Total receipts (excluding transfers) *Total des recettes (non compris les transferts)* Total de ingresos (excl. las transferencias)	Expenditure *Dépenses* Egresos Benefits *Prestations* Prestaciones Medical care *Soins médicaux* Asistencia médica	Benefits in kind other than for medical care *Prestations en nature à d'autres titres que les soins médicaux* Prestaciones en especie, excepto asistencia médica	Cash benefits *Prestations en espèces* Prestaciones monetarias	Total *Total* Total	Administrative expenditure *Frais d'administration* Gastos de administración	Other expenditure *Autres dépenses* Otros egresos	Total expenditure (excluding transfers) *Total des dépenses (non compris les transferts)* Total de egresos (excl. las transferencias)	Difference between receipts and expenditure *Différence entre les recettes et les dépenses* Diferencia entre los ingresos y los egresos In absolute figures *En chiffres absolus* En cifras absolutas	As percentage of total receipts *En pourcentage du total des recettes* En porcentaje del total de ingresos
(10)	(11)	(12)	(13)	(14)	(15)	(16)	(17)	(18)	(19)
6 503	2 201	72	4 230	6 503	—	—	6 503	—	—
9 050	2 642	156	6 252	9 050	—	—	9 050	—	—
12 030	3 313	191	8 526	12 030	—	—	12 030	—	—
14 180	3 573	331	10 276	14 180	—	—	14 180	—	—
14 898	3 797	295	10 806	14 898	—	—	14 898	—	—
15 658	3 922	323	11 413	15 658	—	—	15 658	—	—
16 835	4 120	345	12 370	16 835	—	—	16 835	—	—
34 604	11 798	475	22 331	34 604	—	—	34 604	—	—
49 238	14 604	965	33 669	49 238	—	—	49 238	—	—
64 616	18 988	1 349	44 279	64 616	—	—	64 616	—	—
75 789	20 942	1 605	53 242	75 789	—	—	75 789	—	—
79 969	21 867	1 656	56 446	79 969	—	—	79 969	—	—
83 573	22 531	1 681	59 361	83 573	—	—	83 573	—	—
89 307	23 522	1 906	63 879	89 307	—	—	89 307	—	—
22 770.00	6 692.00	—	11 185.00	19 449.00	411.00	859.00	20 719.00	2 051.00	9.0
271 422.30	87 789.20	—	152 499.50	240 288.70	8 172.70	19 210.20	267 671.60	3 750.70	1.4
462 590.00	142 139.00	—	279 818.00	421 957.00	13 477.00	24 725.00	460 159.00	2 431.00	0.5
659 413.00	162 781.00	32 158.00	374 596.00	569 535.00	11 852.00	49 685.00	631 072.00	28 341.00	4.3
1 205 410.00	308 228.00	59 057.00	675 802.00	1 043 087.00	22 385.00	90 872.00	1 156 344.00	49 066.00	4.1
2 777 651.00	699 128.00	126 325.00	1 642 227.00	2 467 680.00	52 112.00	212 887.00	2 732 679.00	44 972.00	1.6
2 876.40	—	—	—	2 593.90	70.80	14.50	2 679.20	197.20	6.9
8 028.00	—	—	—	7 360.90	295.70	53.00	7 709.60	318.40	4.0
17 235.30	313.30	—	2 051.10	15 182.30	559.00	66.00	15 807.30	1 428.00	8.3
25 538.40	4 678.00	43.10	17 347.10	22 068.20	925.60	91.10	23 084.90	2 453.50	9.6
19 613.30	1 460.80	49.00	18 313.10	19 822.90	221.90	—	20 044.80	− 431.50	−2.2
23 033.40	2 930.40	—	20 393.50	23 323.90	281.00	—	23 604.90	− 571.50	−2.5
24 310.50	3 331.70	—	20 277.80	23 609.50	287.40	—	23 896.90	413.60	1.7
29.16	8.30	0.03	5.42	13.75	2.50	—	16.25	12.91	44.3
57.82	—	—	11.57	11.57	8.94	—	20.51	37.31	64.5
85.35	—	—	24.56	24.56	1.53	—	26.09	59.26	69.4
89.78	—	—	23.03	23.03	1.52	—	24.55	65.23	72.7
111.02	—	—	26.79	26.79	1.74	—	28.53	82.49	74.3
111.57	—	—	32.57	32.57	1.80	—	34.37	77.20	69.2
651.40	202.20	—	377.60	579.80	17.30	11.20	608.30	43.10	6.6
1 822.10	718.50	—	950.00	1 668.50	10.40	8.30	1 687.20	134.90	7.4
4 168.70	1 005.10	—	2 965.90	3 971.00	75.00	6.10	4 052.10	116.60	2.8
6 283.20	1 366.70	—	4 562.00	5 928.70	96.30	17.80	6 042.80	240.40	3.8
6 761.20	1 438.30	—	5 055.40	6 493.70	110.00	23.00	6 626.70	134.50	2.0
8 160.10	1 628.50	—	6 288.90	7 917.40	144.20	25.60	8 087.20	72.90	0.9
9 645.50	2 007.20	—	7 279.20	9 286.40	224.90	23.20	9 534.50	111.00	1.2
3.80	—	—	0.49	0.49	0.13	—	0.62	3.18	83.7
7.52	—	—	1.15	1.15	0.32	—	1.47	6.05	80.5
9.13	—	—	1.45	1.45	0.50	1.57	3.52	5.61	61.4
10.89	—	—	2.02	2.02	0.56	2.34	4.92	5.97	54.8
13.66	—	—	2.77	2.77	0.78	3.24	6.79	6.87	50.3

*Country appears for the first time in this publication. [1] Data for public employees for 1984-86 are not available. [2] Data for 1984, 1985 and 1986 reflect only the schemes for which data were made available, and should therefore be interpreted with caution. [3] Data for 1981-86 reflect only the schemes for which data were made available, and should therefore be interpreted with caution. [4] Financial year ending 30 June. [5] Data are not strictly comparable with those prior to 1984. [6] Excludes other receipts reported for 1985, i.e. 6 million CFA francs. [7] Financial year ending 7 July. [8] Data relate only to Public Employees' Scheme. [9] Data include public undertakings, as well as civil and military personnel. [10] Includes family allowances and estimated pension benefit expenditure for public employees.

[11] Data for public employees and public assistance for 1984-86 are not available. For Italy, data for national health service and benefits for war victims are also not available. [12] Converted from pounds to shillings at the rate of 20 shillings to the pound. [13] The figures prior to 1984 are converted from Mali francs at the rate of 2 Mali francs to 1 CFA franc. [14] Includes public employees, using data of 1986. [15] On 29 June 1973 the ouguiya, equal to 5 CFA francs, was introduced. The necessary conversions have been effected. [16] Including Unemployment Benefit Scheme, which started operating on 1 February 1983. [17] Financial year ending 30 September. [18] On 1 January 1973, the naira, equal to half the Nigerian pound, was introduced. The necessary conversion has been effected. [19] Data relate only to the Social Security Fund, whereas those for the other years include the Social Security Fund as well as the Retirement Insurance Institute. [20] The figures are not strictly comparable with those for other years, due to the impact of social unrest.

[21] These are aggregate figures for 1979-81; no separate figures are available for 1981. [22] Includes insured persons' contributions towards health and welfare benefits. [23] Data for 1984-86 were affected by the economic and social upheavals of the period. [24] Excludes administrative expenditure which was reported to be 105, 142 and 497 million shillings in 1984, 1985 and 1986 respectively. [25] Financial year starting 1 April. [26] On 1 June 1983 the peso argentino, equal to 10,000 pesos, was introduced. On 14 June 1985 the austral, equal to 1,000 pesos argentinos, was introduced. The necessary conversions have been effected. [27] Includes medical benefit branch which came into effect in 1985. [28] Unemployment insurance, which came into effect in 1982, is included in the figures as from 1983. [29] The amount reported in respect of public assistance has been considerably reduced during the recent reports. [30] Data for the Accountant General's Pension Scheme and public assistance are not available.

[31] On 1 January 1963 the Bolivian peso, equal to 1,000 bolivianos, was introduced. On 1 January 1987 the boliviano, equal to 1 million pesos, was introduced. The necessary conversions have been effected. [32] On 28 February 1986 the cruzado, equal to 1,000 cruzeiros, was introduced. The necessary conversions have been effected. [33] Estimates. [34] Includes estimated figures in respect of non-contributory pensions, based on 1977 data (for year 1980), on 1984 data (for year 1983) and on 1985 data (for year 1986). [35] Data prior to 1981 are not strictly comparable with those for subsequent years. A new social insurance system (mandatory private insurance system) has been introduced and a transition from the old social insurance system began in March 1981. [36] As from 1980, the data exclude Public Health Services (Fondo Nacional de Salud). [37] Data include public assistance and administrative expenditure which were not available prior to 1984. [38] The National Insurance Scheme came into effect from 4 April 1983. Prior to this, there was a Provident Fund to which employers alone contributed. No benefits were paid prior to 1983. The figures include provisional data for public employees and public assistance for 1982; figures for the relevant year are not available. [39] Data on public assistance are not available. [40] On 1 February 1985 the inti, equal to 1,000 soles, was introduced. The necessary conversions have been effected.

[41] On 1 July 1975 the new peso, equal to 1,000 old pesos, was introduced. The necessary conversion has been effected. [42] The figures for 1980 are not strictly comparable with those for the later years. The medical care benefit figure for 1980 includes employment injury medical care, which is not available for the other years. [43] Includes Public Employees' Scheme which came into operation in 1986, but no benefits were paid during the period. [44] Includes estimates and data on public employees and public assistance, using data of 1983-84. [45] On 22 February 1980 the shekel was introduced at the rate of 10 Israel pounds to 1 shekel. On 4 September 1985 the new shekel, equal to 1,000 old shekels, was introduced. The necessary conversions have been effected. [46] Includes cash benefits for Employees' Provident Fund, using data of 1984. [47] Formerly Burma. [48] Included data for "urban local councils", using data of 1981/82. [49] Excludes Public Assistance and Veterans' Programmes for which

** Pays qui figurent pour la première fois dans cette publication. [1] On ne dispose pas de données pour les agents publics pour 1984-1986. [2] Pour 1984-1986, les chiffres correspondent aux seuls régimes pour lesquels des données ont été reçues; ils doivent être interprétés avec prudence. [3] Pour 1981-1986, les chiffres correspondent aux seuls régimes pour lesquels des données ont été reçues; ils doivent être interprétés avec prudence. [4] Exercice financier se terminant le 30 juin. [5] Les chiffres ne sont pas rigoureusement comparables à ceux qui sont donnés pour les années antérieures à 1984. [6] A l'exclusion des autres recettes, indiquées pour 1985 (6 millions de francs CFA). [7] Exercice financier se terminant le 7 juillet. [8] Les chiffres se réfèrent uniquement au régime des agents publics. [9] Les chiffres comprennent les entreprises publiques, à côté du personnel civil et militaire. [10] Y compris les prestations familiales et les dépenses afférentes aux pensions des agents publics (estimations).*

[11] Pour 1984-1986, on ne dispose pas de données pour le régime des agents publics et l'assistance publique. Pour l'Italie, on ne dispose pas non plus de données pour le service national de santé et pour le régime de prestations aux victimes de guerre. [12] Les livres ont été converties en shillings à raison de 20 shillings pour 1 livre. [13] Pour les années antérieures à 1984, les chiffres en francs maliens ont été convertis en francs CFA au taux de 2 francs maliens pour 1 franc CFA. [14] Y compris le régime des agents publics, d'après les données reçues pour 1986. [15] Le 29 juin 1973, l'ouguiya, correspondant à 5 francs CFA, a été introduit; les conversions nécessaires ont été faites. [16] Y compris le régime d'indemnisation du chômage, entré en vigueur le 1er février 1983. [17] Exercice financier se terminant le 30 septembre. [18] Le 1er janvier 1973, le naira a été introduit, au taux de 2 naira pour 1 livre nigériane; les conversions nécessaires ont été effectuées. [19] Les chiffres concernent uniquement la Caisse de sécurité sociale; pour les autres années, ils comprennent la Caisse de sécurité sociale ainsi que l'Institution de prévoyance – retraite. [20] Les chiffres ne sont pas exactement comparables selon les années en raison des troubles qu'a connus le pays.

[21] Chiffres agrégés pour la période 1979-1981; on ne dispose pas de chiffres distincts pour 1981. [22] Y compris les cotisations des assurés au titre des prestations de l'action sanitaire et sociale. [23] Pour 1984-1986, les chiffres se ressentent des troubles qu'a connus le pays. [24] A l'exclusion des frais d'administration; les chiffres indiqués sont de 105, 142 et 497 millions de shillings pour 1984, 1985 et 1986. [25] Exercice financier débutant le 1er avril. [26] Le 1er juin 1983, le peso argentin, égal à 10 000 pesos anciens, a été introduit; le 14 juin 1985, il a été remplacé par l'austral, équivalant à 1 000 pesos argentins; les conversions nécessaires ont été faites. [27] Y compris le régime de prestations de maladie, entré en vigueur en 1985. [28] Y compris, depuis 1983, l'assurance chômage, entrée en vigueur en 1982. [29] Les chiffres donnés dans les rapports récents pour l'assistance publique font apparaître une notable réduction. [30] On ne dispose pas de données pour le régime de pensions de la Direction de la comptabilité et pour l'assistance publique.

[31] Le 1er janvier 1963, le peso bolivien, égal à 1 000 bolivianos, a été introduit; le 1er janvier 1987, le boliviano, équivalant à 1 million de pesos, a été mis en circulation; les conversions nécessaires ont été faites. [32] Le 28 février 1986, le cruzado, égal à 1 000 cruzeiros, a été introduit; les conversions nécessaires ont été faites. [33] Estimations. [34] Y compris les pensions non contributives, selon les chiffres estimés pour 1980, 1983 et 1986 d'après les données reçues pour 1977, 1984 et 1985, respectivement. [35] Les chiffres pour les années antérieures à 1981 ne sont pas exactement comparables avec ceux qui sont donnés pour les années suivantes; un nouveau système d'assurances sociales a été introduit (système privé obligatoire), avec une phase de transition à partir de mars 1981. [36] Depuis 1980, les chiffres ne comprennent plus le Fonds national de santé. [37] Y compris l'assistance publique et les frais d'administration, pour lesquels on ne disposait pas de chiffres avant 1984. [38] Le régime d'assurance nationale est entré en vigueur le 4 avril 1983. Auparavant, il existait un fonds de prévoyance auquel seuls les employeurs contribuaient. Aucune prestation n'a été versée avant 1983. Les chiffres comprennent des données provisoires pour le régime des agents publics et l'assistance publique pour 1982; on ne dispose pas de données pour l'année considérée. [39] On ne dispose pas de données pour l'assistance publique. [40] Le 1er février 1985, l'inti, égal à 1 000 soles, a été introduit; les conversions nécessaires ont été faites.

[41] Le 1er janvier 1975, le nouveau peso, égal à 1 000 pesos anciens, a été mis en circulation; les conversions nécessaires ont été faites. [42] Les chiffres pour 1980 ne sont pas exactement comparables avec ceux qui sont donnés pour les années suivantes; le chiffre indiqué pour les soins médicaux pour 1980 comprend les soins en cas de lésion professionnelle, donnée dont on ne dispose pas pour les autres années. [43] Y compris le régime des agents publics, entré en vigueur en 1986; aucune prestation, toutefois, n'a été versée au cours de la période. [44] Y compris les régimes des agents publics et l'assistance publique (estimations ou données), d'après des données pour 1983-84. [45] Le 22 février 1980, le shekel, correspondant à 10 livres israéliennes,

* Países que figuran por primera vez en esta edición. [1] No se dispone de datos relativos a los empleados públicos para 1984-1986. [2] Los datos para 1984, 1985 y 1986 sólo se refieren a los regímenes de los que se proporcionaron informaciones, y, por tanto, deben interpretarse con prudencia. [3] Los datos para 1981-1986 sólo se refieren a los regímenes de los que se proporcionaron informaciones, y, por tanto, deben interpretarse con prudencia. [4] Ejercicio financiero que termina el 30 de junio. [5] Los datos no son estrictamente comparables con los de antes de 1984. [6] Excluidos otros ingresos comunicados para 1985, de 6 millones de francos CFA. [7] Ejercicio financiero que termina el 7 de julio. [8] Los datos sólo se refieren al régimen de empleados públicos. [9] Los datos corresponden a empresas estatales, así como al personal civil y militar. [10] Incluidos los subsidios familiares y los egresos estimados por prestaciones de pensiones para empleados públicos.

[11] No se dispone de datos relativos a los empleados públicos y a la asistencia pública para 1984-1986. [12] Conversión de libras a chelines, a razón de 20 chelines por libra. [13] Las cifras de antes de 1984 se han convertido del franco malí, a razón de 2 francos malíes por 1 franco CFA. [14] Incluidos los empleados públicos, de acuerdo con datos de 1986. [15] El 29 de junio de 1973 se introdujo una nueva moneda, el ouguiya, equivalente a 5 francos CFA; en consecuencia, se han hecho las conversiones pertinentes. [16] Incluido el régimen de prestaciones de desempleo, aplicado desde el 1.° de febrero de 1983. [17] Ejercicio financiero que termina el 30 de septiembre. [18] El 1.° de enero de 1973 se introdujo una nueva moneda, la naira, equivalente a la mitad de 1 libra nigeriana; en consecuencia, se han hecho las conversiones pertinentes. [19] Los datos corresponden exclusivamente al Fondo de Seguridad Social, en tanto que los de otros años incluyen el Fondo de Seguridad Social y el Instituto de Seguro de Jubilaciones. [20] A causa de trastornos sociales, las cifras no son rigurosamente comparables con las de años anteriores.

[21] Total del trienio 1979-1981; no se dispone de cifras separadas para 1981 [22] Incluye las cotizaciones de personas aseguradas con respecto a prestaciones de salud y bienestar. [23] Los datos para 1984-1986 fueron afectados por los trastornos políticos y sociales de ese período. [24] Excluidos los gastos de administración, que, según se comunicó, fueron de 105, 142 y 497 millones de chelines en 1984, 1985 y 1986, respectivamente. [25] Ejercicio financiero que comienza el 1.° de abril. [26] El 1.° de junio de 1983 se introdujo el peso argentino, equivalente a 10 000 pesos. El 14 de junio de 1985 se introdujo el austral, equivalente a 1 000 pesos argentinos. En consecuencia, se han hecho las conversiones pertinentes. [27] Incluye el Servicio de Prestación Médica, que comenzó en 1985. [28] El seguro de desempleo, que entró en vigor en 1982, está incluido en las cifras a partir de 1983. [29] En informes recientes se ha reducido considerablemente el monto comunicado con respecto a la asistencia pública. [30] No se dispone de datos para el régimen de pensiones de contaduría general y la asistencia pública.

[31] El 1.° de enero de 1963 se introdujo el peso boliviano, equivalente a 1 000 bolivianos. El 1.° de enero de 1987 se introdujo el boliviano, equivalente a 1 millón de pesos. En consecuencia, se han hecho las conversiones pertinentes. [32] El 28 de febrero de 1986 se introdujo el cruzado, equivalente a 1 000 cruzeiros. En consecuencia, se han hecho las conversiones pertinentes. [33] Estimaciones. [34] Incluye cifras estimativas respecto de las pensiones no contributivas, basadas sobre datos de 1977 (para 1980), sobre datos de 1984 (para 1983) y sobre datos de 1985 (para 1986). [35] Los datos anteriores a 1981 no son estrictamente comparables con los de años siguientes. Como se creó un nuevo sistema de seguros sociales (sistema privado obligatorio), la transición a partir del antiguo sistema de seguro social comenzó en marzo de 1981. [36] Tal como ocurre a partir de 1980, los datos excluyen los servicios públicos de salud («Fondo Nacional de Salud»). [37] Los datos incluyen la asistencia pública y los gastos de administración, de los que no se disponía antes de 1984. [38] El régimen de seguro nacional entró en vigor el 4 de abril de 1983. Con anterioridad hubo un fondo de previsión al que sólo contribuían los empleadores. No se pagaron prestaciones antes de 1983. Las cifras incluyen datos provisionales acerca de los empleados públicos y la asistencia pública para 1982; no se dispone de cifras para el año pertinente. [39] No se dispone de datos acerca de la asistencia pública. [40] El 1.° de febrero de 1985 se introdujo el inti, equivalente a 1 000 soles; en consecuencia, se han hecho las conversiones pertinentes.

[41] El 1.° de julio de 1975 se introdujo el peso nuevo, equivalente a 1 000 pesos antiguos; en consecuencia, se han hecho las conversiones pertinentes. [42] Las cifras para 1980 no son estrictamente comparables con las de años posteriores. En 1980, las cifras relativas a prestaciones de asistencia médica incluyen las que conciernen a la asistencia médica por riesgos profesionales, de las que no se dispone para los demás años. [43] Incluye el régimen de empleados públicos que comenzó a funcionar en 1986, pero no se pagaron prestaciones durante el período. [44] Incluye estimaciones y datos sobre emplea-

data are not available. [50] Data relate to social assistance only.

[51] Interest credited to Central Provident Fund members was not reflected in the data. [52] Includes public employees. [53] Other receipts include Financial Balancing Fund instituted by the Royal Act No. 214 of 30 September 1983. [54] Includes public assistance which relates to the years 1982; figures for the relevant year are not available. [55] For certain component schemes the figures for medical care include cash benefits which are not available separately, and vice versa. [56] At time of writing the interests of Berlin (West) were represented in the International Labour Organisation by the Federal Republic of Germany. Accordingly the data include West Berlin for which separate figures were not available. [57] Benefits in kind in respect of medical care are included under column 11. [58] Excludes data for war victims, which are not available. [59] Receipts figures are not available; they are assumed to be the same as the expenditure figures. [60] Data are estimates based on the state budget for social security.

[61] Data for war victims are not available. [62] Excludes National Health Service and public assistance, for which data are not available. [63] Data relate to the whole of the USSR (including Byelorussian SSR and Ukrainian SSR which appear separately). [64] Includes, in respect of "childrens' allowances", estimated contributions, which are assumed to be the same as benefit expenditure. [65] Excludes family allowances. [66] Includes insured persons' contributions towards voluntary health insurance and coal miners' pensions. These items are not available for 1984, 1985 and 1986. [67] Data are not strictly comparable with the period prior to 1984. Data for public assistance are not available.

a été introduit; le 4 septembre 1985, il a été remplacé par le nouveau shekel, équivalant à 1 000 shekels anciens; les conversions nécessaires ont été faites. [46] Y compris les prestations en espèces pour la caisse de prévoyance des salariés, d'après des données pour 1984. [47] Ancienne Birmanie. [48] Y compris les données pour les conseils locaux urbains, d'après les chiffres de 1981-82. [49] A l'exclusion de l'assistance publique et des régimes pour les anciens combattants, pour lesquels on ne dispose pas de données. [50] Assistance sociale exclusivement.

[51] Les intérêts crédités aux membres du Fonds central de prévoyance ne sont pas compris dans les chiffres. [52] Y compris le régime des agents publics. [53] Les autres recettes comprennent le Fonds pour l'équilibre financier de la sécurité sociale, institué par l'arrêté royal n° 214 du 30 septembre 1983. [54] Y compris les chiffres de l'assistance publique pour l'année 1982; on ne dispose pas de données pour l'année considérée. [55] Pour certains des régimes entrant en ligne de compte, les chiffres relatifs aux soins médicaux comprennent des prestations en espèces pour lesquelles on ne dispose pas de données distinctes, et inversement. [56] A l'époque considérée, les intérêts de Berlin (Ouest) étaient représentés, au sein de l'Organisation internationale du Travail, par la République fédérale d'Allemagne; les chiffres comprennent Berlin Ouest, zone pour laquelle on ne disposait pas de données distinctes. [57] Les prestations en nature au titre des soins médicaux figurent dans la colonne 11. [58] A l'exclusion du régime pour les victimes de guerre, pour lequel on ne dispose pas de données. [59] On ne dispose pas de données pour les recettes, supposées égales aux dépenses. [60] Estimations fondées sur le budget d'Etat pour la sécurité sociale.

[61] On ne dispose pas de données pour le régime pour les victimes de guerre. [62] A l'exclusion du service national de santé et de l'assistance publique, pour lesquels on ne dispose pas de données. [63] Les données se rapportent à l'ensemble de l'URSS (y compris les RSS de Biélorussie et d'Ukraine, qui figurent séparément dans les tableaux). [64] Y compris, pour les allocations pour enfants, l'estimation des cotisations, supposées égales aux dépenses de prestations. [65] A l'exclusion des prestations familiales. [66] Y compris les cotisations des assurés pour le régime volontaire d'assurance maladie et le régime de pensions des charbonnages; on ne dispose pas des chiffres pour 1984, 1985 et 1986. [67] Les chiffres ne sont pas exactement comparables avec ceux qui sont donnés pour les années antérieures à 1984. On ne dispose pas de données pour l'assistance publique.

dos públicos y asistencia pública, con la utilización de datos de 1983-1984. [45] El 22 de febrero de 1980 se introdujo el shekel, esquivalente a 10 libras israelíes. El 4 de septiembre de 1985 se introdujo el nuevo shekel, equivalente a 1 000 shekels antiguos. En consecuencia, se han hecho las conversiones pertinentes. [46] Incluye las prestaciones monetarias respecto del Fondo de Previsión de Empleados, con la utilización de datos de 1984. [47] Antes Birmania. [48] Incluye datos acerca de «consejos locales urbanos», con la utilización de datos de 1981-1982. [49] Excluye la Asistencia Pública y los Programas para Veteranos, de los que no se dispone de datos. [50] Los datos sólo se refieren a la asistencia social.

[51] Los datos no reflejan los intereses acreditados a los miembros del Fondo Central de Previsión. [52] Incluye los empleados públicos. [53] Entre los demás ingresos figura el Fondo Financiero de Compensación, instituido por la ley real núm. 214 de 30 de septiembre de 1983. [54] Incluye la asistencia pública con referencia al año 1982; no se dispone de cifras para el año pertinente. [55] Respecto de algunos regímenes abarcados, las cifras relativas a asistencia médica incluyen prestaciones monetarias de las que no se dispone en forma desglosada; a la inversa, las prestaciones monetarias pueden incluir gastos de asistencia médica. [56] En el momento de redactar la respuesta, los intereses de Berlín (Oeste) estaban representados en la Organización Internacional del Trabajo por la República Federal de Alemania. Por tanto, los datos incluyen los de Berlín (Oeste), de los que no se dispone por separado. [57] Las prestaciones en especie por concepto de asistencia médica se incluyen en la columna 11. [58] Excluye los datos relativos a víctimas de guerra, por no encontrarse disponibles. [59] No se dispone de cifras sobre ingresos; presuntamente, corresponden a las relativas a ingresos. [60] Los datos son estimaciones basadas sobre el presupuesto estatal para la seguridad social.

[61] No se dispone de datos acerca de víctimas de guerra. [62] Excluye el Servicio Nacional de Salud y la asistencia pública, de los cuales no se dispone de datos. [63] Datos referidos a la totalidad de la URSS (con inclusión de la RSS de Bielorrusia y la RSS de Ucrania, que aparecen por separado). [64] Incluye las contribuciones relativas a las prestaciones por hijos menores, estimadas en el mismo nivel que los egresos por el mismo concepto. [65] Excluye las prestaciones familiares. [66] Incluye las contribuciones de personas aseguradas con respecto al seguro voluntario de salud y las pensiones de mineros de carbón. No se dispone de estos rubros para 1984, 1985 y 1986. [67] Los datos no son estrictamente comparables con los del período anterior a 1984. No se dispone de datos para la asistencia pública.

2. Total social security receipts and expenditure
(in millions of US dollars)

2. Recettes et dépenses totales de la sécurité sociale
(en millions de dollars des Etats-Unis)

2. Ingresos y egresos totales de la seguridad social
(en millones de dólares de los Estados Unidos)

Country Pays País	Financial year Exercice financier Ejercicio financiero	Receipts Recettes Ingresos	Expenditure Dépenses Egresos Total Total Total	Benefits Prestations Prestaciones
(1)	(2)	(3)	(4)	(5)
AFRICA – AFRIQUE – AFRICA				
Bénin	1970	6.62	6.45	6.06
	1975	13.10	12.38	11.32
	1981	19.99	16.76	15.41
	1983	16.78	14.85	14.11
	1984	7.63	7.05	5.08
	1985	10.50	9.37	6.81
	1986	14.06	12.10	7.94
Burkina Faso	1975	12.95	10.31	9.67
	1980	19.18	7.81	4.80
	1983	21.89	13.67	9.49
	1984	14.10	3.52	3.48
	1985	19.15	4.86	4.82
	1986	25.06	6.38	6.33
Burundi	1978	3.69	1.82	1.26
	1980	5.28	2.96	2.18
	1983	7.58	4.28	3.34
	1984	7.68	4.58	3.13
	1985	9.98	5.92	4.45
	1986	11.02	7.51	6.18
Cameroun	1970	19.11	17.68	16.42
	1981	84.95	38.76	38.76
	1983	102.59	36.14	36.14
	1984	80.05	28.70	28.70
	1985	133.25	41.18	41.18
	1986	175.89	61.56	61.56
Cap-Vert	1983	2.79	1.18	0.76
	1984	3.44	1.29	0.85
	1985	4.83	1.89	1.26
	1986	6.53	2.75	1.71
Rép. centrafricaine	1981	7.28	5.90	2.92
	1983	5.47	4.60	2.57
	1984	5.73	6.17	4.29
	1985	8.16	8.41	5.19
	1986	14.09	17.20	7.85
Côte d'Ivoire	1981	91.33	50.71	29.80
	1983	69.78	39.14	30.67
	1984	59.33	45.81	34.15
	1985	101.64	61.54	43.08
	1986	124.79	70.85	56.43
Egypt	1984	3 341	1 305	1 221
	1985	3 970	1 409	1 318
	1986	4 693	1 633	1 529
Ethiopia	1972	35.24	27.59	27.06
	1975	56.55	49.95	49.24
	1980	56.85	38.54	37.86
	1983	61.13	51.36	50.40
	1984	73.16	50.08	49.12
	1985	76.67	55.51	54.55
	1986	78.30	56.19	55.18
Gabon	1980	83.95	81.15	59.90
	1983	94.95	79.90	64.77
	1984	77.99	70.04	56.02
	1985	110.35	100.10	80.31
	1986	117.08	131.14	105.89
Guinée	1981	7.61	2.18	1.74
	1983	7.05	1.90	1.41
	1984	—	—	—
	1985	7.13	6.25	5.62
	1986	1.26	1.14	0.97
Guinée-Bissau	1981	0.92	1.08	0.04
	1983	0.33	0.57	0.02
	1984	0.45	0.19	0.11
	1985	0.48	0.27	0.16
	1986	0.58	0.26	0.15
Kenya	1970	47.57	30.74	29.90
	1975	95.84	59.98	58.06
	1981	47.87	3.80	2.46
	1983	43.52	4.03	2.93
	1984	106.46	12.29	10.14
	1985	114.22	15.72	13.51
	1986	103.48	16.71	14.21
Madagascar	1981	27.62	15.78	15.78
	1983	19.38	13.43	13.43
	1984	12.75	12.96	11.18
	1985	14.02	14.23	12.19
	1986	13.36	13.09	11.39
Mali	1972	6.49	6.79	6.29
	1975	9.70	9.38	8.29
	1980	10.06	10.71	6.25
	1983	10.91	10.55	6.86
	1984	13.31	13.63	10.06
	1985	18.00	19.68	13.47
	1986	25.19	24.55	15.63
Maroc	1970	96.52	86.73	83.88
	1975	165.60	138.69	133.25
	1980	333.80	186.36	166.36
	1983	180.08	101.49	94.67
	1984	273.43	191.09	181.41
	1985	346.33	210.36	199.70
	1986	420.19	287.71	272.05

See note on page 78. *Voir note page 78.* Véase nota pág. 78.

Table 2 *(cont.)*   **Tableau 2** *(suite)*   **Cuadro 2** *(cont.)*

Country / Pays / País	Financial year / Exercice financier / Ejercicio financiero	Receipts / Recettes / Ingresos	Expenditure / Dépenses / Egresos — Total / Total / Total	Expenditure — Benefits / Prestations / Prestaciones
(1)	(2)	(3)	(4)	(5)
Mauritanie	1970	4.41	4.04	3.83
	1981	21.24	17.55	16.06
	1983	20.92	18.56	16.57
	1984	9.91	7.58	6.15
	1985	9.72	6.00	5.02
	1986	7.89	7.87	6.44
Mauritius	1970	13.97	12.68	12.41
	1975	26.73	23.91	23.67
	1981	31.06	18.35	17.59
	1983	35.71	20.38	19.43
	1984	.	.	.
	1985	60.76	39.96	37.70
	1986	75.65	49.79	47.34
Mozambique	1981	7.60	2.83	0.50
	1983	3.71	2.00	0.43
	1984	5.33	3.29	3.29
	1985	5.74	3.90	3.90
	1986	0.57	0.36	0.36
Niger	1970	5.40	4.75	4.49
	1975	9.63	8.25	7.78
	1980	16.93	7.06	5.94
	1983	14.27	10.68	4.24
	1984	28.84	21.96	9.16
	1985	37.98	27.86	11.27
	1986	39.94	31.08	15.23
Nigeria	1970	67.11	49.97	48.63
	1981	110.94	14.36	5.53
	1983	104.70	15.05	6.86
	1984	107.96	16.74	7.55
	1985	99.56	15.88	7.72
	1986	32.68	5.28	2.36
Rwanda	1975	4.75	1.76	1.54
	1981	12.05	1.93	1.04
	1983	14.62	3.91	2.28
	1984	16.58	4.15	2.45
	1985	19.18	5.49	3.36
	1986	25.23	6.96	4.52
Sao Tomé-et-Principe	1981	2.14	0.46	0.46
	1983	1.92	0.46	0.46
	1984	1.69	0.47	0.47
	1985	2.25	0.69	0.69
	1986	1.25	0.64	0.64
Sénégal	1970	31.72	28.63	27.88
	1975	51.89	42.02	37.56
	1980	61.58	49.71	39.17
	1983	18.46	14.58	11.51
	1984	39.15	33.09	27.69
	1985	56.34	46.08	38.74
	1986	68.46	58.33	49.44
Sudan	1980	47.58	6.60	1.84
	1983	25.53	5.80	2.08
	1984	42.69	6.31	3.31
	1985	21.64	3.72	1.92
	1986	16.84	3.40	1.68
Swaziland	1981	7.75	2.75	1.52
	1983	9.09	3.76	1.98
	1984	4.85	0.71	0.71
	1985	4.02	1.30	0.61
	1986	4.91	1.78	0.82
Tanzania, United Rep. of	1980	38.17	10.05	7.50
	1983	31.70	16.16	5.19
	1984	45.84	10.34	6.60
	1985	56.56	17.85	12.05
	1986	24.88	9.43	4.47
Tchad	1979-81	.	.	.
	1983	0.55	0.48	0.11
	1984	1.39	0.64	0.15
	1985	4.41	1.61	0.77
	1986	3.79	2.61	1.08
Togo	1972	7.68	5.27	4.72
	1975	13.49	10.23	8.57
	1980	21.32	10.41	8.13
	1983	16.79	7.65	5.53
	1984	17.05	7.32	5.60
	1985	25.22	10.68	8.01
	1986	29.71	14.47	10.23
Tunisie	1984	437.95	376.70	298.73
	1985	618.89	547.29	403.96
	1986	550.60	490.60	400.00
Uganda	1980	1 080.26	690.79	98.68
	1983	71.25	23.42	1.33
	1984	29.00	0.41	0.41
	1985	10.42	0.14	0.14
	1986	5.36	0.04	0.04
Zaïre	1984	7.97	5.10	0.98
	1985	13.20	7.44	1.66
	1986	17.42	14.69	4.09
Zambia	1970	63.87	43.05	40.99
	1975	165.21	122.63	117.13
	1980	85.94	36.71	25.97
	1983	.	.	.
	1984	46.25	16.63	7.73
	1985	22.46	9.81	5.04
	1986	14.10	5.32	2.16

AMERICA – AMÉRIQUE – AMERICA

Country / Pays / País	Financial year	Receipts	Expenditure Total	Expenditure Benefits
Argentina	1970	.	.	.
	1980			
	1983	2 247	2 176	2 020
	1984	2 417	2 144	2 014
	1985	3 539	2 923	2 846
	1986	3 973	3 580	3 488
Bahamas	1980	32.59	8.12	5.41
	1983	48.50	19.86	15.30
	1984	54.48	23.66	17.83
	1985	71.47	27.62	21.39
	1986	73.56	31.76	24.00
Barbados	1971	10.18	5.66	5.60
	1975	26.77	19.71	19.33
	1980	32.88	18.74	17.54
	1983	67.37	38.93	36.10
	1984	68.66	47.02	43.91
	1985	73.75	51.97	48.64
	1986	73.58	64.38	59.83

See note on page 78.   *Voir note page 78.*   Véase nota pág. 78.

73

Table 2 *(cont.)*   **Tableau 2** *(suite)*   **Cuadro 2** *(cont.)*

Country / Pays / País	Financial year / Exercice financier / Ejercicio financiero	Receipts / Recettes / Ingresos	Expenditure / Dépenses / Egresos — Total / Total / Total	Expenditure — Benefits / Prestations / Prestaciones
(1)	(2)	(3)	(4)	(5)
Belize	1981	3.10	1.98	1.81
	1983	5.77	2.85	2.54
	1984	5.29	0.83	0.47
	1985	5.21	1.10	0.61
	1986	5.62	1.20	0.62
Bolivia	1972	.	.	.
	1975	.	.	.
	1980	.	.	.
	1983	.	.	.
	1984	84.47	92.29	74.61
	1985	41.81	31.30	25.67
Brasil	1970	.	.	.
	1975	.	.	.
	1980	12 618	9 821	9 361
	1983	6 934	6 863	6 384
	1984	6 333	6 276	5 684
	1985	6 836	6 464	6 051
	1986	13 548	12 407	11 376
Canada	1970	14 438	12 579	12 333
	1975	25 740	23 178	22 627
	1980	40 889	35 031	33 942
	1983	58 936	53 188	51 244
	1984	59 509	54 108	51 704
	1985	63 388	55 845	53 738
Colombia	1970	209.37	174.75	161.62
	1975	446.11	376.78	345.78
	1980	1 029.32	867.65	673.06
	1983	801.14	765.98	676.65
	1984	796.79	721.31	375.30
	1985	671.50	575.66	310.74
	1986	775.67	611.13	315.53
Costa Rica	1970	47.40	33.28	28.61
	1975	134.05	100.91	89.91
	1980	397.70	341.59	303.16
	1983	312.17	180.78	160.24
	1984	329.56	240.02	192.86
	1985	375.91	274.21	225.36
	1986	397.24	307.09	251.07
Cuba	1980	1 619	1 619	1 565
	1983	1 714	1 714	1 656
	1984	1 796	1 796	1 730
	1985	1 931	1 931	1 859
	1986	2 380	2 380	2 293
Chile	1971	1 567	1 388	1 255
	1975	579	458	422
	1980	3 588	2 962	2 739
	1983	2 976	2 543	2 315
	1984	2 496	2 169	1 976
	1985	2 491	1 886	1 719
	1986	2 873	2 076	1 910
Dominica	1980	1.84	0.47	0.21
	1983	2.63	0.76	0.43
	1984	3.31	1.20	0.80
	1985	4.17	1.38	0.96
	1986	4.56	1.62	1.10
República Dominicana	1984	58.32	55.07	45.19
	1985	19.86	19.39	15.77
	1986	25.31	24.13	18.32
Ecuador	1972	96.52	62.52	55.76
	1974	168.16	111.52	102.20
	1980	545.72	343.40	247.32
	1983	510.33	375.91	278.60
	1984	697.80	355.37	310.16
	1985	758.97	323.16	284.01
	1986	690.36	284.13	250.23
El Salvador	1970	38.50	29.58	23.50
	1975	69.22	59.84	42.41
	1980	89.38	59.37	50.47
	1983	115.20	67.20	61.48
	1984	81.28	70.00	58.20
	1985	92.12	73.28	63.44
	1986	57.48	42.18	31.62
Grenada	1981	1.30	1.27	1.27
	1983	2.94	1.68	1.60
	1984	4.26	1.92	1.78
	1985	5.31	2.20	2.03
	1986	5.61	2.22	2.02
Guatemala	1970	42.50	40.90	36.50
	1975	73.30	71.30	66.60
	1980	133.40	90.90	80.30
	1983	124.20	90.20	80.00
	1984	138.30	101.50	85.50
	1985	150.90	109.20	92.30
	1986	83.60	53.76	46.24
Guyana	1972	14.02	8.92	7.55
	1975	16.79	8.88	7.37
	1980	35.85	7.44	5.48
	1983	45.44	8.88	6.38
	1984	37.58	7.33	5.34
	1985	42.18	8.59	5.82
	1986	45.51	14.12	11.33
Honduras	1970	13.47	11.96	11.59
	1971	9.20	8.90	8.46
	1981	32.84	22.00	18.56
	1983	38.21	27.39	22.34
	1984	66.71	34.77	27.99
	1985	74.52	37.02	30.11
	1986	83.11	38.40	32.48
Jamaica	1970	57.79	39.72	31.21
	1975	151.28	117.45	104.37
	1980	76.15	36.54	34.32
	1983	57.10	31.61	29.65
	1984	54.39	29.35	27.74
	1985	50.06	27.08	25.35
	1986	60.07	31.18	29.12
México	1970	1 080	1 017	851
	1974	2 503	2 214	1 886
	1980	6 205	5 021	3 659
	1983	3 777	3 171	2 182
	1984	4 586	4 150	3 077
	1985	3 850	3 203	2 512
	1986	2 667	2 290	1 685

See note on page 78.   *Voir note page 78.*   Véase nota pág. 78.

Table 2 *(cont.)*   **Tableau 2** *(suite)*   **Cuadro 2** *(cont.)*

Country / Pays / País (1)	Financial year / Exercice financier / Ejercicio financiero (2)	Receipts / Recettes / Ingresos (3)	Expenditure — Dépenses — Egresos	
			Total / Total / Total (4)	Benefits / Prestations / Prestaciones (5)
Panamá	1972	110.17	95.99	81.01
	1975	177.87	138.40	118.79
	1980	289.97	210.48	189.59
	1983	451.00	335.10	292.40
	1984	427.00	363.60	340.10
	1985	453.20	389.90	365.90
	1986	500.50	425.90	401.60
Perú	1981	486.65	405.63	365.51
	1983	249.78	266.52	236.12
	1984	182.46	193.51	75.26
	1985	228.03	199.21	80.22
	1986	504.73	439.93	173.48
St. Lucia	1981	3.06	0.58	0.27
	1983	2.55	0.80	0.36
	1984	3.87	1.14	0.75
	1985	3.95	0.79	0.32
	1986	5.42	1.25	0.77
Trinidad and Tobago	1970	27.07	26.43	26.43
	1975	76.84	55.56	53.52
	1980	81.72	45.97	39.25
	1983	283.52	190.37	173.80
	1984	218.85	129.46	108.34
	1985	203.75	125.19	104.05
	1986	140.40	106.44	82.02
United States	1970	110 932	93 805	87 544
	1975	219 900	202 156	190 016
	1980	370 597	329 582	316 684
	1983	514 462	451 695	432 879
	1984	539 628	465 992	444 662
	1985	592 112	498 306	476 296
	1986	644 464	525 855	504 468
Uruguay	1975	339.08	319.54	252.29
	1980	975.51	753.17	689.34
	1983	534.77	472.23	437.02
	1984	369.24	424.55	394.87
	1985	383.69	376.37	349.05
	1986	512.98	515.91	478.16
Venezuela	1970	394.54	360.56	267.35
	1975	1 242.40	1 083.13	1 016.17
	1980	992.15	777.92	668.25
	1983	1 187.19	995.40	832.40
	1984	714.76	647.85	552.08
	1985	773.76	685.43	581.83
	1986	514.32	438.32	373.17
ASIA – ASIE – ASIA				
Bahrain	1978	49.73	7.75	6.08
	1980	65.43	9.65	6.81
	1983	125.20	24.36	15.16
	1984	83.00	15.45	9.64
	1985	99.45	15.88	11.77
	1986	95.12	20.10	14.72
Bangladesh	1975	19.79	18.73	18.68
	1980	0.19	0.19	0.19
	1983	1.16	0.52	0.49
	1984	4.94	2.21	2.15
	1985	4.04	1.80	1.74
	1986	4.99	1.88	1.80
Cyprus	1970	20.10	17.29	16.93
	1975	41.98	45.88	45.14
	1980	93.12	75.51	74.08
	1983	170.43	101.71	99.78
	1984	170.84	96.08	94.56
	1985	246.74	131.03	128.90
	1986	276.55	159.63	157.17
India	1970	1 636	1 054	1 037
	1975	3 454	1 996	1 964
	1980	4 620	2 718	2 654
	1983	7 871	3 752	3 697
	1984	6 721	3 159	3 111
	1985	7 217	3 317	3 263
	1986	.	.	.
Indonesia	1981	51.33	9.07	3.88
	1983	56.66	15.96	4.76
	1984	58.14	48.06	5.55
	1985	75.51	71.02	7.07
	1986	59.66	56.19	7.02
Iran, Islamic Rep. of	1981	2 840.68	1 141.25	1 042.91
	1983	3 420.24	1 219.58	1 138.16
	1984	3 104.99	1 258.50	517.06
	1985	3 616.47	1 707.08	690.98
	1986	4 580.14	2 219.33	968.63
Israel	1970	587	486	429
	1975	1 476	1 352	1 176
	1980	2 227	2 117	1 881
	1983	2 503	2 345	1 970
	1984	2 211	2 264	1 887
	1985	3 031	3 042	2 555
	1986	4 524	4 136	3 717
Japan	1970	16 120	11 410	9 851
	1975	57 186	43 352	38 252
	1980	168 475	132 621	118 819
	1983	184 104	148 806	135 079
	1984	174 752	138 993	131 368
	1985	239 059	185 310	174 834
	1986	317 572	252 329	238 742
Jordan	1980	15.78	1.01	0.10
	1983	81.59	9.27	6.93
	1984	99.93	17.56	9.01
	1985	119.95	25.35	14.43
	1986	155.76	27.70	21.45
Kuwait	1980	332.47	156.09	146.86
	1983	727.10	316.59	301.16
	1984	650.10	300.56	280.95
	1985	1 118.93	569.48	549.34
	1986	1 321.13	580.51	559.25
Malaysia	1970	183.20	100.40	97.86
	1975	457.93	261.22	240.57
	1980	958.71	230.72	196.85
	1983	1 871.96	529.63	510.00
	1984	2 074.92	605.98	553.94
	1985	2 352.62	625.93	593.96
	1986	2 421.81	610.58	573.48

See note on page 78.   *Voir note page 78.*   Véase nota pág. 78.

Table 2 *(cont.)* **Tableau 2** *(suite)* **Cuadro 2** *(cont.)*

Country / Pays / País (1)	Financial year / Exercice financier / Ejercicio financiero (2)	Receipts / Recettes / Ingresos (3)	Expenditure / Dépenses / Egresos — Total / Total / Total (4)	Benefits / Prestations / Prestaciones (5)
Myanmar	1970	44.99	42.87	42.58
	1975	48.34	46.78	46.47
	1980	4.50	2.83	2.20
	1983	4.74	3.49	2.16
	1984	4.64	3.27	1.92
	1985	5.42	3.98	2.10
	1986	6.29	5.10	2.63
Pakistan	1965	65.83	65.83	65.83
	1980	25.76	11.51	6.05
	1983	191.64	166.64	162.95
	1984	221.78	201.30	196.42
	1985	383.55	357.30	353.22
	1986	297.67	268.38	264.21
Philippines	1970	115.05	63.72	56.35
	1978	428.37	183.43	153.94
	1980	590.46	227.09	184.45
	1983	482.99	203.56	170.06
	1984	400.52	167.54	139.26
	1985	558.94	196.23	166.15
	1986	521.43	206.76	179.74
Qatar	1984	20.94	20.94	20.94
	1985	21.85	21.85	21.85
	1986	21.98	21.98	21.98
Singapore	1970	102	53	52
	1975	497	162	159
	1980	1 386	439	407
	1983	2 700	1 375	860
	1984	3 163	2 262	1 659
	1985	3 704	2 404	1 665
	1986	3 076	2 575	1 849
Sri Lanka	1970	95.94	72.74	64.84
	1975	113.42	74.65	73.60
	1980	116.27	63.43	60.79
	1983	192.00	107.80	105.54
	1984	284.89	120.58	119.40
	1985	342.62	141.58	140.19
	1986	365.81	141.04	139.38
Rép. arabe syrienne	1984	377.32	176.82	169.04
	1985	400.25	196.69	188.41
	1986	435.41	209.17	199.11
Thailand	1980	12.30	5.04	4.76
	1983	79.67	69.97	69.40
	1984	9.17	9.62	9.10
	1985	10.07	9.46	8.73
	1986	10.90	9.41	8.36

EUROPE – EUROPE – EUROPA

Countries with a market economy – Pays à économie de marché – Países con economía de mercado

Country / Pays / País (1)	Financial year / Exercice financier / Ejercicio financiero (2)	Receipts / Recettes / Ingresos (3)	Expenditure / Dépenses / Egresos — Total / Total / Total (4)	Benefits / Prestations / Prestaciones (5)
Austria	1970	2 735	2 693	2 570
	1975	7 279	7 171	6 843
	1980	16 285	16 182	15 409
	1983	15 610	15 094	14 565
	1984	14 921	14 420	13 908
	1985	20 167	19 684	18 923
	1986	26 882	26 345	25 349
Belgique	1970	4 861	4 661	4 283
	1975	14 288	13 780	12 924
	1980	28 100	28 711	27 037
	1983	21 203	21 054	19 921
	1984	19 528	19 070	18 048
	1985	25 467	24 799	23 508
	1986	33 211	32 730	30 917
Denmark	1970	2 412	2 347	2 289
	1975	7 238	7 065	6 905
	1980	17 168	16 722	16 272
	1983	15 119	14 567	14 147
	1984	13 650	13 151	12 746
	1985	18 391	17 794	17 254
	1986	24 375	23 743	23 055
España	1975	12 242	11 826	11 056
	1980	30 295	30 618	29 305
	1983	25 507	25 656	24 773
	1984	26 720	26 165	25 117
	1985	33 633	33 380	32 052
	1986	44 514	43 817	41 632
Finland	1970	1 496	1 364	1 310
	1975	4 866	4 258	4 099
	1980	10 530	9 022	8 702
	1983	10 645	9 734	9 344
	1984	10 796	9 855	9 514
	1985	15 112	13 717	13 273
	1986	18 859	17 139	16 582
France	1970	21 711	21 707	20 032
	1975	79 192	78 103	67 767
	1980	168 669	163 633	155 702
	1983	142 373	138 728	131 793
	1984	135 064	131 874	125 154
	1985	181 210	178 324	169 615
	1986	221 692	223 050	212 119
Germany, Fed. Rep. of	1970	33 022	31 720	29 857
	1975	91 896	92 836	88 984
	1980	182 599	181 241	174 669
	1983	148 967	149 272	145 286
	1984	133 792	134 215	130 621
	1985	166 079	165 014	160 491
	1986	236 651	232 810	226 201
Grèce	1970	1 192	1 077	1 028
	1975	2 285	2 044	1 924
	1980	5 215	4 500	4 282
	1983	5 772	5 470	5 140
	1984	5 547	5 464	5 115
	1985	5 904	6 082	5 699
Iceland	1984	152.42	149.98	146.97
	1985	209.56	206.99	202.35
	1986	291.15	285.76	279.77
Ireland	1970	404	400	384
	1975	1 451	1 457	1 401
	1980	3 599	3 569	3 392
	1983	3 824	3 870	3 675
	1984	3 621	3 648	3 476
	1985	4 990	5 000	4 780
	1986	6 013	6 017	5 729

See note on page 78. *Voir note page 78.* Véase nota pág. 78.

Table 2 *(cont.)*   **Tableau 2** *(suite)*   **Cuadro 2** *(cont.)*

Country / Pays / País (1)	Financial year / Exercice financier / Ejercicio financiero (2)	Receipts / Recettes / Ingresos (3)	Expenditure / Dépenses / Egresos — Total / Total / Total (4)	Expenditure — Benefits / Prestations / Prestaciones (5)
Italie	1970	15 660	15 173	14 015
	1975	33 291	38 746	35 180
	1980	77 990	78 385	71 406
	1983	85 590	83 484	78 133
	1984	37 923	42 307	37 542
	1985	48 830	54 431	48 427
	1986	66 749	73 822	65 921
Luxembourg	1970	183.68	164.66	159.71
	1975	504.81	462.01	444.70
	1980	1 134.36	1 032.93	990.67
	1983	861.99	798.08	741.43
	1984	806.53	741.99	708.99
	1985	1 079.91	962.43	927.86
	1986	1 470.62	1 277.98	1 237.41
Malta	1970	16.03	17.10	16.94
	1975	46.87	46.42	40.70
	1980	148.62	123.28	122.26
	1983	157.53	151.11	149.76
	1984	138.39	187.01	176.51
	1985	165.92	213.69	201.74
	1986	193.98	254.85	240.47
Netherlands	1970	7 582	6 380	6 156
	1975	24 649	20 874	20 176
	1980	53 430	44 799	43 223
	1983	45 663	39 031	37 339
	1984	39 922	34 441	33 467
	1985	51 594	43 853	42 570
	1986	64 203	56 017	54 332
Norway	1970	1 827	1 729	1 652
	1975	5 396	4 919	4 737
	1980	11 488	11 094	10 857
	1983	11 804	11 378	11 109
	1984	14 671	14 282	14 138
	1985	19 187	18 634	18 437
	1986	21 331	20 709	20 503
Portugal	1970	469	348	302
	1975	1 666	1 509	1 394
	1980	2 394	2 285	2 059
	1983	1 741	1 763	1 670
	1984	1 758	1 695	1 608
	1985	2 329	2 254	2 142
	1986	3 384	3 143	2 997
Suisse	1970	2 436	2 119	1 994
	1975	8 476	8 071	7 646
	1980	14 496	13 274	12 375
	1983	13 922	13 381	12 352
	1984	12 791	12 401	11 399
	1985	16 952	16 139	14 758
	1986	23 154	21 977	20 114
Sweden	1970	7 726	6 205	6 075
	1975	19 311	17 167	16 826
	1980	42 042	38 261	37 300
	1983	31 526	29 318	28 683
	1984	29 394	26 673	25 861
	1985	37 454	34 749	33 328
	1986	46 728	42 815	41 073
Turquie	1970	439	312	289
	1975	2 101	1 176	981
	1980	2 421	2 040	1 947
	1983	1 967	1 530	1 471
	1984	2 006	1 584	1 534
	1985	2 233	1 863	1 808
	1986	2 313	1 871	1 817
United Kingdom	1970	17 449	16 775	15 746
	1975	38 799	36 615	34 301
	1980	104 317	99 477	94 718
	1983	91 805	88 603	84 599
	1984	78 443	75 868	72 314
	1985	105 660	102 828	98 137
	1986	116 131	112 181	106 974

EUROPE – EUROPE – EUROPA

Countries with a centrally planned economy – Pays à économie planifiée – Países con economía centralmente planificada

Country / Pays / País	Financial year	Receipts	Expenditure — Total	Expenditure — Benefits
RSS de Biélorussie	1970	1 228	1 228	1 228
	1975	2 181	2 182	2 182
	1980	3 398	3 398	3 398
	1983	3 492	3 492	3 492
	1984	3 321	3 321	3 321
	1985	3 820	3 820	3 820
	1986	4 676	4 676	4 676
Bulgarie	1970	1 254	1 232	1 201
	1975	2 414	2 359	2 196
	1980	2 948	2 948	2 948
	1983	3 013	3 013	3 013
	1984	3 399	3 000	2 994
	1985	3 331	3 220	3 212
	1986	3 014	2 921	2 914
Czechoslovakia	1970	3 456	3 456	3 441
	1975	6 844	6 844	6 816
	1980	8 351	8 351	8 321
	1983	8 192	8 192	8 166
	1984	8 954	8 954	8 927
	1985	10 108	10 108	10 079
	1986	12 429	12 429	12 393
German Democratic Rep.	1970	3 932	3 932	3 913
	1975	8 331	8 331	8 288
	1980	15 193	15 193	15 137
	1983	11 418	11 418	11 378
	1984	10 228	10 228	10 192
	1985	12 586	12 586	12 541
	1986	17 157	17 157	17 094
Hongrie	1970	1 003	1 008	998
	1975	1 351	1 349	1 336
	1980	3 310	3 310	3 292
	1983	3 061	3 061	3 047
	1984	2 359	2 359	2 345
	1985	2 857	2 795	2 776
	1986	3 252	3 112	3 090
Pologne	1984	12 065	10 324	10 263
	1985	11 860	9 725	9 648
	1986	11 441	9 337	9 260

See note on page 78. *Voir note page 78.* Véase nota pág. 78.

Table 2 *(concl.)* **Tableau 2** *(fin)* **Cuadro 2** *(fin)*

Country / Pays / País	Financial year / Exercice financier / Ejercicio financiero	Receipts / Recettes / Ingresos	Expenditure / Dépenses / Egresos	
			Total	Benefits / Prestations / Prestaciones
(1)	(2)	(3)	(4)	(5)
RSS d'Ukraine	1970	7 225	7 225	7 225
	1975	12 066	12 066	12 066
	1980	18 227	18 227	18 227
	1983	18 415	18 415	18 415
	1984	17 527	17 527	17 527
	1985	20 335	20 335	20 335
	1986	24 612	24 612	24 612
URSS	1970	38 448	38 448	38 448
	1975	65 650	65 650	65 650
	1980	97 903	97 903	97 903
	1983	98 427	98 427	98 427
	1984	94 081	94 081	94 081
	1985	108 536	108 536	108 536
	1986	130 565	130 565	130 565
Yugoslavia	1970	1 821	1 657	1 555
	1981	6 489	6 400	5 745
	1983	3 680	3 661	3 357
	1984	3 114	2 980	2 689
	1985	3 853	3 696	3 334
	1986	6 075	5 977	5 397

Country / Pays / País	Financial year / Exercice financier / Ejercicio financiero	Receipts / Recettes / Ingresos	Expenditure / Dépenses / Egresos	
			Total	Benefits / Prestations / Prestaciones
(1)	(2)	(3)	(4)	(5)
OCEANIA – OCÉANIE – OCEANIA				
Australia	1970	3 207	2 987	2 892
	1975	10 098	9 698	9 259
	1980	20 348	18 662	17 924
	1983	23 028	20 815	19 899
	1984	16 236	16 593	16 409
	1985	15 679	16 068	15 877
	1986	16 163	15 888	15 697
Fiji	1975	33.79	18.83	15.94
	1980	73.09	25.93	14.63
	1983	81.60	24.95	23.48
	1984	78.55	21.48	20.15
	1985	99.13	25.47	23.92
	1986	97.44	30.02	28.45
New Zealand	1970	727	678	647
	1975	1 901	1 761	1 741
	1980	4 012	3 900	3 821
	1983	4 112	3 954	3 880
	1984	3 228	3 164	3 101
	1985	4 067	4 031	3 946
	1986	5 050	4 991	4 861
Solomon Islands	1981	4.27	0.70	0.55
	1983	6.16	1.20	0.94
	1984	6.79	2.62	1.08
	1985	6.75	3.05	1.25
	1986	6.88	3.42	1.39

The footnotes to table 1 equally apply to this table. For exchange rate conversions, consult appendix table 1.

Les notes du tableau 1 sont aussi valables pour ce tableau. Pour les taux de change appliqués, voir le tableau 1 de l'annexe.

Los notas del cuadro 1 son igualmente válidas para el presente cuadro. Para tasas de conversión de divisas, consúltese el cuadro anexo 1.

3. Receipts and expenditure of social security schemes
(as percentages of total gross domestic product in purchasers' values)

3. Recettes et dépenses de la sécurité sociale
(en pourcentage du produit intérieur brut aux valeurs d'acquisition)

3. Ingresos y egresos de los regímenes de seguridad social
(en porcentaje del producto interno bruto a precios de comprador)

Country / Pays / País	Financial year / Exercice financier / Ejercicio financiero	Receipts / Recettes / Ingresos	Expenditure / Dépenses / Egresos Total / Total / Total	Benefits / Prestations / Prestaciones
(1)	(2)	(3)	(4)	(5)
AFRICA – AFRIQUE – AFRICA				
Bénin	1970	2.6	2.6	2.4
	1975	2.6	2.5	2.2
	1981	1.9	1.6	1.5
	1983	1.6	1.4	1.3
	1984	0.8	0.7	0.5
	1985	0.8	0.7	0.5
	1986	0.9	0.8	0.5
Burkina Faso	1975	2.3	1.8	1.7
	1980	1.6	0.6	0.4
	1983	2.4	1.5	1.0
	1984	1.7	0.4	0.4
	1985	1.5	0.4	0.4
	1986	1.6	0.4	0.4
Burundi	1978	0.6	0.3	0.2
	1980	0.6	0.3	0.2
	1983	0.9	0.5	0.4
	1984	0.8	0.5	0.3
	1985	0.8	0.5	0.4
	1986	1.0	0.7	0.5
Cameroun	1970	1.6	1.5	1.4
	1981	1.1	0.5	0.5
	1983	1.3	0.5	0.5
	1984	1.0	0.4	0.4
	1985	1.2	0.4	0.4
	1986	1.4	0.5	0.5
Cap-Vert	1983	3.6	1.5	1.0
	1984	4.0	1.5	1.0
	1985	4.2	1.7	1.1
	1986	4.5	1.9	1.2
Rép. centrafricaine	1981	1.0	0.8	0.4
	1983	0.9	0.8	0.4
	1984	1.0	1.1	0.7
	1985	1.0	1.0	0.6
	1986	1.4	1.7	0.8
Côte d'Ivoire	1981	1.1	0.6	0.4
	1983	1.1	0.6	0.5
	1984	1.0	0.8	0.6
	1985	1.2	0.7	0.5
	1986	1.2	0.7	0.6
Egypt	1984	6.8	2.7	2.5
	1985	7.3	2.6	2.4
	1986	7.5	2.6	2.4
Ethiopia	1972	1.7	1.3	1.3
	1975	2.1	1.9	1.8
	1980	1.4	0.9	0.9
	1983	1.3	1.1	1.0
	1984	1.5	1.0	1.0
	1985	1.6	1.2	1.1
	1986	1.5	1.1	1.1
Gabon	1980	2.1	2.0	1.5
	1983	3.1	2.6	2.1
	1984	2.4	2.2	1.7
	1985	2.5	2.3	1.8
	1986	3.2	3.6	2.9
Guinée	1981	.	.	.
	1983	.	.	.
	1984	.	.	.
	1985	.	.	.
	1986	.	.	.
Guinée-Bissau	1981	.	.	.
	1983	.	.	.
	1984	.	.	.
	1985	.	.	.
	1986	0.3	0.1	0.1
Kenya	1970	3.0	1.9	1.9
	1975	3.3	2.1	2.0
	1981	0.8	0.1	0.0
	1983	0.8	0.1	0.1
	1984	1.9	0.2	0.2
	1985	1.9	0.3	0.2
	1986	1.4	0.2	0.2
Madagascar	1981	1.0	0.6	0.6
	1983	0.8	0.5	0.5
	1984	0.6	0.6	0.5
	1985	0.6	0.6	0.5
	1986	0.6	0.6	0.5
Mali	1972	1.8	1.8	1.7
	1975	1.7	1.6	1.4
	1980	0.8	0.8	0.5
	1983	1.1	1.1	0.7
	1984	1.4	1.4	1.0
	1985	1.4	1.6	1.1
	1986	1.5	1.5	0.9
Maroc	1970	2.4	2.2	2.1
	1975	1.9	1.6	1.5
	1980	2.1	1.2	1.0
	1983	1.5	0.9	0.8
	1984	2.5	1.7	1.6
	1985	2.8	1.7	1.6
	1986	2.7	1.9	1.8
Mauritanie	1970	2.2	2.0	1.9
	1981	2.4	2.0	1.8
	1983	2.6	2.3	2.1
	1984	1.5	1.1	0.9
	1985	.	.	.
	1986	.	.	.

See note on page 85. *Voir note page 85.* Véase nota pág. 85.

Table 3 *(cont.)*   **Tableau 3** *(suite)*   **Cuadro 3** *(cont.)*

Country / Pays / País (1)	Financial year / Exercice financier / Ejercicio financiero (2)	Receipts / Recettes / Ingresos (3)	Expenditure / Dépenses / Egresos — Total / Total / Total (4)	Benefits / Prestations / Prestaciones (5)	Country / Pays / País (1)	Financial year / Exercice financier / Ejercicio financiero (2)	Receipts / Recettes / Ingresos (3)	Expenditure / Dépenses / Egresos — Total / Total / Total (4)	Benefits / Prestations / Prestaciones (5)
Mauritius	1970	7.3	6.6	6.5	Tchad	1979-81	.	.	.
	1975	5.2	4.6	4.6		1983	.	.	.
	1981	3.1	1.9	1.8		1984	.	.	.
	1983	3.6	2.0	1.9		1985	.	.	.
	1984	.	.	.		1986	.	.	.
	1985	5.2	3.4	3.2	Togo	1972	2.2	1.5	1.4
	1986	5.0	3.3	3.2		1975	2.4	1.8	1.5
Mozambique	1981	0.25	0.09	0.02		1980	2.0	1.0	0.8
	1983	0.17	0.09	0.02		1983	2.5	1.1	0.8
	1984	0.21	0.13	0.13		1984	2.0	0.9	0.7
	1985	0.16	0.11	0.11		1985	2.9	1.2	0.9
	1986	0.14	0.09	0.09		1986	2.6	1.3	0.9
Niger	1970	1.3	1.2	1.1	Tunisie	1984	6.1	5.2	4.1
	1975	1.2	1.0	1.0		1985	6.8	6.0	4.4
	1980	0.7	0.3	0.3		1986	6.6	5.9	4.8
	1983	0.9	0.6	0.3	Uganda	1980	0.060	0.038	0.005
	1984	2.2	1.6	0.7		1983	0.036	0.012	0.001
	1985	2.2	1.6	0.7		1984	0.023	0.000	0.000
	1986	2.0	1.6	0.8		1985	.	.	.
Nigeria	1970	0.853	0.635	0.618		1986	.	.	.
	1981	0.145	0.019	0.007	Zaïre	1984	0.323	0.207	0.040
	1983	0.124	0.018	0.008		1985	0.500	0.282	0.063
	1984	0.125	0.019	0.009		1986	0.609	0.513	0.143
	1985	0.126	0.020	0.010	Zambia	1970	3.6	2.4	2.3
	1986	0.136	0.022	0.010		1975	6.7	5.0	4.8
Rwanda	1975	0.8	0.3	0.3		1980	2.3	1.0	0.7
	1981	0.9	0.1	0.1		1983	.	.	.
	1983	1.0	0.3	0.2		1984	2.1	0.7	0.3
	1984	1.1	0.3	0.2		1985	1.8	0.8	0.4
	1985	1.0	0.3	0.2		1986	1.5	0.6	0.2
	1986	1.3	0.3	0.2					
Sao Tomé-et-Principe	1981	.	.	.					
	1983	.	.	.					
	1984	.	.	.	AMERICA – AMÉRIQUE – AMERICA				
	1985	.	.	.					
	1986	.	.	.	Argentina	1975	7.6	6.8	6.6
Sénégal	1970	3.6	3.3	3.2		1980	9.7	9.3	8.9
	1975	2.9	2.3	2.1		1983	7.6	7.3	6.8
	1980	2.2	1.8	1.4		1984	8.2	7.3	6.8
	1983	0.8	0.7	0.5		1985	7.2	5.9	5.8
	1984	1.8	1.6	1.3		1986	6.7	6.1	5.9
	1985	1.8	1.5	1.3	Bahamas	1980	2.2	0.6	0.4
	1986	1.7	1.4	1.2		1983	2.8	1.1	0.9
Sudan	1980	0.4	0.1	0.0		1984	2.7	1.2	0.9
	1983	0.3	0.1	0.0		1985	3.2	1.2	0.9
	1984	0.4	0.1	0.0		1986	3.3	1.4	1.1
	1985	0.2	0.0	0.0	Barbados	1971	5.9	3.3	3.3
	1986	0.1	0.0	0.0		1975	6.6	4.9	4.8
Swaziland	1981	1.5	0.5	0.3		1980	3.8	2.2	2.0
	1983	1.9	0.8	0.4		1983	6.4	3.7	3.4
	1984	1.5	0.2	0.2		1984	6.0	4.1	3.8
	1985	1.4	0.4	0.2		1985	6.2	4.3	4.1
	1986	1.1	0.4	0.2		1986	5.6	4.9	4.5
Tanzania, United Rep. of	1980	0.7	0.2	0.1	Belize	1981	1.7	1.1	1.0
	1983	0.6	0.3	0.1		1983	3.3	1.6	1.4
	1984	0.9	0.2	0.1		1984	2.7	0.4	0.2
	1985	0.8	0.2	0.2		1985	2.7	0.6	0.3
	1986	0.8	0.3	0.1		1986	2.6	0.6	0.3

See note on page 85.   *Voir note page 85.*   Véase nota pág. 85.

Table 3 *(cont.)*   **Tableau 3** *(suite)*   **Cuadro 3** *(cont.)*

Country Pays País (1)	Financial year Exercice financier Ejercicio financiero (2)	Receipts Recettes Ingresos (3)	Expenditure Dépenses Egresos Total Total Total (4)	Benefits Prestations Prestaciones (5)	Country Pays País (1)	Financial year Exercice financier Ejercicio financiero (2)	Receipts Recettes Ingresos (3)	Expenditure Dépenses Egresos Total Total Total (4)	Benefits Prestations Prestaciones (5)
Bolivia	1972	3.4	3.2	2.9	Ecuador	1972	5.1	3.3	3.0
	1975	3.4	3.1	2.8		1974	4.5	3.0	2.8
	1980	2.9	3.0	2.4		1980	4.7	2.9	2.1
	1983	2.8	2.1	1.8		1983	4.9	3.6	2.7
	1984	3.5	3.9	3.1		1984	5.8	2.9	2.6
	1985	2.6	1.9	1.6		1985	6.5	2.8	2.5
						1986	7.3	3.0	2.7
Brasil	1970	5.9	5.9	4.9	El Salvador	1970	3.7	2.9	2.3
	1975	5.6	5.2	4.5		1975	3.9	3.3	2.4
	1980	6.8	5.3	5.1		1980	2.5	1.7	1.4
	1983	5.7	5.7	5.3		1983	2.8	1.7	1.5
	1984	5.1	5.1	4.6		1984	1.7	1.5	1.2
	1985	5.1	4.8	4.5		1985	1.6	1.3	1.1
	1986	5.4	5.0	4.6		1986	1.5	1.1	0.8
Canada	1970	16.5	14.4	14.1	Grenada	1981	1.61	1.58	1.58
	1975	15.4	13.8	13.5		1983	3.14	1.79	1.71
	1980	15.9	13.6	13.2		1984	4.20	1.89	1.76
	1983	18.2	16.5	15.9		1985	4.61	1.91	1.76
	1984	17.8	16.2	15.5		1986	4.35	1.72	1.57
	1985	18.4	16.2	15.6					
Colombia	1970	3.0	2.5	2.3	Guatemala	1970	2.2	2.1	1.9
	1975	3.6	3.1	2.8		1975	2.0	2.0	1.8
	1980	3.3	2.8	2.2		1980	1.7	1.2	1.0
	1983	2.3	2.2	2.0		1983	1.4	1.0	0.9
	1984	2.4	2.1	1.1		1984	1.5	1.1	0.9
	1985	2.3	2.0	1.1		1985	1.3	1.0	0.8
	1986	2.5	2.0	1.0		1986	1.3	0.8	0.7
Costa Rica	1970	4.8	3.4	2.9	Guyana	1972	5.8	3.7	3.1
	1975	6.8	5.1	4.6		1975	3.6	1.9	1.6
	1980	8.2	7.1	6.3		1980	6.1	1.3	0.9
	1983	10.5	6.1	5.4		1983	9.4	1.8	1.3
	1984	9.7	7.0	5.6		1984	9.2	1.8	1.3
	1985	10.2	7.4	6.1		1985	8.9	1.8	1.2
	1986	9.4	7.3	6.0		1986	9.0	2.8	2.2
Cuba	1980	11.7	11.7	11.3	Honduras	1970	2.0	1.7	1.7
	1983	11.5	11.5	11.1		1971	0.8	0.8	0.8
	1984	11.8	11.8	11.4		1981	1.3	0.9	0.7
	1985	12.5	12.5	12.0		1983	1.3	0.9	0.7
	1986	14.7	14.7	14.1		1984	2.1	1.1	0.9
						1985	2.1	1.1	0.9
						1986	2.2	1.0	0.9
Chile	1971	19.7	17.5	15.8	Jamaica	1970	4.1	2.8	2.2
	1975	13.9	11.0	10.1		1975	5.3	4.1	3.6
	1980	13.0	10.7	9.9		1980	2.9	1.4	1.3
	1983	16.7	14.3	13.0		1983	2.7	1.5	1.4
	1984	16.9	14.7	13.4		1984	2.9	1.6	1.5
	1985	17.8	13.5	12.3		1985	2.4	1.3	1.2
	1986	18.1	13.1	12.0		1986	2.5	1.3	1.2
Dominica	1980	3.1	0.8	0.4	México	1970	3.0	2.9	2.4
	1983	3.3	0.9	0.5		1974	2.8	2.5	2.1
	1984	3.7	1.3	0.9		1980	3.2	2.6	1.9
	1985	4.2	1.4	1.0		1983	3.0	2.6	1.8
	1986	4.0	1.4	1.0		1984	3.0	2.7	2.0
República Dominicana	1984	0.6	0.5	0.4		1985	3.0	2.5	2.0
	1985	0.4	0.4	0.3		1986	3.1	2.7	2.0
	1986	0.5	0.5	0.4					

See note on page 85.   *Voir note page 85.*   Véase nota pág. 85.

Table 3 *(cont.)* **Tableau 3** *(suite)* **Cuadro 3** *(cont.)*

Country / Pays / País (1)	Financial year / Exercice financier / Ejercicio financiero (2)	Receipts / Recettes / Ingresos (3)	Expenditure / Dépenses / Egresos — Total / Total / Total (4)	Expenditure — Benefits / Prestations / Prestaciones (5)	Country / Pays / País (1)	Financial year / Exercice financier / Ejercicio financiero (2)	Receipts / Recettes / Ingresos (3)	Expenditure — Total / Total / Total (4)	Expenditure — Benefits / Prestations / Prestaciones (5)
Panamá	1972	8.7	7.6	6.4	Cyprus	1970	3.7	3.2	3.1
	1975	9.7	7.5	6.5		1975	6.4	7.0	6.9
	1980	8.1	5.9	5.3		1980	4.5	3.6	3.6
	1983	10.3	7.7	6.7		1983	8.3	5.0	4.9
	1984	9.4	8.0	7.4		1984	8.2	4.6	4.6
	1985	9.2	8.0	7.5		1985	9.1	4.8	4.7
	1986	9.7	8.3	7.8		1986	8.9	5.2	5.1
Perú	1981	2.3	1.9	1.7	India	1970	3.1	2.0	2.0
	1983	1.7	1.9	1.6		1975	4.2	2.4	2.4
	1984	1.4	1.5	0.6		1980	2.7	1.6	1.5
	1985	1.6	1.4	0.6		1983	4.0	1.9	1.9
	1986	1.8	1.6	0.6		1984	3.6	1.7	1.7
St. Lucia	1981	2.4	0.5	0.2		1985	3.4	1.5	1.5
	1983	1.8	0.6	0.3		1986	.	.	.
	1984	2.6	0.8	0.5	Indonesia	1981	0.057	0.010	0.004
	1985	2.7	0.5	0.2		1983	0.076	0.022	0.006
	1986	3.4	0.8	0.5		1984	0.072	0.059	0.007
Trinidad and Tobago	1970	3.3	3.2	3.2		1985	0.090	0.084	0.008
	1975	3.4	2.5	2.4		1986	0.102	0.096	0.012
	1980	1.3	0.7	0.6	Iran, Islamic Rep. of	1981	2.7	1.1	1.0
	1983	3.6	2.4	2.2		1983	2.2	0.8	0.7
	1984	2.8	1.7	1.4		1984	1.9	0.8	0.3
	1985	2.8	1.7	1.4		1985	1.8	0.9	0.4
	1986	2.9	2.2	1.7		1986	1.9	0.9	0.4
United States	1970	11.0	9.3	8.7	Israel	1970	10.5	8.5	7.5
	1975	13.9	12.8	12.0		1975	13.1	12.0	10.4
	1980	13.8	12.3	11.8		1980	15.4	14.6	13.0
	1983	15.3	13.5	12.9		1983	16.6	15.5	13.0
	1984	14.5	12.5	11.9		1984	17.6	18.1	15.1
	1985	14.9	12.6	12.0		1985	15.1	15.2	12.7
	1986	15.4	12.5	12.0		1986	14.3	13.0	11.7
Uruguay	1975	11.3	10.7	8.4	Japan	1970	7.9	5.6	4.8
	1980	10.6	8.2	7.5		1975	11.8	8.9	7.9
	1983	12.5	11.0	10.2		1980	14.2	11.2	10.0
	1984	9.3	10.7	10.0		1983	15.3	12.3	11.2
	1985	9.1	8.9	8.3		1984	14.7	11.7	11.1
	1986	9.6	9.6	8.9		1985	15.2	11.7	11.1
Venezuela	1970	3.4	3.1	2.3		1986	15.3	12.2	11.5
	1975	4.5	3.9	3.7	Jordan	1980	0.494	0.032	0.003
	1980	1.7	1.3	1.1		1983	2.127	0.242	0.181
	1983	1.8	1.5	1.2		1984	2.700	0.474	0.243
	1984	1.3	1.2	1.0		1985	2.755	0.582	0.331
	1985	1.2	1.1	0.9		1986	3.285	0.584	0.452
	1986	1.5	1.3	1.1	Kuwait	1980	1.2	0.5	0.5
ASIA – ASIE – ASIA						1983	3.5	1.5	1.4
						1984	3.1	1.4	1.3
Bahrain	1978	2.1	0.3	0.3		1985	5.5	2.8	2.7
	1980	1.8	0.3	0.2		1986	8.0	3.5	3.4
	1983	2.8	0.5	0.3	Malaysia	1970	5.3	2.9	2.8
	1984	1.8	0.3	0.2		1975	5.3	3.0	2.8
	1985	2.3	0.4	0.3		1980	4.0	1.0	0.8
	1986	2.6	0.5	0.4		1983	6.3	1.8	1.7
Bangladesh	1975	0.273	0.258	0.258		1984	6.3	1.8	1.7
	1980	0.001	0.001	0.001		1985	7.4	2.0	1.9
	1983	0.008	0.004	0.004		1986	8.9	2.2	2.1
	1984	0.031	0.014	0.013					
	1985	0.027	0.012	0.012					
	1986	0.029	0.011	0.011					

See note on page 85. *Voir note page 85.* Véase nota pág. 85.

Table 3 *(cont.)* **Tableau 3** *(suite)* **Cuadro 3** *(cont.)*

Country / Pays / País	Financial year / Exercice financier / Ejercicio financiero	Receipts / Recettes / Ingresos	Expenditure / Dépenses / Egresos — Total / Total / Total	Benefits / Prestations / Prestaciones
(1)	(2)	(3)	(4)	(5)
Myanmar	1970	2.106	2.007	1.993
	1975	1.375	1.331	1.322
	1980	0.079	0.050	0.038
	1983	0.078	0.058	0.036
	1984	0.076	0.053	0.031
	1985	0.076	0.056	0.029
	1986	0.075	0.061	0.031
Pakistan	1965	0.947	0.947	0.947
	1980	0.092	0.041	0.022
	1983	0.619	0.538	0.526
	1984	0.713	0.647	0.631
	1985	1.136	1.058	1.046
	1986	0.853	0.769	0.757
Philippines	1970	1.8	1.0	0.9
	1978	1.8	0.8	0.6
	1980	1.7	0.7	0.5
	1983	1.8	0.7	0.6
	1984	1.5	0.6	0.5
	1985	1.7	0.6	0.5
	1986	1.7	0.7	0.6
Qatar	1984	0.305	0.305	0.305
	1985	0.355	0.355	0.355
	1986	0.438	0.438	0.438
Singapore	1970	5.4	2.8	2.8
	1975	9.2	3.0	3.0
	1980	11.6	3.7	3.4
	1983	15.6	8.0	5.0
	1984	17.2	12.3	9.0
	1985	20.0	13.0	9.0
	1986	17.5	14.7	10.5
Sri Lanka	1970	4.0	3.1	2.7
	1975	3.2	2.1	2.1
	1980	3.1	1.7	1.6
	1983	4.0	2.3	2.2
	1984	5.1	2.2	2.1
	1985	6.0	2.5	2.4
	1986	6.1	2.3	2.3
Rép. arabe syrienne	1984	2.0	0.9	0.9
	1985	1.9	0.9	0.9
	1986	1.7	0.8	0.8
Thailand	1980	0.037	0.015	0.014
	1983	0.198	0.174	0.173
	1984	0.025	0.026	0.025
	1985	0.026	0.024	0.022
	1986	0.026	0.022	0.020

EUROPE – EUROPE – EUROPA

Countries with a market economy – Pays à économie de marché –
Países con economía de mercado

Country / Pays / País	Financial year	Receipts	Expenditure Total	Benefits
Austria	1970	18.8	18.5	17.7
	1975	20.5	20.2	19.3
	1980	22.6	22.5	21.4
	1983	25.1	24.3	23.5
	1984	25.8	24.9	24.0
	1985	25.9	25.2	24.3
	1986	25.9	25.4	24.4

Country / Pays / País	Financial year / Exercice financier / Ejercicio financiero	Receipts / Recettes / Ingresos	Expenditure / Dépenses / Egresos — Total / Total / Total	Benefits / Prestations / Prestaciones
(1)	(2)	(3)	(4)	(5)
Belgique	1970	18.9	18.1	16.6
	1975	24.9	24.0	22.5
	1980	25.7	26.2	24.7
	1983	28.7	28.5	26.9
	1984	27.9	27.2	25.8
	1985	27.1	26.4	25.1
	1986	26.8	26.4	24.9
Denmark	1970	15.2	14.8	14.5
	1975	20.7	20.2	19.7
	1980	27.6	26.9	26.2
	1983	29.1	28.1	27.3
	1984	27.2	26.2	25.4
	1985	26.8	25.9	25.2
	1986	27.0	26.3	25.5
España	1975	12.2	11.7	11.0
	1980	15.8	16.0	15.3
	1983	18.0	18.1	17.5
	1984	18.5	18.1	17.3
	1985	18.6	18.4	17.7
	1986	18.4	18.1	17.2
Finland	1970	13.7	12.5	12.0
	1975	18.0	15.7	15.1
	1980	21.0	18.0	17.3
	1983	22.5	20.6	19.7
	1984	22.8	20.8	20.1
	1985	24.3	22.1	21.3
	1986	25.1	22.8	22.1
France	1970	15.1	15.1	13.9
	1975	24.2	23.9	20.7
	1980	27.1	26.3	25.0
	1983	29.7	28.9	27.5
	1984	29.7	29.0	27.5
	1985	29.2	28.7	27.3
	1986	28.4	28.6	27.2
Germany, Fed. Rep. of	1970	17.8	17.1	16.1
	1975	23.5	23.7	22.7
	1980	24.2	24.0	23.1
	1983	24.2	24.3	23.6
	1984	24.0	24.1	23.4
	1985	24.0	23.8	23.2
	1986	23.8	23.4	22.7
Grèce	1970	12.0	10.8	10.3
	1975	12.1	10.8	10.2
	1980	14.2	12.2	11.6
	1983	18.5	17.5	16.5
	1984	18.7	18.5	17.3
	1985	18.9	19.5	18.3
Iceland	1984	7.0	6.9	6.8
	1985	7.4	7.3	7.1
	1986	7.4	7.2	7.1
Ireland	1970	10.4	10.3	9.9
	1975	18.9	19.0	18.3
	1980	20.3	20.1	19.1
	1983	22.8	23.1	21.9
	1984	22.2	22.3	21.3
	1985	22.8	22.8	21.8
	1986	23.2	23.2	22.1

See note on page 85. *Voir note page 85.* Véase nota pág. 85.

Table 3 *(cont.)*   Tableau 3 *(suite)*   Cuadro 3 *(cont.)*

Country / Pays / País (1)	Financial year / Exercice financier / Ejercicio financiero (2)	Receipts / Recettes / Ingresos (3)	Expenditure / Dépenses / Egresos — Total / Total / Total (4)	Benefits / Prestations / Prestaciones (5)
Italie	1970	14.5	14.1	13.0
	1975	16.5	19.2	17.4
	1980	18.7	18.8	17.1
	1983	22.4	21.9	20.5
	1984	10.1	11.3	10.0
	1985	10.1	11.2	10.0
	1986	10.1	11.2	10.0
Luxembourg	1970	16.6	14.9	14.4
	1975	23.0	21.1	20.3
	1980	26.9	24.5	23.5
	1983	27.5	25.4	23.6
	1984	26.3	24.2	23.1
	1985	26.2	23.4	22.5
	1986	27.0	23.4	22.7
Malta	1970	7.0	7.5	7.4
	1975	11.4	11.3	9.9
	1980	13.4	11.1	11.0
	1983	15.3	14.7	14.6
	1984	14.8	20.0	18.8
	1985	14.8	19.0	18.0
	1986	14.0	18.4	17.3
Netherlands	1970	22.5	18.9	18.3
	1975	30.1	25.5	24.7
	1980	33.8	28.3	27.3
	1983	36.7	31.4	30.5
	1984	35.4	30.6	29.7
	1985	34.2	29.1	28.2
	1986	32.7	28.6	27.7
Norway	1970	16.3	15.5	14.8
	1975	20.3	18.5	17.8
	1980	20.9	20.2	19.7
	1983	22.7	21.8	21.3
	1984	29.5	28.7	28.4
	1985	29.1	28.3	28.0
	1986	30.7	29.8	29.5
Portugal	1970	7.6	5.7	4.9
	1975	12.3	11.1	10.3
	1980	10.1	9.7	8.7
	1983	9.9	10.1	9.5
	1984	10.6	10.2	9.7
	1985	10.4	10.1	9.6
	1986	11.2	10.4	9.9
Suisse	1970	11.6	10.1	9.5
	1975	15.8	15.1	14.3
	1980	15.0	13.7	12.8
	1983	14.9	14.3	13.2
	1984	15.5	15.0	13.8
	1985	15.4	14.7	13.5
	1986	15.5	14.7	13.4
Sweden	1970	23.2	18.6	18.2
	1975	28.2	25.0	24.5
	1980	35.0	31.9	31.1
	1983	35.8	33.3	32.5
	1984	33.5	30.4	29.4
	1985	33.1	30.7	29.5
	1986	34.2	31.3	30.1

Country / Pays / País (1)	Financial year / Exercice financier / Ejercicio financiero (2)	Receipts / Recettes / Ingresos (3)	Expenditure / Dépenses / Egresos — Total / Total / Total (4)	Benefits / Prestations / Prestaciones (5)
Turquie	1970	4.5	3.2	3.0
	1975	6.1	3.4	2.9
	1980	5.0	4.2	4.1
	1983	4.8	3.8	3.6
	1984	4.9	3.9	3.7
	1985	4.7	3.9	3.8
	1986	4.5	3.6	3.5
United Kingdom	1970	14.2	13.7	12.8
	1975	18.1	17.1	16.0
	1980	19.0	18.1	17.2
	1983	21.1	20.3	19.4
	1984	21.3	20.6	19.6
	1985	20.8	20.3	19.4
	1986	21.1	20.4	19.4

EUROPE – EUROPE – EUROPA

Countries with a centrally planned economy – Pays à économie planifiée – Países con economía centralmente planificada

Country / Pays / País (1)	Financial year / Exercice financier / Ejercicio financiero (2)	Receipts / Recettes / Ingresos (3)	Expenditure / Dépenses / Egresos — Total / Total / Total (4)	Benefits / Prestations / Prestaciones (5)
RSS de Biélorussie	1970	.	.	.
	1975	.	.	.
	1980	.	.	.
	1983	.	.	.
	1984	.	.	.
	1985	.	.	.
Bulgarie	1970	13.9	13.7	13.4
	1975	16.4	16.0	14.9
	1980	12.2	12.2	12.2
	1983	12.6	12.6	12.6
	1984	13.4	11.8	11.8
	1985	13.1	12.7	12.6
	1986	13.8	13.4	13.4
Czechoslovakia	1970	18.0	18.0	17.9
	1975	17.2	17.2	17.1
	1980	18.9	18.9	18.9
	1983	20.9	20.9	20.8
	1984	20.3	20.3	20.2
	1985	20.9	20.9	20.8
	1986	21.5	21.5	21.4
German Democratic Rep.	1970	12.3	12.3	12.2
	1975	14.3	14.3	14.2
	1980	16.0	16.0	16.0
	1983	14.8	14.8	14.8
	1984	13.8	13.8	13.7
	1985	13.6	13.6	13.5
	1986	14.2	14.2	14.1
Hongrie	1970	10.9	11.0	10.9
	1975	14.9	14.9	14.7
	1980	18.3	18.3	18.2
	1983	18.7	18.7	18.7
	1984	15.0	15.0	14.9
	1985	16.1	15.7	15.6
	1986	17.0	16.2	16.1
Pologne	1984	20.5	17.5	17.4
	1985	20.7	17.0	16.8
	1986	21.0	17.1	17.0

See note on page 85.   *Voir note page 85.*   Véase nota pág. 85.

Table 3 *(concl.)*　**Tableau 3** *(fin)*　**Cuadro 3** *(fin)*

Country / Pays / País (1)	Financial year / Exercice financier / Ejercicio financiero (2)	Receipts / Recettes / Ingresos (3)	Expenditure / Dépenses / Egresos — Total / Total / Total (4)	Expenditure / Dépenses / Egresos — Benefits / Prestations / Prestaciones (5)	Country / Pays / País (1)	Financial year / Exercice financier / Ejercicio financiero (2)	Receipts / Recettes / Ingresos (3)	Expenditure / Dépenses / Egresos — Total / Total / Total (4)	Expenditure / Dépenses / Egresos — Benefits / Prestations / Prestaciones (5)
RSS d'Ukraine	1970	11.9	11.9	11.9	*OCEANIA – OCÉANIE – OCEANIA*				
	1975	13.8	13.8	13.8	Australia	1970	8.5	8.0	7.7
	1980	15.5	15.5	15.5		1975	11.0	10.3	10.1
	1983	15.4	15.4	15.4		1980	12.4	11.4	10.9
	1984	15.5	15.5	15.5		1983	13.4	12.1	11.6
	1985	16.2	16.2	16.2		1984	9.3	9.5	9.4
	1986	17.3	17.3	17.3		1985	9.8	10.0	9.9
	1986	.	.	.		1986	9.3	9.2	9.1
URSS	1970	12.1	12.1	12.1	Fiji	1975	5.2	2.9	2.4
	1975	13.6	13.6	13.6		1980	5.9	2.1	1.2
	1980	14.2	14.2	14.2		1983	7.5	2.3	2.2
	1983	14.1	14.1	14.1		1984	7.0	1.9	1.8
	1984	14.3	14.3	14.3		1985	8.5	2.2	2.0
	1985	14.7	14.7	14.7		1986	7.7	2.4	2.2
	1986	15.5	15.5	15.5	New Zealand	1970	11.2	10.4	9.9
Yugoslavia	1970	12.5	11.4	10.7		1975	15.6	14.5	14.3
	1981	11.3	11.1	10.0		1980	18.2	17.7	17.3
	1983	10.8	10.7	9.9		1983	18.3	17.6	17.3
	1984	9.9	9.5	8.6		1984	17.4	17.1	16.7
	1985	10.1	9.7	8.7		1985	18.2	18.0	17.6
	1986	11.9	11.7	10.5		1986	18.1	17.9	17.4
					Solomon Islands	1981	2.7	0.4	0.3
						1983	4.3	0.8	0.7
						1984	4.2	1.6	0.7
						1985	4.6	2.1	0.9
						1986	5.5	2.7	1.1

For general footnotes, see table 1.   For further notes on the corresponding denominators, consult footnotes of appendix table 1.

Pour les notes de caractère général, se reporter au tableau 1.   Pour des précisions sur l'agrégat utilisé comme dénominateur (produit intérieur brut, produit matériel net), consulter les notes du tableau 1 de l'annexe.

Véanse las notas generales del cuadro 1.   En lo que concierne a otras notas sobre los denominadores correspondientes, consúltense las notas del cuadro anexo 1.

4. Average annual social security receipts and expenditure per head of population
(in national currency units)

4. Moyennes annuelles des recettes et des dépenses de la sécurité sociale par habitant
(en unités monétaires nationales)

4. Ingresos y egresos anuales medios de la seguridad social por habitante
(en unidades monetarias nacionales)

Country and currency unit / Pays et unité monétaire / País y unidad monetaria	Financial year / Exercice financier / Ejercicio financiero	Per head of total population / Par habitant (population totale) / Por habitante (población total)			Per head of population between 15 and 64 years of age / Par habitant de 15 à 64 ans / Por habitante entre 15 y 64 años de edad		
		Receipts / Recettes / Ingresos	Expenditure Total / Dépenses Total / Egresos Total	Benefits / Prestations / Prestaciones	Receipts / Recettes / Ingresos	Expenditure Total / Dépenses Total / Egresos Total	Benefits / Prestations / Prestaciones
(1)	(2)	(3)	(4)	(5)	(6)	(7)	(8)
AFRICA – AFRIQUE – AFRICA							
Bénin (Franc CFA)	1970	672.0	654.8	615.0	1 296.3	1 263.3	1 186.3
	1975	944.1	891.9	815.9	1 829.5	1 728.4	1 581.1
	1981	1 607.2	347.2	239.1	3 157.1	2 646.4	2 433.9
	1983	1 840.1	629.4	548.0	3 633.4	3 217.5	3 056.8
	1984	932.4	861.2	620.9	1 845.5	1 704.6	1 228.9
	1985	982.2	876.4	636.7	1 949.4	1 739.4	1 263.8
	1986	1 088.7	936.9	614.5	2 166.6	1 864.5	1 222.8
Burkina Faso (Franc CFA)	1975	515.0	410.1	384.5	964.0	767.6	719.8
	1980	704.9	287.1	176.3	1 321.8	538.4	330.7
	1983	1 424.2	889.3	617.6	2 669.9	1 667.1	1 157.8
	1984	1 035.9	258.3	255.6	1 942.1	484.3	479.3
	1985	1 090.7	276.8	274.3	2 044.4	518.9	514.1
	1986	1 000.6	254.9	252.7	1 876.4	478.0	473.9
Burundi (Franc burundais)	1978	83.5	41.2	28.5	155.4	76.7	53.1
	1980	115.3	64.7	47.5	217.1	121.9	89.5
	1983	199.5	112.6	87.8	381.1	215.1	167.7
	1984	209.3	124.8	85.3	401.5	239.5	163.6
	1985	236.7	140.5	105.5	456.2	270.9	203.4
	1986	281.8	192.1	157.9	544.9	371.4	305.3
Kenya (Shilling)	1970	30.2	19.5	19.0	64.5	41.6	40.5
	1975	59.0	36.9	35.7	132.3	82.8	80.1
	1981	28.3	2.2	1.4	61.2	4.8	3.1
	1983	31.9	2.9	2.1	69.4	6.4	4.6
	1984	85.9	9.9	8.1	187.3	21.6	17.8
	1985	91.4	12.5	10.8	199.9	27.5	23.6
	1986	78.4	12.6	10.7	171.8	27.7	23.6
Madagascar (Franc malgache)	1981	886.3	506.4	506.4	1 674.1	956.5	956.5
	1983	1 014.4	703.0	703.0	1 924.5	1 333.8	1 333.8
	1984	846.9	860.4	742.2	1 609.0	1 634.6	1 409.9
	1985	892.9	905.7	776.3	1 698.9	1 723.3	1 477.0
	1986	975.4	955.2	831.0	1 860.4	1 821.9	1 584.9
Mali (Franc CFA)	1972	315.8	330.5	306.3	602.7	630.6	584.5
	1975	374.5	362.4	320.2	666.9	645.3	570.2
	1980	320.0	340.8	199.0	624.2	664.9	388.2
	1983	588.1	568.6	369.9	1 150.8	1 112.7	723.9
	1984	800.5	819.6	605.0	1 567.7	1 605.3	1 184.9
	1985	829.1	906.7	620.5	1 625.8	1 778.0	1 216.7
	1986	963.3	939.1	597.8	1 891.2	1 843.7	1 173.6

(Left page)

Cameroun (Franc CFA)

	787.3	728.3	676.3	1 430.3	1 323.2	1 228.6
1970	787.3	728.3	676.3	1 430.3	1 323.2	1 228.6
1981	2 722.9	1 242.4	1 242.4	5 266.1	2 402.9	2 402.9
1983	4 471.7	1 575.3	1 575.2	8 542.8	3 009.5	3 009.3
1984	3 889.4	1 394.5	1 394.5	7 453.5	2 672.4	2 672.4
1985	4 955.4	1 531.2	1 531.2	9 526.6	2 943.8	2 943.8
1986	5 428.8	1 900.0	1 900.0	1 044.1	3 654.4	3 654.4

Cap-Vert (Escudo)

1983	711.1	301.8	194.7	1 386.9	588.6	379.8
1984	993.9	372.9	246.4	1 905.0	714.8	472.3
1985	1 234.5	484.1	322.5	2 329.5	913.5	608.5
1986	1 474.5	620.3	386.7	2 761.7	1 161.8	724.2

Rép. centrafricaine (Franc CFA)

1981	889.7	721.1	356.6	1 636.6	1 326.6	655.7
1983	928.2	781.1	435.5	1 719.5	1 447.0	806.8
1984	1 091.3	1 175.3	817.2	2 028.8	2 184.9	1 519.2
1985	1 182.5	1 218.5	751.9	2 206.0	2 273.2	1 402.7
1986	1 660.2	2 025.5	924.0	3 105.1	3 788.3	1 728.3

Côte d'Ivoire (Franc CFA)

1981	3 022.8	1 678.5	986.4	6 126.7	3 402.2	1 999.3
1983	3 131.7	1 756.7	1 376.5	6 375.8	3 576.5	2 802.4
1984	2 892.9	2 233.8	1 665.2	5 902.9	4 558.0	3 397.8
1985	3 747.5	2 269.1	1 588.4	7 664.8	4 641.0	3 248.7
1986	3 768.4	2 139.4	1 703.9	7 724.8	4 385.5	3 492.8

Egypt (Pound)

1984	49.5	19.3	18.1	90.2	35.2	32.9
1985	57.3	20.3	19.0	104.4	37.0	34.6
1986	66.9	23.3	21.8	120.6	41.9	39.2

Ethiopia (Birr)

1972	3.1	2.4	2.4	5.9	4.6	4.5
1975	4.2	3.7	3.7	8.1	7.2	7.1

Gabon (Franc CFA)

1980	23 490.7	22 706.3	16 760.8	38 219.8	36 943.5	27 270.2
1983	43 408.5	36 527.9	29 607.9	71 797.1	60 416.7	48 971.0
1984	39 412.0	35 395.2	28 311.9	65 502.6	64 032.1	47 054.3
1985	42 311.4	38 380.3	30 794.1	70 590.5	68 711.0	51 375.6
1986	36 974.6	41 414.9	33 439.3	61 344.2		55 478.9

Guinée (Syli)

1981	29.1	8.3	6.6	53.8	15.4	12.2
1983	28.7	7.7	5.7	53.0	14.2	10.6
1984						
1985	26.3	23.1	20.7	48.8	42.7	38.4
1986	47.5	43.1	36.7	88.3	80.1	68.2

Guinée-Bissau (Peso)

1981	41.7	48.8	1.7	75.3	88.0	3.0
1983	32.3	55.3	1.9	58.5	100.1	3.4
1984	65.7	28.1	15.6	119.2	51.0	28.3
1985	93.3	51.8	31.1	169.5	94.2	56.6
1986	152.1	68.2	40.6	277.1	124.2	74.0

(Right page)

Maroc (Dirham)

	57.0	59.0	65.6	27.1	28.1	31.2
1970	57.0	59.0	65.6	27.1	28.1	31.2
1975	65.5	68.1	81.4	32.2	33.5	40.0
1980	68.2	76.4	136.8	35.9	40.2	72.1
1983	68.1	73.0	129.5	36.3	39.0	69.2
1984	149.8	157.8	225.8	80.4	84.7	121.2
1985	161.0	169.6	279.2	86.8	91.4	150.6
1986	192.2	203.3	296.9	104.3	110.3	161.1

Mauritanie (Ouguiya)

1970	323.6	341.2	372.5	170.0	179.2	195.6
1981	930.2	1 016.5	1 229.9	494.0	539.9	653.2
1983	1 064.2	1 192.1	1 343.3	563.8	631.6	711.7
1984	454.8	560.2	733.0	240.6	296.3	387.8
1985	414.1	494.8	802.0	218.9	261.5	423.9
1986	498.7	609.4	610.8	262.9	321.3	322.1

Mauritius (Rupee)

1970	160.7	164.1	181.0	81.9	83.7	92.3
1975	309.4	312.6	349.4	176.6	178.4	199.4
1981	307.4	320.6	542.8	187.3	195.3	330.7
1983	385.6	404.5	708.8	249.4	261.6	458.5
1984						
1985	801.6	849.6	1 291.9	528.4	560.0	851.6
1986	952.3	1 001.6	1 521.8	603.7	635.0	964.8

Mozambique (Metical)

1981	2.2	12.9	34.8	1.2	6.9	18.5
1983	2.5	11.8	22.0	1.3	6.3	11.7
1984	20.1	20.1	32.5	10.7	10.7	17.3
1985	22.0	22.0	32.4	11.7	11.7	17.2
1986	19.2	19.2	30.3	10.2	10.2	16.0

Niger (Franc CFA)

1970	600.2	634.8	721.3	310.2	328.1	372.8
1975	747.1	791.6	924.1	380.5	403.1	470.6
1980	505.5	600.7	1 440.6	252.5	300.1	719.7
1983	615.1	1 551.2	2 071.9	308.3	777.6	1 038.6
1984	1 487.9	3 565.0	4 681.7	739.9	1 772.9	2 328.2
1985	1 402.7	3 467.8	4 727.8	696.5	1 722.0	2 347.6
1986	1 572.2	3 209.2	4 123.6	780.4	1 592.9	2 046.7

Nigeria (Naira)

1970	1.217	1.251	1.680	0.616	0.633	0.850
1981	0.086	0.224	1.730	0.043	0.111	0.855
1983	0.117	0.256	1.783	0.058	0.127	0.881
1984	0.134	0.298	1.920	0.066	0.147	0.948
1985	0.164	0.338	2.120	0.081	0.167	1.046
1986	0.162	0.361	2.233	0.080	0.178	1.101

Rwanda (Franc rwandais)

1975	68.3	78.4	211.5	33.9	38.9	105.1
1981	36.9	68.4	428.0	18.0	33.4	208.9
1983	79.9	137.1	513.3	38.9	66.8	250.2
1984	88.9	150.7	602.2	43.3	73.4	293.2
1985	105.7	172.7	604.1	51.4	84.0	293.8
1986	123.9	190.7	691.5	60.2	92.8	336.4

Sao Tomé-et-Principe (Dobra)

1981	429.0	429.0	1 981.1	207.1	207.1	956.4
1983	437.6	437.6	1 841.8	214.0	214.0	900.8
1984	466.7	466.7	1 691.3	226.0	226.0	818.9
1985	536.6	536.6	1 752.2	263.3	263.3	859.9
1986	483.2	483.2	947.1	236.8	236.8	464.1

See note on page 95.   Voir note page 95.   Véase nota pág. 95.

Table 4 (cont.)   **Tableau 4** (suite)   **Cuadro 4** (cont.)

Country and currency unit / Pays et unité monétaire / País y unidad monetaria	Financial year / Exercice financier / Ejercicio financiero	Per head of total population / Par habitant (population totale) / Por habitante (población total) — Receipts / Recettes / Ingresos	Expenditure / Dépenses / Egresos — Total	Benefits / Prestations / Prestaciones — Total	Per head of population between 15 and 64 years of age / Par habitant de 15 à 64 ans / Por habitante entre 15 y 64 años de edad — Receipts / Recettes / Ingresos	Expenditure / Dépenses / Egresos — Total	Benefits / Prestations / Prestaciones — Total
(1)	(2)	(3)	(4)	(5)	(6)	(7)	(8)
Belize (Dollar)	1981	42.4	27.1	24.8	63.9	40.8	37.4
	1983	72.9	36.0	32.1	109.8	54.2	48.3
	1984	65.3	10.2	5.8	98.9	15.4	8.8
	1985	62.8	13.2	7.3	94.7	20.0	11.1
	1986	65.7	14.0	7.2	99.4	21.2	11.0
Bolivia (Peso)	1972	111.3	104.3	94.1	207.7	194.5	175.5
	1975	346.1	313.4	284.6	646.3	585.3	531.4
	1980	647.9	655.9	527.1	1 215.9	1 230.9	989.3
	1983	6 794.6	5 208.6	4 415.6	12 786.3	9 801.7	8 309.3
	1984	121 572.0	132 835.0	107 381.0	228 973.0	250 186.0	202 245.0
	1985	11 002 801.0	8 237 463.0	6 756 803.0	20 737 909.0	15 525 843.0	12 735 118.0
Brasil (Cruzado)	1970	0.1	0.1	0.1	0.2	0.2	0.1
	1975	0.5	0.5	0.4	1.0	0.9	0.8
	1980	6.7	5.2	5.0	11.6	9.0	8.6
	1983	52.5	52.0	48.4	89.3	88.4	82.2
	1984	152.0	150.6	136.4	257.3	255.0	230.9
	1985	529.0	500.2	468.2	892.3	843.7	789.8
	1986	1 457.1	1 334.4	1 223.5	2 451.0	2 244.6	2 058.0
Canada (Dollar)	1970	684.5	596.3	584.7	1 117.0	973.1	954.1
	1975	1 150.6	1 036.1	1 011.5	1 792.2	1 613.8	1 575.4
	1980	2 032.3	1 741.1	1 687.0	2 998.1	2 568.5	2 488.7
	1983	2 945.6	2 658.3	2 561.2	4 334.9	3 912.1	3 769.2
	1984	3 128.4	2 844.5	2 718.1	4 600.4	4 182.9	3 997.0
	1985	3 451.9	3 041.2	2 926.4	5 072.0	4 468.5	4 299.9
Colombia (Peso)	1970	194.7	162.5	150.3	376.8	314.5	290.8
	1975	621.8	525.2	482.0	1 147.0	968.7	889.0
	1980	2 024.2	1 706.3	1 323.6	3 547.1	2 990.0	2 319.4
	1983	2 585.8	2 472.4	2 184.0	4 437.6	4 242.8	3 748.0
	1984	3 234.4	2 928.0	1 523.4	6 172.7	5 588.0	2 907.4
	1985	4 039.7	3 463.1	1 869.4	6 838.9	5 862.8	3 164.7
	1986	5 819.9	4 585.3	2 367.4	9 827.7	7 742.9	3 997.8

Country and currency unit / Pays et unité monétaire / País y unidad monetaria	Financial year / Exercice financier / Ejercicio financiero	Per head of total population / Par habitant (population totale) / Por habitante (población total) — Receipts / Recettes / Ingresos	Expenditure / Dépenses / Egresos — Total	Benefits / Prestations / Prestaciones — Total	Per head of population between 15 and 64 years of age / Par habitant de 15 à 64 ans / Por habitante entre 15 y 64 años de edad — Receipts / Recettes / Ingresos	Expenditure / Dépenses / Egresos — Total	Benefits / Prestations / Prestaciones — Total
(1)	(2)	(3)	(4)	(5)	(6)	(7)	(8)
Sénégal (Franc CFA)	1970	2 051.7	1 851.7	1 803.2	3 833.1	3 459.5	3 368.8
	1975	2 405.5	1 947.8	1 740.9	4 445.3	3 599.6	3 217.3
	1980	2 438.0	1 968.0	1 550.7	4 700.4	3 794.4	2 989.8
	1983	1 219.7	963.4	760.9	2 394.0	1 890.9	1 493.4
	1984	2 933.4	2 479.8	2 075.3	5 564.3	4 703.9	3 936.5
	1985	3 305.4	2 703.1	2 272.5	6 275.7	5 132.2	4 314.6
	1986	3 340.4	2 846.5	2 412.7	6 345.2	5 406.9	4 582.9
Sudan (Pound)	1980	1.273	0.177	0.049	2.431	0.337	0.094
	1983	1.617	0.367	0.132	3.099	0.704	0.252
	1984	2.622	0.387	0.203	5.032	0.743	0.390
	1985	2.479	0.426	0.220	4.766	0.819	0.423
	1986	1.874	0.378	0.187	3.602	0.727	0.359
Swaziland (Lilangeni)	1981	13.1	4.6	2.5	26.0	9.2	5.1
	1983	18.3	7.5	3.9	36.3	15.0	7.9
	1984	15.4	2.2	2.2	30.6	4.4	4.4
	1985	15.8	5.1	2.4	31.6	10.2	4.8
	1986	15.9	5.8	2.6	31.8	11.5	5.2
Tanzania, United Rep. of (Shilling)	1980	16.8	4.4	3.3	34.0	8.9	6.7
	1983	19.3	9.8	3.1	39.3	20.0	6.4
	1984	39.4	8.8	5.6	80.1	18.0	11.5
	1985	42.9	13.5	9.1	87.4	27.5	18.6
	1986	57.2	21.7	10.3	116.8	44.3	21.0
Tchad (Franc CFA)	1979–81		41.8	9.8		77.0	18.0
	1983	47.5	62.1	14.9	87.6	114.6	27.6
	1984	136.5	121.3	57.8	251.8	224.3	106.8
	1985	332.5	163.6	67.7	614.4	303.1	125.5
	1986	237.6			440.1		

AFRICA (continued) — AFRIQUE — ÁFRICA

Country	Year	(1)	(2)	(3)	(4)	(5)	(6)
Togo (Franc CFA)	1972	951.5	653.4	584.7	1 784.0	1 225.0	1 096.1
	1975	1 356.5	1 028.7	862.3	2 563.5	1 944.0	1 629.6
	1980	1 884.1	919.7	718.2	3 589.8	1 752.4	1 368.3
	1983	2 514.5	1 146.0	828.4	4 819.8	2 196.6	1 588.0
	1984	2 847.1	1 223.1	935.9	5 465.9	2 348.2	1 796.7
	1985	3 220.5	1 363.3	1 023.3	6 192.2	2 621.4	1 967.5
	1986	3 140.5	1 529.9	1 081.5	6 053.0	2 948.8	2 084.5
Tunisie (Dinar)	1984	53.9	46.4	36.8	96.1	82.6	65.5
	1985	64.5	57.0	42.1	114.1	100.9	74.4
	1986	61.9	55.2	45.0	108.9	97.0	79.1
Uganda (Shilling)	1980	6.258	4.002	0.572	12.464	7.970	1.139
	1983	11.807	3.880	0.221	23.863	7.843	0.447
	1984	10.069	0.142	0.142	20.365	0.288	0.288
	1985	9.420	0.129	0.129	19.068	0.260	0.260
	1986	4.682	0.033	0.033	9.494	0.066	0.066
Zaïre (Zaïre)	1984	10.7	6.8	1.3	20.9	13.4	2.5
	1985	23.7	13.4	2.9	46.2	26.1	5.8
	1986	39.3	33.1	9.2	76.5	64.5	18.0
Zambia (Kwacha)	1970	10.7	7.2	6.8	21.1	14.2	13.5
	1975	21.3	15.8	15.1	42.5	31.5	30.1
	1980	11.8	5.0	3.5	23.5	10.0	7.1
	1983			.			
	1984	14.5	5.2	2.4	30.5	11.0	5.1
	1985	17.5	7.6	3.9	36.9	16.1	8.2
	1986	23.6	8.9	3.6	49.8	18.8	7.6

AMERICA – AMÉRIQUE – AMERICA

Country	Year	(1)	(2)	(3)	(4)	(5)	(6)
Argentina (Austral)	1975	0.000	0.000	0.000	0.001	0.001	0.001
	1980	0.097	0.093	0.089	0.157	0.151	0.144
	1983	1.745	1.690	1.569	2.859	2.769	2.570
	1984	14.3	12.7	11.9	23.6	21.0	19.7
	1985	92.6	76.5	74.5	153.2	126.5	123.2
	1986	160.9	145.0	141.3	266.6	240.2	234.1
Bahamas (Dollar)	1980	155.1	38.6	25.7	278.5	69.4	46.2
	1983	216.5	88.6	68.2	367.4	150.4	115.8
	1984	237.9	103.3	77.8	394.7	171.4	129.2
	1985	308.0	119.0	92.1	503.3	194.5	150.6
	1986	311.6	134.5	101.6	500.4	216.0	163.2
Barbados (Dollar)	1971	79.7	44.3	43.8	146.1	81.2	80.3
	1975	219.8	161.8	158.7	388.6	286.2	280.6
	1980	265.5	151.3	141.6	443.8	252.8	236.7
	1983	539.8	311.9	289.2	879.8	508.3	471.3
	1984	547.9	375.1	350.4	890.8	609.9	569.7
	1985	586.2	413.1	386.6	944.6	665.7	622.9
	1986	584.8	511.7	475.5	936.4	819.4	761.5
Costa Rica (Colón)	1970	182.1	127.8	109.9	358.6	251.7	216.4
	1975	584.6	440.1	392.1	1 068.6	804.4	716.7
	1980	1 518.1	1 303.9	1 157.2	2 633.9	2 262.2	2 007.8
	1983	5 563.9	3 222.0	2 856.0	9 487.6	5 494.1	4 870.0
	1984	6 510.6	4 741.8	3 810.0	11 043.0	8 042.8	6 462.4
	1985	8 110.3	5 916.0	4 862.0	13 676.5	9 976.2	8 198.9
	1986	8 607.8	6 654.4	5 440.5	14 499.3	11 209.0	9 164.2
Cuba (Peso)	1980	118.2	118.2	114.2	192.5	192.5	186.1
	1983	150.7	150.7	145.6	234.1	234.1	226.2
	1984	161.8	161.8	155.8	247.5	247.5	238.4
	1985	172.1	172.1	165.7	259.4	259.4	249.7
	1986	185.0	185.0	178.3	276.1	276.1	266.1
Chile (Peso)	1971	2.6	2.3	2.1	4.5	4.0	3.6
	1975	480.7	380.3	350.1	810.6	641.4	590.4
	1980	12 557.2	10 367.5	9 584.8	20 580.9	16 992.0	15 709.3
	1983	22 235.9	18 997.9	17 296.6	35 847.2	30 627.2	27 884.5
	1984	26 861.0	23 337.5	21 267.6	43 072.2	37 422.3	34 103.1
	1985	37 787.1	28 615.5	26 080.7	60 262.5	45 635.7	41 593.2
	1986	47 716.8	34 485.2	31 728.6	75 946.4	54 886.9	50 499.4
Dominica (EC Dollar)	1980	67.2	17.0	7.7	127.6	32.3	14.6
	1983	87.8	25.1	14.2	165.3	47.4	26.9
	1984	109.0	39.3	26.3	207.9	75.1	50.2
	1985	146.2	48.4	33.5	274.6	90.9	62.9
	1986	159.7	56.7	38.5	300.0	106.5	72.4
República Dominicana (Peso)	1984	9.5	9.0	7.4	16.8	15.9	13.0
	1985	9.3	9.1	7.4	16.3	15.9	13.0
	1986	12.1	11.5	8.7	21.1	20.1	15.3
Ecuador (Sucre)	1972	378.3	245.0	218.5	740.1	479.4	427.6
	1974	615.5	408.1	374.0	1 198.0	794.5	728.1
	1980	1 679.5	1 056.8	761.1	3 166.8	1 992.8	1 435.2
	1983	3 117.1	2 296.1	1 701.7	5 780.7	4 258.1	3 155.7
	1984	5 142.5	2 618.9	2 285.7	9 483.0	4 829.4	4 215.0
	1985	7 749.1	3 299.5	2 899.7	14 213.1	6 051.8	5 318.6
	1986	10 483.8	4 314.8	3 799.9	19 147.6	7 880.5	6 940.1
El Salvador (Colón)	1970	27.2	20.9	16.6	53.7	41.2	32.7
	1975	43.2	37.3	26.4	84.8	73.1	51.9
	1980	49.5	32.9	27.9	97.2	64.6	54.9
	1983	60.9	35.5	32.5	120.1	70.0	64.1
	1984	42.5	36.6	30.4	83.9	72.2	60.0
	1985	47.7	38.0	32.9	94.5	75.1	65.0
	1986	58.4	42.9	32.1	115.0	84.4	63.2
Grenada (EC Dollar)	1981	37.6	36.8	36.8	70.0	68.6	68.6
	1983	84.4	48.1	46.0	155.6	88.7	84.8
	1984	71.6	4.9	1.2	133.4	9.2	2.2
	1985	95.4	8.1	3.3	176.2	15.0	6.0
	1986	105.7	12.4	6.9	195.4	23.0	12.8

See note on page 95.   *Voir note page 95.*   *Véase nota pág. 95.*

Table 4 *(cont.)*   **Tableau 4** *(suite)*   **Cuadro 4** *(cont.)*

Country and currency unit / Pays et unité monétaire / País y unidad monetaria (1)	Financial year / Exercice financier / Ejercicio financiero (2)	Per head of total population / Par habitant (population totale) / Por habitante (población total)			Per head of population between 15 and 64 years of age / Par habitant de 15 à 64 ans / Por habitante entre 15 y 64 años de edad		
		Receipts / Recettes / Ingresos (3)	Expenditure / Dépenses / Egresos — Total (4)	Benefits / Prestations / Prestaciones — Total (5)	Receipts / Recettes / Ingresos (6)	Expenditure / Dépenses / Egresos — Total (7)	Benefits / Prestations / Prestaciones — Total (8)
Venezuela (Bolivar)	1970	170.8	156.1	115.7	322.0	294.3	218.2
	1975	443.9	386.9	363.0	786.5	685.7	643.3
	1980	283.5	222.0	190.9	508.8	398.6	342.7
	1983	311.3	261.0	218.3	550.7	461.1	386.1
	1984	318.1	288.3	245.7	559.9	507.5	432.4
	1985	335.1	296.8	251.9	586.9	519.9	441.3
	1986	419.1	357.2	304.1	731.7	623.5	530.8
ASIA – ASIE – ASIA							
Bahrain (Dinar)	1978	55.3	8.6	6.7	99.9	15.5	12.2
	1980	70.6	10.4	7.3	111.3	16.4	11.5
	1983	122.5	23.8	14.8	190.5	37.0	23.0
	1984	78.0	14.5	9.0	120.9	22.5	14.0
	1985	89.6	14.3	10.6	137.9	22.0	16.3
	1986	86.8	18.3	13.4	133.4	28.1	20.6
Bangladesh (Taka)	1975	3.717	3.517	3.507	7.364	6.967	6.948
	1980	0.035	0.035	0.035	0.070	0.070	0.070
	1983	0.306	0.137	0.130	0.602	0.269	0.255
	1984	1.329	0.593	0.577	2.603	1.162	1.131
	1985	1.271	0.566	0.548	2.483	1.106	1.070
	1986	1.527	0.575	0.551	2.960	1.115	1.068
Cyprus (Pound)	1970	13.8	11.9	11.6	23.7	20.4	20.0
	1975	26.7	29.2	28.7	41.4	45.3	44.5
	1980	54.2	43.9	43.1	82.9	67.2	65.9
	1983	146.0	87.1	85.4	226.1	134.9	132.4
	1984	167.4	94.1	92.6	260.0	146.2	143.9
	1985	201.4	106.9	105.2	314.5	167.0	164.3
	1986	210.3	121.4	119.5	328.5	189.6	186.7

Country and currency unit / Pays et unité monétaire / País y unidad monetaria (1)	Financial year / Exercice financier / Ejercicio financiero (2)	Per head of total population / Par habitant (population totale) / Por habitante (población total)			Per head of population between 15 and 64 years of age / Par habitant de 15 à 64 ans / Por habitante entre 15 y 64 años de edad		
		Receipts / Recettes / Ingresos (3)	Expenditure / Dépenses / Egresos — Total (4)	Benefits / Prestations / Prestaciones — Total (5)	Receipts / Recettes / Ingresos (6)	Expenditure / Dépenses / Egresos — Total (7)	Benefits / Prestations / Prestaciones — Total (8)
Guatemala (Quetzal)	1970	8.0	7.7	6.9	15.7	15.1	13.4
	1975	12.0	11.7	10.9	22.5	21.9	20.4
	1980	19.2	13.1	11.6	37.6	25.6	22.6
	1983	16.5	11.9	10.6	32.2	23.4	20.7
	1984	17.8	13.1	11.0	34.9	25.6	21.5
	1985	18.9	13.7	11.5	37.0	26.8	22.6
	1986	25.5	16.4	14.1	49.8	32.0	27.5
Guyana (Dollar)	1972	41.9	26.7	22.6	83.4	53.0	44.9
	1975	54.8	29.0	24.0	103.9	54.9	45.6
	1980	105.6	21.9	16.1	185.7	38.5	28.3
	1983	148.4	29.0	20.8	254.8	49.7	35.7
	1984	166.6	32.4	23.6	283.5	55.2	40.2
	1985	221.6	45.1	30.5	374.0	76.1	51.6
	1986	205.9	63.9	51.2	345.8	107.3	86.0
Honduras (Lempira)	1970	10.2	9.0	8.7	20.3	18.0	17.5
	1971	6.7	6.5	6.2	13.5	13.1	12.4
	1981	17.1	11.5	9.7	35.8	23.9	20.2
	1983	18.6	13.3	10.9	37.3	26.7	21.8
	1984	31.5	16.4	13.2	62.8	32.7	26.3
	1985	34.0	16.9	13.7	67.7	33.6	27.3
	1986	36.8	17.0	14.3	72.6	33.5	28.3
Jamaica (Dollar)	1970	25.8	17.7	13.9	54.1	37.1	29.2
	1975	67.3	52.2	46.4	138.9	107.8	95.8
	1980	63.5	30.5	28.6	117.4	56.3	52.9
	1983	81.3	45.0	42.2	143.4	79.3	74.4
	1984	114.7	61.9	58.5	199.8	107.8	101.9
	1985	115.5	62.5	58.5	199.6	108.0	101.1
	1986	137.1	71.1	66.4	239.9	124.5	116.3

Country (Currency)	Year	1	2	3	4	5	6
India (Rupee)	1970	27.0	27.5	42.7	14.5	14.8	22.9
	1975	53.1	54.0	93.4	29.2	29.7	51.3
	1980	55.9	57.2	97.3	31.1	31.9	54.2
	1983	92.6	93.9	197.1	53.8	54.6	114.7
	1984	90.3	91.7	195.0	52.6	53.4	113.7
	1985	90.4	91.9	200.1	52.8	53.7	116.9
	1986	.	.	.	.	.	.
Indonesia (Rupiah)	1981	30.4	71.1	402.7	16.6	38.9	220.8
	1983	53.0	178.0	632.2	30.2	101.3	360.0
	1984	64.9	562.6	680.6	37.2	322.7	390.5
	1985	83.8	842.5	895.7	48.4	487.0	517.8
	1986	117.9	944.8	1 003.0	68.9	552.3	586.4
Iran, Islamic Rep. of (Rial)	1981	3 865.2	4 229.6	10 528.2	2 028.2	2 219.4	5 524.4
	1983	4 284.4	4 590.9	12 875.0	2 271.1	2 433.6	6 824.9
	1984	1 984.7	4 830.7	11 918.4	1 057.4	2 573.7	6 350.0
	1985	2 272.9	5 615.2	11 896.0	1 217.0	3 006.7	6 369.8
	1986	2 756.6	6 315.9	13 034.6	1 472.3	3 373.4	6 961.9
Israel (New Shekel)	1970	0.08	0.09	0.11	0.05	0.05	0.07
	1975	0.41	0.47	0.51	0.24	0.27	0.30
	1980	6.7	7.6	8.0	3.8	4.3	4.5
	1983	88.2	105.1	112.1	51.1	60.9	65.0
	1984	492.7	591.2	577.1	284.9	341.9	333.7
	1985	1 535.4	1 828.5	1 821.7	891.5	1 061.6	1 057.7
	1986	2 168.2	2 412.4	2 638.5	1 264.5	1 406.9	1 538.7
Japan (Yen)	1970	49 535	57 375	81 057	33 766	39 110	55 254
	1975	155 762	176 532	232 862	104 619	118 569	156 404
	1980	308 192	343 992	436 989	206 497	230 485	292 795
	1983	386 493	425 770	526 765	262 897	289 613	358 312
	1984	402 944	426 333	536 015	274 699	290 643	365 417
	1985	424 401	449 831	580 305	290 095	307 478	396 662
	1986	455 338	481 253	605 686	312 645	330 439	415 877
Jordan (Dinar)	1980	0.022	0.223	3.501	0.010	0.106	1.663
	1983	1.633	2.186	19.231	0.792	1.060	9.328
	1984	2.216	4.317	24.572	1.082	2.108	11.998
	1985	3.080	5.412	25.603	1.515	2.661	12.590
	1986	4.109	5.306	29.833	2.025	2.615	14.700
Kuwait (Dinar)	1980	51.9	55.2	117.6	29.0	30.8	65.7
	1983	98.3	103.4	237.5	56.3	59.2	136.0
	1984	90.8	97.2	210.2	52.1	55.8	120.7
	1985	161.1	167.0	328.2	92.7	96.1	188.8
	1986	157.9	163.9	373.0	91.1	94.6	215.3
Malaysia (Ringgit)	1970	56.1	57.5	105.0	34.3	35.2	64.2
	1975	96.5	104.8	183.8	62.2	67.6	118.5
	1980	56.0	65.6	272.7	31.9	37.4	155.5
	1983	139.7	145.0	512.7	80.8	83.9	296.7
	1984	153.0	167.3	573.1	89.0	97.3	333.3
	1985	157.2	165.7	622.9	91.9	96.8	364.1
	1986	157.6	167.8	665.9	92.6	98.6	391.3

Country (Currency)	Year	1	2	3	4	5	6
México (Peso)	1970	266.4	250.9	209.9	529.4	498.7	417.2
	1974	538.5	476.3	405.7	1 074.0	949.8	809.2
	1980	2 079.9	1 683.3	1 226.5	3 969.6	3 212.6	2 340.8
	1983	7 284.2	6 115.8	4 208.2	13 427.6	11 273.9	7 757.3
	1984	11 576.7	10 474.7	7 768.4	21 099.8	19 091.3	14 158.9
	1985	18 362.2	15 276.3	11 981.5	33 095.4	27 533.4	21 595.2
	1986	30 964.8	26 589.9	19 567.9	55 121.4	47 333.6	34 833.4
Panamá (Balboa)	1972	71.0	61.9	52.2	136.0	118.5	100.0
	1975	106.6	82.9	71.2	201.2	156.5	134.3
	1980	148.2	107.6	96.9	266.5	193.4	174.2
	1983	215.8	160.4	139.9	379.3	281.8	245.9
	1984	200.0	170.3	159.3	348.2	296.5	277.4
	1985	207.8	178.8	167.8	358.5	308.4	289.4
	1986	224.7	191.2	180.3	484.5	412.2	388.7
Perú (Inti)	1981	13.9	11.6	10.4	25.5	21.3	19.2
	1983	30.3	32.3	28.6	54.9	58.6	51.9
	1984	54.1	57.4	22.3	97.7	103.6	40.3
	1985	161.4	141.0	56.8	289.9	253.3	102.0
	1986	348.4	303.7	119.7	620.1	540.5	213.1
St. Lucia (EC Dollar)	1981	65.4	12.4	5.7	137.5	26.1	12.0
	1983	52.4	16.4	7.4	107.3	33.6	15.3
	1984	77.9	23.0	15.0	158.2	46.8	30.6
	1985	77.9	15.4	6.3	157.0	31.1	12.7
	1986	104.4	24.0	14.7	211.9	48.8	30.0
Trinidad and Tobago (Dollar)	1970	52.8	51.6	51.6	96.0	93.8	93.8
	1975	169.5	122.6	118.1	293.0	211.8	204.1
	1980	181.2	101.9	87.0	302.6	170.2	145.3
	1983	597.4	401.1	366.2	980.4	658.3	601.0
	1984	450.0	266.2	222.8	734.6	434.5	363.6
	1985	422.6	259.7	215.8	685.7	421.3	350.1
	1986	421.5	319.5	246.2	682.0	517.1	398.5
United States (Dollar)	1970	541.4	457.8	427.2	885.7	748.9	698.9
	1975	1 029.6	946.6	889.7	1 586.9	1 458.8	1 371.2
	1980	1 627.1	1 447.0	1 390.4	2 458.3	2 186.2	2 100.7
	1983	2 191.0	1 923.7	1 843.6	3 305.1	2 901.9	2 781.0
	1984	2 276.9	1 966.2	1 876.2	3 432.8	2 964.4	2 828.7
	1985	2 474.5	2 082.4	1 990.5	3 728.8	3 138.1	2 999.4
	1986	2 667.5	2 176.5	2 088.0	4 034.5	3 292.0	3 158.1
Uruguay (Nuevo peso)	1975	328.8	309.8	244.6	524.4	494.2	390.2
	1980	3 362.9	2 596.4	2 376.4	5 376.3	4 150.9	3 799.1
	1983	7 792.7	6 881.4	6 368.2	12 475.2	11 016.2	10 194.7
	1984	9 169.2	10 542.8	9 805.6	14 692.4	16 893.4	15 712.2
	1985	15 944.5	15 640.3	14 505.0	25 551.9	25 064.5	23 245.1
	1986	30 693.9	30 869.1	28 610.6	49 178.5	49 459.2	45 840.6

Table 4 *(cont.)* **Tableau 4** *(suite)* **Cuadro 4** *(cont.)*

Country and currency unit / Pays et unité monétaire / País y unidad monetaria (1)	Financial year / Exercice financier / Ejercicio financiero (2)	Per head of total population — Par habitant (population totale) — Por habitante (población total)			Per head of population between 15 and 64 years of age — Par habitant de 15 à 64 ans — Por habitante entre 15 y 64 años de edad		
		Receipts / Recettes / Ingresos (3)	Expenditure Total / Dépenses Total / Egresos Total (4)	Benefits Total / Prestations / Prestaciones (5)	Receipts / Recettes / Ingresos (6)	Expenditure Total / Dépenses Total / Egresos Total (7)	Benefits Total / Prestations / Prestaciones (8)
Finland (Markka)	1970	1 358.0	1 238.0	1 189.5	2 048.2	1 867.1	1 794.0
	1975	3 977.0	3 479.8	3 349.9	5 904.7	5 166.6	4 973.7
	1980	8 459.2	7 248.1	6 991.5	12 495.4	10 706.5	10 327.4
	1983	12737.5	11 646.6	11 180.7	18 743.4	17 138.2	16 452.6
	1984	14 440.7	13 183.0	12 726.4	21 228.4	19 379.5	18 708.3
	1985	16 700.2	15 159.1	14 668.3	24 517.7	22 255.2	21 534.6
	1986	18 384.2	16 707.0	16 164.3	27 037.5	24 570.8	23 772.7
France (Franc français)	1970	2 361.1	2 360.6	2 178.5	3 789.5	3 788.7	3 496.4
	1975	6 740.4	6 647.8	5 768.0	10 763.8	10 615.8	9 210.8
	1980	14 137.2	13 715.1	13 050.4	22 175.7	21 513.6	20 470.9
	1983	21 717.1	21 161.1	20 103.2	33 406.5	32 551.2	30 923.9
	1984	23 577.9	23 021.1	21 848.0	36 036.1	35 185.1	33 392.2
	1985	24 834.7	24 439.2	23 245.6	37 715.6	37 115.0	35 302.3
	1986	25 833.6	25 991.8	24 718.1	39 208.3	39 448.4	37 515.3
Germany, Fed. Rep. of (Deutsche Mark)	1970	1 984.1	1 905.9	1 793.9	3 117.5	2 994.5	2 818.6
	1975	3 896.8	3 936.7	3 773.4	6 093.9	6 156.1	5 900.8
	1980	5 810.6	5 767.4	5 558.3	8 762.0	8 696.9	8 381.5
	1983	6 606.6	6 620.1	6 443.3	9 664.1	9 683.9	9 425.3
	1984	6 884.1	6 905.9	6 721.0	9 970.6	10 002.1	9 734.3
	1985	7 188.6	7 142.5	6 946.7	10 309.7	10 243.6	9 962.8
	1986	7 524.2	7 402.1	7 192.0	10 790.5	10 615.4	10 314.0
Grèce (Drachme)	1970	4 067.6	3 675.7	3 508.0	6 359.7	5 746.9	5 484.7
	1975	9 007.1	8 056.3	7 585.2	14 095.8	12 607.9	11 870.6
	1980	25 170.0	21 719.7	20 666.9	39 299.5	33 912.4	32 268.6
	1983	57 846.8	54 817.2	51 506.5	89 183.8	84 513.1	79 409.0
	1984	72 029.3	70 942.4	66 420.6	110 581.0	108 912.0	101 970.0
	1985	87 830.0	90 478.6	84 778.3	134 273.0	138 322.0	129 607.0
Iceland (Króna)	1984	25 857.7	25 443.5	24 933.1	40 927.2	40 271.5	39 463.6
	1985	36 572.6	36 124.5	35 315.4	57 986.8	57 276.3	55 993.4
	1986	48 214.0	47 321.0	46 329.2	76 077.9	74 668.8	73 103.9

Country and currency unit / Pays et unité monétaire / País y unidad monetaria (1)	Financial year / Exercice financier / Ejercicio financiero (2)	Per head of total population — Par habitant (population totale) — Por habitante (población total)			Per head of population between 15 and 64 years of age — Par habitant de 15 à 64 ans — Por habitante entre 15 y 64 años de edad		
		Receipts / Recettes / Ingresos (3)	Expenditure Total / Dépenses Total / Egresos Total (4)	Benefits Total / Prestations / Prestaciones (5)	Receipts / Recettes / Ingresos (6)	Expenditure Total / Dépenses Total / Egresos Total (7)	Benefits Total / Prestations / Prestaciones (8)
Myanmar (Kyat)	1970	7.9	7.6	7.5	14.5	13.8	13.7
	1975	10.7	10.3	10.2	19.3	18.6	18.5
	1980	0.9	0.5	0.4	1.6	1.0	0.7
	1983	1.0	0.7	0.4	1.8	1.3	0.8
	1984	1.0	0.7	0.4	1.8	1.3	0.7
	1985	1.1	0.8	0.4	1.9	1.4	0.7
	1986	1.1	0.9	0.4	2.4	1.9	1.0
Pakistan (Rupee)	1965	5.9	5.9	5.9	12.1	12.1	12.1
	1980	3.0	1.3	0.7	6.0	2.6	1.4
	1983	28.5	24.8	24.3	55.1	47.9	46.8
	1984	36.5	33.1	32.3	70.4	63.9	62.4
	1985	63.7	59.3	58.6	123.2	114.7	113.4
	1986	51.7	46.6	45.9	100.5	90.6	89.2
Philippines (Peso)	1970	20.0	11.1	9.8	39.3	21.7	19.2
	1978	68.1	29.1	24.4	124.6	53.3	44.8
	1980	92.8	35.7	29.0	170.2	65.4	53.1
	1983	129.9	54.7	45.7	235.7	99.3	82.9
	1984	148.3	62.0	51.5	268.2	112.2	93.2
	1985	194.5	68.3	57.8	350.6	123.1	104.2
	1986	191.1	75.7	65.8	343.1	136.0	118.2
Qatar (Riyal)	1984	267.4	267.4	267.4	412.0	412.0	412.0
	1985	266.0	266.0	266.0	412.1	412.1	412.1
	1986	255.6	255.6	255.6	398.0	398.0	398.0
Singapore (Dollar)	1970	151.4	79.3	78.0	263.5	137.6	135.2
	1975	550.9	179.4	176.9	869.8	283.3	279.4
	1980	1 202.8	381.6	353.0	1 764.0	559.7	517.8
	1983	2 295.8	1 169.5	731.1	3 303.2	1 682.7	1 052.0
	1984	2 724.8	1 948.7	1 429.0	3 895.4	2 786.0	2 043.0
	1985	3 048.3	1 979.0	1 370.8	4 331.9	2 812.4	1 948.1
	1986	2 587.3	2 165.9	1 555.7	3 664.2	3 067.4	2 203.2

EUROPE – EUROPE – EUROPA
Countries with a market economy – Pays à économie de marché – Países con economía de mercado

Country (Currency)	Year	(1)	(2)	(3)	(4)	(5)	(6)
Ireland (Pound)	1970	57.4	56.8	54.5	100.1	99.1	95.1
	1975	229.3	230.3	221.4	390.4	392.0	376.9
	1980	557.6	553.1	525.7	951.2	943.4	896.6
	1983	961.5	973.0	924.1	1 621.3	1 640.8	1 558.3
	1984	1 035.4	1 043.2	994.0	1 739.2	1 752.2	1 669.6
	1985	1 133.5	1 135.8	1 085.7	1 896.3	1 900.1	1 816.4
	1986	1 214.2	1 214.9	1 156.9	2 016.6	2 017.9	1 921.5
Italie Lire (milliers)	1970	181.8	176.1	162.7	279.8	271.1	250.4
	1975	409.6	476.7	432.9	641.2	746.3	677.6
	1980	1 286.6	1 293.1	1 177.9	1 985.5	1 995.5	1 817.9
	1983	2 499.8	2 438.3	2 282.0	3 757.5	3 665.0	3 430.1
	1984	1 287.9	1 436.8	1 275.0	1 919.3	2 141.1	1 900.0
	1985	1 435.1	1 599.7	1 423.2	2 120.4	2 363.6	2 102.9
	1986	1 584.1	1 751.9	1 564.4	2 333.9	2 581.2	2 305.0
Luxembourg (Franc luxembourgeois)	1970	26 915.3	24 128.3	23 402.4	40 916.1	36 679.4	35 575.8
	1975	55 737.4	51 012.6	49 100.8	84 550.8	77 383.5	74 483.5
	1980	98 237.6	89 453.0	85 794.0	146 551.0	133 446.0	127 988.0
	1983	131 042.0	121 326.0	112 713.0	191 080.0	176 914.0	164 355.0
	1984	139 006.0	127 881.0	122 195.0	201 092.0	184 998.0	176 772.0
	1985	148 591.0	132 426.0	127 669.0	213 272.0	190 070.0	183 243.0
	1986	161 489.0	140 334.0	135 879.0	231 237.0	200 946.0	194 567.0
Malta (Lira)	1970	20.5	21.8	21.6	32.6	34.776	34.4
	1975	57.7	57.1	50.1	89.3	88.453	77.5
	1980	164.9	136.8	135.6	245.8	203.9	202.2
	1983	213.7	205.0	203.1	321.5	308.4	305.6
	1984	205.7	277.9	262.3	310.9	420.1	396.5
	1985	209.3	269.6	254.5	316.8	408.1	385.3
	1986	208.0	273.3	257.9	313.9	412.4	389.1
Netherlands (Guilder)	1970	2 092.9	1 761.1	1 699.3	3 346.2	2 815.7	2 716.9
	1975	4 854.7	4 111.3	3 973.7	7 613.3	6 447.5	6 231.7
	1980	8 046.3	6 746.5	6 509.2	12 160.2	10 195.9	9 837.2
	1983	9 745.0	8 329.6	8 096.6	14 424.3	12 329.3	11 984.3
	1984	9 874.4	8 478.9	8 239.3	14 450.0	12 465.9	11 897.0
	1985	9 663.1	8 392.9	8 147.3	14 418.9	12 255.6	11 914.5
	1986		8 431.1	8 177.4	14 079.0	12 284.0	
Norway (Krone)	1970	3 364.9	3 185.1	3 044.1	5 366.5	5 079.6	4 854.7
	1975	7 522.2	6 856.3	6 603.2	12 023.0	10 958.6	10 554.1
	1980	14 565.0	14 064.4	13 764.1	23 093.8	22 300.0	21 823.8
	1983	22 082.0	21 284.6	20 782.0	34 685.9	33 433.4	32 643.9
	1984	32 194.8	31 342.0	31 025.9	50 423.1	49 087.5	48 592.4
	1985	35 035.4	34 025.2	33 664.4	54 700.0	53 122.9	52 559.5
	1986	37 881.9	36 777.0	36 411.4	58 988.7	57 268.2	56 699.0
Portugal (Escudo)	1970	1 491.8	1 108.1	960.4	2 411.0	1 790.9	1 552.2
	1975	4 858.1	4 399.0	4 063.0	7 810.4	7 072.3	6 532.1
	1980	13 004.2	12 412.7	11 186.3	20 447.4	19 517.5	17 589.0
	1983	22 866.2	23 157.4	21 934.7	35 649.2	36 103.2	34 197.0
	1984	29 501.4	28 453.1	26 993.6	45 868.3	44 238.5	41 969.2
	1985	36 118.5	34 962.6	33 215.5	55 999.9	54 207.8	51 499.1
	1986	48 445.0	44 999.4	42 909.8	74 792.3	69 472.7	66 246.7

Country (Currency)	Year	(1)	(2)	(3)	(4)	(5)	(6)
Sri Lanka (Rupee)	1970	45.6	34.6	30.8	83.8	63.5	56.6
	1975	64.7	42.6	42.0	114.3	75.2	74.2
	1980	141.9	77.4	74.1	234.9	128.2	122.8
	1983	311.3	174.8	171.1	511.2	287.0	281.0
	1984	479.9	203.1	201.1	786.0	332.7	329.4
	1985	592.9	245.0	242.6	968.5	400.2	396.2
	1986	647.3	249.5	246.6	1 321.6	509.5	503.5
Rép. arabe syrienne (Livre syrienne)	1984	149.0	69.8	66.7	303.1	142.0	135.7
	1985	153.0	75.1	72.0	311.2	152.9	146.5
	1986	161.0	77.3	73.6	327.3	157.2	149.7
Thailand (Baht)	1980	5.4	2.2	2.1	9.6	3.9	3.7
	1983	36.8	32.3	32.0	62.9	55.3	54.8
	1984	4.9	5.1	4.8	8.2	8.6	8.2
	1985	5.1	4.8	4.5	8.6	8.1	7.5
	1986	5.4	4.6	4.1	8.9	7.7	6.8

EUROPE – EUROPE – EUROPA
Countries with a market economy – Pays à économie de marché – Países con economía de mercado

Country (Currency)	Year	(1)	(2)	(3)	(4)	(5)	(6)
Austria (Schilling)	1970	9 531.9	9 386.0	8 958.1	15 516.0	15 278.6	14 582.0
	1975	17 918.8	17 651.6	16 844.5	29 028.2	28 595.4	27 288.0
	1980	29 790.6	29 602.1	28 187.2	46 426.3	46 132.5	43 927.5
	1983	39 978.4	38 658.9	37 303.4	60 516.5	58 519.1	56 467.2
	1984	43 567.3	42 102.9	40 610.4	65 333.6	63 137.6	60 899.5
	1985	46 109.6	45 005.0	43 264.2	68 493.7	66 853.0	64 267.1
	1986	48 719.4	47 745.0	45 941.4	72 380.6	70 933.0	68 253.5
Belgique (Franc belge)	1970	25 000	23 972	22 027	39 682	38 050	34 963
	1975	57 627	55 577	52 126	90 340	87 126	81 716
	1980	89 956	91 914	86 554	137 313	140 301	132 119
	1983	119 701	118 856	112 465	179 953	178 683	169 075
	1984	124 999	122 068	115 525	186 957	182 575	172 788
	1985	130 102	126 688	120 096	193 622	188 540	178 729
	1986	135 412	133 451	126 059	201 542	198 624	187 622
Denmark (Krone)	1970	3 649.0	3 550.4	3 462.8	5 720.8	5 566.2	5 428.8
	1975	8 837.8	8 626.4	8 431.2	13 823.7	13 493.0	13 187.7
	1980	20 157.9	19 634.5	19 106.3	31 133.3	30 324.8	29 509.0
	1983	29 195.9	28 128.7	27 319.0	44 410.4	42 787.1	41 555.4
	1984	30 066.7	28 967.6	28 076.6	45 500.6	43 837.4	42 489.0
	1985	32 255.5	31 207.4	30 261.1	48 558.9	46 981.1	45 556.5
	1986	34 952.5	34 046.0	33 059.6	52 444.2	51 084.0	49 604.0
España (Peseta)	1975	20 558	19 859	18 566	32 970	31 849	29 775
	1980	63 953	64 634	61 863	101 925	103 010	98 593
	1983	104 712	105 322	101 698	163 146	164 096	158 449
	1984	120 843	118 331	113 592	186 881	182 997	175 669
	1985	134 646	133 635	128 320	206 695	205 144	196 984
	1986	152 412	150 025	142 544	232 962	229 313	217 878

See note on page 95. *Voir note page 95.* Véase nota pág. 95.

Table 4 *(concl.)* **Tableau 4** *(fin)* **Cuadro 4** *(fin)*

Country and currency unit / *Pays et unité monétaire* / País y unidad monetaria	Financial year / *Exercice financier* / Ejercicio financiero	Per head of total population / *Par habitant (population totale)* / Por habitante (población total)			Per head of population between 15 and 64 years of age / *Par habitant de 15 à 64 ans* / Por habitante entre 15 y 64 años de edad		
		Receipts / *Recettes* / Ingresos	Expenditure / *Dépenses* / Egresos Total	Benefits / *Prestations* / Prestaciones	Receipts / *Recettes* / Ingresos	Expenditure / *Dépenses* / Egresos Total	Benefits / *Prestations* / Prestaciones
(1)	(2)	(3)	(4)	(5)	(6)	(7)	(8)
Suisse (Franc suisse)	1970	1 678.2	1 459.4	1 373.2	2 601.3	2 262.2	2 128.6
	1975	3 467.4	3 301.6	3 127.9	5 301.6	5 048.1	4 782.7
	1980	4 046.7	3 705.6	3 454.7	6 088.3	5 575.1	5 197.7
	1983	4 728.3	4 544.5	4 195.2	6 985.3	6 713.7	6 197.7
	1984	5 133.0	4 976.2	4 574.2	7 537.4	7 307.3	6 716.9
	1985	5 442.1	5 181.1	4 737.9	7 944.5	7 563.6	6 916.5
	1986	5 781.4	5 487.5	5 022.5	8 444.3	8 015.0	7 335.8
Sweden (Krona)	1970	4 966.6	3 988.9	3 905.2	7 587.2	6 093.7	5 965.8
	1975	10 338.4	9 190.2	9 007.5	16 112.3	14 322.9	14 038.2
	1980	22 124.2	20 134.3	19 628.9	34 506.7	31 403.1	30 615.0
	1983	30 285.0	28 163.6	27 553.7	47 025.4	43 731.2	42 784.2
	1984	31 696.9	28 763.0	27 887.3	49 136.6	44 588.6	43 231.0
	1985	34 161.7	31 695.2	30 398.6	52 882.9	49 064.7	47 057.5
	1986	38 074.1	34 886.1	33 466.4	58 833.4	53 907.3	51 713.5
Turquie (Livre turque)	1970	188.2	134.0	123.9	341.0	242.8	224.4
	1975	789.2	441.8	368.5	1 434.7	803.2	669.9
	1980	4 911.6	4 138.8	3 950.9	8 764.2	7 385.2	7 049.9
	1983	11 768.8	9 155.3	8 799.0	20 273.2	15 771.3	15 157.4
	1984	18 489.4	14 603.6	14 143.4	31 487.6	24 870.1	24 086.4
	1985	26 149.7	21 813.5	21 170.8	44 029.9	36 728.8	35 646.7
	1986	34 856.0	28 189.1	27 383.4	58 297.4	47 146.8	45 799.3
United Kingdom (Pound)	1970	149.8	144.0	135.2	209.9	201.8	189.4
	1975	389.9	367.9	344.7	546.5	515.7	483.1
	1980	775.9	739.9	704.5	1 220.4	1 163.7	1 108.1
	1983	1 122.5	1 083.4	1 034.4	1 724.1	1 664.0	1 588.8
	1984	1 201.8	1 162.3	1 107.8	1 836.3	1 776.0	1 692.8
	1985	1 291.4	1 256.7	1 199.4	1 966.3	1 913.6	1 826.3
	1986	1 387.1	1 339.9	1 277.7	2 112.7	2 040.9	1 946.1
Hongrie (Forint)	1970	2 911.1	2 927.9	2 898.5	4 302.9	4 327.8	4 284.3
	1975	5 577.7	5 569.6	5 515.8	8 329.0	8 317.0	8 236.7
	1980	9 956.6	9 956.6	9 902.8	15 406.5	15 406.8	15 323.5
	1983	12 945.6	12 945.6	12 883.7	19 753.7	19 753.7	19 659.4
	1984	11 323.7	11 323.7	11 255.8	17 198.3	17 198.3	17 095.2
	1985	12 705.4	12 427.6	12 344.4	19 207.8	18 787.9	18 662.0
	1986	14 053.2	13 445.5	13 349.9	21 206.5	20 289.4	20 145.2
Pologne (Zloty)	1984	39 875.0	34 123.8	33 919.4	61 188.4	52 363.0	52 049.4
	1985	48 138.7	39 475.1	39 162.4	73 998.2	60 680.6	60 200.0
	1986	59 868.7	48 861.7	48 456.1	92 080.8	75 151.4	74 527.7
RSS d'Ukraine (Rouble)	1970	137.4	137.4	137.4	205.1	205.1	205.1
	1975	185.0	185.0	185.0	275.5	275.5	275.5
	1980	240.3	240.3	240.3	360.1	360.1	360.1
	1983	280.4	280.4	280.4	420.1	420.1	420.1
	1984	293.5	293.5	293.5	439.7	439.7	439.7
	1985	307.5	307.5	307.5	460.7	460.7	460.7
	1986	329.4	329.4	329.4	493.6	493.6	493.6
URSS (Rouble)	1970	142.5	142.5	142.5	224.3	224.3	224.3
	1975	193.5	193.5	193.5	298.2	298.2	298.2
	1980	243.3	243.3	243.3	374.4	374.4	374.4
	1983	278.0	278.0	278.0	427.1	427.1	427.1
	1984	290.7	290.7	290.7	446.2	446.2	446.2
	1985	301.1	301.1	301.1	461.8	461.8	461.8
	1986	317.5	317.5	317.5	487.4	487.4	487.4
Yugoslavia (Dinar)	1970	1 117.8	1 017.1	954.7	1 725.5	1 570.0	1473.8
	1981	12 078.8	11 911.9	10 693.3	18 174.8	17 923.6	16 090.0
	1983	20 284.6	20 178.0	18 502.8	30 319.9	30 160.5	27 656.6
	1984	28 712.6	27 478.5	24 799.1	42 774.6	40 936.2	36 944.4
	1985	52 128.1	50 006.2	45 108.4	77 403.8	74 253.1	66 980.5
	1986	119 376.0	117 444.0	106 055.0	176 932.0	174 067.0	157 187.0

EUROPE – EUROPE – EUROPA

Countries with a centrally planned economy – Pays à économie planifiée – Paises con economía centralmente planificada

Country	Year	(1)	(2)	(3)	(4)	(5)	(6)
RSS de Biélorussie (Rouble)	1970	122.3	122.3		197.3	197.3	
	1975	174.9	175.0		281.6	281.8	
	1980	232.6	232.6		347.5	347.5	
	1983	273.1	273.1		408.1	408.1	
	1984	284.8	284.8		425.5	425.5	
	1985	294.9	294.9		440.6	440.6	
	1986	318.5	318.5		475.9	475.9	
Bulgarie (Lev)	1970	172.9	169.8	165.6	265.4	260.7	254.3
	1975	268.5	262.4	244.2	412.2	402.9	375.0
	1980	282.8	282.8	282.8	428.5	428.5	428.5
	1983	330.3	330.3	330.3	494.2	494.2	494.2
	1984	371.8	328.1	327.5	553.9	488.9	487.9
	1985	371.8	359.4	358.5	547.2	528.9	527.7
	1986	413.8	401.0	400.1	609.0	590.2	588.9
Czechoslovakia (Koruna)	1970	3 906.7	3 906.7	3 889.9	5 952.3	5 952.3	5 926.6
	1975	4 693.2	4 693.2	4 673.8	7 276.6	7 276.6	7 246.5
	1980	5 967.4	5 967.4	5 945.8	9 433.8	9 433.8	9 399.7
	1983	6 824.3	6 824.3	6 802.7	10 660.8	10 660.8	10 627.1
	1984	7 015.2	7 015.2	6 993.5	10 915.0	10 915.0	10 881.3
	1985	7 383.1	7 383.1	7 361.8	11 443.1	11 443.1	11 410.2
	1986	7 769.5	7 769.5	7 746.9	12 016.3	12 016.3	11 981.4
German Democratic Rep. (Mark)	1970	843.8	843.8	839.6	1 381.8	1 381.8	1 374.9
	1975	1 295.4	1 295.4	1 288.7	2 085.3	2 085.3	2 074.6
	1980	1 770.1	1 770.1	1 763.6	2 747.0	2 747.0	2 736.9
	1983	1 846.1	1 846.1	1 839.7	2 793.7	2 793.7	2 783.9
	1984	1 871.3	1 871.3	1 864.8	2 808.5	2 808.5	2 798.7
	1985	1 966.1	1 966.1	1 959.1	2 926.7	2 926.7	2 916.4
	1986	2 064.1	2 064.1	2 056.5	3 072.5	3 072.5	3 061.2

OCEANIA – OCÉANIE – OCEANIA

Country	Year	(1)	(2)	(3)	(4)	(5)	(6)
Australia (Dollar)	1970	259.6	220.3	209.6	417.3	354.2	337.0
	1975	795.7	228.6	197.6	1 245.5	357.9	309.4
	1980	1 172.8	1 075.6	1 033.1	1 812.5	1 662.3	1 596.6
	1983	1 660.6	1 501.0	1 434.9	2 539.6	2 295.6	2 194.5
	1984	1 260.8	1 288.5	1 274.2	1 919.8	1 962.0	1 940.3
	1985	1 461.6	1 497.9	1 480.1	2 219.6	2 274.7	2 247.6
	1986	1 521.8	1 495.9	1 477.9	2 307.8	2 268.5	2 241.2
Fiji (Dollar)	1975	51.2	28.5	24.1	89.1	49.7	42.0
	1980	91.1	32.3	18.2	153.7	54.5	30.7
	1983	127.0	38.8	36.5	214.4	65.5	61.7
	1984	130.8	35.7	33.5	221.1	60.4	56.7
	1985	159.2	40.9	38.4	268.8	69.0	64.8
	1986	158.4	48.8	46.2	267.5	82.4	78.1
New Zealand (Dollar)	1970	231.7	216.4	206.2	388.6	362.9	345.9
	1975	593.3	549.3	543.3	979.0	906.6	896.5
	1980	1 339.1	1 301.6	1 275.6	2 115.0	2 055.8	2 014.7
	1983	1 964.1	1 888.9	1 853.2	3 048.6	2 931.9	2 876.6
	1984	2 095.1	2 053.5	2 012.3	3 233.4	3 169.1	3 105.5
	1985	2 513.1	2 490.6	2 438.3	3 856.3	3 821.9	3 741.6
	1986	2 969.6	2 935.4	2 859.1	4 536.9	4 484.7	4 368.0
Solomon Islands (Dollar)	1981	16.3	2.6	2.1	33.9	5.5	4.3
	1983	30.0	5.8	4.6	62.1	12.1	9.5
	1984	35.1	13.5	5.5	73.0	28.1	11.6
	1985	40.3	18.2	7.4	83.7	37.8	15.5
	1986	48.6	24.1	9.8	100.4	49.9	20.3

For general footnotes, see table 1. For further notes on the corresponding denominators, consult footnotes of appendix table 1.

Pour les notes de caractère général, se reporter au tableau 1. Pour des précisions sur les chiffres relatifs à la population, consulter les notes du tableau 1 de l'annexe.

Véanse las notas generales del cuadro 1. En lo que concierne a otras notas sobre los denominadores correspondientes, consúltense las notas del cuadro 1 del anexo.

5. Average annual social security receipts and expenditure per head of population
(in US dollars)

5. Moyennes annuelles des recettes et des dépenses de la sécurité sociale par habitant
(en dollars des Etats-Unis)

5. Ingresos y egresos anuales medios de la seguridad social por habitante
(en dólares de los Estados Unidos)

Country / Pays / País	Financial year / Exercice financier / Ejercicio financiero	Per head of total population — Par habitant (population totale) — Por habitante (población total)			Per head of population between 15 and 64 years of age — Par habitant de 15 à 64 ans — Por habitante entre 15 y 64 años de edad		
		Receipts / Recettes / Ingresos — Expenditure Total / Dépenses Total / Egresos Total — Benefits Total / Prestations Total / Prestaciones Total			Receipts / Recettes / Ingresos — Expenditure Total / Dépenses Total / Egresos Total — Benefits Total / Prestations Total / Prestaciones Total		
(1)	(2)	(3)	(4)	(5)	(6)	(7)	(8)

AFRICA – AFRIQUE – AFRICA

Country	Financial year	(3)	(4)	(5)	(6)	(7)	(8)
Bénin	1970	2.43	2.37	2.23	4.70	4.58	4.30
	1975	4.21	3.98	3.64	8.16	7.71	7.05
	1981	5.59	4.69	4.31	10.98	9.21	8.47
	1983	4.41	3.90	3.71	8.70	7.71	7.32
	1984	1.94	1.80	1.29	3.85	3.55	2.56
	1985	2.60	2.32	1.68	5.16	4.60	3.34
	1986	3.37	2.90	1.90	6.71	5.78	3.79
Burkina Faso	1975	2.30	1.83	1.71	4.30	3.42	3.21
	1980	3.12	1.27	0.78	5.85	2.38	1.46
	1983	3.41	2.13	1.48	6.40	3.99	2.77
	1984	2.16	0.54	0.53	4.05	1.01	1.00
	1985	2.88	0.73	0.73	5.41	1.37	1.36
	1986	3.10	0.79	0.78	5.81	1.48	1.47
Burundi	1978	0.93	0.46	0.32	1.73	0.85	0.59
	1980	1.28	0.72	0.53	2.41	1.35	1.00
	1983	1.70	0.96	0.75	3.25	1.83	1.43
	1984	1.67	1.00	0.68	3.21	1.92	1.31
	1985	2.11	1.26	0.94	4.07	2.42	1.82
	1986	2.27	1.55	1.27	4.39	2.99	2.46
Kenya	1970	4.24	2.74	2.66	9.03	5.84	5.68
	1975	7.15	4.48	4.33	16.02	10.03	9.71
	1981	2.76	0.22	0.14	5.95	0.47	0.31
	1983	2.32	0.21	0.16	5.03	0.47	0.34
	1984	5.45	0.63	0.52	11.87	1.37	1.13
	1985	5.62	0.77	0.66	12.28	1.69	1.45
	1986	4.89	0.79	0.67	10.71	1.73	1.47
Madagascar	1981	3.08	1.76	1.76	5.82	3.33	3.33
	1983	2.06	1.43	1.43	3.91	2.71	2.71
	1984	1.29	1.31	1.13	2.44	2.48	2.14
	1985	1.40	1.42	1.22	2.67	2.71	2.32
	1986	1.27	1.24	1.08	2.42	2.37	2.06
Mali	1972	1.23	1.29	1.20	2.35	2.46	2.28
	1975	1.67	1.62	1.43	2.97	2.88	2.54
	1980	1.42	1.51	0.88	2.76	2.94	1.72
	1983	1.41	1.36	0.89	2.76	2.67	1.73
	1984	1.67	1.71	1.26	3.27	3.35	2.47
	1985	2.19	2.40	1.64	4.30	4.70	3.22
	1986	2.98	2.91	1.85	5.86	5.71	3.64

Maroc / Mauritanie / Mauritius / Mozambique / Niger / Nigeria / Rwanda

Pays	Année	(1)	(2)	(3)	(4)	(5)	(6)
Maroc	1970	11.35	11.74	13.06	5.40	5.59	6.22
	1975	15.66	16.30	19.46	7.70	8.01	9.57
	1980	15.74	17.63	31.58	8.30	9.29	16.65
	1983	8.45	9.06	16.07	4.51	4.84	8.59
	1984	15.69	16.52	23.64	8.42	8.87	12.69
	1985	16.74	17.63	29.03	9.03	9.51	15.66
	1986	22.07	23.34	34.08	11.98	12.67	18.50
Mauritanie	1970	5.86	6.18	6.75	3.08	3.25	3.54
	1981	19.01	20.77	25.13	10.09	11.03	13.35
	1983	18.66	20.90	23.55	9.89	11.08	12.48
	1984	6.76	8.32	10.89	3.58	4.40	5.76
	1985	5.37	6.42	10.41	2.84	3.39	5.50
	1986	6.73	8.23	8.25	3.55	4.34	4.35
Mauritius	1970	28.86	29.48	32.50	14.72	15.04	16.57
	1975	46.96	47.45	53.04	26.80	27.08	30.27
	1981	29.76	31.04	52.55	18.13	18.91	32.02
	1983	30.31	31.79	55.72	19.61	20.57	36.04
	1984	·	·	·	·	·	·
	1985	56.02	59.37	90.28	36.92	39.14	59.51
	1986	72.50	76.25	115.85	45.96	48.34	73.45
Mozambique	1981	0.07	0.43	1.14	0.04	0.23	0.61
	1983	0.06	0.29	0.53	0.03	0.15	0.28
	1984	0.46	0.46	0.74	0.24	0.24	0.40
	1985	0.53	0.53	0.78	0.28	0.28	0.42
	1986	0.05	0.05	0.08	0.03	0.03	0.04
Niger	1970	2.17	2.30	2.61	1.12	1.19	1.35
	1975	3.33	3.53	4.12	1.70	1.80	2.10
	1980	2.24	2.66	6.38	1.12	1.33	3.19
	1983	1.47	3.72	4.96	0.74	1.86	2.49
	1984	3.10	7.43	9.76	1.54	3.70	4.85
	1985	3.71	9.17	12.51	1.84	4.55	6.21
	1986	4.87	9.94	12.78	2.42	4.93	6.34
Nigeria	1970	1.70	1.75	2.35	0.86	0.89	1.19
	1981	0.13	0.35	2.72	0.07	0.17	1.34
	1983	0.16	0.34	2.38	0.08	0.17	1.18
	1984	0.17	0.37	2.38	0.08	0.18	1.17
	1985	0.16	0.34	2.12	0.08	0.17	1.05
	1986	0.05	0.11	0.67	0.02	0.05	0.33
Rwanda	1975	0.74	0.84	2.28	0.37	0.42	1.13
	1981	0.40	0.74	4.61	0.19	0.36	2.25
	1983	0.81	1.39	5.21	0.39	0.68	2.54
	1984	0.85	1.44	5.77	0.41	0.70	2.81
	1985	1.13	1.85	6.46	0.55	0.90	3.14
	1986	1.47	2.27	8.21	0.72	1.10	4.00

Cameroun / Cap-Vert / Rép. centrafricaine / Côte d'Ivoire / Egypt / Ethiopia / Gabon / Guinée / Guinée-Bissau

Pays	Année	(1)	(2)	(3)	(4)	(5)	(6)
Cameroun	1970	4.45	4.79	5.18	2.45	2.64	2.85
	1981	8.36	8.36	18.32	4.32	4.32	9.47
	1983	7.21	7.21	20.47	3.77	3.77	10.71
	1984	5.57	5.57	15.54	2.91	2.91	8.11
	1985	7.79	7.79	25.20	4.05	4.05	13.11
	1986	11.32	11.32	32.35	5.89	5.89	16.82
Cap-Vert	1983	4.75	7.36	17.34	2.43	3.77	8.89
	1984	5.08	7.69	20.48	2.65	4.01	10.69
	1985	7.13	10.70	27.29	3.78	5.67	14.46
	1986	9.46	15.17	36.07	5.05	8.10	19.26
Rép. centrafricaine	1981	2.28	4.62	5.69	1.24	2.51	3.10
	1983	1.93	3.47	4.12	1.04	1.87	2.22
	1984	3.17	4.56	4.23	1.70	2.45	2.28
	1985	3.71	6.01	5.83	1.99	3.22	3.13
	1986	5.35	11.74	9.62	2.86	6.28	5.14
Côte d'Ivoire	1981	6.96	11.84	21.32	3.43	5.84	10.52
	1983	6.71	8.57	15.28	3.30	4.21	7.50
	1984	7.08	9.50	12.31	3.47	4.66	6.03
	1985	8.59	12.28	20.27	4.20	6.00	9.91
	1986	10.82	13.59	23.93	5.28	6.63	11.68
Egypt	1984	47.12	50.36	128.93	25.88	27.66	70.81
	1985	49.56	52.96	149.24	27.18	29.05	81.87
	1986	56.13	59.96	172.28	31.17	33.30	95.68
Ethiopia	1972	1.99	2.03	2.60	1.04	1.07	1.36
	1975	3.44	3.49	3.95	1.79	1.82	2.06
	1980	1.85	1.88	2.77	0.98	0.99	1.47
	1983	2.42	2.46	2.93	1.23	1.26	1.50
	1984	2.35	2.39	3.50	1.18	1.20	1.76
	1985	2.53	2.58	3.56	1.26	1.28	1.77
	1986	2.45	2.50	3.48	1.23	1.25	1.74
Gabon	1980	120.77	163.61	169.26	74.23	100.56	104.03
	1983	117.33	144.75	172.02	70.94	87.52	104.00
	1984	98.11	122.66	136.58	59.03	73.80	82.18
	1985	135.90	169.38	186.72	81.45	101.52	111.92
	1986	171.89	212.89	190.07	103.61	128.32	114.56
Guinée	1981	0.58	0.73	2.54	0.31	0.39	1.38
	1983	0.45	0.60	2.25	0.24	0.33	1.22
	1984	·	·	·	·	·	·
	1985	1.71	1.90	2.17	0.92	1.03	1.17
	1986	0.29	0.34	0.38	0.16	0.18	0.20
Guinée-Bissau	1981	0.08	2.33	1.99	0.04	1.29	1.10
	1983	0.04	1.19	0.69	0.02	0.66	0.38
	1984	0.22	0.40	0.93	0.12	0.22	0.51
	1985	0.33	0.54	0.98	0.18	0.30	0.54
	1986	0.31	0.52	1.16	0.17	0.29	0.64

See note on page 105. *Voir note page 105.* *Véase nota pág. 105.*

Table 5 *(cont.)* **Tableau 5** *(suite)* **Cuadro 5** *(cont.)*

Country / Pays / País (1)	Financial year / Exercice financier / Ejercicio financiero (2)	Per head of total population — Par habitant (population totale) — Por habitante (población total)			Per head of population between 15 and 64 years of age — Par habitant de 15 à 64 ans — Por habitante entre 15 y 64 años de edad		
		Receipts / Recettes / Ingresos (3)	Expenditure / Dépenses / Egresos — Total (4)	Benefits / Prestations / Prestaciones — Total (5)	Receipts / Recettes / Ingresos (6)	Expenditure / Dépenses / Egresos — Total (7)	Benefits / Prestations / Prestaciones — Total (8)
Barbados	1971	42.42	23.57	23.32	77.72	43.18	42.73
	1975	109.70	80.78	79.21	193.96	142.83	140.05
	1980	132.06	75.25	70.46	220.70	125.75	117.74
	1983	268.42	155.10	143.81	437.50	252.80	234.39
	1984	272.47	186.57	174.26	442.98	303.33	283.32
	1985	291.50	205.43	192.24	469.75	331.04	309.79
	1986	290.81	254.47	236.49	465.67	407.48	378.68
Belize	1981	21.23	13.56	12.43	31.96	20.41	18.71
	1983	36.49	18.03	16.06	54.91	27.13	24.17
	1984	32.68	5.11	2.91	49.48	7.73	4.41
	1985	31.40	6.64	3.69	47.39	10.02	5.56
	1986	32.87	7.01	3.64	49.75	10.61	5.51
Bolivia	1972	.	.	.	.	.	.
	1975	.	.	.	.	.	.
Brasil	1980	.	.	.	.	.	.
	1983	.	.	.	.	.	.
	1984	13.51	14.76	11.93	25.44	27.80	22.47
	1985	6.50	4.87	3.99	12.26	9.18	7.53
Canada	1970	677.11	589.90	578.40	1 104.89	962.59	943.81
	1975	1 132.58	1 019.85	995.63	1 763.98	1 588.42	1 550.68
	1980	1 700.70	1 457.04	1 411.73	2 508.89	2 149.44	2 082.60
	1983	2 367.89	2 136.96	2 058.86	3 484.70	3 144.85	3 029.91
	1984	2 368.25	2 153.32	2 057.66	3 482.52	3 166.47	3 025.79
	1985	2 499.63	2 202.18	2 119.11	3 672.75	3 235.70	3 113.65

Table 5 *(cont.)* **Tableau 5** *(suite)* **Cuadro 5** *(cont.)*

Country / Pays / País (1)	Financial year / Exercice financier / Ejercicio financiero (2)	Per head of total population — Par habitant (population totale) — Por habitante (población total)			Per head of population between 15 and 64 years of age — Par habitant de 15 à 64 ans — Por habitante entre 15 y 64 años de edad		
		Receipts / Recettes / Ingresos (3)	Expenditure / Dépenses / Egresos — Total (4)	Benefits / Prestations / Prestaciones — Total (5)	Receipts / Recettes / Ingresos (6)	Expenditure / Dépenses / Egresos — Total (7)	Benefits / Prestations / Prestaciones — Total (8)
Sao Tomé-et-Principe	1981	24.60	5.33	5.33	50.96	11.04	11.04
	1983	20.84	4.95	4.95	42.61	10.13	10.13
	1984	17.74	4.90	4.90	36.64	10.11	10.11
	1985	20.87	6.39	6.39	42.53	13.03	13.03
	1986	12.55	6.40	6.40	25.60	13.06	13.06
Sénégal	1970	7.43	6.71	6.53	13.89	12.53	12.20
	1975	10.73	8.68	7.76	19.82	16.05	14.34
	1980	10.80	8.72	6.87	20.82	16.80	13.24
	1983	2.92	2.31	1.82	5.74	4.53	3.58
	1984	6.12	5.17	4.33	11.60	9.81	8.21
	1985	8.74	7.15	6.01	16.60	13.58	11.41
	1986	10.35	8.82	7.48	19.66	16.75	14.20
Sudan	1980	2.55	0.35	0.10	4.86	0.67	0.19
	1983	1.24	0.28	0.10	2.38	0.54	0.19
	1984	2.02	0.30	0.16	3.87	0.57	0.30
	1985	0.99	0.17	0.09	1.91	0.33	0.17
	1986	0.75	0.15	0.07	1.44	0.29	0.14
Swaziland	1981	13.69	4.86	2.69	27.10	9.61	5.32
	1983	15.03	6.22	3.27	29.81	12.34	6.48
	1984	7.75	1.13	1.13	15.39	2.25	2.25
	1985	6.21	2.02	0.95	12.36	4.01	1.89
	1986	7.33	2.66	1.22	14.61	5.31	2.43
Tanzania, United Rep. of	1980	2.05	0.54	0.40	4.17	1.10	0.82
	1983	1.55	0.79	0.25	3.16	1.61	0.52
	1984	2.18	0.49	0.31	4.43	1.00	0.64
	1985	2.60	0.82	0.55	5.30	1.67	1.13
	1986	1.11	0.42	0.20	2.26	0.86	0.41

Country	Year	1	2	3	4	5	6
Tchad	1979-81	.	.	.	.	.	.
	1983	0.04	0.18	0.21	0.02	0.10	0.11
	1984	0.06	0.24	0.52	0.03	0.13	0.28
	1985	0.28	0.59	1.63	0.15	0.32	0.88
	1986	0.39	0.94	1.36	0.21	0.51	0.74
Togo	1972	4.28	4.78	6.97	2.28	2.55	3.72
	1975	7.27	8.67	11.43	3.84	4.59	6.05
	1980	6.06	7.76	15.90	3.18	4.07	8.34
	1983	3.80	5.26	11.55	1.98	2.75	6.02
	1984	3.75	4.90	11.40	1.95	2.55	5.94
	1985	5.20	6.93	16.38	2.71	3.61	8.52
	1986	6.46	9.14	18.75	3.35	4.74	9.73
Tunisie	1984	75.63	95.37	110.87	42.47	53.55	62.26
	1985	98.38	133.29	150.73	55.63	75.37	85.23
	1986	94.21	115.54	129.67	53.58	65.72	73.76
Uganda	1980	14.98	104.87	164.00	7.52	52.65	82.34
	1983	0.19	3.27	9.94	0.09	1.62	4.92
	1984	0.05	0.05	3.92	0.03	0.03	1.94
	1985	0.02	0.02	1.36	0.01	0.01	0.67
	1986	0.00	0.00	0.68	0.00	0.00	0.33
Zaïre	1984	0.06	0.33	0.52	0.03	0.17	0.27
	1985	0.10	0.47	0.83	0.05	0.24	0.43
	1986	0.25	0.91	1.08	0.13	0.47	0.55
Zambia	1970	19.03	19.99	29.65	9.64	10.13	15.02
	1975	46.93	49.13	66.19	23.51	24.62	33.17
	1980	8.85	12.51	29.28	4.45	6.30	14.74
	1984	2.32	5.00	13.90	1.10	2.37	6.60
	1985	1.45	2.83	6.48	0.69	1.35	3.08
	1986	0.60	1.48	3.92	0.29	0.70	1.86

AMERICA – AMÉRIQUE – AMERICA

Country	Year	1	2	3	4	5	6
Argentina	1975	.	.	.	.	.	.
	1980	.	.	.	.	.	.
	1983	111.74	120.38	124.32	68.20	73.46	75.87
	1984	110.20	117.33	132.24	66.93	71.26	80.32
	1985	154.06	158.24	191.56	93.13	95.66	115.81
	1986	186.26	191.15	212.15	112.42	115.38	128.05
Bahamas	1980	69.40	155.19	278.55	25.76	38.67	46.24
	1983	150.49	216.51	367.42	68.29	88.68	115.89
	1984	171.45	237.90	394.78	77.86	103.82	129.20
	1985	194.51	308.06	503.31	92.20	119.05	150.63
	1986	216.05	311.69	500.41	101.69	134.58	163.26

Country	Year	1	2	3	4	5	6
Colombia	1970	15.24	16.47	19.74	7.87	8.51	10.20
	1975	26.97	29.39	34.80	14.62	15.94	18.87
	1980	45.55	58.72	69.66	25.99	33.51	39.75
	1983	42.22	47.80	49.99	24.60	27.85	29.13
	1984	25.53	49.06	54.20	13.38	25.71	28.40
	1985	18.38	34.05	39.71	10.86	20.11	23.46
	1986	18.25	35.36	44.88	10.81	20.94	26.57
Costa Rica	1970	32.62	37.94	54.05	16.56	19.27	27.45
	1975	83.63	93.87	124.70	45.75	51.35	68.22
	1980	234.28	263.98	307.34	135.04	152.15	177.15
	1983	112.21	126.59	218.61	65.81	74.24	128.20
	1984	135.34	168.44	231.27	79.79	99.30	136.35
	1985	152.68	185.78	254.68	90.54	110.17	151.03
	1986	155.66	190.39	246.27	92.41	113.03	146.20
Cuba	1980	262.25	271.24	271.24	160.98	166.50	166.50
	1983	260.05	269.13	269.13	167.38	173.22	173.22
	1984	264.99	275.07	275.07	173.19	179.79	179.79
	1985	277.53	288.29	288.29	184.14	191.28	191.28
	1986	335.57	348.22	348.22	224.92	233.40	233.40
Chile	1971	228.21	252.41	284.90	131.55	145.49	164.22
	1975	69.46	75.46	95.38	41.19	44.75	56.56
	1980	402.80	435.69	527.71	245.77	265.83	321.98
	1983	318.57	349.91	409.54	197.61	217.04	254.04
	1984	265.93	291.81	335.87	165.84	181.98	209.46
	1985	226.22	248.21	327.76	141.85	155.64	205.52
	1986	246.66	268.09	370.96	154.98	168.44	233.07
Dominica	1980	5.41	11.97	47.29	2.85	6.31	24.92
	1983	9.97	17.58	61.26	5.29	9.33	32.52
	1984	18.60	27.82	77.00	9.76	14.59	40.38
	1985	23.31	33.69	101.72	12.41	17.94	54.16
	1986	26.83	39.48	111.11	14.29	21.02	59.16
República Dominicana	1984	13.09	15.95	16.89	7.41	9.02	9.56
	1985	4.42	5.44	5.57	2.52	3.11	3.18
	1986	4.97	6.55	6.87	2.85	3.76	3.94
Ecuador	1972	17.10	19.18	29.61	8.74	9.80	15.13
	1974	29.13	31.78	47.92	14.96	16.33	24.62
	1980	57.41	79.71	126.68	30.45	42.27	67.18
	1983	58.33	78.71	106.85	31.45	42.44	57.62
	1984	62.75	71.89	141.17	34.03	38.99	76.55
	1985	55.55	63.20	148.44	30.28	34.46	80.93
	1986	47.37	53.79	130.70	25.94	29.45	71.56
El Salvador	1970	13.11	16.51	21.48	6.65	8.37	10.89
	1975	20.79	29.33	33.93	10.59	14.94	17.28
	1980	21.97	25.85	38.91	11.19	13.17	19.83
	1983	25.65	28.03	48.06	13.01	14.22	24.39
	1984	24.04	28.91	33.57	12.18	14.64	17.00
	1985	26.03	30.07	37.80	13.16	15.21	19.12
	1986	12.66	16.89	23.01	6.44	8.58	11.70

See note on page 105.   *Voir note page 105.*   Véase nota pág. 105.

Table 5 *(cont.)*   **Tableau 5** *(suite)*   **Cuadro 5** *(cont.)*

Country / Pays / País (1)	Financial year / Exercice financier / Ejercicio financiero (2)	Per head of total population / Par habitant (population totale) / Por habitante (población total)			Per head of population between 15 and 64 years of age / Par habitant de 15 à 64 ans / Por habitante entre 15 y 64 años de edad		
		Receipts / Recettes / Ingresos (3)	Expenditure / Dépenses / Egresos — Total (4)	Benefits / Prestations / Prestaciones (5)	Receipts / Recettes / Ingresos (6)	Expenditure / Dépenses / Egresos — Total (7)	Benefits / Prestations / Prestaciones (8)
Uruguay	1975	120.45	113.51	89.62	192.11	181.04	142.94
	1980	335.46	259.00	237.05	536.29	414.06	378.96
	1983	180.18	159.11	147.24	288.44	254.71	235.72
	1984	123.49	141.99	132.06	197.88	227.52	211.61
	1985	127.56	125.12	116.04	204.42	200.52	185.96
	1986	169.58	170.55	158.07	271.70	273.25	253.26
Venezuela	1970	38.40	35.09	26.02	72.38	66.15	49.05
	1975	103.59	90.31	84.73	183.57	160.04	150.14
	1980	66.04	51.73	44.48	118.54	92.86	79.84
	1983	72.42	60.72	50.77	128.08	107.39	89.80
	1984	42.42	38.45	32.76	74.66	67.67	57.66
	1985	44.68	39.58	33.60	78.26	69.33	58.85
	1986	28.91	24.64	20.97	50.46	43.01	36.61

ASIA – ASIE – ASIA

Country	Financial year	Receipts (3)	Expenditure Total (4)	Benefits (5)	Receipts (6)	Expenditure Total (7)	Benefits (8)
Bahrain	1978	144.15	22.47	17.63	260.38	40.59	31.85
	1980	188.00	27.74	19.56	296.04	43.68	30.81
	1983	326.05	63.45	39.47	506.89	98.64	61.36
	1984	207.51	38.64	24.09	321.72	59.90	37.35
	1985	238.49	38.07	28.23	366.98	58.58	43.44
	1986	230.89	48.78	35.72	354.94	74.98	54.91
Bangladesh	1975	0.25	0.24	0.24	0.50	0.47	0.47
	1980	0.00	0.00	0.00	0.00	0.00	0.00
	1983	0.01	0.00	0.00	0.02	0.01	0.01
	1984	0.05	0.02	0.02	0.10	0.04	0.04
	1985	0.04	0.02	0.02	0.08	0.04	0.03
	1986	0.05	0.02	0.02	0.10	0.04	0.03

Country (1)	Financial year (2)	Receipts (3)	Expenditure Total (4)	Benefits (5)	Receipts (6)	Expenditure Total (7)	Benefits (8)
Grenada	1981	13.94	13.66	13.66	25.93	25.41	25.41
	1983	31.27	17.84	17.05	57.64	32.88	31.43
	1984	44.86	20.16	18.78	83.57	37.55	34.98
	1985	55.30	22.97	21.17	102.09	42.40	39.08
	1986	57.26	22.68	20.65	105.88	41.94	38.18
Guatemala	1970	8.06	7.76	6.92	15.71	15.11	13.49
	1975	12.05	11.72	10.95	22.53	21.91	20.47
	1980	19.29	13.14	11.61	37.61	25.63	22.64
	1983	16.51	11.99	10.63	32.24	23.42	20.77
	1984	17.87	13.11	11.05	34.91	25.63	21.58
	1985	18.95	13.73	11.59	37.05	26.83	22.66
	1986	10.20	6.56	5.64	19.92	12.81	11.02
Guyana	1972	18.93	12.04	10.19	37.60	23.91	20.25
	1975	21.50	11.38	9.44	40.76	21.56	17.90
	1980	41.44	8.60	6.33	72.86	15.11	11.13
	1983	49.50	9.67	6.95	84.93	16.59	11.92
	1984	40.15	7.83	5.70	68.32	13.32	9.70
	1985	53.40	10.87	7.37	90.14	18.36	12.44
	1986	46.82	14.53	11.65	78.59	24.39	19.56
Honduras	1970	5.11	4.53	4.39	10.18	9.04	8.76
	1971	3.38	3.27	3.11	6.77	6.55	6.22
	1981	8.60	5.76	4.86	17.91	12.00	10.12
	1983	9.34	6.69	5.46	18.67	13.38	10.91
	1984	15.76	8.22	6.61	31.41	16.37	13.18
	1985	17.05	8.47	6.89	33.86	16.82	13.68
	1986	18.41	8.51	7.19	36.31	16.78	14.19

Jamaica	1970	30.92	21.25	16.70	64.71	44.48	34.94
	1975	74.05	57.49	51.09	152.81	118.63	105.42
	1980	35.70	17.13	16.09	65.93	31.64	29.72
	1983	24.80	13.73	12.88	43.75	24.22	22.72
	1984	23.27	12.56	11.87	40.53	21.87	20.67
	1985	21.09	11.41	10.68	36.43	19.71	18.45
	1986	24.93	12.94	12.09	43.62	22.64	21.15
México	1970	21.32	20.08	16.80	42.36	39.90	33.38
	1974	43.08	38.10	32.46	85.92	75.99	64.74
	1980	89.42	72.37	52.73	170.66	138.12	100.64
	1983	50.61	42.49	29.24	93.29	78.33	53.90
	1984	60.12	54.40	40.34	109.57	99.14	73.53
	1985	49.40	41.10	32.23	89.04	74.07	58.10
	1986	33.53	28.79	21.19	59.69	51.25	37.72
Panamá	1972	71.08	61.93	52.26	136.01	118.51	100.01
	1975	106.64	82.97	71.22	201.21	156.56	134.38
	1980	148.25	107.61	96.93	266.52	193.46	174.26
	1983	215.89	160.41	139.97	379.31	281.83	245.92
	1984	200.09	170.38	159.37	348.29	296.57	277.41
	1985	207.89	178.85	167.84	358.54	308.46	289.48
	1986	224.74	191.24	180.33	484.51	412.29	388.77
Perú	1981	27.41	22.85	20.59	50.16	41.81	37.68
	1983	13.35	14.25	12.62	24.21	25.83	22.88
	1984	9.50	10.08	3.92	17.15	18.19	7.07
	1985	11.58	10.11	4.07	20.79	18.16	7.31
	1986	24.98	21.77	8.58	44.45	38.75	15.28
St. Lucia	1981	24.25	4.61	2.12	50.93	9.69	4.44
	1983	19.43	6.09	2.77	39.77	12.47	5.68
	1984	28.87	8.54	5.58	58.61	17.34	11.34
	1985	28.86	5.73	2.35	58.15	11.55	4.74
	1986	38.69	8.91	5.48	78.50	18.09	11.11
Trinidad and Tobago	1970	26.36	25.74	25.74	47.91	46.79	46.79
	1975	71.48	51.69	49.79	123.53	89.33	86.05
	1980	75.52	42.49	36.28	126.11	70.95	60.58
	1983	248.92	167.14	152.59	408.54	274.31	250.44
	1984	187.53	110.94	92.84	306.08	181.07	151.53
	1985	172.52	106.00	88.10	279.88	171.97	142.92
	1986	117.09	88.77	68.41	189.47	143.65	110.69
United States	1970	541.45	457.86	427.30	885.72	748.97	698.98
	1975	1 029.69	946.60	889.76	1 586.90	1 458.85	1 371.24
	1980	1 627.16	1 447.08	1 390.45	2 458.37	2 186.30	2 100.74
	1983	2 191.07	1 923.75	1 843.61	3 305.16	2 901.92	2 781.03
	1984	2 276.90	1 966.20	1 876.20	3 432.83	2 964.40	2 828.71
	1985	2 474.53	2 082.50	1 990.51	3 728.85	3 138.10	2 999.50
	1986	2 667.53	2 176.59	2 088.06	4 034.56	3 292.03	3 158.14

Cyprus	1970	33.27	28.63	28.03	56.93	48.98	47.96
	1975	68.05	74.36	73.16	105.49	115.27	113.42
	1980	148.52	120.43	118.15	227.13	184.16	180.69
	1983	262.61	156.72	153.75	406.76	242.75	238.15
	1984	260.03	146.23	143.93	403.88	227.13	223.55
	1985	371.03	197.03	193.83	579.19	307.58	302.58
	1986	410.92	237.20	233.53	641.64	370.38	364.66
India	1970	3.04	1.96	1.92	5.64	3.63	3.57
	1975	5.75	3.32	3.27	10.46	6.05	5.95
	1980	6.85	4.03	3.93	12.27	7.22	7.05
	1983	10.93	5.21	5.14	18.79	8.96	8.83
	1984	9.13	4.29	4.23	15.67	7.36	7.25
	1985	9.61	4.42	4.35	16.45	7.56	7.44
	1986	.	.	.	.	.	.
Indonesia	1981	0.34	0.06	0.03	0.63	0.11	0.05
	1983	0.36	0.10	0.03	0.64	0.18	0.05
	1984	0.36	0.30	0.03	0.63	0.52	0.06
	1985	0.46	0.43	0.04	0.80	0.75	0.07
	1986	0.36	0.34	0.04	0.61	0.58	0.07
Iran, Islamic Rep. of	1981	69.53	27.93	25.53	132.51	53.24	48.65
	1983	77.41	27.60	25.76	146.04	52.07	48.60
	1984	67.56	27.38	11.25	126.80	51.39	21.12
	1985	75.63	35.70	14.45	141.23	66.67	26.98
	1986	92.03	44.60	19.46	172.31	83.50	36.44
Israel	1970	200.00	142.86	142.86	314.29	257.14	228.57
	1975	422.54	380.28	338.03	718.31	661.97	577.46
	1980	574.39	546.03	485.11	1 001.12	951.68	845.51
	1983	602.00	563.93	473.76	1 038.88	973.18	817.58
	1984	522.35	535.07	445.97	903.23	925.22	771.16
	1985	705.14	707.78	594.34	1 214.50	1 219.04	1 023.66
	1986	1 035.53	946.78	850.97	1 775.60	1 623.42	1 459.14
Japan	1970	154.49	109.35	94.41	226.64	160.42	138.50
	1975	512.55	388.56	342.84	763.11	578.51	510.44
	1980	1 442.34	1 135.39	1 017.23	2 152.65	1 694.54	1 518.19
	1983	1 543.12	1 247.26	1 132.20	2 268.58	1 833.63	1 664.48
	1984	1 455.26	1 157.48	1 093.98	2 134.67	1 697.86	1 604.72
	1985	1 978.36	1 533.55	1 446.86	2 894.29	2 243.54	2 116.71
	1986	2 613.93	2 076.92	1 965.08	3 806.95	3 024.85	2 861.96
Jordan	1980	5.40	0.34	0.03	11.37	0.72	0.07
	1983	25.14	2.86	2.13	51.84	5.89	4.40
	1984	29.63	5.20	2.67	60.67	10.66	5.47
	1985	34.21	7.23	4.12	69.57	14.71	8.37
	1986	42.73	7.60	5.89	86.72	15.42	11.94
Kuwait	1980	242.68	113.93	107.20	434.04	203.77	191.73
	1983	464.30	202.16	192.31	810.59	352.94	335.74
	1984	397.13	183.60	171.63	691.59	319.74	298.89
	1985	653.58	332.64	320.88	1 135.97	578.15	557.71
	1986	737.65	324.13	312.25	1 277.69	561.42	540.86

See note on page 105. *Voir note page 105.* Véase nota pág. 105.

Table 5 (*cont.*)   **Tableau 5** (*suite*)   **Cuadro 5** (*cont.*)

Country / Pays / País (1)	Financial year / Exercice financier / Ejercicio financiero (2)	Per head of total population — Receipts / Recettes / Ingresos (3)	Expenditure / Dépenses / Egresos Total (4)	Benefits / Prestations / Prestaciones Total (5)	Per head of population between 15 and 64 years of age — Receipts / Recettes / Ingresos (6)	Expenditure / Dépenses / Egresos Total (7)	Benefits / Prestations / Prestaciones Total (8)
Denmark	1970	487.26	474.09	462.39	763.90	743.26	724.91
	1975	1 430.54	1 396.32	1 364.73	2 237.57	2 184.05	2 134.63
	1980	3 351.28	3 264.25	3 176.44	5 175.94	5 041.53	4 905.91
	1983	2 956.54	2 848.48	2 766.48	4 497.25	4 332.87	4 208.15
	1984	2 670.22	2 572.61	2 493.48	4 040.90	3 893.19	3 773.44
	1985	3 596.33	3 479.48	3 373.97	5 414.08	5 238.16	5 079.32
	1986	4 759.98	4 636.53	4 502.19	7 142.06	6 956.83	6 755.27
España	1975	343.94	332.25	310.61	551.58	532.83	498.14
	1980	806.98	815.58	780.61	1 286.12	1 299.81	1 244.08
	1983	668.23	672.13	649.00	1 041.13	1 047.20	1 011.16
	1984	696.90	682.41	655.09	1 077.75	1 055.34	1 013.08
	1985	873.47	866.92	832.43	1 340.87	1 330.81	1 277.87
	1986	1 151.19	1 133.16	1 076.66	1 759.60	1 732.03	1 645.67
Finland	1970	324.90	296.18	284.58	490.01	446.69	429.20
	1975	1 033.00	903.87	870.12	1 533.71	1 341.99	1 291.88
	1980	2 202.93	1 887.54	1 820.71	3 254.02	2 788.15	2 689.43
	1983	2 192.33	2 004.58	1 924.40	3 226.05	2 949.77	2 831.78
	1984	2 211.44	2 018.83	1 948.91	3 250.90	2 967.76	2 864.98
	1985	3 082.93	2 798.44	2 707.82	4 526.06	4 108.40	3 975.37
	1986	3 834.83	3 484.97	3 371.77	5 639.86	5 125.33	4 958.84
France	1970	427.67	427.58	394.59	686.39	686.24	633.31
	1975	1 502.56	1 481.90	1 285.78	2 399.41	2 366.42	2 053.24
	1980	3 130.47	3 037.01	2 889.81	4 910.47	4 763.86	4 532.96
	1983	2 601.48	2 534.87	2 408.15	4 001.73	3 899.28	3 704.34
	1984	2 458.08	2 400.03	2 277.73	3 756.89	3 668.18	3 481.26
	1985	3 284.58	3 232.27	3 074.41	4 988.18	4 908.74	4 668.99
	1986	4 002.10	4 026.61	3 829.29	6 074.10	6 111.30	5 811.82
Malaysia	1970	20.88	11.44	11.15	34.14	18.71	18.24
	1975	45.81	26.13	24.06	71.03	40.52	37.31
	1980	69.99	16.84	14.37	122.77	29.54	25.21
	1983	126.94	35.91	34.58	219.33	62.05	59.75
	1984	137.48	40.15	36.70	236.35	69.03	63.10
	1985	150.03	39.92	37.88	256.67	68.29	64.80
	1986	150.34	37.90	35.60	255.84	64.50	60.58
Myanmar	1970	1.66	1.59	1.57	3.02	2.88	2.86
	1975	1.60	1.55	1.54	2.89	2.80	2.78
	1980	0.13	0.08	0.06	0.24	0.15	0.12
	1983	0.13	0.09	0.06	0.23	0.17	0.10
	1984	0.12	0.09	0.05	0.22	0.15	0.09
	1985	0.14	0.11	0.06	0.25	0.19	0.10
	1986	0.16	0.13	0.07	0.35	0.28	0.15
Pakistan	1965	1.25	1.25	1.25	2.54	2.54	2.54
	1980	0.31	0.14	0.07	0.61	0.27	0.14
	1983	2.12	1.84	1.80	4.08	3.55	3.47
	1984	2.38	2.16	2.11	4.59	4.16	4.06
	1985	3.99	3.71	3.67	7.71	7.18	7.10
	1986	3.00	2.71	2.66	5.83	5.25	5.17
Philippines	1970	3.12	1.73	1.53	6.11	3.38	2.99
	1978	9.24	3.96	3.32	16.90	7.24	6.07
	1980	12.22	4.70	3.82	22.40	8.61	7.00
	1983	9.28	3.91	3.27	16.83	7.09	5.93
	1984	7.51	3.14	2.61	13.57	5.68	4.72
	1985	10.22	3.59	3.04	18.42	6.47	5.48
	1986	9.31	3.69	3.21	16.72	6.63	5.76
Qatar	1984	73.47	73.47	73.47	113.19	113.19	113.19
	1985	73.08	73.08	73.08	113.22	113.22	113.22
	1986	70.23	70.23	70.23	109.36	109.36	109.36

Country / Pays	Year	(1)	(2)	(3)	(4)	(5)	(6)
Singapore	1970	43.92	44.68	85.23	25.34	25.78	49.17
	1975	112.22	113.78	349.35	71.07	72.06	221.26
	1980	247.28	267.31	842.43	168.61	182.27	574.42
	1983	494.60	791.13	1 552.99	343.77	549.87	1 079.40
	1984	938.02	1 279.17	1 788.54	656.13	894.76	1 251.06
	1985	925.49	1 336.07	2 057.95	651.24	940.16	1 448.13
	1986	1 013.00	1 410.34	1 684.72	715.29	995.86	1 189.60
Sri Lanka	1970	9.51	10.67	14.07	5.18	5.81	7.66
	1975	9.63	9.76	14.83	5.45	5.52	8.39
	1980	6.83	7.12	13.05	4.12	4.30	7.88
	1983	11.24	11.48	20.45	6.85	6.99	12.45
	1984	12.54	12.66	29.91	7.65	7.73	18.26
	1985	14.46	14.60	35.34	8.85	8.94	21.63
	1986	17.66	17.87	46.34	8.65	8.75	22.70
Rép. arabe syrienne	1984	34.60	36.19	77.23	17.02	17.80	37.98
	1985	37.33	38.97	79.30	18.35	19.16	38.98
	1986	38.14	40.07	83.41	18.76	19.71	41.03
Thailand	1980	0.18	0.19	0.47	0.10	0.11	0.26
	1983	2.38	2.40	2.74	1.39	1.41	1.60
	1984	0.30	0.32	0.30	0.18	0.19	0.18
	1985	0.28	0.31	0.32	0.17	0.18	0.19
	1986	0.26	0.29	0.34	0.16	0.18	0.21

EUROPE – EUROPE – EUROPA

*Countries with a market economy – Pays à économie de marché –
Países con economía de mercado*

Country / Pays	Year	(1)	(2)	(3)	(4)	(5)	(6)
Austria	1970	563.45	590.36	599.54	346.14	362.68	368.31
	1975	1 474.23	1 544.86	1 568.24	910.02	953.63	968.06
	1980	3 181.08	3 340.76	3 362.03	2 041.22	2 143.68	2 157.33
	1983	2 919.56	3 025.65	3 128.92	1 928.72	1 928.81	2 067.03
	1984	2 761.88	2 863.38	2 962.97	1 841.74	1 909.43	1 975.84
	1985	3 719.16	3 868.81	3 963.76	2 503.72	2 604.46	2 668.38
	1986	4 978.38	5 173.82	5 279.40	3 350.94	3 482.49	3 553.56
Belgique	1970	703.85	765.99	798.84	443.44	482.59	503.29
	1975	2 067.29	2 204.16	2 285.49	1 318.71	1 406.02	1 457.90
	1980	4 191.18	4 450.75	4 355.95	2 745.74	2 915.79	2 853.69
	1983	3 038.73	3 211.42	3 234.24	2 021.30	2 136.17	2 151.35
	1984	2 739.19	2 894.33	2 963.81	1 831.41	1 935.14	1 981.59
	1985	3 549.03	3 743.83	3 844.75	2 384.74	2 515.64	2 583.45
	1986	4 642.96	4 915.21	4 987.44	3 119.51	3 302.43	3 350.96
Germany, Fed. Rep. of	1970	772.67	820.88	854.58	491.77	522.46	543.91
	1975	2 250.50	2 347.90	2 324.14	1 439.14	1 501.42	1 486.23
	1980	4 278.49	4 439.47	4 472.73	2 837.34	2 944.09	2 966.15
	1983	3 460.10	3 555.04	3 547.78	2 365.42	2 430.32	2 425.35
	1984	3 092.23	3 177.30	3 167.29	2 135.01	2 193.74	2 186.83
	1985	3 772.36	3 878.68	3 903.72	2 630.36	2 704.49	2 721.95
	1986	5 313.77	5 469.01	5 559.24	3 705.31	3 813.56	3 876.48
Grèce	1970	182.82	191.57	211.99	116.93	122.52	135.59
	1975	332.98	353.66	395.39	212.77	225.98	252.66
	1980	693.43	728.75	844.52	444.11	466.74	540.88
	1983	804.79	856.52	903.86	522.01	555.56	586.26
	1984	793.66	847.69	860.68	516.97	552.17	560.63
	1985	877.15	936.12	908.72	573.76	612.33	594.41
Iceland	1984	973.33	993.25	1 009.42	614.95	627.54	637.75
	1985	1 331.27	1 361.78	1 378.67	839.64	858.88	869.53
	1986	1 816.70	1 855.59	1 890.60	1 151.32	1 175.97	1 198.16
Ireland	1970	227.62	237.25	239.66	130.59	136.11	137.49
	1975	763.10	793.63	790.32	448.30	466.23	464.29
	1980	1 701.50	1 790.28	1 804.94	997.59	1 049.64	1 058.23
	1983	1 768.88	1 862.46	1 840.39	1 049.01	1 104.51	1 091.42
	1984	1 654.74	1 736.61	1 723.71	985.16	1 033.90	1 026.22
	1985	2 259.25	2 363.41	2 358.62	1 350.44	1 412.70	1 409.84
	1986	2 687.43	2 822.24	2 820.56	1 618.08	1 699.24	1 698.23
Italie	1970	402.02	435.24	449.21	261.18	282.76	291.84
	1975	986.36	1 086.35	933.39	630.14	694.01	596.29
Luxembourg	1970	716.17	738.39	823.68	471.11	485.72	541.83
	1975	1 884.32	1 957.69	2 139.01	1 242.18	1 290.54	1 410.07
	1980	4 060.14	4 233.30	4 649.02	2 721.63	2 837.71	3 116.38
	1983	2 953.89	3 179.61	3 434.23	2 025.76	2 180.55	2 355.17
	1984	2 802.34	2 932.75	3 187.88	1 937.14	2 027.28	2 203.65
	1985	3 638.66	3 774.23	4 234.94	2 535.13	2 629.59	2 950.58
	1986	4 814.81	4 972.67	5 722.27	3 362.52	3 472.76	3 996.26
Malta	1970	82.66	83.39	78.20	51.98	52.44	49.17
	1975	191.99	218.94	221.07	124.09	141.51	142.88
	1980	571.31	576.06	694.47	383.26	386.45	465.88
	1983	686.96	693.14	722.60	456.58	460.69	480.26
	1984	805.96	853.92	631.92	533.25	564.98	418.10
	1985	908.73	962.58	747.38	600.41	635.99	493.80
	1986	1 054.71	1 117.75	850.81	699.05	740.84	563.91

See note on page 105. Voir note page 105. Véase nota pág. 105.

Table 5 *(concl.)* **Tableau 5** *(fin)* **Cuadro 5** *(fin)*

Country / Pays / País (1)	Financial year / Exercice financier / Ejercicio financiero (2)	Per head of total population — Par habitant (population totale) — Por habitante (población total)			Per head of population between 15 and 64 years of age — Par habitant de 15 à 64 ans — Por habitante entre 15 y 64 años de edad		
		Receipts / Recettes / Ingresos — Total (3)	Expenditure / Dépenses / Egresos — Total (4)	Benefits / Prestations / Prestaciones — Total (5)	Receipts / Recettes / Ingresos — Total (6)	Expenditure / Dépenses / Egresos — Total (7)	Benefits / Prestations / Prestaciones — Total (8)
Czechoslovakia	1970	241.16	241.16	240.12	367.43	367.43	365.84
	1975	462.39	462.39	460.48	716.91	716.91	713.95
	1980	545.47	545.47	543.50	862.33	862.33	859.21
	1983	531.49	531.49	529.81	830.28	830.28	827.66
	1984	579.29	579.29	577.50	901.32	901.32	898.54
	1985	652.22	652.22	650.34	1 010.88	1 010.88	1 007.97
	1986	800.16	800.16	797.83	1 237.52	1 237.52	1 233.92
German Democratic Rep.	1970	230.56	230.56	229.42	377.55	377.55	375.67
	1975	494.43	494.43	491.88	795.95	795.95	791.83
	1980	907.77	907.77	904.43	1 408.75	1 408.75	1 403.56
	1983	683.77	683.76	681.37	1 034.74	1 034.72	1 031.11
	1984	613.55	613.56	611.42	920.82	920.84	917.62
	1985	756.20	756.20	753.53	1 125.68	1 125.68	1 121.70
	1986	1 032.07	1 032.08	1 028.29	1 536.28	1 536.29	1 530.65
Hongrie	1970	97.04	97.60	96.62	143.43	144.26	142.81
	1975	128.20	128.01	126.78	191.44	191.16	189.31
	1980	309.08	309.09	307.42	478.27	478.28	475.69
	1983	286.45	286.45	285.08	437.10	437.10	435.01
	1984	221.17	221.17	219.84	335.91	335.91	333.90
	1985	268.35	262.48	260.72	405.68	396.81	394.15
	1986	305.99	292.76	290.68	461.74	441.78	438.63
Pologne	1984	326.84	279.70	278.03	501.54	429.20	426.63
	1985	318.80	261.42	259.35	490.05	401.86	398.67
	1986	305.45	249.29	247.22	469.80	383.43	380.24
RSS d'Ukraine	1970	152.74	152.74	152.74	227.96	227.96	227.96
	1975	246.76	246.76	246.76	367.40	367.40	367.40
	1980	364.23	364.23	364.23	545.69	545.69	545.69
	1983	364.20	364.20	364.20	545.66	545.66	545.66
	1984	345.33	345.33	345.33	517.39	517.39	517.39
	1985	399.38	399.38	399.38	598.34	598.34	598.34
	1986	481.68	481.68	481.68	721.65	721.65	721.65

Country / Pays / País (1)	Financial year / Exercice financier / Ejercicio financiero (2)	Per head of total population — Par habitant (population totale) — Por habitante (población total)			Per head of population between 15 and 64 years of age — Par habitant de 15 à 64 ans — Por habitante entre 15 y 64 años de edad		
		Receipts / Recettes / Ingresos — Total (3)	Expenditure / Dépenses / Egresos — Total (4)	Benefits / Prestations / Prestaciones — Total (5)	Receipts / Recettes / Ingresos — Total (6)	Expenditure / Dépenses / Egresos — Total (7)	Benefits / Prestations / Prestaciones — Total (8)
Netherlands	1970	581.85	489.62	472.44	930.28	782.81	755.35
	1975	1 805.41	1 528.96	1 477.77	2 831.30	2 397.76	2 317.49
	1980	3 777.63	3 167.42	3 055.99	5 709.03	4 786.83	4 618.44
	1983	3 179.47	2 717.68	2 641.65	4 706.13	4 022.60	3 910.06
	1984	2 768.57	2 388.43	2 320.93	4 070.43	3 511.53	3 412.30
	1985	3 562.20	3 027.75	2 939.15	5 201.62	4 421.20	4 291.83
	1986	4 408.37	3 846.32	3 730.61	6 422.92	5 604.02	5 435.43
Norway	1970	471.29	446.09	426.34	751.62	711.44	679.94
	1975	1 346.87	1 227.63	1 182.31	2 152.73	1 962.15	1 889.72
	1980	2 811.78	2 715.14	2 657.16	4 458.25	4 305.03	4 213.09
	1983	2 859.63	2 756.36	2 691.28	4 491.83	4 329.63	4 227.40
	1984	3 542.95	3 449.11	3 414.32	5 548.93	5 401.95	5 347.47
	1985	4 620.26	4 487.04	4 439.46	7 213.51	7 005.52	6 931.23
	1986	5 119.17	4 969.86	4 920.46	7 971.44	7 738.94	7 662.02
Portugal	1970	51.89	38.54	33.41	83.86	62.29	53.99
	1975	176.84	160.13	147.90	284.30	257.44	237.78
	1980	245.18	234.03	210.90	385.51	367.98	331.62
	1983	173.95	176.17	166.87	271.20	274.65	260.15
	1984	174.28	168.08	159.46	270.96	261.33	247.93
	1985	229.34	222.00	210.91	355.58	344.20	327.00
	1986	331.55	307.97	293.67	511.87	475.46	453.38
Suisse	1970	388.83	338.14	318.18	602.72	524.14	493.20
	1975	1 323.43	1 260.16	1 193.89	2 023.54	1 926.79	1 825.46
	1980	2 294.05	2 100.69	1 958.48	3 451.45	3 160.54	2 946.58
	1983	2 168.96	2 084.64	1 924.41	3 204.27	3 079.71	2 842.99
	1984	1 985.69	1 925.07	1 769.53	2 915.84	2 826.82	2 598.43
	1985	2 620.17	2 494.52	2 281.13	3 825.03	3 641.60	3 330.08
	1986	3 560.02	3 379.05	3 092.69	5 199.72	4 935.40	4 517.14

Sweden

Year						
1970	960.67	771.56	755.37	1 467.56	1 178.67	1 153.93
1975	2 357.13	2 095.36	2 053.71	3 673.58	3 265.60	3 200.69
1980	5 059.26	4 604.22	4 488.67	7 890.85	7 181.14	7 000.90
1983	3 785.16	3 520.01	3 443.78	5 877.44	5 465.72	5 347.36
1984	3 525.79	3 199.45	3 102.04	5 465.70	4 959.80	4 808.79
1985	4 485.52	4 161.66	3 991.41	6 943.65	6 442.32	6 178.77
1986	5 583.53	5 116.02	4 907.82	8 627.87	7 905.46	7 583.74

Turquie

Year						
1970	12.61	8.98	8.30	22.85	16.27	15.03
1975	52.10	29.17	24.32	94.70	53.02	44.22
1980	54.48	45.91	43.83	97.22	81.92	78.20
1983	41.61	32.37	31.11	71.69	55.77	53.60
1984	41.57	32.84	31.80	70.80	55.92	54.16
1985	45.33	37.81	36.70	76.33	63.67	61.79
1986	46.00	37.20	36.14	76.93	62.22	60.44

United Kingdom

Year						
1970	358.46	344.60	323.47	502.31	482.89	453.28
1975	789.30	744.87	697.80	1 106.38	1 044.09	978.12
1980	1 851.90	1 765.97	1 681.49	2 912.67	2 777.53	2 644.66
1983	1 629.29	1 572.47	1 501.40	2 502.40	2 415.13	2 305.98
1984	1 389.37	1 343.75	1 280.81	2 122.97	2 053.27	1 957.09
1985	1 866.20	1 816.17	1 733.32	2 841.56	2 765.38	2 639.23
1986	2 045.90	1 976.31	1 884.59	3 116.20	3 010.21	2 870.50

EUROPE – EUROPE – EUROPA

Countries with a centrally planned economy – Pays à économie planifiée – Países con economía centralmente planificada

RSS de Biélorussie

Year						
1970	135.97	135.97	135.97	219.29	219.29	219.29
1975	233.41	233.41	233.41	375.74	375.74	375.74
1980	352.43	352.43	352.43	526.57	526.57	526.57
1983	354.79	354.79	354.79	530.09	530.09	530.09
1984	335.13	335.13	335.13	500.70	500.70	500.70
1985	383.04	383.04	383.04	572.23	572.23	572.23
1986	465.69	465.69	465.69	695.76	695.76	695.76

Bulgarie

Year						
1970	147.81	145.15	141.57	226.92	222.84	217.35
1975	276.80	270.58	251.85	425.00	415.44	386.69
1980	332.72	332.72	332.72	504.20	504.20	504.20
1983	337.13	337.13	337.13	504.35	504.35	504.35
1984	379.41	334.88	334.19	565.24	498.89	497.87
1985	371.86	359.42	358.58	547.29	528.97	527.74
1986	336.44	326.06	325.31	495.18	479.90	478.80

URSS

Year						
1970	158.38	158.38	158.38	249.25	249.25	249.25
1975	258.07	258.07	258.07	397.66	397.66	397.66
1980	368.69	368.69	368.69	567.40	567.40	567.40
1983	361.15	361.15	361.15	554.69	554.69	554.69
1984	342.03	342.03	342.03	524.98	524.98	524.98
1985	391.07	391.07	391.07	599.85	599.85	599.85
1986	464.26	464.26	464.26	712.65	712.65	712.65

Yugoslavia

Year						
1970	89.43	81.37	76.38	138.04	125.61	117.91
1981	288.81	284.82	255.68	434.56	428.56	384.72
1983	161.41	160.56	147.23	241.26	239.99	220.07
1984	135.60	129.77	117.11	202.01	193.32	174.47
1985	166.65	159.86	144.21	247.45	237.38	214.13
1986	261.11	256.89	231.98	387.01	380.74	343.82

OCEANIA – OCÉANIE – OCEANIA

Australia

Year						
1970	258.86	241.14	233.44	412.15	383.95	371.68
1975	731.45	702.52	695.85	1 147.80	1 102.26	1 052.45
1980	1 384.73	1 270.00	1 219.79	2 139.93	1 962.63	1 885.03
1983	1 497.39	1 353.53	1 293.92	2 290.01	2 070.00	1 978.84
1984	1 043.72	1 066.69	1 054.88	1 589.29	1 624.25	1 606.27
1985	995.03	1 019.72	1 007.58	1 511.00	1 548.49	1 530.06
1986	1 011.89	994.67	982.71	1 534.45	1 508.34	1 490.20

Fiji

Year						
1975	59.38	33.10	28.01	103.33	57.59	48.73
1980	115.29	40.89	23.07	194.40	68.95	38.91
1983	121.42	37.12	34.94	205.02	62.68	58.99
1984	114.50	31.31	29.38	193.47	52.91	49.64
1985	142.22	36.55	34.32	240.01	61.68	57.92
1986	138.41	42.64	40.40	233.67	71.98	68.21

New Zealand

Year						
1970	258.63	241.52	230.20	433.78	405.07	386.10
1975	619.34	573.48	567.13	1 022.02	946.36	935.87
1980	1 288.86	1 252.81	1 227.74	2 035.63	1 978.69	1 939.09
1983	1 285.41	1 236.23	1 212.89	1 995.17	1 918.83	1 882.60
1984	1 000.57	980.67	960.98	1 544.16	1 513.44	1 483.07
1985	1 252.80	1 241.61	1 215.54	1 922.42	1 905.25	1 865.24
1986	1 554.80	1 536.91	1 496.92	2 375.35	2 348.02	2 286.92

Solomon Islands

Year						
1981	18.34	2.99	2.37	38.16	6.23	4.92
1983	24.64	4.82	3.77	50.90	9.95	7.78
1984	26.13	10.07	4.15	54.34	20.95	8.63
1985	25.00	11.30	4.64	51.93	23.46	9.63
1986	24.48	12.17	4.96	50.57	25.14	10.26

For general footnotes, see table 1. For further notes on the corresponding denominators and for exchange rate conversions, consult appendix table 1.

Pour les notes de caractère général, se reporter au tableau 1. Pour des précisions sur les chiffres relatifs à la population et pour les taux de change appliqués, voir le tableau 1 de l'annexe.

Véanse las notas generales del cuadro 1. En lo que concierne a otras notas sobre los denominadores correspondientes y para tasas de conversión de divisas, consúltese el cuadro anexo 1.

6. **Indices of annual average benefit expenditure per head of the total population**
(values adjusted according to cost-of-living indices: 1970 = 100 for former series, 1980 = 100 for new or continuous series[1])

6. **Indices des moyennes annuelles des dépenses en prestations par habitant (population totale)**
(valeurs ajustées d'après l'indice du coût de la vie : 1970 = 100 pour les anciennes séries; 1980 = 100 pour les nouvelles séries et les séries continues[1])

6. **Indices de promedios anuales de egresos en prestaciones por habitante (población total)**
(valores ajustados de acuerdo con los índices del costo de la vida: 1970 = 100 para las series anteriores y 1980 = 100 para las series nuevas[1])

Country – Pays – País	Year – Année – Año						
(1)	1970 (2)	1975 (3)	1980 (4)	1983 (5)	1984 (6)	1985 (7)	1986 (8)
Dominica	.	.	100	151	271	337	379
República Dominicana[5]	.	.	.	.	100	73	78
Ecuador	100	123[11] I	100	111	114	113	120
El Salvador	100	104 I	100	80	67	59	44
Grenada	—	—	100[3]	109	114	125	122
Guatemala	100	105 I	100	78	79	70	62
Guyana	100	77 I	100	76	69	77	120
Honduras[2]	.	.	100[3]	95	102	101	100
Jamaica[9]	100	171 I	100	110	119	95	94
México	100	129[11] I	100	84	93	91	80
Panamá	100	106 I	100	127	142	148	159
Perú	.	.	100[3]	78	29	28	33
St. Lucia[4]	.	.	100[3]	124	247	102	232
Trinidad and Tobago[4]	100	121 I	100[2]	322[2]	303[2]	271[2]	285[2]
United States[4]	100	163 I	100	110	107	109	113
Uruguay[2]	.	.	100	75	112	96	107
Venezuela	100	239 I	100	85	85	78	84

Country – Pays – País	Year – Année – Año						
(1)	1970 (2)	1975 (3)	1980 (4)	1983 (5)	1984 (6)	1985 (7)	1986 (8)
AFRICA – AFRIQUE – AFRICA							
Bénin	.	.	.	.	.	.	.
Burkina Faso[2]	.	.	100[3]	108	106	107	100
Burundi	.	.	100	143	123	146	214
Cameroun[2,4]	.	.	100[3]	95	119	130	156
Cap-Vert	.	.	.	100	113	142	153
Rép. centrafricaine	.	.	100[3]	96	165	139	159
Côte d'Ivoire	.	.	100[3]	123	143	134	134
Egypt[4,5]	100[6]	.	.	.	100	93	87
Ethiopia[4]	.	122 I	100[3,7]	113[7] I	100	89	97
Gabon[2]	.	.	100	110	114	115	118
Guinée	.	.	.	.	.	.	.
Guinée-Bissau	.	.	.	.	.	.	.
Kenya	100	111 I	100[3]	110	381	444	426
Madagascar	.	.	100[3]	88	85	80	75
Mali	100	52 I	100	148	214	204	204
Maroc	100	83 I	100	77 I	150	151	167
Mauritanie[2]	.	.	100[3]	115	113	91	101
Mauritius[4]	100	122 I	100[3]	113	.	211	236

(Africa, continued)							
Mozambique	.	.	.	.	.	.	.
Niger[4]	100	86 ❙	100[3]	73	441	374	279
Nigeria	.	.	100[3]	102	84	98	91
Rwanda	.	.	100[3]	180	190	223	263
Sao Tomé-et-Principe	.	.	.	.	.	.	.
Sénégal[4]	100	51 ❙	100	35	86	84	83
Sudan	.	.	100	130	151	112	75
Swaziland[2,4]	.	.	100[3]	135	142	128	125
Tanzania, United Rep. of[4]	.	.	100	47	61	74	63
Tchad[8]	.	.	.	100	127	468	629
Togo	100[6]	108 ❙	100	79	93	103	105
Tunisie[5]	.	.	.	.	100	105	106
Uganda[4,8]	.	.	.	100	45	18	2
Zaïre[5]	.	.	.	.	100	183	386
Zambia[9]	100	166 ❙	100	84	37	44	26

AMERICA – AMÉRIQUE – AMERICA

Argentina	.	.	100	73	77	62	62
Bahamas	.	.	100	216	238	269	282
Barbados	100[10]	175 ❙	100	153	178	188	228
Belize[2]	.	.	100[3]	611	609	743	729
Bolivia	100	131 ❙	100	76	133	706	.
Brasil	100	154 ❙	100	98	93	98	104
Canada[9]	100	121 ❙	100	110	113	116	.
Colombia	100	141 ❙	100	87	52	52	55
Costa Rica[2]	100	191 ❙	100	71	85	94	94
Cuba	.	4 753 ❙	100	.	.	.	.
Chile	100	.	100	107	110	104	106

ASIA – ASIE – ASIA

Bahrain[2]	.	.	100	250	319	383	497
Bangladesh[2]	.	.	100	256	286	265	254
Cyprus	100	173 ❙	100	160	164	177	198
India[9]	100	117 ❙	100	127	114	109	.
Indonesia	.	.	100[3]	148	165	205	276
Iran, Islamic Rep. of[12]	.	.	100[3]	128	161	188	203
Israel[9]	100	160 ❙	100	112	132	102	98
Japan[9]	100	178 ❙	100	116	119	122	132
Jordan[2]	.	.	.	100	132	136	134
Kuwait[2,4]	.	.	100	190	201	355	343
Malaysia	100	127 ❙	100	211	223	228	230
Myanmar[9]	100	59 ❙	100	.	87	80	79
Pakistan[2,4]	.	– ❙	100	129	139	157	202
Philippines	100[4]	97[4] ❙	100	115	86	78	89
Qatar[5]	.	– ❙	.	.	100	98	92
Singapore	100	146 ❙	100	182	346	332	380
Sri Lanka[2]	100[4]	156 ❙	100	121	150	144	100
Rép. arabe syrienne[5]	.	.	.	.	.	92	69
Thailand[2]	.	.	100	89	187	168	153

EUROPE – EUROPE – EUROPA

Countries with a market economy – Pays à économie de marché – Países con economía de mercado

Austria	100	132 ❙	.	114	117	121	126
Belgique	100	157 ❙	.	100	103	98	103
Denmark	46[4]	72[4] ❙	100	108	105	108	114
España	100	.	100	112	112	117	119

See notes on page 108.   *Voir notes page 108.*   *Véanse notas pág. 108.*

Table 6 *(concl.)* **Tableau 6** *(fin)* **Cuadro 6** *(fin)*

Country – Pays – Pais (1)	Year – Année – Año 1970 (2)	1975 (3)	1980 (4)	1983 (5)	1984 (6)	1985 (7)	1986 (8)
Finland	49	80	100	120	128	139	148
France	42	72	100	111	112	113	117
Germany, Fed. Rep. of	100	156	100	100	102	103	107
Grèce	100	120	100	138	149	160	.
Iceland[5]	.	.	.	.	100	107	116
Ireland	37	81	100	113	112	116	119
Italie[2]	100	140	100	120	73	75	78
Luxembourg	51	76	100	103	105	106	112
Malta	100	172	100	128	165	162	160
Netherlands	53	81	100	107	105	102	102
Norway	49	72	100	110	154	159	160
Portugal	100	212	100	107	101	105	121
Suisse	100	159	100	105	111	111	117
Sweden	49	75	100	106	99	101	107
Turquie[2]	100	135	100	114	107	108	116
United Kingdom[9]	69	96	100	116	117	120	124

Country – Pays – Pais (1)	Year – Année – Año 1970 (2)	1975 (3)	1980 (4)	1983 (5)	1984 (6)	1985 (7)	1986 (8)
EUROPE – EUROPE – EUROPA							
Countries with a centrally planned economy – Pays à économie planifiée – Países con economía centralmente planificada							
RSS de Biélorussie	53	76	100	110	114	116	119
Bulgarie	72	105	100	115	112	121	131
Czechoslovakia	74	87	100	104	106	109	114
German Democratic Rep.	47	74	100	104	106	111	117
Hongrie	46	75	100	108	87	90	92
Pologne[5]	.	.	.	.	100	101	110
RSS d'Ukraine	59	80	100	111	116	120	122
URSS	60	82	100	107	112	114	114
Yugoslavia	69	.	100	94	81	86	106
OCEANIA – OCÉANIE – OCEANIA							
Australia[4]	100	154	100	104	88	96	88
Fiji[2,4]	.	.	100	197	260	285	339
New Zealand[9]	52	85	100	101	103	109	112
Solomon Islands[4]	.	.	100[3]	181	198	243	282

[1] See the explanations in the introduction concerning table 6. For countries with a different financial year from the calendar year, see footnotes to table 1. [2] The indices relate to social insurance and assimilated schemes only (including family allowances, if any). [3] 1981 base equals 100. [4] For the financial year ending during the calendar year. [5] 1984 base equals 100. [6] Financial year 1972, or ending in 1972. [7] Data relate only to Public Employees' Scheme. [8] The figures reflect the effect of the economic and social upheavals of the period. [9] For the financial year starting during the calendar year. [10] Financial year 1971.

[11] Financial year 1974. [12] The indices relate to medical care benefit expenditure.

[1] Voir, pour le tableau 6, les explications figurant dans l'introduction. Pour les pays dont l'exercice financier ne correspond pas à l'année civile, voir les notes du tableau 1. [2] Les indices se rapportent uniquement aux prestations sociales et aux régimes assimilés (y compris les prestations familiales, le cas échéant). [3] Base: 1981 = 100. [4] Pour l'exercice financier se terminant au cours de l'année civile. [5] Base: 1984 = 100. [6] Exercice financier de 1972 ou se terminant en 1972. [7] Les chiffres se rapportent uniquement au régime des agents publics. [8] Les chiffres se ressentent des troubles qu'a connus le pays. [9] Pour l'exercice financier débutant au cours de l'année civile. [10] Exercice financier de 1971.

[11] Exercice financier 1974. [12] Les indices se rapportent aux dépenses de soins médicaux.

[1] Véanse, acerca del cuadro 6, las explicaciones que figuran en la introducción. Respecto de países que tienen un año financiero diferente del año civil, véanse las notas del cuadro 1. [2] Los índices corresponden sólo al seguro social y regímenes asimilados (incluidos los subsidios familiares, si los hubiera). [3] La base 1981 equivale a 100. [4] Para el año financiero que termina durante el año civil. [5] La base 1984 equivale a 100. [6] Ejercicio financiero de 1972, o que terminó en 1972. [7] Los datos corresponden sólo al Régimen de Empleados Públicos. [8] Las cifras reflejan los efectos de los trastornos económicos y sociales del período. [9] Para el ejercicio financiero que comienza durante el año civil. [10] Ejercicio financiero de 1971.

[11] Ejercicio financiero de 1974. [12] Los índices corresponden a los egresos por concepto de prestaciones de asistencia médica.

7. Distribution of social security benefit expenditure among the different schemes
(as percentages of total benefit expenditure)

7. Répartition des dépenses de la sécurité sociale en prestations entre les différents régimes
(en pourcentage du total des dépenses en prestations)

7. Distribución de los egresos de la seguridad social en prestaciones entre los distintos regímenes
(en porcentaje del total de gastos en prestaciones)

Country and currency unit *Pays et unité monétaire* País y unidad monetaria	Financial year *Exercice financier* Ejercicio financiero	Social insurance and assimilated schemes *Assurances sociales et régimes assimilés* Seguros sociales y regímenes asimilados	Family allowances *Prestations familiales* Asignaciones familiares	Special schemes for public employees *Agents publics (régimes spéciaux)* Empleados públicos (regímenes especiales)	Public health services *Services publics de santé* Servicios públicos de salud	Public assistance and assimilated schemes *Assistance publique et régimes assimilés* Asistencia pública y regímenes asimilados	War victims *Victimes de guerre* Victimas de guerra	Absolute total benefit expenditure (in millions of national currency units) *Total (millions d'unités monétaires nationales)* Total en millones de unidades monetarias nacionales
(1)	(2)	(3)	(4)	(5)	(6)	(7)	(8)	(9)

AFRICA – AFRIQUE – AFRICA

Bénin	1970	5.1	23.9	—	70.9	—	—	1 671.60
(Franc CFA)	1975	12.1	31.6	—	56.4	—	—	2 539.30
	1981	19.7	27.0	53.2	x	—	—	4 429.84
	1983	20.2	21.6	58.2	x	—	—	5 890.52
	1984	53.4	46.6	.	x	—	—	2 437.10
	1985	65.6	34.4	.	x	—	—	2 573.10
	1986	69.3	30.7	.	x	—	—	2 561.90
Burkina Faso	1975	9.7	18.4	29.2	42.6	—	—	2 169.00
(Franc CFA)	1980	48.3	51.7	.	x	—	—	1 083.90
	1983	22.2	18.3	59.5	x	—	—	3 962.00
	1984	54.5	45.5	.	x	—	—	1 668.50
	1985	61.1	38.9	.	x	—	—	1 821.10
	1986	61.8	38.2	.	x	—	—	2 042.90
Burundi	1978	20.9	—	21.9	x	57.2	—	113.62
(Franc burundais)	1980	21.8	—	16.1	x	62.2	—	195.95
	1983	29.0	—	71.0	x	—	—	391.58
	1984	42.7	—	57.3	x	—	—	391.20
	1985	40.6	—	59.4	x	—	—	498.10
	1986	35.1	—	64.9	x	—	—	767.10
Cameroun	1970	6.6	23.2	8.2	62.0	—	—	4 531.40
(Franc CFA)	1981	14.8	49.1	36.0	x	—	—	11 140.00
	1983	15.6	47.2	37.2	x	—	—	15 083.00
	1984	30.7	69.3	.	x	—	—	13 766.00
	1985	34.5	65.5	.	x	—	—	15 567.00
	1986	34.2	65.8	.	x	—	—	19 869.00
Cap-Vert	1983	46.4	53.6	—	x	—	—	61.15
(Escudo)	1984	50.3	49.7	—	x	—	—	79.36
	1985	57.8	42.2	—	x	—	—	107.72
	1986	64.0	36.0	—	x	—	—	131.09
Rép. centrafricaine	1981	28.4	71.6	—	x	—	—	838.10
(Franc CFA)	1983	30.5	69.5	—	x	—	—	1 071.50
	1984	37.2	62.8	—	x	—	—	2 057.00
	1985	41.9	58.1	—	x	—	—	1 961.00
	1986	45.6	54.4	—	x	—	—	2 532.00
Côte d'Ivoire	1981	54.7	45.3	—	x	—	—	8 565.09
(Franc CFA)	1983	57.0	43.0	—	x	—	—	12 801.70
	1984	50.4	49.6	—	x	—	—	16 377.60
	1985	55.8	44.2	—	x	—	—	16 286.00
	1986	55.1	44.9	—	x	—	—	18 211.70
Egypt	1984	56.7	—	43.3	x	—	—	854.80
(Pound)	1985	59.9	—	40.1	x	—	—	923.00
	1986	58.9	—	41.1	x	—	—	1 070.40

See notes on page 122. *Voir notes page 122.* Véanse notas pág. 122.

Table 7 *(cont.)*   **Tableau 7** *(suite)*   **Cuadro 7** *(cont.)*

Country and currency unit / Pays et unité monétaire / País y unidad monetaria	Financial year / Exercice financier / Ejercicio financiero	Social insurance and assimilated schemes / Assurances sociales et régimes assimilés / Seguros sociales y regímenes asimilados	Family allowances / Prestations familiales / Asignaciones familiares	Special schemes for public employees / Agents publics (régimes spéciaux) / Empleados públicos (regímenes especiales)	Public health services / Services publics de santé / Servicios públicos de salud	Public assistance and assimilated schemes / Assistance publique et régimes assimilés / Asistencia pública y regímenes asimilados	War victims / Victimes de guerre / Víctimas de guerra	Absolute total benefit expenditure (in millions of national currency units) / Total (millions d'unités monétaires nationales) / Total en millones de unidades monetarias nacionales
(1)	(2)	(3)	(4)	(5)	(6)	(7)	(8)	(9)
Ethiopia (Birr)	1972	2.1	—	38.4	59.5	—	—	62.23
	1975	3.4	—	43.5	53.2	—	—	101.93
	1980	3.7	—	89.6	x	6.7	—	78.36
	1983[1]	.	—	100.0	x	.	—	104.32
	1984	7.8	—	92.2	x	.	—	101.67
	1985	8.3	—	91.7	x	.	—	112.91
	1986	8.8	—	91.2	x	.	—	114.22
Gabon (Franc CFA)	1980	88.3	11.7	.	x	.	—	13 526.00
	1983	73.0	13.9	12.8	x	0.4	—	27 032.00
	1984	84.9	15.1	.	x	.	—	26 868.00
	1985	84.5	15.5	.	x	.	—	30 363.00
	1986	87.0	13.0	.	x	.	—	34 175.00
Guinée (Syli)	1981	100.0[2]	.	—	x	—	—	36.86
	1983	100.0[2]	.	—	x	—	—	33.34
	1984	.		—	x	—	—	.
	1985	43.3	56.7	—	x	—	—	126.29
	1986	44.0	56.0	—	x	—	—	229.00
Guinée-Bissau (Peso)	1981	100.0[2]	—	—	x	.	—	1.43
	1983	100.0[2]	—	—	x	.	—	1.64
	1984	59.8	—[3]	—	x	40.2	—	13.68
	1985	62.5	—[3]	—	x	37.5	—	27.77
	1986	64.5	—[3]	—	x	35.5	—	36.89
Kenya (Shilling)	1970	12.6	—	35.9	51.5	—	—	213.60
	1975	11.4	—	18.1	70.5	—	—	479.60
	1981	100.0[1]	—	.	x	—	—	25.30
	1983	100.0[1]	—	.	x	—	—	40.40
	1984	100.0[1]	—	.	x	—	—	160.00
	1985	100.0[1]	—	.	x	—	—	220.00
	1986	100.0[1]	—	.	x	—	—	228.00
Madagascar (Franc malgache)	1981	39.6	60.4	—	x	—	—	4 535.00
	1983	50.2	49.8	—	x	—	—	6 609.00
	1984	56.0	44.0	—	x	—	—	7 354.50
	1985	56.8	43.2	—	x	—	—	7 751.50
	1986	59.0	41.0	—	x	—	—	8 764.60
Mali (Franc CFA)	1972	12.4	20.8	.	66.8	—	—	1 610.50
	1975	18.9	17.4	.	63.7	—	—	1 859.50
	1980	56.7	43.3	.	x	—	—	1 412.00
	1983	39.5	23.5	37.0	x	—	—	2 863.80
	1984	27.6	13.1	59.3[4]	x	—	—	4 824.10
	1985	30.4	13.5	56.1[4]	x	—	—	5 092.20
	1986	30.2	13.1	56.7	x	—	—	5 044.40
Maroc (Dirham)	1970	15.2	34.4	.	50.3	0.2	—	421.85
	1975	29.2	31.7	.	38.9	0.2	—	557.53
	1980	51.5	48.1	.	x	0.4	—	721.00
	1983	49.1	50.9	.	x	.	—	763.10
	1984	24.6	23.5	52.0	x	.	—	1 732.60
	1985	25.1	21.8	53.1	x	.	—	1 921.30
	1986	22.7	18.0	59.3	x	.	—	2 370.10
Mauritanie (Ouguiya)	1970	7.9	19.7	26.4	46.0	—	—	211.68
	1981	9.8	25.5	64.7	x	—	—	786.02
	1983	12.0	28.3	59.7	x	—	—	945.03
	1984	34.2	65.8	.	x	—	—	413.91
	1985	35.8	64.2	.	x	—	—	386.82
	1986	41.7	58.3	.	x	—	—	477.27

See notes on page 122.   *Voir notes page 122.*   Véanse notas pág. 122.

Table 7 *(cont.)*   **Tableau 7** *(suite)*   **Cuadro 7** *(cont.)*

Country and currency unit *Pays et unité monétaire* País y unidad monetaria	Financial year *Exercice financier* Ejercicio financiero	Social insurance and assimilated schemes *Assurances sociales et régimes assimilés* Seguros sociales y regímenes asimilados	Family allowances *Prestations familiales* Asignaciones familiares	Special schemes for public employees *Agents publics (régimes spéciaux)* Empleados públicos (regímenes especiales)	Public health services *Services publics de santé* Servicios públicos de salud	Public assistance and assimilated schemes *Assistance publique et régimes assimilés* Asistencia pública y regímenes asimilados	War victims *Victimes de guerre* Víctimas de guerra	Absolute total benefit expenditure (in millions of national currency units) *Total (millions d'unités monétaires nationales)* Total en millones de unidades monetarias nacionales
(1)	(2)	(3)	(4)	(5)	(6)	(7)	(8)	(9)
Mauritius (Rupee)	1970	19.7	8.0	24.6	35.3	12.5	—	69.12
	1975	19.6	6.2	23.2	42.7	8.3	—	155.94
	1981	80.0	11.4	.	x	8.6	—	181.70
	1983	86.5	6.8	.	x	6.8	—	247.20
	1985	55.8	2.3	38.2	x	3.7	—	539.50
	1986	57.0	1.8	36.8	x	4.4	—	621.90
Mozambique (Metical)	1981	100.0[3]	—	.	x	—	—	15.24
	1983	100.0[3]	—	.	x	—	—	17.75
	1984	49.3	—	50.7[4]	x	—	—	144.00
	1985	54.9	—	45.1[4]	x	—	—	162.00
	1986	49.7	—	50.3	x	—	—	145.00
Niger (Franc CFA)	1970	4.8	24.7	.	70.6	—	—	1 240.10
	1975	6.0	29.9	.	64.0	—	—	1 745.40
	1980	12.2	87.8	.	x	—	—	1 341.80
	1983	22.2	77.8	.	x	—	—	1 767.80
	1984	11.0	32.6	56.3[4]	x	—	—	4 395.50
	1985	12.9	29.0	58.1[4]	x	—	—	4 260.00
	1986	15.9	33.7	50.4	x	—	—	4 915.00
Nigeria (Naira)	1970	3.5	—	20.9	75.5[5,6]	—	0.2	34.72
	1981	100.0[7]	—	.	x	—	.	3.52
	1983	100.0[7]	—	.	x	—	.	5.14
	1984	100.0[7]	—	.	x	—	.	6.10
	1985	100.0[7]	—	.	x	—	.	7.72
	1986	100.0[7]	—	.	x	—	.	7.84
Rwanda (Franc rwandais)	1975	13.2	—	—	85.4	1.4	—	142.65
	1981	100.0	—	—	x	.	—	96.60
	1983	100.0	—	—	x	.	—	224.30
	1984	100.0	—	—	x	.	—	255.60
	1985	100.0	—	—	x	.	—	314.00
	1986	100.0	—	—	x	.	—	380.60
Sao Tomé-et-Principe (Dobra)	1981	100.0	—	—	x	—	—	18.02
	1983	100.0	—	—	x	—	—	19.70
	1984	100.0	—	—	x	—	—	21.47
	1985	100.0	—	—	x	—	—	28.44
	1986	100.0	—	—	x	—	—	23.68
Sénégal (Franc CFA)	1970	3.0	25.5	24.2	47.3	—	—	7 694.50
	1975	5.8	15.5	25.5	53.2	—	—	8 422.90
	1980	64.8	35.2	.	x	—	—	8 844.00
	1983	21.6	78.4	.	x	—	—	4 806.00
	1984	73.9	26.1	.	x	—	—	13 282.00
	1985	76.7	23.3	.	x	—	—	14 644.00
	1986	78.6	21.4	.	x	—	—	15 958.00
Sudan (Pound)	1980	100.0	—	—	x	—	—	0.92
	1983	100.0	—	—	x	—	—	2.70
	1984	100.0	—	—	x	—	—	4.30
	1985	100.0	—	—	x	—	—	4.80
	1986	100.0	—	—	x	—	—	4.20
Swaziland (Lilangeni)	1981	43.8	—	56.2	x	—	—	1.46
	1983	47.7	—	52.3	x	—	—	2.41
	1984	100.0[7]	—	.	x	—	—	1.41
	1985	100.0[7]	—	.	x	—	—	1.57
	1986	100.0[7]	—	.	x	—	—	1.78

See notes on page 122.   *Voir notes page 122.*   Véanse notas pág. 122.

Table 7 *(cont.)*   **Tableau 7** *(suite)*   **Cuadro 7** *(cont.)*

Country and currency unit / *Pays et unité monétaire* / País y unidad monetaria	Financial year / *Exercice financier* / Ejercicio financiero	Social insurance and assimilated schemes / *Assurances sociales et régimes assimilés* / Seguros sociales y regímenes asimilados	Family allowances / *Prestations familiales* / Asignaciones familiares	Special schemes for public employees / *Agents publics (régimes spéciaux)* / Empleados públicos (regímenes especiales)	Public health services / *Services publics de santé* / Servicios públicos de salud	Public assistance and assimilated schemes / *Assistance publique et régimes assimilés* / Asistencia pública y regimenes asimilados	War victims / *Victimes de guerre* / Víctimas de guerra	Absolute total benefit expenditure (in millions of national currency units) / *Total (millions d'unités monétaires nationales)* / Total en millones de unidades monetarias nacionales
(1)	(2)	(3)	(4)	(5)	(6)	(7)	(8)	(9)
Tanzania, United Rep. of (Shilling)	1980	90.4	—	9.6	x	—	—	61.40
	1983	100.0[7]	—	.	x	—	—	64.70
	1984	100.0[7]	—	.	x	—	—	119.43
	1985	100.0[7]	—	.	x	—	—	198.74
	1986	100.0[7]	—	.	x	—	—	231.43
Tchad (Franc CFA)	1979-81	23.8	76.2	—	x	—	—	74.19
	1983	16.9	83.1	—	x	—	—	47.03
	1984	30.6	69.4	—	x	—	—	73.35
	1985	40.6	59.4	—	x	—	—	290.14
	1986	76.1	23.9	—	x	—	—	348.45
Togo (Franc CFA)	1972	11.8	28.5	—	59.7	—	—	1208.00
	1975	12.6	22.3	—	65.1	—	—	1923.00
	1980	30.7	69.3	—	x	—	—	1835.00
	1983	46.8	53.2	—	x	—	—	2309.00
	1984	52.2	47.8	—	x	—	—	2688.00
	1985	56.4	43.6	—	x	—	—	3030.00
	1986	59.2	40.8	—	x	—	—	3302.00
Tunisie (Dinar)	1984	57.6	15.2	27.2	x	—	—	259.00
	1985	61.5	12.8	25.7	x	—	—	305.80
	1986	54.3	16.1	29.6	x	—	—	336.00
Uganda[7] (Shilling)	1980	100.0	—	—	x	—	—	7.50
	1983	100.0	—	—	x	—	—	3.20
	1984	100.0	—	—	x	—	—	2.13
	1985	100.0	—	—	x	—	—	1.99
	1986	100.0	—	—	x	—	—	0.52
Zaïre (Zaïre)	1984	87.2	12.8	—	x	—	—	39.51
	1985	63.9	36.1	—	x	—	—	92.52
	1986	68.5	31.5	—	x	—	—	291.13
Zambia (Kwacha)	1970	14.7	—	14.6	70.7	—	—	29.27
	1975	13.8	—	21.5	64.7	—	—	75.31
	1980	100.0[7]	—	.	x	—	—	20.85
	1983	.	—	.	x	—	—	.
	1984	100.0[7]	—	.	x	—	—	17.02
	1985	100.0[7]	—	.	x	—	—	28.72
	1986	100.0[7]	—	.	x	—	—	27.45

AMERICA – AMÉRIQUE – AMERICA

Argentina (Austral)	1975	68.6	25.7	—	5.7	—	—	0.01
	1980	82.1	17.9	—	x	—	—	2.51
	1983	85.7	14.3	—	x	—	—	46.47
	1984	85.1	14.9	—	x	—	—	360.60
	1985	81.4	18.6	—	x	—	—	2277.20
	1986	77.4	22.6	—	x	—	—	4384.90
Bahamas[2] (Dollar)	1980	100.0	—	—	x	—	—	5.41
	1983	100.0	—	—	x	—	—	15.30
	1984	100.0	—	—	x	—	—	17.83
	1985	100.0	—	—	x	—	—	21.39
	1986	100.0	—	—	x	—	—	24.00

See notes on page 122.   *Voir notes page 122.*   Véanse notas pág. 122.

Table 7 *(cont.)*   **Tableau 7** *(suite)*   **Cuadro 7** *(cont.)*

Country and currency unit / *Pays et unité monétaire* / País y unidad monetaria	Financial year / *Exercice financier* / Ejercicio financiero	Social insurance and assimilated schemes / *Assurances sociales et régimes assimilés* / Seguros sociales y regímenes asimilados	Family allowances / *Prestations familiales* / Asignaciones familiares	Special schemes for public employees / *Agents publics (régimes spéciaux)* / Empleados públicos (regímenes especiales)	Public health services / *Services publics de santé* / Servicios públicos de salud	Public assistance and assimilated schemes / *Assistance publique et régimes assimilés* / Asistencia pública y regímenes asimilados	War victims / *Victimes de guerre* / Victimas de guerra	Absolute total benefit expenditure (in millions of national currency units) / *Total (millions d'unités monétaires nationales)* / Total en millones de unidades monetarias nacionales
(1)	(2)	(3)	(4)	(5)	(6)	(7)	(8)	(9)
Barbados	1971	12.2	—	—	87.8	.	—	10.53
(Dollar)	1975	12.9	—	—	65.9	21.2	—	38.73
	1980	42.0	—	—	x	58.0	—	35.28
	1983	94.4	—	—	x	5.6	—	72.59
	1984	93.2	—	—	x	6.8	—	88.31
	1985	94.1	—	—	x	5.9	—	97.81
	1986	94.5	—	—	x	5.5	—	120.32
Belize	1981	3.3	—	87.3[8]	x	9.4[9]	—	3.63
(Dollar)	1983	17.6	—	75.6[8]	x	6.8[9]	—	5.07
	1984	100.0	—	.	x	.	—	0.94
	1985	100.0	—	.	x	.	—	1.22
	1986	100.0	—	.	x	.	—	1.25
Bolivia	1972	67.6	5.0	—	27.4	—	—	489.00
(Peso)	1975	56.3	6.5	—	37.2	—	—	1 391.80
	1980	98.9	1.1	—	x	—	—	2 952.30
	1983	96.2	3.8	—	x	—	—	26 855.70
	1984	98.5	1.5	—	x	—	—	671 452.00
	1985	97.8	2.2	—	x	—	—	43 439 487.00
Brasil	1970	73.4	6.9	16.9	2.8	.	—	9.85
(Cruzado)	1975	83.1	6.6	8.8	1.2	0.3	—	49.53
	1980[2]	100.0	.	—	x	.	—	608.51
	1983	97.0	.[3]	3.0	x	.	—	6 282.80
	1984	98.4	.[3]	1.6	x	.	—	18 100.40
	1985	97.9	.[3]	2.1	x	.	—	63 482.70
	1986	97.6	.	2.4	x	.	—	169 448.80
Canada	1970	53.8	5.7	2.4	19.2	15.8	3.1	12 469.40
(Dollar)	1975	69.3	9.0	1.6	17.4	2.7	.	22 989.60
	1980	69.3	7.5	1.8	x	2.3	.	40 560.90
	1983	71.9	6.2	1.5	x	18.4	2.0	63 748.70
	1984	72.2	6.0	1.5	x	18.3	1.9	68 302.00
	1985	73.1	5.6	1.6	x	17.9	1.8	74 212.90
Colombia	1970	28.8	17.0	11.8	42.4	—	—	3 085.27
(Peso)	1975	29.4	3.8	36.6	30.3	—	—	11 396.80
	1980	47.9	11.5	40.6	x	—	—	34 272.20
	1983	77.4	.	22.6	x	—	—	60 066.00
	1984	52.9	.	47.1	x	—	—	42 743.00
	1985	56.1	.	43.9	x	—	—	53 510.00
	1986	58.3	.	41.7	x	—	—	69 102.00
Costa Rica	1970	77.8	—	—	22.2	—	—	189.80
(Colón)	1975	78.6	—	—	21.4	—	—	770.50
	1980	100.0[2]	—	—	x	—	—	2 598.10
	1983	100.0[2]	—	—	x	—	—	6 954.50
	1984	100.0[2]	—	—	x	—	—	9 209.00
	1985	100.0[2]	—	—	x	—	—	12 101.60
	1986	100.0[2]	—	—	x	—	—	14 781.90
Cuba	1980[2]	100.0	—	—	x	—	—	1 111.40
(Peso)	1983	.	.	—	x	—	—	1 441.20
	1984	.	.	—	x	—	—	1 557.80
	1985	.	.	—	x	—	—	1 673.50
	1986	.	.	—	x	—	—	1 819.10

See notes on page 122.   *Voir notes page 122.*   Véanse notas pág. 122.

Table 7 *(cont.)*   **Tableau 7** *(suite)*   **Cuadro 7** *(cont.)*

Country and currency unit / Pays et unité monétaire / País y unidad monetaria	Financial year / Exercice financier / Ejercicio financiero	Social insurance and assimilated schemes / Assurances sociales et régimes assimilés / Seguros sociales y regímenes asimilados	Family allowances / Prestations familiales / Asignaciones familiares	Special schemes for public employees / Agents publics (régimes spéciaux) / Empleados públicos (regímenes especiales)	Public health services / Services publics de santé / Servicios públicos de salud	Public assistance and assimilated schemes / Assistance publique et régimes assimilés / Asistencia pública y regímenes asimilados	War victims / Victimes de guerre / Víctimas de guerra	Absolute total benefit expenditure (in millions of national currency units) / Total (millions d'unités monétaires nationales) / Total en millones de unidades monetarias nacionales
(1)	(2)	(3)	(4)	(5)	(6)	(7)	(8)	(9)
Chile (Peso)	1971	33.1	21.6	42.3	3.1	—	—	20.09
	1975	35.5	19.9	40.5	4.0	—	—	3 589.90
	1980	43.3	12.4	44.3	x	—	—	106 823.40
	1983	90.4	9.6	.	x	—	—	202 664.50
	1984	90.9	9.1	.	x	—	—	253 488.00
	1985	91.6	8.4	.	x	—	—	316 150.00
	1986	93.2	6.8	.	x	—	—	391 118.00
Dominica[2] (EC Dollar)	1980	100.0	—	—	x	—	—	0.57
	1983	100.0	—	—	x	—	—	1.16
	1984	100.0	—	—	x	—	—	2.16
	1985	100.0	—	—	x	—	—	2.58
	1986	100.0	—	—	x	—	—	2.97
República Dominicana[2] (Peso)	1984	100.0	—	—	x	—	—	45.19
	1985	100.0	—	—	x	—	—	46.35
	1986	100.0	—	—	x	—	—	56.37
Ecuador (Sucre)	1972	88.9	—	.	11.1	.	—	1 394.00
	1974	67.8	—	.	32.2	.	—	2 555.00
	1980	74.0	—	26.0	x	.	—	6 183.00
	1983	66.1	—	33.9	x	.	—	15 072.00
	1984[10]	84.1	—	1.8	x	14.1	—	20 835.00
	1985[10]	82.5	—	1.9	x	15.6	—	27 194.00
	1986[10]	80.0	—	2.8	x	17.2	—	36 658.00
El Salvador (Colón)	1970	24.1	—	31.9	40.6	3.5	—	58.74
	1975	32.2	—	21.6	46.3	.	—	106.02
	1980	73.7	—	26.3	x	.	—	126.17
	1983	79.6	—	20.4	x	.	—	153.70
	1984[10]	94.9	—	5.1	x	.	—	145.50
	1985[10]	93.9	—	6.1	x	.	—	158.60
	1986[10]	90.9	—	9.1	x	.	—	158.10
Grenada (EC Dollar)	1981	.	—	89.5[11]	x	10.5[12]	—	3.43
	1983	0.2	—	88.7[11]	x	11.1	—	4.33
	1984	2.4	—	97.6	x	.	—	4.82
	1985	5.8	—	94.2	x	.	—	5.49
	1986	12.5	—	87.5	x	.	—	5.46
Guatemala (Quetzal)	1970	41.9	—	12.6	45.5	—	—	36.50
	1975	44.3	—	15.5	40.2[13]	—	—	66.60
	1980	82.6	—	17.4	x	—	—	80.30
	1983	100.0[2]	—	.	x	—	—	80.00
	1984	100.0[2]	—	.	x	—	—	85.50
	1985	100.0[2]	—	.	x	—	—	92.30
	1986	100.0[2]	—	.	x	—	—	115.60
Guyana (Dollar)	1972	21.2	—	2.1	76.7	.	—	16.76
	1975	16.4	—	2.3	81.3	.	—	18.81
	1980	88.6	—	11.4	x	.	—	13.97
	1983	85.9	—	6.8	x	7.3	—	19.14
	1984	84.8	—	3.2	x	12.0	—	22.15
	1985	82.0	—	5.8	x	12.2	—	24.16
	1986	93.7	—	3.4	x	2.9	—	49.83
Honduras (Lempira)	1970	16.9	—	—	34.7	48.4	—	23.19
	1971	27.0	—	—	.	73.0	—	16.92
	1981	100.0[2]	—	—	x	—	—	37.13
	1983	100.0[2]	—	—	x	—	—	44.67
	1984	92.7	—	7.3	x	—	—	55.99
	1985	91.7	—	8.3	x	—	—	60.22
	1986	90.8	—	9.2	x	—	—	64.95

See notes on page 122. *Voir notes page 122.* Véanse notas pág. 122.

114

Table 7 *(cont.)*   Tableau 7 *(suite)*   Cuadro 7 *(cont.)*

Country and currency unit / Pays et unité monétaire / País y unidad monetaria	Financial year / Exercice financier / Ejercicio financiero	Social insurance and assimilated schemes / Assurances sociales et régimes assimilés / Seguros sociales y regimenes asimilados	Family allowances / Prestations familiales / Asignaciones familiares	Special schemes for public employees / Agents publics (régimes spéciaux) / Empleados públicos (regimenes especiales)	Public health services / Services publics de santé / Servicios públicos de salud	Public assistance and assimilated schemes / Assistance publique et régimes assimilés / Asistencia pública y regimenes asimilados	War victims / Victimes de guerre / Victimas de guerra	Absolute total benefit expenditure (in millions of national currency units) / Total (millions d'unités monétaires nationales) / Total en millones de unidades monetarias nacionales
(1)	(2)	(3)	(4)	(5)	(6)	(7)	(8)	(9)
Jamaica (Dollar)	1970	4.8	—	23.6	71.6	.	—	26.09
	1975	7.2	—	14.5	70.1	8.1	—	94.87
	1980[14]	35.4	—	48.1	x	16.5	—	61.13
	1983	39.4	—	47.5	x	13.1	—	97.19
	1984	30.3	—	32.2	x	37.5	—	136.77
	1985	33.2	—	29.3	x	37.5	—	138.94
	1986	31.1	—	35.2	x	33.7	—	160.18
México (Peso)	1970	64.9	—	22.2	7.6	5.4	—	10 645.53
	1974	65.0	—	24.4	8.7	1.8	—	23 583.67
	1980	73.7	—	26.3	x	.	—	85 113.00
	1983	83.2	—	16.8	x	.	—	314 070.00
	1984	70.4	—	29.6	x	.	—	592 676.00
	1985	68.0	—	32.0	x	.	—	933 818.00
	1986	65.6	—	34.4	x	.	—	1 556 878.00
Panamá (Balboa)	1972	68.7	—	13.8	17.5	—	—	81.01
	1975	72.3	—	11.9	15.8	—	—	118.79
	1980	92.9	—	7.1	x	—	—	189.59
	1983	94.8	—	5.2	x	—	—	292.40
	1984	94.6	—	5.4	x	—	—	340.10
	1985	93.5	—	6.5	x	—	—	365.90
	1986	94.6	—	5.4	x	—	—	401.60
Perú[2] (Inti)	1981	100.0	—	—	x	—	—	186.41
	1983	100.0	—	—	x	—	—	536.00
	1984	100.0	—	—	x	—	—	429.00
	1985	100.0	—	—	x	—	—	1 119.00
	1986	100.0	—	—	x	—	—	2 420.00
St. Lucia[2] (EC Dollar)	1981	100.0	—	—	x	—	—	0.72
	1983	100.0	—	—	x	—	—	0.98
	1984	100.0	—	—	x	—	—	2.02
	1985	100.0	—	—	x	—	—	0.87
	1986	100.0	—	—	x	—	—	2.07
Trinidad and Tobago (Dollar)	1970	9.1	—	16.2	71.1	3.6	—	53.00
	1975	13.1	—	6.1	65.4	15.4	—	126.96
	1980	45.2	—	17.9	x	36.8	—	94.21
	1983	50.9	—	41.5	x	7.6	—	417.13
	1984	88.9	—	.	x	11.1	—	260.02
	1985	88.6	—	.	x	11.4	—	254.92
	1986	87.8	—	.	x	12.2	—	295.29
United States (Dollar)	1970	50.5	—	9.8	8.4	22.7	8.7	87 544.00
	1975	52.4	—	10.5	7.0	24.0	6.1	190 016.00
	1980	57.7	—	12.3	x	24.7	5.3	316 684.00
	1983	63.4	—	12.5	x	18.8	5.3	432 879.00
	1984	62.4	—	13.1	x	19.3	5.2	444 662.00
	1985	62.6	—	13.1	x	19.2	5.1	476 296.00
	1986	62.6	—	13.1	x	19.3	4.9	504 468.00
Uruguay (Nuevo peso)	1975	55.1	11.2	21.6	12.2	—	—	688.75
	1980	92.5	7.5	.	x	—	—	6 910.60
	1983	59.1	7.1	33.8	x	—	—	18 901.00
	1984	80.4	19.6	.	x	—	—	29 319.00
	1985	92.5	7.5	.	x	—	—	43 631.00
	1986	93.4	6.6	.	x	—	—	86 547.00

See notes on page 122.   *Voir notes page 122.*   Véanse notas pág. 122.

Table 7 *(cont.)*   **Tableau 7** *(suite)*   **Cuadro 7** *(cont.)*

Country and currency unit / *Pays et unité monétaire* / País y unidad monetaria	Financial year / *Exercice financier* / Ejercicio financiero	Social insurance and assimilated schemes / *Assurances sociales et régimes assimilés* / Seguros sociales y regimenes asimilados	Family allowances / *Prestations familiales* / Asignaciones familiares	Special schemes for public employees / *Agents publics (régimes spéciaux)* / Empleados públicos (regimenes especiales)	Public health services / *Services publics de santé* / Servicios públicos de salud	Public assistance and assimilated schemes / *Assistance publique et régimes assimilés* / Asistencia pública y regimenes asimilados	War victims / *Victimes de guerre* / Victimas de guerra	Absolute total benefit expenditure (in millions of national currency units) / *Total (millions d'unités monétaires nationales)* / Total en millones de unidades monetarias nacionales
(1)	(2)	(3)	(4)	(5)	(6)	(7)	(8)	(9)
Venezuela (Bolívar)	1970	47.7	—	—	52.3	—	—	1 189.70
	1975	26.9	—	—	73.1	—	—	4 354.30
	1980	100.0[2]	—	—	x	—	—	2 868.80
	1983	100.0[2]	—	—	x	—	—	3 579.30
	1984	100.0[2]	—	—	x	—	—	4 140.60
	1985	100.0[2]	—	—	x	—	—	4 363.70
	1986	100.0[2]	—	—	x	—	—	5 410.90

ASIA – ASIE – ASIA

Country and currency unit	Financial year	(3)	(4)	(5)	(6)	(7)	(8)	(9)
Bahrain (Dinar)	1978	30.4	—	69.6	x	—	—	2.34
	1980	30.9	—	69.1	x	—	—	2.56
	1983	47.9	—	52.1	x	—	—	5.70
	1984	100.0[2]	—	.	x	—	—	3.62
	1985	100.0[2]	—	.	x	—	—	4.43
	1986	100.0[2]	—	.	x	—	—	5.53
Bangladesh (Taka)	1975	1.0	—	0.4	98.6	—	—	276.91
	1980	100.0[2]	—	.	x	—	—	3.14
	1983	100.0[2]	—	.	x	—	—	12.29
	1984	27.7	—	72.3	x	—	—	55.85
	1985	29.9	—	70.1	x	—	—	54.04
	1986	31.6	—	68.4	x	—	—	55.45
Cyprus (Pound)	1970	46.6	—	18.1	31.2	4.1	—	7.06
	1975	46.3	—	15.3	22.2	16.1	—	17.74
	1980	65.2	—	22.9	x	11.9	—	27.04
	1983	69.6	—	22.7	x	7.6	—	55.48
	1984	75.9	—	20.9	x	3.2	—	60.90
	1985	76.2	—	20.5	x	3.2	—	69.99
	1986	78.8	—	18.3	x	2.9	—	80.47
India (Rupee)	1970	22.4	—	34.4	42.6	0.6	—	7 861.60
	1975	19.9	—	43.2	36.2	0.7	—	17 556.90
	1980	30.4	—	66.8	x	2.8	—	21 048.40
	1983	24.8	—	70.6	x	4.6	—	38 800.97
	1984	24.7	—	70.7[15]	x	4.7[15]	—	38 743.92
	1985	26.5	—	69.0[15]	x	4.5[15]	—	39 702.67
Indonesia (Rupiah)	1981	100.0[2]	—	—	x	—	—	2 497.00
	1983	100.0[2]	—	—	x	—	—	4 729.00
	1984	89.1	—	—	x	10.9	—	5 956.53
	1985	84.6	—	—	x	15.4	—	7 948.56
	1986	78.8	—	—	x	21.2	—	11 515.92
Iran, Islamic Rep. of[2] (Rial)	1981	100.0	—	—	x	—	—	82 859.00
	1983	100.0	—	—	x	—	—	100 341.00
	1984	100.0	—	—	x	—	—	48 600.00
	1985	100.0	—	—	x	—	—	58 200.00
	1986	100.0	—	—	x	—	—	73 271.00
Israel (New Shekel)	1970	52.0	11.3	4.7	13.3	11.3	7.3	1.50
	1975	49.9	21.1	4.2	9.3	6.9	8.5	8.35
	1980	61.4	15.4	9.0	x	6.6	7.6	15.05
	1983	64.6	14.8	7.8	x	5.4	7.5	212.80
	1984	68.1	12.7	8.3	x	3.7	7.1	1 206.30
	1985	68.1	14.8	7.4	x	3.3	6.4	3 832.60
	1986	66.5	15.3	8.2	x	3.4	6.7	5 524.80

See notes on page 122.   *Voir notes page 122.*   Véanse notas pág. 122.

Table 7 *(cont.)*   Tableau 7 *(suite)*   Cuadro 7 *(cont.)*

Country and currency unit *Pays et unité monétaire* País y unidad monetaria	Financial year *Exercice financier* Ejercicio financiero	Social insurance and assimilated schemes *Assurances sociales et régimes assimilés* Seguros sociales y regímenes asimilados	Family allowances *Prestations familiales* Asignaciones familiares	Special schemes for public employees *Agents publics (régimes spéciaux)* Empleados públicos (regímenes especiales)	Public health services *Services publics de santé* Servicios públicos de salud	Public assistance and assimilated schemes *Assistance publique et régimes assimilés* Asistencia pública y regímenes asimilados	War victims *Victimes de guerre* Víctimas de guerra	Absolute total benefit expenditure (in millions of national currency units) *Total (millions d'unités monétaires nationales)* Total en millones de unidades monetarias nacionales
(1)	(2)	(3)	(4)	(5)	(6)	(7)	(8)	(9)
Japan (Yen)	1970	60.6	—	14.1	5.1	11.6	8.7	3 523 411.00
	1975	63.7	1.2	13.8	2.8	12.3	6.2	11 672 623.00
	1980	67.3	0.7	14.0	x	11.4	6.5	24 120 351.00
	1983	70.8	0.5	14.1	x	9.0	5.6	31 365 423.00
	1984	70.9	0.5	14.3	x	8.9	5.4	32 986 628.00
	1985	71.1	0.5	14.6	x	8.7	5.1	35 054 218.00
	1986	72.9	0.4	13.7	x	8.2	4.8	37 983 864.00
Jordan[2] (Dinar)	1980	100.0	—	—	x	—	—	0.03
	1983	100.0	—	—	x	—	—	2.57
	1984	100.0	—	—	x	—	—	3.65
	1985	100.0	—	—	x	—	—	5.31
	1986	100.0	—	—	x	—	—	7.38
Kuwait (Dinar)	1980	72.6	—	—	x	27.4	—	39.80
	1983	85.9	—	—	x	14.1	—	88.24
	1984	100.0[2]	—	—	x	.	—	85.41
	1985	100.0[2]	—	—	x	.	—	158.76
	1986	100.0[2]	—	—	x	.	—	163.30
Malaysia (Ringgit)	1970	27.4	—	20.0	51.4	1.2	—	301.22
	1975	20.6	—	28.4	50.3	0.7	—	622.60
	1980	58.2	—	40.5	x	1.3	—	437.39
	1983	45.2	—	52.8	x	2.1	—	1 192.39
	1984	47.3	—	50.7	x	2.0	—	1 343.31
	1985	44.4	—	53.8	x	1.8	—	1 441.54
	1986	43.3	—	54.7	x	2.0	—	1 492.78
Myanmar (Kyat)	1970	2.3	—	42.1	55.6	—	—	204.48
	1975	1.6	—	37.4	61.0	—	—	310.33
	1980	100.0[2]	—	.	x	—	—	14.85
	1983	100.0[2]	—	.	x	—	—	17.80
	1984	100.0[2]	—	.	x	—	—	16.80
	1985	100.0[2]	—	.	x	—	—	16.50
	1986	100.0[2]	—	.	x	—	—	18.50
Pakistan (Rupee)	1965	5.9	—	44.8	49.3	—	—	314.80
	1980	96.6	—	3.4	x	—	—	59.10
	1983	4.6	—	61.3	x	34.1	—	2 199.83
	1984	4.0	—	96.0	x	—	—	3 017.00
	1985	2.6	—	97.4	x	—	—	5 644.50
	1986	4.4	—	95.6	x	—	—	4 557.70
Philippines[16] (Peso)	1970	17.8	—	23.6	50.8	—	7.8	362.60
	1978	42.1	—	57.9	x	—	.	1 135.30
	1980	47.0	—	53.0	x	—	.	1 401.80
	1983	49.3	—	50.7	x	—	.	2 381.20
	1984	47.8	—	52.2	x	—	.	2 751.70
	1985	48.4	—	51.6	x	—	.	3 162.10
	1986	49.6	—	50.4	x	—	.	3 690.00
Qatar[17] (Riyal)	1984	—	—	—	x	100.0	—	76.22
	1985	—	—	—	x	100.0	—	79.54
	1986	—	—	—	x	100.0	—	80.02
Singapore (Dollar)	1970	28.9	—	14.8	54.2	2.2	—	161.93
	1975	55.6	—	8.4	35.2	0.8	—	398.20
	1980	93.3	—	6.3	x	0.3	—	852.32
	1983	95.1	—	4.7	x	0.2	—	1 829.44
	1984	96.8	—	3.1	x	0.1	—	3 614.09
	1985	95.7	—	4.2	x	0.1	—	3 506.69
	1986	96.0	—	3.9	x	0.1	—	4 023.19

See notes on page 122.   *Voir notes page 122.*   Véanse notas pág. 122.

Table 7 *(cont.)*   Tableau 7 *(suite)*   Cuadro 7 *(cont.)*

Country and currency unit / *Pays et unité monétaire* / País y unidad monetaria	Financial year / *Exercice financier* / Ejercicio financiero	Social insurance and assimilated schemes / *Assurances sociales et régimes assimilés* / Seguros sociales y regimenes asimilados	Family allowances / *Prestations familiales* / Asignaciones familiares	Special schemes for public employees / *Agents publics (régimes spéciaux)* / Empleados públicos (regimenes especiales)	Public health services / *Services publics de santé* / Servicios públicos de salud	Public assistance and assimilated schemes / *Assistance publique et régimes assimilés* / Asistencia pública y regimenes asimilados	War victims / *Victimes de guerre* / Victimas de guerra	Absolute total benefit expenditure (in millions of national currency units) / *Total (millions d'unités monétaires nationales)* / Total en millones de unidades monetarias nacionales
(1)	(2)	(3)	(4)	(5)	(6)	(7)	(8)	(9)
Sri Lanka (Rupee)	1970	9.3	—	20.4	62.0	8.3	—	386.30
	1975	15.4	—	16.8	61.9	5.8	—	567.70
	1980	18.8	—	78.0	x	3.2	—	1 094.20
	1983	14.7	—	82.4	x	2.9	—	2 638.60
	1984	18.1	—	81.7	x	0.2	—	3 137.76
	1985	14.6	—	85.2	x	0.2	—	3 842.42
	1986	10.7	—	89.1	x	0.2	—	3 975.01
Rép. arabe syrienne (Livre syrienne)	1984	56.7	—	43.3[4]	x	—	—	663.50
	1985	61.1	—	38.9[4]	x	—	—	739.50
	1986	63.2	—	36.8	x	—	—	781.50
Thailand (Baht)	1980[18]	100.0	—	.	x	—	—	98.28
	1983	7.1	—	92.9	x	—	—	1 596.23
	1984[18]	100.0	—	.	x	—	—	247.18
	1985[18]	100.0	—	.	x	—	—	232.61
	1986[18]	100.0	—	.	x	—	—	218.48

EUROPE – EUROPE – EUROPA

Countries with a market economy – Pays à économie de marché – Países con economía de mercado

Austria (Schilling)	1970	62.1	10.7	20.6	0.5	2.5	3.5	66 523.00
	1975	63.3	9.6	20.9	0.5	2.6	3.1	126 671.00
	1980	63.4	11.6	19.3	x	3.1	2.7	212 785.00
	1983	62.6	12.2	20.0	x	3.0	2.2	281 715.00
	1984	65.3	10.0	19.5	x	3.2	2.0	306 690.00
	1985	65.7	9.8	19.7	x	3.0	1.9	326 991.00
	1986	66.2	9.4	19.6	x	3.1	1.8	347 547.00
Belgique (Franc belge)	1970	58.3	16.7	15.2	3.2	2.9	3.7	212 789.60
	1975	64.5	12.9	12.9	3.5	4.2	2.0	510 888.30
	1980	70.8	10.6	13.7	x	2.9	1.9	852 297.30
	1983	72.9	10.7	11.6	x	3.0	1.8	1 108 456.00
	1984	72.3	10.4	12.2	x	3.2	1.9	1 138 501.00
	1985	72.4	10.2	12.4	x	3.2	1.8	1 183.902.00
	1986	72.6	9.9	12.4	x	3.3	1.7	1 249 375.00
Denmark (Krone)	1970	45.9	6.6	5.5	23.5	18.5	0.2	17 144.40
	1975	46.9	5.9	3.6	18.9	24.4	0.3	42 662.30
	1980	68.3	3.0	4.2	x	24.2	0.3	97 881.50
	1983	68.7	2.1	4.1	x	24.8	0.3	139 709.40
	1984	69.9	2.0	2.4	x	25.4	0.3	143 527.70
	1985	68.2	1.8	4.0	x	25.7	0.3	154 755.30
	1986	69.3	1.6	4.0	x	24.8	0.3	169 298.30
España (Peseta)	1975	73.2	9.1	10.3	3.0	4.3	.	660 900.90
	1980	85.0	2.5	9.3	x	3.2	.	2 322 464.60
	1983	82.8	1.6	10.1	x	4.2[19]	1.2	3 882 008.00
	1984	83.5	1.6	8.6	x	5.1	1.1	4 355 362.00
	1985	84.4	1.3	8.7	x	4.6	0.9	4 940 950.00
	1986	84.5	1.1	8.8	x	4.5	1.1	5 511 884.00
Finland (Markka)	1970	55.9	5.9	—	23.2	10.8	4.2	5 479.00
	1975	59.3	4.5	—	22.7	10.6	2.9	15 781.70
	1980	80.3	4.3	—	x	13.0	2.4	33 419.50
	1983	81.0	4.1	—	x	12.6	2.3	54 293.70
	1984	81.5	3.8	—	x	12.8	2.0	62 130.30
	1985	81.4	3.4	—	x	13.3	1.8	71 903.90
	1986	81.7	3.3	—	x	13.3	1.8	79 495.80

See notes on page 122.   *Voir notes page 122.*   Véanse notas pág. 122.

118

Table 7 *(cont.)*   **Tableau 7** *(suite)*   **Cuadro 7** *(cont.)*

Country and currency unit / Pays et unité monétaire / País y unidad monetaria	Financial year / Exercice financier / Ejercicio financiero	Social insurance and assimilated schemes / Assurances sociales et régimes assimilés / Seguros sociales y regímenes asimilados	Family allowances / Prestations familiales / Asignaciones familiares	Special schemes for public employees / Agents publics (régimes spéciaux) / Empleados públicos (regímenes especiales)	Public health services / Services publics de santé / Servicios públicos de salud	Public assistance and assimilated schemes / Assistance publique et régimes assimilés / Asistencia pública y regímenes asimilados	War victims / Victimes de guerre / Víctimas de guerra	Absolute total benefit expenditure (in millions of national currency units) / Total (millions d'unités monétaires nationales) / Total en millones de unidades monetarias nacionales
(1)	(2)	(3)	(4)	(5)	(6)	(7)	(8)	(9)
France (Franc français)	1975	66.1	11.8	12.3	—	9.8	—	304 003.40
	1980	62.6	10.6	11.0	x	15.8	—	703 153.70
	1983	65.3	10.8	9.6	x	14.3	—	1 100 209.40
	1984	66.4	10.8	9.8	x	13.1	—	1 200 483.30
	1985	65.7	11.2	9.9	x	13.2	—	1 282 460.60
	1986	65.8	11.4	9.7	x	13.1	—	1 369 233.40
Germany, Fed. Rep. of (Deutsche Mark)	1970	70.2	2.6	15.5	0.6	4.7	6.3	108 920.00
	1975	70.9	6.2	13.9	0.5	4.2	4.4	233 318.00
	1980	75.4	5.0	11.9	x	4.1	3.6	342 177.00
	1983	77.5	3.7	11.0	x	4.5	3.3	395 760.00
	1984	78.2	3.5	10.6	x	4.6	3.1	411 198.00
	1985	78.3	3.3	10.6	x	4.9	2.9	423 858.00
	1986	78.1	3.1	10.7	x	5.2	2.9	439 058.00
Grèce (Drachme)	1970	69.7	—[3]	19.4	4.8	2.2	4.0	30 846.00
	1975	65.8	—[3]	22.8	5.9	2.2	3.3	68 624.00
	1980	73.4	—[3]	21.3	x	3.1	2.2	199 291.00
	1983	75.7	—[3]	17.1	x	5.2	2.0	507 185.00
	1984	76.4	—[3]	16.4	x	5.3	1.8	657 298.00
	1985	77.3	—[3]	15.8	x	5.0	1.8	842 188.00
Iceland (Króna)	1984	99.0	1.0	—	x	—	—	5 959.00
	1985	98.9	1.1	—	x	—	—	8 511.00
	1986	99.0	1.0	—	x	—	—	11 258.00
Ireland (Pound)	1970	47.3	8.6	12.4	26.6	5.1	—	160.70
	1975	45.0	6.8	10.6	35.1	2.5	—	692.50
	1980	81.7	4.9	10.8	x	2.5	—	1 788.00
	1983	88.1	.[3]	9.1	x	2.9	—	3 238.33
	1984	88.3	.[3]	8.8	x	2.9	—	3 507.91
	1985	88.7	.[3]	8.4	x	2.9	—	3 843.58
	1986	88.5	.[3]	8.6	x	2.9	—	4 096.67
Italie (Lire (milliards))	1970	69.2	9.2	15.2	0.4	1.8	4.4	8 731.59
	1975	70.0	.[3]	8.5	14.4	5.6	1.5	24 169.00
	1980	83.8	.[3]	11.1	x	3.4	1.6	66 479.00
	1983	83.2	.[3]	11.3	x	3.8	1.7	129 701.00
	1984[20]	93.9	6.1	.	x	.	.	72 682.00
	1985[20]	94.9	5.1	.	x	.	.	81 309.00
	1986[20]	95.7	4.3	.	x	.	.	89 522.00
Luxembourg (Franc luxembourgeois)	1970	68.2	11.6	18.3	—	0.0	1.8	7 933.40
	1975	70.8	8.8	19.0	—	0.2	1.2	17 578.10
	1980	71.8	8.3	18.3	x	0.8	0.8	31 229.00
	1983	69.7	7.8	17.9	x	3.9	0.7	41 253.00
	1984	69.4	7.6	17.6	x	4.7	0.6	44 723.30
	1985	69.7	7.2	17.5	x	5.0	0.6	46 726.90
	1986	69.9	7.7	17.3	x	4.5	0.6	50 003.60
Malta (Lira)	1970	36.9	—	19.7	36.6	6.6	0.2	7.07
	1975	56.6	—	17.1	18.6	7.5	0.3	16.44
	1980	79.5	—	14.3	x	6.1	0.1	43.28
	1983	80.5	—	11.4	x	8.0	0.1	66.64
	1984	79.3	—	8.9	x	11.7	.	86.84
	1985	78.7	—	9.2	x	12.1	.	85.54
	1986	78.2	—	9.3	x	12.4	.	88.73
Netherlands (Guilder)	1970	69.4	10.3	14.8	—	4.8	0.6	22 146.10
	1975	71.3	7.3	13.6	—	6.9	0.9	54 253.40
	1980	73.7	7.5	11.7	x	6.2	0.8	92 067.10
	1983	72.3	6.3	11.6	x	9.0	0.7	116 284.00
	1984	75.2	7.2	11.8	x	5.1	0.6	118 811.00
	1985	76.5	7.2	12.2	x	3.5	0.6	118 006.00
	1986	76.8	6.8	12.4	x	3.3	0.6	119 097.00

See notes on page 122.   *Voir notes page 122.*   Véanse notas pág. 122.

Table 7 *(cont.)* **Tableau 7** *(suite)* **Cuadro 7** *(cont.)*

Country and currency unit *Pays et unité monétaire* País y unidad monetaria	Financial year *Exercice financier* Ejercicio financiero	Social insurance and assimilated schemes *Assurances sociales et régimes assimilés* Seguros sociales y regímenes asimilados	Family allowances *Prestations familiales* Asignaciones familiares	Special schemes for public employees *Agents publics (régimes spéciaux)* Empleados públicos (regímenes especiales)	Public health services *Services publics de santé* Servicios públicos de salud	Public assistance and assimilated schemes *Assistance publique et régimes assimilés* Asistencia pública y regímenes asimilados	War victims *Victimes de guerre* Victimas de guerra	Absolute total benefit expenditure (in millions of national currency units) *Total (millions d'unités monétaires nationales)* Total en millones de unidades monetarias nacionales
(1)	(2)	(3)	(4)	(5)	(6)	(7)	(8)	(9)
Norway (Krone)	1970	66.0	10.2	7.4	8.8	5.2	2.4	11 802.00
	1975	70.9	5.2	6.1	9.4	6.9	1.6	26 459.10
	1980	80.7	5.0	4.5	x	8.8	1.0	56 240.00
	1983	79.5	5.1	3.9	x	10.7	0.8	85 788.30
	1984	63.0	3.6	2.8	x	30.2	0.4	128 478.40
	1985	62.5	3.6	2.7	x	30.7	0.5	139 808.30
	1986	61.3	3.6	2.8	x	31.7	0.5	151 726.40
Portugal (Escudo)	1970	52.2	24.0	14.4	9.4	.	—	8 686.50
	1975	64.7	17.4	11.6	3.4	3.0	—	38 298.20
	1980	82.9	.[3]	12.6	x	4.5	—	109 245.50
	1983	77.6	.[3]	18.3	x	4.2	—	219 544.80
	1984	76.8	.[3]	19.1	x	4.1	—	272 338.10
	1985	75.0	.[3]	20.6	x	4.4	—	337 370.30
	1986	75.6	.[3]	19.9	x	4.5	—	438 022.90
Suisse (Franc suisse)	1970	67.9	0.6	7.8	13.8	9.9	—	8 606.20
	1975	73.1	0.4	5.1	13.3	8.1	—	20 034.80
	1980	84.8	0.3	6.5	x	8.4	—	21 830.60
	1983	87.4	0.3	3.7	x	8.5	—	26 929.10
	1984	87.7	0.3	3.7	x	8.3	—	29 467.20
	1985	87.2	0.3	3.8	x	8.7	—	30 654.30
	1986	87.1	0.3	3.8	x	8.8	—	32 666.50
Sweden (Krona)	1970	51.6	5.1	—	28.6	14.7	0.1	31 410.00
	1975	53.1	5.7	—	24.9	16.4	0.0	73 799.00
	1980	77.9	5.2	—	x	16.8	—	163 116.50
	1983	78.6	4.6	—	x	16.8	—	229 494.50
	1984	84.7	15.0	—	x	0.2	—	232 496.50
	1985	84.5	15.3	—	x	0.3	—	253 828.40
	1986	84.1	15.5	—	x	0.5	—	280 080.50
Turquie (Livre turque)	1970	36.4	—	60.2	3.1	0.3	—	4 317.90
	1975	33.1	—	58.1	8.6[21]	0.2	—	14 869.30
	1980	50.5	—	48.8	x	0.1	0.6	175 572.30
	1983	61.5	—	38.3	x	0.2	.	416 010.00
	1984	53.0	—	28.3	x	18.7	.	682 633.00
	1985	52.2	—	27.3	x	20.6	.	1 043 130.00
	1986	58.1	—	26.3	x	15.6	.	1 377 413.00
United Kingdom (Pound)	1970	41.8	5.4	7.1	28.7	15.0	1.9	6 582.00
	1975	41.8	3.3	7.7	29.6	16.1	1.5	16 945.00
	1980	67.3	7.8	8.1	x	15.6	1.1	39 687.00
	1983	60.8	7.3	8.8	x	22.2	0.9	58 289.00
	1984	59.7	7.3	8.9	x	23.2	0.9	62 552.00
	1985	58.8	7.0	8.8	x	24.5	0.9	67 911.00
	1986	59.1	6.7	8.9	x	24.4	0.8	72 529.00

EUROPE – EUROPE – EUROPA

Countries with a centrally planned economy – Pays à économie planifiée – Países con economía centralmente planificada

RSS de Biélorussie (Rouble)	1970	64.6	0.8	—	34.6	—	—	1 106.00
	1975	68.2	2.6[22]	—	29.1	—	—	1 637.00
	1980	98.9	1.1	—	x	—	—	2 243.00
	1983	99.0	1.0	—	x	—	—	2 689.00
	1984	99.1	0.9	—	x	—	—	2 823.00
	1985	99.2	0.8	—	x	—	—	2 942.00
	1986	99.2	0.8	—	x	—	—	3 199.00

See notes on page 122. *Voir notes page 122.* Véanse notas pág. 122.

Table 7 *(cont.)*   Tableau 7 *(suite)*   Cuadro 7 *(cont.)*

Country and currency unit *Pays et unité monétaire* País y unidad monetaria	Financial year *Exercice financier* Ejercicio financiero	Social insurance and assimilated schemes *Assurances sociales et régimes assimilés* Seguros sociales y regímenes asimilados	Family allowances *Prestations familiales* Asignaciones familiares	Special schemes for public employees *Agents publics (régimes spéciaux)* Empleados públicos (regímenes especiales)	Public health services *Services publics de santé* Servicios públicos de salud	Public assistance and assimilated schemes *Assistance publique et régimes assimilés* Asistencia pública y regímenes asimilados	War victims *Victimes de guerre* Victimas de guerra	Absolute total benefit expenditure (in millions of national currency units) *Total (millions d'unités monétaires nationales)* Total en millones de unidades monetarias nacionales
(1)	(2)	(3)	(4)	(5)	(6)	(7)	(8)	(9)
Bulgarie (Lev)	1970	62.6	16.1	—	20.1	—	1.2	1 406.30
	1975	63.3	11.9	—	24.1	—	0.7	2 130.50
	1980	79.6	19.7	—	x	.	0.7	2 506.30
	1983	82.4	17.1	—	x	.	0.5	2 953.70
	1984	82.9	16.8	—	x	0.3	.	2 934.80
	1985	82.2	17.6	—	x	0.3	.	3 212.90
	1986	81.4	18.4	—	x	0.2	.	3 584.80
Czechoslovakia (Koruna)	1970	59.4	13.6	—	25.0	1.9	—	55 758.00
	1975	61.4	14.2	—	22.3	2.1	—	69 183.00
	1980	82.9	14.6	—	x	2.4	—	91 037.00
	1983	82.5	14.8	—	x	2.7	—	104 858.00
	1984	82.9	14.4	—	x	2.7	—	108 106.00
	1985	82.8	14.4	—	x	2.8	—	114 102.00
	1986	83.6	13.6	—	x	2.8	—	120 341.00
German Democratic Rep. (Mark)	1970	99.1	0.9	—	—	—	—	14 323.00
	1975	93.3	6.7	—	—	—	—	21 714.90
	1980	95.5	4.5	—	x	—	—	29 517.90
	1983	95.5	4.5	—	x	—	—	30 721.30
	1984	95.6	4.4	—	x	—	—	31 088.50
	1985	95.9	4.1	—	x	—	—	32 608.50
	1986	96.1	3.9	—	x	—	—	34 188.50
Hongrie (Forint)	1970	86.6	13.4	—	.	—	—	29 965.00
	1975	59.9	16.2	—	23.9	—	—	58 143.00
	1980	83.5	16.5	—	x	—	—	106 069.00
	1983	85.9	14.1	—	x	—	—	137 714.00
	1984	100.0[2]	.[3]	—	x	—	—	120 077.00
	1985	100.0[2]	.[3]	—	x	—	—	131 455.00
	1986	100.0[2]	.[3]	—	x	—	—	141 923.00
Pologne (Zloty)	1984	95.8	.[3]	1.8	x	0.9	1.5	1 252 101.00
	1985	95.9	.[3]	1.8	x	0.9	1.5	1 456 960.00
	1986	95.9	.[3]	1.8	x	0.8	1.5	1 814 972.00
RSS d'Ukraine (Rouble)	1970	65.7	0.5	—	33.8	—	—	6 503.00
	1975	69.1	1.7	—	29.2	—	—	9 050.00
	1980	99.1	0.9	—	x	—	—	12 030.00
	1983	99.0	1.0	—	x	—	—	14 180.00
	1984	99.1	0.9	—	x	—	—	14 898.00
	1985	99.1	0.9	—	x	—	—	15 658.00
	1986	99.2	0.8	—	x	—	—	16 835.00
URSS (Rouble)	1970	64.6	1.3	—	34.1	—	—	34 604.00
	1975	67.1	3.3	—	29.7	—	—	49 238.00
	1980	97.8	2.2	—	x	—	—	64 616.00
	1983	98.0	2.0	—	x	—	—	75 789.00
	1984	98.1	1.9	—	x	—	—	79 969.00
	1985	98.1	1.9	—	x	—	—	83 573.00
	1986	98.2	1.8	—	x	—	—	89 307.00
Yugoslavia (Dinar)	1970	84.8	8.1	—	2.3[23]	0.6	4.2	19 449.00
	1981	95.2	4.8	—	x	—	—	240 288.70
	1983	95.4	4.6	—	x	—	—	421 957.00
	1984	100.0[2]	.	—	x	—	—	569 535.00
	1985	100.0[2]	.	—	x	—	—	1 043 087.00
	1986	100.0[2]	.	—	x	—	—	2 467 680.00

See notes on page 122.   *Voir notes page 122.*   Véanse notas pág. 122.

Table 7 *(concl.)* Tableau 7 *(fin)* Cuadro 7 *(fin)*

Country and currency unit / *Pays et unité monétaire* / País y unidad monetaria	Financial year / *Exercice financier* / Ejercicio financiero	Social insurance and assimilated schemes / *Assurances sociales et régimes assimilés* / Seguros sociales y regimenes asimilados	Family allowances / *Prestations familiales* / Asignaciones familiares	Special schemes for public employees / *Agents publics (régimes spéciaux)* / Empleados públicos (regimenes especiales)	Public health services / *Services publics de santé* / Servicios públicos de salud	Public assistance and assimilated schemes / *Assistance publique et régimes assimilés* / Asistencia pública y regimenes asimilados	War victims / *Victimes de guerre* / Victimas de guerra	Absolute total benefit expenditure (in millions of national currency units) / *Total (millions d'unités monétaires nationales)* / Total en millones de unidades monetarias nacionales
(1)	(2)	(3)	(4)	(5)	(6)	(7)	(8)	(9)

OCEANIA – OCÉANIE – OCEANIA

Country and currency unit	Financial year	(3)	(4)	(5)	(6)	(7)	(8)	(9)
Australia (Dollar)	1970	63.9	—[3]	8.5	13.1	3.2	11.3	2 593.90
	1975	64.3	—[3]	7.8	15.8	3.5	8.6	7 360.90
	1980	80.2	—[3]	7.2	x	4.2	8.4	15 182.30
	1983	79.6	—[3]	5 7	x	4.6	10.0	22 068.20
	1984	80.4	—[3]	6.5	x	—	13.1	19 822.90
	1985	80.9	—[3]	6.5	x	—	12.6	23 323.90
	1986	78.7	—[3]	7.5	x	—	13.8	23 609.50
Fiji (Dollar)	1975	18.8	—	20.9	60.4	—	—	13.75
	1980	52.7	—	47.3	x	—	—	11.57
	1983	65.7	—	34.3	x	—	—	24.56
	1984	100.0[7]	—	.	x	—	—	23.03
	1985	100.0[7]	—	.	x	—	—	26.79
	1986	100.0[7]	—	.	x	—	—	32.57
New Zealand (Dollar)	1970	60.6	.[3]	7.7	26.2	—	5.4	579.80
	1975	57.0	.[3]	4.8	35.2	—	3.0	1 668.50
	1980	93.7	.[3]	4.4	x	—	1.9	3 971.00
	1983	94.7	.[3]	3.9	x	—	1.3	5 928.70
	1984	94.2	.[3]	4.5	x	—	1.3	6 493.70
	1985	93.8	.[3]	5.2	x	—	1.1	7 917.40
	1986	92.6	2.0[3,24]	4.5	x	—	0.9	9 286.40
Solomon Islands[7] (Dollar)	1981	100.0	—	—	x	—	—	0.49
	1983	100.0	—	—	x	—	—	1.15
	1984	100.0	—	—	x	—	—	1.45
	1985	100.0	—	—	x	—	—	2.02
	1986	100.0	—	—	x	—	—	2.77

For general footnotes, see table 1. [1] Only data in respect of Public Employees' Scheme are available. [2] Only data in respect of social insurance and assimilated schemes are available. [3] Included in column (3). [4] Estimated by using absolute figures of 1986. [5] Excludes the three eastern states. [6] The numerator relates to the social security benefit expenditure for 1968-69. [7] Only data in respect of Provident Fund are available. [8] The figures relate to the financial year ended 31 March. [9] The figures relate to those of 1981-82. [10] Data are not strictly comparable with those prior to 1984.

[11] The figures are provisional. [12] The figures relate to 1982. [13] Estimated on the basis of the total benefit expenditure on public health services for 1974. [14] Estimates. [15] Data relate to the period 1983-84. [16] As from 1978 onwards data on public assistance and veterans' programmes are not available. [17] Only data in respect of "social assistance" are available. [18] Only data in respect of "employment injuries" are available. [19] Data relate to the year 1982. [20] No data were reported in respect of public employees, public assistance and war victims.

[21] Includes part of the administrative expenditure. [22] Figure represents payments for "children's allowances" and benefits payable to mothers with numerous children and to unmarried mothers. [23] Absolute figures for "public assistance and assimilated schemes" are the amount for 1968 since the figures for the relevant years are not available. [24] The 2 per cent shown is the family support tax credit and the Homestart Deposit Assistance.

Pour les notes de caractère général, se reporter au tableau 1. [1] On ne dispose de données que pour le régime des agents publics. [2] On ne dispose de données que pour les assurances sociales et les régimes assimilés. [3] Compris dans la colonne 3. [4] Estimations fondées sur les chiffres absolus pour 1986. [5] A l'exclusion des trois États de l'Est. [6] Le chiffre utilisé au numérateur se rapporte aux dépenses en prestations pour 1968-69. [7] On ne dispose de données que pour le Fonds de prévoyance. [8] Les chiffres se rapportent à l'exercice financier se terminant le 31 mars. [9] Se rapporte aux chiffres de 1981-82. [10] Les chiffres ne sont pas exactement comparables avec ceux qui sont donnés pour les années antérieures à 1984.

[11] Chiffres provisoires. [12] Les chiffres se rapportent à 1982. [13] Estimations fondées sur les dépenses totales en prestations des services publics de santé pour 1974. [14] Estimations. [15] Les chiffres se rapportent à la période 1983-84. [16] Depuis 1978, on ne dispose plus de données pour l'assistance publique et pour les régimes des anciens combattants. [17] On ne dispose de données que pour la réparation des accidents du travail et des maladies professionnelles. [18] On ne dispose de données que pour la réparation des accidents du travail et des maladies professionnelles. [19] Les chiffres se rapportent à 1982. [20] Aucune donnée n'a été reçue pour les régimes des agents publics, l'assistance publique et les prestations aux victimes de guerre.

[21] Comprend une partie des frais d'administration. [22] Correspond aux allocations pour enfants et aux prestations aux mères de familles nombreuses et aux mères célibataires. [23] Les chiffres absolus pour l'assistance publique et les régimes assimilés sont ceux de 1968, les chiffres pour 1970 n'étant pas disponibles. [24] Correspond au crédit d'impôt pour l'aide aux familles et au régime d'assistance aux jeunes foyers.

Véanse las notas generales del cuadro 1. [1] Sólo se dispuso de datos sobre regimenes de empleados públicos. [2] Sólo se dispuso de datos sobre seguros sociales y regimenes asimilados. [3] Incluido en la columna 3. [4] Estimación fundada en cifras absolutas de 1986. [5] Excluye los tres Estados orientales. [6] El numerador corresponde a los egresos por prestaciones de la seguridad social en 1968-1969. [7] Sólo se dispuso de datos sobre el Fondo de Previsión. [8] Las cifras corresponden al ejercicio financiero terminado el 31 de marzo. [9] Las cifras son del período 1981-1982. [10] Los datos no son estrictamente comparables con los anteriores a 1984.

[11] Se trata de cifras provisionales. [12] Las cifras corresponden a 1982. [13] Estimación sobre la base de egresos totales por prestaciones en servicios públicos de salud en 1974. [14] Estimaciones. [15] Los datos corresponden al período 1983-1984. [16] No se dispone de datos sobre asistencia pública y programas de veteranos a partir de 1978. [17] Sólo se dispuso de datos con respecto a «asistencia social». [18] Sólo se dispuso de datos con respecto a «riesgos profesionales». [19] Los datos corresponden al año 1982. [20] No se comunicaron datos con respecto a empleados públicos, asistencia pública y víctimas de guerra.

[21] Incluye parte de los gastos de administración. [22] La cifra refleja los pagos de «asignaciones por hijos» y de prestaciones pagaderas a madres de numerosos hijos o madres solteras. [23] Las cifras absolutas respecto de «asistencia pública y regímenes asimilados» son las de 1968, pues no se dispuso de las cifras para los años pertinentes. [24] El 2 por ciento indicado corresponde al crédito fiscal de ayuda familiar y la ayuda de depósito para nuevos hogares.

8. Distribution of social security receipts according to origin
(as percentages of total receipts)

8. Répartition des recettes de la sécurité sociale d'après leur provenance
(en pourcentage du total des recettes)

8. Distribución de los ingresos de la seguridad social según su procedencia
(en porcentaje del total de ingresos)

Country and currency unit / Pays et unité monétaire / País y unidad monetaria	Financial year / Exercice financier / Ejercicio financiero	Contributions / Cotisations / Cotizaciones — From insured persons / Des assurés / De los asegurados	From employers / Des employeurs / De los empleadores	Special taxes allocated to social security / Taxes et impôts spéciaux / Impuestos y derechos especiales	State participation / Participation de l'Etat / Participación del Estado	Participation of other public authorities / Participation d'autres pouvoirs publics / Participación de otras entidades públicas	Income from capital / Revenu des capitaux / Renta del capital	Other receipts / Autres recettes / Otros ingresos	Absolute total receipts (in millions of national currency units) / Total (millions d'unités monétaires nationales) / Total en millones de unidades monetarias nacionales
(1)	(2)	(3)	(4)	(5)	(6)	(7)	(8)	(9)	(10)

AFRICA – AFRIQUE – AFRICA

Bénin (Franc CFA)	1970	2.3	32.6	—	64.9	—	—	0.2	1 826.60
	1975	6.1	41.0	—	52.1	—	0.8	0.0	2 938.30
	1981	22.1	77.8	—	—	—	—	0.1	5 745.94
	1983	21.3	78.6	—	—	—	—	0.0	7 001.73
	1984	15.1	75.0	—	—	—	7.9	2.0	3 659.80
	1985	15.6	77.4	—	—	—	5.5	1.5	3 969.10
	1986	15.9	78.4	—	—	—	4.4	1.3	4 539.20
Burkina Faso (Franc CFA)	1975	7.4	57.7	—	33.4	—	1.5	0.0	2 904.70
	1980	17.8	72.0	—	—	—	1.5	8.7	4 331.80
	1983	23.9	75.6	0.1	—	—	0.4	—	9 136.70
	1984	15.3	63.1	—	—	—	21.6	0.1	6 760.70
	1985	15.7	62.7	—	—	—	21.6	0.0	7 241.30
	1986	15.6	64.3	—	—	—	20.1	0.0	8 087.50
Burundi (Franc burundais)	1978	23.0	43.1	—	19.5	—	1.3	13.1	332.49
	1980	21.1	39.3	—	25.7	—	1.0	12.9	474.96
	1983	32.1	41.0	—	11.2	—	14.7	1.0	890.01
	1984	32.7	48.9	—	—	—	18.3	0.1	959.70
	1985	32.3	49.0	—	—	—	18.6	0.1	1 117.00
	1986	30.9	51.1	—	—	—	17.8	0.1	1 368.90
Cameroun (Franc CFA)	1970	2.4	44.0	—	53.3	—	0.3	0.0	5 275.10
	1981	13.8	86.2	—	—	—	—	0.0	24 414.00
	1983	11.1	69.0	—	—	—	19.9	0.0	42 817.00
	1984	16.4	80.9	—	—	—	2.7	—	38 393.00
	1985	13.1	68.1	—	—	—	18.8	—	50 377.00
	1986	14.0	68.2	—	—	—	17.8	—	56 770.00
Cap-Vert (Escudo)	1983	28.8	70.2	—	—	—	0.1	0.8	223.29
	1984	29.4	68.9	—	—	—	1.1	0.6	320.05
	1985	28.8	66.7	—	1.5	—	2.5	0.5	412.32
	1986	27.5	62.5	—	1.5	—	8.0	0.4	499.87
Rép. centrafricaine (Franc CFA)	1981	11.4	88.5	—	—	—	—	0.1	2 091.70
	1983	9.9	88.7	—	—	—	1.4	0.1	2 283.50
	1984	10.0	90.0	—	—	—	—	—	2 747.00
	1985	9.8	87.9	—	—	—	1.4	0.9	3 084.00
	1986	9.8	88.5	—	—	—	1.3	0.3	4 549.00
Côte d'Ivoire (Franc CFA)	1981	32.0	49.1	—	—	—	18.9	—	26 247.00
	1983	31.7	47.9	—	—	—	20.4	—	29 125.00
	1984	12.4	61.2	—	—	—	26.4	0.0	28 452.40
	1985	12.7	54.7	—	—	—	32.6	0.0	38 423.70
	1986	13.6	53.1	—	—	—	33.3	0.0	40 277.40
Egypt (Pound)	1984	27.9	40.2	—	13.5	—	12.0	6.4	2 339.00
	1985	26.7	39.0	—	12.5	—	12.9	9.0	2 779.60
	1986	26.0	39.8	—	11.8	—	13.1	9.3	3 285.50

See notes on page 136. *Voir notes page 136.* Véanse notas pág. 136.

Table 8 (cont.)   Tableau 8 (suite)   Cuadro 8 (cont.)

| Country and currency unit / Pays et unité monétaire / País y unidad monetaria | Financial year / Exercice financier / Ejercicio financiero | Contributions / Cotisations / Cotizaciones | | Special taxes allocated to social security / Taxes et impôts spéciaux / Impuestos y derechos especiales | State participation / Participation de l'Etat / Participación del Estado | Participation of other public authorities / Participation d'autres pouvoirs publics / Participación de otras entidades públicas | Income from capital / Revenu des capitaux / Renta del capital | Other receipts / Autres recettes / Otros ingresos | Absolute total receipts (in millions of national currency units) / Total (millions d'unités monétaires nationales) / Total en millones de unidades monetarias nacionales |
		From insured persons / Des assurés / De los asegurados	From employers / Des employeurs / De los empleadores						
(1)	(2)	(3)	(4)	(5)	(6)	(7)	(8)	(9)	(10)
Ethiopia (Birr)	1972	9.7	36.9	—	51.6	—	1.5	0.4	81.06
	1975	8.8	38.4	—	50.6	—	1.7	0.5	117.05
	1980	21.8	70.7	—	4.5	—	3.0	—	117.67
	1983	31.7	65.3	—	—	—	3.1	—	126.54
	1984	31.7	65.2	—	—	—	3.0	—	151.45
	1985	32.7	64.6	—	—	—	2.7	—	158.70
	1986	32.5	63.2	—	—	—	4.2	—	162.08
Gabon (Franc CFA)	1980	8.6	86.3	—	—	—	2.9	2.2	18 957.00
	1983	16.0	65.1	—	12.8	—	5.5	0.6	39 632.00
	1984	8.6	84.9	—	—	—	—	6.6	37 402.00
	1985	8.5	84.7	—	—	—	—	6.8	41 719.00
	1986	8.3	84.8	—	—	—	—	6.9	37 788.00
Guinée (Syli)	1981	—	82.8	17.2	—	—	—	—	161.32
	1983	—	78.7	21.3	—	—	—	—	166.32
	1984	.	.	—	—	—	—	.	.
	1985	3.0	90.4	—	—	—	—	6.6	160.20
	1986	3.0	90.9	—	—	—	—	6.1	296.19
Guinée-Bissau (Peso)	1981	24.4	42.7	—	—	—	11.5	21.4	34.81
	1983	25.8	44.5	—	—	—	19.7	10.0	27.91
	1984	18.1	61.5	—	10.4	—	10.1	—	57.60
	1985	18.5	59.0	—	16.2	—	6.3	—	83.10
	1986	22.8	63.0	—	10.3	—	3.8	—	138.00
Kenya (Shilling)	1970	21.6	45.1	0.1	32.4	—	—	0.8	339.80
	1975	17.2	26.6	0.0	42.7	—	11.6	1.9	791.60
	1981	32.5	32.5	—	—	—	35.0	—	492.40
	1983	25.3	25.3	—	—	—	49.4	—	600.40
	1984	22.6	22.6	1.2	—	—	53.6	—	1 680.00
	1985	22.6	22.6	1.1	—	—	53.8	—	1 860.00
	1986	27.7	27.7	1.2	—	—	43.4	—	1 660.00
Madagascar (Franc malgache)	1981	6.6	86.4	—	—	—	6.9	—	7 937.20
	1983	5.4	69.6	—	—	—	25.1	—	9 536.10
	1984	22.2	77.8	—	—	—	—	—	8 392.60
	1985	22.2	77.8	—	—	—	—	—	8 916.10
	1986	22.2	77.8	—	—	—	—	—	10 288.20
Mali (Franc CFA)	1972	1.7	33.0	—	64.9	—	—	0.4	1 660.50
	1975	4.0	34.1	0.0	55.5	—	0.1	6.2	2 175.00
	1980	8.5	79.4	—	10.7	—	0.2	1.2	2 270.50
	1983	13.7	75.5	—	1.9	—	—	8.8	4 552.60
	1984	19.8	75.8	—	—	—	—	4.4	6 382.40
	1985	18.6	77.2	—	—	—	—	4.1	6 804.20
	1986	16.6	74.3	—	—	—	0.0	9.1	8 128.80
Maroc (Dirham)	1970	5.2	48.6	—	43.8	—	2.4	—	485.38
	1975	5.1	62.3	—	31.5	—	1.1	0.1	692.86
	1980	—	89.8	—	0.2	—	9.7	0.3	1 446.70
	1983	8.4	78.4	—	—	—	13.2	—	1 451.60
	1984	31.8	49.1	—	—	—	14.1	5.0	2 611.50
	1985	26.9	41.9	—	—	—	14.2	17.1	3 332.00
	1986	27.6	41.2	—	—	—	14.7	16.5	3 660.70
Mauritanie (Ouguiya)	1970	10.3	47.6	—	40.0	—	1.4	0.7	243.64
	1981	8.8	56.4	—	33.4	—	1.4	0.1	1 039.28
	1983	9.3	57.7	—	30.1	—	2.7	0.1	1 192.86
	1984	6.8	88.8	—	—	—	4.1	0.4	667.03
	1985	6.4	86.3	—	—	—	4.6	2.7	749.08
	1986	6.3	87.7	—	—	—	6.1	—	584.62

See notes on page 136.   *Voir notes page 136.*   Véanse notas pág. 136.

Table 8 *(cont.)*   **Tableau 8** *(suite)*   **Cuadro 8** *(cont.)*

Country and currency unit / Pays et unité monétaire / País y unidad monetaria	Financial year / Exercice financier / Ejercicio financiero	Contributions / Cotisations / Cotizaciones — From insured persons / Des assurés / De los asegurados	From employers / Des employeurs / De los empleadores	Special taxes allocated to social security / Taxes et impôts spéciaux / Impuestos y derechos especiales	State participation / Participation de l'Etat / Participación del Estado	Participation of other public authorities / Participation d'autres pouvoirs publics / Participación de otras entidades públicas	Income from capital / Revenu des capitaux / Renta del capital	Other receipts / Autres recettes / Otros ingresos	Absolute total receipts (in millions of national currency units) / Total (millions d'unités monétaires nationales) / Total en millones de unidades monetarias nacionales
(1)	(2)	(3)	(4)	(5)	(6)	(7)	(8)	(9)	(10)
Mauritius (Rupee)	1970	4.0	23.9	—	66.6	—	4.3	1.1	77.83
	1975	5.6	25.8	—	64.9	—	3.6	0.2	176.14
	1981	11.1	22.1	—	56.3	—	8.8	1.7	320.80
	1983	10.1	20.2	—	54.3	—	13.8	1.6	454.40
	1984	.	.	—	.	—	.	.	.
	1985	9.8	35.5	—	37.2	—	15.1	2.4	869.50
	1986	9.6	35.0	—	37.7	—	17.2	0.5	993.80
Mozambique (Metical)	1981	—	99.9	—	—	—	0.1	—	231.36
	1983	—	99.8	—	—	—	0.2	—	153.96
	1984	—	86.5	—	13.4	—	0.1	—	233.20
	1985	—	86.7	—	13.1	—	0.1	—	238.35
	1986	—	86.2	—	13.7	—	0.1	—	228.19
Niger (Franc CFA)	1970	4.6	35.8	—	58.7	—	0.6	0.3	1 490.40
	1975	4.7	38.8	—	51.7	—	4.8	—	2 158.90
	1980	8.4	80.4	—	—	—	11.2	0.0	3 823.50
	1983	8.6	82.8	—	—	—	8.6	0.0	5 954.70
	1984	11.5	36.2	—	35.3	—	6.2	10.8	13 830.00
	1985	11.1	35.9	—	34.0	—	8.6	10.4	14 358.50
	1986	12.3	39.2	—	37.8	—	10.7	—	12 890.60
Nigeria (Naira)	1970	10.0	26.0	0.1	54.8	—	9.1	—	47.92
	1981	33.1	22.3	—	—	—	44.4	0.2	70.67
	1983	28.2	20.2	—	—	—	51.4	0.3	78.42
	1984	17.8	27.5	—	—	—	54.7	0.0	87.23
	1985	19.1	26.5	—	—	—	54.0	0.4	99.56
	1986	17.9	24.4	—	—	—	57.2	0.5	108.38
Rwanda (Franc rwandais)	1975	23.2	38.7	—	29.0	—	8.3	0.7	441.36
	1981	30.8	51.3	—	—	—	16.5	1.4	1 118.50
	1983	26.9	44.8	—	—	—	26.2	2.1	1 440.50
	1984	26.7	44.5	—	—	—	27.8	1.1	1 730.20
	1985	25.0	41.6	—	—	—	32.6	0.8	1 793.60
	1986	24.6	41.0	—	—	—	33.1	1.3	2 123.80
Sao Tomé-et-Principe (Dobra)	1981	40.1	59.8	—	—	—	—	0.1	83.21
	1983	40.0	59.8	—	—	—	—	0.3	82.88
	1984	40.1	59.8	—	—	—	—	0.1	77.80
	1985	38.8	58.1	—	—	—	—	3.1	92.87
	1986	37.7	56.4	—	—	—	—	6.0	46.41
Sénégal (Franc CFA)	1970	14.3	38.4	5.6	41.5	—	0.0	0.2	8 755.00
	1975	9.6	42.8	—	44.6	—	0.3	2.6	11 637.90
	1980	18.1	67.0	—	5.5	—	7.8	1.7	13 904.00
	1983	—	95.8	—	—	—	1.2	3.1	7 704.00
	1984	21.9	69.4	—	—	—	8.5	0.3	18 774.00
	1985	20.8	70.9	—	—	—	8.1	0.3	21 300.00
	1986	21.3	69.9	—	—	—	8.5	0.2	22 094.00
Sudan (Pound)	1980	21.9	43.7	—	—	—	12.5	21.9	23.79
	1983	16.8	37.3	—	—	—	14.8	31.0	33.19
	1984	11.7	23.4	—	—	—	16.9	47.9	55.50
	1985	12.2	24.6	—	—	—	35.3	27.9	54.10
	1986	14.3	28.7	—	—	—	37.1	20.0	42.10
Swaziland (Lilangeni)	1981	35.6	46.6	—	—	—	17.7	—	7.44
	1983	29.5	40.9	—	—	—	29.7	—	11.09
	1984	33.9	33.9	—	—	—	31.7	0.5	9.65
	1985	32.2	32.2	—	—	—	35.2	0.4	10.28
	1986	31.4	31.4	—	—	—	36.7	0.5	10.70

See notes on page 136.   *Voir notes page 136.*   Véanse notas pág. 136.

Table 8 *(cont.)*   Tableau 8 *(suite)*   Cuadro 8 *(cont.)*

Country and currency unit / Pays et unité monétaire / País y unidad monetaria	Financial year / Exercice financier / Ejercicio financiero	Contributions / Cotisations / Cotizaciones		Special taxes allocated to social security / Taxes et impôts spéciaux / Impuestos y derechos especiales	State participation / Participation de l'Etat / Participación del Estado	Participation of other public authorities / Participation d'autres pouvoirs publics / Participación de otras entidades públicas	Income from capital / Revenu des capitaux / Renta del capital	Other receipts / Autres recettes / Otros ingresos	Absolute total receipts (in millions of national currency units) / Total (millions d'unités monétaires nationales) / Total en millones de unidades monetarias nacionales
		From insured persons / Des assurés / De los asegurados	From employers / Des employeurs / De los empleadores						
(1)	(2)	(3)	(4)	(5)	(6)	(7)	(8)	(9)	(10)
Tanzania, United Rep. of (Shilling)	1980	32.7	32.7	—	—	—	34.6	—	312.30
	1983	32.2	32.2	—	—	—	35.6	0.1	394.80
	1984	32.7	43.9	—	2.5	—	10.2	10.8	829.93
	1985	31.7	39.9	—	2.8	—	12.5	13.1	933.24
	1986	26.9	33.7	—	2.0	—	20.6	16.8	1 286.63
Tchad (Franc CFA)	1979-81	13.9	86.1	—	—	—	—	—	211.14
	1983	14.0	86.0	—	—	—	—	—	227.69
	1984	29.5	59.5	2.9	—	—	1.2	6.9	669.01
	1985	31.8	64.1	—	—	—	1.4	2.8	1 668.87
	1986	26.4	65.9	—	—	—	4.0	3.8	1 221.90
Togo (Franc CFA)	1972	9.9	50.1	—	36.7	—	1.9	1.4	1 966.00
	1975	8.0	49.3	—	41.4	—	1.3	—	3 025.00
	1980	10.4	77.8	—	—	—	11.7	0.2	4 814.00
	1983	9.9	75.2	—	—	—	14.9	—	7 008.00
	1984	9.6	73.4	—	—	—	17.0	—	8 177.00
	1985	9.1	69.3	—	—	—	21.6	—	9 536.00
	1986	9.3	70.9	—	—	—	19.8	—	9 588.00
Tunisie (Dinar)	1984	31.5	54.0	—	—	—	7.1	7.5	379.70
	1985	32.4	50.8	—	—	—	7.5	9.4	468.50
	1986	33.0	52.0	—	—	—	7.8	7.2	462.50
Uganda (Shilling)	1980	27.4	27.4	—	—	—	45.2	—	82.10
	1983	24.3	24.3	—	—	—	51.5	—	171.00
	1984	21.0	21.0	—	—	—	58.0	—	150.78
	1985	26.7	26.7	—	—	—	46.6	—	145.93
	1986	44.6	44.6	—	—	—	10.9	—	75.06
Zaïre (Zaïre)	1984	25.9	61.6	—	—	—	—	12.5	322.36
	1985	25.0	67.9	—	—	—	—	7.2	736.33
	1986	28.6	60.2	—	—	—	—	11.2	1 238.25
Zambia (Kwacha)	1970	25.1	21.0	—	45.4	—	7.3	1.2	45.60
	1975	28.0	15.4	—	45.8	—	9.3	1.5	106.23
	1980	38.1	30.6	—	—	—	31.3	0.1	69.01
	1983	.	.	.	.	.	.	.	.
	1984	29.8	29.8	—	—	—	40.4	—	101.79
	1985	30.2	30.2	—	—	—	39.7	—	128.05
	1986	28.4	28.4	—	—	—	43.2	—	179.21

AMERICA – AMÉRIQUE – AMERICA

Country and currency unit	Financial year	From insured persons	From employers	Special taxes	State participation	Other public authorities	Income from capital	Other receipts	Absolute total receipts
Argentina (Austral)	1975	22.8	70.3	—	5.0	—	1.0	0.9	0.01
	1980	38.3	49.3	2.9	7.3	—	2.2	0.0	2.74
	1983	34.5	27.2	2.9	33.1	—	2.0	0.3	51.70
	1984	33.0	31.9	2.3	26.6	—	5.8	0.3	432.72
	1985	30.6	41.4	—	19.6	—	7.7	0.7	2 831.60
	1986	31.3	45.6	—	19.5	—	3.3	0.3	4 994.50
Bahamas (Dollar)	1980	26.3	44.6	—	3.1	—	26.1	0.0	32.59
	1983	23.2	38.0	—	5.2	—	33.6	0.1	48.50
	1984	23.8	39.1	—	4.6	—	32.3	0.2	54.48
	1985	26.6	40.2	—	3.4	—	29.6	0.2	71.47
	1986	26.8	40.7	—	1.4	—	30.7	0.5	73.56

See notes on page 136.   *Voir notes page 136.*   Véanse notas pág. 136.

Table 8 *(cont.)*   **Tableau 8** *(suite)*   **Cuadro 8** *(cont.)*

Country and currency unit *Pays et unité monétaire* País y unidad monetaria	Financial year *Exercice financier* Ejercicio financiero	Contributions *Cotisations* Cotizaciones		Special taxes allocated to social security *Taxes et impôts spéciaux* Impuestos y derechos especiales	State participation *Participation de l'Etat* Participación del Estado	Participation of other public authorities *Participation d'autres pouvoirs publics* Participación de otras entidades públicas	Income from capital *Revenu des capitaux* Renta del capital	Other receipts *Autres recettes* Otros ingresos	Absolute total receipts (in millions of national currency units) *Total (millions d'unités monétaires nationales)* Total en millones de unidades monetarias nacionales
		From insured persons *Des assurés* De los asegurados	From employers *Des employeurs* De los empleadores						
(1)	(2)	(3)	(4)	(5)	(6)	(7)	(8)	(9)	(10)
Barbados (Dollar)	1971	43.0	—	—	48.3	—	8.7	—	19.15
	1975	12.2	14.3	—	62.9	—	10.6	—	53.64
	1980	22.7	28.8	—	31.0	—	17.5	—	66.13
	1983	35.0	36.2	—	3.3	—	21.6	3.9	135.49
	1984	37.6	39.2	—	5.3	—	17.3	0.6	138.08
	1985	37.0	38.5	—	4.9	—	19.3	0.3	148.31
	1986	37.7	39.4	—	5.6	—	16.7	0.6	147.96
Belize (Dollar)	1981	6.0	87.1	—	5.5	—	1.3	0.2	6.20
	1983	7.3	77.3	—	3.0	—	9.1	3.2	11.53
	1984	12.2	73.2	—	—	—	14.2	0.4	10.59
	1985	10.1	60.6	—	—	—	28.9	0.3	10.43
	1986	9.4	56.4	—	—	—	33.9	0.3	11.24
Bolivia (Peso)	1972	25.0	35.9	1.0	23.2	—	2.0	12.9	578.70
	1975	17.8	43.9	0.2	30.6	—	2.4	5.1	1 692.70
	1980	28.8	53.6	6.2	—	—	7.9	3.6	3 628.40
	1983	25.5	34.8	3.3	20.9	—	12.4	3.1	41 325.30
	1984	25.0	35.8	0.7	30.0	—	7.4	1.1	760 189.00
	1985	25.6	39.4	0.0	21.2	2.2	8.3	3.2	70 737 008.00
Brasil (Cruzado)	1970	—	5.7	—	2.4	—	—	—	11.88
	1975	—	5.4	—	1.4	—	—	0.2	61.46
	1980	—	—	—	—	—	—	—	820.18
	1983	15.2	74.7	—	8.0	—	0.0	2.1	6 823.40
	1984	21.2	65.0	—	10.9	—	1.0	2.0	20 166.90
	1985	17.2	72.6	—	4.3	—	4.2	1.7	71 715.00
	1986	38.5	53.5	—	3.8	—	2.8	1.4	201 807.60
Canada (Dollar)	1970	13.1	10.9	13.1	28.3	29.5	5.0	0.0	14 597.60
	1975	10.9	12.6	—	49.0	21.7	5.8	—	26 151.90
	1980	11.4	14.3	—	47.2	19.4	7.7	—	48 863.50
	1983	12.2	16.2	—	43.3	19.2	8.9	0.2	73 317.30
	1984	11.8	16.1	—	43.4	18.7	9.7	0.2	78 611.80
	1985	11.7	16.6	—	43.1	18.0	10.4	0.2	87 538.90
Colombia (Peso)	1970	14.6	39.5	0.1	42.6	—	2.9	0.2	3 996.84
	1975	16.6	33.7	0.5	39.6	—	3.3	6.3	14 703.80
	1980	16.0	49.8	—	16.2	—	6.4	11.6	52 412.90
	1983	25.2	54.1	0.2	11.6	—	8.6	0.3	71 117.00
	1984	23.9	61.8	—	1.5	—	6.8	6.1	90 746.00
	1985	22.9	59.4	—	1.5	—	8.6	7.6	115 633.00
	1986	21.5	56.5	—	1.7	—	7.2	13.1	169 872.00
Costa Rica (Colón)	1970	23.2	36.0	—	28.9	—	10.6	1.2	314.50
	1975	23.8	47.8	3.9	16.2	—	6.5	1.8	1 148.80
	1980	27.6	45.9	18.6	1.8	—	5.2	0.9	3 408.30
	1983	24.5	51.2	7.1	4.3	—	4.6	8.3	13 548.30
	1984	25.0	52.5	1.2	3.1	—	6.6	11.7	15 736.30
	1985	24.2	52.1	0.8	2.1	—	9.1	11.7	20 186.57
	1986	25.5	49.2	1.0	1.6	—	11.3	11.3	23 387.40
Cuba (Peso)	1980	—	.	—	.	—	—	—	1 149.50
	1983	—	44.3	—	55.7	—	—	—	1 491.50
	1984	—	44.6	—	55.4	—	—	—	1 617.10
	1985	—	43.0	—	57.0	—	—	—	1 738.40
	1986	—	41.8	—	58.2	—	—	—	1 887.70

See notes on page 136.   *Voir notes page 136.*   Véanse notas pág. 136.

Table 8 *(cont.)*   Tableau 8 *(suite)*   Cuadro 8 *(cont.)*

Country and currency unit / Pays et unité monétaire / País y unidad monetaria	Financial year / Exercice financier / Ejercicio financiero	Contributions / Cotisations / Cotizaciones — From insured persons / Des assurés / De los asegurados	From employers / Des employeurs / De los empleadores	Special taxes allocated to social security / Taxes et impôts spéciaux / Impuestos y derechos especiales	State participation / Participation de l'Etat / Participación del Estado	Participation of other public authorities / Participation d'autres pouvoirs publics / Participación de otras entidades públicas	Income from capital / Revenu des capitaux / Renta del capital	Other receipts / Autres recettes / Otros ingresos	Absolute total receipts (in millions of national currency units) / Total (millions d'unités monétaires nationales) / Total en millones de unidades monetarias nacionales
(1)	(2)	(3)	(4)	(5)	(6)	(7)	(8)	(9)	(10)
Chile (Peso)	1971	20.5	37.5	1.9	35.3	—	1.1	3.7	25.08
	1975	16.3	46.5	1.3	30.9	—	1.6	3.4	4 929.00
	1980	20.5	38.3	1.4	32.8	—	2.0	5.0	139 950.10
	1983	31.1	2.1	0.0	48.9	—	15.9	2.0	260 537.60
	1984	31.8	2.1	—	52.6	—	12.0	1.4	320 156.00
	1985	29.1	2.0	0.0	48.6	—	19.4	0.8	458 055.00
	1986	30.1	2.0	0.0	48.9	—	18.3	0.7	588 205.00
Dominica (EC Dollar)	1980	29.3	48.6	—	—	—	21.3	0.8	4.98
	1983	27.4	45.6	—	—	—	26.2	0.8	7.11
	1984	28.7	47.9	—	—	—	22.7	0.7	8.94
	1985	22.0	54.2	—	—	—	23.0	0.8	11.26
	1986	22.6	50.9	—	—	—	25.4	1.1	12.30
República Dominicana (Peso)	1984	20.1	75.3	—	0.2	—	2.3	2.1	58.32
	1985	20.0	76.4	—	—	—	2.5	1.1	58.39
	1986	20.1	72.9	—	—	—	1.3	5.6	77.87
Ecuador (Sucre)	1972	32.9	35.4	—	6.7	—	23.2	1.7	2 413.00
	1974	30.2	32.2	—	20.4	—	16.3	0.9	4 204.00
	1980	36.9	43.0	—	0.1	—	19.9	—	13 643.00
	1983	32.1	44.2	—	0.9	—	22.8	—	27 609.00
	1984	21.4	23.6	—	6.4	—	46.6	2.0	46 874.60
	1985	18.4	26.2	—	6.0	—	36.5	12.9	72 671.50
	1986	16.4	24.3	—	11.0	—	39.8	8.5	101 137.50
El Salvador (Colón)	1970	8.5	37.2	—	53.1	—	1.0	0.2	96.24
	1975	11.0	35.7	—	50.1	—	2.8	0.5	173.05
	1980	27.8	39.3	—	17.9	—	13.9	1.1	223.45
	1983	27.9	35.9	—	8.3	3.9	23.1	0.9	288.00
	1984	24.5	53.4	—	—	—	21.3	0.8	203.20
	1985	23.5	52.8	—	—	—	22.4	1.3	230.30
	1986	23.3	54.0	—	—	—	22.2	0.6	287.40
Grenada (EC Dollar)	1981	—	88.3	—	10.3	—	1.4	—	3.50
	1983	22.0	70.4	—	6.1	—	1.5	0.1	7.94
	1984	25.2	63.6	—	—	—	8.0	3.2	11.51
	1985	29.5	64.5	—	—	—	4.9	1.1	14.33
	1986	27.7	57.9	—	—	—	13.0	1.5	15.15
Guatemala (Quetzal)	1970	23.1	36.9	—	39.1	—	0.7	0.2	42.50
	1975	23.6	34.0	—	41.1	—	—	1.4	73.30
	1980	31.6	53.1	—	8.2	—	6.9	0.2	133.40
	1983	29.5	51.0	—	3.6	—	13.2	2.7	124.20
	1984	28.0	55.0	—	—	—	—	17.0	138.30
	1985	28.0	54.5	—	—	—	—	17.5	150.90
	1986	26.8	55.9	—	—	—	—	17.2	209.00
Guyana (Dollar)	1972	21.0	27.8	—	41.3	—	10.0	—	31.12
	1975	21.1	28.6	—	35.7	—	14.6	—	42.82
	1980	31.9	40.4	—	0.2	—	27.2	0.4	91.41
	1983	22.7	27.9	—	1.0	—	43.9	4.4	136.32
	1984	20.5	24.5	—	1.7	—	49.5	3.9	155.94
	1985	18.0	22.2	—	1.7	—	54.3	3.9	175.07
	1986	17.3	21.4	—	0.7	—	56.5	4.1	200.22
Honduras (Lempira)	1970	7.6	11.8	—	79.9	—	0.6	0.2	26.95
	1971	11.6	17.1	—	70.2	—	0.9	0.2	18.40
	1981	28.1	51.1	—	8.4	—	11.5	0.9	65.69
	1983	25.9	47.9	—	7.2	—	16.8	2.2	76.42
	1984	24.6	44.7	—	4.1	—	26.3	0.3	133.42
	1985	24.3	43.2	—	3.7	—	28.5	0.3	149.05
	1986	23.9	40.8	—	3.3	—	31.7	0.3	166.23

See notes on page 136.   *Voir notes page 136.*   Véanse notas pág. 136.

Table 8 *(cont.)*   **Tableau 8** *(suite)*   **Cuadro 8** *(cont.)*

Country and currency unit / Pays et unité monétaire / País y unidad monetaria	Financial year / Exercice financier / Ejercicio financiero	Contributions / Cotisations / Cotizaciones		Special taxes allocated to social security / Taxes et impôts spéciaux / Impuestos y derechos especiales	State participation / Participation de l'Etat / Participación del Estado	Participation of other public authorities / Participation d'autres pouvoirs publics / Participación de otras entidades públicas	Income from capital / Revenu des capitaux / Renta del capital	Other receipts / Autres recettes / Otros ingresos	Absolute total receipts (in millions of national currency units) / Total (millions d'unités monétaires nationales) / Total en millones de unidades monetarias nacionales
		From insured persons / Des assurés / De los asegurados	From employers / Des employeurs / De los empleadores						
(1)	(2)	(3)	(4)	(5)	(6)	(7)	(8)	(9)	(10)
Jamaica (Dollar)	1970	12.6	26.4	—	48.8	4.6	7.7	—	48.31
	1975	9.1	10.6	—	72.0	—	8.3	—	137.51
	1980	19.2	22.9	—	27.6	—	30.3	0.0	135.62
	1983	19.6	23.5	—	32.7	—	24.1	0.1	187.16
	1984	13.9	16.8	—	38.4	—	30.9	0.0	268.14
	1985	14.0	16.9	—	36.7	—	32.4	0.1	274.31
	1986	11.8	14.3	—	36.1	—	37.8	0.1	330.37
México (Peso)	1970	63.9	11.6	—	17.6	—	3.9	2.9	13 507.73
	1974	64.4	9.9	—	19.6	—	2.5	3.5	31 299.69
	1980	25.0	51.8	—	7.3	—	2.1	13.8	144 335.00
	1983	19.7	60.1	—	6.9	—	1.9	11.4	543 643.00
	1984	20.3	61.8	—	7.0	—	2.0	8.9	883 218.00
	1985	19.4	62.7	—	7.2	—	1.5	9.3	1 431 113.00
	1986	19.6	63.1	—	5.0	—	1.8	10.4	2 463 649.00
Panamá (Balboa)	1972	20.3	45.0	0.8	24.3	—	7.8	1.8	110.17
	1975	22.8	49.8	0.4	20.1	—	6.3	0.6	177.87
	1980	28.6	45.1	0.5	3.8	—	9.6	12.4	289.97
	1983	27.6	43.8	0.4	2.8	—	12.8	12.6	451.00
	1984	30.7	46.1	0.6	3.0	—	13.8	5.7	427.00
	1985	30.8	46.0	0.6	3.0	—	13.5	6.1	453.20
	1986	30.0	44.9	0.4	3.0	—	15.2	6.5	500.50
Perú (Inti)	1981	87.3		—	—	—	11.1	1.7	248.19
	1983	88.5		—	—	—	10.2	1.2	567.00
	1984	30.7	69.3	—	—	—	—	—	1 040.00
	1985	31.2	68.8	—	—	—	—	—	3 181.00
	1986	31.1	68.9	—	—	—	—	—	7 041.00
St. Lucia (EC Dollar)	1981	37.3	37.3	—	—	—	25.3	—	8.25
	1983	43.5	43.5	—	—	—	13.0	—	6.87
	1984	27.5	27.5	—	—	—	44.9	0.0	10.44
	1985	24.4	24.4	—	—	—	51.1	0.0	10.68
	1986	28.6	28.6	—	—	—	42.7	0.0	14.62
Trinidad and Tobago (Dollar)	1970	4.3	15.0	—	72.0	8.7	—	—	54.27
	1975	11.2	23.2	—	60.5	—	5.1	—	182.26
	1980	18.2	36.0	—	26.9	—	18.9	—	196.12
	1983	12.6	27.3	—	47.1	—	12.9	—	680.46
	1984	16.9	33.9	—	31.2	—	18.0	—	525.24
	1985	16.2	32.3	—	30.1	—	21.4	—	499.19
	1986	15.7	31.5	—	34.9	—	18.0	—	505.43
United States (Dollar)	1970	24.3	33.3	—	24.1	12.8	5.4	—	110 932
	1975	22.7	34.1	—	25.7	12.2	5.4	—	219 900
	1980	23.4	40.4	—	21.4	8.4	6.4	—	370 597
	1983	22.6	34.3	—	28.6	6.3	8.2	0.1	514 462
	1984	24.4	34.2	0.5	25.9	6.0	9.0	0.0	539 628
	1985	24.7	34.4	0.6	24.4	6.0	9.9	0.1	592 112
	1986	24.5	33.7	0.6	23.7	5.9	11.7	−0.1	644 464
Uruguay (Nuevo peso)	1975	68.0		5.6	25.2	—	0.4	0.7	925.69
	1980	25.1	34.0	8.1	30.2	—	1.5	1.1	9 779.50
	1983	24.7	24.6	1.5	46.4	—	1.2	1.7	23 129.00
	1984	27.8	29.9	1.0	36.4	—	1.0	3.8	27 416.00
	1985	30.3	35.0	1.0	28.7	—	0.9	4.0	47 961.00
	1986	33.3	37.2	0.9	23.1	—	0.7	4.7	92 849.00

See notes on page 136.   *Voir notes page 136.*   Véanse notas pág. 136.

Table 8 *(cont.)*   **Tableau 8** *(suite)*   **Cuadro 8** *(cont.)*

Country and currency unit *Pays et unité monétaire* País y unidad monetaria	Financial year *Exercice financier* Ejercicio financiero	Contributions *Cotisations* Cotizaciones		Special taxes allocated to social security *Taxes et impôts spéciaux* Impuestos y derechos especiales	State participation *Participation de l'Etat* Participación del Estado	Participation of other public authorities *Participation d'autres pouvoirs publics* Participación de otras entidades públicas	Income from capital *Revenu des capitaux* Renta del capital	Other receipts *Autres recettes* Otros ingresos	Absolute total receipts (in millions of national currency units) *Total (millions d'unités monétaires nationales)* Total en millones de unidades monetarias nacionales
		From insured persons *Des assurés* De los asegurados	From employers *Des employeurs* De los empleadores						
(1)	(2)	(3)	(4)	(5)	(6)	(7)	(8)	(9)	(10)
Venezuela (Bolívar)	1970	13.6	26.3	—	57.3	—	2.8	0.1	1 755.70
	1975	9.5	19.1	—	66.5	—	4.9	0.0	5 323.70
	1980	26.8	53.5	—	6.8	—	12.7	0.2	4 259.30
	1983	22.7	45.3	—	13.7	—	18.3	—	5 104.90
	1984	22.4	44.9	—	13.4	—	19.3	—	5 360.70
	1985	21.4	42.8	—	13.4	—	22.3	—	5 803.20
	1986	21.3	40.7	—	12.7	—	25.3	—	7 457.60
ASIA – ASIE – ASIA									
Bahrain (Dinar)	1978	11.5	40.2	—	18.7	—	10.3	19.3	19.10
	1980	12.6	43.5	—	21.1	—	21.9	1.0	24.60
	1983	24.9	49.9	—	—	—	25.0	0.2	47.08
	1984	25.2	50.4	—	—	—	24.3	0.0	31.21
	1985	22.5	45.0	—	—	—	31.2	1.4	37.39
	1986	21.1	42.2	—	—	—	36.7	0.0	35.77
Bangladesh (Taka)	1975	2.4	2.7	—	93.0	—	1.8	0.1	293.48
	1980	—	100.0	—	—	—	—	—	3.14
	1983	19.4	43.4	4.3	—	—	32.9	—	28.98
	1984	49.2	29.1	1.1	0.2	—	20.3	—	128.51
	1985	32.9	32.7	1.6	0.2	—	32.7	—	125.39
	1986	37.6	41.9	1.2	0.2	—	19.1	—	153.66
Cyprus (Pound)	1970	23.3	26.7	—	43.3	—	4.7	2.0	8.38
	1975	18.7	24.9	—	52.1	—	2.6	1.6	16.50
	1980	30.0	36.3	—	29.2	—	3.6	0.9	33.99
	1983	28.7	42.5	—	20.5	—	7.8	0.6	94.76
	1984	31.2	40.5	—	18.2	—	9.3	0.7	110.02
	1985	28.8	43.0	—	16.8	—	10.5	0.9	133.98
	1986	29.3	39.9	—	17.2	—	12.8	0.7	141.59
India (Rupee)	1970	48.8	15.3	0.3	2.8	25.1	7.7	0.0	12 398.00
	1975	66.1	—	0.5	2.8	19.4	10.9	0.2	30 870.40
	1980	13.8	70.0	0.4	1.7	0.4	13.0	0.6	36 643.20
	1983	8.9	68.9	0.1	3.5	6.5	11.6	0.5	82 593.44
	1984	9.1	68.4	0.1	3.5	6.4	11.9	0.5	83 685.22
	1985	9.8	66.9	0.1	3.4	6.1	13.2	0.5	87 807.66
	1986	.	.	.	.	.	.	.	.
Indonesia (Rupiah)	1981	21.1	60.9	—	—	—	—	18.0	33 054.00
	1983	16.5	48.4	—	—	—	—	35.1	56 324.00
	1984	19.0	60.3	—	—	—	20.4	0.3	62 446.47
	1985	18.2	59.9	—	—	—	21.0	0.9	84 946.74
	1986	17.3	58.1	—	—	—	23.7	0.9	97 894.94
Iran, Islamic Rep. of (Rial)	1981	17.3	49.4	—	14.8	—	5.1	13.4	225 692.00
	1983	17.4	49.8	—	25.8	—	6.2	0.7	301 532.00
	1984	79.0	0.0	—	8.8	—	12.1	0.0	291 847.00
	1985	85.2	0.0	—	9.7	—	5.1	0.0	304 608.00
	1986	83.2	0.0	—	8.2	—	8.5	0.1	346 460.00
Israel (New Shekel)	1970	22.0	38.3	—	27.3	7.7	4.3	0.5	2.09
	1975	12.7	31.3	—	45.0	1.5	6.5	3.0	10.48
	1980	19.4	42.0	—	24.4	2.2	10.5	1.5	17.82
	1983	18.5	36.2	—	32.4	1.3	10.2	1.4	270.40
	1984	18.7	36.9	—	31.0	1.5	11.3	0.7	1 412.90
	1985	21.0	35.5	—	32.0	1.3	9.7	0.5	4 547.10
	1986	23.9	37.3	—	29.4	1.3	7.7	0.4	6 723.00

See notes on page 136.   *Voir notes page 136.*   Véanse notas pág. 136.

Table 8 *(cont.)*   **Tableau 8** *(suite)*   **Cuadro 8** *(cont.)*

Country and currency unit *Pays et unité monétaire* País y unidad monetaria	Financial year *Exercice financier* Ejercicio financiero	Contributions *Cotisations* Cotizaciones From insured persons *Des assurés* De los asegurados	From employers *Des employeurs* De los empleadores	Special taxes allocated to social security *Taxes et impôts spéciaux* Impuestos y derechos especiales	State participation *Participation de l'Etat* Participación del Estado	Participation of other public authorities *Participation d'autres pouvoirs publics* Participación de otras entidades públicas	Income from capital *Revenu des capitaux* Renta del capital	Other receipts *Autres recettes* Otros ingresos	Absolute total receipts (in millions of national currency units) *Total (millions d'unités monétaires nationales)* Total en millones de unidades monetarias nacionales
(1)	(2)	(3)	(4)	(5)	(6)	(7)	(8)	(9)	(10)
Japan (Yen)	1970	27.0	29.5	—	25.0	3.5	8.2	6.7	5 765 517
	1975	25.3	29.1	—	27.8	4.0	8.2	5.5	17 450 443
	1980	26.0	28.4	—	27.3	3.2	9.5	5.5	34 200 482
	1983	26.4	29.1	—	25.0	3.0	11.6	4.9	42 749 123
	1984	27.1	30.1	—	25.2	3.2	12.6	1.9	43 880 330
	1985	27.5	30.3	—	23.5	3.8	12.9	2.2	47 931 468
	1986	27.2	30.6	—	22.7	4.1	13.6	1.8	50 525 725
Jordan (Dinar)	1980	32.9	65.0	—	—	—	2.1	—	4.86
	1983	30.8	59.0	—	—	—	9.6	0.7	30.27
	1984	30.6	58.7	—	—	—	9.9	0.7	40.47
	1985	29.7	57.2	—	—	—	13.3	0.8	44.14
	1986	28.7	55.3	—	—	—	15.2	0.8	53.58
Kuwait (Dinar)	1980	11.2	22.4	—	43.8	—	20.5	2.0	90.10
	1983	9.0	17.7	—	39.9	—	20.6	12.8	213.04
	1984	10.2	20.2	—	39.6	—	17.4	12.5	197.63
	1985	6.5	12.8	—	61.8	—	12.9	6.1	323.37
	1986	6.3	12.4	—	54.6	—	21.1	5.6	385.77
Malaysia (Ringgit)	1970	19.0	30.2	—	28.1	—	22.5	0.2	563.90
	1975	34.4	14.9	—	26.8	—	22.9	0.9	1 185.12
	1980	63.6		—	0.3	—	34.4	1.7	2 130.25
	1983	24.3	45.3	—	0.6	—	29.2	0.5	4 376.64
	1984	22.9	42.7	—	3.0	—	31.1	0.3	5 031.69
	1985	22.0	41.7	—	2.8	—	32.9	0.7	5 709.81
	1986	21.6	40.5	—	2.5	—	34.7	0.7	6 303.98
Myanmar (Kyat)	1970	1.4	44.7	—	53.9	—	—	0.0	216.04
	1975	1.3	40.1	—	58.6	—	—	0.0	322.81
	1980	20.1	60.4	—	17.8	—	1.3	0.3	30.39
	1983	20.3	60.8	17.2	—	—	1.3	0.5	39.00
	1984	20.2	60.1	18.0	—	—	1.2	0.5	40.60
	1985	19.8	59.3	19.1	—	—	1.4	0.5	42.50
	1986	19.9	59.6	18.5	—	—	1.6	0.5	44.30
Pakistan (Rupee)	1965	—	50.7	—	49.3	—	—	—	314.80
	1980	—	74.7	—	8.2	—	16.3	0.8	254.99
	1983	—	10.7	33.1	52.1	—	4.0	0.1	2 587.18
	1984	1.0	10.9	—	83.8	—	4.1	0.1	3 406.60
	1985	0.7	7.0	—	88.8	—	3.4	0.0	6 129.20
	1986	1.0	10.1	—	83.6	—	5.3	0.1	5 134.80
Philippines (Peso)	1970	21.7	30.3	—	31.3	—	16.5	0.2	740.37
	1978	30.5	43.6	—	—	—	23.4	2.5	3 159.20
	1980	30.3	42.2	—	—	—	25.6	1.9	4 487.50
	1983	26.0	36.1	—	—	—	35.8	2.0	6 762.80
	1984	22.1	31.4	—	—	—	44.9	1.6	7 914.20
	1985	17.7	25.3	—	—	—	56.2	0.8	10 637.80
	1986	18.6	26.6	—	—	—	53.1	1.8	10 705.00
Qatar (Riyal)	1984	—	—	100.0	—	—	—	—	76.22
	1985	—	—	100.0	—	—	—	—	79.54
	1986	—	—	100.0	—	—	—	—	80.02
Singapore (Dollar)	1970	19.5	38.2	—	29.0	—	13.1	0.2	314.23
	1975	33.7	40.9	—	11.6	—	13.6	0.2	1 239.60
	1980	37.2	44.3	—	0.1	—	17.9	0.4	2 903.63
	1983	39.1	41.2	—	0.1	—	19.2	0.5	5 744.30
	1984	39.1	41.2	—	0.0	—	19.2	0.4	6 891.03
	1985	38.4	40.8	—	0.0	—	20.4	0.3	7 797.58
	1986	51.0	23.2	—	0.1	—	25.3	0.4	6 690.97

See notes on page 136.   *Voir notes page 136.*   Véanse notas pág. 136.

Table 8 *(cont.)* Tableau 8 *(suite)* Cuadro 8 *(cont.)*

Country and currency unit *Pays et unité monétaire* País y unidad monetaria	Financial year *Exercice financier* Ejercicio financiero	Contributions *Cotisations* Cotizaciones From insured persons *Des assurés* De los asegurados	From employers *Des employeurs* De los empleadores	Special taxes allocated to social security *Taxes et impôts spéciaux* Impuestos y derechos especiales	State participation *Participation de l'Etat* Participación del Estado	Participation of other public authorities *Participation d'autres pouvoirs publics* Participación de otras entidades públicas	Income from capital *Revenu des capitaux* Renta del capital	Other receipts *Autres recettes* Otros ingresos	Absolute total receipts (in millions of national currency units) *Total (millions d'unités monétaires nationales)* Total en millones de unidades monetarias nacionales
(1)	(2)	(3)	(4)	(5)	(6)	(7)	(8)	(9)	(10)
Sri Lanka (Rupee)	1970	15.1	31.2	—	44.8	—	7.5	1.4	571.60
	1975	13.8	27.6	—	42.3	—	14.4	1.8	874.80
	1980	1.7	37.1	—	43.6	—	17.6	0.0	2 092.80
	1983	19.1	20.4	—	37.8	—	22.4	0.3	4 800.00
	1984	22.5	25.1	—	32.1	0.7	19.5	0.0	7 486.79
	1985	21.8	24.6	—	32.8	0.4	20.4	0.1	9 390.65
	1986	20.9	24.2	—	31.7	0.5	22.6	0.1	10 432.84
Rép. arabe syrienne (Livre syrienne)	1984	31.1	58.0	—	—	—	8.8	2.1	1 481.00
	1985	30.8	58.5	—	—	—	8.3	2.4	1 571.00
	1986	29.1	60.3	—	—	—	7.6	3.0	1 709.00
Thailand (Baht)	1980	—	60.0	—	2.2	—	18.0	19.8	253.71
	1983	—	93.1	—	0.7	—	6.2	—	1 832.49
	1984	—	100.0	—	—	—	—	—	248.99
	1985	—	100.0	—	—	—	—	—	268.30
	1986	—	100.0	—	—	—	—	—	284.76

EUROPE – *EUROPE* – EUROPA

Countries with a market economy – Pays à économie de marché – Países con economía de mercado

Country and currency unit	Financial year	From insured persons	From employers	Special taxes	State participation	Participation of other public authorities	Income from capital	Other receipts	Absolute total receipts
Austria (Schilling)	1970	25.5	50.4	—	21.9	0.2	0.6	1.4	70 784.00
	1975	26.2	49.2	—	22.1	—	0.7	2.0	134 749.00
	1980	27.2	48.5	4.1	16.6	0.3	0.7	2.7	224 889.00
	1983	28.7	46.8	3.2	18.1	0.4	0.5	2.3	301 917.00
	1984	28.6	46.4	4.0	17.7	0.4	0.4	2.5	329 020.00
	1985	29.3	47.0	3.8	17.0	0.4	0.5	2.0	348 496.00
	1986	29.5	46.8	3.7	17.1	0.4	0.4	2.1	368 562.00
Belgique (Franc belge)	1970	20.8	46.6	—	24.8	1.5	3.3	3.0	241 507.30
	1975	19.3	42.9	—	31.0	1.2	2.5	3.1	564 810.10
	1980	18.4	43.2	0.7	33.0	1.5	2.3	0.9	885 804.00
	1983	19.6	38.1	0.5	36.0	1.5	1.8	2.5[1]	1 179 773.00
	1984	20.6	38.9	1.0	33.8	1.5	2.1	2.1[1]	1 231 861.00
	1985	24.1	39.2	0.6	30.3	1.5	2.0	2.3[1]	1 282 549.00
	1986	24.4	39.7	0.5	29.6	1.5	2.1	2.2[1]	1 342 070.00
Denmark (Krone)	1970	14.1	8.9	—	57.1	18.7	1.2	—	18 066.50
	1975	1.1	5.6	—	68.8	23.1	1.4	0.0	44 719.70
	1980	1.8	5.9	—	57.5	32.7	2.1	—	103 269.10
	1983	3.3	8.1	—	53.3	32.6	2.8	—	149 307.60
	1984	3.4	6.3	—	54.5	33.1	2.8	—	153 700.90
	1985	3.1	7.8	—	52.7	33.4	3.0	—	164 954.50
	1986	3.5	8.0	—	53.5	32.2	2.8	—	178 991.90
España (Peseta)	1975	14.2	72.6	0.6	8.3	2.3	1.3	0.6	731 810.20
	1980	12.4	70.7	0.3	14.6	0.8	0.6	0.4	2 400 940.90
	1983	16.2	59.4	0.3	21.0	1.8	0.8	0.6	3 997 066.00
	1984	16.6	54.4	0.4	24.5	1.8	0.7	1.6	4 633 345.00
	1985	16.2	55.0	0.4	23.6	1.9	0.9	2.0	5 184 538.00
	1986	16.4	54.1	—	25.4	1.7	0.8	1.6	5 893 481.00
Finland (Markka)	1970	11.1	38.6	—	27.2	17.5	5.6	0.0	6 255.40
	1975	11.0	47.9	—	21.8	15.0	4.2	0.0	18 735.90
	1980	7.9	44.9	—	26.3	15.1	5.8	0.0	40 435.20
	1983	7.1	39.7	—	30.6	15.9	6.7	0.0	61 853.10
	1984	8.3	39.8	—	27.9	16.7	7.4	—	70 499.50
	1985	8.7	40.2	—	26.9	17.0	7.2	—	81 864.50
	1986	8.3	39.7	—	27.1	17.6	7.3	—	90 413.30

See notes on page 136. *Voir notes page 136.* Véanse notas pág. 136.

Table 8 *(cont.)*   **Tableau 8** *(suite)*   **Cuadro 8** *(cont.)*

| Country and currency unit / Pays et unité monétaire / País y unidad monetaria | Financial year / Exercice financier / Ejercicio financiero | Contributions / Cotisations / Cotizaciones | | Special taxes allocated to social security / Taxes et impôts spéciaux / Impuestos y derechos especiales | State participation / Participation de l'Etat / Participación del Estado | Participation of other public authorities / Participation d'autres pouvoirs publics / Participación de otras entidades públicas | Income from capital / Revenu des capitaux / Renta del capital | Other receipts / Autres recettes / Otros ingresos | Absolute total receipts (in millions of national currency units) / Total (millions d'unités monétaires nationales) / Total en millones de unidades monetarias nacionales |
		From insured persons / Des assurés / De los asegurados	From employers / Des employeurs / De los empleadores						
(1)	(2)	(3)	(4)	(5)	(6)	(7)	(8)	(9)	(10)
France	1970	18.9	68.4	2.6	7.7	—	0.5	1.9	119 871.00
(Franc français)	1975	17.3	56.1	2.2	21.3	1.5	1.0	0.8	355 257.60
	1980	21.0	53.4	1.9	20.9	1.3	1.0	0.6	761 712.20
	1983	21.5	50.4	2.7	21.4	1.3	1.4	1.3	1 188 535.90
	1984	22.3	49.8	3.2	20.5	1.4	1.5	1.4	1 295 535.10
	1985	23.0	50.3	2.4	20.0	1.3	1.6	1.3	1 370 132.60
	1986	23.4	50.6	2.1	19.6	1.3	1.7	1.3	1 431 025.00
Germany, Fed. Rep. of	1970	28.9	42.3	0.8	25.1	—	1.9	0.9	120 467.00
(Deutsche Mark)	1975	28.2	39.6	0.4	28.1	—	1.8	1.8	240 953.00
	1980	34.0	34.2	—	28.9	—	0.8	2.0	357 712.00
	1983	35.7	34.2	—	27.4	—	0.7	2.0	405 788.00
	1984	36.0	34.5	—	26.7	—	0.6	2.1	421 179.00
	1985	36.3	34.7	—	26.4	—	0.6	2.1	438 617.00
	1986	36.6	35.0	—	25.8	—	0.5	2.1	459 340.00
Grèce	1970	27.5	41.4	11.4	14.2	—	4.3	1.2	35 767.00
(Drachme)	1975	25.9	44.9	10.2	14.2	—	3.6	1.2	81 488.00
	1980	29.7	47.3	8.2	8.9	—	4.9	1.1	242 714.00
	1983	28.4	42.1	10.6	12.6	—	5.2	1.3	569 617.00
	1984	28.9	42.4	8.4	13.4	—	5.2	1.7	712 802.00
	1985	29.4	42.6	8.9	12.5	—	5.1	1.6	872 503.00
Iceland	1984	—	11.5	—	79.7	7.6	1.2	—	6 180.00
(Króna)	1985	—	10.2	—	81.1	7.3	1.4	—	8 814.00
	1986	—	10.9	—	80.4	7.9	0.8	—	11 716.00
Ireland	1970	10.6	22.8	—	52.1	13.6	0.6	0.3	169.20
(Pound)	1975	11.9	22.8	—	60.5	1.5	0.4	3.0	717.20
	1980	11.6	26.3	—	60.5	0.5	0.2	0.8	1 896.70
	1983	13.1	24.6	—	60.6	0.4	0.2	1.1	3 369.23
	1984	13.4	24.7	—	60.5	0.4	0.1	0.8	3 654.12
	1985	13.1	24.7	—	60.8	0.4	0.1	0.8	4 012.64
	1986	13.0	24.4	—	61.7	0.0	0.1	0.8	4 299.60
Italie	1970	14.2	61.5	0.2	19.4	—	2.4	2.3	9 756.39
(Lire (milliards))	1975	12.3	66.7	—	11.1	6.0	2.3	1.6	22 871.00
	1980	15.3	53.5	—	26.9	1.6	1.5	1.3	72 609.00
	1983	15.4	48.3	—	32.7	1.3	1.2	1.0	142 081.00
	1984	19.1	52.1	—	17.8	—	0.3	10.8	73 419.00
	1985	19.1	52.3	—	18.3	—	0.3	9.9	81 986.00
	1986	19.5	51.7	—	17.6	—	0.3	10.9	90 646.00
Luxembourg	1970	26.1	38.0	—	25.4	1.2	8.6	0.6	9 124.30
(Franc luxembourgeois)	1975	25.1	39.0	—	24.6	1.0	6.6	3.8	19 954.00
	1980	23.8	37.2	—	24.4	0.8	7.3	6.4	35 758.50
	1983	25.9	34.2	—	26.7	0.9	7.6	4.7	47 961.20
	1984	26.8	35.5	—	29.2	—	7.9	0.6	50 876.20
	1985	26.7	35.3	—	31.2	—	4.7	2.1	54 384.30
	1986	24.8	34.2	—	34.5	—	4.7	1.9	59 427.90
Malta	1970	7.3	24.7	—	65.8	—	1.3	0.9	6.68
(Lira)	1975	15.8	26.7	—	56.7	—	—	0.8	18.93
	1980	28.1	33.9	—	38.1	—	—	—	52.61
	1983	27.6	33.2	—	39.2	—	—	—	70.10
	1984	27.4	33.0	—	39.6	—	—	—	68.09
	1985	27.5	33.1	—	39.4	—	—	—	70.35
	1986	26.8	33.6	—	39.7	—	—	—	71.58

See notes on page 136.   *Voir notes page 136.*   Véanse notas pág. 136.

Table 8 *(cont.)*   **Tableau 8** *(suite)*   **Cuadro 8** *(cont.)*

Country and currency unit	Financial year	Contributions *Cotisations* Cotizaciones		Special taxes allocated to social security *Taxes et impôts spéciaux*	State participation *Participation de l'Etat*	Participation of other public authorities *Participation d'autres pouvoirs publics*	Income from capital *Revenu des capitaux*	Other receipts *Autres recettes*	Absolute total receipts (in millions of national currency units)
Pays et unité monétaire País y unidad monetaria	*Exercice financier* Ejercicio financiero	From insured persons *Des assurés* De los asegurados	From employers *Des employeurs* De los empleadores	Impuestos y derechos especiales	Participación del Estado	Participación de otras entidades públicas	Renta del capital	Otros ingresos	*Total (millions d'unités monétaires nationales)* Total en millones de unidades monetarias nacionales
(1)	(2)	(3)	(4)	(5)	(6)	(7)	(8)	(9)	(10)
Netherlands (Guilder)	1970	38.5	42.9	—	8.6	3.7	6.2	0.1	27 274.90
	1975	36.5	39.1	—	15.7	1.2	7.0	0.5	66 282.00
	1980	33.2	33.3	—	23.3	1.3	8.9	—	113 807.60
	1983	39.9	31.7	—	17.9	0.0	10.5	—	139 959.00
	1984	39.1	31.0	—	18.4	0.0	11.5	—	141 726.00
	1985	39.5	31.8	—	16.3	0.0	12.3	—	143 021.00
	1986	38.0	33.4	—	15.5	0.0	13.0	—	140 734.00
Norway (Krone)	1970	22.9	33.2	0.3	25.3	16.2	2.0	0.2	13 046.10
	1975	22.8	39.9	0.3	18.4	17.2	1.3	0.0	30 141.70
	1980	21.0	34.6	0.2	26.3	16.3	1.4	0.0	59 512.60
	1983	20.9	32.1	0.2	28.8	16.2	1.9	0.1	91 154.60
	1984	15.0	23.5	0.2	35.3	24.2	1.5	0.4	133 318.80
	1985	15.8	23.7	0.1	34.4	23.9	1.7	0.4	145 502.10
	1986	17.5	24.6	0.1	22.1	33.5	1.8	0.4	157 853.70
Portugal (Escudo)	1970	21.5	57.7	—	4.4	—	7.8	8.6	13 492.50
	1975	21.8	67.7	—	7.4	—	2.7	0.5	45 792.60
	1980	26.2	64.2	—	5.7	3.6	0.0	0.3	126 998.70
	1983	27.9	61.6	—	7.6	2.5	0.0	0.3	228 867.60
	1984	25.4	56.5	—	10.9	3.5	1.8	1.8	297 639.60
	1985	25.3	58.2	—	8.8	3.8	1.7	2.3	366 855.30
	1986	24.6	66.0	—	7.0	—	0.1	2.3	494 527.00
Suisse (Franc suisse)	1970	34.1	20.8	—	12.3	21.4	8.2	3.2	10 517.30
	1975	36.0	21.6	—	11.4	22.4	6.1	2.4	22 208.70
	1980	41.2	25.5	—	13.9	11.6	6.0	1.8	25 571.10
	1983	44.4	23.3	—	14.2	12.3	4.7	1.1	30 351.20
	1984	44.8	23.1	—	14.4	12.2	4.3	1.2	33 066.80
	1985	45.4	22.9	—	13.8	12.4	4.3	1.2	35 210.40
	1986	45.1	23.2	—	13.5	12.8	4.3	1.2	37 602.70
Sweden (Krona)	1970	11.4	27.7	—	27.7	26.9	6.3	0.1	39 947.10
	1975	0.8	35.6	—	29.1	27.2	7.3	—	84 702.40
	1980	1.0	45.9	—	21.5	23.8	7.8	—	183 851.70
	1983	1.0	43.8	—	19.6	26.4	9.3	—	252 244.10
	1984	1.0	38.4	—	23.3	27.5	9.7	—	264 256.70
	1985	1.3	36.4	—	24.8	27.4	10.1	—	285 250.10
	1986	1.7	38.5	—	22.7	26.6	10.5	—	318 641.90
Turquie (Livre turque)	1970	28.4	54.3	—	2.3	—	11.1	3.9	6 561.60
	1975	32.4	50.4	—	4.5	0.0	7.7	5.0	31 844.90
	1980	27.9	49.9	—	7.1	4.2	6.3	4.5	218 265.00
	1983	32.1	41.6	—	3.7	3.9	14.3	4.4	556 419.00
	1984	27.9	32.7	—	17.8	1.7	16.2	3.8	892 389.00
	1985	28.3	31.5	—	19.3	2.8	11.9	6.2	1 288 448.00
	1986	28.2	32.5	—	13.2	2.8	16.4	7.0	1 753 294.00
United Kingdom (Pound)	1970	19.9	24.9	—	45.2	7.8	2.0	0.2	7 294.00
	1975	17.4	28.7	—	44.7	7.1	1.9	0.2	19 167.00
	1980	15.6	26.2	—	49.1	5.9	2.7	0.4	43 709.00
	1983	18.0	23.9	—	50.5	5.0	2.1	0.5	63 254.00
	1984	18.2	23.5	—	50.8	4.9	2.2	0.4	67 854.00
	1985	18.3	23.5	—	50.2	5.3	2.3	0.4	73 117.00
	1986	18.3	23.4	—	50.2	4.8	2.8	0.4	78 737.00

See notes on page 136.   *Voir notes page 136.*   Véanse notas pág. 136.

Table 8 *(cont.)*   **Tableau 8** *(suite)*   **Cuadro 8** *(cont.)*

Country and currency unit / Pays et unité monétaire / País y unidad monetaria	Financial year / Exercice financier / Ejercicio financiero	Contributions / Cotisations / Cotizaciones		Special taxes allocated to social security / Taxes et impôts spéciaux / Impuestos y derechos especiales	State participation / Participation de l'Etat / Participación del Estado	Participation of other public authorities / Participation d'autres pouvoirs publics / Participación de otras entidades públicas	Income from capital / Revenu des capitaux / Renta del capital	Other receipts / Autres recettes / Otros ingresos	Absolute total receipts (in millions of national currency units) / Total (millions d'unités monétaires nationales) / Total en millones de unidades monetarias nacionales
		From insured persons / Des assurés / De los asegurados	From employers / Des employeurs / De los empleadores						
(1)	(2)	(3)	(4)	(5)	(6)	(7)	(8)	(9)	(10)

EUROPE – EUROPE – EUROPA

Countries with a centrally planned economy – Pays à économie planifiée – Países con economía centralmente planificada

RSS de Biélorussie (Rouble)	1970	—	—	—	95.9	—	—	4.1	1 106.00
	1975	—	—	—	28.7	—	—	0.4	1 636.00
	1980	—	—	—	95.2	—	—	4.8	2 243.00
	1983	—	—	—	96.1	—	—	3.9	2 689.00
	1984	—	—	—	93.6	—	—	6.4	2 823.00
	1985	—	—	—	93.0	—	—	7.0	2 942.00
	1986	—	—	—	93.2	—	—	6.8	3 199.00
Bulgarie (Lev)	1970	1.0	42.2	3.4	47.5	2.9	—	3.0	1 468.20
	1975	0.6	54.9	2.7	27.2	0.3	—	14.3	2 341.60
	1980	—	—	—	—	—	—	—	2 506.30[2]
	1983[3]	.	17.1	—	0.5	—	—	—	2 953.70
	1984[3]	.	14.8	—	0.4	—	—	—	3 331.90
	1985[3]	.	16.9	—	0.5	—	—	—	3 331.90
	1986[3]	—	17.8	—	0.4	—	—	—	3 707.40
Czechoslovakia (Koruna)	1970	0.1	2.8	—	96.7	—	—	0.5	56 000.00
	1975	0.0	2.9	—	95.5	—	—	1.6	69 470.00
	1980	0.0	3.7	—	94.6	—	—	1.7	91 367.00
	1983	0.0	3.7	—	94.6	—	—	1.7	105 190.00
	1984	0.0	3.9	—	94.4	—	—	1.7	108 441.00
	1985	0.0	3.9	—	94.4	—	—	1.7	114 431.00
	1986	0.0	3.7	—	94.5	—	—	1.7	120 692.00
German Democratic Rep. (Mark)	1970	29.3	31.9	—	38.5	—	—	0.2	14 394.60
	1975	25.0	27.6	—	47.2	—	—	0.2	21 827.80
	1980	21.9	28.3	—	49.7	—	—	0.1	29 627.00
	1983	23.1	29.5	—	47.3	—	—	0.1	30 829.50
	1984	23.4	29.9	—	46.6	—	—	0.1	31 196.90
	1985	22.7	29.1	—	48.1	—	—	0.1	32 724.20
	1986	22.3	28.3	—	49.3	—	—	0.1	34 314.30
Hongrie (Forint)	1970	18.1	53.5	—	27.8	—	0.1	0.5	30 095.00
	1975	16.1	40.5	—	42.9	—	0.1	0.5	58 795.00
	1980	14.6	41.1	—	43.6	—	0.0	0.6	106 644.00
	1983	14.9	47.1	—	38.0	—	—	—	138 375.00
	1984	19.6	80.4	—	—	—	—	—	120 801.00
	1985	20.2	79.8	—	—	—	—	—	135 300.00
	1986	21.2	78.8	—	—	—	—	—	149 400.00
Pologne (Zloty)	1984	2.3	63.1	4.9	28.7	—	0.2	0.8	1 471 947.00
	1985	2.2	63.2	5.0	28.5	—	0.3	0.8	1 790 905.00
	1986	2.6	60.7	4.9	30.4	—	0.5	0.9	2 242 443.00
RSS d'Ukraine (Rouble)	1970	—	—	—	93.8	—	—	6.2	6 503.00
	1975	—	—	—	27.7	—	—	1.5	9 050.00
	1980	—	—	—	94.4	—	—	5.6	12 030.00
	1983	—	—	—	95.6	—	—	4.4	14 180.00
	1984	—	—	—	94.0	—	—	6.0	14 898.00
	1985	—	—	—	94.2	—	—	5.8	15 658.00
	1986	—	—	—	94.7	—	—	5.3	16 835.00
URSS (Rouble)	1970	—	—	—	96.5	—	—	3.5	34 604.00
	1975	—	—	—	29.0	—	—	0.7	49 238.00
	1980	—	—	—	96.7	—	—	3.3	64 616.00
	1983	—	—	—	97.2	—	—	2.8	75 789.00
	1984	—	—	—	96.0	—	—	4.0	79 969.00
	1985	—	—	—	96.1	—	—	3.9	83 573.00
	1986	—	—	—	96.4	—	—	3.6	89 307.00

See notes on page 136.   *Voir notes page 136.*   Véanse notas pág. 136.

Table 8 *(concl.)*   **Tableau 8** *(fin)*   **Cuadro 8** *(fin)*

Country and currency unit / Pays et unité monétaire / País y unidad monetaria	Financial year / Exercice financier / Ejercicio financiero	Contributions / Cotisations / Cotizaciones		Special taxes allocated to social security / Taxes et impôts spéciaux / Impuestos y derechos especiales	State participation / Participation de l'Etat / Participación del Estado	Participation of other public authorities / Participation d'autres pouvoirs publics / Participación de otras entidades públicas	Income from capital / Revenu des capitaux / Renta del capital	Other receipts / Autres recettes / Otros ingresos	Absolute total receipts (in millions of national currency units) / Total (millions d'unités monétaires nationales) / Total en millones de unidades monetarias nacionales
		From insured persons / Des assurés / De los asegurados	From employers / Des employeurs / De los empleadores						
(1)	(2)	(3)	(4)	(5)	(6)	(7)	(8)	(9)	(10)
Yugoslavia (Dinar)	1970	72.6	13.0	—	13.7	0.3	—	0.5	22 770.00
	1981	66.3[4]	23.4	0.8	7.3	0.3	1.0	0.9	271 422.30
	1983	66.7[4]	24.5	0.8	6.3	0.1	0.9	0.6	462 590.00
	1984	64.9	26.4	—	7.0	0.3	—	1.5	659 413.00
	1985	65.1	28.8	—	4.5	0.2	—	1.4	1 205 410.00
	1986	63.3	32.2	—	2.7	0.6	—	1.1	2 777 651.00

OCEANIA – OCÉANIE – OCEANIA

		(3)	(4)	(5)	(6)	(7)	(8)	(9)	(10)
Australia (Dollar)	1970	11.8	11.1	—	59.0	14.1	3.7	0.4	2 876.40
	1975	11.5	12.3	—	56.2	16.8	2.8	0.3	8 028.00
	1980	13.0	12.3	—	70.0	0.5	4.0	0.3	17 235.30
	1983	13.6	13.4	—	69.5	—	3.0	0.5	25 538.40
	1984	1.9	8.3	2.1	86.7	—	1.0	—	19 613.30
	1985	1.7	14.0	4.6	78.6	—	1.0	—	23 033.40
	1986	1.8	12.5	5.0	79.8	—	0.9	—	24 310.50
Fiji (Dollar)	1975	23.3	23.9	—	37.3	—	9.6	5.8	29.16
	1980	28.7	30.8	—	9.5	—	21.3	9.8	57.82
	1983	28.8	29.1	—	9.9	—	32.0	0.3	85.35
	1984	30.5	30.5	—	—	—	38.1	1.0	89.78
	1985	30.8	30.8	—	—	—	37.7	0.8	111.02
	1986	26.5	26.5	—	—	—	46.3	0.8	111.57
New Zealand (Dollar)	1970	4.7	4.7	—	88.2	—	2.5	—	651.40
	1975	4.6	6.3	—	87.1	—	2.1	—	1 822.10
	1980	2.6	4.0	—	91.8	—	1.2	0.4	4 168.70
	1983	2.0	4.5	—	90.9	—	2.3	0.3	6 283.20
	1984[5]	1.8	3.5	—	91.9	—	2.5	0.4	6 761.20
	1985[5]	1.7	3.2	—	92.4	—	2.4	0.4	8 160.10
	1986[5]	1.6	3.1	—	92.5	—	2.5	0.3	9 645.50
Solomon Islands (Dollar)	1981	39.5	39.5	—	—	—	16.6	4.5	3.80
	1983	30.3	45.5	—	—	—	21.0	3.2	7.52
	1984	29.8	44.6	—	—	—	25.6	—	9.13
	1985	28.7	43.2	—	—	—	28.1	—	10.89
	1986	27.9	41.8	—	—	—	30.3	—	13.66

For general footnotes, see table 1. [1] Including Financial Balancing Fund. [2] Receipts figures are not available; they are assumed to be the same as the expenditure figures. Breakdown is not available. [3] Data are not strictly comparable with those prior to 1983. [4] Including, in respect of "children's allowances", estimated contributions, which are assumed to be the same as benefit expenditure. [5] Data are not strictly comparable with those prior to 1984.

Pour les notes de caractère général, se reporter au tableau 1. [1] Y compris le Fonds pour l'équilibre financier de la sécurité sociale. [2] On ne dispose pas des chiffres des recettes, supposées égales aux dépenses; la ventilation des données n'est pas connue. [3] Les chiffres ne sont pas exactement comparables avec ceux qui sont donnés pour les années antérieures à 1983. [4] Y compris, pour les allocations pour enfants, l'estimation des cotisations, supposées égales aux dépenses de prestations. [5] Les chiffres ne sont pas exactement comparables avec ceux qui sont donnés pour les années antérieures à 1984.

Véanse las notas generales del cuadro 1. [1] Incluido el Fondo Financiero de Compensación. [2] No se dispone de cifras sobre los ingresos; se ha supuesto que coinciden con las cifras de egresos. La repartición no pudo conocerse. [3] Los datos no son estrictamente comparables con los de antes de 1983. [4] Respecto de las «asignaciones por hijos», se han incluido cifras estimativas de las cotizaciones percibidas, que se supone corresponden a los egresos por prestaciones. [5] Los datos no son estrictamente comparables con los de antes de 1984.

9. Distribution of receipts relating to social insurance and assimilated schemes and family allowances
(as percentages of total receipts)

9. Répartition des recettes au titre des assurances sociales et régimes assimilés et des prestations familiales
(en pourcentage du total des recettes)

9. Distribución de los ingresos relativos a los seguros sociales y regímenes asimilados y a las asignaciones familiares
(en porcentaje del total de ingresos)

Country and currency unit / Pays et unité monétaire / País y unidad monetaria	Financial year / Exercice financier / Ejercicio financiero	Contributions / Cotisations / Cotizaciones		Special taxes allocated to social security / Taxes et impôts spéciaux / Impuestos y derechos especiales	State participation / Participation de l'Etat / Participación del Estado	Participation of other public authorities / Participation d'autres pouvoirs publics / Participación de otras entidades públicas	Income from capital / Revenu des capitaux / Renta del capital	Other receipts / Autres recettes / Otros ingresos	Absolute total receipts (in millions of national currency units) / Total (millions d'unités monétaires nationales) / Total en millones de unidades monetarias nacionales
		From insured persons / Des assurés / De los asegurados	From employers / Des employeurs / De los empleadores						
(1)	(2)	(3)	(4)	(5)	(6)	(7)	(8)	(9)	(10)
AFRICA – AFRIQUE – AFRICA									
Bénin (Franc CFA)	1970	6.5	92.9	—	—	—	—	0.6	640.60
	1975	11.9	79.9	—	6.6	—	1.6	0.0	1 507.20
	1981	19.3	80.7	—	—	—	.	.	3 367.64
	1983	20.9	79.1	—	—	—	.	.	3 542.69
	1984	15.1	75.0	—	—	—	7.9	2.0	3 659.80
	1985	15.6	77.4	—	—	—	5.5	1.5	3 969.10
	1986	15.9	78.4	—	—	—	4.4	1.3	4 539.20
Burkina Faso (Franc CFA)	1975	16.1	77.4	—	3.3	—	3.2	0.1	1 345.60
	1980	17.8	72.0	—	—	—	1.5	8.7	4 331.80
	1983	19.1	80.0	0.2	—	—	0.7	—	5 133.70
	1984	15.3	63.1	—	—	—	21.6	0.1	6 760.70
	1985	15.7	62.7	—	—	—	21.6	0.0	7 241.30
	1986	15.6	64.3	—	—	—	20.1	0.0	8 087.50
Burundi[1] (Franc burundais)	1978	31.5	48.7	—	—	—	1.8	18.0	242.65
	1980	31.2	48.2	—	—	—	1.5	19.0	321.66
	1983	30.3	45.6	—	—	—	22.3	1.8	519.13
	1984	26.6	50.1	—	—	—	23.3	.	658.70
	1985	26.6	50.2	—	—	—	23.2	.	790.00
	1986	24.0	45.2	—	—	—	30.8	.	711.90
Cameroun (Franc CFA)	1970	—	99.2	—	—	—	0.8	0.0	2 081
	1981	16.5	83.5	—	—	—	.	0.0	20 401
	1983	12.8	64.4	—	—	—	22.8	0.0	37 201
	1984	16.4	80.9	—	—	—	2.7	—	38 393
	1985	13.1	68.1	—	—	—	18.8	—	50 377
	1986	14.0	68.2	—	—	—	17.8	—	56 770
Cap-Vert (Escudo)	1983	28.8	70.2	—	—	—	0.1	0.8	223.29
	1984	29.4	68.9	—	—	—	1.1	0.6	320.05
	1985	28.8	66.7	—	1.5	—	2.5	0.5	412.32
	1986	27.5	62.5	—	1.5	—	8.0	0.4	499.87
Rép. centrafricaine (Franc CFA)	1981	11.4	88.5	—	—	—	—	0.1	2 091.7
	1983	9.9	88.7	—	—	—	1.4	0.1	2 283.5
	1984	10.0	90.0	—	—	—	—	—	2 747.0
	1985	9.8	87.9	—	—	—	1.4	0.9	3 084.0
	1986	9.8	88.5	—	—	—	1.3	0.3	4 549.0
Côte d'Ivoire (Franc CFA)	1981	32.0	49.1	—	—	—	18.9	—	26 247.0
	1983	31.7	47.9	—	—	—	20.4	—	29 125.0
	1984	12.4	61.2	—	—	—	26.4	0.0	28 452.4
	1985	12.7	54.7	—	—	—	32.6	0.0	38 423.7
	1986	13.6	53.1	—	—	—	33.3	0.0	40 277.4
Egypt[1] (Pound)	1984	21.7	32.4	—	18.5	—	17.8	9.5	1 572.0
	1985	21.3	32.5	—	16.0	—	17.8	12.4	2 012.6
	1986	20.2	33.3	—	15.1	—	18.3	13.0	2 353.6

See notes on page 149. *Voir notes page 149.* Véanse notas pág. 149.

Table 9 *(cont.)*   Tableau 9 *(suite)*   Cuadro 9 *(cont.)*

Country and currency unit / Pays et unité monétaire / País y unidad monetaria	Financial year / Exercice financier / Ejercicio financiero	Contributions / Cotisations / Cotizaciones — From insured persons / Des assurés / De los asegurados	From employers / Des employeurs / De los empleadores	Special taxes allocated to social security / Taxes et impôts spéciaux / Impuestos y derechos especiales	State participation / Participation de l'Etat / Participación del Estado	Participation of other public authorities / Participation d'autres pouvoirs publics / Participación de otras entidades públicas	Income from capital / Revenu des capitaux / Renta del capital	Other receipts / Autres recettes / Otros ingresos	Absolute total receipts (in millions of national currency units) / Total (millions d'unités monétaires nationales) / Total en millones de unidades monetarias nacionales
(1)	(2)	(3)	(4)	(5)	(6)	(7)	(8)	(9)	(10)
Ethiopia[1] (Birr)	1972	—	88.6	—	—	—	—	11.4	2.80
	1975	—	83.5	—	—	—	—	16.5	3.76
	1980	—	100.0	—	—	—	—	—	8.19
	1983	—	.	—	—	—	—	.	.
	1984	36.7	55.0	—	—	—	8.4	—	40.70
	1985	37.2	55.7	—	—	—	7.1	—	44.06
	1986	35.1	52.7	—	—	—	12.3	—	45.45
Gabon (Franc CFA)	1980	8.9	88.9	—	—	—	—	2.2	18 408
	1983	8.5	77.4	—	6.8	—	6.5	0.8	33 332
	1984	8.6	84.9	—	—	—	—	6.6	37 402
	1985	8.5	84.7	—	—	—	—	6.8	41 719
	1986	8.3	84.8	—	—	—	—	6.9	37 788
Guinée (Syli)	1981	—	82.8	17.2	—	—	—	—	161.32
	1983	—	78.7	21.3	—	—	—	—	166.32
	1984	.	.	.	—	—	—	—	.
	1985	3.0	90.4	—	—	—	—	6.6	160.20
	1986	3.0	90.9	—	—	—	—	6.1	296.19
Guinée-Bissau (Peso)	1981	24.4	42.7	—	—	—	11.5	21.4	34.81
	1983	25.8	44.5	—	—	—	19.7	10.0	27.91
	1984	20.2	68.6	—	—	—	11.2	—	51.60
	1985	22.1	70.4	—	—	—	7.5	—	69.60
	1986	25.4	70.3	—	—	—	4.3	—	123.80
Kenya[1] (Shilling)	1970	47.9	50.1	0.1	—	—	—	1.8	153.2
	1975	38.3	31.9	0.0	—	—	25.7	4.2	356.6
	1981	32.5	32.5	.	—	—	35.0	.	492.4
	1983	25.3	25.3	.	—	—	49.4	.	600.4
	1984	22.6	22.6	1.2	—	—	53.6	.	1 680.0
	1985	22.6	22.6	1.1	—	—	53.8	.	1 860.0
	1986	27.7	27.7	1.2	—	—	43.4	.	1 660.0
Madagascar (Franc malgache)	1981	6.6	86.4	—	—	—	6.9	—	7 937.2
	1983	5.4	69.6	—	—	—	25.1	—	9 536.1
	1984	22.2	77.8	—	—	—	.	—	8 392.6
	1985	22.2	77.8	—	—	—	.	—	8 916.1
	1986	22.2	77.8	—	—	—	.	—	10 288.2
Mali (Franc CFA)	1972	4.7	93.9	—	0.3	—	—	1.1	584.0
	1975	8.8	74.9	0.1	2.4	—	0.3	13.5	991.0
	1980	8.5	79.4	—	10.7	—	0.2	1.2	2 270.5
	1983	8.5	80.0	—	.	—	.	11.6	3 470.5
	1984	10.5	88.5	—	.	—	.	1.0	3 433.3
	1985	9.5	89.6	—	.	—	.	0.9	3 855.1
	1986	8.7	81.9	—	.	—	0.0	9.4	5 179.7
Maroc (Dirham)	1970	9.2	86.5	—	—	—	4.3	—	272.55
	1975	7.4	90.9	—	—	—	1.5	0.1	474.69
	1980	—	90.0	—	—	—	9.7	0.3	1 444.10
	1983	8.4	78.4	—	—	—	13.2	.	1 451.60
	1984	8.4	77.8	—	—	—	13.8	.	1 592.20
	1985	8.2	76.0	—	—	—	15.8	.	1 759.40
	1986	8.2	76.1	—	—	—	15.7	.	1 870.70
Mauritanie (Ouguiya)	1970	8.8	85.9	—	—	—	3.6	1.7	96.76
	1981	7.0	90.1	—	—	—	2.7	0.2	530.76
	1983	6.8	87.9	—	—	—	5.2	0.2	628.41
	1984	6.8	88.8	—	—	—	4.1	0.4	667.03
	1985	6.4	86.3	—	—	—	4.6	2.7	749.08
	1986	6.3	87.7	—	—	—	6.1	—	584.62

See notes on page 149.   *Voir notes page 149.*   Véanse notas pág. 149.

Table 9 *(cont.)*   **Tableau 9** *(suite)*   **Cuadro 9** *(cont.)*

Country and currency unit *Pays et unité monétaire* País y unidad monetaria	Financial year *Exercice financier* Ejercicio financiero	Contributions *Cotisations* Cotizaciones From insured persons *Des assurés* De los asegurados	From employers *Des employeurs* De los empleadores	Special taxes allocated to social security *Taxes et impôts spéciaux* Impuestos y derechos especiales	State participation *Participation de l'Etat* Participación del Estado	Participation of other public authorities *Participation d'autres pouvoirs publics* Participación de otras entidades públicas	Income from capital *Revenu des capitaux* Renta del capital	Other receipts *Autres recettes* Otros ingresos	Absolute total receipts (in millions of national currency units) *Total (millions d'unités monétaires nationales)* Total en millones de unidades monetarias nacionales
(1)	(2)	(3)	(4)	(5)	(6)	(7)	(8)	(9)	(10)
Mauritius	1970	6.3	12.4	—	67.9	—	13.4	—	25.23
(Rupee)	1975	11.5	19.7	—	58.3	—	10.5	—	59.99
	1981	11.7	23.2	—	54.0	—	9.3	1.8	304.90
	1983	10.6	21.2	—	52.2	—	14.4	1.7	434.40
	1984	.	.	—	.	—	.	3.3	.
	1985	9.8	19.2	—	47.2	—	20.5	3.3	641.80
	1986	9.8	19.2	—	47.1	—	23.2	0.6	735.70
Mozambique[1]	1981	—	99.9	—	—	—	0.1	—	231.36
(Metical)	1983	—	99.8	—	—	—	0.2	—	153.96
	1984	—	99.9	—	—	—	0.1	—	160.20
	1985	—	99.8	—	—	—	0.2	—	165.35
	1986	—	99.9	—	—	—	0.1	—	155.19
Niger	1970	11.2	86.7	—	—	—	1.4	0.7	615.40
(Franc CFA)	1975	9.7	80.4	—	—	—	9.9	—	1 041.70
	1980	8.4	80.4	—	—	—	11.2	0.0	3 823.50
	1983	8.6	82.8	—	—	—	8.6	0.0	5 954.70
	1984	6.3	62.6	—	—	—	11.4	19.8	7 588.40
	1985	6.0	60.2	—	—	—	15.3	18.5	8 116.90
	1986	7.2	72.1	—	—	—	20.7	—	6 649.00
Nigeria[1]	1970	33.1	36.5	0.3	—	—	30.1	—	14.40
(Naira)	1981	33.1	22.3	—	—	—	44.4	0.2	70.67
	1983	28.2	20.2	—	—	—	51.4	0.3	78.42
	1984	17.8	27.5	—	—	—	54.7	0.0	87.23
	1985	19.1	26.5	—	—	—	54.0	0.4	99.56
	1986	17.9	24.4	—	—	—	57.2	0.5	108.38
Rwanda[1]	1975	32.7	54.6	—	—	—	11.7	1.0	313.3
(Franc rwandais)	1981	30.8	51.3	—	—	—	16.5	1.4	1 118.5
	1983	26.9	44.8	—	—	—	26.2	2.1	1 440.5
	1984	26.7	44.5	—	—	—	27.8	1.1	1 730.2
	1985	25.0	41.6	—	—	—	32.6	0.8	1 793.6
	1986	24.6	41.0	—	—	—	33.1	1.3	2 123.8
Sao Tomé-et-Principe[1]	1981	40.1	59.8	—	—	—	—	0.1	83.21
(Dobra)	1983	40.0	59.8	—	—	—	—	0.3	82.88
	1984	40.1	59.8	—	—	—	—	0.1	77.80
	1985	38.8	58.1	—	—	—	—	3.1	92.87
	1986	37.7	56.4	—	—	—	—	6.0	46.41
Sénégal	1970	—	79.7	19.7	—	—	0.0	0.6	2 483.7
(Franc CFA)	1975	—	77.6	—	15.2	—	0.8	6.4	4 706.0
	1980	18.1	67.0	—	5.5	—	7.8	1.7	13 904.0
	1983	.	95.8	—	.	—	1.2	3.1	7 704.0
	1984	21.9	69.4	—	.	—	8.5	0.3	18 774.0
	1985	20.8	70.9	—	.	—	8.1	0.3	21 300.0
	1986	21.3	69.9	—	.	—	8.5	0.2	22 094.0
Sudan[1]	1980	21.9	43.7	—	—	—	12.5	21.9	23.79
(Pound)	1983	16.8	37.3	—	—	—	14.8	31.0	33.19
	1984	11.7	23.4	—	—	—	16.9	47.9	55.50
	1985	12.2	24.6	—	—	—	35.3	27.9	54.10
	1986	14.3	28.7	—	—	—	37.1	20.0	42.10
Swaziland[1]	1981	40.0	40.0	—	—	—	19.9	—	6.62
(Lilangeni)	1983	33.3	33.3	—	—	—	33.5	—	9.83
	1984	33.9	33.9	—	—	—	31.7	0.5	9.65
	1985	32.2	32.2	—	—	—	35.2	0.4	10.28
	1986	31.4	31.4	—	—	—	36.7	0.5	10.70
Tanzania, United Rep. of[1]	1980	33.3	33.3	—	—	—	33.5	—	295.20
(Shilling)	1983	32.2	32.2	—	—	—	35.6	0.1	394.80
	1984	32.7	43.9	—	2.5	—	10.2	10.8	829.93
	1985	31.7	39.9	—	2.8	—	12.5	13.1	933.24
	1986	26.9	33.7	—	2.0	—	20.6	16.8	1 286.63

See notes on page 149.   *Voir notes page 149.*   Véanse notas pág. 149.

Table 9 *(cont.)*   Tableau 9 *(suite)*   Cuadro 9 *(cont.)*

Country and currency unit / Pays et unité monétaire / País y unidad monetaria	Financial year / Exercice financier / Ejercicio financiero	Contributions / Cotisations / Cotizaciones		Special taxes allocated to social security / Taxes et impôts spéciaux / Impuestos y derechos especiales	State participation / Participation de l'Etat / Participación del Estado	Participation of other public authorities / Participation d'autres pouvoirs publics / Participación de otras entidades públicas	Income from capital / Revenu des capitaux / Renta del capital	Other receipts / Autres recettes / Otros ingresos	Absolute total receipts (in millions of national currency units) / Total (millions d'unités monétaires nationales) / Total en millones de unidades monetarias nacionales
		From insured persons / Des assurés / De los asegurados	From employers / Des employeurs / De los empleadores						
(1)	(2)	(3)	(4)	(5)	(6)	(7)	(8)	(9)	(10)
Tchad (Franc CFA)	1979-81	13.9	86.1	—	—	—	—	—	211.14
	1983	14.0	86.0	—	—	—	—	—	227.69
	1984	29.5	59.5	2.9	—	—	1.2	6.9	669.01
	1985	31.8	64.1	.	—	—	1.4	2.8	1 668.87
	1986	26.4	65.9	.	—	—	4.0	3.8	1 221.90
Togo (Franc CFA)	1972	15.7	79.0	—	—	—	3.1	2.2	1 245
	1975	13.7	84.1	—	—	—	2.2	.	1 773
	1980	10.4	77.8	—	—	—	11.7	0.2	4 814
	1983	9.9	75.2	—	—	—	14.9	. .	7 008
	1984	9.6	73.4	—	—	—	17.0	.	8 177
	1985	9.1	69.3	—	—	—	21.6	.	9 536
	1986	9.3	70.9	—	—	—	19.8	.	9 588
Tunisia (Dinar)	1984	27.8	55.5	—	—	—	6.8	9.8	287.60
	1985	29.1	51.4	—	—	—	7.4	12.1	364.20
	1986	28.1	55.0	—	—	—	6.7	10.1	326.40
Uganda[1] (Shilling)	1980	27.4	27.4	—	—	—	45.2	—	82.10
	1983	24.3	24.3	—	—	—	51.5	—	171.00
	1984	21.0	21.0	—	—	—	58.0	—	150.78
	1985	26.7	26.7	—	—	—	46.6	—	145.93
	1986	44.6	44.6	—	—	—	10.9	—	75.06
Zaïre (Zaïre)	1984	25.9	61.6	—	—	—	—	12.5	322.36
	1985	25.0	67.9	—	—	—	—	7.2	736.33
	1986	28.6	60.2	—	—	—	—	11.2	1 238.25
Zambia[1] (Kwacha)	1970	34.9	46.4	—	—	—	16.1	2.6	20.62
	1975	32.7	39.5	—	—	—	23.9	3.9	41.34
	1980	38.1	30.6	—	—	—	31.3	0.1	69.01
	1983	.	.	.	.	.	.	.	
	1984	29.8	29.8	—	—	—	40.4	.	101.79
	1985	30.2	30.2	—	—	—	39.7	.	128.05
	1986	28.4	28.4	—	—	—	43.2	.	179.21
AMERICA – AMÉRIQUE – AMERICA									
Argentina (Austral)	1975	24.0	74.0	—	—	—	1.1	1.0	0.01
	1980	38.3	49.3	2.9	7.3	—	2.2	0.0	2.74
	1983	34.5	27.2	2.9	33.1	—	2.0	0.3	51.70
	1984	33.0	31.9	2.3	26.6	—	5.8	0.3	432.72
	1985	30.6	41.4	.	19.6	—	7.7	0.7	2 831.60
	1986	31.3	45.6	.	19.5	—	3.3	0.3	4 994.50
Bahamas[1] (Dollar)	1980	26.3	44.6	—	3.1	—	26.1	0.0	32.59
	1983	23.2	38.0	—	5.2	—	33.6	0.1	48.50
	1984	23.8	39.1	—	4.6	—	32.3	0.2	54.48
	1985	26.6	40.2	—	3.4	—	29.6	0.2	71.47
	1986	26.8	40.7	—	1.4	—	30.7	0.5	73.56
Barbados[1] (Dollar)	1971	83.1	—	—	—	—	16.9	—	9.90
	1975	32.9	38.5	—	—	—	28.6	—	19.91
	1980	32.9	41.7	—	—	—	25.4	—	45.65
	1983	36.2	37.5	—	—	—	22.3	4.1	130.96
	1984	39.7	41.4	—	—	—	18.3	0.6	130.83
	1985	38.9	40.5	—	—	—	20.3	0.3	141.07
	1986	39.9	41.7	—	—	—	17.7	0.7	139.68
Belize[1] (Dollar)	1981	13.8	82.9	—	—	—	3.0	0.4	2.69
	1983	11.5	69.1	—	—	—	14.3	5.0	7.35
	1984	12.2	73.2	—	—	—	14.2	0.4	10.59
	1985	10.1	60.6	—	—	—	28.9	0.3	10.43
	1986	9.4	56.4	—	—	—	33.9	0.3	11.24

See notes on page 149.   *Voir notes page 149.*   Véanse notas pág. 149.

Country and currency unit *Pays et unité monétaire* País y unidad monetaria	Financial year *Exercice financier* Ejercicio financiero	Contributions *Cotisations* Cotizaciones From insured persons *Des assurés* De los asegurados	From employers *Des employeurs* De los empleadores	Special taxes allocated to social security *Taxes et impôts spéciaux* Impuestos y derechos especiales	State participation *Participation de l'Etat* Participación del Estado	Participation of other public authorities *Participation d'autres pouvoirs publics* Participación de otras entidades públicas	Income from capital *Revenu des capitaux* Renta del capital	Other receipts *Autres recettes* Otros ingresos	Absolute total receipts (in millions of national currency units) *Total (millions d'unités monétaires nationales)* Total en millones de unidades monetarias nacionales
(1)	(2)	(3)	(4)	(5)	(6)	(7)	(8)	(9)	(10)
Bolivia	1972	32.6	46.7	1.3	—	—	2.5	16.8	444.6
(Peso)	1975	25.6	63.3	0.4	—	—	3.4	7.3	1 175.5
	1980	28.8	53.6	6.2	—	—	7.9	3.6	3 628.4
	1983	25.5	34.8	3.3	20.9	—	12.4	3.1	41 325.3
	1984	25.0	35.8	0.7	30.0	—	7.4	1.1	760 189.0
	1985	25.6	39.4	0.0	21.2	2.2	8.3	3.2	70 737 008.0
Brasil	1970	.	7.0	—	—	—	—	—	9.72
(Cruzado)	1975	.	6.0	—	—	—	—	—	54.42
	1980	.		—	—	—	—	—	820.18
	1983	15.6	74.0	—	8.2	—	0.0	2.2	6 636.90
	1984	21.5	64.5	—	11.1	—	1.0	2.0	19 873.40
	1985	17.6	72.1	—	4.4	—	4.2	1.7	70 365.00
	1986	39.3	52.5	—	3.9	—	2.8	1.5	197 691.60
Canada	1970	19.2	12.1	21.8	29.1	12.9	4.8	0.0	8 766.8
(Dollar)	1975	12.7	14.8	—	51.9	15.8	4.8	—	20 369.5
	1980	12.4	16.6	—	53.3	10.8	6.9	—	36 739.4
	1983	13.8	19.4	—	48.0	11.3	7.3	0.2	55 025.8
	1984	13.4	19.3	—	48.2	11.2	7.6	0.3	58 712.8
	1985	13.4	19.5	—	48.1	10.8	8.0	0.2	65 734.3
Colombia[1]	1970	19.2	70.6	—	4.9	—	5.1	0.2	2 198.62
(Peso)	1975	20.5	61.7	0.2	3.0	—	6.9	7.6	6 687.00
	1980	16.9	59.5	—	1.1	—	7.3	15.2	36 103.30
	1983	26.6	62.8	—	—	—	10.2	0.4	55 257.00
	1984	25.4	58.9	—	—	—	8.5	7.2	69 460.00
	1985	24.5	56.3	—	—	—	10.7	8.5	90 937.00
	1986	22.9	52.7	—	—	—	8.5	15.9	139 774.00
Costa Rica[1]	1970	26.8	41.6	—	17.9	—	12.2	1.4	272.3
(Colón)	1975	27.7	55.8	4.5	2.2	—	7.6	2.1	984.2
	1980	27.6	45.9	18.6	1.8	—	5.2	0.9	3 408.3
	1983	24.5	51.2	7.1	4.3	—	4.6	8.3	13 548.3
	1984	25.0	52.5	1.2	3.1	—	6.6	11.7	15 736.3
	1985	24.2	52.1	0.8	2.1	—	9.1	11.7	20 186.5
	1986	25.5	49.2	1.0	1.6	—	11.3	11.3	23 387.4
Cuba[1]	1980	—	.	—	.	—	—	—	1 149.5
(Peso)	1983	—	.	—	.	—	—	—	.
	1984	—	.	—	.	—	—	—	.
	1985	—	.	—	.	—	—	—	.
	1986	—	.	—	.	—	—	—	.
Chile	1971	19.2	57.5	2.6	14.7	—	1.1	4.8	15.12
(Peso)	1975	13.7	58.3	2.0	18.9	—	2.0	5.1	2 875.90
	1980	18.9	50.7	2.0	20.1	—	1.8	6.4	90 466.50
	1983	31.1	2.1	0.0	48.9	—	15.9	2.0	260 537.60
	1984	31.8	2.1	—	52.6	—	12.0	1.4	320 156.00
	1985	29.1	2.0	0.0	48.6	—	19.4	0.8	458 055.00
	1986	30.1	2.0	0.0	48.9	—	18.3	0.7	588 205.00
Dominica[1]	1980	29.3	48.6	—	—	—	21.3	0.8	4.98
(EC Dollar)	1983	27.4	45.6	—	—	—	26.2	0.8	7.11
	1984	28.7	47.9	—	—	—	22.7	0.7	8.94
	1985	22.0	54.2	—	—	—	23.0	0.8	11.26
	1986	22.6	50.9	—	—	—	25.4	1.1	12.30
República Dominicana[1]	1984	20.1	75.3	—	0.2	—	2.3	2.1	58.32
(Peso)	1985	20.0	76.4	—	—	—	2.5	1.1	58.39
	1986	20.1	72.9	—	—	—	1.3	5.6	77.87

See notes on page 149.   *Voir notes page 149.*   Véanse notas pág. 149.

141

Table 9 *(cont.)*   **Tableau 9** *(suite)*   **Cuadro 9** *(cont.)*

Country and currency unit *Pays et unité monétaire* País y unidad monetaria	Financial year *Exercice financier* Ejercicio financiero	Contributions *Cotisations* Cotizaciones From insured persons *Des assurés* De los asegurados	From employers *Des employeurs* De los empleadores	Special taxes allocated to social security *Taxes et impôts spéciaux* Impuestos y derechos especiales	State participation *Participation de l'Etat* Participación del Estado	Participation of other public authorities *Participation d'autres pouvoirs publics* Participación de otras entidades públicas	Income from capital *Revenu des capitaux* Renta del capital	Other receipts *Autres recettes* Otros ingresos	Absolute total receipts (in millions of national currency units) *Total (millions d'unités monétaires nationales)* Total en millones de unidades monetarias nacionales
(1)	(2)	(3)	(4)	(5)	(6)	(7)	(8)	(9)	(10)
Ecuador[1] (Sucre)	1972	35.2	37.8	—	0.3	—	24.8	1.8	2 258.0
	1974	37.5	40.0	—	1.1	—	20.3	1.2	3 381.0
	1980	41.7	40.5	—	0.2	—	17.7	.	10 692.0
	1983	38.6	38.1	—	1.3	—	22.1	.	19 880.0
	1984	24.7	20.3	—	.	—	54.4	0.5	38 328.3
	1985	22.4	18.1	—	.	—	44.6	14.8	56 038.1
	1986	19.9	15.9	—	6.0	—	48.9	9.3	78 732.8
El Salvador[1] (Colón)	1970	18.8	45.2	—	33.0	—	2.4	0.6	38.85
	1975	26.8	63.9	—	0.3	—	7.6	1.4	63.31
	1980	25.6	58.7	—	1.0	—	13.6	1.0	146.87
	1983	23.7	55.8	—	—	—	20.0	0.6	185.20
	1984	24.0	53.1	—	—	—	22.1	0.9	195.80
	1985	23.2	52.1	—	—	—	23.3	1.3	220.60
	1986	23.2	52.9	—	—	—	23.3	0.6	273.00
Grenada[1] (EC Dollar)	1981	—	33.8	—	—	—	66.2	—	0.07
	1983	48.2	48.3	—	—	—	3.3	0.2	3.62
	1984	42.6	42.6	—	—	—	13.5	1.3	6.81
	1985	46.1	46.1	—	—	—	7.7	0.1	9.16
	1986	40.4	40.4	—	—	—	19.0	0.2	10.37
Guatemala[1] (Quetzal)	1970	30.5	67.6	—	—	—	1.4	0.5	21.3
	1975	30.9	57.2	—	9.1	—	.	2.8	36.2
	1980	28.8	54.1	—	9.1	—	7.7	0.3	119.4
	1983	29.5	51.0	—	3.6	—	13.2	2.7	124.2
	1984	28.0	55.0	—	.	—	.	17.0	138.3
	1985	28.0	54.5	—	.	—	.	17.5	150.9
	1986	26.8	55.9	—	.	—	.	17.2	209.0
Guyana[1] (Dollar)	1972	35.7	52.2	—	—	—	12.1	—	16.56
	1975	32.2	47.4	—	—	—	20.4	—	25.89
	1980	29.2	43.9	—	—	—	26.7	0.3	84.04
	1983	20.6	30.9	—	—	—	48.5	0.1	123.42
	1984	18.0	27.1	—	—	—	54.8	0.1	140.88
	1985	16.2	24.3	—	—	—	59.5	0.0	159.72
	1986	15.5	23.2	—	—	—	61.3	0.0	184.56
Honduras[1] (Lempira)	1970	37.9	58.4	—	—	—	2.8	0.9	5.43
	1971	39.1	57.5	—	—	—	2.9	0.5	5.48
	1981	28.1	51.1	—	8.4	—	11.5	0.9	65.69
	1983	25.9	47.9	—	7.2	—	16.8	2.2	76.42
	1984	25.6	49.9	—	7.0	—	17.0	0.4	78.72
	1985	25.5	48.8	—	6.3	—	18.9	0.6	87.44
	1986	25.7	46.6	—	5.9	—	21.3	0.5	92.60
Jamaica[1] (Dollar)	1970	33.5	42.3	—	5.6	—	18.5	—	14.85
	1975	29.7	35.3	—	4.9	—	30.1	—	37.91
	1980	25.4	31.0	—	—	—	43.6	0.0	94.23
	1983	27.1	33.2	—	3.2	—	36.3	0.1	124.24
	1984	21.1	25.8	—	2.9	—	50.1	0.0	165.22
	1985	20.7	25.3	—	2.8	—	51.0	0.2	173.97
	1986	17.3	21.2	—	2.8	—	58.5	0.1	213.23
México[1] (Peso)	1970	85.9	—	—	10.6	—	2.4	1.2	9 067.00
	1974	85.2	—	—	10.6	—	1.6	2.5	21 357.42
	1980	20.6	63.7	—	10.7	—	—	5.0	99 050.00
	1983	16.8	65.7	—	10.3	—	—	7.2	364 662.00
	1984	17.5	67.6	—	11.0	—	—	4.0	561 790.00
	1985	17.4	67.5	—	10.7	—	—	4.4	969 272.00
	1986	18.1	68.8	—	7.5	—	—	5.5	1 660 051.00

See notes on page 149.   *Voir notes page 149.*   Véanse notas pág. 149.

142

Table 9 *(cont.)*   **Tableau 9** *(suite)*   **Cuadro 9** *(cont.)*

Country and currency unit *Pays et unité monétaire* País y unidad monetaria	Financial year *Exercice financier* Ejercicio financiero	Contributions *Cotisations* Cotizaciones		Special taxes allocated to social security *Taxes et impôts spéciaux* Impuestos y derechos especiales	State participation *Participation de l'Etat* Participación del Estado	Participation of other public authorities *Participation d'autres pouvoirs publics* Participación de otras entidades públicas	Income from capital *Revenu des capitaux* Renta del capital	Other receipts *Autres recettes* Otros ingresos	Absolute total receipts (in millions of national currency units) *Total (millions d'unités monétaires nationales)* Total en millones de unidades monetarias nacionales
		From insured persons *Des assurés* De los asegurados	From employers *Des employeurs* De los empleadores						
(1)	(2)	(3)	(4)	(5)	(6)	(7)	(8)	(9)	(10)
Panamá[1]	1972	29.6	50.7	1.1	4.7	—	11.3	2.5	75.75
(Balboa)	1975	30.3	55.7	0.6	4.2	—	8.3	0.9	133.60
	1980	29.9	42.4	0.5	4.0	—	10.1	13.0	276.49
	1983	28.8	44.6	0.4	2.9	—	13.3	10.0	433.60
	1984	28.9	48.7	0.6	3.2	—	14.6	4.0	404.30
	1985	28.8	48.5	0.6	3.2	—	14.2	4.5	429.50
	1986	28.1	47.2	0.4	3.1	—	16.0	5.2	475.50
Perú[1]	1981	—	87.3	—	—	—	11.1	1.7	248.19
(Inti)	1983	—	88.5	—	—	—	10.2	1.2	567.00
	1984	30.7	69.3	—	—	—	.	.	1 040.00
	1985	31.2	68.8	—	—	—	.	.	3 181.00
	1986	31.1	68.9	—	—	—	.	.	7 041.00
St. Lucia[1]	1981	37.3	37.3	—	—	—	25.3	—	8.25
(EC Dollar)	1983	43.5	43.5	—	—	—	13.0	—	6.87
	1984	27.5	27.5	—	—	—	44.9	—	10.44
	1985	24.4	24.4	—	—	—	51.1	—	10.68
	1986	28.6	28.6	—	—	—	42.7	—	14.62
Trinidad and Tobago[1]	1970	—	13.0	—	87.0	—	—	—	4.83
(Dollar)	1975	24.9	51.4	—	10.8	—	12.9	—	71.96
	1980	23.3	47.5	—	.	—	29.3	—	126.52
	1983	18.1	36.2	—	27.3	—	18.5	—	475.52
	1984	17.9	35.9	—	27.2	—	19.0	—	496.34
	1985	17.2	34.3	—	25.8	—	22.7	—	470.09
	1986	16.9	33.9	—	29.9	—	19.3	—	469.53
United States[1]	1970	40.9	50.2	—	3.9	0.3	4.6	—	54 739
(Dollar)	1975	41.0	50.4	—	4.2	0.3	4.2	—	104 548
	1980	39.0	53.1	—	5.2	0.1	2.6	—	196 604
	1983	34.9	45.1	—	17.6	0.0	2.3	0.1	295 358
	1984	38.4	50.4	0.8	7.4	0.0	2.8	0.1	308 106
	1985	38.9	50.5	1.1	6.3	0.0	3.1	0.1	339 176
	1986	39.0	50.3	1.1	6.7	0.0	3.0	−0.1	364 810
Uruguay	1975	—	71.7	9.1	18.3	—	0.6	0.3	575.67
(Nuevo peso)	1980	25.1	34.0	8.1	30.2	—	1.5	1.1	9 779.50
	1983	23.5	23.3	2.0	47.2	—	1.6	2.3	16 599.00
	1984	27.8	29.9	1.0	36.4	—	1.0	3.8	27 416.00
	1985	30.3	35.0	1.0	28.7	—	0.9	4.0	47 961.00
	1986	33.3	37.2	0.9	23.1	—	0.7	4.7	92 849.00
Venezuela[1]	1970	27.2	52.6	—	14.5	—	5.6	0.1	876.0
(Bolívar)	1975	23.7	47.4	—	16.6	—	12.2	0.0	2 138.7
	1980	26.8	53.5	—	6.8	—	12.7	0.2	4 259.3
	1983	22.7	45.3	—	13.7	—	18.3	—	5 104.9
	1984	22.4	44.9	—	13.4	—	19.3	—	5 360.7
	1985	21.4	42.8	—	13.4	—	22.3	—	5 803.2
	1986	20.2	40.4	—	13.2	—	26.3	—	7 177.6
ASIA – ASIE – ASIA									
Bahrain[1]	1978	24.1	64.5	—	—	—	11.4	0.0	9.13
(Dinar)	1980	22.3	58.6	—	—	—	19.0	0.1	13.85
	1983	25.7	51.4	—	—	—	22.9	0.0	28.28
	1984	25.2	50.4	—	—	—	24.3	0.0	31.21
	1985	22.5	45.0	—	—	—	31.2	1.4	37.39
	1986	21.1	42.2	—	—	—	36.7	0.0	35.77
Bangladesh	1975	23.3	34.8	—	—	—	38.7	3.2	6.92
(Taka)	1980	—	100.0	—	—	—	—	—	3.14
	1983	19.4	43.4	4.3	—	—	32.9	—	28.98
	1984	16.8	44.1	3.9	—	—	35.2	—	37.13
	1985	15.5	32.8	3.5	—	—	48.2	—	56.47
	1986	15.3	35.7	3.5	—	—	45.5	—	54.37

See notes on page 149.   *Voir notes page 149.*   Véanse notas pág. 149.

Table 9 *(cont.)*   **Tableau 9** *(suite)*   **Cuadro 9** *(cont.)*

Country and currency unit / Pays et unité monétaire / País y unidad monetaria	Financial year / Exercice financier / Ejercicio financiero	Contributions / Cotisations / Cotizaciones		Special taxes allocated to social security / Taxes et impôts spéciaux / Impuestos y derechos especiales	State participation / Participation de l'Etat / Participación del Estado	Participation of other public authorities / Participation d'autres pouvoirs publics / Participación de otras entidades públicas	Income from capital / Revenu des capitaux / Renta del capital	Other receipts / Autres recettes / Otros ingresos	Absolute total receipts (in millions of national currency units) / Total (millions d'unités monétaires nationales) / Total en millones de unidades monetarias nacionales
		From insured persons / Des assurés / De los asegurados	From employers / Des employeurs / De los empleadores						
(1)	(2)	(3)	(4)	(5)	(6)	(7)	(8)	(9)	(10)
Cyprus[1] (Pound)	1970	39.7	22.0	—	30.4	—	7.9	0.0	4.31
	1975	39.9	23.5	—	31.6	—	4.4	0.6	6.42
	1980	39.5	27.3	—	29.2	—	2.7	1.3	22.94
	1983	35.1	35.3	—	20.6	—	8.2	0.7	73.43
	1984	35.9	33.5	—	20.2	—	9.5	0.9	89.37
	1985	35.2	32.6	—	19.8	—	11.3	1.1	102.69
	1986	34.2	32.4	—	19.4	—	13.1	0.9	113.26
India[1] (Rupee)	1970	42.8	46.3	0.9	1.6	—	8.4	0.1	4 086.50
	1975	80.9	—	1.5	0.9	—	16.3	0.5	11 481.00
	1980	31.7	35.8	0.9	0.3	0.0	29.8	1.4	15 975.50
	1983	27.3	30.9	0.4	4.2	—	35.7	1.5	26 772.54
	1984	27.4	30.8	0.4	4.0	—	35.9	1.5	27 864.32
	1985	26.8	31.5	0.3	3.8	—	36.2	1.5	31 986.76
Indonesia[1] (Rupiah)	1981	21.1	60.9	—	—	—	—	18.0	33 054.00
	1983	16.5	48.4	—	—	—	—	35.1	56 324.00
	1984	19.9	58.4	—	—	—	21.4	0.3	59 608.89
	1985	19.5	56.9	—	—	—	22.5	1.0	79 163.02
	1986	18.8	54.5	—	—	—	25.7	1.0	90 282.47
Iran, Islamic Rep. of[1] (Rial)	1981	17.3	49.4	—	14.8	—	5.1	13.4	225 692
	1983	17.4	49.8	—	25.8	—	6.2	0.7	301 532
	1984	79.0	0.0	—	8.8	—	12.1	0.0	291 847
	1985	85.2	0.0	—	9.7	—	5.1	0.0	304 608
	1986	83.2	0.0	—	8.2	—	8.5	0.1	346 460
Israel (New Shekel)	1970	32.4	51.4	—	9.2	0.0	6.3	0.7	1.42
	1975	18.8	41.5	—	28.8	0.7	9.6	0.6	7.06
	1980	24.7	43.8	—	15.8	0.7	13.3	1.7	14.01
	1983	22.6	36.5	—	27.0	0.1	12.4	1.4	222.00
	1984	22.7	36.1	—	26.9	0.2	13.7	0.4	1 163.60
	1985	24.8	34.7	—	28.5	0.2	11.5	0.4	3 839.50
	1986	28.5	36.4	—	25.6	0.1	9.1	0.3	5 644.60
Japan (Yen)	1970	33.4	31.2	—	16.2	0.7	8.6	9.9	3 907 789
	1975[2]	30.8	30.7	—	21.3	1.2	8.7	7.4	12 228 641
	1980	31.4	28.5	—	21.9	0.9	10.0	7.3	24 677 033
	1983	31.4	28.3	—	20.2	1.6	12.3	6.2	31 824 265
	1984	32.4	29.2	—	20.7	1.8	13.4	2.6	32 298 664
	1985	32.3	29.1	—	19.8	1.9	13.9	2.9	35 477 296
	1986	31.9	29.4	—	19.7	2.0	14.6	2.4	37 724 839
Jordan[1] (Dinar)	1980	32.9	65.0	—	—	—	2.1	—	4.86
	1983	30.8	59.0	—	—	—	9.6	0.7	30.27
	1984	30.6	58.7	—	—	—	9.9	0.7	40.47
	1985	29.7	57.2	—	—	—	12.3	0.8	44.14
	1986	28.7	55.3	—	—	—	15.2	0.8	53.58
Kuwait[1] (Dinar)	1980	12.8	25.5	—	36.1	—	23.4	2.3	79.20
	1983	9.5	18.8	—	36.2	—	21.9	13.6	200.57
	1984	10.2	20.2	—	39.6	—	17.4	12.5	197.63
	1985	6.5	12.8	—	61.8	—	12.9	6.1	323.37
	1986	6.3	12.4	—	54.6	—	21.1	5.6	385.77
Malaysia[1] (Ringgit)	1970	30.4	32.5	—	—	—	36.8	0.3	345.38
	1975	59.1	—	—	—	—	39.3	1.6	690.03
	1980	—	60.5	—	—	—	37.6	1.8	1 945.85
	1983	28.6	36.4	—	—	—	34.4	0.6	3 719.94
	1984	27.4	34.9	—	0.2	—	37.2	0.3	4 208.61
	1985	26.3	33.5	—	0.1	—	39.3	0.8	4 781.58
	1986	25.5	32.6	—	—	—	41.1	0.8	5 329.17

See notes on page 149. *Voir notes page 149.* Véanse notas pág. 149.

Table 9 *(cont.)*   **Tableau 9** *(suite)*   **Cuadro 9** *(cont.)*

Country and currency unit / Pays et unité monétaire / País y unidad monetaria	Financial year / Exercice financier / Ejercicio financiero	Contributions / Cotisations / Cotizaciones — From insured persons / Des assurés / De los asegurados	From employers / Des employeurs / De los empleadores	Special taxes allocated to social security / Taxes et impôts spéciaux / Impuestos y derechos especiales	State participation / Participation de l'Etat / Participación del Estado	Participation of other public authorities / Participation d'autres pouvoirs publics / Participación de otras entidades públicas	Income from capital / Revenu des capitaux / Renta del capital	Other receipts / Autres recettes / Otros ingresos	Absolute total receipts (in millions of national currency units) / Total (millions d'unités monétaires nationales) / Total en millones de unidades monetarias nacionales
(1)	(2)	(3)	(4)	(5)	(6)	(7)	(8)	(9)	(10)
Myanmar[1] (Kyat)	1970	18.3	64.7	—	16.6	—	—	0.4	16.21
	1975	23.2	76.3	—	—	—	—	0.6	17.53
	1980	20.1	60.4	—	17.8	—	1.3	0.3	30.39
	1983	20.3	60.8	17.2	—	—	1.3	0.5	39.00
	1984	20.2	60.1	18.0	—	—	1.2	0.5	40.60
	1985	19.8	59.3	19.1	—	—	1.4	0.5	42.50
	1986	19.9	59.6	18.5	—	—	1.6	0.5	44.30
Pakistan[1] (Rupee)	1965	—	100.0	—	—	—	—	—	18.50
	1980	—	81.4	—	—	—	17.7	0.8	233.98
	1983	—	72.4	0.1	—	—	27.0	0.5	382.51
	1984	—	71.3	—	—	—	28.0	0.7	483.70
	1985	—	65.8	—	—	—	33.7	0.5	587.30
	1986	—	64.4	—	—	—	35.1	0.4	724.90
Philippines[1] (Peso)	1970	27.4	47.4	—	—	—	24.6	0.6	235.77
	1978	25.2	42.3	—	—	—	31.7	0.9	1 638.00
	1980	24.4	39.7	—	—	—	35.2	0.7	2 521.60
	1983	20.0	31.4	—	—	—	48.1	0.5	3 865.00
	1984	15.5	25.5	—	—	—	58.8	0.3	5 156.20
	1985	11.1	18.3	—	—	—	70.4	0.2	7 437.70
	1986	11.9	19.6	—	—	—	68.3	0.2	7 049.80
Qatar[1] (Riyal)		—	—		—	—	—	—	—
Singapore[1] (Dollar)	1970	30.5	48.6	—	—	—	20.6	0.2	199.73
	1975	39.2	44.7	—	—	—	15.9	0.2	1 062.96
	1980	37.9	43.3	—	—	—	18.3	0.4	2 846.27
	1983	39.7	40.3	—	—	—	19.5	0.5	5 654.38
	1984	39.7	40.3	—	—	—	19.5	0.4	6 774.94
	1985	39.2	39.7	—	—	—	20.8	0.3	7 647.75
	1986	52.3	21.4	—	—	—	25.9	0.4	6 528.04
Sri Lanka[1] (Rupee)	1970	32.1	48.6	—	—	—	19.3	—	208.50
	1975	26.5	39.9	—	—	—	33.4	0.2	353.60
	1980	—	68.2	—	—	—	31.8	—	1 102.50
	1983	28.7	29.9	—	—	—	41.4	0.1	2 434.80
	1984	32.6	38.3	—	—	—	29.0	0.1	4 853.04
	1985	31.8	37.4	—	—	—	30.7	0.0	6 034.03
	1986	30.2	36.1	—	—	—	33.7	0.0	6 779.79
Rép. arabe syrienne[1] (Livre syrienne)	1984	27.4	70.0	—	—	—	—	2.7	936.00
	1985	27.3	69.6	—	—	—	—	3.1	1 026.00
	1986	25.1	71.0	—	—	—	—	4.0	1 164.00
Thailand[1] (Baht)	1980	—	60.0	—	2.2	—	18.0	19.8	253.71
	1983	—	64.0	—	3.8	—	32.3	—	350.19
	1984	—	100.0	—	—	—	—	—	248.99
	1985	—	100.0	—	—	—	—	—	268.30
	1986	—	100.0	—	—	—	—	—	284.76

EUROPE – EUROPE – EUROPA

Countries with a market economy – Pays à économie de marché – Países con economía de mercado

Austria (Schilling)	1970	32.5	44.6	—	20.0	0.2	0.8	1.9	52 341
	1975	32.2	42.7	—	21.6	—	0.9	2.6	100 629
	1980	32.6	42.9	5.4	14.4	0.3	0.9	3.5	171 711
	1983	34.6	39.8	4.2	17.8	0.6	0.6	2.4	230 702
	1984	34.1	39.9	5.1	17.1	0.5	0.6	2.6	252 738
	1985	34.9	40.6	5.0	16.6	0.5	0.6	2.0	267 774
	1986	34.9	40.6	4.8	16.8	0.5	0.6	2.0	282 986

See notes on page 149.   *Voir notes page 149.*   Véanse notas pág. 149.

145

Table 9 *(cont.)*   Tableau 9 *(suite)*   Cuadro 9 *(cont.)*

Country and currency unit *Pays et unité monétaire* País y unidad monetaria	Financial year *Exercice financier* Ejercicio financiero	Contributions *Cotisations* Cotizaciones From insured persons *Des assurés* De los asegurados	From employers *Des employeurs* De los empleadores	Special taxes allocated to social security *Taxes et impôts spéciaux* Impuestos y derechos especiales	State participation *Participation de l'Etat* Participación del Estado	Participation of other public authorities *Participation d'autres pouvoirs publics* Participación de otras entidades públicas	Income from capital *Revenu des capitaux* Renta del capital	Other receipts *Autres recettes* Otros ingresos	Absolute total receipts (in millions of national currency units) *Total (millions d'unités monétaires nationales)* Total en millones de unidades monetarias nacionales
(1)	(2)	(3)	(4)	(5)	(6)	(7)	(8)	(9)	(10)
Belgique	1970	25.1	48.7	—	21.1	0.0	4.4	0.7	180 957.3
(Franc belge)	1975	22.2	44.3	—	28.4	0.0	3.1	1.9	443 707.7
	1980	20.2	41.2	0.9	34.0	—	2.8	0.9	723 835.1
	1983	21.2	36.4	0.6	36.9	—	2.2	2.8	992 194.0
	1984	22.5	37.1	1.1	34.4	—	2.5	2.3	1 030 184.0
	1985	26.7	37.4	0.7	30.1	—	2.4	2.6	1 069 280.0
	1986	27.2	37.8	0.6	29.4	—	2.5	2.5	1 118 318.0
Denmark	1970	25.7	7.3	—	54.7	10.0	2.3	—	9 695.3
(Krone)	1975	2.0	4.2	—	82.3	8.9	2.6	0.0	23 744.4
	1980	2.5	2.7	—	63.9	27.8	3.0	—	72 888.8
	1983	4.6	6.0	—	59.4	26.0	3.9	—	105 092.4
	1984	4.7	5.7	—	59.9	25.7	3.9	—	109 728.1
	1985	4.4	5.8	—	58.9	26.6	4.3	—	114 640.9
	1986	5.0	6.0	—	59.9	25.1	4.1	—	125 631.2
España	1975	16.1	76.5	0.8	4.3	—	1.6	0.7	608 907.5
(Peseta)	1980	12.9	71.6	0.4	13.9	0.1	0.7	0.5	2 080 148.2
	1983	17.7	60.6	0.4	19.8	—	0.8	0.7	3 403 704.0
	1984	18.3	55.6	0.5	24.5	—	0.6	0.5	3 951 266.0
	1985	17.8	55.8	0.5	24.9	—	0.7	0.4	4 357 735.0
	1986	17.9	54.7	—	26.6	—	0.6	0.3	5 051 704.0
Finland	1970	20.4	49.9	—	15.5	3.8	10.3	0.0	3 388.3
(Markka)	1975	19.2	63.9	—	6.8	2.7	7.3	0.0	10 729.4
	1980	10.5	44.7	—	25.4	11.7	7.7	0.0	30 362.0
	1983	8.3	46.2	—	26.5	11:1	7.9	0.1	53 068.3
	1984	9.6	46.0	—	23.0	12.9	8.5	—	60 979.8
	1985	10.1	46.7	—	21.9	13.0	8.3	—	70 544.5
	1986	9.6	46.0	—	22.4	13.4	8.5	—	77 980.5
France	1975	22.3	66.2	3.1	6.3	—	1.3	1.0	252 741.6
(Franc français)	1980	26.2	60.2	2.6	9.2	—	1.1	0.7	562 882.2
	1983	25.8	55.6	3.4	11.8	—	1.6	1.7	917 197.2
	1984	26.4	54.0	4.0	12.1	—	1.7	1.7	1 012 634.6
	1985	27.1	55.0	3.1	11.1	—	1.9	1.7	1 067 426.9
	1986	27.7	55.6	2.7	10.3	—	1.9	1.7	1 107 522.9
Germany, Fed. Rep. of	1970	39.4	40.5	—	16.8	—	2.6	0.7	88 347
(Deutsche Mark)	1975	36.7	37.4	—	22.8	—	2.3	0.7	185 158
	1980	42.4	36.6	—	19.5	—	1.0	0.5	286 684
	1983	43.9	36.0	—	18.6	—	0.9	0.6	329 907
	1984	44.1	36.3	—	18.1	—	0.8	0.7	344 245
	1985	44.4	36.4	—	17.8	—	0.7	0.7	358 710
	1986	44.8	36.9	—	17.1	—	0.6	0.7	375 037
Grèce	1970	37.2	33.4	15.4	6.5	—	5.8	1.6	26 422
(Drachme)	1975	36.3	36.1	14.3	6.4	—	5.0	1.8	58 031
	1980	38.0	38.2	10.5	5.7	—	6.2	1.4	189 709
	1983	35.6	34.9	13.5	7.9	—	6.6	1.6	446 188
	1984	36.4	35.3	10.8	8.7	—	6.7	2.2	557 744
	1985	37.1	35.4	11.4	7.5	—	6.5	2.1	681 725
Iceland	1984	—	11.4	—	79.7	7.7	1.2	—	6 123
(Króna)	1985	—	10.1	—	81.1	7.4	1.5	—	8 710
	1986	—	10.8	—	80.4	8.0	0.8	—	11 601
Ireland	1970	15.6	22.5	—	59.9	0.4	1.0	0.5	96.10
(Pound)	1975	15.6	26.8	—	56.9	0.1	0.5	0.1	371.70
	1980	11.4	20.1	—	67.3	0.0	0.2	1.0	1 646.00
	1983	13.1	19.5	—	66.0	—	0.3	1.2	2 967.63
	1984	13.3	20.0	—	65.6	—	0.2	0.9	3 228.32
	1985	12.9	20.3	—	65.7	—	0.1	0.9	3 561.74
	1986	12.8	19.9	—	66.3	—	0.1	0.9	3 810.20

See notes on page 149.   *Voir notes page 149.*   Véanse notas pág. 149.

Table 9 (cont.)   Tableau 9 (suite)   Cuadro 9 (cont.)

Country and currency unit / Pays et unité monétaire / Pais y unidad monetaria	Financial year / Exercice financier / Ejercicio financiero	Contributions / Cotisations / Cotizaciones — From insured persons / Des assurés / De los asegurados	From employers / Des employeurs / De los empleadores	Special taxes allocated to social security / Taxes et impôts spéciaux / Impuestos y derechos especiales	State participation / Participation de l'Etat / Participación del Estado	Participation of other public authorities / Participation d'autres pouvoirs publics / Participación de otras entidades públicas	Income from capital / Revenu des capitaux / Renta del capital	Other receipts / Autres recettes / Otros ingresos	Absolute total receipts (in millions of national currency units) / Total (millions d'unités monétaires nationales) / Total en millones de unidades monetarias nacionales
(1)	(2)	(3)	(4)	(5)	(6)	(7)	(8)	(9)	(10)
Italie (Lire (milliards))	1970	14.9	63.4	0.2	16.6	—	2.1	2.7	7 688.06
	1975	14.4	74.1	—	7.4	0.0	2.8	1.3	18 107.00
	1980	16.8	52.1	—	28.0	0.0	1.7	1.3	61 759.00
	1983	16.9	46.1	—	34.5	0.0	1.4	1.1	120 602.00
	1984	19.1	52.1	—	17.8	—	0.3	10.8	73 419.00
	1985	19.1	52.3	—	18.3	—	0.3	9.9	81 986.00
	1986	19.5	51.7	—	17.6	—	0.3	10.9	90 646.00
Luxembourg (Franc luxembourgeois)	1970	30.5	35.3	—	21.4	1.5	10.5	0.8	7 456.1
	1975	29.3	36.9	—	19.9	1.2	8.1	4.7	16 269.8
	1980	26.8	33.5	—	22.0	1.0	8.8	7.9	28 687.5
	1983	27.8	31.4	—	23.9	1.0	10.0	6.0	35 932.8
	1984	27.0	31.7	—	30.2	—	10.2	0.7	38 938.6
	1985	27.2	31.8	—	33.2	—	6.1	1.8	41 533.7
	1986	26.5	31.0	—	34.6	—	6.1	1.8	45 208.1
Malta (Lira)	1970	20.0	14.5	—	61.4	—	4.1	—	2.16
	1975	30.8	24.5	—	44.6	—	—	—	9.48
	1980	33.5	26.8	—	39.7	—	—	—	43.72
	1983	33.9	27.4	—	38.7	—	—	—	57.08
	1984	37.3	29.4	—	33.3	—	—	—	50.13
	1985	37.1	29.6	—	33.3	—	—	—	52.12
	1986	36.7	30.1	—	33.2	—	—	—	52.22
Netherlands (Guilder)	1970	47.6	39.8	—	8.7	0.0	3.9	—	20 165.1
	1975	45.4	37.3	—	12.4	0.3	4.1	0.5	48 692.4
	1980	39.9	31.3	—	23.4	0.4	5.0	—	86 793.6
	1983	50.0	31.8	—	12.6	0.0	5.6	—	104 484.0
	1984	46.9	30.4	—	16.8	0.0	5.9	—	110 508.0
	1985	47.1	31.0	—	15.5	0.0	6.3	—	113 510.0
	1986	45.6	33.0	—	14.8	0.0	6.7	—	111 378.0
Norway (Krone)	1970	28.4	37.5	0.4	23.9	8.3	1.3	0.2	9 977.9
	1975	28.3	48.2	0.4	15.3	7.4	0.4	0.0	23 127.2
	1980	23.8	37.6	0.3	24.0	13.9	0.3	0.1	49 715.3
	1983	24.4	35.4	0.3	26.5	13.1	0.3	0.1	74 636.0
	1984	22.0	32.5	0.2	25.9	18.6	0.2	0.5	87 042.0
	1985	23.3	33.1	0.2	24.4	18.2	0.2	0.7	94 390.0
	1986	26.4	35.1	0.2	20.4	17.0	0.2	0.6	100 502.9
Portugal (Escudo)	1970	21.4	61.7	—	—	—	9.3	7.6	11 022.4
	1975	21.6	73.2	—	1.9	—	3.1	0.2	38 457.9
	1980	25.3	68.2	—	2.2	4.2	—	—	106 379.5
	1983	28.1	64.1	—	4.6	3.1	—	—	179 917.4
	1984	25.9	58.5	—	8.8	4.5	2.3	—	232 089.6
	1985	24.7	60.3	—	8.0	4.9	2.1	—	284 747.9
	1986	23.9	69.0	—	7.0	—	0.1	0.0	396 218.9
Suisse (Franc suisse)	1970	46.0	22.7	—	16.4	6.6	7.4	0.9	7 112.6
	1975	47.5	24.6	—	14.9	6.8	5.4	0.8	15 938.3
	1980	47.8	24.9	—	16.1	6.4	4.0	0.8	20 895.5
	1983	50.2	23.7	—	15.5	6.2	3.8	0.6	26 291.6
	1984	50.5	23.3	—	15.7	6.3	3.4	0.8	28 718.5
	1985	51.3	22.9	—	15.2	6.3	3.4	0.8	30 383.2
	1986	51.0	23.1	—	14.8	6.8	3.4	0.8	32 293.0
Sweden (Krona)	1970	18.9	37.3	—	29.7	3.5	10.4	0.1	24 081.2
	1975	1.4	51.3	—	31.9	3.0	12.4	—	50 084.6
	1980	1.4	50.1	—	17.6	20.8	10.1	—	141 478.5
	1983	1.2	52.1	—	14.3	21.4	11.0	—	211 769.9
	1984	1.1	39.1	—	22.7	27.2	9.9	—	259 397.3
	1985	1.4	36.7	—	24.3	27.4	10.4	—	276 869.8
	1986	1.8	38.9	—	22.0	26.5	10.9	—	308 753.5

See notes on page 149.   *Voir notes page 149.*   Véanse notas pág. 149.

Table 9 *(cont.)*   **Tableau 9** *(suite)*   **Cuadro 9** *(cont.)*

Country and currency unit / Pays et unité monétaire / País y unidad monetaria	Financial year / Exercice financier / Ejercicio financiero	Contributions / Cotisations / Cotizaciones — From insured persons / Des assurés / De los asegurados	From employers / Des employeurs / De los empleadores	Special taxes allocated to social security / Taxes et impôts spéciaux / Impuestos y derechos especiales	State participation / Participation de l'Etat / Participación del Estado	Participation of other public authorities / Participation d'autres pouvoirs publics / Participación de otras entidades públicas	Income from capital / Revenu des capitaux / Renta del capital	Other receipts / Autres recettes / Otros ingresos	Absolute total receipts (in millions of national currency units) / Total (millions d'unités monétaires nationales) / Total en millones de unidades monetarias nacionales
(1)	(2)	(3)	(4)	(5)	(6)	(7)	(8)	(9)	(10)
Turquie[1] (Livre turque)	1970	34.6	50.4	—	—	—	13.1	1.9	3 592.8
	1975	37.8	48.8	—	—	—	11.5	1.9	16 878.3
	1980	36.0	40.5	—	11.6	—	8.7	3.3	124 084.0
	1983	36.9	39.9	—	5.1	—	17.6	0.5	387 411.0
	1984	35.2	42.0	—	—	—	22.1	0.6	567 825.0
	1985	39.0	43.4	—	—	—	16.9	0.7	780 723.0
	1986	35.7	41.4	—	—	—	22.0	0.9	1 158 957.0
United Kingdom (Pound)	1970	34.4	39.2	—	23.8	—	2.1	0.4	3 292
	1975	30.4	46.5	—	20.6	—	2.4	0.2	8 334
	1980	17.9	25.9	—	53.6	—	2.0	0.6	31 586
	1983	23.5	24.9	—	49.7	—	1.2	0.7	41 687
	1984	24.2	24.7	—	49.2	—	1.2	0.6	44 006
	1985	24.9	25.6	—	47.7	—	1.2	0.6	46 665
	1986	25.0	25.8	—	47.3	—	1.3	0.6	50 034

EUROPE – EUROPE – EUROPA

Countries with a centrally planned economy – Pays à économie planifiée – Países con economía centralmente planificada

RSS de Biélorussie (Rouble)	1970	—	—	—	93.9[3]	—	—	6.1[4]	723
	1975	—	—	—	.	—	—	.	1 160
	1980	—	—	—	.	—	—	.	2 243
	1983	—	—	—	.	—	—	.	2 689
	1984	—	—	—	.	—	—	.	2 823
	1985	—	—	—	.	—	—	.	2 942
	1986	—	—	—	.	—	—	.	3 199
Bulgarie (Lev)	1970	1.3	53.0	4.3	34.0	3.7	—	3.7	1 168.9
	1975	0.7	70.9	3.5	6.0	0.3	—	18.5	1 813.3
	1980	.	.	—	.	—	—	—	2 488.7
	1983	—	.	—	.	—	—	—	2 939.5
	1984	—	.	—	.	—	—	—	3 318.1
	1985	—	.	—	.	—	—	—	3 316.0
	1986	—	.	—	.	—	—	—	3 691.4
Czechoslovakia (Koruna)	1970	0.1	3.8	—	96.1	—	—	—	40 965
	1975	0.0	3.8	—	96.2	—	—	—	52 605
	1980	0.0	3.8	—	95.0	—	—	1.2	89 164
	1983	0.0	3.8	—	95.0	—	—	1.2	102 407
	1984	0.0	4.0	—	94.7	—	—	1.3	105 501
	1985	0.0	4.0	—	94.7	—	—	1.3	111 231
	1986	0.0	3.9	—	94.8	—	—	1.3	117 321
German Democratic Rep. (Mark)	1970	29.3	31.9	—	38.5	—	—	0.2	14 394.6
	1975	25.0	27.6	—	47.2	—	—	0.2	21 827.8
	1980	21.9	28.3	—	49.7	—	—	0.1	29 627.0
	1983	23.1	29.5	—	47.3	—	—	0.1	30 829.5
	1984	23.4	29.9	—	46.6	—	—	0.1	31 196.9
	1985	22.7	29.1	—	48.1	—	—	0.1	32 724.2
	1986	22.3	28.3	—	49.3	—	—	0.1	34 314.3
Hongrie (Forint)	1970	18.1	53.5	—	27.8	—	0.1	0.5	30 095
	1975	21.1	53.0	—	25.2	—	0.1	0.6	44 917
	1980	.	.	—	—	—	0.9	99.1	698
	1983	100.0	—	—	—	—	.	.	20 602
	1984	.	.	—	—	—	.	.	.
	1985	.	.	—	—	—	.	.	.
	1986	.	.	—	—	—	.	.	.
Pologne (Zloty)	1984	3.1	84.6	6.6	4.5	—	0.2	1.0	1 099 121
	1985	2.9	84.4	6.7	4.5	—	0.4	1.0	1 340 536
	1986	3.5	81.4	6.5	6.7	—	0.6	1.3	1 671 856

See notes on page 149.   *Voir notes page 149.*   Véanse notas pág. 149.

Table 9 *(concl.)*   **Tableau 9** *(fin)*   **Cuadro 9** *(fin)*

Country and currency unit / Pays et unité monétaire / País y unidad monetaria	Financial year / Exercice financier / Ejercicio financiero	Contributions / Cotisations / Cotizaciones		Special taxes allocated to social security / Taxes et impôts spéciaux / Impuestos y derechos especiales	State participation / Participation de l'Etat / Participación del Estado	Participation of other public authorities / Participation d'autres pouvoirs publics / Participación de otras entidades públicas	Income from capital / Revenu des capitaux / Renta del capital	Other receipts / Autres recettes / Otros ingresos	Absolute total receipts (in millions of national currency units) / Total (millions d'unités monétaires nationales) / Total en millones de unidades monetarias nacionales
		From insured persons / Des assurés / De los asegurados	From employers / Des employeurs / De los empleadores						
(1)	(2)	(3)	(4)	(5)	(6)	(7)	(8)	(9)	(10)
RSS d'Ukraine (Rouble)	1970	—	—	—	93.0[3]	—	—	7.0[4]	4 302
	1975	—	—	—	.	—	—	.	6 408
	1980	—	—	—	.	—	—	.	12 030
	1983	—	—	—	.	—	—	.	14 180
	1984	—	—	—	.	—	—	.	14 898
	1985	—	—	—	.	—	—	.	15 658
	1986	—	—	—	.	—	—	.	16 835
URSS (Rouble)	1970	—	—	—	95.8[3]	—	—	4.2[4]	22 806
	1975	—	—	—	.	—	—	.	34 634
	1980	—	—	—	.	—	—	.	64 616
	1983	—	—	—	.	—	—	.	75 789
	1984	—	—	—	.	—	—	.	79 969
	1985	—	—	—	.	—	—	.	83 573
	1986	—	—	—	.	—	—	.	89 307
Yugoslavia (Dinar)	1970	77.2[5]	13.8	—	8.1	0.3	—	0.6	21 390.0
	1981	66.3[5]	23.4	0.8	7.3	0.3	1.0	0.9	271 422.3
	1983	66.7[5]	24.5	0.8	6.3	0.1	0.9	0.6	462 590.0
	1984	64.9	26.4	—	7.0	0.3	—	1.5	659 413.0
	1985	65.1	28.8	—	4.5	0.2	—	1.4	1 205 410.0
	1986	63.3	32.2	—	2.7	0.6	—	1.1	2 777 651.0

OCEANIA – OCÉANIE – OCEANIA

Country and currency unit	Financial year	From insured persons	From employers	Special taxes	State participation	Participation of other public authorities	Income from capital	Other receipts	Absolute total receipts
Australia (Dollar)	1970	11.7	9.6	—	77.9	—	0.8	—	1 757.6
	1975	11.5	12.1	—	75.9	—	0.5	0.1	4 966.7
	1980	12.7	6.6	—	80.2	—	0.5	—	12 655.6
	1983	13.9	9.8	—	75.5	—	0.8	0.0	19 097.2
	1984	—	7.2	2.6	90.2	—	—	—	15 539.7
	1985	—	13.7	5.8	80.4	—	—	—	18 264.4
	1986	—	11.5	6.4	82.1	—	—	—	19 053.0
Fiji[1] (Dollar)	1975	37.2	38.2	—	—	—	15.3	9.3	18.28
	1980	31.7	34.0	—	—	—	23.5	10.8	52.34
	1983	32.0	32.2	—	—	—	35.5	0.3	76.92
	1984	30.5	30.5	—	—	—	38.1	1.0	89.78
	1985	30.8	30.8	—	—	—	37.7	0.8	111.02
	1986	26.5	26.5	—	—	—	46.3	0.8	111.57
New Zealand (Dollar)	1970	—	5.1	—	94.9	—	—	—	374.2
	1975	—	6.4	—	93.6	—	—	—	975.0
	1980	—	3.3	—	96.4	—	—	0.4	3 816.3
	1983	—	3.5	—	95.4	—	0.7	0.3	5 788.0
	1984	—	2.5	—	96.4	—	0.7	0.4	6 221.3
	1985	—	2.3	—	96.8	—	0.5	0.4	7 504.7
	1986	—	2.3	—	97.1	—	0.3	0.4	8 865.3
Solomon Islands[1] (Dollar)	1981	39.5	39.5	—	—	—	16.6	4.5	3.80
	1983	30.3	45.5	—	—	—	21.0	3.2	7.52
	1984	29.8	44.6	—	—	—	25.6	—	9.13
	1985	28.7	43.2	—	—	—	28.1	—	10.89
	1986	27.9	41.8	—	—	—	30.3	—	13.66

10. Distribution of benefit expenditure by social security branch, relating to schemes classified under the headings "social insurance and assimilated schemes" and "family allowances"

(as percentages of total benefit expenditure)

10. Répartition des dépenses en prestations par branche de la sécurité sociale, pour les régimes entrant dans les rubriques «assurances sociales et régimes assimilés» et «prestations familiales»

(en pourcentage du total des dépenses en prestations)

10. Distribución de los egresos por prestaciones por ramas de la seguridad social, en lo relativo únicamente a los regímenes clasificados en las rúbricas «Seguros sociales y regímenes asimilados» y «Asignaciones familiares»

(en porcentaje del total de egresos por prestaciones)

Country and currency unit / Pays et unité monétaire / Países y unidades monetarias	Financial year / Exercice financier / Ejercicio financiero	Sickness-maternity / Maladie-maternité / Enfermedad, maternidad				Employment injuries / Accidents du travail et maladies professionnelles / Riesgos profesionales				Pensions / Pensions / Pensiones	Unemployment / Chômage / Desempleo	Family allowances / Prestations familiales / Asignaciones familiares	Total amount of benefit expenditure (in millions of national currency units) / Total des dépenses en prestations (millions d'unités monétaires nationales) / Total de egresos por prestaciones (en millones de unidades monetarias nacionales)
		Medical care / Soins médicaux / Asistencia médica	Benefits in kind other than for medical care / Prestations en nature à titres que les soins médicaux / Prestaciones en especie, excepto asistencia médica	Cash benefits / Prestations en espèces / Prestaciones monetarias	Total / Total / Total	Medical care / Soins médicaux / Asistencia médica	Benefits in kind other than for medical care / Prestations en nature à d'autres titres que les soins médicaux / Prestaciones en especie, excepto asistencia médica	Cash benefits / Prestations en espèces / Prestaciones monetarias	Total / Total / Total				
(1)	(2)	(3)	(4)	(5)	(6)	(7)	(8)	(9)	(10)	(11)	(12)	(13)	(14)

AFRICA – AFRIQUE – AFRICA

(1)	(2)	(3)	(4)	(5)	(6)	(7)	(8)	(9)	(10)	(11)	(12)	(13)	(14)
Bénin (Franc CFA)	1970	—	—	—	—	3.7	—	5.4	9.1	8.6	—	82.3[1]	485.60
	1975	—	—	—	—	—	—	7.9[2]	7.9	19.7	—	72.4[1]	1 108.10
	1981	—	—	—	—	—	0.4	8.6	9.0	33.3	—	57.8	2 071.45
	1983	—	—	—	—	—	0.4	8.9	9.3	39.0	—	51.7	2 459.42
	1984	—	—	—	—	2.8	—	3.9	6.7	46.7	—	46.6	2 437.12
	1985	—	—	—	—	2.5	—	3.7	6.2	59.4	—	34.4	2 573.10
	1986	—	—	—	—	2.7	—	3.8	6.5	62.8	—	30.7	2 561.77
Burkina Faso (Franc CFA)	1975	—	—	0.3	0.3	1.8	—	6.4	8.2	26.1	—	65.4	609.80
	1980	—	—	1.5	1.5	3.4	—	8.5	11.9	34.9	—	51.7	1 083.90
	1983	—	0.0	1.3	1.3	2.3	—	8.3	10.6	42.7	—	45.2	1 604.00
	1984	0.7	—	—	0.7	—	—	9.0	9.0	44.7	—	45.5	1 668.50
	1985	0.4	—	—	0.4	—	—	8.2	8.2	52.5	—	38.9	1 821.10
	1986	0.7	—	—	0.7	—	—	8.2	8.2	52.9	—	38.2	2 042.90

Country (Currency)	Year													
Burundi (Franc burundais)	1978	—	—	—	—	—	—	—	—	56.7	43.3	—	—	23.77
	1980	—	—	—	—	—	—	—	38.3	45.8	54.2	—	—	42.65
	1983	—	—	—	—	—	11.8	—	51.4	50.1	49.9	—	—	113.70
	1984	—	—	—	—	—	—	—	50.5	51.4	48.6	—	—	167.20
	1985	—	—	—	—	—	—	—	39.7	50.5	49.5	—	—	202.10
	1986	—	—	—	—	—	—	—	—	39.7	60.3	—	—	269.10
Cameroun (Franc CFA)	1970	—	—	—	—	—	—	—	—	22.1	—	—	77.9[3]	1 349
	1981	—	—	—	—	—	—	—	12.1	15.8	8.6	—	75.6	8 114
	1983	—	—	—	—	—	—	—	12.0	14.9	10.0	—	75.2	9 467
	1984	0.1	—	—	9.6	9.5	—	—	10.3	12.5	8.6	—	69.3	13 766
	1985	0.1	—	—	10.1	10.0	3.6	0.0	11.6	13.4	11.0	—	65.5	15 567
	1986	0.1	—	—	9.5	9.3	2.8	0.1	10.0	11.6	13.0	—	65.8	19 869
Cap-Vert (Escudo)	1983	8.9	17.6	—	35.6	9.1	—	—	—	—	8.2	—	56.3	58.27
	1984	9.3	22.1	—	43.7	12.4	—	—	—	—	6.6	—	49.7	79.36
	1985	13.0	24.4	—	50.7	13.4	—	—	—	—	7.2	—	42.2	107.71
	1986	14.1	26.6	—	52.8	12.0	—	—	—	—	11.2	—	36.0	131.06
Rép. centrafricaine (Franc CFA)	1981	—	—	—	—	—	0.4	—	8.7	9.1	19.4	—	71.6	838.00
	1983	—	—	—	—	—	0.4	—	7.3	7.7	22.9	—	69.5	1 071.00
	1984	—	—	—	—	—	0.5	—	6.3	6.8	30.4	—	62.8	2 057.00
	1985	—	—	—	—	—	1.2	—	6.5	7.7	34.2	—	58.1	1 961.00
	1986	—	—	—	—	—	1.1	—	10.0	11.1	34.5	—	54.4	2 532.00
Côte d'Ivoire (Franc CFA)	1981	—	—	—	—	—	—	9.4	20.1	29.5	25.3	—	45.3	8 565.10
	1983	—	—	—	—	—	—	6.4	17.7	24.1	32.9	—	43.0	12 801.70
	1984	—	—	—	—	—	5.8	—	18.1	23.9	26.4	—	49.6	16 377.60
	1985	—	—	—	—	—	6.2	—	16.1	22.3	33.4	—	44.2	16 286.10
	1986	—	—	—	—	—	6.8	—	15.1	21.9	33.2	—	44.9	18 211.80
Egypt (Pound)	1984	—	—	—	0.2	0.2	—	—	3.0	3.0	96.8	0.1	—	484.50
	1985	—	—	—	0.2	0.2	—	—	2.9	2.9	96.9	0.0	—	552.70
	1986	—	—	—	0.2	0.2	—	—	2.9	2.9	96.8	0.0	—	631.00
Ethiopia (Birr)	1972[4]	—	—	—	—	—	—	—	100	100	—	—	—	2.31
	1975[4]	—	—	—	—	—	—	—	100	100	—	—	—	3.50
	1980[4]	—	—	—	—	—	—	—	100	100	—	—	—	2.87
	1983[5]	—	—	—	...	...	—	—	...	...	—	—	—	...
	1984	—	—	—	—	—	—	—	—	—	100[6]	—	—	7.90
	1985	—	—	—	—	—	—	—	—	—	100[6]	—	—	9.34
	1986	—	—	—	—	—	—	—	—	—	100[6]	—	—	10.01
Gabon (Franc CFA)	1980	57.1	—	—	57.1	1.5	3.2	—	5.0	8.2	23.0	—	11.7	13 525
	1983	54.9	0.4	—	56.8	—	0.9	—	3.3	4.2	23.0	—	16.0	23 468
	1984	57.1	3.5	—	60.6	—	0.9	—	2.9	3.8	20.5	—	15.1	26 868
	1985	55.8	4.1	—	59.9	—	0.6	—	3.1	3.7	20.9	—	15.5	30 363
	1986	55.5	3.8	—	59.3	—	0.8	—	3.4	4.2	23.6	—	13.0	34 175
Guinée (Syli)	1981[7]	...	—	—	...	...	...	—	...	...	...	—	...	33.86
	1983[7]	...	—	—	...	...	...	—	...	...	...	—	...	33.34
	1984[5]	...	—	—	...	...	...	—	...	...	...	—	...	...
	1985	2.1	—	—	2.2	0.1	0.1	—	10.2	10.3	30.8	—	56.7	126.29
	1986	5.4	—	—	6.0	0.6	0.1	—	12.9	13.0	25.3	—	55.7	229.00

See notes on page 169.   *Voir notes page 169.*   Véanse notas pág. 169.

Table 10 (cont.) **Tableau 10** (suite) **Cuadro 10** (cont.)

Country and currency unit / Pays et unité monétaire / Países y unidades monetarias	Financial year / Exercice financier / Ejercicio financiero	Sickness-maternity / Maladie-maternité / Enfermedad, maternidad				Employment injuries / Accidents du travail et maladies professionnelles / Riesgos profesionales				Pensions / Pensions / Pensiones	Unemployment / Chômage / Desempleo	Family allowances / Prestations familiales / Asignaciones familiares	Total amount of benefit expenditure (in millions of national currency units) / Total des dépenses en prestations (millions d'unités monétaires nationales) / Total de egresos por prestaciones (en millones de unidades monetarias nacionales)
		Medical care / Soins médicaux / Asistencia médica	Benefits in kind other than for medical care / Prestations en nature à d'autres titres que les soins médicaux / Prestaciones en especie, excepto asistencia médica	Cash benefits / Prestations en espèces / Prestaciones monetarias	Total	Medical care / Soins médicaux / Asistencia médica	Benefits in kind other than for medical care / Prestations en nature à d'autres titres que les soins médicaux / Prestaciones en especie, excepto asistencia médica	Cash benefits / Prestations en espèces / Prestaciones monetarias	Total				
(1)	(2)	(3)	(4)	(5)	(6)	(7)	(8)	(9)	(10)	(11)	(12)	(13)	(14)
Guinée-Bissau[8] (Peso)	1981	55.6	43.4	1.0	100	—	—	—	—	—	—	—	1.44
	1983	100	—	—	100	—	—	—	—	—	—	—	1.64
	1984	29.4	—	2.4	31.8	3.7	—	—	3.7	3.4	—	61.2	8.18
	1985	30.5	—	2.1	32.6	2.3	—	—	2.3	47.8	—	17.3	17.37
	1986	23.1	—	1.5	24.6	2.6	—	—	2.6	49.6	—	23.1	23.78
Kenya[8] (Shilling)	1970	69.7	—	—	69.7	—	—	19.1	19.1	11.2	—	—	17.8
	1975	47.6	—	—	47.6	—	—	6.2	6.2	46.2	—	—	55.0
	1981	1.6	—	—	1.6	—	—	—	—	98.4	—	—	25.3
	1983	1.0	—	—	1.0	—	—	—	—	99.0	—	—	40.4
	1984	—	—	—	—	—	—	—	—	100[9]	—	—	160.0
	1985	—	—	—	—	—	—	—	—	100[9]	—	—	220.0
	1986	—	—	—	—	—	—	—	—	100[9]	—	—	228.0
Madagascar (Franc malgache)	1981	—	—	—	—	—	—	9.9	9.9	29.7	—	60.4	4 535.0
	1983	—	—	—	—	—	—	8.0	8.0	42.2	—	49.8	6 609.0
	1984	—	—	—	—	0.7	—	7.4	8.1	47.9	—	44.0	7 354.5
	1985	—	—	—	—	0.8	—	7.5	8.3	48.5	—	43.2	7 751.5
	1986	—	—	—	—	0.7	—	7.4	8.1	50.9	—	41.0	8 764.6
Mali (Franc CFA)	1972	5.3	—	0.2	5.5	0.4	—	3.5	3.9	26.1	—	64.5	1 068.0
	1975	7.2	—	3.1	10.3	0.9	—	4.2	5.1	34.2	—	50.4	1 351.3
	1980	1.2	—	23.9	25.1	—	—	4.1	4.1	27.6	—	43.3	2 824.0
	1983	9.3	—	1.9	11.2[10]	—	2.9	3.5	6.4	45.3	—	37.3	1 803.3
	1984	16.6	—	1.5	18.1[10]	0.8	—	3.9	4.7	45.0	—	32.2	1 965.3
	1985	13.5	—	3.3	16.8[10]	0.4	—	5.1	5.5	46.9	—	30.7	2 233.4
	1986	7.5	—	2.3	9.8[10]	0.7	—	6.1	6.8	53.1	—	30.2	2 185.6
Maroc (Dirham)	1970	—	—	1.9	1.9	—	—	25.0	25.0	3.7	—	69.4	209.00
	1975	—	—	1.5	1.5	—	—	28.1	28.1	18.4	—	52.1	339.40
	1980	—	—	1.3	1.3	1.0	—	21.4	22.4	28.0	—	48.3	718.40
	1983	—	—	2.5	2.5	—	—	—	—	46.6	—	50.9	763.10
	1984	—	—	2.3	2.3	—	—	—	—	48.8	—	48.9	831.90
	1985	—	—	1.8	1.8	—	—	—	—	51.7	—	46.4	900.70
	1986	—	—	1.7	1.7	—	—	—	—	54.1	—	44.2	965.00

	1	2	3	4	5	6	7	8	9	10	11	12
Mauritanie (Ouguiya)												
1970	58.38	77.7	—	7.4	14.9	10.7	—	4.2	—	—	—	—
1981	277.50	72.1	—	11.6	16.4	13.0	2.5	0.9	—	—	—	—
1983	380.57	70.3	—	13.4	16.4	12.5	2.7	1.2	7.9	—	—	7.9
1984	413.91	65.8	—	12.6	13.7	12.3	0.8	0.6	6.3	—	—	6.3
1985	386.82	64.2	—	14.5	15.1	12.9	0.9	1.3	6.2	—	—	6.2
1986	477.27	58.3	—	23.1	12.4	10.7	1.2	0.5	—	—	—	—
Mauritius (Rupee)												
1970	19.13	28.9	—	67.4	3.7	3.7	—	—	—	—	—	—
1975	40.16	23.9	—	74.2	1.9	1.9	—	—	—	—	—	—
1981	166.00	12.5	—	87.5[11]	—	—	—	—	—	—	—	—
1983	230.50	7.2	0.7[12]	92.0[11]	—	—	—	—	—	—	—	—
1984[5]	—	—	—	—	—	—	—	—	—	—	—	—
1985	313.30	4.0	5.5	89.5	1.0	1.0	—	—	—	—	—	—
1986	365.30	3.0	5.3	90.7	1.0	1.0	—	—	—	—	—	—
Mozambique (Metical)												
1981	12.25	—	—	—	100	94.4	4.9	0.7	—	—	—	—
1983	17.75	—	—	—	100	92.7	6.1	1.2	—	—	—	—
1984	71.00	—	—	—	100	28.2	45.1	26.8	—	—	—	—
1985	89.00	—	—	—	100	39.3	37.1	23.6	—	—	—	—
1986	72.00	—	—	—	100	26.4	43.1	30.6	—	—	—	—
Niger (Franc CFA)												
1970	365.10	89.5	—	3.5	7.0	5.4	0.1	1.5	—	—	—	—
1975	628.20	88.6	—	6.2	5.2	4.2	—	1.0	—	—	—	—
1980	1 341.80	89.4	—	5.5	5.1	4.4	0.6	0.1	—	—	—	—
1983	1 767.81	77.8	—	12.4	6.6	5.0	1.5	0.1	3.3	—	—	3.2
1984	1 918.70	74.7	—	15.3	7.4	6.5	0.2	0.7	2.6	0.0	0.1	2.6
1985	1 783.20	69.3	—	21.7	5.7	4.7	0.2	0.8	3.5	0.0	0.1	3.4
1986	2 438.20	68.0	—	19.6	9.7	7.3	0.5	1.9	2.7	0.0	0.1	2.6
Nigeria (Naira)												
1970	1.20	—	—	93.3	6.7	6.7	—	—	—	—	—	—
1981[13]	3.52	—	—	100	—	—	—	—	—	—	—	—
1983[13]	5.14	—	—	100	—	—	—	—	—	—	—	—
1984[13]	6.10	—	—	100	—	—	—	—	—	—	—	—
1985[13]	7.72	—	—	100	—	—	—	—	—	—	—	—
1986[13]	7.84	—	—	100	—	—	—	—	—	—	—	—
Rwanda (Franc rwandais)												
1975	7.5	—	—	19.6	80.4	80.4	—	—	—	—	—	—
1981	96.6	—	—	52.2	47.8	21.7	26.1	—	—	—	—	—
1983	224.3	—	—	61.2	38.7	32.5	6.2	—	—	—	—	—
1984	255.6	—	—	70.8	29.2	29.2	—	—	—	—	—	—
1985	314.0	—	—	74.2	24.6	24.2	1.6	—	—	—	—	—
1986	380.6	—	—	75.5	24.6	21.0	3.6	—	—	—	—	—
Sao Tomé-et-Principe (Dobra)												
1981	17.94	—	—	93.2	0.1	0.1	—	—	6.6	—	—	6.6
1983	19.67	—	—	88.5	0.1	0.1	—	—	11.4	—	—	11.4
1984	21.47	—	—	88.1	2.1	2.1	—	—	9.8	—	—	9.8
1985	28.25	—	—	77.7	0.9	0.9	—	—	21.4	—	—	21.4
1986	23.18	—	—	98.8	0.5	0.5	—	—	0.6	—	—	0.6
Sénégal (Franc CFA)												
1970	2 186	89.4	—	—	10.6	6.9	—	3.7	—	—	—	—
1975	1 784	72.7	—	—	27.3	20.6	—	6.7	—	—	—	—
1980	8 845	35.1	—	55.7	9.2	8.2	0.3	0.7	—	—	—	—
1983	4 806	78.4	—	—	21.6	16.8	4.8	—	—	—	—	—
1984	13 282	26.1	—	65.6	8.2	6.1	2.1	—	—	—	—	—
1985	14 644	23.3	—	69.4	7.3	5.5	1.8	—	—	—	—	—
1986	15 958	21.4	—	71.9	6.7	5.1	1.6	—	—	—	—	—

See notes on page 169.   *Voir notes page 169.*   *Véanse notas pág. 169.*

Table 10 *(cont.)* **Tableau 10** *(suite)* **Cuadro 10** *(cont.)*

| Country and currency unit / Pays et unité monétaire / Países y unidades monetarias (1) | Financial year / Exercice financier / Ejercicio financiero (2) | Sickness-maternity / Maladie-maternité / Enfermedad, maternidad | | | | Employment injuries / Accidents du travail et maladies professionnelles / Riesgos profesionales | | | | Pensions / Pensions / Pensiones (11) | Unemployment / Chômage / Desempleo (12) | Family allowances / Prestations familiales / Asignaciones familiares (13) | Total amount of benefit expenditure (in millions of national currency units) / Total des dépenses en prestations (millions d'unités monétaires nationales) / Total de egresos por prestaciones (en millones de unidades monetarias nacionales) (14) |
		Medical care / Soins médicaux / Asistencia médica (3)	Benefits in kind other than for medical care / Prestations en nature à d'autres titres que les soins médicaux / Prestaciones en especie, excepto asistencia médica (4)	Cash benefits / Prestations en espèces / Prestaciones monetarias (5)	Total / Total / Total (6)	Medical care / Soins médicaux / Asistencia médica (7)	Benefits in kind other than for medical care / Prestations en nature à d'autres titres que les soins médicaux / Prestaciones en especie, excepto asistencia médica (8)	Cash benefits / Prestations en espèces / Prestaciones monetarias (9)	Total / Total / Total (10)				
Sudan (Pound)	1980	—	—	—	—	—	—	18.4	18.4	81.6	—	—	0.92
	1983	—	—	—	—	—	—	15.6	15.6	84.4	—	—	2.70
	1984	—	—	—	—	—	—	14.0	14.0	86.0	—	—	4.30
	1985	—	—	—	—	—	—	12.5	12.5	87.5	—	—	4.80
	1986	—	—	—	—	—	—	11.9	11.9	88.1	—	—	4.20
Swaziland[13] (Lilangeni)	1981	—	—	—	—	—	—	—	—	100	—	—	0.64
	1983	—	—	—	—	—	—	—	—	100	—	—	1.15
	1984	—	—	—	—	—	—	—	—	100	—	—	1.41
	1985	—	—	—	—	—	—	—	—	100	—	—	1.56
	1986	—	—	—	—	—	—	—	—	100	—	—	1.78
Tanzania, United Rep. of[13] (Shilling)	1980	—	—	—	—	—	—	—	—	100	—	—	55.5
	1983	—	—	—	—	—	—	—	—	100	—	—	64.7
	1984	—	—	—	—	—	—	—	—	100	—	—	119.4
	1985	—	—	—	—	—	—	—	—	100	—	—	198.7
	1986	—	—	—	—	—	—	—	—	100	—	—	231.4
Tchad (Franc CFA)	1979-81[14]	—	—	—	—	4.3	0.0	18.8	23.1	—	—	76.9	74.19[1]
	1983	—	—	—	—	8.3	1.2	1.5	11.0	—	—	89.0[1]	47.03
	1984	—	4.7	—	4.7	1.2	—	24.6	25.8	—	—	69.4	73.35
	1985	—	2.4	—	2.4	0.3	—	32.5	32.8	5.4	—	59.4	290.14
	1986	—	8.7	—	8.7	0.5	—	56.1	56.6	10.8	—	23.9	348.45
Togo (Franc CFA)	1972	—	—	—	—	1.4	—	5.6	7.0	16.4	—	76.6[2]	487
	1975	—	—	—	—	0.6	—	6.3	6.9	21.1	—	72.0[3]	670
	1980	—	—	—	—	1.2	0.6	5.5	7.3	23.4	—	69.3	1 835
	1983	—	—	—	—	—	—	13.1	13.1	31.8	—	55.1[10]	2 309
	1984	—	—	—	—	0.3	—	14.2	14.5	37.6	—	47.8[10]	2 688
	1985	—	—	—	—	0.5	—	15.5	16.0	40.4	—	43.6[10]	3 030
	1986	—	—	—	—	0.2	—	16.1	16.3	42.9	—	40.8[10]	3 302
Tunisie (Dinar)	1984	17.7	1.1	5.1	23.9	—	—	—	—	55.2	—	20.9	188.50
	1985	17.4	0.9	5.4	23.7	—	—	—	—	59.1	—	17.2	227.10
	1986	18.0	0.8	4.6	23.4	—	—	—	—	53.8	—	22.8	236.40

Country (Currency)	Year	(1)	(2)	(3)	(4)	(5)	(6)	(7)	(8)	(9)	(10)	(11)	(12)
Uganda[13] (Shilling)	1980	7.50	—	—	100	—	—	—	—	—	—	—	—
	1983	3.20	—	—	100	—	—	—	—	—	—	—	—
	1984	2.13	—	—	100	—	—	—	—	—	—	—	—
	1985	1.99	—	—	100	—	—	—	—	—	—	—	—
	1986	0.52	—	—	100	—	—	—	—	—	—	—	—
Zaïre (Zaïre)	1984	39.51	12.8	—	80.1	7.0	4.5	0.8	1.7	—	—	0.8	—
	1985	92.52	36.1	—	63.0	0.9	0.6	—	0.3	—	—	—	—
	1986	291.13	31.5	—	67.8	0.7	0.4	—	0.3	—	—	—	—
Zambia[13] (Kwacha)	1970	4.29	—	—	37.0	63.0	62.2	—	0.8	—	—	—	—
	1975	10.43	—	—	85.6	14.4	14.4	—	0.0	—	—	—	—
	1980	20.85	—	—	98.9	—	—	—	—	—	—	—	—
	1983[5]	.	—	—	.	—	—	—	—	1.1	1.1	—	—
	1984	17.02	—	—	97.7	—	—	—	—	2.3	2.3	—	—
	1985	28.72	—	—	98.3	—	—	—	—	1.7	1.7	—	—
	1986	27.45	—	—	98.7	—	—	—	—	1.3	1.3	—	—

AMERICA – AMÉRIQUE – AMERICA

Country (Currency)	Year	(1)	(2)	(3)	(4)	(5)	(6)	(7)	(8)	(9)	(10)	(11)	(12)
Argentina (Austral)	1975	0.01	27.2	.	58.3	.	.	.	.	14.5	.	0.6	13.9
	1980	2.50	17.8	—	58.1	—	—	—	—	24.1	—	1.8	22.3
	1983	46.47	14.3	—	58.6	—	—	—	—	27.1	—	0.9	26.2
	1984[8]	360.50	14.9	0.7	58.8	—	—	—	—	26.3	—	1.0	25.3
	1985[8]	2 277.20	18.6	0.7	80.7	—	—	—	—	—	—	—	—
	1986[8]	4 421.10	22.4	0.8	76.8	—	—	—	—	—	—	—	—
Bahamas (Dollar)	1980	5.41	—	—	72.5	0.1	0.1	—	0.1	27.4	27.4	—	—
	1983	15.30	—	—	81.1	0.7	0.6	—	0.7	18.2	18.2	—	—
	1984	17.82	—	—	80.4	2.4	1.7	—	0.1	17.2	17.2	—	—
	1985	21.39	—	—	66.9	2.2	2.1	—	0.3	30.8	30.8	—	—
	1986	30.12	—	—	53.1	22.9	22.6	—	—	24.1	24.1	—	—
Barbados (Dollar)	1971	1.28	—	—	25.2	9.4	6.3	—	3.1	65.4	65.4	—	—
	1975	5.00	—	—	63.2	5.4	4.4	—	1.0	31.4	31.4	—	—
	1980	14.80	—	—	74.3	3.7	3.0	—	0.7	22.0	22.0	—	0.2
	1983	68.53	—	3.2[15]	82.5	1.4	1.4	—	—	12.9	12.7	—	—
	1984	82.00	—	6.0	82.0	1.1	1.1	—	—	10.9	10.9	—	—
	1985	91.69	—	9.4	78.1	1.1	1.1	—	—	11.3	11.3	—	—
	1986	113.26	—	14.2	75.0	0.9	0.9	—	—	9.8	9.8	—	—
Belize (Dollar)	1981	0.12	—	—	—	100	84.9	0.8	15.1	52.7	52.7	—	—
	1983	0.89	—	—	5.8	41.4	37.7	1.8	2.9	53.8	53.8	—	—
	1984	0.94	—	—	6.7	39.5	32.1	—	5.6	41.9	41.9	—	—
	1985	1.22	—	—	10.9	47.2	40.9	—	6.3	40.9	40.9	—	—
	1986	1.25	—	—	26.2	33.0	26.6	—	6.4	40.9	40.9	—	—

See notes on page 169.   Voir notes page 169.   Véanse notas pág. 169.

Table 10 *(cont.)*   **Tableau 10** *(suite)*   **Cuadro 10** *(cont.)*

Country and currency unit / Pays et unité monétaire / Países y unidades monetarias	Financial year / Exercice financier / Ejercicio financiero	Sickness-maternity / Maladie-maternité / Enfermedad, maternidad				Employment injuries / Accidents du travail et maladies professionnelles / Riesgos profesionales				Pensions / Pensions / Pensiones	Unemployment / Chômage / Desempleo	Family allowances / Prestations familiales / Asignaciones familiares	Total amount of benefit expenditure (in millions of national currency units) / Total des dépenses en prestations (millions d'unités monétaires nationales) / Total de egresos por prestaciones (en millones de unidades monetarias nacionales)
		Medical care / Soins médicaux / Asistencia médica	Benefits in kind other than for medical care / Prestations en nature à d'autres titres que les soins médicaux / Prestaciones en especie, excepto asistencia médica	Cash benefits / Prestations en espèces / Prestaciones monetarias	Total	Medical care / Soins médicaux / Asistencia médica	Benefits in kind other than for medical care / Prestations en nature à d'autres titres que les soins médicaux / Prestaciones en especie, excepto asistencia médica	Cash benefits / Prestations en espèces / Prestaciones monetarias	Total				
(1)	(2)	(3)	(4)	(5)	(6)	(7)	(8)	(9)	(10)	(11)	(12)	(13)	(14)
Bolivia (Peso)	1972	59.2	—	2.2	61.7	—	—	11.2	11.2	23.0	—	6.8	354.9
	1975	53.8	—	2.2	56.0	—	—	7.9	7.9	25.8	—	10.3	874.6
	1980	54.2	—	2.4	56.6	—	—	6.0	6.0	36.3	—	1.1	2 952.3
	1983	40.5	—	0.4	40.9	—	—	9.9	9.9	44.7	0.7	3.8	26 855.2
	1984	59.7	—	0.2	59.9	—	—	7.2	7.2	31.3	0.1	1.5	671 450.0
	1985	54.9	—	0.3	55.2	—	—	5.8	5.8	36.4	0.3	2.2	43 367 313.0
Brasil (Cruzado)	1970	30.0	—	17.2	47.2	.	—	3.4	3.4	40.2	—	9.2	7.47
	1975	25.6	—	14.4	40.0	.	—	0.8	0.8	51.6	—	7.6	43.30
	1980	29.1	—	8.8	37.9	—	—	2.6	2.6	53.7	—	5.8	599.40
	1983	21.9	—	11.8	33.7	—	—	0.6	0.6	62.3	—	3.3	6 071.20
	1984	23.4	—	8.8	32.2	—	—	1.6	1.6	62.6	—	3.7	17 737.40
	1985	27.7	—	7.0	34.7	—	—	1.1	1.1	60.4	—	3.8	61 877.20
	1986	25.1	—	7.0	32.1	—	—	0.9	0.9	63.3	—	3.7	164 635.20
Canada (Dollar)	1970	48.2	—	—	48.2	1.0	—	3.1	4.1	27.8	10.2	9.7	7 423.9
	1975	38.8	—	—	38.8	0.8	—	2.9	3.7	26.1	19.9	11.5	17 997.5
	1980	38.1	—	—	38.1	0.8	—	3.5	4.3	32.5	15.3	9.7	31 157.3
	1983	36.3	—	—	36.3	0.8	—	3.7	4.5	30.8	20.4	7.9	49 778.2
	1984	35.8	—	—	35.8	0.8	—	3.9	4.7	32.3	19.5	7.7	53 446.1
	1985	35.0	—	—	35.0	0.8	—	3.9	4.7	33.1	20.1	7.1	58 406.6
Colombia (Peso)	1970	51.2	0.9	4.4	56.5	1.9	—	2.5	4.4	2.1	—	37.0	1 411
	1975	54.2	6.2	4.8	65.2	4.9	1.3	2.8	9.0	14.4	—	11.4	3 779
	1980	40.6	10.8	4.0	55.4	0.5	0.2	2.1	2.8	22.4	—	19.4	20 350
	1983	58.9	—	4.0	62.9	—	—	8.3	8.3	28.8	—	—	46 462
	1984[8]	—	—	9.1	9.1	—	—	7.1	7.1	83.8	—	—	22 607
	1985[8]	—	—	9.6	9.6	—	—	7.5	7.5	82.8	—	—	28 013
	1986[8]	—	—	8.9	8.9	—	—	6.7	6.7	84.4	—	—	40 294

Table (currency values and percentages by country and year; column headers appear on the facing page):

Costa Rica (Colón)

Year	(1)	(2)	(3)	(4)	(5)	(6)	(7)	(8)	(9)	(10)	(11)	(12)
1970	147.6	—	—	6.6	14.9	9.3	1.2	4.4	78.4	7.0	0.2	71.2
1975	605.9	—	—	15.3	7.3	4.4	0.8	2.1	77.4	6.0	0.1	71.3
1980	2 598.1	—	—	15.1[16]	5.1	3.2	0.4	1.5	79.8	3.9	—	75.9
1983	6 954.5	—	—	25.5[16]	4.6	2.9	0.7	1.0	69.9	3.7	—	66.2
1984	9 209.0	—	—	25.0	8.5	5.7	0.3	2.5	66.5	4.4	—	62.1
1985	12 101.6	—	—	25.9	8.3	5.3	0.3	2.7	65.8	3.8	—	62.0
1986	14 781.9	—	—	26.7[16]	7.8	5.3	0.2	2.3	65.5	3.9	—	61.6

Cuba (Peso)

Year	(1)	(2)	(3)	(4)	(5)	(6)	(7)	(8)	(9)	(10)	(11)	(12)
1980	1 111.4	—	...	85.2	1.8	...	...	...	13.0	...	...	...
1983	1 441.2	—	...	...	...	...	...	...	...	...	...	...
1984	1 557.8	—	...	...	...	...	...	...	...	...	...	...
1985	1 673.5	—	...	...	...	...	...	...	...	...	...	...
1986	1 819.1	—	...	...	...	...	...	...	...	...	...	...

Chile (Peso)

Year	(1)	(2)	(3)	(4)	(5)	(6)	(7)	(8)	(9)	(10)	(11)	(12)
1971	10.7	40.7	0.8	35.4	3.2	1.5	—	1.7	19.9	3.6	—	16.3
1975	1 974.3	36.2	1.8	34.0	2.9	1.3	0.3	1.3	25.1	0.3	6.6	18.2
1980	57 989.6	22.9	4.3	43.9	4.9	2.1	0.5	2.3	24.0[17]	3.2	3.4	17.4
1983	195 315.8	10.0	3.6	68.4	2.6	1.1	0.3	1.2	15.4[17]	2.0	1.4	12.0
1984	24 835.0	9.3	2.6	70.4	2.6	1.2	0.3	1.1	15.1[17]	2.1	1.7	11.3
1985	307 000.0	8.7	1.8	70.7	2.5	1.2	0.3	1.0	16.2[17]	2.1	1.4	12.7
1986	376 604.0	7.0	1.1	70.8	2.6	1.2	0.3	1.2	17.4[17]	2.6	1.2	13.6

Dominica (EC Dollar)

Year	(1)	(2)	(3)	(4)	(5)	(6)	(7)	(8)	(9)	(10)	(11)	(12)
1980	0.57	—	—	30.9	—	—	—	—	69.1	69.1	—	—
1983	1.15	—	—	40.8	—	—	—	—	59.2	47.3	—	11.9
1984	2.17	—	—	38.5	—	—	—	—	61.4	33.1	—	28.3
1985	2.57	—	—	40.5	0.9	0.9	—	—	58.6	31.8	—	26.8
1986	2.97	—	—	45.4	3.8	3.8	—	—	50.8	26.5	—	24.3

República Dominicana (Peso)

Year	(1)	(2)	(3)	(4)	(5)	(6)	(7)	(8)	(9)	(10)	(11)	(12)
1984	45 194	—	—	26.6	—	—	—	—	73.4	—	—	73.4
1985	46 343	—	—	27.5	—	—	—	—	72.5	—	—	72.5
1986	56 365	—	—	32.6	—	—	—	—	67.4	—	—	67.4

Ecuador (Sucre)

Year	(1)	(2)	(3)	(4)	(5)	(6)	(7)	(8)	(9)	(10)	(11)	(12)
1972	1 239	—	10.5	59.2	0.7	0.7	—	—	29.6	1.8	0.2	27.6
1974	1 732	—	9.5	60.6	0.8	0.8	—	—	29.1	1.7	0.2	27.2
1980	4 573	—	6.4	76.7	2.2	2.2	—	—	14.7	2.2	—	12.5
1983	9 957	—	5.7	75.8	1.6	1.6	—	—	16.9	1.9	—	15.0
1984	14 615	—	3.7	60.8	1.3	1.3	—	—	34.2	—	—	34.2
1985	18 581	—	3.9	58.2	1.2	1.2	—	—	36.7	—	—	36.7
1986	24 375	—	3.9	59.0	1.4	1.4	—	—	35.8	—	—	35.8

El Salvador (Colón)

Year	(1)	(2)	(3)	(4)	(5)	(6)	(7)	(8)	(9)	(10)	(11)	(12)
1970	14.18	—	—	1.3	9.8	5.7	—	4.1	88.9	15.7	1.1	72.1
1975	34.09	—	—	7.8	1.2	0.7	—	0.5	91.0	19.0	0.7	71.3
1980	93.05	—	—	12.1	—	—	—	—	87.9	21.8	0.4	65.7
1983	122.28	—	—	17.8	—	—	—	—	75.8	16.3	0.3	59.2
1984	138.10	—	—	26.4	6.4	6.4	—	—	73.5	15.1	0.2	58.2
1985	148.90	—	—	24.5	—	—	—	—	75.5	16.4	0.1	59.0
1986	143.70	—	—	34.5	—	—	—	—	65.4	16.6	0.2	48.6

Grenada (EC Dollar)

Year	(1)	(2)	(3)	(4)	(5)	(6)	(7)	(8)	(9)	(10)	(11)	(12)
1981	—	—	—	—	—	—	—	—	—	100	—	—
1983[18]	0.01	—	—	21.4	—	—	—	—	100	—	—	—
1984	0.12	—	—	36.6	—	—	—	—	—	—	—	—
1985	0.32	—	—	58.6	—	—	—	—	—	—	—	—
1986	0.68	—	—	—	—	—	—	—	—	—	—	—

See notes on page 169.   *Voir notes page 169.*   *Véanse notas pág. 169.*

Table 10 *(cont.)* **Tableau 10** *(suite)* **Cuadro 10** *(cont.)*

Country and currency unit / Pays et unité monétaire / Países y unidades monetarias	Financial year / Exercice financier / Ejercicio financiero	Sickness-maternity / Maladie-maternité / Enfermedad, maternidad				Employment injuries / Accidents du travail et maladies professionnelles / Riesgos profesionales				Pensions / Pensions / Pensiones	Unemployment / Chômage / Desempleo	Family allowances / Prestations familiales / Asignaciones familiares	Total amount of benefit expenditure (in millions of national currency units) / Total des dépenses en prestations (millions d'unités monétaires nationales) / Total de egresos por prestaciones (en millones de unidades monetarias nacionales)
		Medical care / Soins médicaux / Asistencia médica	Benefits in kind other than for medical care / Prestations en nature à d'autres titres que les soins médicaux / Prestaciones en especie, excepto asistencia médica	Cash benefits / Prestations en espèces / Prestaciones monetarias	Total / Total / Total	Medical care / Soins médicaux / Asistencia médica	Benefits in kind other than for medical care / Prestations en nature à d'autres titres que les soins médicaux / Prestaciones en especie, excepto asistencia médica	Cash benefits / Prestations en espèces / Prestaciones monetarias	Total / Total / Total				
(1)	(2)	(3)	(4)	(5)	(6)	(7)	(8)	(9)	(10)	(11)	(12)	(13)	(14)
Guatemala (Quetzal)	1970	42.9	—	7.4	50.3	25.2	—	24.5	49.7	—	—	—	15.3
	1975	44.3	—	6.9	51.2	25.8	—	22.8	48.6	0.2	—	—	29.5
	1980	43.4	—	6.2	49.6	27.3	—	18.1	45.4	5.0	—	—	66.3
	1983	36.8	—	5.9	42.7	21.6	—	19.4	41.0	16.4	—	—	80.0
	1984	35.9	—	5.4	41.3	20.6	—	17.5	38.1	20.6	—	—	85.5
	1985	35.4	—	5.4	40.8	20.4	—	16.3	36.7	22.5	—	—	92.3
	1986	34.3	—	5.2	39.5	19.9	—	13.9	33.8	26.6	—	—	115.6
Guyana (Dollar)	1972	—	—	25.6	25.6	14.5	—	54.6	69.1	5.3	—	—	3.55
	1975	—	—	32.2	32.2	11.8	—	37.9	49.7	18.1	—	—	3.09
	1980	—	—	18.7	18.7	4.9	—	16.6	21.5	59.8	—	—	12.38
	1983	—	—	15.1	15.1	10.5	—	14.7	25.2	59.6	—	—	16.44
	1984	—	—	13.9	13.9	11.7	—	13.1	24.8	61.3	—	—	18.79
	1985	—	—	12.5	12.5	11.6	—	12.2	23.8	63.7	—	—	19.82
	1986	—	—	6.5	6.5	5.3	—	11.0	16.3	77.2	—	—	46.67
Honduras (Lempira)	1970	88.7	—	8.7	97.4	.	—	2.6	2.6	—	—	—	3.91
	1971	90.4	—	8.1	98.5	.	—	1.5	1.5	—	—	—	4.56
	1981	81.7	—	12.0	93.7	—	—	—	—	6.3	—	—	37.14
	1983	80.1	—	11.2	91.3	—	—	—	—	8.7	—	—	44.67
	1984	77.6	—	12.3	89.9	—	—	—	—	10.1	—	—	51.89
	1985	75.7	—	12.4	88.1	—	—	—	—	11.8	—	—	55.22
	1986	74.3	—	11.9	86.2	—	—	—	—	13.8	—	—	58.95
Jamaica (Dollar)	1970	—	—	—	—	0.3	—	2.2	2.5	97.5	—	—	1.26
	1975	—	—	—	—	0.8	—	6.4	7.2	92.8	—	—	6.87
	1980[19]	—	—	0.2	0.2	0.1	—	8.1	8.2	91.6	—	—	21.66
	1983	—	—	0.1	0.1	0.1	—	5.8	5.9	94.0	—	—	38.31
	1984	—	—	0.1	0.1	0.2	—	5.7	5.9	94.0	—	—	41.49
	1985	—	—	0.1	0.1	0.1	—	5.5	5.6	94.2	—	—	46.14
	1986	—	—	12.6	12.6	0.2	—	4.7	4.9	82.4	—	—	56.95

Country / Year	(1)	(2)	(3)	(4)	(5)	(6)	(7)	(8)	(9)	(10)	(11)	(12)
México (Peso)												
1970	6 908	—	—	19.1	9.1	4.3	—	4.8	71.8	4.9	—	66.9
1974	15 336	—	—	19.1	10.0	4.5	—	5.5	70.9	4.8	0.0	66.1
1980	62 764	—	—	19.4	11.3	5.9	1.6	5.4	69.3	5.3	1.2	62.8
1983	261 233	0.4	—	22.5	10.1	5.0	—	3.5	67.0	4.7	31.0	31.3
1984	410 088	—	—	26.2	10.9	5.1	—	5.8	62.9	4.7	—	58.2
1985	623 612	—	—	28.7	12.3	5.9	—	6.4	58.9	5.3	—	53.6
1986	1 000 051	—	—	30.0	11.4	6.3	—	5.1	58.6	5.9	—	52.7
Panamá (Balboa)												
1972	55.6	—	—	34.6	7.3	3.4	—	3.9	58.1	6.7	0.1	51.3
1975	85.9	—	—	36.1	9.7	3.6	—	6.1	54.2	5.6	—	48.6
1980	176.1	—	0.4	40.0	4.7	2.8	—	1.9	55.3	4.4	—	50.9
1983	277.1	—	—	41.9	3.3	3.3	—	—	54.5	3.9	—	50.6
1984	321.6	—	—	41.3	4.7	3.3	—	1.4	54.0	3.4	—	50.6
1985	342.0	—	—	43.5	4.5	3.3	—	1.2	52.1	3.6	—	48.5
1986	380.1	—	—	46.8	6.4	3.2	—	3.2	46.8	3.3	—	43.5
Perú (Inti)												
1981	186.27	—	—	32.1	7.8	0.4	—	7.4	60.0	—	—	60.0
1983	535.68	—	—	34.1	7.2	0.4	—	6.8	58.7	—	—	58.7
1984	—	—	—	...	...	...	—	...	...	—	—	...
1985	—	—	—	...	...	...	—	...	...	—	—	...
1986	—	—	—	...	...	...	—	...	...	—	—	...
St. Lucia (EC Dollar)												
1981	0.72	—	—	65.0	4.3	4.3	—	—	30.7	30.7	—	—
1983	0.98	—	—	66.0	1.0	1.0	—	—	33.0	33.0	—	—
1984	2.02	—	—	50.5[20]	—	—	—	—	49.5	—	—	49.5
1985	0.87	—	—	100[20]	...	...	—	—	...	...	—	...
1986	2.07	—	—	51.7	...	...	—	—	48.3	—	—	48.3
Trinidad and Tobago (Dollar)												
1970	4.83	—	—	87.0	13.0	13.0	—	—	—	—	—	—
1975	16.66	—	—	71.4	7.2	7.2	—	—	21.4	21.4	—	—
1980	42.61	—	—	79.0	7.9	7.9	—	—	13.1	13.1	—	—
1983	211.77	—	—	89.4	3.3[21]	3.3	—	—	7.3	7.3	—	—
1984	231.12	—	—	90.2	3.2[21]	3.2	—	—	6.6	6.6	—	—
1985	225.82	—	—	89.7	3.5[21]	3.5	—	—	6.8	6.8	—	—
1986	259.39	—	—	91.3	3.0[21]	3.0	—	—	5.6	5.6	—	—
United States (Dollar)												
1970	44 117	—	7.2	69.5	6.3	4.1	—	2.2	17.0	1.5	—	15.5
1975	99 587	—	12.7	65.9	6.3	4.4	—	1.9	15.1	0.9	—	14.2
1980	182 794	—	8.1	55.1	7.0	5.0	—	2.0	29.8	0.7	—	29.1
1983	274 614	—	10.7[22]	53.8	6.2	4.3	—	1.9	29.2	9.0	—	20.2
1984	27 559	—	6.2[22]	59.5	6.9	4.7	—	2.2	29.6	7.1	—	22.5
1985	298 265	—	5.4[22]	57.3	7.1	4.7	—	2.4	30.2	6.9	0.0	23.3
1986	315 745	—	5.1[22]	57.1	7.6	5.0	—	2.6	30.3	6.8	—	23.5
Uruguay (Nuevo peso)												
1975	456	16.9	4.0	73.6	1.9	1.0	—	0.9	3.6	1.4	—	2.2
1980	6 911	7.5	1.6	79.9	4.7	3.7	—	1.0	6.3	1.5	—	4.8
1983	12 510	10.7	4.5	76.1	...	...	—	...	8.8	8.8	—	—
1984	29 011	19.8	1.7	73.3	...	...	—	...	5.3	0.9	—	4.4
1985	43 140	7.6	1.5	81.4	...	...	—	...	9.5	1.6	—	7.9
1986	85 666	6.7	1.4	81.8	...	...	—	...	10.1	1.6	—	8.5
Venezuela (Bolivar)												
1970	568	—	—	5.3	...	...	—	...	94.7	14.1	—	80.6
1975	1 169	—	—	28.0	...	...	—	...	72.0	12.3	—	59.7
1980	2 869	—	—	34.2	...	...	—	...	65.8	8.9	—	56.9
1983	3 666[7]	—	—	...	...	...	—	...	...	...	—	...
1984	4 045.00	—	—	40.7	...	...	—	...	59.3	5.4	—	53.9
1985	4 363.70	—	—	42.3	...	...	—	...	57.7	4.9	—	52.8
1986	5 410.90	—	—	34.1	...	...	—	...	65.9	4.2	—	61.7

See notes on page 169.   *Voir notes page 169.*   *Véanse notas pág. 169.*

Table 10 (*cont.*) **Tableau 10** (*suite*) **Cuadro 10** (*cont.*)

Country and currency unit / Pays et unité monétaire / Paises y unidades monetarias	Financial year / Exercice financier / Ejercicio financiero	Sickness-maternity / Maladie-maternité / Enfermedad, maternidad				Employment injuries / Accidents du travail et maladies professionnelles / Riesgos profesionales				Pensions / Pensions / Pensiones	Unemploy-ment / Chômage / Desempleo	Family allowances / Prestations familiales / Asignaciones familiares	Total amount of benefit expenditure (in millions of national currency units) / Total des dépenses en prestations (millions d'unités monétaires nationales) / Total de egresos por prestaciones (en millones de unidades monetarias nacionales)
		Medical care / Soins médicaux / Asistencia médica	Benefits in kind other than for medical care / Prestations en nature à d'autres titres que les soins médicaux / Prestaciones en especie, excepto asistencia médica	Cash benefits / Prestations en espèces / Prestaciones monetarias	Total / Total / Total	Medical care / Soins médicaux / Asistencia médica	Benefits in kind other than medical care / Prestations en nature à d'autres titres que les soins médicaux / Prestaciones en especie, excepto asistencia médica	Cash benefits / Prestations en espèces / Prestaciones monetarias	Total / Total / Total				
(1)	(2)	(3)	(4)	(5)	(6)	(7)	(8)	(9)	(10)	(11)	(12)	(13)	(14)

ASIA – ASIE – ASIA

Bahrain (Dinar)	1978	—	—	—	—	4.5	4.9	7.8	17.2	82.8	—	—	0.71
	1980	—	—	—	—	6.2	10.9	12.2	29.3	70.7	—	—	0.79
	1983	—	—	—	—	5.2	6.6	7.7	19.5	80.6	—	—	2.73
	1984	—	—	—	—	0.7	1.5	12.1	14.3	85.7	—	—	3.62
	1985	—	—	—	—	0.6	1.7	12.0	14.3	85.7	—	—	4.43
	1986	—	—	—	—	0.3	1.4	12.6	14.3	85.7	—	—	5.53
Bangladesh[8] (Taka)	1975	—	—	17.1	17.1	—	—	11.9	11.9	71.0	—	—	2.86
	1980	—	—	93.3	93.3	—	—	6.7	6.7	.	—	—	3.14
	1983	—	—	46.3	46.3	—	—	10.3	10.3	43.4	—	—	12.29
	1984	—	—	43.7	43.7	—	—	21.9	21.9	34.3	—	—	15.49
	1985	—	—	30.9	30.9	—	—	29.7	29.7	39.5	—	—	16.17
	1986	—	—	33.5	33.5	—	—	29.6	29.6	36.8	—	—	17.54
Cyprus (Pound)	1970	—	—	2.5	2.5	0.3	—	2.8	3.1	92.3	2.1	—	3.26
	1975	—	—	2.1	2.1	0.0	—	2.0	2.0	85.6	10.3	—	8.21
	1980	—	—	2.7	2.7	0.0	—	1.8	1.8	94.4	1.1	—	17.61
	1983	—	—	4.9	4.9	0.0	—	1.7	1.7	86.2	7.2	—	38.47
	1984	—	—	5.6	5.6	0.0	—	1.8	1.8	85.0	7.7	—	45.98
	1985	—	—	5.9	5.9	0.0	—	1.8	1.8	84.7	7.5	—	53.10
	1986	—	—	6.2	6.2	0.0	—	1.8	1.8	81.7	10.3	—	63.11
India (Rupee)	1970	11.8	0.1	8.7	20.6	—	—	4.4	4.4	75.0	—	—	1 761.8
	1975	9.6	0.0	4.8	14.4	—	—	3.0	3.0	82.6	—	—	3 418.7
	1980	11.9	1.0	9.1	22.0	—	—	4.4	4.4	73.6	—	—	6 402.7
	1983	9.8	0.2	10.5	20.5	—	—	0.3	0.3	79.2	—	—	9 609.8
	1984	10.1	—	—	10.1	—	—	0.3	0.3	89.6	—	—	8 608.5
	1985	10.5	—	—	10.5	—	—	0.3	0.3	89.2	—	—	9 639.4
Indonesia (Rupiah)	1981	—	—	—	—	—	—	72.0	72.0	28.0	—	—	2.50
	1983	—	—	—	—	—	—	61.5	61.5	38.5	—	—	4.73
	1984	—	—	—	—	—	—	50.6	50.6	49.4	—	—	5 305.66
	1985	—	—	—	—	—	—	47.7	47.7	52.3	—	—	6 721.21
	1986	—	—	—	—	—	—	40.8	40.8	59.2	—	—	9 075.25

Country (currency)	Year												
Iran, Islamic Rep. of[8] (Rial)	1981	46.6	—	2.9	49.5	—	—	0.6	0.6	49.9	—	—	82 859
	1983	48.0	—	3.3	51.3	—	—	0.8	0.8	47.9	—	—	100 600
	1984	100	—	—	100	—	—	—	—	—	—	—	48 600
	1985	100	—	—	100	—	—	—	—	—	—	—	58 200
	1986	100	—	—	100	—	—	—	—	—	—	—	73 271
Israel (New Shekel)	1970	42.0	1.2	4.3	47.5	—	0.2	5.0	5.2	29.3	—	18.0	0.9
	1975	26.7	0.9	2.9	30.5	—	0.1	3.6	3.7	35.7	0.5	29.6	5.9
	1980	37.5	0.0	1.9	39.4	—	0.0	2.6	2.6	36.8[23]	1.0	20.1	11.5
	1983	34.4	0.0	1.9	36.3	—	0.0	2.5	2.5	41.5	1.0	18.6	168.6
	1984	40.1	0.0	1.6	41.7	—	0.0	2.5	2.5	38.8	1.3	15.7	974.9
	1985	33.7	0.0	1.6	35.3	—	0.0	2.6	2.6	42.5	1.7	17.9	3 174.8
	1986	32.3	0.0	1.7	34.0	—	0.0	3.1	3.1	42.1	1.9	18.7	4 509.8
Japan (Yen)	1970	70.0	—	5.0	75.0	2.6	—	3.2	5.8	11.6	7.6	—	2 116 852
	1975	54.7	—	4.0	58.7	1.5	—	2.3	3.8	26.2	9.4	1.9	7 517 034
	1980	49.0	—	3.4	52.4	1.2	—	2.2	3.4	37.3	5.8	1.1	16 413 757
	1983	47.7	—	3.0	50.7	1.0	—	2.5	3.5	39.3	5.8	0.7	22 378 239
	1984	46.8	—	2.1	48.9	1.0	—	2.5	3.4	41.2	5.7	0.7	23 545 441
	1985	46.8	—	2.1	48.9	0.9	—	2.4	3.3	42.7	4.4	0.6	25 071 236
	1986	45.3	—	1.9	47.2	0.8	—	2.2	3.1	44.8	4.3	0.6	27 848 036
Jordan (Dinar)	1980	—	—	—	—	33.3	—	—	33.3	66.7	—	—	0.03
	1983	—	—	—	—	7.8	3.5	8.6	19.9	80.1	—	—	2.56
	1984	—	—	—	—	4.9	—	10.2	15.1	84.9	—	—	3.64
	1985	—	—	—	—	4.5	—	9.6	14.1	85.9	—	—	5.32
	1986	—	—	—	—	3.8	—	9.8	13.6	86.4	—	—	7.38
Kuwait (Dinar)	1980	—	—	—	—	—	—	—	—	100	—	—	28.90
	1983	—	—	—	—	—	—	—	—	100	—	—	75.77
	1984	—	—	—	—	—	—	—	—	100	—	—	75.77
	1985	—	—	—	—	—	—	—	—	100	—	—	85.41
	1986	—	—	—	—	—	—	—	—	100	—	—	158.76
Malaysia (Ringgit)	1970	—	—	—	—	—	—	5.1	5.1	94.9	—	—	82.53
	1975	—	—	—	—	0.5	—	4.3	4.8	95.2	—	—	128.24
	1980	—	—	—	—	0.4	—	5.0	5.4	94.6	—	—	254.59
	1983	—	—	—	—	0.3	0.0	3.8	4.1	95.9	—	—	538.79
	1984	—	—	—	—	0.3	0.0	3.6	3.9	96.1	—	—	635.18
	1985	—	—	—	—	0.4	0.0	4.2	4.6	95.4	—	—	640.14
	1986	—	—	—	—	0.3	0.0	4.9	5.2	94.7	—	—	646.41
Myanmar (Kyat)	1970	1.1[24]	—	50.3	51.4	—	—	48.6	48.6	—	—	—	4.65
	1975	1.6	—	50.1	51.7	—	—	48.3	48.3	—	—	—	5.05
	1980	59.6	—	29.6	89.2	—	—	9.1	9.1	—	—	—	14.86
	1983	62.6	—	27.3	89.9	—	—	8.5	8.5	—	—	—	17.87
	1984	62.9	—	28.2	91.1	—	—	8.9	8.9	—	—	—	17.85
	1985	59.7	—	30.5	90.2	—	—	9.8	9.8	—	—	—	16.72
	1986	62.6	—	28.3	90.9	—	—	9.1	9.1	—	—	—	18.49
Pakistan (Rupee)	1965	—	—	—	—	—	—	100	100	—	—	—	1.50
	1980	81.1	—	18.9	100[26]	—	—	—	—	—	1.7[25]	—	57.09
	1983	85.3	—	14.6	100[27]	—	—	—	—	0.0	1.5[25]	—	102.06
	1984	85.3	0.1	7.1	92.4	—	—	2.0	2.0	5.7	—	—	120.20
	1985	74.1	—	5.7	79.8	—	—	1.3	1.3	18.9	—	—	146.80
	1986	60.3	—	4.5	64.8	—	—	1.0	1.0	34.2	—	—	202.40

See notes on page 169.   *Voir notes page 169.*   *Véanse notas pág. 169.*

Table 10 *(cont.)* **Tableau 10** *(suite)* **Cuadro 10** *(cont.)*

Country and currency unit / Pays et unité monétaire / Países y unidades monetarias	Financial year / Exercice financier / Ejercicio financiero	Sickness-maternity / Maladie-maternité / Enfermedad, maternidad				Employment injuries / Accidents du travail et maladies professionnelles / Riesgos profesionales				Pensions / Pensions / Pensiones	Unemployment / Chômage / Desempleo	Family allowances / Prestations familiales / Asignaciones familiares	Total amount of benefit expenditure (in millions of national currency units) / Total des dépenses en prestations (millions d'unités monétaires nationales) / Total de egresos por prestaciones (en millones de unidades monetarias nacionales)
		Medical care / Soins médicaux / Asistencia médica	Benefits in kind other than for medical care / Prestations en nature d'autres titres que les soins médicaux / Prestaciones en especie, excepto asistencia médica	Cash benefits / Prestations en espèces / Prestaciones monetarias	Total / Total / Total	Medical care / Soins médicaux / Asistencia médica	Benefits in kind other than for medical care / Prestations en nature d'autres titres que les soins médicaux / Prestaciones en especie, excepto asistencia médica	Cash benefits / Prestations en espèces / Prestaciones monetarias	Total / Total / Total				
(1)	(2)	(3)	(4)	(5)	(6)	(7)	(8)	(9)	(10)	(11)	(12)	(13)	(14)
Philippines[8] (Peso)	1970	—	—	29.2	29.2	1.7	—	26.6	28.3	42.5	—	—	64.4
	1978	—	—	—	—	40.0	—	1.2	41.2	58.8	—	—	478.5
	1980	—	—	—	—	33.6	—	1.7	35.3	64.7	—	—	659.4
	1983	—	—	—	—	23.3[27]	—	3.0	26.3	73.7[27]	—	—	1 174.2
	1984	18.2	—	11.7	29.9	1.5	—	3.0	4.5	65.6	—	—	1 315.7
	1985	17.3	—	11.5	28.8	—	—	4.2	4.2	66.8	—	—	1 531.5
	1986	15.3	—	9.4	24.7	1.3	—	3.1	4.4	71.0	—	—	1 829.7
Singapore (Dollar)	1970	—	—	—	—	—	—	3.4	3.4	96.6	—	—	46.73
	1975	—	—	—	—	—	—	2.1	2.1	97.9	—	—	221.56
	1980	—	—	—	—	—	—	2.1	2.1	97.9	—	—	795.60
	1983	—	—	—	—	—	—	1.9	1.9	98.1	—	—	1 737.12
	1984	—	—	—	—	—	—	1.0	1.0	99.0	—	—	3 497.76
	1985	—	—	—	—	—	—	1.1	1.1	98.8	—	—	3 356.92
	1986	—	—	—	—	—	—	0.8	0.8	99.2	—	—	3 834.74
Sri Lanka (Rupee)	1970	—	—	—	—	—	—	3.3	3.3	96.7	—	—	36.0
	1975	—	—	—	—	—	—	0.2	0.2	99.8	—	—	87.7
	1980	—	—	—	—	—	—	0.3	0.3	99.7	—	—	205.5
	1983	—	—	—	—	—	—	0.3	0.3	99.7[28]	—	—	387.7
	1984	—	—	—	—	—	—	0.5	0.5	99.5	—	—	568.86
	1985	—	—	—	—	—	—	0.5	0.5	99.5	—	—	559.93
	1986	—	—	—	—	—	—	0.3	0.3	99.7	—	—	426.09
Rép. arabe syrienne (Livre syrienne)	1984	—	—	—	—	—	—	—	—	—	100[29]	—	376
	1985	—	—	—	—	—	—	—	—	—	100[29]	—	452
	1986	—	—	—	—	—	—	—	—	—	100[29]	—	494
Thailand (Baht)	1980	—	—	—	—	42.2	1.8	56.0	100	—	—	—	98.28
	1983	—	—	—	—	41.0	—	59.0	100	—	—	—	113.93
	1984	—	—	—	—	24.7	—	75.3	100	—	—	—	247.18
	1985	—	—	—	—	27.7	—	72.3	100	—	—	—	232.61
	1986	—	—	—	—	30.4	—	69.6	100	—	—	—	218.48

EUROPE – EUROPE – EUROPA

Countries with a market economy – Pays à économie de marché – Países con economía de mercado

Austria (Shilling)

Year												
1970	48 454	14.7	2.9	56.2	3.3	2.3	0.1	0.9	22.9	4.2	5.1	13.6
1975	92 379	13.2	4.0	56.8	3.2	2.0	0.2	1.0	22.8	2.9	5.0	14.9
1980	159 482	15.4	3.5	55.0	3.1	2.0	0.2	0.9	23.0	2.9	4.7	15.4
1983	210 744	16.3	6.2	53.9	2.9	1.8	0.2	0.9	20.7	2.2	4.0	14.5
1984	230 827	13.2	6.0	58.2	2.6	1.6	0.3	0.7	20.0	2.0	3.9	14.1
1985	246 715	12.9	6.3	58.0	2.6	1.6	0.3	0.7	20.2	2.0	4.0	14.1
1986	262 511	12.4	6.6	58.2	2.6	1.6	0.3	0.7	20.3	2.0	4.1	14.2

Belgique (Franc belge)

Year												
1970	159 518.2	22.3	5.1	33.8	5.9	5.1	—	0.8	32.9	10.1	0.1	22.7
1975	395 566.4	16.7	11.4	33.9	5.2	4.8	—	0.4	32.8	9.8	0.1	22.9
1980	693 917.3	13.1	17.8	32.9	4.5	4.2	—	0.3	31.7	9.5	—	22.2
1983	926 573.7	12.8	21.1	31.7	3.7	3.5	—	0.2	30.7	8.7	—	22.0
1984	942 012.0	12.6	20.3	33.4	3.8	3.5	—	0.3	29.9	8.7	—	21.2
1985	977 987.0	12.4	20.5	33.8	3.7	3.4	—	0.3	29.6	8.8	—	20.8
1986	1 030 982.0	12.0	20.3	33.5	3.5	3.2	—	0.3	30.7	8.4	—	22.3

Denmark (Krone)

Year												
1970	8 989.0	12.5	5.9	59.7	2.8	2.8	—	—	19.1	5.2	—	13.9
1975	22 536.2	11.1	13.3	55.2	1.3	1.3	—	—	19.1	8.7	0.1	10.3
1980	69 819.6	4.3	16.9	42.0	0.8	0.8	—	—	36.0	6.8	0.1	29.1
1983	98 884.6	3.0	22.1	41.6	0.9	0.9	—	—	32.5	4.7	0.1	27.7
1984	103 170.6	2.7	21.0	43.4	0.9	0.9	—	—	32.0	4.6	0.0	27.4
1985	108 297.1	2.5	18.8	44.5	1.0	1.0	—	—	33.1	5.5	0.0	27.6
1986	119 952.4	2.2	22.4	42.4	1.6	1.6	—	—	31.5	5.7	0.0	25.8

España (Peseta)

Year												
1975	544 158.8	11.1	5.3	37.9	5.3	4.0	0.0	1.3	40.4	10.1	—	30.3
1980	2 031 787.5	2.8	15.7	43.1	3.4	2.7	0.1	0.7	35.0	8.8	—	26.2
1983	2 277 565.9	1.9	15.0	50.4	3.6	2.6	0.1	0.9	29.2	5.6	—	23.6
1984	3 690 880.0	1.9	17.5	50.8	3.6	2.5	0.0	1.0	26.2	4.2	—	22.0
1985	4 213 362.0	1.6	19.5	50.3	3.4	2.4	0.0	1.0	25.3	3.9	—	21.4
1986	4 688 525.0	1.3	18.5	51.1	3.4	2.4	0.0	1.0	25.6	3.8	—	21.8

Finland (Markka)

Year												
1970	2 660.6	12.1	3.5	62.7	5.0	4.5	—	0.5	16.7	8.7	—	8.0
1975	7 956.3	8.9	2.6	67.4	4.0	3.7	—	0.3	17.1	9.1	—	8.0
1980	23 694.2	5.3	4.3	48.9	1.8	1.6	—	0.2	39.7	4.2	—	35.5
1983	39 503.4	5.7	3.7	47.2	2.1	1.9	—	0.2	41.4	7.8	—	33.6
1984	52 952.4	4.4	2.6	55.9	2.0	1.8	—	0.2	35.1	6.6	—	28.5
1985	61 045.0	4.1	4.7	54.5	1.7	1.6	—	0.1	34.9	6.3	—	28.6
1986	67 525.4	3.9	4.8	54.7	1.8	1.7	—	0.1	34.9	6.4	—	28.5

France (Franc français)

Year												
1970	95 343.4	20.7[35]	1.1[34]	35.5[33]	35.5[32]	0.5	0.0	—	42.2	10.1[31]	.	32.1[30]
1975	236 703.9	15.1[35]	2.6[34]	42.1[33]	0.1[32]	0.0	0.1	—	40.1	8.5[31]	0.9	30.7[30]
1980	514 792.1	14.1[35]	6.5[34]	41.3[33]	—	—	—	—	37.8	7.4[31]	0.7	29.7[30]
1983	837 211.7	14.2[35]	10.4[34]	44.5[33]	—	—	—	—	30.9	—	0.6	30.3[36]
1984	925 725.8	14.0[35]	10.6[34]	44.3[33]	—	—	—	—	31.2	—	0.5	30.7[36]
1985	986 488.4	14.6[35]	10.6[34]	43.9[33]	—	—	—	—	30.9	—	0.5	30.4[36]
1986	1 056 491.0	14.8[35]	10.0[34]	44.1[33]	—	—	—	—	31.2	—	0.3	30.9[36]

See notes on page 169.   *Voir notes page 169.*   Véanse notas pág. 169.

Table 10 *(cont.)* **Tableau 10** *(suite)* **Cuadro 10** *(cont.)*

Country and currency unit / Pays et unité monétaire / Países y unidades monetarias (1)	Financial year / Exercice financier / Ejercicio financiero (2)	Sickness-maternity — Maladie-maternité — Enfermedad, maternidad: Medical care / Soins médicaux / Asistencia médica (3)	Benefits in kind other than for medical care / Prestations en nature à d'autres titres que les soins médicaux / Prestaciones en especie, excepto asistencia médica (4)	Cash benefits / Prestations en espèces / Prestaciones monetarias (5)	Total (6)	Employment injuries — Accidents du travail et maladies professionnelles — Riesgos profesionales: Medical care / Soins médicaux / Asistencia médica (7)	Benefits in kind other than for medical care / Prestations en nature à d'autres titres que les soins médicaux / Prestaciones en especie, excepto asistencia médica (8)	Cash benefits / Prestations en espèces / Prestaciones monetarias (9)	Total (10)	Pensions / Pensions / Pensiones (11)	Unemployment / Chômage / Desempleo (12)	Family allowances / Prestations familiales / Asignaciones familiares (13)	Total amount of benefit expenditure (in millions of national currency units) / Total des dépenses en prestations (millions d'unités monétaires nationales) / Total de egresos por prestaciones (en millones de unidades monetarias nacionales) (14)
Germany, Fed. Rep. of (Deutsche Mark)	1970	25.6	—	4.3	29.9	—	0.7	3.9	4.6	58.6	3.3	3.6	79 293
	1975	29.5	—	3.1	32.6	—	0.8	2.7	3.5	48.3	7.6	8.0	179 860
	1980	27.4	1.1	3.1	31.6	0.5	0.3	2.5	3.3	51.5	7.4	6.2	274 918
	1983	26.6	1.2	2.3	30.1	0.5	0.3	2.3	3.1	50.4	11.7	4.6	321 388
	1984	27.5	1.3	2.3	31.1	0.5	0.3	2.3	3.1	50.9	10.6	4.2	335 822
	1985	28.2	1.4	2.2	31.8	0.5	0.3	2.2	3.0	50.6	10.6	4.0	345 738
	1986	28.7	1.4	2.2	32.3	0.5	0.3	2.2	3.0	50.1	10.8	3.8	356 613
Grèce (Drachme)	1970	16.8[26]	—	3.0[26]	19.8[26]	—	—	—	—[26]	73.3	—[37]	6.9[38]	19 544
	1975	19.6[26]	—	3.0[26]	22.6[26]	—	—	—	—[26]	69.4	—[37]	8.0[38]	42 304
	1980	19.8[26]	—	5.0[26]	24.8[26]	—	—	—	—[26]	67.8	—[37]	7.4[38]	138 189
	1983	13.4[26]	—	3.5[26]	16.9[26]	—	—	—	—[26]	76.5	6.6	—	355 815
	1984	12.2[26]	—	3.5[26]	15.7[26]	—	—	—	—[26]	78.4	5.9	—	491 743
	1985	11.2[26]	—	3.6[26]	14.8[26]	—	—	—	—[26]	79.0	6.3	—	637 473
Iceland (Króna)	1984	51.7	—	6.3	58.0	—	—	0.5	0.5	37.4	3.1	1.1	5 871
	1985	51.0	—	6.5	57.5	—	—	0.5	0.5	38.7	2.2	1.1	8 386
	1986	52.5	—	6.2	58.7	—	—	0.6	0.6	38.0	1.8	1.0	11 092
Ireland (Pound)	1970	0.8	—	16.5	17.3	—	—	3.0	3.0	47.6	16.7	15.5	89.9
	1975	0.7	—	13.3	14.0	—	—	3.7	3.7	46.2	22.9	13.2	357.6
Italie (Lire (milliards))	1970	27.8	0.2	3.3	31.3	1.0	0.0	4.2	5.2	50.1	1.7	11.7	6 840
	1975	11.8	—	5.3	17.1	0.1	0.0	3.6	3.7	64.4	3.3	11.5	16 930
	1980	36.1	—	3.6	39.7	—	0.0	3.5	3.5	48.0	3.4	5.4	45 857
	1983[39]	33.3	—	4.2	37.5	—	0.0	3.3	3.3	49.7	4.8	4.7	89 741
	1984[39]	—	—	3.7	3.7	—	—	.	.[5]	86.2	4.1	6.1	72 681
	1985[39]	—	—	3.6	3.6	—	—	.	.[5]	87.9	3.4	5.1	81 310
	1986[39]	—	—	3.7	3.7	—	—	.	.[5]	88.5	3.6	4.3	89 521

Country (Currency)	Year												
Luxembourg (Franc luxembourgeois)	1970	17.5	—	3.8	21.3	0.8	—	8.4	9.2	55.0	0.0	14.5	6 332.3
	1975	21.3	0.4	8.3	30.0	0.7	—	7.1	7.8	51.1	—	11.1	13 992.3
	1980	24.4	0.8	5.4	30.6	0.5	0.0	5.9	6.4	52.7	—	10.3	24 998.1
	1983	24.5	0.9	5.0	30.4	—	0.8	5.6	6.4	53.3	—	10.1	31 992.4
	1984	25.6	0.3	5.0	30.9	0.8	0.0	5.5	6.3	52.9	—	9.9	34 461.6
	1985	26.5	0.3	5.4	32.2	0.8	0.0	5.5	6.3	52.1	—	9.4	35 924.7
	1986	27.1	0.3	5.0	32.4	0.9	0.0	5.2	6.1	51.6	—	10.0	38 823.0
Malta (Lira)	1970	—	—	7.4	7.4	—	—	1.3	1.3	87.6	3.7	—	2.60
	1975	—	—	6.6	6.6	—	—	1.0	1.0	87.9	4.5	—	9.30
	1980	—	—	2.3	2.3	—	—	0.8	0.8	69.4	1.0	26.5	34.39
	1983	—	—	2.1	2.1	—	—	1.0	1.0	70.8	2.0	24.0	53.36
	1984	21.0	—	1.5	22.5	—	—	0.8	0.8	57.7	1.1	17.9	72.15
	1985	22.1	—	1.5	23.6	—	—	1.1	1.1	55.6	1.0	18.6	70.39
	1986	22.7	—	1.6	24.3	—	—	1.1	1.1	55.6	0.9	18.2	72.31
Netherlands (Guilder)	1970	23.3	—	12.3	35.6	—	—	—	—	47.8	3.4	13.2	17 352
	1975	26.3	—	10.8	37.1	—	—	—	—	47.0	6.4	9.5	41 659
	1980	25.0	—	9.3	34.3	—	—	—	—	51.2	5.0	9.5	73 226
	1983	23.9	—	6.8	30.7	—	—	—	—	49.4	11.8	8.0	91 571
	1984	22.5	—	6.4	28.9	—	—	—	—	46.9	15.5	8.8	97 908
	1985	23.0	—	6.5	29.4	—	—	—	—	47.5	14.4	8.6	98 796
	1986	23.0	—	6.9	29.9	—	—	—	—	48.7	13.3	8.1	99 569
Norway (Krone)	1970	26.6	—	4.6	31.2	0.3	—	1.3	1.6	52.2	1.5	13.4	8 992.6
	1975	32.7	—	5.8	38.2	—	—	0.5	0.5	52.6	1.5	6.9	20 134.7
	1980	37.3	—	10.6	47.9	—	—	0.2	0.2	43.9	2.2	5.8	48 224.7
	1983	36.0[40]	—	9.6	45.6	—	0.5	2.4	2.9	41.7	3.7	6.0	72 584.1
	1984	40.1[40]	—	8.9	49.0	—	0.5	2.2	2.7	39.4	3.5	5.4	85 552.2
	1985	39.5[40]	—	9.1	48.6	—	0.5	2.2	2.7	40.5	2.8	5.4	92 363.0
	1986	37.3[40]	—	9.5	46.8	—	0.7	2.4	3.1	42.5	2.0	5.6	98 545.4
Portugal (Escudo)	1970	25.7	—	13.3	39.0	2.6	—	3.3	5.9	23.6	—	31.5	6 617.2
	1975	24.2	—	13.0	37.2	1.3	—	1.4	2.7	38.9	—	21.2	31 443.9
	1980	—	—	9.9	9.9	0.0	—	3.9	3.9	72.1	5.0	9.1	90 558.3
	1983	—	—	9.6	9.6	0.0	—	—	—	77.0	3.3	10.0	170 306.3
	1984	—	—	9.5	9.5	0.0	—	0.5	0.5	74.9	4.2	10.8	209 111.7
	1985	—	—	8.9	8.9	—	—	0.5	0.5	75.6	5.0	10.0	253 098.7
	1986	—	—	8.1	8.1	—	—	0.4	0.4	74.2	6.7	10.5	331 166.5
Suisse (Franc suisse)	1970	21.1	—	5.3	26.4	2.0	—	6.9	8.9	63.8	0.0	0.9	5 894.6
	1975	18.9	—	3.0	21.9	1.4	—	4.8	6.2	69.8	1.6	0.5	14 717.5
	1980	21.3	—	2.8	24.1	1.3	—	4.7	6.0	68.9	0.6	0.4	18 576.5
	1983	24.3	—	2.7	27.0	1.3	—	4.6	5.9	63.7	3.2	0.3	23 618.3
	1984	23.2	—	2.4	25.6	1.2	—	4.4	5.6	65.7	2.8	0.3	25 939.0
	1985	24.2	—	2.4	26.6	1.3	—	4.6	5.9	64.9	2.3	0.3	26 820.6
	1986	24.6	—	2.3	26.9	1.3	—	4.6	5.9	64.9	2.0	0.3	28 539.9
Sweden (Krona)	1970	9.1	—	19.4	28.5	0.1	—	1.1	1.2	57.7	2.5	10.1	15 719.6
	1975	10.0	—	23.7	33.7	—	—	1.0	1.0	52.9	1.8	10.6	39 563.4
	1980	31.7	4.0	13.2	48.9	—	—	1.0	1.0	41.4	1.7	7.0	122 244.8
	1983	33.3	3.5	10.6	47.4	—	—	1.0	1.0	42.0	3.5	6.0	174 254.7
	1984	27.0	0.0	8.8	35.8	—	—	0.8	0.8	41.1	7.1	15.0	231 905.2
	1985	26.2	0.3	9.5	36.0	—	—	0.8	0.8	41.9	6.0	15.3	253 099.6
	1986	24.7	0.3	9.8	34.8	—	—	0.9	0.9	42.1	6.7	15.5	278 752.9

See notes on page 169.   *Voir notes page 169.*   *Véanse notas pág. 169.*

Table 10 *(cont.)*   **Tableau 10** *(suite)*   **Cuadro 10** *(cont.)*

Country and currency unit / Pays et unité monétaire / Países y unidades monetarias (1)	Financial year / Exercice financier / Ejercicio financiero (2)	Sickness-maternity / Maladie-maternité / Enfermedad, maternidad — Medical care / Soins médicaux / Asistencia médica (3)	Benefits in kind other than medical care / Prestations en nature à d'autres titres que les soins médicaux / Prestaciones en especie, excepto asistencia médica (4)	Cash benefits / Prestations en espèces / Prestaciones monetarias (5)	Total (6)	Employment injuries / Accidents du travail et maladies professionnelles / Riesgos profesionales — Medical care / Soins médicaux / Asistencia médica (7)	Benefits in kind other than medical care / Prestations en nature à d'autres titres que les soins médicaux / Prestaciones en especie, excepto asistencia médica (8)	Cash benefits / Prestations en espèces / Prestaciones monetarias (9)	Total (10)	Pensions / Pensions / Pensiones (11)	Unemployment / Chômage / Desempleo (12)	Family allowances / Prestations familiales / Asignaciones familiares (13)	Total amount of benefit expenditure (in millions of national currency units) / Total des dépenses en prestations (millions d'unités monétaires nationales) / Total de egresos por prestaciones (en millones de unidades monetarias nacionales) (14)
Turquie (Livre turque)	1970	38.9	—	15.8	54.7	1.6	—	2.7	4.3	41.0	—	—	1 555
	1975	55.0	—	10.2	65.2	1.4	—	3.0	4.4	30.4	—	—	4 915
	1980	22.4	—	3.5	25.9	0.5	—	3.1	3.6	70.5	—	—	88 731
	1983	16.6	—	2.4	19.0	0.4	—	2.9	3.3	77.8	—	—	255 984
	1984	17.9	—	2.4	20.3	0.3	—	3.0	3.3	76.5	—	—	361 976
	1985	18.0	—	2.1	20.1	0.2	—	2.7	2.9	77.0	—	—	544 113
	1986	18.6	—	2.0	20.6	0.2	—	2.7	2.9	76.5	—	—	800 479
United Kingdom (Pound)	1970	—	—	15.0	15.0	—	—	3.7	3.7	63.3	5.8	12.2	2 911
	1975	—	—	6.5	6.5	—	—	2.8	2.8	75.8	7.6	7.3	7 638
	1980	37.3	—	2.7	40.0	—	—	1.3	1.3	42.8	5.5	10.4	29 827
	1983	36.0	—	2.3	38.3	—	—	1.1	1.1	44.9	5.0	10.7	39 700
	1984	36.0	—	2.5	38.5	—	—	1.1	1.1	44.8	4.7	10.9	41 932
	1985	35.8	—	2.5	38.3	—	—	1.1	1.1	45.5	4.4	10.7	44 728
	1986	36.0	—	2.5	38.6	—	—	1.1	1.1	46.0	4.3	10.1	47 736

EUROPE – EUROPE – EUROPA

Countries with a centrally planned economy – *Pays à économie planifiée* – *Países con economía centralmente planificada*

Country (1)	Year (2)	(3)	(4)	(5)	(6)	(7)	(8)	(9)	(10)	(11)	(12)	(13)	(14)
RSS de Biélorussie (Rouble)	1970		—	26.4	26.4	—[41]	—	—[41]	—	72.3	—	1.3	704
	1975		—	22.7	22.7	—[41]	—	—[41]	—	73.5	—	3.8	1 125
	1980	29.2	—	15.9	45.1		—		—	53.8	—	1.1	2 171
	1983	27.2	—	17.0	44.2		—		—	54.8	—	1.0	2 606
	1984	26.5	—	16.0	42.5		—		—	56.5	—	0.9	2 823
	1985[8]		—	19.4	19.4		—		—	79.5	—	1.1	2 152
	1986	26.1	—	13.7	39.8		—		—	59.4	—	0.8	3 199
Bulgarie (Lev)	1970	[41]	—	12.5	12.5	[41]	—	[41]		66.1		21.4	1 062.0
	1975	[41]	—	17.5	17.5	[41]	—	[41]		66.2		16.3	1 554.2
	1980	19.3	—	12.2	31.5	[26]	—	[26]		52.3		16.2	3 052.8
	1983	.	—	13.0	13.0	[41]	—	[41]		69.7		17.4	2 902.6
	1984	.	—	12.0	12.0		—	0.3	0.3	70.9		16.8	2 927.0
	1985	.	—	12.9	12.9		—	0.3	0.3	69.0	0.3	17.5	3 213.2
	1986	.	—	14.4	14.4		—	0.3	0.3	66.9		18.4	3 577.0

Czechoslovakia (Koruna)	1970	.[41]	1.9	18.7	20.6	.	.	.	.	60.8	—	18.6	40 723
	1975	.[41]	1.7	19.5	21.2	.	.	.	.	60.0	—	18.8	52 318
	1980	22.6	1.0	7.8	31.4	.	.	.	.	53.6	—	15.0	88 834
	1983	23.0	1.2	7.5	31.7	—	—	—	—	53.2	—	15.2	102 075
	1984	23.5	1.2	12.6	37.3	—	—	—	—	48.0	—	14.8	105 166
	1985	23.6	1.1	12.7	37.4	—	—	—	—	47.7	—	14.8	110 902
	1986	24.4	1.3	12.7	38.4	—	—	—	—	47.6	—	14.0	116 970
German Democratic Rep. (Mark)	1970	26.7	—	8.0	34.7	—	—	1.3	1.3	54.1	—	9.9	15 759.2
	1975	28.6	—	8.4	37.0	—	—	—	.[42]	56.4	—	6.6	21 827.8
	1980	28.2	—	12.7	40.9	—	—	—	.[42]	54.6	—	4.5	29 517.9
	1983[8]	—	—	11.4	11.4	—	—	—	—	84.1	—	4.5	30 721.7
	1984	33.2	—	13.4	46.6	—	—	—	—[43]	48.9	—	4.6	29 529.7
	1985	33.0	—	13.3	46.3	—	—	—	—[43]	49.4	—	4.3	30 963.1
	1986	33.3	—	13.6	46.8	—	—	—	—[43]	48.8	—	4.9	32 277.4
Hongrie (Forint)	1970	27.7	—	15.6	43.3	—[25]	—	0.4	0.4	43.0	—	13.3	29 965
	1975	.	—	17.5	17.5	.[41]	—	0.4	0.4	60.8	—	21.3	44 265
	1980	21.1	0.4	9.1	30.6	—[41]	—	0.4	0.4	52.4	—	16.5	106 069
	1983	22.2	0.2	9.1	31.5	—[41]	—	—	—	54.5	—	14.1	137 714
	1984	—	0.2	10.8	11.0	—	—	0.5	0.5	69.5	—	19.0	120 077
	1985	—	0.2	10.4	10.6	—	—	0.5	0.5	69.3	—	19.6	131 455
	1986	—	0.2	10.9	11.1	—	—	0.5	0.5	69.5	—	18.9	141 923
Pologne (Zloty)	1984	26.7	—	10.7	37.4	—	—	0.1	0.1	49.0	—	13.4	1 198 906
	1985	27.9	—	10.5	38.4	—	—	0.1	0.1	49.4	—	12.0	1 396 847
	1986	28.5	—	10.0	38.5	—	—	0.1	0.1	51.0	—	10.4	1 740 244
RSS d'Ukraine (Rouble)	1970	—	—	23.4	23.4	—	—	—	.	75.9	—	0.7	4 230
	1975	—	—	19.8	19.8	—	—	—	.	77.7	—	2.5	6 265
	1980	28.0	—	13.3	41.3	—	—	—	.	57.7	—	1.0	11 839
	1983	25.8	—	14.2	40.0	—	—	—	—	59.0	—	1.0	13 849
	1984	25.5	—	13.7	39.2	—	—	—	—	59.9	—	0.9	14 898
	1985	25.0	—	13.1	38.1	—	—	—	—	61.0	—	0.9	15 658
	1986	24.5	—	12.2	36.7	—	—	—	—	62.5	—	0.8	16 807
URSS (Rouble)	1970	—[41]	—	25.5	25.5	—[41]	—	—[41]	—	72.6	—	1.9	22 331
	1975	—[41]	—	22.6	22.6	—[41]	—	—[41]	—	72.6	—	4.8	33 669
	1980	30.0	—	15.1	45.1	—	—	—	—	52.7	—	2.2	63 267
	1983	28.2	—	15.8	44.0	—	—	—	—	53.9	—	2.1	74 184
	1984	27.3	—	15.9	43.2	—	—	—	—	54.8	—	1.9	79 969
	1985	27.0	—	15.3	42.3	—	—	—	—	55.8	—	1.9	83 573
	1986	26.3	—	14.5	40.8	—	—	—	—	57.3	—	1.8	89 307
Yugoslavia (Dinar)	1970	34.5	—	6.6	41.1	.	.	.	.[42]	50.2	.	8.7	18 069.0
	1981	36.5	—	7.6	44.1	—	—	0.4	0.4	50.7	—	4.8	240 288.7
	1983	33.7	—	8.1	41.8	—	—	0.3	0.3	53.3	—	4.6	421 957.0
	1984	28.6	5.6	8.3	42.5	—	—	—	—	57.5	—	—	569 535.0
	1985	29.5	5.7	6.6	41.8	—	—	—	—	58.2	—	—	1 043 087.0
	1986	28.3	5.1	5.3	38.7	—	—	—	—	61.2	—	—	2 467 680.0

See notes on page 169. *Voir notes page 169.* Véanse notas pág. 169.

Table 10 (concl.) **Tableau 10** (fin) **Cuadro 10** (fin)

Country and currency unit / Pays et unité monétaire / Países y unidades monetarias	Financial year / Exercice financier / Ejercicio financiero	Sickness-maternity / Maladie-maternité / Enfermedad, maternidad — Medical care / Soins médicaux / Asistencia médica	Benefits in kind other than for medical care / Prestations en nature à d'autres titres que les soins médicaux / Prestaciones en especie, excepto asistencia médica	Cash benefits / Prestations en espèces / Prestaciones monetarias	Total	Employment injuries / Accidents du travail et maladies professionnelles / Riesgos profesionales — Medical care / Soins médicaux / Asistencia médica	Benefits in kind other than for medical care / Prestations en nature à d'autres titres que les soins médicaux / Prestaciones en especie, excepto asistencia médica	Cash benefits / Prestations en espèces / Prestaciones monetarias	Total	Pensions / Pensions / Pensiones	Unemployment / Chômage / Desempleo	Family allowances / Prestations familiales / Asignaciones familiares	Total amount of benefit expenditure (in millions of national currency units) / Total des dépenses en prestations (millions d'unités monétaires nationales) / Total de egresos por prestaciones (en millones de unidades monetarias nacionales)
(1)	(2)	(3)	(4)	(5)	(6)	(7)	(8)	(9)	(10)	(11)	(12)	(13)	(14)

OCEANIA – OCÉANIE – OCEANIA

(1)	(2)	(3)	(4)	(5)	(6)	(7)	(8)	(9)	(10)	(11)	(12)	(13)	(14)
Australia[8] (Dollar)	1970	33.1	—	1.0	34.1	—	—	—	7.2	44.8	0.5	13.4	1 642.2
	1975	29.4	—	1.5	30.9	—	—	—	10.7	46.7	5.3	6.4	4 705.4
	1980	25.1	—	1.2	26.3	—	—	—	6.5	46.7	8.6	11.9	10 717.4
	1983	23.8	—	1.5	25.3	—	—	8.8	8.8	45.1	12.8	8.0	17 570.0
	1984	5.6	—	2.1	7.7	—	—	9.3	9.3	54.0	18.9	10.0	15 698.1
	1985	12.2	—	1.9	14.1	—	—	12.5	12.5	49.0	16.0	8.4	18 823.0
	1986	14.2	—	2.1	16.3	—	—	4.5	4.5	53.4	17.0	8.7	18 546.6
Fiji (Dollar)	1975	—	—	—	—	—	—	4.1	4.1	95.9	—	—	6.10
	1980	—	—	—	—	—	—	3.1	3.1	96.9	—	—	7.84
	1983	—	—	—	—	—	—	1.3	1.3	98.7	—	—	16.13
	1984	—	—	—	—	—	—	.	—	100	—	—	23.03
	1985	—	—	—	—	—	—	.	—	100	—	—	26.79
	1986	—	—	—	—	—	—	.	—	100	—	—	32.56
New Zealand (Dollar)	1970	14.2	—	2.0	16.2	—	—	3.8	3.8	59.6	0.3	20.1	351.5
	1975	13.8	—	2.0	15.8	—	—	4.8	4.8	61.2	0.9	17.3	950.7
	1980	27.0	—	8.4	35.4	—	—	2.4	2.4	50.8	3.2	8.2	3 720.5
	1983	23.8	—	7.0	30.8	0.5	—	2.5	3.0	55.4	5.6	5.2	5 617.4
	1984	23.0	—	7.2	30.2	0.5	—	2.8	3.3	56.3	4.5	5.6	6 114.9
	1985	21.3	—	8.0	29.3	0.6	—	3.0	3.6	57.2	3.9	6.0	7 424.3
	1986	22.6	—	8.8	31.4	0.7	—	3.3	4.0	55.2	5.3	4.0	8 599.9
Solomon Islands[13] (Dollar)	1981	—	—	—	—	—	—	—	—	100	—	—	0.72
	1983	—	—	—	—	—	—	—	—	100	—	—	1.15
	1984	—	—	—	—	—	—	—	—	100	—	—	1.45
	1985	—	—	—	—	—	—	—	—	100	—	—	2.02
	1986	—	—	—	—	—	—	—	—	100	—	—	2.77

1 Including "maternity". 2 The figures may also include the "medical care". 3 Including "maternity" and "health and welfare benefits". 4 Data are available only for Public Employees' Scheme. 5 Data are not available. 6 Includes "old-age, survivors, invalidity and employment injury". 7 Breakdown by branch is not available. 8 The figures reflect the available data. 9 Only data in respect of "employment injury" are available. 10 Including "health and welfare benefits".

11 "Employment injuries" included under "pensions". 12 Unemployment Benefit Scheme started operating on 1 February 1983. 13 Only data in respect of "Provident Fund" are available. 14 The figures relate to the three-year period 1979-81. 15 Unemployment insurance came into effect in 1982. 16 Includes estimated figures in respect of non-contributory pensions, based on 1977 data (for year 1980), on 1984 data (for year 1983) and on 1985 data (for year 1986). 17 Excluding "Public Health Services" (Fondo Nacional de Salud). 18 The National Insurance Scheme came into effect on 4 April 1983. No benefits were paid prior to 1983. 19 Estimates. 20 Including "sickness and maternity".

21 Excludes "employment injury" (private sector), for which data are not available. 22 Including "temporary disability". 23 Including "income support benefit". 24 The medical service of the social security scheme was taken over by the Ministry of Health on 1 October 1969. The expenses indicated are the amounts reimbursed to insured persons by the Social Security Board. 25 Death grant. 26 "Employment injuries" included under "sickness and maternity". 27 Including "medical care for sickness". 28 From 1981, including "Employees' Trust Fund". 29 May include employment injuries. 30 Includes the general sickness insurance scheme and the special schemes for employees in agriculture, occupiers of agricultural holdings, workers in mines and on the railways, employees of the Paris transport board, seafarers, self-employed workers, etc.

31 Includes only cash benefits under the general sickness insurance scheme. Cash benefits under the special schemes mentioned in note 30 are included under "pensions" because breakdown by type of benefit is not available for those schemes. 32 Relates to employment injuries in agriculture only. 33 Includes the general old-age insurance scheme and special schemes (for agriculture, the national electricity board, the railways, mines, the Paris transport board, shopkeepers, craftsmen, seafarers and the liberal professions, the special old-age fund and various other special schemes). 34 Relates to the joint labour-management scheme (UNEDIC) applicable to most persons in private employment, dockers and construction workers. 35 Relates to the National Family Allowances Fund only. The figures relating to the special schemes (employees in agriculture, occupiers of agricultural holdings, the railways, the Paris transport board and various other special schemes) are included under "pensions" because breakdowns by type of benefit are not available for those schemes. 36 Figures for medical care may include cash benefits which are not available separately, and vice versa. 37 Included under "unemployment"; figures are not separable. 38 Includes "unemployment" and "family allowances". 39 Figures do not include professional and voluntary schemes. 40 Figures include benefits in kind.

41 Included in column 5. 42 Included under "sickness and maternity" and "pensions". 43 Included in "pensions".

1 Y compris les prestations de maternité. 2 Les chiffres peuvent aussi comprendre les soins médicaux. 3 Y compris les prestations de maternité et les prestations de l'action sanitaire et sociale. 4 On ne possède de données que pour le régime des agents publics. 5 On ne dispose pas de données. 6 Y compris les prestations de vieillesse, d'invalidité et de survivants et les prestations en cas d'accidents du travail ou de maladies professionnelles. 7 On ne dispose pas de la ventilation par branche. 8 Les chiffres correspondent aux données disponibles. 9 On ne possède de données que pour les accidents du travail et les maladies professionnelles. 10 Y compris les prestations de l'action sanitaire et sociale.

11 Les prestations en cas d'accidents du travail et de maladies professionnelles sont comprises dans la rubrique «pensions». 12 Le régime d'indemnisation du chômage est entré en vigueur le 1er février 1983. 13 Seules sont disponibles les données relatives au Fonds de prévoyance. 14 Les chiffres se rapportent à la période 1979-1981. 15 L'assurance chômage est entrée en vigueur en 1982. 16 Comprend les chiffres estimés pour les pensions non contributives sur la base des données de 1977, de 1984 et de 1985 pour les années 1980, 1983 et 1986 respectivement. 17 A l'exclusion des services publics de santé (Fondo Nacional de Salud). 18 Le régime national d'assurance est entré en vigueur le 4 avril 1983; aucune prestation n'a été versée avant 1983. 19 Estimations. 20 Y compris les prestations de maladie et maternité.

21 A l'exclusion des prestations en cas d'accidents du travail et de maladies professionnelles (secteur privé) pour lesquelles on ne dispose pas de données. 22 Y compris l'incapacité temporaire. 23 Y compris les prestations de maintien du revenu. 24 Le service médical du régime de sécurité sociale a été repris par le ministère de la Santé le 1er octobre 1969. Les dépenses indiquées correspondent aux remboursements effectués par le Conseil de la sécurité sociale en faveur des assurés. 25 Allocations de décès. 26 Les prestations en cas d'accidents du travail ou de maladies professionnelles sont comprises dans la rubrique «maladie-maternité». 27 Y compris les soins en cas de maladie. 28 Y compris, depuis 1981, le Fonds fiduciaire des salariés. 29 Pourrait comprendre les prestations en cas d'accidents du travail et de maladies professionnelles. 30 Comprend le régime général d'assurance maladie et les régimes spéciaux ou autonomes pour les salariés agricoles, les exploitants agricoles, les mineurs, les salariés des transports publics (SNCF et RATP), les marins, les non-salariés, etc.

31 Comprend exclusivement les prestations en espèces du régime général d'assurance maladie. Les prestations en espèces des régimes spéciaux ou autonomes mentionnés dans la note 30 sont comprises dans la rubrique «pensions», les chiffres n'étant pas ventilés. 32 Risques professionnels de l'agriculture seulement. 33 Comprend le régime général d'assurance vieillesse et les régimes spéciaux ou autonomes (pour l'agriculture, l'électricité (EDF), les mines, les transports publics (SNCF et RATP), les professions industrielles et commerciales, les artisans, les marins, les professions libérales, etc. 34 Régime de l'UNEDIC (Union nationale interprofessionnelle pour l'emploi dans l'industrie et le commerce), géré paritairement par les employeurs et les salariés et applicable à la plus grande partie des salariés du secteur privé, régime des dockers, régime des ouvriers du bâtiment. 35 Caisse nationale d'allocations familiales uniquement. Les chiffres pour les régimes spéciaux ou autonomes (pour l'agriculture, l'électricité (EDF), les transports publics (SNCF et RATP), etc., sont inclus dans la rubrique «pensions», la ventilation n'étant pas connue. 36 Les chiffres pour les soins médicaux peuvent comprendre des prestations en espèces pour lesquelles on ne possède pas de chiffres séparés, et inversement. 37 Compris dans les prestations familiales. 38 Comprend les prestations de chômage (chiffres non ventilés). 39 Les chiffres ne comprennent pas les régimes professionnels et les régimes volontaires. 40 Y compris les prestations en nature.

41 Compris dans la colonne 5. 42 Compris dans les rubriques «maladie-maternité» et «pensions». 43 Compris dans les pensions.

1 Incluida la «maternidad». 2 Las cifras pueden abarcar datos relativos a la «asistencia médica». 3 Incluidas la «maternidad» y las «prestaciones sanitarias y sociales». 4 Sólo se dispuso de datos sobre el régimen de empleados públicos. 5 No se dispuso de datos. 6 Incluye «personas de edad avanzada, sobrevivientes, invalidez y riesgos profesionales». 7 No se dispuso de una repartición por ramas. 8 Las cifras reflejan los datos disponibles. 9 Sólo se dispuso de datos respecto de «riesgos profesionales». 10 Incluye las «prestaciones sanitarias y sociales».

11 Los «riesgos profesionales» aparecen incluidos en la rúbrica «pensiones». 12 El régimen de prestaciones de desempleo entró en vigor el 1.° de febrero de 1983. 13 Sólo se dispuso de datos sobre el Fondo de Previsión. 14 Las cifras se refieren al trienio 1979-1981. 15 El seguro de desempleo entró en vigor en 1982. 16 Incluye cifras estimativas acerca de las pensiones no contributivas, basadas en datos de 1977 (para el año 1980), en datos de 1984 (para el año 1983) y en datos de 1985 (para el año 1986). 17 Excluidos los «servicios públicos de salud» (Fondo Nacional de Salud). 18 El régimen nacional de seguros entró en vigor el 4 de abril de 1983; antes de ese año no se pagó prestación alguna. 19 Estimaciones. 20 Incluidas «enfermedad y maternidad».

21 Excluye «riesgos profesionales» (sector privado), sobre los que no se dispone de datos. 22 Incluida la «incapacidad temporal». 23 Incluidas las «prestaciones de mantenimiento de ingresos». 24 El Ministerio de Salud absorbió el 1.° de octubre de 1969 al servicio médico del régimen de seguridad social. Los gastos indicados corresponden a los montos reembolsados a las personas aseguradas por el Consejo de Seguridad Social. 25 Asignación por muerte. 26 Los «riesgos profesionales están incluidos en la rúbrica «enfermedad y maternidad». 27 Incluye la «asistencia médica en caso de enfermedad». 28 Desde 1981 incluye al Fondo Fiduciario para Empleados. 29 Puede incluir riesgos profesionales. 30 Incluye el régimen general de seguro de enfermedad y los regímenes especiales para empleados agrícolas, productores agrícolas independientes, trabajadores de minas, ferrocarriles y transportes públicos de la ciudad de París, marinos, trabajadores por cuenta propia, etc.

31 Sólo incluye las prestaciones monetarias del régimen general de seguro de enfermedad. Las prestaciones monetarias pagadas por los regímenes especiales mencionados en la nota 30 se incluyeron en la rúbrica «pensiones» debido a que en esos regímenes no aparecen desglosadas según los tipos de prestación de cue se trate. 32 Sólo se refiere a «riesgos profesionales» en la agricultura. 33 Comprende el régimen general de seguro de vejez y regímenes especiales (para la agricultura, la empresa eléctrica del Estado, los ferrocarriles, las minas, los transportes públicos de la ciudad de París, los comerciantes, los artesanos, los marinos, las profesiones liberales, la caja especial de vejez y otros regímenes especiales). 34 Se refiere al UNEDIC (régimen paritario obrero-patronal aplicable a la mayoría del personal de las profesiones privadas), a los trabajadores portuarios y a los obreros de la construcción. 35 Se refiere únicamente al Fondo Nacional de Asignaciones Familiares. Las cifras relativas a los regímenes especiales (empleados agrícolas, productores agrícolas independientes, servicios públicos de electricidad, ferrocarriles, transportes públicos de la ciudad de París y otros diversos regímenes especiales) aparecen en la columna «pensiones», pues los datos relativos a esos regímenes no están desglosados por tipos de prestación. 36 Es posible que las cifras para asistencia médica incluyan prestaciones monetarias de las que no se dispone por separado, y vice versa. 37 Incluido en la rúbrica «asignaciones familiares». 38 Incluye «desempleo»; las cifras no pueden presentarse separadamente. 39 Las cifras no comprenden los regímenes profesionales y voluntarios. 40 Las cifras comprenden las prestaciones en especie.

41 Incluido en la columna 5. 42 Incluido en «enfermedad y maternidad» y «pensiones». 43 Incluido en «pensiones».

Appendix tables

Tableaux annexes

Cuadros anexos

1. National accounts data, population data, consumer price indices and exchange rates

1. Données de la comptabilité nationale, données démographiques, indices des prix à la consommation et taux de change

1. Datos sobre las cuentas nacionales y la población, índices de los precios del consumo y tasas de cambio

AFRICA – AFRIQUE – AFRICA

Country and currency unit / Pays et unité monétaire / País y unidad monetaria	Financial year / Exercice financier / Ejercicio financiero	Gross domestic product in purchasers' values[1] (in millions of national currency units) / PIB aux valeurs d'acquisition[1] (millions d'unités monétaires nationales) / Producto interno bruto a precios de comprador[1] (en millones de unidades monetarias nacionales)	Population in thousands — Total / Population (milliers) — Total / Población (millares) — Total	Population in thousands — Between 15 and 64 years of age / Entre 15 et 64 ans / Entre 15 y 64 años de edad	Consumer price index 1980 = 100 / Indices des prix à la consommation 1980 = 100 / Índice de los precios del consumo 1980 = 100	Exchange rate (national currency per US dollar)[2] / Taux de change (en monnaie nationale pour 1 dollar des Etats-Unis)[2] / Tasa de cambio (moneda nacional por dólar EUA)[2]
(1)	(2)	(3)	(4)	(5)	(6)	(7)
Bénin (Franc CFA)	1970	69 700	2 718	1 409	.	276.030
	1975	113 100	3 112	1 606	.	224.280
	1981	301 000	3 575	1 820	.	287.400
	1983	439 400	3 805	1 927	.	417.380
	1984	466 200	3 925	1 983	.	479.600
	1985	499 800	4 041	2 036	.	378.050
	1986	502 700	4 169	2 095	.	322.750
Burkina Faso (Franc CFA)	1975	127 000	5 640	3 013	60	224.280
	1980	272 000	6 145	3 277	100	225.800
	1983	381 000	6 415	3 422	131	417.380
	1984	390 600	6 526	3 481	137	479.600
	1985	469 313	6 639	3 542	146	378.050
	1986	503 500	8 082	4 310	143	322.750
Burundi (Franc burundais)	1978	55 226	3 980	2 139	67	90.000
	1980	85 607	4 118	2 187	100	90.000
	1983	102 892	4 459	2 335	129	117.410
	1984	120 451	4 585	2 390	146	124.950
	1985	141 347	4 718	2 448	152	111.970
	1986	140 842	4 857	2 512	155	124.170
Cameroun (Franc CFA)	1970	321 300	6 700	3 688	37	276.030
	1981	2 172 800	8 966	4 636	111	287.400
	1983	3 195 000	9 575	5 012	146	417.380
	1984	3 838 900	9 871	5 151	163	479.600
	1985	4 135 100	10 166	5 288	165	378.050
	1986	4 004 900	10 457	5 437	170	322.750

Country and currency unit	Financial year	Gross domestic product in purchasers' values[1] (in millions of national currency units)	Population in thousands — Total	Population in thousands — Between 15 and 64 years of age	Consumer price index 1980 = 100	Exchange rate (national currency per US dollar)[2]
(1)	(2)	(3)	(4)	(5)	(6)	(7)
Madagascar (Franc malgache)	1981	789 000	8 955	4 741	131	287.400
	1983	1 221 100	9 400	4 955	205	492.160
	1984	1 369 100	9 909	5 216	226	658.020
	1985	1 553 400	9 985	5 248	249	635.790
	1986	1 806 900	10 547	5 530	286	769.810
Mali (Franc CFA)	1972	94 050[3]	5 257	2 755	34	256.050
	1975	129 500[3]	5 807	3 261	68	224.280
	1980	300 600[3]	7 095	3 637	100	225.800
	1983	411 300[3]	7 741	3 956	126	417.380
	1984	463 500	7 973	4 071	142	479.600
	1985	475 000	8 206	4 185	153	378.050
	1986	542 900	8 438	4 298	147	322.750
Maroc (Dirham)	1970	20 000	15 520	7 388	44	5.029
	1975	36 400	17 305	8 510	63	4.184
	1980	70 200	20 050	10 569	100	4.334
	1983	94 600	20 965	11 205	132	8.061
	1984	105 500	21 538	11 564	149	9.551
	1985	119 300	22 121	11 931	160	9.621
	1986	134 300	22 710	12 329	174	8.712
Mauritanie (Ouguiya)	1970	11 300	1 245	654	39	55.205
	1981	43 200	1 591	845	119	48.940
	1983	45 900	1 676	888	135	57.030
	1984	44 500	1 720	910	145	67.290
	1985	.	1 767	934	165	77.070
	1986	.	1 815	957	177	74.080

Left panel

Country (currency)	Year	Col 1	Col 2	Col 3	Col 4	Rate
Cap-Vert (Escudo)	1983	6 164	314	161	100	79.975
	1984	8 026	322	168	112	93.015
	1985	9 744	334	177	117	85.375
	1986	11 220	339	181	130	76.565
Rép. centrafricaine (Franc CFA)	1981	216 300	2 351	1 278	113	287.400
	1983	251 000	2 460	1 328	144	417.380
	1984	278 700	2 517	1 354	157	479.600
	1985	316 200	2 608	1 398	171	378.050
	1986	330 900	2 740	1 465	184	322.750
Côte d'Ivoire (Franc CFA)	1981	2 291 400	8 683	4 284	109	287.400
	1983	2 605 900	9 300	4 568	124	417.380
	1984	2 883 400	9 835	4 820	129	479.600
	1985	3 137 600	10 253	5 013	131	378.050
	1986	3 244 400	10 688	5 214	140	322.750
Egypt (Pound)	1984	34 211	47 191	25 916	172	0.700
	1985	38 211	48 503	26 607	195	0.700
	1986	44 050	49 056	27 243	239	0.700
Ethiopia (Birr)	1972	4 744	25 890	13 575	38	2.300
	1975	5 551	27 465	14 325	48	2.070
	1980	8 534	38 751	20 502	100	2.070
	1983	10 031	40 876	20 840	112	2.070
	1984	10 001	41 553	20 919	121	2.070
	1985	9 881	43 350	21 546	144	2.070
	1986	10 804	44 927	22 499	130	2.070
Gabon (Franc CFA)	1980	904 500	807	496	100	225.800
	1983	1 292 600	913	552	140	417.380
	1984	1 535 800	949	571	148	479.600
	1985	1 645 800	986	591	159	378.050
	1986	1 176 300	1 022	616	169	322.750
Guinée (Syli)	1981	..	5 531	2 998	..	21.208
	1983	..	5 793	3 134	..	23.578
	1985	..	6 076	3 282	..	22.473
	1986	46 973	6 225	3 354	..	235.630
Guinée-Bissau (Peso)	1981	..	833	462	..	37.802
	1983	..	863	477	..	84.163
	1984	..	876	483	..	128.580
	1985	..	890	490	..	173.610
	1986	..	907	498	..	238.980
Kenya (Shilling)	1970	11 454	11 225	5 268	32	7.143
	1975	23 850	13 399	5 982	54	8.260
	1981	60 468	17 342	8 041	112	10.286
	1983	78 532	18 775	8 648	150	13.796
	1984	87 780	19 536	8 969	165	15.781
	1985	98 286	20 333	9 304	187	16.284
	1986	116 634	21 163	9 658	194	16.042

Right panel

Country (currency)	Year	Col 1	Col 2	Col 3	Col 4	Rate
Mauritius (Rupee)	1970	1 067	843	430	26	5.570
	1975	3 416	883	504	46	6.589
	1981	10 209	970	591	115	10.329
	1983	12 763	991	641	135	12.723
	1984	14 360	1 012	661	145	15.603
	1985	16 618	1 021	673	154	14.310
	1986	19 700	1 030	653	157	13.137
Mozambique (Metical)	1981	92 000	12 449	6 645	102	30.431[4]
	1983	91 000	13 112	6 983	155	41.508[4]
	1984	109 000	13 456	7 158	202	43.723[4]
	1985	147 000	13 810	7 338	261	41.500[4]
	1986	167 000	14 174	7 520	305	399.500
Niger (Franc CFA)	1970	111 000	3 997	2 066	35	276.030
	1975	180 300	4 587	2 336	50	224.280
	1980	536 208	5 312	2 654	100	225.800
	1983	687 100	5 733	2 874	134	417.380
	1984	638 406	5 940	2 954	145	479.600
	1985	647 141	6 116	3 037	144	378.050
	1986	643 362	6 298	3 126	139	322.750
Nigeria (Naira)	1970	5 621	56 346	28 524	24	0.714
	1981	48 643	82 623	40 851	121	0.637
	1983	63 293	89 043	43 974	160	0.749
	1984	69 950	92 055	45 435	224	0.808
	1985	78 776	95 199	46 959	236	1.000
	1986	79 704	98 484	48 538	249	3.317
Rwanda (Franc rwandais)	1975	52 800	4 198	2 086	58	92.840
	1981	122 600	5 353	2 613	107	92.840
	1983	142 200	5 757	2 806	128	98.540
	1984	159 100	5 900	2 873	135	104.360
	1985	173 700	6 103	2 969	137	93.490
	1986	169 000	6 312	3 071	136	84.180
Sao Tomé-et-Principe (Dobra)	1981	..	87	42	..	38.876
	1983	..	92	45	..	43.221
	1984	..	95	46	..	46.164
	1985	..	108	53	..	41.196
	1986	..	100	49	..	36.993
Sénégal (Franc CFA)	1970	240 100	4 267	2 284	38	276.030
	1975	406 400	4 838	2 618	72	224.280
	1980	627 500	5 703	2 958	100	225.800
	1983	924 900	6 316	3 218	139	417.380
	1984	1 015 500	6 400	3 374	155	479.600
	1985	1 152 000	6 444	3 394	175	378.050
	1986	1 307 000	6 614	3 482	187	322.750
Sudan (Pound)	1980	6 398	18 681	9 788	100	0.500
	1983	11 311	20 528	10 710	205	1.300
	1984	13 913	21 171	11 030	274	1.300
	1985	22 009	21 819	11 352	399	2.500
	1986	31 157	22 471	11 687	504	2.500

See notes on page 181.   Voir notes page 181.   Véanse notas pág. 181.

Appendix *(cont.)*   **Annexe** *(suite)*   **Anexo** *(cont.)*

Country and currency unit / Pays et unité monétaire / País y unidad monetaria (1)	Financial year / Exercice financier / Ejercicio financiero (2)	Gross domestic product in purchasers' values[1] (in millions of national currency units) / PIB aux valeurs d'acquisition[1] (millions d'unités monétaires nationales) / Producto interno bruto a precios de comprador[1] (en millones de unidades monetarias nacionales) (3)	Population in thousands / Population (milliers) / Población (millares) — Total (4)	Between 15 and 64 years of age / Entre 15 et 64 ans / Entre 15 y 64 años de edad (5)	Consumer price index 1980 = 100 / Indices des prix à la consommation 1980 = 100 / Indice de los precios del consumo 1980 = 100 (6)	Exchange rate (national currency per US dollar)[2] / Taux de change (en monnaie nationale pour 1 dollar des Etats-Unis)[2] / Tasa de cambio (moneda nacional por dólar EUA)[2] (7)
Canada (Dollar)	1970	88 500	21 324	13 068	46	1.011
	1975	170 100	22 727	14 592	66	1.016
	1980	307 700	24 043	16 298	100	1.195
	1983	402 200	24 890	16 913	138	1.244
	1984	441 300	25 128	17 088	143	1.321
	1985	475 100	25 359	17 259	149	1.381
Colombia (Peso)	1970	132 800	20 527	10 607	15	19.090
	1975	405 100	23 644	12 819	34	32.960
	1980	1 579 100	25 892	14 776	100	50.920
	1983	3 054 100	27 502	16 026	190	88.770
	1984	3 856 600	28 056	14 701	221	113.890
	1985	4 965 900	28 624	16 908	274	172.200
	1986	6 701 400	29 188	17 285	326	219.000
Costa Rica (Colón)	1970	6 525	1 727	877	36	6.635
	1975	16 805	1 965	1 075	68	8.570
	1980	41 406	2 245	1 294	100	8.570
	1983	129 314	2 435	1 428	346	43.400
	1984	163 011	2 417	1 425	387	47.750
	1985	197 920	2 489	1 476	445	53.700
	1986	247 752	2 717	1 613	498	58.875
Cuba (Peso)	1980	9 853	9 724	5 969	.	0.710
	1983	12 926	9 897	6 370	.	0.870
	1984	13 695	9 994	6 532	.	0.900
	1985	13 952	10 098	6 700	.	0.900
	1986	12 857	10 199	6 836	.	0.793
Chile (Peso)	1971	127	9 545	5 502	2	0.016
	1975	35 400	10 253	6 080	7	8.500
	1980	1 075 300	11 145	6 800	100	39.000
	1983	1 557 700	11 717	7 268	168	87.530
	1984	1 893 400	11 919	7 433	201	128.240
	1985	2 576 600	12 122	7 601	262	183.860
	1986	3 246 100	12 327	7 745	313	204.730

Appendix *(cont.)*   **Annexe** *(suite)*   **Anexo** *(cont.)*

Country and currency unit / Pays et unité monétaire / País y unidad monetaria (1)	Financial year / Exercice financier / Ejercicio financiero (2)	Gross domestic product in purchasers' values[1] (in millions of national currency units) / PIB aux valeurs d'acquisition[1] (millions d'unités monétaires nationales) / Producto interno bruto a precios de comprador[1] (en millones de unidades monetarias nacionales) (3)	Population in thousands / Population (milliers) / Población (millares) — Total (4)	Between 15 and 64 years of age / Entre 15 et 64 ans / Entre 15 y 64 años de edad (5)	Consumer price index 1980 = 100 / Indices des prix à la consommation 1980 = 100 / Indice de los precios del consumo 1980 = 100 (6)	Exchange rate (national currency per US dollar)[2] / Taux de change (en monnaie nationale pour 1 dollar des Etats-Unis)[2] / Tasa de cambio (moneda nacional por dólar EUA)[2] (7)
Swaziland (Lilangeni)	1981	501	566	286	120	0.960
	1983	580	605	305	149	1.220
	1984	662	626	315	168	1.990
	1985	743	647	325	201	2.560
	1986	956	670	336	225	2.180
Tanzania, United Rep. of (Shilling)	1980	42 118	18 580	9 161	100	8.182
	1983	70 509	20 412	10 042	206	12.456
	1984	88 892	21 062	10 353	280	18.103
	1985	120 621	21 733	10 675	374	16.499
	1986	161 889	22 462	11 007	495	51.719
Tchad (Franc CFA)	1983	.	4 789	2 599	112	417.380
	1984	.	4 901	2 656	134	479.600
	1985	.	5 019	2 716	141	378.050
	1986	.	5 141	2 776	123	322.750
Togo (Franc CFA)	1972	87 555	2 066	1 102	44	256.050
	1975	128 300	2 230	1 180	60	224.280
	1980	238 900	2 555	1 341	100	225.800
	1983	281 300	2 787	1 454	146	417.380
	1984	404 800	2 872	1 496	140	479.600
	1985	332 500	2 961	1 540	138	378.050
	1986	363 600	3 053	1 584	144	322.750
Tunisie (Dinar)	1984	6 241	7 034	3 950	146	0.867
	1985	6 910	7 261	4 106	158	0.757
	1986	7 025	7 465	4 246	167	0.840
Uganda (Shilling)	1980	137 674	13 120	6 587	.	0.076
	1983	475 185	14 483	7 166	188	2.400
	1984	648 190	14 975	7 404	269	5.200
	1985	.	15 492	7 653	625	14.000
	1986	.	16 033	7 906	1 681	14.000
Zaïre (Zaïre)	1984	99 723	29 992	15 393	496	40.450
	1985	147 263	30 981	15 904	614	55.793
	1986	203 416	31 499	16 166	900	71.100

Country (Currency)	Year					
Zambia (Kwacha)	1970	1 278	4 251	2 154	34	0.714
	1975	1 583	4 981	2 496	45	0.643
	1980	3 064	5 830	2 935	100	0.803
	1983					
	1984	4 931	7 007	3 327	184	2.201
	1985	7 049	7 283	3 469	253	5.700
	1986	12 098	7 564	3 598	384	12.710
AMERICA – AMÉRIQUE – AMERICA						
Argentina (Austral)	1975	0	25 384	16 039		0.000
	1980	28	28 237	17 451	100	0.000
	1983	683	29 627	18 081	2 403	0.023
	1984	5 281	30 097	18 280	17 462	0.179
	1985	39 593	30 564	18 477	134 833	0.800
	1986	74 309	31 030	18 729	256 308	1.257
Bahamas (Dollar)	1980	1 475	210	117	100	1.000
	1983	1 744	224	132	123	1.000
	1984	2 018	229	138	127	1.000
	1985	2 258	232	142	133	1.000
	1986	2 216	236	147	140	1.000
Barbados (Dollar)	1971	322	240	131	30	1.881
	1975	812	244	138	62	2.004
	1980	1 731	249	149	100	2.011
	1983	2 113	251	154	133	2.011
	1984	2 303	252	155	139	2.011
	1985	2 410	253	157	145	2.011
	1986	2 646	253	158	147	2.011
Belize (Dollar)	1981	359	146	97	111	2.000
	1983	351	158	105	125	2.000
	1984	386	162	107	129	2.000
	1985	390	166	110	134	2.000
	1986	425	171	113	135	2.000
Bolivia (Peso)	1972					
	1975	17 000	5 195	2 786	20	
	1980	49 201	4 890	2 619	46	0.000
	1983	123 000	5 600	2 984	100	0.000
	1984	1 501 000	6 082	3 232	1 107	0.000
	1985	21 507 000	6 253	3 320	15 320	0.009
	1986	2 768 888 000	6 429	3 411	181 580	1.692
Brasil (Cruzado)	1970	200	90 065	50 244	5	
	1975	1 100	104 940	58 975	14	
	1980	12 000	121 286	70 634	100	0.065
	1983	119 000	129 760	76 385	984	0.984
	1984	394 000	132 659	78 370	2 924	3.184
	1985	1 413 000	135 564	80 370	9 556	10.490
	1986	3 709 000	138 493	82 336	23 436	14.895
Dominica (EC Dollar)	1980	159	74	39	100	2.700
	1983	216	81	43	123	2.700
	1984	243	82	43	126	2.700
	1985	270	77	41	129	2.700
	1986	308	77	41	132	2.700
República Dominicana (Peso)	1984	10 335	6 102	3 453	154	1.000
	1985	13 972	6 243	3 563	212	2.940
	1986	15 780	6 416	3 683	233	3.077
Ecuador (Sucre)	1972	46 859	6 378	3 260	36	25.000
	1974	92 763	6 830	3 509	50	25.000
	1980	293 337	8 123	4 308	100	25.000
	1983	560 271	8 857	4 776	201	54.100
	1984	812 629	9 115	4 943	264	67.175
	1985	1 109 940	9 378	5 113	337	95.750
	1986	1 382 143	9 647	5 282	415	146.500
El Salvador (Colón)	1970	2 571	3 534	1 792	36	2.500
	1975	4 478	4 005	2 040	55	2.500
	1980	8 917	4 508	2 297	100	2.500
	1983	10 152	4 724	2 397	145	2.500
	1984	11 657	4 780	2 421	162	2.500
	1985	14 331	4 819	2 437	198	2.500
	1986	19 763	4 913	2 498	262	5.000
Grenada (EC Dollar)	1981	217	93	50	119	2.700
	1983	253	94	51	136	2.700
	1984	274	95	51	144	2.700
	1985	311	96	52	147	2.700
	1986	348	98	53	148	2.700
Guatemala (Quetzal)	1970	1 904	5 272	2 706	40	1.000
	1975	3 646	6 082	3 254	60	1.000
	1980	7 879	6 917	3 547	100	1.000
	1983	9 050	7 524	3 852	117	1.000
	1984	9 470	7 740	3 961	121	1.000
	1985	11 180	7 963	4 073	143	1.000
	1986	15 838	8 195	4 196	196	2.500
Guyana (Dollar)	1972	536	741	373	40	2.219
	1975	1 188	781	412	55	2.550
	1980	1 508	865	492	100	2.550
	1983	1 455	918	535	170	3.000
	1984	1 700	936	550	213	4.150
	1985	1 964	790	468	245	4.150
	1986	2 219	972	579	264	4.400
Honduras (Lempira)	1970	1 382	2 639	1 323	46	2.000
	1971	2 248	2 720	1 359	47	2.000
	1981	5 088	3 821	1 834	100	2.000
	1983	6 035	4 092	2 047	109	2.000
	1984	6 462	4 232	2 124	129	2.000
	1985	6 977	4 372	2 201	135	2.000
	1986	7 565	4 514	2 289	146	2.000

See notes on page 181. *Voir notes page 181.* Véanse notas pág. 181.

Appendix (cont.)   **Annexe** (suite)   **Anexo** (cont.)

Country and currency unit / Pays et unité monétaire / País y unidad monetaria (1)	Financial year / Exercice financier / Ejercicio financiero (2)	Gross domestic product in purchasers' values[1] (in millions of national currency units) / PIB aux valeurs d'acquisition[1] (millions d'unités monétaires nationales) / Producto interno bruto a precios de comprador[1] (en millones de unidades monetarias nacionales) (3)	Population in thousands / Population (milliers) / Población (millares) — Total (4)	Between 15 and 64 years of age / Entre 15 et 64 ans / Entre 15 y 64 años de edad (5)	Consumer price index 1980 = 100 / Indices des prix à la consommation 1980 = 100 / Índice de los precios del consumo 1980 = 100 (6)	Exchange rate (national currency per US dollar)[2] / Taux de change (en monnaie nationale pour 1 dollar des Etats-Unis)[2] / Tasa de cambio (moneda nacional por dólar EUA)[2] (7)
Cyprus (Pound)	1970	227	604	353	47	0.417
	1975	257	617	398	67	0.393
	1980	760	627	410	100	0.365
	1983	1 137	649	419	124	0.556
	1984	1 336	657	423	131	0.644
	1985	1 479	665	426	138	0.543
	1986	1 585	673	431	140	0.512
India (Rupee)	1970	402 600	539 075	290 245	48	7.576
	1975	743 400	600 763	330 180	82	8.937
	1980	1 358 100	675 000	376 459	100	7.930
	1983	2 072 700	720 000	418 851	136	10.493
	1984	2 295 400	736 000	428 969	148	12.451
	1985	2 617 300	750 859	438 776	156	12.166
	1986	2 927 900	766 135	449 056	170	13.122
Indonesia (Rupiah)	1981	58 127 200	149 701	82 074	112	644.000
	1983	73 697 600	156 446	89 084	137	994.000
	1984	87 054 800	159 895	91 740	152	1 074.000
	1985	94 720 800	164 047	94 833	159	1 125.000
	1986	95 823 100	166 940	97 601	168	1 641.000
Iran, Islamic Rep. of (Rial)	1981	8 323 000	40 853	21 437	124	79.450
	1983	13 749 500	44 181	23 420	147	88.161
	1984	15 029 600	45 960	24 487	177	93.993
	1985	16 555 800	47 820	25 606	199	84.228
	1986	18 125 500	49 765	26 580	207	75.644
Israel (New Shekel)	1970	20	2 974	1 747	3	0.00035
	1975	80	3 455	2 018	9	0.00071
	1980	116	3 878	2 225	100	0.008
	1983	1 632	4 159	2 410	1 174	0.108
	1984	8 013	4 233	2 448	5 560	0.639
	1985	30 086	4 299	2 496	22 498	1.500
	1986	47 178	4 369	2 548	33 330	1.486

Country and currency unit (1)	Financial year (2)	Gross domestic product in purchasers' values[1] (millions national currency units) (3)	Population — Total (4)	Between 15 and 64 years of age (5)	Consumer price index 1980 = 100 (6)	Exchange rate (national currency per US dollar)[2] (7)
Jamaica (Dollar)	1970	1 166	1 869	893	19	0.836
	1975	2 601	2 043	990	37	0.909
	1980	4 751	2 133	1 155	100	1.781
	1983	6 979	2 302	1 305	134	3.278
	1984	9 323	2 337	1 342	171	4.930
	1985	11 244	2 373	1 374	215	5.480
	1986	13 329	2 409	1 377	248	5.500
México (Peso)	1970	444 300	50 695	25 513	22	12.500
	1974	1 100 000	58 118	29 143	33	12.500
	1980	4 470 100	69 393	36 360	100	23.260
	1983	17 878 700	74 633	40 487	410	143.930
	1984	29 471 600	76 293	41 859	679	192.560
	1985	47 402 500	77 938	43 242	1 071	371.700
	1986	79 353 400	79 563	44 695	1 995	923.500
Panamá (Balboa)	1972	1 265	1 550	810	56	1.000
	1975	1 841	1 668	884	72	1.000
	1980	3 559	1 956	1 088	100	1.000
	1983	4 374	2 089	1 189	114	1.000
	1984	4 566	2 134	1 226	116	1.000
	1985	4 901	2 180	1 264	117	1.000
	1986	5 145	2 227	1 033	117	1.000
Perú (Inti)	1981	10 658	17 755	9 701	175	0.510
	1983	32 565	18 707	10 319	609	2.270
	1984	72 845	19 198	10 640	1 280	5.700
	1985	199 845	19 698	10 969	3 372	13.950
	1986	381 022	20 207	11 354	5 999	13.950
St. Lucia (EC Dollar)	1981	341	126	60	115	2.700
	1983	380	131	64	122	2.700
	1984	408	134	66	123	2.700
	1985	389	137	68	125	2.700
	1986	427	140	69	128	2.700

Country (Currency)	Year					
Trinidad and Tobago (Dollar)	1970	1 644	1 027	565	29	2.005
	1975	5 300	1 075	622	55	2.372
	1980	14 966	1 082	648	100	2.400
	1983	18 719	1 139	694	147	2.400
	1984	18 829	1 167	715	166	2.400
	1985	18 077	1 181	728	179	2.450
	1986	17 242	1 199	741	193	3.600
United States (Dollar)	1970	1 009 200	204 878	125 245	47	1.000
	1975	1 583 900	213 559	138 572	60	1.000
	1980	2 688 500	227 757	150 749	100	1.000
	1983	3 353 500	234 799	155 654	121	1.000
	1984	3 722 300	237 001	157 196	126	1.000
	1985	3 967 500	239 283	158 792	131	1.000
	1986	4 191 500	241 596	159 736	133	1.000
Uruguay (Nuevo peso)	1975	8 166	2 815	1 765	11	2.730
	1980	92 204	2 908	1 819	100	10.025
	1983	185 006	2 968	1 854	238	43.250
	1984	294 359	2 990	1 866	370	74.250
	1985	528 152	3 008	1 877	637	125.000
	1986	971 734	3 025	1 888	1 124	181.000
Venezuela (Bolívar)	1970	52 000	10 275	5 451	45	4.450
	1975	118 100	11 993	6 768	59	4.285
	1980	254 200	15 024	8 370	100	4.293
	1983	290 500	16 394	9 269	135	4.300
	1984	409 500	16 851	9 574	152	7.500
	1985	464 600	17 317	9 887	169	7.500
	1986	493 800	17 791	10 192	189	14.500

ASIA – ASIE – ASIA

Country (Currency)	Year					
Bahrain (Dinar)	1978	915	345	191	94	0.384
	1980	1 344	348	221	100	0.376
	1983	1 711	384	247	125	0.376
	1984	1 734	400	258	125	0.376
	1985	1 603	417	271	122	0.376
	1986	1 383	412	268	119	0.376
Bangladesh (Taka)	1975	107 500	78 961	39 855	68	14.826
	1980	233 300	88 678	44 713	100	16.251
	1983	349 900	94 651	48 158	143	25.000
	1984	417 000	96 730	49 363	158	26.000
	1985	459 900	98 657	50 497	175	31.000
	1986	521 600	100 616	51 907	194	30.800
Japan (Yen)	1970	73 345 000	104 345	71 129	42	357.650
	1975	148 327 000	111 573	74 939	73	305.150
	1980	240 176 000	116 807	78 264	100	203.000
	1983	280 257 000	119 307	81 154	110	232.200
	1984	297 948 000	120 083	81 864	112	251.100
	1985	316 304 000	120 837	82 597	115	200.500
	1986	330 024 000	121 492	83 419	115	159.100
Jordan (Dinar)	1980	984	2 923	1 388	100	0.308
	1983	1 423	3 245	1 574	122	0.371
	1984	1 499	3 373	1 647	126	0.405
	1985	1 602	3 506	1 724	130	0.368
	1986	1 631	3 645	1 796	130	0.344
Kuwait (Dinar)	1980	7 741	1 370	766	100	0.271
	1983	6 134	1 566	897	121	0.293
	1984	6 381	1 637	940	123	0.304
	1985	5 830	1 712	985	124	0.289
	1986	4 816	1 791	1 034	126	0.292
Malaysia (Ringgit)	1970	10 588	8 775	5 366	56	3.078
	1975	22 332	9 997	6 447	80	2.588
	1980	53 308	13 697	7 809	100	2.222
	1983	69 565	14 747	8 535	120	2.338
	1984	79 550	15 093	8 779	125	2.425
	1985	77 547	15 681	9 166	126	2.427
	1986	71 144	16 109	9 466	126	2.603
Myanmar (Kyat)	1970	10 260	27 034	14 895	37	4.802
	1975	23 477	30 170	16 726	85	6.678
	1980	38 609	33 637	18 967	100	6.757
	1983	49 823	36 747	20 850	110	8.223
	1984	53 597	37 614	21 387	116	8.751
	1985	55 989	37 544	21 391	124	7.842
	1986	58 759	39 411	17 964	135	7.039
Pakistan (Rupee)	1965	33 250	52 579	25 957	25	4.782
	1980	278 000	82 581	42 402	100	9.900
	1983	418 200	90 480	46 915	126	13.500
	1984	478 000	93 286	48 343	134	15.360
	1985	539 500	96 180	49 737	141	15.980
	1986	602 200	99 163	51 091	146	17.250
Philippines (Peso)	1970	41 500	36 852	18 827	26	6.435
	1978	177 700	46 351	25 339	72	7.375
	1980	264 400	48 317	26 360	100	7.600
	1983	384 100	52 055	28 692	137	14.002
	1984	540 500	53 351	29 506	206	19.760
	1985	612 700	54 668	30 337	254	19.032
	1986	632 200	56 004	31 194	256	20.530
Qatar (Riyal)	1984	25 008	285	185	119	3.640
	1985	22 398	299	193	121	3.640
	1986	18 263	313	201	123	3.640

See notes on page 181.   *Voir notes page 181.*   *Véanse notas pág. 181.*

Appendix *(cont.)* **Annexe** *(suite)* **Anexo** *(cont.)*

Country and currency unit / *Pays et unité monétaire* / País y unidad monetaria (1)	Financial year / *Exercice financier* / Ejercicio financiero (2)	Gross domestic product in purchasers' values[1] (in millions of national currency units) / *PIB aux valeurs d'acquisition[1] (millions d'unités monétaires nationales)* / Producto interno bruto a precios de comprador[1] (en millones de unidades monetarias nacionales) (3)	Population in thousands / *Population (milliers)* / Población (millares) — Total (4)	Between 15 and 64 years of age / *Entre 15 et 64 ans* / Entre 15 y 64 años de edad (5)	Consumer price index 1980 = 100 / *Indices des prix à la consommation 1980 = 100* / Indice de los precios del consumo 1980 = 100 (6)	Exchange rate (national currency per US dollar)[2] / *Taux de change (en monnaie nationale pour 1 dollar des Etats-Unis)[2]* / Tasa de cambio (moneda nacional por dólar EUA)[2] (7)
Iceland (Króna)	1984	88 125	239	151	542	40.545
	1985	119 910	241	152	718	42.060
	1986	158 980	243	154	870	40.240
Ireland (Pound)	1970	1 620	2 944	1 689	28	0.418
	1975	3 790	3 127	1 837	52	0.494
	1980	9 361	3 401	1 994	100	0.527
	1983	14 786	3 504	2 078	156	0.881
	1984	16 483	3 529	2 101	169	1.009
	1985	17 619	3 540	2 116	178	0.804
	1986	18 543	3 541	2 132	185	0.715
Italie (Lire (milliards))	1970	67 178	53 661	34 862	27	0.623
	1975	138 632	55 830	35 667	46	0.687
	1980	387 669	56 434	36 569	100	0.931
	1983	633 441	56 836	37 812	160	1.660
	1984	727 225	57 005	38 253	177	1.936
	1985	812 751	57 128	38 665	193	1.679
	1986	896 321	57 221	38 838	204	1.358
Luxembourg (Franc luxembourgeois)	1970	55 000	339	223	53	49.675
	1975	86 700	358	236	75	39.528
	1980	132 900	364	244	100	31.523
	1983	174 700	366	251	128	55.640
	1984	193 700	366	253	136	63.080
	1985	207 500	366	255	141	50.360
	1986	220 500	368	257	142	40.410
Malta (Lira)	1970	95	326	205	52	0.417
	1975	166	328	212	70	0.404
	1980	392	319	214	100	0.354
	1983	458	328	218	117	0.445
	1984	461	331	219	117	0.492
	1985	476	336	222	116	0.424
	1986	512	344	228	119	0.369

Country and currency unit / *Pays et unité monétaire* / País y unidad monetaria (1)	Financial year / *Exercice financier* / Ejercicio financiero (2)	Gross domestic product in purchasers' values[1] (in millions of national currency units) / *PIB aux valeurs d'acquisition[1] (millions d'unités monétaires nationales)* / Producto interno bruto a precios de comprador[1] (en millones de unidades monetarias nacionales) (3)	Population in thousands — Total (4)	Between 15 and 64 years of age / *Entre 15 et 64 ans* / Entre 15 y 64 años de edad (5)	Consumer price index 1980 = 100 (6)	Exchange rate (national currency per US dollar)[2] (7)
Singapore (Dollar)	1970	5 805	2 075	1 197	54	3.080
	1975	13 443	2 250	1 425	84	2.490
	1980	25 091	2 414	1 646	100	2.094
	1983	36 733	2 502	1 739	114	2.127
	1984	40 048	2 529	1 769	117	2.178
	1985	38 924	2 558	1 800	117	2.105
	1986	38 155	2 586	1 826	116	2.175
Sri Lanka (Rupee)	1970	14 161	12 516	6 816	43	5.958
	1975	27 041	13 514	7 647	62	7.713
	1980	68 338	14 747	8 906	100	18.000
	1983	119 202	15 417	9 388	149	25.000
	1984	147 344	15 599	9 524	174	26.280
	1985	157 763	15 837	9 696	176	27.408
	1986	172 440	16 117	7 894	190	28.520
Rép. arabe syrienne (Livre syrienne)	1984	75 342	9 934	4 886	157	3.925
	1985	83 225	10 267	5 047	184	3.925
	1986	100 300	10 612	5 220	251	3.925
Thailand (Baht)	1980	684 900	46 718	26 375	100	20.630
	1983	924 900	49 734	29 102	123	23.000
	1984	988 900	50 714	30 023	124	27.150
	1985	1 041 400	51 683	30 951	127	26.650
	1986	1 098 400	52 654	31 909	129	26.130

EUROPE – EUROPE – EUROPA

Countries with a market economy – Pays à économie de marché – Países con economía de mercado

Austria (Schilling)	1970	375 900	7 426	4 562	54	25.880
	1975	656 100	7 520	4 642	77	18.510
	1980	994 700	7 549	4 844	100	13.809
	1983	1 201 200	7 552	4 989	116	19.341
	1984	1 276 800	7 552	5 036	123	22.050
	1985	1 348 100	7 558	5 088	127	17.280
	1986	1 423 000	7 565	5 092	129	13.710

Belgique (Franc belge)

Année					
1970	1 280 900	9 660	6 086	49	49.675
1975	2 271 100	9 801	6 252	74	39.528
1980	3 450 900	9 847	6 451	100	31.523
1983	4 117 400	9 856	6 556	126	55.640
1984	4 416 800	9 855	6 589	134	63.080
1985	4 725 800	9 858	6 624	141	50.360
1986	5 011 100	9 911	6 659	142	40.410

Denmark (Krone)

Année					
1970	118 600	4 951	3 158	39	7.489
1975	216 300	5 060	3 235	61	6.178
1980	373 800	5 123	3 317	100	6.015
1983	512 500	5 114	3 362	132	9.875
1984	565 300	5 112	3 378	140	11.260
1985	615 100	5 114	3 397	146	8.969
1986	663 600	5 121	3 413	152	7.343

España (Peseta)

Année					
1975	6 023 100	35 596	22 196	44	59.774
1980	15 209 100	37 542	23 556	100	79.250
1983	22 234 700	38 172	24 500	147	156.700
1984	25 111 300	38 342	24 793	164	173.400
1985	27 913 200	38 505	25 083	178	154.150
1986	31 981 500	38 668	25 298	194	132.395

Finland (Markka)

Année					
1970	45 700	4 606	3 054	35	4.180
1975	104 300	4 711	3 173	60	3.850
1980	192 800	4 780	3 236	100	3.840
1983	275 200	4 856	3 300	133	5.810
1984	309 600	4 882	3 321	142	6.530
1985	336 800	4 902	3 339	151	5.417
1986	360 300	4 918	3 344	156	4.794

France (Franc français)

Année					
1970	793 500	50 768	31 632	40	5.521
1975	1 467 900	52 705	33 005	61	4.486
1980	2 808 300	53 880	34 349	100	4.516
1983	4 006 500	54 728	35 578	139	8.348
1984	4 361 900	54 947	35 951	149	9.592
1985	4 695 000	55 170	36 328	158	7.561
1986	5 034 900	55 394	36 498	162	6.455

Germany, Fed. Rep. of[5] (Deutsche Mark)

Année					
1970	675 300	60 714	38 642	61	3.648
1975	1 026 900	61 832	39 540	82	2.622
1980	1 478 900	61 561	40 825	100	1.959
1983	1 674 800	61 421	41 989	116	2.724
1984	1 755 800	61 181	42 242	118	3.148
1985	1 830 500	61 015	42 544	121	2.641
1986	1 931 500	61 048	42 569	121	1.941

Grèce (Drachme)

Année					
1970	298 900	8 793	5 624	26	30.000
1975	672 200	9 047	5 781	47	35.650
1980	1 710 900	9 643	6 176	100	46.535
1983	3 077 800	9 847	6 387	181	98.670
1984	3 804 700	9 896	6 446	215	128.480
1985	4 614 200	9 934	6 498	256	147.760

Netherlands (Guilder)

Année					
1970	121 200	13 032	8 151	49	3.597
1975	220 000	13 653	8 706	75	2.689
1980	336 700	14 144	9 359	100	2.130
1983	381 000	14 362	9 703	116	3.065
1984	400 200	14 420	9 808	120	3.550
1985	418 900	14 484	9 919	123	2.772
1986	429 900	14 564	9 996	123	2.192

Norway (Krone)

Année					
1970	79 900	3 877	2 431	45	7.140
1975	148 700	4 007	2 507	67	5.585
1980	285 000	4 086	2 577	100	5.180
1983	402 200	4 128	2 628	137	7.722
1984	452 500	4 141	2 644	146	9.087
1985	500 200	4 153	2 660	154	7.583
1986	514 600	4 167	2 676	165	7.400

Portugal (Escudo)

Année					
1970	177 300	9 044	5 596	19	28.750
1975	372 200	9 426	5 863	38	27.472
1980	1 256 000	9 766	6 211	100	53.040
1983	2 301 710	10 009	6 420	184	131.450
1984	2 815 730	10 089	6 489	238	169.280
1985	3 523 950	10 157	6 551	284	157.487
1986	4 420 400	10 208	6 612	318	146.117

Suisse (Franc suisse)

Année					
1970	90 700	6 267	4 043	62	4.316
1975	140 200	6 405	4 189	89	2.620
1980	170 300	6 319	4 200	100	1.764
1983	203 900	6 419	4 345	116	2.180
1984	213 200	6 442	4 387	119	2.585
1985	227 900	6 470	4 432	123	2.077
1986	243 300	6 504	4 453	124	1.624

Sweden (Krona)

Année					
1970	172 200	8 043	5 265	41	5.170
1975	300 800	8 193	5 257	61	4.386
1980	525 100	8 310	5 328	100	4.373
1983	705 400	8 329	5 364	133	8.001
1984	789 600	8 337	5 378	143	8.990
1985	860 900	8 350	5 394	154	7.616
1986	931 800	8 369	5 416	160	6.819

Turquie (Livre turque)

Année					
1970	145 500	34 848	19 237	7	14.930
1975	519 200	40 348	22 195	14	15.150
1980	4 328 000	44 438	24 904	100	90.150
1983	11 532 000	47 279	27 446	238	282.800
1984	18 212 000	48 265	28 341	352	444.740
1985	27 552 000	49 272	29 263	511	576.860
1986	39 155 000	50 301	30 075	688	757.790

United Kingdom (Pound)

Année					
1970	51 300	48 680	34 739	28	0.418
1975	106 000	49 157	35 069	51	0.494
1980	230 100	56 330	35 815	100	0.419
1983	300 100	56 347	36 687	127	0.689
1984	319 100	56 460	36 950	134	0.865
1985	350 700	56 618	37 184	142	0.692
1986	373 700	56 763	37 267	146	0.678

See notes on page 181. *Voir notes page 181.* Véanse notas pág. 181.

Appendix *(concl.)*   **Annexe** *(fin)*   **Anexo** *(fin)*

Country and currency unit / Pays et unité monétaire / País y unidad monetaria	Financial year / Exercice financier / Ejercicio financiero	Gross domestic product in purchasers' values[1] (in millions of national currency units) / PIB aux valeurs d'acquisition[1] (millions d'unités monétaires nationales) / Producto interno bruto a precios de comprador[1] (en millones de unidades monetarias nacionales)	Population in thousands / Population (milliers) / Población (millares) Total	Between 15 and 64 years of age / Entre 15 et 64 ans / Entre 15 y 64 años de edad	Consumer price index 1980 = 100 / Indices des prix à la consommation 1980 = 100 / Indice de los precios del consumo 1980 = 100	Exchange rate (national currency per US dollar)[2] / Taux de change (en monnaie nationale pour 1 dollar des Etats-Unis)[2] / Tasa de cambio (moneda nacional por dólar EUA)[2]
(1)	(2)	(3)	(4)	(5)	(6)	(7)
EUROPE – EUROPE – EUROPA						
Countries with a centrally planned economy – Pays à économie planifiée – Países con economía centralmente planificada[6]						
RSS de Biélorussie (Rouble)	1970	...	9 038	5 604	100	0.900
	1975	...	9 351	5 809	99	0.750
	1980	...	9 643	6 454	100	0.660
	1983	...	9 843	6 588	107	0.770
	1984	...	9 910	6 633	107	0.850
	1985	...	9 975	6 677	109	0.770
	1986	...	10 043	6 722	115	0.684
Bulgarie (Lev)	1970	10 527	8 490	5 530	81	1.170
	1975	14 289	8 721	5 680	82	0.970
	1980	20 509	8 862	5 848	100	0.850
	1983	23 479	8 940	5 976	102	0.980
	1984	24 907	8 961	6 015	103	0.980
	1985	25 451	8 960	6 088	105	1.000
	1986	26 851	8 959	6 087	108	1.230
Czechoslovakia (Koruna)	1970	311 100	14 334	9 408	89	16.200
	1975	404 000	14 802	9 547	90	10.150
	1980	482 500	15 311	9 685	100	10.940
	1983	503 300	15 414	9 867	110	12.840
	1984	534 000	15 458	9 935	111	12.110
	1985	548 700	15 499	10 000	114	11.320
	1986	562 200	15 534	10 044	114	9.710
German Democratic Rep. (Mark)	1970	117 430	17 058	10 417	101	3.660
	1975	152 780	16 850	10 467	99	2.620
	1980	184 890	16 737	10 785	100	1.950
	1983	207 800	16 699	11 035	100	2.700
	1984	226 500	16 671	11 108	100	3.050
	1985	241 200	16 644	11 181	100	2.600
	1986	242 360	16 624	11 168	100	2.000

Country and currency unit / Pays et unité monétaire / País y unidad monetaria	Financial year / Exercice financier / Ejercicio financiero	Gross domestic product in purchasers' values[1] (in millions of national currency units) / PIB aux valeurs d'acquisition[1] (millions d'unités monétaires nationales) / Producto interno bruto a precios de comprador[1] (en millones de unidades monetarias nacionales)	Population in thousands / Population (milliers) / Población (millares) Total	Between 15 and 64 years of age / Entre 15 et 64 ans / Entre 15 y 64 años de edad	Consumer price index 1980 = 100 / Indices des prix à la consommation 1980 = 100 / Indice de los precios del consumo 1980 = 100	Exchange rate (national currency per US dollar)[2] / Taux de change (en monnaie nationale pour 1 dollar des Etats-Unis)[2] / Tasa de cambio (moneda nacional por dólar EUA)[2]
(1)	(2)	(3)	(4)	(5)	(6)	(7)
URSS[7] (Rouble)	1970	285 500	242 757	154 260	97	0.900
	1975	363 000	254 393	165 091	97	0.750
	1980	454 100	265 542	172 546	100	0.660
	1983	536 400	272 540	177 446	107	0.770
	1984	559 000	275 066	179 210	107	0.850
	1985	568 700	277 537	180 939	109	0.770
	1986	576 000	281 236	183 211	114	0.684
Yugoslavia (Dinar)	1970	181 900[8]	20 370	13 196	18	12.500
	1981	2 410 200[8]	22 471	14 934	140	41.823
	1983	4 282 900[8]	22 805	15 257	258	125.673
	1984	6 653 500[8]	22 966	15 416	399	211.749
	1985	11 951 000[8]	23 124	15 573	687	312.805
	1986	23 400 000[8]	23 268	15 699	1 304	457.180
OCEANIA – OCÉANIE – OCEANIA						
Australia (Dollar)	1970	35 100	12 507	7 780	39	0.897
	1975	76 700	13 771	8 798	61	0.795
	1980	138 700	14 695	9 509	100	0.847
	1983	190 600	15 379	10 056	134	1.109
	1984	211 500	15 556	10 216	140	1.208
	1985	236 200	15 758	10 377	149	1.469
	1986	260 400	15 974	10 534	162	1.504
Fiji (Dollar)	1975	562	569	327	64	0.863
	1980	984	634	376	100	0.791
	1983	1 142	672	398	127	1.046
	1984	1 275	686	406	134	1.143
	1985	1 311	697	413	140	1.120
	1986	1 456	704	417	142	1.145

Pays (Monnaie)	Année	(3)	(4)	(5)	(6)	(7)
Hongrie (Forint)	1970	274 900	10 338	6 994	64	30.000
	1975	395 000	10 541	7 059	74	43.508
	1980	582 900	10 711	6 922	100	32.213
	1983	738 100	10 689	7 005	120	45.193
	1984	804 100	10 649	7 024	130	51.199
	1985	842 900	10 631	7 044	139	47.347
	1986	881 300		7 045	146	45.927
Pologne (Zloty)	1984	7 181 800	36 914	24 056	352	122.000
	1985	8 657 900	37 203	24 202	404	151.000
	1986	10 697 100	37 456	24 353	458	196.000
RSS d'Ukraine (Rouble)	1970	54 800	47 307	31 696	97	0.900
	1975	65 800	48 900	32 843	96	0.750
	1980	77 500	50 043	33 402	100	0.660
	1983	92 300	50 564	33 749	105	0.770
	1984	96 200	50 754	33 876	105	0.850
	1985	96 600	50 917	33 986	107	0.770
	1986	97 400	51 097	34 106	112	0.684
New Zealand (Dollar)	1970	5 832	·	1 676	31	0.896
	1975	11 668	2 811	1 861	50	0.958
	1980	22 947	3 071	1 971	100	1.039
	1983	34 307	3 113	2 061	144	1.528
	1984	38 838	3 199	2 091	153	2.094
	1985	44 861	3 227	2 116	176	2.006
	1986	53 382	3 248	2 126	200	1.910
Solomon Islands (Dollar)	1981	141	233	112	116	0.889
	1983	175	250	121	140	1.221
	1984	220	260	125	155	1.344
	1985	235	270	130	170	1.613
	1986	250	281	136	193	1.986

[1] Gross domestic product computed in accordance with the new System of National Accounts (unless otherwise indicated). [2] Foreign exchange rates are shown in units of national currency per US dollar and refer to end-of-period quotations. [3] Converted from Mali francs at the rate of 2 Mali francs to 1 CFA franc. [4] Source: Union Bank of Switzerland. [5] At the time of writing the interests of Berlin (West) were represented in the International Labour Organisation by the Federal Republic of Germany. Accordingly the data include West Berlin for which separate figures were not available. [6] For these countries, except Yugoslavia, the aggregate in column 3 is the net material product. [7] Data relate to the whole of the USSR (including Byelorussian SSR and Ukrainian SSR which appear separately). [8] Gross domestic product.

Sources: col. (3) United Nations: Yearbook of National Accounts Statistics; Monthly Bulletin of Statistics; Statistical Yearbook; cols. (4) and (5) United Nations: Demographic Yearbook; Monthly Bulletin of Statistics; Global Estimates and Projections of Population by Sex and Age, The 1988 Revision; col. (6) ILO: Year Book of Labour Statistics; International Financial Statistics Yearbook; col. (7) International Monetary Fund: International Financial Statistics Yearbook; United Nations: Monthly Bulletin of Statistics; Statistical Yearbook.

[1] Produit intérieur brut calculé selon le nouveau Système de comptabilité nationale (sauf indication contraire). [2] Montant en monnaie nationale pour 1 dollar des Etats-Unis; taux en vigueur à la fin de la période. [3] Convertis au taux de 2 francs maliens pour 1 franc CFA. [4] Source: Union de banques suisses. [5] A l'époque de l'enquête, les intérêts de Berlin (Ouest) étaient représentés au sein de l'Organisation internationale du Travail par la République fédérale d'Allemagne; on ne dispose pas de données distinctes pour Berlin (Ouest), ces données étant comprises dans celles relatives à la République fédérale d'Allemagne. [6] Pour ces pays, à l'exception de la Yougoslavie, l'agrégat donné dans la colonne 3 est le produit matériel net. [7] Les données se rapportent à l'ensemble de l'URSS (y compris les RSS de Biélorussie et d'Ukraine, qui figurent séparément dans les tableaux). [8] Produit matériel brut.

Sources: Colonne 3: Nations Unies: Yearbook of National Accounts Statistics; Bulletin mensuel de statistique; Annuaire statistique. Colonnes 4 et 5: Nations Unies: Annuaire démographique; Bulletin mensuel de statistique; Global estimates and projections of population by sex and age. The 1988 revision. Colonne 6: BIT: Annuaire des statistiques du travail; Fonds monétaire international: Statistiques financières internationales. Colonne 7: Fonds monétaire international: Statistiques financières internationales; Nations Unies: Bulletin mensuel de statistique; Annuaire statistique.

[1] Producto interno bruto computado de conformidad con el nuevo sistema de cuentas nacionales (salvo indicación en contrario). [2] Las tasas de cambio de divisas se presentan en unidades monetarias nacionales por dólar de los Estados Unidos y corresponden a cotizaciones de fines del período. [3] A razón de 2 francos malíes por 1 franco CFA. [4] Fuente: Unión Bank of Switzerland. [5] En el momento de redactar la respuesta, los intereses de Berlín (Oeste) estaban representados en la Organización Internacional del Trabajo por la República Federal de Alemania. Por tanto, los datos incluyen los de Berlín (Oeste), de los que no se dispone por separado. [6] Con excepción de Yugoslavia, los totales relativos a estos países que figuran en la columna 3 son los del producto material neto. [7] Los datos se refieren a toda la URSS (incluidas la RSS de Bielorrusia y la RSS de Ucrania, que figuran por separado). [8] Producto interno bruto.

Fuentes: Columna 3: Naciones Unidas: Yearbook of National Accounts Statistics; Monthly Bulletin of Statistics; Statistical Yearbook. Columnas 4 y 5: Naciones Unidas: Demographic Yearbook; Monthly Bulletin of Statistics; Global Estimates and Projections of Population by Sex and Age, The 1988 Revision. Columna 6: OIT: Year Book of Labour Statistics; Fondo Monetario Internacional: International Financial Statistics Yearbook. Columna 7: Fondo Monetario Internacional: International Financial Statistics Yearbook; Naciones Unidas: Monthly Bulletin of Statistics; Statistical Yearbook.

2. Key to country names in three languages

2. Index des noms des pays dans les trois langues

2. Clave de nombres de países en tres idiomas

Ordre de présentation	English	Français	Español
AFRICA – AFRIQUE – AFRICA			
1 Bénin	Benin	Bénin	Benin
2 Burkina Faso	Burkina Faso	Burkina Faso	Burkina Faso
3 Burundi	Burundi	Burundi	Burundi
—	—	—	Cabo Verde (5)
4 Cameroon	Cameroon	Cameroun	Camerún
5 Cap-Vert	Cape Verde	Cap-Vert	*Cabo Verde*
6 Rép. centrafricaine	Central African Rep.	Rép. centrafricaine	Rep. Centroafricana
	Chad (28)	—	Chad (28)
7 Côte d'Ivoire	Côte d'Ivoire	Côte d'Ivoire	Côte d'Ivoire
8 Egypt	Egypt	Egypte	Egipto
9 Ethiopia	Ethiopia	Ethiopie	Etiopía
10 Gabon	Gabon	Gabon	Gabón
11 Guinée	Guinea	Guinée	Guinea
12 Guinée-Bissau	Guinea-Bissau	Guinée-Bissau	Guinea-Bissau
13 Kenya	Kenya	Kenya	Kenya
14 Madagascar	Madagascar	Madagascar	Madagascar
15 Mali	Mali	Mali	Malí
16 Maroc	*Morocco*	Maroc	Marruecos
	—	Maurice (18)	Mauricio (18)
17 Mauritanie	Mauritania	Mauritanie	Mauritania
18 Mauritius	Mauritius	*Maurice*	*Mauricio*
	Morocco (16)	—	—
19 Mozambique	Mozambique	Mozambique	Mozambique
20 Niger	Niger	Niger	Níger
21 Nigeria	Nigeria	Nigéria	Nigeria
	—	Ouganda (31)	—
22 Rwanda	Rwanda	Rwanda	Rwanda
23 Sao Tomé-et-Principe	Sao Tome and Principe	Sao Tomé-et-Principe	Santo Tomé y Príncipe
24 Sénégal	Senegal	Sénégal	Senegal
25 Sudan	Sudan	Soudan	Sudán
26 Swaziland	Swaziland	Swaziland	Swazilandia
27 Tanzania, United Rep. of	Tanzania, United Rep. of	Tanzanie, Rép.-Unie	Tanzanía, Rep. Unida de
28 Tchad	*Chad*	Tchad	*Chad*
29 Togo	Togo	Togo	Togo
30 Tunisie	Tunisia	Tunisie	Túnez
31 Uganda	Uganda	*Ouganda*	Uganda
32 Zaïre	Zaire	Zaïre	Zaire
33 Zambia	Zambia	Zambie	Zambia
AMERICA – AMÉRIQUE – AMERICA			
34 Argentina	Argentina	Argentine	Argentina
35 Bahamas	Bahamas	Bahamas	Bahamas
36 Barbados	Barbados	Barbade	Barbados
37 Belize	Belize	Belize	Belice
38 Bolivia	Bolivia	Bolivie	Bolivia
39 Brasil	Brazil	Brésil	Brasil
40 Canada	Canada	Canada	Canadá
	Chile (44)	Chili (44)	—
41 Colombia	Colombia	Colombie	Colombia
42 Costa Rica	Costa Rica	Costa Rica	Costa Rica
43 Cuba	Cuba	Cuba	Cuba
44 Chile	*Chile*	*Chili*	Chile
	—	Rép. dominicaine (46)	—
45 Dominica	Dominica	Dominique	Dominica
46 República Dominicana	Dominican Rep.	*Rép. dominicaine*	República Dominicana
	—	El Salvador (48)	—
47 Ecuador	Ecuador	Equateur	Ecuador
48 El Salvador	El Salvador	*El Salvador*	El Salvador
	—	Etats-Unis (59)	Estados Unidos (59)
49 Grenada	Grenada	Grenade	Granada
50 Guatemala	Guatemala	Guatemala	Guatemala
51 Guyana	Guyana	Guyana	Guyana
52 Honduras	Honduras	Honduras	Honduras
53 Jamaica	Jamaica	Jamaïque	Jamaica
54 México	Mexico	Mexique	México
55 Panamá	Panama	Panama	Panamá
56 Perú	Peru	Pérou	Perú
57 St. Lucia	St Lucia	Sainte-Lucie	Santa Lucía
58 Trinidad and Tobago	Trinidad and Tobago	Trinité-et-Tobago	Trinidad y Tabago
59 United States	United States	*Etats-Unis*	*Estados Unidos*
60 Uruguay	Uruguay	Uruguay	Uruguay
61 Venezuela	Venezuela	Venezuela	Venezuela

Ordre de présentation	English	Français	Español

ASIA – ASIE – ASIA

62 Bahrain	Bahrain	Bahreïn	Bahrein
63 Bangladesh	Bangladesh	Bangladesh	Bangladesh
64 Cyprus	Cyprus	Chypre	Chipre
	—	—	Filipinas (75)
65 India	India	Inde	India
66 Indonesia	Indonesia	Indonésie	Indonesia
67 Iran, Islamic Rep. of	Iran, Islamic Rep. of	Iran, Rép. islamique	Irán, Rep. Islámica del
68 Israel	Israel	Israël	Israel
69 Japan	Japan	Japon	Japón
70 Jordan	Jordan	Jordanie	Jordania
71 Kuwait	Kuwait	Koweit	Kuwait
72 Malaysia	Malaysia	Malaisie	Malasia
73 Myanmar	Myanmar	Myanmar	Myanmar
74 Pakistan	Pakistan	Pakistan	Pakistán
75 Philippines	Philippines	Philippines	*Filipinas*
76 Qatar	Qatar	Qatar	Qatar
77 Singapore	Singapore	Singapour	Singapur
78 Sri Lanka	Sri Lanka	Sri Lanka	Sri Lanka
79 Rép. arabe syrienne	Syrian Arab Rep.	Rép. arabe syrienne	*República Arabe Siria*
80 Thailand	Thailand	Thaïlande	Tailandia

EUROPE – EUROPE – EUROPA
Countries with a market economy – Pays à économie de marché – Países con economía de mercado

	—	Allemagne, Rép. féd. (87)	Alemania, Rep. Fed. de (87)
81 Austria	Austria	Autriche	Austria
82 Belgique	Belgium	Belgique	Bélgica
83 Denmark	Denmark	Danemark	Dinamarca
84 España	*Spain*	Espagne	España
85 Finland	Finland	Finlande	Finlandia
86 France	France	France	Francia
87 Germany, Fed. Rep. of	Germany, Fed. Rep. of	*Allemagne, Rép. féd.*	*Alemania, Rep. Fed. de*
88 Grèce	Greece	Grèce	Grecia
89 Iceland	Iceland	*Islande*	*Islandia*
90 Ireland	Ireland	Irlande	Irlanda
	—	Islande (89)	Islandia (89)
91 Italie	Italy	Italie	Italia
92 Luxembourg	Luxembourg	Luxembourg	Luxemburgo
93 Malta	Malta	Malte	Malta
94 Netherlands	Netherlands	*Pays-Bas*	*Países Bajos*
95 Norway	Norway	Norvège	Noruega
	—	Pays-Bas (94)	Países Bajos (94)
96 Portugal	Portugal	Portugal	Portugal
		Royaume-Uni (100)	Reino Unido (100)
	Spain (84)	—	—
	Sweden (98)	Suède (98)	Suecia (98)
97 Suisse	*Switzerland*	Suisse	Suiza
98 Sweden	Sweden	*Suède*	*Suecia*
	Switzerland (97)	—	—
99 Turquie	Turkey	Turquie	Turquía
100 United Kingdom	United Kingdom	*Royaume-Uni*	*Reino Unido*

EUROPE – EUROPE – EUROPA
Countries with a centrally planned economy – Pays à économie planifiée – Países con economía centralmente planificada

101 RSS de Biélorussie	*Byelorussian SSR*	RSS de Biélorussie	RSS de Bielorrusia
102 Bulgarie	Bulgaria	Bulgarie	Bulgaria
	Byelorussian SSR (101)	—	—
103 Czechoslovakia	Czechoslovakia	*Tchécoslovaquie*	Checoslovaquia
104 German Democratic Rep.	German Democratic Rep.	*Rép. dém. allemande*	*Rep. Dem. Alemana*
105 Hongrie	Hungary	Hongrie	Hungría
106 Pologne	Poland	Pologne	Polonia
	—	Rép. dém. allemande (103)	Rep. Dem. Alemana (103)
107 RSS d'Ukraine	Ukrainian SSR	RSS d'Ukraine	RSS de Ucrania
	—	Tchécoslovaquie (102)	—
108 URSS	USSR	URSS	URSS
109 Yugoslavia	Yugoslavia	Yougoslavie	Yugoslavia

OCEANIA – OCÉANIE – OCEANIA

110 Australia	Australia	Australie	Australia
111 Fiji	Fiji	Fidji	Fiji
	—	Iles Salomon (113)	Islas Salomón (113)
112 New Zealand	New Zealand	Nouvelle-Zélande	Nueva Zelandia
113 Solomon Islands	Solomon Islands	*Iles Salomon*	*Islas Salomón*

Supplementary inquiry
Special schemes for
central government employees

Enquête complémentaire
Régimes spéciaux
des agents de l'Etat

Encuesta suplementaria
Regímenes especiales para
empleados del gobierno central

INTRODUCTION

A supplementary inquiry relating to special social security schemes for central government employees has been conducted concurrently with the 13th international inquiry into the cost of social security. This inquiry requested data on receipts and expenditure of the schemes concerned, as well as on the number of insured persons and their wages and salaries.

Special schemes for central government employees are social security schemes or arrangements for these employees which are separate from the general and other specific social security schemes. For the purpose of the supplementary inquiry, the special schemes for central government employees are defined to be those schemes covering public employees (including military personnel) whose wages and salaries are paid from the central government budget.

The period covered was the calendar year 1986 or the latest available calendar year, or the financial year of which the greater part fell in the calendar year concerned.

The contingencies for which data were requested were defined as in the basic inquiry, but were grouped as follows:

- pensions;
- sickness and maternity cash benefits and medical care;
- employment injuries;
- family allowances;
- others.

The requested presentation of the data on receipts and expenditure was as follows:

Receipts	Expenditure
Contributions:	Benefits:
From insured persons	Medical care
From government as employer	Benefits in kind other than for medical care
Income from capital	Cash benefit
Other receipts (state participation, transfer from other schemes, etc.)	Total benefits
	Administrative expenditure
Total receipts	Other expenditure
	Total expenditure

In addition to the above, the following two items of information were also requested:

(a) the number of central government employees covered by the respective schemes at the end of the reference year; and

(b) their total wages and salaries in the reference year.

Thirty countries have provided replies to this supplementary inquiry and they are presented in table A. The countries covered, classified by region, are as follows:

Africa (7 countries): Burundi, Mali, Mauritius, Morocco, Mozambique, Niger and Tunisia.

America (9 countries): Canada, Colombia, El Salvador, Grenada, Honduras, Mexico, Panama, the United States and Venezuela.

Asia (3 countries): Japan, Malaysia and Pakistan.

Europe (9 countries): Belgium, Federal Republic of Germany, Greece, Ireland, Netherlands, Portugal, Spain, Turkey and the United Kingdom.

Oceania (2 countries): Australia and New Zealand.

It should be noted that for certain countries, where all government employees are employed by the central government, a separate reply to the supplementary inquiry was not submitted because the relevant financial data were already included in the basic inquiry under the item "Special schemes for public employees".

Using the data of table A, tables B, C and D have been derived. Countries or schemes for which data on wages and salaries and/or number of employees covered were not available do not appear in the tables which are based on the respective data.

Table B gives average social security contributions in 1986 per head of employee, in national currency units and in US dollars. The contributions refer to the aggregate contributions by the government and the employee. The exchange rates are those given in appendix table 1.

Table C gives total benefit expenditure in 1986 as a percentage of the wages and salaries of economically active persons covered by the respective scheme.

Table D gives the distribution of benefit expenditure in 1986 among the main branches of social security, namely pensions, sickness and maternity, employment injury, family allowances and others. In this table, whenever "100%" is indicated against one of the heads of classification, caution should be exercised as this could be due to incomplete reporting.

As this is the first inquiry on this topic, the Office has had considerable difficulty in verifying whether all schemes within the scope of the inquiry were reported with the necessary breakdowns by the responding countries. The results should therefore be interpreted with caution.

INTRODUCTION

En même temps que la treizième enquête sur le coût de la sécurité sociale, le BIT a conduit une enquête complémentaire sur les régimes spéciaux des agents de l'Etat, c'est-à-dire les régimes ou arrangements de sécurité sociale institués pour ces agents qui sont distincts du régime général et des autres régimes particuliers de la sécurité sociale. Les régimes en question sont définis aux fins de l'enquête comme les régimes couvrant les agents publics (y compris le personnel militaire) qui émargent au budget de l'Etat (à l'exclusion des agents qui émargent aux budgets des Etats constituants pour les Etats fédératifs).

Les Etats Membres de l'OIT ont été invités à fournir des données sur les recettes et les dépenses de ces régimes, sur le nombre d'agents protégés ainsi que sur le montant des salaires et traitements de ces agents.

La période considérée est l'année civile 1986 ou la dernière année civile pour laquelle il existe des données, ou l'exercice financier compris en majeure partie dans l'année en question.

Les éventualités pour lesquelles des données ont été demandées sont définies comme pour l'enquête de base, les prestations étant regroupées par branche comme suit:

– pensions;
– prestations de maladie et de maternité: prestations en espèces et soins médicaux;
– prestations en cas d'accidents du travail et de maladies professionnelles;
– allocations familiales;
– autres.

Les données sur les recettes et les dépenses sont présentées selon la ventilation suivante:

Recettes	Dépenses
Cotisations:	Prestations:
– des assurés	soins médicaux
– de l'Etat en tant qu'employeur	prestations en nature à d'autres titres que les soins médicaux
Revenu des capitaux	prestations en espèces
Autres recettes (participation de l'Etat, transferts provenant d'autres régimes, etc.)	total des prestations
	Frais d'administration
	Autres dépenses
Total des recettes	Total des dépenses

Les gouvernements ont été invités en outre à fournir des données sur les deux points suivants:

a) nombre d'agents de l'Etat protégés par les régimes considérés à la fin de l'année de référence;

b) montant total des salaires et traitements versés aux agents protégés au cours de l'année de référence.

Pour cette enquête complémentaire, des réponses ont été reçues des 30 pays suivants, regroupés par région:

Afrique (7 pays): Burundi, Mali, Maroc, Maurice, Mozambique, Niger, Tunisie.

Amérique (9 pays): Canada, Colombie, El Salvador, Etats-Unis, Grenade, Honduras, Mexique, Panama, Venezuela.

Asie (3 pays): Japon, Malaisie, Pakistan.

Europe (9 pays): République fédérale d'Allemagne, Belgique, Espagne, Grèce, Irlande, Pays-Bas, Portugal, Turquie, Royaume-Uni.

Océanie (2 pays): Australie, Nouvelle-Zélande.

On se souvient que l'enquête de base couvre les régimes spéciaux des agents publics. Dans certains pays, tous les agents publics sont des agents de l'Etat au sens de l'enquête complémentaire. Ces pays n'ont donc pas nécessairement fourni une réponse distincte pour cette dernière, les données financières demandées apparaissant déjà dans la réponse communiquée pour l'enquête de base.

Les données reçues pour l'enquête complémentaire sont présentées ci-après dans le tableau A. A partir de ces chiffres, on a établi les tableaux B, C et D. Pour certains pays ou certains régimes, les réponses ne contenaient pas de données sur le nombre des agents protégés ou sur le montant total des salaires et traitements; ces pays ou ces régimes n'apparaissent pas dans les tableaux B ou C.

Le tableau B indique le montant moyen des cotisations de sécurité sociale par agent protégé en 1986, en unités monétaires nationales et en dollars des Etats-Unis. Il s'agit de la cotisation totale (part de l'Etat et part de l'assuré). Les taux de change appliqués sont ceux qui sont indiqués pour l'enquête de base dans le tableau 1 de l'annexe.

Le tableau C donne le total des dépenses en prestations pour 1986 en pourcentage du montant total des salaires et traitements des agents couverts par les différents régimes.

Le tableau D donne la répartition des dépenses en prestations pour 1986 entre les principales branches considérées: pensions, prestations de maladie et de maternité, prestations en cas d'accidents du travail et de maladies professionnelles, allocations familiales, autres prestations. L'indication 100 pour cent sous l'une ou l'autre de ces rubriques doit être considérée avec prudence; elle pourrait s'expliquer en effet par le fait que les données reçues n'étaient pas complètes.

C'est la première enquête que le BIT conduit sur les régimes spéciaux des agents de l'Etat. Il a été très difficile de ce fait de déterminer si des données avaient été reçues des Etats Membres pour tous les régimes visés avec toutes les ventilations nécessaires. Il convient donc d'interpréter avec prudence les résultats de l'enquête.

INTRODUCCION

Conjuntamente con la decimotercera encuesta internacional sobre el costo de la seguridad social, se ha efectuado una encuesta suplementaria en relación con los regímenes especiales de seguridad social para empleados del gobierno central. Para ello se requirieron datos sobre ingresos y egresos de los regímenes comprendidos en esta encuesta, así como sobre el número de personas aseguradas y sus sueldos y salarios.

Los regímenes especiales para empleados del gobierno central son regímenes o arreglos de la seguridad social para dichos empleados, que son también distintos de los regímenes generales y otros regímenes específicos de la seguridad social. Para los fines de la encuesta suplementaria, los regímenes especiales para empleados del gobierno central se definen como aquellos regímenes que abarcan empleados públicos (incluido el personal militar) cuyos sueldos y salarios se cargan al presupuesto del gobierno central.

El período comprendido fue el del año civil de 1986 o el último año civil con datos disponibles, o el ejercicio financiero cuya mayor parte correspondió al año civil pertinente.

Las contingencias para las cuales se requirieron los datos se definieron tal como en la encuesta básica, pero se las agrupó de la siguiente manera:
- pensiones;
- asistencia médica y prestaciones monetarias de enfermedad y de maternidad;
- accidentes del trabajo y enfermedades profesionales;
- prestaciones familiares;
- otros.

Se requirió que la presentación de datos sobre ingresos y egresos fuera la siguiente:

Ingresos

Cotizaciones:
  de los asegurados
  del gobierno como empleador
Renta del capital
Otros ingresos (participación del Estado, transferencias de otros regímenes, etc.)
Total de ingresos

Egresos

Prestaciones:
  Asistencia médica
  Prestaciones en especie distintas de la asistencia médica
  Prestaciones monetarias
  Total de prestaciones
Gastos de administración
Otros egresos
Total de egresos

Asimismo, se requirió información sobre:
a) el número de empleados del gobierno central comprendidos por los respectivos regímenes al finalizar el año de referencia; y
b) sus sueldos y salarios totales en el año de referencia.

En el cuadro A se presentan los 30 países que suministraron respuestas a esta encuesta suplementaria. Los países comprendidos, según su clasificación por región, san los siguientes:

Africa (7 países): Burundi, Malí, Marruecos, Mauricio, Mozambique, Níger y Túnez.

América (9 países): Canadá, Colombia, El Salvador, Estados Unidos, Granada, Honduras, México, Panamá y Venezuela.

Asia (3 países): Japón, Malasia y Pakistán.

Europa (9 países): República Federal de Alemania, Bélgica, España, Grecia, Irlanda, Países Bajos, Portugal, Reino Unido y Turquía.

Oceanía (2 países): Australia y Nueva Zelandia.

Procede señalar que en ciertos países, en donde todos los empleados del gobierno son empleados del gobierno central, no se remitió una respuesta por separado para la encuesta suplementaria, ya que los datos financieros pertinentes se habían incluido en la encuesta básica bajo el rubro de «regímenes especiales para empleados públicos».

A partir de los datos del cuadro A, se confeccionaron los cuadros B, C y D. Los países o regímenes de los que no se dispuso de datos acerca de sueldos y salarios y/o del número de empleados comprendidos no aparecen en los cuadros basados sobre los respectivos datos.

En el cuadro B se presentan los promedios de cotizaciones de la seguridad social en 1986 por cada empleado, en unidades monetarias nacionales y en dólares de los Estados Unidos. Las cotizaciones se refieren a las cotizaciones totales del gobierno y de los empleados. Las tasas del cambio de divisas son las consignadas en el apéndice 1.

En el cuadro C se presentan los egresos totales por prestaciones en 1986 como un porcentaje de los sueldos y salarios de personas económicamente activas, abarcadas por los regímenes respectivos.

En el cuadro D se presenta la distribución de los egresos por prestaciones en 1986 entre las principales ramas de la seguridad social: pensiones, enfermedad y maternidad, riesgos profesionales, prestaciones familiares y otros egresos. En este cuadro, cada vez que se indique «100%» en uno de los rubros de la clasificación, la interpretación debe hacerse en forma prudente, ya que ello puede deberse a una información incompleta.

Dado que ésta es la primera encuesta sobre el tema, la Oficina ha tenido considerables dificultades para verificar si todos los regímenes comprendidos en el ámbito de la encuesta figuraban con los necesarios desgloses en las comunicaciones de los países que han respondido. Por tanto, los resultados deben interpretarse con prudencia.

Tables

Tableaux

Cuadros

A. Total social security receipts and expenditure, wages and salaries and number of employees covered, by main item, 1986
(financial data in millions of national currency units)

A. Recettes et dépenses totales des régimes, total des salaires et traitements et nombre d'agents couverts, par branche principale, 1986
(données financières en millions d'unités monétaires nationales)

A. Ingresos y egresos totales de la seguridad social, sueldos y salarios y número de empleados comprendidos, por rubros principales, 1986
(datos financieros en millones de unidades monetarias nacionales)

Country, currency unit and scheme / Pays et unité monétaire, régime / País, unidad monetaria y régimen	Receipts / Recettes / Ingresos					Expenditure / Dépenses / Egresos			
	Contributions / Cotisations / Cotizaciones		Income from capital / Revenu des capitaux / Renta del capital	Other receipts / Autres recettes / Otros ingresos	Total receipts / Total des recettes / Total de ingresos	Benefits / Prestations / Prestaciones			
	From insured persons / Des assurés / De los asegurados	From government as employer / De l'Etat (employeur) / Del gobierno como empleador				Medical care / Soins médicaux / Asistencia médica	Benefits in kind other than for medical care / Prestations en nature à d'autres titres que les soins médicaux / Prestaciones en especie distintas de la asistencia médica	Cash benefits / Prestations en espèces / Prestaciones monetarias	Total / Total / Total
(1)	(2)	(3)	(4)	(5)	(6)	(7)	(8)	(9)	(10)
AFRICA – AFRIQUE – AFRICA									
Burundi (Franc burundais) Sickness and maternity	252	378	25	2	657	498	.	.	498
Mali (Franc CFA) Pensions	900.6	1 801.1	.	247.4	2 949.1	.	.	2 858.8	2 858.8
Maroc (Dirham) Pensions:									
1. Moroccan Pension Fund (CMR)	545	85	.	605	1 235	.	.	1 359	1 359
2. General Retirement Benefits Scheme (RCAR)	311	.	244	.	555	.	.	47	47
Total	856	85	244	605	1 790	.	.	1 405	1 405
Mauritius[1] (Rupee)									
1. Widows' and Children's Pension Scheme	24	16	.	.	39	.	.	38	38
2. Pensions and children's allowances	.	133	.	.	133	.	.	133	133
3. Gratuities	.	58	.	.	58	.	.	58	58
Total	24	207	.	.	231	.	.	229	229
Mozambique (Metical) Pensions:									
1. Old-age	.	41.0	.	24.0	65.0	.	.	65.0	65.0
2. Survivors	.	0.7	.	7.3	8.0	.	.	8.0	8.0
Total	.	41.7	.	31.3	73.0	.	.	73.0	73.0

See notes on page 206.   *Voir notes page 206.*   Véanse notas pág. 206.

(11) Administrative expenditure / Frais d'administration / Gastos de administración	(12) Other expenditure / Autres dépenses / Otros egresos	(13) Total expenditure / Total des dépenses / Total de egresos	(14) Difference between receipts and expenditure in financial year / Différence entre les recettes et les dépenses au cours de l'exercice / Diferencia entre ingresos y egresos en ejercicio financiero	(15) Total wages and salaries / Total des salaires et traitements / Total de sueldos y salarios	(16) No. of employees covered / Nombre d'agents couverts / Núm. de empleados comprendidos	(17) Régime	(18) Régimen
40	.	538	119	8 400	65 000	*Maladie et maternité*	Enfermedad y maternidad
56.5	3.2	2 918.5	30.6	25 782.5	12 000	*Pensions*	Pensiones
						Pensions:	Pensiones:
.	.	1 359	− 124	.	477 891	*1. Caisse marocaine de retraite*	1. Caja Marroquí de Pensiones (CMB)
9	48	103	452	.	117 345	*2. Régime collectif d'allocations de retraite*	2. Régimen General de Prestaciones de Pensiones (RCAR)
9	.	1 462	328	.	.	*Total*	Total
1	0	39	.	.	48 323	*1. Pensions (veuves et enfants)*	1. Régimen de Pensión para Viudas e Hijos
.	.	133	.	.	.	*2. Pensions et allocations familiales*	2. Pensiones y asignaciones por hijos
.	.	58	.	.	.	*3. Gratifications*	3. Gratificaciones
1	0	231	.	.	.	*Total*	Total
.	.	65.0	.	.	1 042	*Pensions:* *1. Vieillesse*	Pensiones: 1. Vejez
.	.	8.0	.	.	224	*2. Survivants*	2. Sobrevivientes
.	.	73.0	.	.	.	*Total*	Total

Table A *(cont.)* Tableau A *(suite)* Cuadro A *(cont.)*

Country, currency unit and scheme / Pays et unité monétaire, régime / País, unidad monetaria y régimen	Receipts / Recettes / Ingresos					Expenditure / Dépenses / Egresos			
	Contributions / Cotisations / Cotizaciones		Income from capital / Revenu des capitaux / Renta del capital	Other receipts / Autres recettes / Otros ingresos	Total receipts / Total des recettes / Total de ingresos	Benefits / Prestations / Prestaciones			
	From insured persons / Des assurés / De los asegurados	From government as employer / De l'Etat (employeur) / Del gobierno como empleador				Medical care / Soins médicaux / Asistencia médica	Benefits in kind other than for medical care / Prestations en nature à d'autres titres que les soins médicaux / Prestaciones en especie distintas de la asistencia médica	Cash benefits / Prestations en espèces / Prestaciones monetarias	Total / Total / Total
(1)	(2)	(3)	(4)	(5)	(6)	(7)	(8)	(9)	(10)
Niger[2] (Franc CFA) Pensions	1 106.3	5 135.3[3]	.	.	6 241.6	1 306.3	.	1 170.5	2 476.8
Tunisie (Dinar) National Retirement and Social Benefits Fund:									
1. Social benefits (medical care):									
Compulsory scheme	8.5	7.4	2.4	.	18.3	8.3	2.0	.	10.3
Voluntary	1.0	.	.	.	1.0	1.5	.	.	1.5
Subtotal 1	9.5	7.4	2.4	.	19.3	9.8	2.0	.	11.8
2. Pensions	46.7	53.5	11.6	.	111.8	.	.	82.1	82.1
3. Death indemnity	4.8	.	0.2	.	5.0	.	.	5.7	5.7
Subtotal 2-3	51.5	53.5	11.8	.	116.8	.	.	87.8	87.8
Total	61.0	60.9	14.2	.	136.1	9.8	2.0	87.8	99.6
AMERICA – AMÉRIQUE – AMERICA									
Canada[4] (Dollar)									
1. Public service	524.1	512.7	1 992.6	9.7	3 039.1	.	.	739.8	739.8
2. Canadian forces	125.3	223.0	1 350.2	1.9	1 700.4	.	.	394.7	394.7
3. Royal Canadian Mounted Police (RCMP)	34.3	68.3	196.1	.	298.7	.	.	27.4	27.4
4. Supplementary retirement	126.2	126.4	268.3	0.3	521.2	.	.	26.9	26.9
Total	809.9	930.4	3 807.2	11.9	5 559.4	.	.	1 188.8	1 188.8
Colombia (Peso) Special schemes for central government employees	4 592	23 837	200	1 469	30 098	6 755	.	22 053	28 808
El Salvador (Colón) Sickness, maternity and employment injuries	3.6	10.8	.	.	14.4	.	.	14.4	14.4
Grenada (EC dollar) Pensions and gratuities	.	4.581	.	0.199	4.780	.	.	4.780	4.780

See notes on page 206. *Voir notes page 206.* Véanse notas pág. 206.

Administrative expenditure	Other expenditure	Total expenditure	Difference between receipts and expenditure in financial year	Total wages and salaries	No. of employees covered	Régime	Régimen
Frais d'administration	*Autres dépenses*	*Total des dépenses*	*Différence entre les recettes et les dépenses au cours de l'exercice*	*Total des salaires et traitements*	*Nombre d'agents couverts*		
Gastos de administración	Otros egresos	Total de egresos	Diferencia entre ingresos y egresos en ejercicio financiero	Total de sueldos y salarios	Núm. de empleados comprendidos		
(11)	(12)	(13)	(14)	(15)	(16)	(17)	(18)
2 598.4	1 166.4	6 241.6	.	6 950.0	54 000	*Pensions*	Pensiones
						Caisse nationale de retraite et de prévoyance sociale	Caja Nacional de Pensiones y Prestaciones Sociales:
						1. Prévoyance sociale (soins médicaux)	1. Prestaciones sociales (asistencia medica):
2.0	.	12.3	6.0	.	.	*Régime obligatoire*	Régimen obligatorio
0.2	.	1.7	−0.7	.	.	*Régime facultatif*	Régimen voluntario
2.2	.	14.0	5.3	.	.	*Sous-total 1*	Subtotal 1
13.6	.	95.7	16.1	.	.	*2. Pensions*	2. Pensiones
0.8	.	6.5	−1.5	.	.	*3. Capital décès*	3. Indemnización por muerte
14.4	.	102.2	14.6	.	.	*Sous-total 2-3*	Subtotal 2-3
16.6	.	116.2	19.9	.	.	*Total*	Total
.	64.8	804.6	2 234.5	.	.	*1. Fonction publique*	1. Administración pública
.	15.9	410.6	1 289.8	.	.	*2. Forces canadiennes*	2. Fuerzas armadas
.	2.4	29.8	268.9	.	.	*3. Gendarmerie royale du Canada*	3. Real Policía Montada del Canadá (RCMP)
.	14.9	41.8	479.4	.	.	*4. Retraites complémentaires*	4. Pensión suplementaria
.	98.0	1 286.8	4 272.6	.	.	*Total*	Total
1 290	.	30 098	.	.	310 000	*Régimes spéciaux*	Regímenes especiales para empleados del Gobierno central
.	.	14.4	.	.	.	*Maladie et maternité, lésions professionnelles*	Enfermedad, maternidad y lesiones profesionales
.	.	4.780	.	.	.	*Pensions et gratifications*	Pensiones y gratificaciones

Table A *(cont.)*   Tableau A *(suite)*   Cuadro A *(cont.)*

Country, currency unit and scheme / *Pays et unité monétaire, régime* / País, unidad monetaria y régimen	Receipts / *Recettes* / Ingresos — Contributions / *Cotisations* / Cotizaciones — From insured persons / *Des assurés* / De los asegurados	From government as employer / *De l'Etat (employeur)* / Del gobierno como empleador	Income from capital / *Revenu des capitaux* / Renta del capital	Other receipts / *Autres recettes* / Otros ingresos	Total receipts / *Total des recettes* / Total de ingresos	Expenditure / *Dépenses* / Egresos — Benefits / *Prestations* / Prestaciones — Medical care / *Soins médicaux* / Asistencia médica	Benefits in kind other than for medical care / *Prestations en nature à d'autres titres que les soins médicaux* / Prestaciones en especie distintas de la asistencia médica	Cash benefits / *Prestations en espèces* / Prestaciones monetarias	Total / *Total* / Total
(1)	(2)	(3)	(4)	(5)	(6)	(7)	(8)	(9)	(10)
Honduras (Lempira) Pensions	16.0	24.7	32.9	0.0	73.6	.	.	6.0	6.0
México (Peso)									
1. Pensions	123 170	123 169	37 130	160 576	444 045	.	170 479	104 534	275 013
2. Medical care	49 116	174 140	.	731	223 987	158 096	.	.	158 096
3. Housing	10 323	113 553	8 250	3 440	135 566	.	103 230	.	103 230
Total	182 609	410 862	45 380	164 747	803 598	158 096	273 709	104 534	536 339
Panamá (Balboa) Complementary Fund:									
1. Invalidity	.	.	.	.	.	.	.	1.3	1.3
2. Old-age	.	.	.	.	.	.	.	1.3	1.3
3. Early retirement	.	.	.	.	.	.	.	0.5	0.5
4. Physical incapacity	.	.	.	.	.	.	.	0.3	0.3
5. Long service	.	.	.	.	.	.	.	17.5	17.5
6. Grants	.	.	.	.	.	.	.	0.6	0.6
Total	16.9	.	.	8.1	25.0	.	.	21.5	21.5
United States[5] (Dollar) Federal government pensions	4 723	5 154	15 262	34 975[6]	60 114	.	.	41 816	41 816
Venezuela (Bolivar) Pensions	140	140	.	.	280	.	.	.[7]	.

ASIA – ASIE – ASIA

Japan[4] (Yen)									
1. National Public Service Mutual Aid Association:									
Pensions	.	.	.	.	.	187 800	.	878 822	1 066 622
Sickness, maternity and medical care	.	.	.	.	.	.	.	10 837	10 837
Employment injuries	.	.	.	.	.	.	.	2 731	2 731
Others	.	.	.	.	.	.	.	3 768	3 768
Subtotal 1	383 452	868 126	282 613	143 392[8]	1 677 583	187 800	.	896 158	1 083 958

See notes on page 206.   *Voir notes page 206.*   Véanse notas pág. 206.

(11) Administrative expenditure / Frais d'administration / Gastos de administración	(12) Other expenditure / Autres dépenses / Otros egresos	(13) Total expenditure / Total des dépenses / Total de egresos	(14) Difference between receipts and expenditure in financial year / Différence entre les recettes et les dépenses au cours de l'exercice / Diferencia entre ingresos y egresos en ejercicio financiero	(15) Total wages and salaries / Total des salaires et traitements / Total de sueldos y salarios	(16) No. of employees covered / Nombre d'agents couverts / Núm. de empleados comprendidos	(17) Régime	(18) Régimen
0.7	.	6.7	66.9	221.9	28 793	*Pensions*	Pensiones
74 931	.	349 944	94 101	2 239 445	1 816 171	*1. Pensions*	1. Pensiones
10 473	.	168 569	55 418	2 455 800	1 954 633	*2. Soins médicaux*	2. Asistencia médica
6 109	.	109 339	26 227	2 064 600	1 785 708	*3. Logement*	3. Vivienda
91 513	.	627 852	175 746	.	.	*Total*	Total
						Régime complémentaire:	Caja complementaria:
.	.	1.3	.	.	.	*1. Invalidité*	1. Invalidez
.	.	1.3	.	.	.	*2. Vieillesse*	2. Vejez
.	.	0.5	.	.	.	*3. Retraite anticipée*	3. Jubilación anticipada
.	.	0.3	.	.	.	*4. Invalidité*	4. Incapacidad física
.	.	17.5	.	.	.	*5. Ancienneté*	5. Servicio prolongado
.	.	0.6	.	.	.	*6. Gratifications*	6. Subvenciones
.	.	21.5	3.5	427.37	153 788	*Total*	Total
53	586	42 455	17 659	125 000	5 300 000	*Pensions (fonctionnaires fédéraux)*	Pensiones del Gobierno federal
.	.	.	280	85 000	1 200 000	*Pensions*	Pensiones
						1. Mutuelle (fonction publique nationale):	1. Asociación Nacional de Socorros Mutuos de los Servicios Públicos:
.	.	.	.	.	.	*Pensions* / *Maladie, maternité, soins médicaux*	Pensiones / Enfermedad, maternidad y asistencia médica
.	.	.	.	.	.	*Lésions professionnelles*	Lesiones profesionales
2 685	202 479[9]	1 289 122	388 461	.	.	*Autres prestations* / *Sous-total 1*	Otros / Subtotal 1

Country, currency unit and scheme / *Pays et unité monétaire, régime* / País, unidad monetaria y régimen	Receipts / *Recettes* / Ingresos — Contributions / *Cotisations* / Cotizaciones — From insured persons / *Des assurés* / De los asegurados	From government as employer / *De l'Etat (employeur)* / Del gobierno como empleador	Income from capital / *Revenu des capitaux* / Renta del capital	Other receipts / *Autres recettes* / Otros ingresos	Total receipts / *Total des recettes* / Total de ingresos	Expenditure / *Dépenses* / Egresos — Benefits / *Prestations* / Prestaciones — Medical care / *Soins médicaux* / Asistencia médica	Benefits in kind other than for medical care / *Prestations en nature à d'autres titres que les soins médicaux* / Prestaciones en especie distintas de la asistencia médica	Cash benefits / *Prestations en espèces* / Prestaciones monetarias	Total / *Total* / Total
(1)	(2)	(3)	(4)	(5)	(6)	(7)	(8)	(9)	(10)
2. National public service accident compensation	.	9 609	.	.	9 609	4 333	.	5 195	9 528
3. National public employees' pensions	859	121 000	.	1 219[6]	123 078	.	.	121 859	121 859
Total	384 311	998 735	282 613	144 611	1 810 270	192 133	.	1 023 212	1 215 345
Malaysia (Ringgit)									
Pensions	.	817	.	.	817	.	.	817	817
Pakistan[1] (Rupee)									
1. Pensions	.	617	.	.	617	.	.	617	617
2. Sickness and maternity	.	314	.	.	314	314	.	.	314
3. Group insurance	7	36	.	.	43	.	.	26	26
4. Benevolent Fund	44	.	15	.	59	.	.	36	36
Total	50	967	15	.	1 032	314	.	679	993
EUROPE – EUROPE – EUROPA									
Belgique (Franc belge)									
1. Pensions[11]	.	66 882	.	.	66 882	.	.	66 882	66 882
2. Military pensions (including police pensions)	.	22 067	.	.	22 067	.	.	22 067	22 067
3. Widows' and orphans' pensions	19 529	.	.	.	19 529	.	.	19 529	19 529
4. Family allowances[12]	.	14 082	.	32	14 114	.	.	14 082	14 082
Total	19 529	103 031	.	32	122 592	.	.	122 560	122 560
España (Peseta)									
1. State Retirement Scheme: Pensions	.	.	.	.	.	.	.	324 044	324 044
Family allowances (pensioners)	.	.	.	.	.	.	.	808	808
Others	.	.	.	.	.	.	.	1 400	1 400
Subtotal 1	34 340	291 912	.	4 256	330 508	.	.	326 252	326 252
2. Public assistance to families	.	3 944	.	51	3 995	.	.	3 944	3 944

See notes on page 206.   *Voir notes page 206.*   Véanse notas pág. 206.

200

			Difference between receipts and expenditure in financial year	Total wages and salaries	No. of employees covered	*Régime*	Régimen
			Différence entre les recettes et les dépenses au cours de l'exercice	*Total des salaires et traitements*	*Nombre d'agents couverts*		
Administrative expenditure	Other expenditure	Total expenditure	Diferencia entre ingresos y egresos en ejercicio financiero	Total de sueldos y salarios	Núm. de empleados comprendidos		
Frais d'administration	*Autres dépenses*	*Total des dépenses*					
Gastos de administración	Otros egresos	Total de egresos					
(11)	(12)	(13)	(14)	(15)	(16)	(17)	(18)
.	81	9 609	.	.	.	*2. Indemnisation des accidents (fonction publique nationale)*	2. Indemnizaciones por accidentes del trabajo a los empleados públicos
1 219	.	123 078	.	.	.	*3. Pensions (personnel national)*	3. Pensiones a los empleados públicos nacionales
3 904	202 560	1 421 809	388 461	3 957 252	1 151 062	*Total*	Total
.	.	817	.	7 486	.	*Pensions*	Pensiones
.	.	617	.	.	.	*1. Pensions*	1. Pensiones
.	.	314	.	.	.	*2. Maladie et maternité*	2. Enfermedad y maternidad
.	.	43	.	.	426 600[10]	*3. Assurance de groupe*	3. Seguro colectivo
2	.	38	21	.	.	*4. Caisse de secours*	4. Fondo de Beneficencia
2	.	1 012	21	.	.	*Total*	Total
.	.	66 882	.	.	.	*1. Pensions[11]*	1. Pensiones[11]
.	.	22 067	.	.	.	*2. Pensions militaires (y compris la gendarmerie)*	2. Pensiones militares (incluidas las pensiones policiales)
.	.	19 529	.	.	.	*3. Pensions (veuves et orphelins)*	3. Pensiones para viudas y huérfanos
32	.	14 114	.	.	.	*4. Allocations familiales[12]*	4. Asignaciones familiares[12]
32	.	122 592	.	403 374	609 648	*Total*	Total
						1. Régime de pensions de l'Etat:	1. Régimen de Pensiones del Estado:
.	.	.	.	.	.	*Pensions*	Pensiones
.	.	.	.	.	.	*Allocations familiales (pour les pensionnés)*	Asignaciones familiares (pensionados)
						Autres prestations	Otros
4 256	.	330 508	.	1 131 356	595 518	*Sous-total 1*	Subtotal 1
51	.	3 995	.	.	.	*2. Assistance publique aux familles*	2. Asistencia pública familiar

Table A *(cont.)*   **Tableau A** *(suite)*   **Cuadro A** *(cont.)*

Country, currency unit and scheme / *Pays et unité monétaire, régime* / País, unidad monetaria y régimen	Receipts / *Recettes* / Ingresos					Expenditure / *Dépenses* / Egresos			
	Contributions / *Cotisations* / Cotizaciones		Income from capital / *Revenu des capitaux* / Renta del capital	Other receipts / *Autres recettes* / Otros ingresos	Total receipts / *Total des recettes* / Total de ingresos	Benefits / *Prestations* / Prestaciones			
	From insured persons / *Des assurés* / De los asegurados	From government as employer / *De l'Etat (employeur)* / Del gobierno como empleador				Medical care / *Soins médicaux* / Asistencia médica	Benefits in kind other than for medical care / *Prestations en nature à d'autres titres que les soins médicaux* / Prestaciones en especie distintas de la asistencia médica	Cash benefits / *Prestations en espèces* / Prestaciones monetarias	Total / *Total* / Total
(1)	(2)	(3)	(4)	(5)	(6)	(7)	(8)	(9)	(10)
3. General Mutual Benefit Society for Public Employees:									
Pensions	.	.	.	.	.	.	.	5 953	5 953
Sickness and maternity	.	.	.	.	.	30 535	.	907	31 442
Family allowances	.	.	.	.	.	.	.	539	539
Others	.	.	.	.	.	.	195	1 688	1 883
Subtotal 3	10 363	26 475	1 974	6 999	45 811	30 535	195	9 087	39 817
4. Social Institute for Military Forces (ISFAS):									
Old-age, invalidity and others	.	.	.	.	.	.	151	1 577	1 728
Sickness and maternity	.	.	.	.	.	17 956	.	260	18 216
Family allowances	.	.	.	.	.	.	.	1 198	1 198
Subtotal 4	5 869	18 014	1 493	374	25 750	17 956	151	3 035	21 142
5. General Mutual Benefit Society for the Judiciary:									
Pensions	.	.	.	.	.	.	4	85	89
Sickness and maternity	.	.	.	.	.	1 020	.	83	1 103
Family allowances	.	.	.	.	.	.	.	28	28
Subtotal 5	440	1 265	57	.	1 762	1 020	4	196	1 220
Total	51 012	341 610	3 524	11 680	407 826	49 511	350	342 514	392 375
Germany, Fed. Rep. of (Deutsche Mark)									
1. Civil Servants' Pension Scheme (Federal government)	.	3 880	.	3 960	7 840	.	.	7 840	7 840
2. Other allowances for federal civil servants	.	340	.	.	340	.	.	340	340
Subtotal 1-2	.	4 220	.	3 960	8 180	.	.	8 180	8 180
3. Supplementary benefits (Federal government)	.	6 490	.	.	6 490	.	.	6 490	6 490
4. Other social assistance for federal government employees	.	.	.	420	420	.	.	420	420
Total	.	10 710	.	4 380	15 090	.	.	15 090	15 090

See notes on page 206.   *Voir notes page 206.*   Véanse notas pág. 206.

Administrative expenditure *Frais d'administration* Gastos de administración	Other expenditure *Autres dépenses* Otros egresos	Total expenditure *Total des dépenses* Total de egresos	Difference between receipts and expenditure in financial year *Différence entre les recettes et les dépenses au cours de l'exercice* Diferencia entre ingresos y egresos en ejercicio financiero	Total wages and salaries *Total des salaires et traitements* Total de sueldos y salarios	No. of employees covered *Nombre d'agents couverts* Núm. de empleados comprendidos	*Régime*	Régimen
(11)	(12)	(13)	(14)	(15)	(16)	(17)	(18)
						3. Mutuelle des fonctionnaires civils de l'Etat	3. Mutualidad General de Funcionarios Civiles del Estado
.	.	5 953	.	.	.	*Pensions*	Pensiones
.	.	31 442	.	.	.	*Maladie et maternité*	Enfermedad y maternidad
.	.	539	.	.	.	*Allocations familiales*	Asignaciones familiares
.	.	1 883	.	.	.	*Autres prestations*	Otros
2 169	.	41 986	3 825	.	.	*Sous-total 3*	Subtotal 3
						4. Institut social des forces armées:	4. Instituto Social de las Fuerzas Armadas:
.	.	.	.	.	.	*Vieillesse, invalidité et autres prestations*	Vejez, invalidez y otros
.	.	.	.	.	.	*Maladie et maternité*	Enfermedad y maternidad
.	.	.	.	.	.	*Allocations familiales*	Asignaciones familiares
1 777	.	22 919	2 831	.	.	*Sous-total 4*	Subtotal 4
						5. Mutuelle de l'ordre judiciaire:	5. Mutualidad General Judicial:
.	.	.	.	.	.	*Pensions*	Pensiones
.	.	.	.	.	.	*Maladie et maternité*	Enfermedad y maternidad
.	.	.	.	.	.	*Allocations familiales*	Asignaciones familiares
79	.	1 299	463	.	.	*Sous-total 5*	Subtotal 5
8 332	.	400 707	7 119	.	.	*Total*	Total
.	.	7 840	.	.	.	*1. Pensions (fonctionnaires fédéraux)*	1. Régimen de Pensiones para Funcionarios Públicos (Gobierno federal)
.	.	340	.	.	.	*2. Autres prestations (fonctionnaires fédéraux)*	2. Otras asignaciones para funcionarios civiles federales
.	.	8 180	.	15 421[13]	377 000[13]	*Sous-total 1-2*	Subtotal 1-2
.	.	6 490[14]	.	.	.	*3. Prestations supplémentaires (services fédéraux)*	3. Prestaciones suplementarias (Gobierno federal)
.	.	420	.	.	.	*4. Autres prestations d'assistance sociale (personnel fédéral)*	4. Otra asistencia social para empleados del Gobierno federal
.	.	15 090	.	.	.	*Total*	Total

Country, currency unit and scheme / *Pays et unité monétaire, régime* / País, unidad monetaria y régimen	Receipts / *Recettes* / Ingresos					Expenditure / *Dépenses* / Egresos			
	Contributions / *Cotisations* / Cotizaciones		Income from capital / *Revenu des capitaux* / Renta del capital	Other receipts / *Autres recettes* / Otros ingresos	Total receipts / *Total des recettes* / Total de ingresos	Benefits / *Prestations* / Prestaciones			
	From insured persons / *Des assurés* / De los asegurados	From government as employer / *De l'Etat (employeur)* / Del gobierno como empleador				Medical care / *Soins médicaux* / Asistencia médica	Benefits in kind other than for medical care / *Prestations en nature à d'autres titres que les soins médicaux* / Prestaciones en especie distintas de la asistencia médica	Cash benefits / *Prestations en espèces* / Prestaciones monetarias	Total / *Total* / Total
(1)	(2)	(3)	(4)	(5)	(6)	(7)	(8)	(9)	(10)
Grèce[15] (Drachme)									
1. Pensions	.	116 582	.	.	116 582	.	.	116 582	116 582
2. Sickness, maternity and medical care	3 359	13 137	.	.	16 496	16 496	.	.	16 496
Total	3 359	129 719	.	.	133 078	16 496	.	116 582	133 078
Ireland (Pound)									
Special schemes for central government employees	70.8	292.8	.	3.8	367.4			352.3	352.3
Netherlands (Guilder)									
1. Pensions	2 106	5 183	10 926	669[16]	18 884	.	.	9 069	9 069
2. Sickness and maternity	81	3 804	.	33[17]	3 918	171	.	3 742	3 913
3. Employment injuries	.	855	.	.	855	.	.	855	855
4. Family allowances	.	.	.	5	5	.	.	5	5
Total	2 187	9 842	10 926	707	23 662	171	.	13 671	13 842
Portugal (Escudo)									
1. Sickness	.	11 926	.	712	12 638	.	9 446	2 288	11 734
2. Survivor' pensions	5 563	7 833	12	635	14 043	.	.	13 340[18]	13 340
3. General Retirement Fund									
Retirement pension	21 423	32 364	63	9 957	63 807	.	.	61 553	61 553
Death grant	.	438	.	.	438	.	.	438	438
Family allowances	.	210	.	.	210	.	.	210	210
Subtotal 2-3	26 986	40 845	75	10 592	78 498	.	.	75 541	75 541
4. Employment injuries	.	21	.	.	21	.	.	18	18
Total	26 986	52 792	75	11 304	91 157	.	9 446	77 847	87 293
Turquie (Livre turque)									
1. Pensions	80 792	137 931	32 175	112 521	363 419	24 351	.	321 666	346 017
2. Medical care and funeral benefit	.	16 454	.	.	16 454	16 454	.	.	16 454
Total	80 792	154 385	32 175	112 521	379 873	.	.	321 666	362 471

See notes on page 206.   *Voir notes page 206.*   Véanse notas pág. 206.

(11) Administrative expenditure / Frais d'administration / Gastos de administración	(12) Other expenditure / Autres dépenses / Otros egresos	(13) Total expenditure / Total des dépenses / Total de egresos	(14) Difference between receipts and expenditure in financial year / Différence entre les recettes et les dépenses au cours de l'exercice / Diferencia entre ingresos y egresos en ejercicio financiero	(15) Total wages and salaries / Total des salaires et traitements / Total de sueldos y salarios	(16) No. of employees covered / Nombre d'agents couverts / Núm. de empleados comprendidos	(17) Régime	(18) Régimen
.	.	116 582	.	.	.	1. Pensions	1. Pensiones
.	.	16 496	.	.	.	2. Maladie, maternité, soins médicaux	2. Enfermedad, maternidad y asistencia médica
.	.	133 078	.	.	.	Total	Total
15.2	.	367.5	−0.1	1 345.8	172 389	Régimes spéciaux	Regímenes especiales para empleados del Gobierno central
240	.	9 309	9 575	.	.	1. Pensions	1. Pensiones
5	.	3 918	.	.	.	2. Maladie et maternité	2. Enfermedad y maternidad
.	.	855	.	.	.	3. Lésions professionnelles	3. Lesiones profesionales
.	.	5	.	.	.	4. Allocations familiales	4. Asignaciones familiares
245	.	14 087	9 575	16 210	607 000	Total	Total
282	.	12 016	622	.	664 464	1. Maladie	1. Enfermedad
498	.	13 838	205	.	791 672	2. Pensions de survivants	2. Pensiones de sobrevivientes
.	.	.	.	.	.	3. Caisse de retraite	3. Caja General de Jubilaciones
982	.	62 535	1 272	.	.	Retraites	Pensión de jubilación
.	.	438	.	.	.	Allocations de décès	Subvención por muerte
.	.	210	.	.	791 672	Allocations familiales	Asignaciones familiares
1 480	.	77 021	1 477	.	.	Sous-total 2-3	Subtotal 2-3
.	.	18	3	.	.	4. Lésions professionnelles	4. Lesiones profesionales
1 762	.	89 055	2 102	.	.	Total	Total
7 635	.	353 652	9 767	.	.	1. Pensions	1. Pensiones
.	.	16 454	.	.	.	2. Soins médicaux, prestations de décès	2. Prestaciones de asistencia médica y funerarias
7 635	.	370 106	9 767	.	.	Total	Total

Table A (concl.)   Tableau A (fin)   Cuadro A (fin)

Country, currency unit and scheme / Pays et unité monétaire, régime / País, unidad monetaria y régimen	Receipts / Recettes / Ingresos					Expenditure / Dépenses / Egresos			
	Contributions / Cotisations / Cotizaciones		Income from capital / Revenu des capitaux / Renta del capital	Other receipts / Autres recettes / Otros ingresos	Total receipts / Total des recettes / Total de ingresos	Benefits / Prestations / Prestaciones			
	From insured persons / Des assurés / De los asegurados	From government as employer / De l'Etat (employeur) / Del gobierno como empleador				Medical care / Soins médicaux / Asistencia médica	Benefits in kind other than for medical care / Prestations en nature à d'autres titres que les soins médicaux / Prestaciones en especie distintas de la asistencia médica	Cash benefits / Prestations en espèces / Prestaciones monetarias	Total / Total / Total
(1)	(2)	(3)	(4)	(5)	(6)	(7)	(8)	(9)	(10)
United Kindom[4] (Pound)									
1. Civil service	.	1 284	.	.	1 284	.	.	1 341	1 341
2. Armed forces	.	983	.	.	983	.	.	983	983
Total	.	2 267	.	.	2 267	.	.	2 324	2 324
OCEANIA – OCÉANIE – OCEANIA									
Australia[1] (Dollar)									
1. C/w public service superannuation	340.8	629.7	221.9	.	1 192.4	.	.	1 104.2	1 104.2
2. Defence force retirement and death benefits	91.5	.	.	.	91.5	.	.	431.1	431.1
3. C/w pensions for members of the South Australia and Tasmania state schemes	.	8.7	.	.	8.7	.	.	22.6	22.6
4. C/w employees' compensation	.	203.3	.	.	203.3	28.8	.	174.5	203.3
Total	432.3	841.7	221.9	.	1 495.9	28.8	.	1 732.4	1 761.2
New Zealand[4] (Dollar)									
Superannuation	155.5	313.5	218.9	.	687.9	.	.	416.7	416.7

C/w = Commonwealth.

[1] Financial year ending 30 June. [2] Financial year ending 30 September. [3] Includes state participation of 4,875.3 million CFA francs. [4] Financial year starting 1 April. [5] Financial year ending 30 September. [6] State participation. [7] The scheme started operating from 1986 and benefits will be payable as from 1989. [8] State participation: 59,546 million yen; transfers from other schemes: 74,504 million yen; and others: 9,343 million yen. [9] Transfers to other schemes: 202,385 million yen and others: 94 million yen. [10] Number of employees covered in group insurance and benevolent fund. [11] Of which an amount of 26,943 million francs was paid by the State in respect of pensions for ministers of religion and teachers. [12] Estimates. [13] Includes professional military personnel but excludes draftees for compulsory service. [14] All government expenditure, federal rail, federal post offices and churches. [15] Financial year 1985. [16] Contributions by the State and other public authorities. [17] Contributions by the State. [18] Includes public enterprises.

[1] Exercice financier se terminant le 30 juin. [2] Exercice financier se terminant le 30 septembre. [3] Y compris une participation de l'Etat de 4 875,3 millions de francs CFA. [4] Exercice financier commençant le 1er avril. [5] Exercice financier se terminant le 30 septembre. [6] Participation de l'Etat. [7] Ce régime est entré en vigueur en 1986; le paiement des prestations devait commencer en 1989. [8] Participation de l'Etat: 59 546 millions de yen; transferts d'autres régimes: 74 504 millions de yen; autres recettes: 9 343 millions de yen. [9] Transferts à d'autres régimes: 202 385 millions de yen; autres dépenses: 94 millions de yen. [10] Pour l'assurance de groupe et la caisse de secours. [11] Comprend 26 943 millions de francs versés par l'Etat au titre des pensions pour les ministres des cultes et les enseignants. [12] Estimations. [13] Comprend le personnel militaire de carrière, mais non les appelés du service militaire obligatoire. [14] Ensemble des dépenses de l'Etat, chemins de fer fédéraux, postes fédérales et églises. [15] Exercice financier de 1985. [16] Participation de l'Etat et d'autres collectivités publiques. [17] Participation de l'Etat. [18] Y compris les entreprises publiques.

[1] Ejercicio financiero que termina el 30 de junio. [2] Ejercicio financiero que termina el 30 de septiembre. [3] Incluye participación del Estado de 4 875,3 millones de francos CFA. [4] Ejercicio financiero que comienza el 1.º de abril. [5] Ejercicio financiero que termina el 30 de septiembre. [6] Participación del Estado. [7] El régimen entró en vigor a partir de 1986, y las prestaciones serían pagaderas a partir de 1989. [8] Participación del Estado: 59 546 millones de yen; transferencias de otros regímenes: 74 504 millones de yen, y otros: 9 343 millones de yen. [9] Transferencia a otros regímenes: 202 385 millones de yen, y otros: 94 millones de yen. [10] Número de empleados comprendidos en seguro colectivo y fondo de beneficencia. [11] De las cuales, el Gobierno pagó un importe de 26 943 millones de francos en concepto de pensiones para los ministros de culto y personal docente. [12] Estimaciones. [13] Incluye al personal militar profesional y excluye a los reclutas del servicio militar obligatorio. [14] Total de gastos gubernamentales, ferrocarril federal, oficinas de correo federales y templos. [15] Ejercicio financiero de 1985. [16] Cotizaciones del Estado y otras autoridades públicas. [17] Cotizaciones del Estado. [18] Incluye empresas públicas.

Administrative expenditure *Frais d'administration* Gastos de administración	Other expenditure *Autres dépenses* Otros egresos	Total expenditure *Total des dépenses* Total de egresos	Difference between receipts and expenditure in financial year *Différence entre les recettes et les dépenses au cours de l'exercice* Diferencia entre ingresos y egresos en ejercicio financiero	Total wages and salaries *Total des salaires et traitements* Total de sueldos y salarios	No. of employees covered *Nombre d'agents couverts* Núm. de empleados comprendidos	*Régime*	Régimen
(11)	(12)	(13)	(14)	(15)	(16)	(17)	(18)
.	.	1 341	− 57	.	610 000	*1. Fonction publique*	1. Administración civil
.	.	983	.	.	322 000	*2. Forces armées*	2. Fuerzas armadas
.	.	2 324	− 57	.	932 000	*Total*	Total
8.8	.	1 113.0	79.4	.	324 671	*1. Retraites (fonctionnaires fédéraux)*	1. Jubilaciones (funcionarios federales)
3.0	.	434.1	− 342.6	.	70 363	*2. Retraites, prestations de décès (forces armées)*	2. Jubilaciones, prestaciones por defunción (fuerzas armadas)
.	.	22.6	− 13.9	44.6	2 152	*3. Pensions fédérales (régimes d'Australie du Sud et de Tasmanie)*	3. Pensiones federales (regímenes de Australia del Sur y de Tasmania)
.	.	203.3	0.0	.	546 386	*4. Lésions professionnelles (personnel fédéral)*	4. Lesiones profesionales (personal federal)
11.8	.	1 773.0	− 277.1	.	.	*Total*	Total
3.4	.	420.1	267.8	2 371.2	84 301	*Retraites*	Jubilación

B. Average social security contributions per employee, 1986
(in national currency units and in US dollars)

B. Cotisation moyenne par agent, 1986
(en unités monétaires nationales et en dollars des Etats-Unis)

B. Promedio de cotizaciones de la seguridad social por empleado, 1986
(en unidades monetarias nacionales y en dólares de los Estados Unidos)

Country, currency unit and scheme / Pays et unité monétaire, régime / País, unidad monetaria y régimen	Contributions per head / Cotisation par agent / Cotizaciones por empleado	
	In national currency units / En unités monétaires nationales / En unidades monetarias nacionales	In US dollars / En dollars des E.-U. / En dólares EUA
(1)	(2)	(3)

AFRICA – AFRIQUE – AFRICA

Burundi
(Franc burundais)
Sickness and maternity — 9 692 — 78
Maladie et maternité
Enfermedad y maternidad

Mali
(Franc CFA)
Pensions — 225 142 — 698
Pensions
Pensiones

Maroc
(Dirham)
1. Moroccan Pension Fund — 1 317 — 151
   Caisse marocaine de retraite
   Caja Marroquí de Pensiones
2. General Retirement Benefits Scheme — 2 651 — 304
   Régime collectif d'allocations de retraite
   Régimen General de Prestaciones de Pensiones

Mauritius
(Rupee)
Widows' and Children's Pension Scheme — 817 — 62
Pensions (veuves et enfants)
Régimen de Pensión para Viudas e Hijos

Mozambique
(Metical)
Old-age — 62 380 — 156
Vieillesse
Vejez
Survivors — 35 714 — 89
Survivants
Sobrevivientes

Niger
(Franc CFA)
Pensions — 115 585 — 358
Pensions
Pensiones

AMERICA – AMÉRIQUE – AMERICA

Colombia
(Peso)
Central government — 91 706 — 419
Régimes spéciaux
Gobierno central

Honduras
(Lempiras)
Pensions — 1 414 — 707
Pensions
Pensiones

México
(Peso)
1. Pensions — 135 636 — 147
   Pensions
   Pensiones
2. Medical care — 114 219 — 124
   Soins médicaux
   Asistencia médica
3. Housing — 69 371 — 75
   Logement
   Vivienda

Panamá
(Balboa)
Complementary Fund — 110 — 110
Régime complémentaire
Fondo complementario

United States
(Dollar)
Pensions (Federal government) — 8 463 — 8 463
Pensions (fonctionnaires fédéraux)
Pensiones (Gobierno federal)

Venezuela
(Bolivar)
Pensions — 233 — 16
Pensions
Pensiones

ASIA – ASIE – ASIA

Japan
(Yen)
National public employees' pensions — 106 926 — 672
Pensions (personnel national)
Pensiones de empleados publicos nacionales

C/w = Commonwealth.
For general footnotes and financial years, see table A.

Pour les notes de caractère général et pour les exercices financiers, se reporter au tableau A.

Para notas generales y ejercicios financieros, véase el cuadro A.

Table B *(concl.)*   **Tableau B** *(fin)*   **Cuadro B** *(fin)*

Country, currency unit and scheme / Pays et unité monétaire, régime / País, unidad monetaria y régimen (1)	Contributions per head / Cotisation par agent / Cotizaciones por empleado	
	In national currency units / En unités monétaires nationales / En unidades monetarias nacionales (2)	In US dollars / En dollars des E.-U. / En dólares EUA (3)
Pakistan (Rupee)		
Group Insurance and Benevolent Fund *Assurance de groupe, caisse de secours* Seguro Colectivo y Fondo de Beneficencia	203	11
EUROPE – EUROPE – EUROPA		
Belgique (Franc belge)		
Central government *Agents de l'Etat* Gobierno central	201 034	4 975
España (Peseta)		
State Retirement Scheme *Régime de pensions de l'Etat* Régimen de Pensiones del Estado	547 846	4 138
Germany, Fed. Rep. of (Deutsche Mark)		
Civil Servants' Pension Scheme (Federal government) *Pensions (fonctionnaires fédéraux)* Régimen de Pensiones para Funcionarios Públicos (Gobierno federal)	11 194	5 767
Ireland (Pound)		
Central government *Régimes spéciaux* Gobierno central	2 109	2 950
Netherlands (Guilder)		
Pensions, sickness and maternity, employment injuries and family allowances *Pensions, maladie et maternité, lésions professionnelles, allocations familiales* Pensiones, enfermedad y maternidad, lesiones profesionales y asignaciones familiares	19 817	9 041
Portugal (Escudo)		
1. Sickness *Maladie* Enfermedad	17 948	123
2. General Retirement Fund *Caisse de retraite* Caja General de Pensiones	85 680	586
United Kingdom (Pound)		
1. Civil service *Fonction publique* Administración pública	2 105	3 105
2. Armed forces *Forces armées* Fuerzas armadas	3 053	4 503
OCEANIA – OCÉANIE – OCEANIA		
Australia (Dollar)		
1. C/w public service superannuation *Retraites (fonctionnaires fédéraux)* Jubilaciones (funcionarios federales)	2 989	1 987
2. Defence force retirement and death benefits *Retraites, prestations de décès (forces armées)* Jubilaciones, prestaciones por defunción (fuerzas armadas)	1 300	865
3. C/w pensions (South Australia and Tasmania) superannuation *Pensions fédérales (régimes d'Australie du Sud et de Tasmanie)* Pensiones federales (regímenes de Australia del Sur y Tasmania)	4 043	2 688
4. C/w employees' compensation *Lésions professionnelles (personnel fédéral)* Lesiones profesionales (personal federal)	372	247
New Zealand (Dollar)		
Superannuation *Retraites* Jubilación	5 563	2 913

C/w = Commonwealth.
For general footnotes and financial years, see table A.

Pour les notes de caractère général et pour les exercices financiers, se reporter au tableau A.

Para notas generales y ejercicios financieros, véase el cuadro A.

C. Benefit expenditure, 1986
(as percentages of wages and salaries[1])

C. Dépenses en prestations, 1986
(en pourcentage des salaires et traitements[1])

C. Egresos por prestaciones, 1986
(como porcentajes de sueldos y salarios[1])

Country and scheme / *Pays, régime* / País y régimen	Benefit expenditure as percentage of wages and salaries / *Dépenses en pourcentage des salaires et traitements* / Egresos como porcentaje de sueldos y salarios
(1)	(2)
AFRICA – AFRIQUE – AFRICA	
Burundi	
Sickness and maternity	5.9
Maladie et maternité	
Enfermedad y maternidad	
Mali	
Pensions	11.1
Pensions	
Pensiones	
Niger	
Pensions	35.6
Pensions	
Pensiones	
AMERICA – AMÉRIQUE – AMERICA	
Honduras	
Pensions	2.7
Pensions	
Pensiones	
México	
1. Pensions	12.3
Pensiones	
Pensiones	
2. Medical care	6.4
Soins médicaux	
Asistencia médica	
Panamá	
Complementary Fund	5.0
Régime complémentaire	
Fondo complementario	
United States	
Federal government	33.5
Pensions (fonctionnaires fédéraux)	
Gobierno federal	
ASIA – ASIE – ASIA	
Japan	
Central government	30.7
Agents de l'Etat	
Gobierno central	
Malaysia	
Pensions	10.9
Pensions	
Pensiones	

Country and scheme / *Pays, régime* / País y régimen	Benefit expenditure as percentage of wages and salaries / *Dépenses en pourcentage des salaires et traitements* / Egresos como porcentaje de sueldos y salarios
(1)	(2)
EUROPE – EUROPE – EUROPA	
Belgique	
Central government	30.4
Agents de l'Etat	
Gobierno central	
España	
State Retirement Scheme	28.8
Régime de pensions de l'Etat	
Régimen de Pensiones del Estado	
Germany, Fed. Rep. of	
Civil Servants' Pension Scheme (Federal government)	53.0
Pensions (fonctionnaires fédéraux)	
Régimen de Pensiones para Funcionarios Públicos (Gobierno federal)	
Ireland	
Central government	26.2
Régimes spéciaux	
Gobierno central	
Netherlands	
Pensions, sickness and maternity, employment injuries and family allowances	85.4
Pensions, maladie et maternité, lésions professionnelles, allocations familiales	
Pensiones, enfermedad y maternidad, lesiones profesionales y asignaciones familiares	
OCEANIA – OCÉANIE – OCEANIA	
Australia	
C/w pensions for South Australia and Tasmania	50.7
Pensions fédérales (régimes d'Australie du Sud et de Tasmanie)	
Pensiones federales (regímenes de Australia del Sur y Tasmania)	
New Zealand	
Superannuation	17.6
Retraites	
Jubilación	

For general footnotes and financial years, see table A.
[1] Wages and salaries refer to the active persons covered by the respective scheme.

Pour les notes de caractère général et les exercices financiers, se reporter au tableau A.
[1] *Salaires et traitements des agents actifs couverts par les régimes considérés.*

Para notas generales y ejercicios financieros, consúltese el cuadro A.
[1] Los sueldos y salarios corresponden a personas activas comprendidas en el régimen respectivo.

Country and currency unit / Pays et unité monétaire / País y unidad monetaria	Pensions / Pensions / Pensiones	Sickness and maternity / Maladie et maternité / Enfermedad y maternidad	Employment injuries / Accidents du travail et maladies professionnelles / Riesgos profesionales	Family allowances / Allocations familiales / Asignaciones familiares	Others / Autres prestations / Otros	Total amount of benefit expenditure (in millions of national currency units) / Total des dépenses en prestations (millions d'unités monétaires nationales) / Total de egresos por prestaciones (en millones de unidades monetarias nacionales)
(1)	(2)	(3)	(4)	(5)	(6)	(7)
AFRICA – AFRIQUE – AFRICA						
Burundi (Franc burundais)	.	100	.	.	.	498.0
Mali (Franc CFA)	100	.	.	.	.	2 858.8
Maroc (Dirham)	.	.	.	.	.	1 405.1
Mauritius (Rupee)	100	.	.	.	.	229.0
Mozambique (Metical)	100	.	.	.	.	73.0
Niger (Franc CFA)	100	.	.	.	.	2 476.8
Tunisie (Dinar)	88.2	11.8	.	.	.	99.6
AMERICA – AMÉRIQUE – AMERICA						
Canada (Dollar)	100	.	.	.	.	1 188.8
Colombia (Peso)	76.6	23.4	.	.	.	28 808.0
El Salvador (Colón)	.	100	.	.	.	94.1
Grenada (EC Dollar)	100	.	.	.	.	4.8
Honduras (Lempira)	100	.	.	.	.	6.0
México (Peso)	51.3	29.5	.	.	19.2	536 339.0
Panamá (Balboa)	100	.	.	.	.	21.5
United States (Dollar)	100	.	.	.	.	66 258.0

For general footnotes and financial years, see table A.
[1] Financial year 1985.

Pour les notes de caractère général et les exercices financiers, se reporter au tableau A.
[1] Exercice financier de 1985.

Para notas generales y ejercicios financieros, véase el cuadro A.
[1] Ejercicio financiero 1985.

Table D *(concl.)* **Tableau D** *(fin)* **Cuadro D** *(fin)*

Country and currency unit / Pays et unité monétaire / País y unidad monetaria	Pensions / Pensions / Pensiones	Sickness and maternity / Maladie et maternité / Enfermedad y maternidad	Employment injuries / Accidents du travail et maladies professionnelles / Riesgos profesionales	Family allowances / Allocations familiales / Asignaciones familiares	Others / Autres prestations / Otros	Total amount of benefit expenditure (in millions of national currency units) / Total des dépenses en prestations (millions d'unités monétaires nationales) / Total de egresos por prestaciones (en millones de unidades monetarias nacionales)
(1)	(2)	(3)	(4)	(5)	(6)	(7)
ASIA – ASIE – ASIA						
Japan (Yen)	97.8	0.9	1.0	.	0.3	1 215 345.0
Malaysia (Ringgit)	100	.	.	.	.	817.0
Pakistan (Rupee)	68.0	32.0	.	.	.	993.0
EUROPE – EUROPE – EUROPA						
Belgique (Franc belge)	88.5	.	.	11.5	.	122 560.0
España (Peseta)	84.6	12.9	.	1.7	0.8	392 375.0
Germany, Fed. Rep. of (Deutsche Mark)	95.0	.	.	.	5.0	15 090.0
Grèce[1] (Drachme)	87.6	12.4	.	.	.	133 078.0
Ireland (Pound)	100	.	.	.	.	352.3
Netherlands (Guilder)	65.5	28.3	6.2	0.0	.	13 842.0
Portugal (Escudo)	86.3	13.4	.	0.2	.	87 293.0
Turquie (Livre turque)	95.5	4.5	.	.	.	362 471.0
United Kingdom (Pound)	100	.	.	.	.	2 324.0
OCEANIA – OCÉANIE – OCEANIA						
Australia (Dollar)	88.5	.	11.5	.	.	1 761.2
New Zealand (Dollar)	100	.	.	.	.	416.7

For general footnotes and financial years, see table A.
[1] Financial year 1985.

Pour les notes de caractère général et les exercices financiers, se reporter au tableau A.
[1] Exercice financier de 1985.

Para notas generales y ejercicios financieros, véase el cuadro A.
[1] Ejercicio financiero 1985.